Lecture Notes in Computer Science　　10539

Commenced Publication in 1973
Founding and Former Series Editors:
Gerhard Goos, Juris Hartmanis, and Jan van Leeuwen

More information about this series at http://www.springer.com/series/7409

Giovanni Luca Ciampaglia · Afra Mashhadi
Taha Yasseri (Eds.)

Social Informatics

9th International Conference, SocInfo 2017
Oxford, UK, September 13–15, 2017
Proceedings, Part I

 Springer

Editors
Giovanni Luca Ciampaglia
Indiana University
Bloomington, IN
USA

Taha Yasseri
University of Oxford
Oxford
UK

Afra Mashhadi
University of Washington
Seattle, WA
USA

ISSN 0302-9743   ISSN 1611-3349 (electronic)
Lecture Notes in Computer Science
ISBN 978-3-319-67216-8   ISBN 978-3-319-67217-5 (eBook)
DOI 10.1007/978-3-319-67217-5

Library of Congress Control Number: 2017952387

LNCS Sublibrary: SL3 – Information Systems and Applications, incl. Internet/Web, and HCI

Printed on acid-free paper

This Springer imprint is published by Springer Nature
The registered company is Springer International Publishing AG
The registered company address is: Gewerbestrasse 11, 6330 Cham, Switzerland

Preface

This volume contains the proceedings of the 9th Conference on Social Informatics (SocInfo 2017), held in Oxford, UK on September 13–15, 2017. Continuing the tradition of this conference series, SocInfo 2017 brought together researchers from the computational and the social sciences with the intent of closing the chasm that has traditionally separated the two communities. The goal of the conference was in fact to provide a forum for practitioners from the two disciplines to define common research objectives and explore new methodological advances in both fields. The organizers welcomed a broad range of contributions, ranging from those that apply the methods of the social sciences in the study of socio-technical systems, to those that employ computer science methods to analyze complex social processes, as well as those that make use of social concepts in the design of information systems.

This year SocInfo received 142 submitted papers from a total of 451 distinct authors, located in 41 different countries covering 6 continents. We were glad to have a broad and diverse Program Committee of 218 experts with a strong interdisciplinary background from all over the world. The Program Committee reviewed all submissions and provided the authors with in-depth feedback on how to improve their work. In line with previous events, this year SocInfo continued to employ a single-blind peer review process. Papers received at least two reviews by the Program Committee; some submissions received up to five.

The Program Committee selected 40 submissions for oral presentation (28% acceptance rate) and 44 submissions to be presented as posters (30% acceptance rate). In line with the goal of fostering participation from fields with different publication practices than those of computer science, authors were given the chance to present their work without having it included in the proceedings. Four submissions opted out from the proceedings, taking the total number of contributions included in these volumes to 80.

In addition to posters and paper presentations, SocInfo 2017 hosted six great keynotes delivered by Licia Capra (University College London), Jennifer Golbeck (University of Maryland), Filippo Menczer (Indiana University), Gina Neff (University of Oxford), Daniele Quercia (Bell Labs), and Markus Strohmaier (RWTH Aachen University).

We would like to congratulate and thank all the authors and attendees for selecting this venue to present and discuss their research. We would like to thank everybody involved in the conference organization that helped us in making this event successful. We owe special thanks to the Steering Committee of this conference for their input and support, particularly Adam Wierzbicki, the chair of the Steering Committee.

The organizers are extremely grateful to all the reviewers and the members of the Program Committee for their tireless efforts in making sure that the contributions adhered to the highest standards of scientific rigor and originality. We thank our two hardworking program co-chairs Afra Mashhadi and Giovanni Luca Ciampaglia, who oversaw the process and put together a great program for this event. They both went out of their way to guarantee the quality of these proceedings and their support in other aspects of the conference organization was a great help to us. We are grateful to our publicity chair Julia Proskurnia, and our web chair Adam Tamer. This event would not have been possible without the generous support of the staff of the Oxford Internet Institute; in particular we would like to thank our sponsorship chair Victoria Nash, our finance chair Duncan Passey, and, last but not least, the local organizer Jordan Davies. We are extremely grateful to Wolfson College and in particular to Louise Gordon, who kindly provided us with the venue and amazing logistic support.

We are very thankful to our sponsors, particularly the Alan Turing Institute, Springer, and the American Association for the Advancement of Science.

September 2017   Taha Yasseri

Organization

Program Committee

Palakorn Achananuparp	Singapore Management University, Singapore
Eytan Adar	University of Washington, USA
Thomas Ågotnes	University of Bergen, Norway
Luca Maria Aiello	Bell Labs, UK
Harith Alani	KMi, The Open University, UK
Merve Alanyali	University of Warwick, UK
Laura Maria Alessandretti	City University of London, UK
Fred Amblard	University of Toulouse, UK
Stuart Anderson	University of Edinburgh, UK
Pablo Aragón	Universitat Pompeu Fabra, Spain
Alex Arenas	URV, Spain
Yasuhito Asano	Kyoto University, Japan
Ching Man Au Yeung	Axon Labs Ltd., Hong Kong, China
Francois Bar	USC - Annenberg School, USA
Vladimir Barash	Graphika Inc., USA
Alain Barrat	CNRS, France
Dominik Batorski	University of Warsaw, Poland
Ginestra Bianconi	Queen Mary University, UK
Livio Bioglio	University of Turin, Italy
Arnim Bleier	GESIS-Leibniz Institute for the Social Sciences, Germany
Javier Borge-Holthoefer	Internet Interdisciplinary Institute (IN3-UOC), Spain
Ulrik Brandes	University of Konstanz, Germany
Colin Campbell	Washington College, USA
Nan Cao	IBM T.J. Watson Research Center, USA
Adrián Carro	INET, University of Oxford, UK
Claudio Castellano	Instituto dei Sistemi Complessi (ISC-CNR), Italy
Michael Castelle	University of Chicago, USA
James Caverlee	Texas A&M University, USA
Fabio Celli	University of Trento, Italy
Nina Cesare	University of Washington, USA
Meeyoung Cha	KAIST & Facebook, South Korea
Freddy Chong Tat Chua	Hewlett Packard Labs, USA
David Corney	Signal Media, UK
Michele Coscia	Harvard University, USA
Andrew Crooks	George Mason University, USA
Manlio De Domenico	Universitat Rovira i Virgili, Spain
Jean-Charles Delvenne	University of Leuven, Belgium

Bruce Desmarais	Pennsylvania State University, USA
Jana Diesner	University of Illinois at Urbana-Champaign, USA
Victor M. Eguiluz	IFISC (CSIC-UIB), Spain
Young-Ho Eom	University of Strathclyde, UK
Tim Evans	Imperial College London, UK
Katayoun Farrahi	Goldsmiths, University of London, UK
Rosta Farzan	University of Pittsburgh, USA
Diego Fregolente Mendes de Oliveira	Indiana University, USA
Seth Frey	Dartmouth College, USA
Vanessa Frias-Martinez	University of Maryland, USA
Gerhard Fuchs	University of Stuttgart, Germany
Matteo Gagliolo	Université libre de Bruxelles (ULB), Belgium
Bharath Ganesh	Oxford Internet Institute, UK
David Garcia	ETH Zurich, Switzerland
Ruth Garcia Gavilanes	Skyscanner, UK
Manuel Garcia-Herranz	UNICEF, USA
Floriana Gargiulo	CNRS and University of Paris Sorbonne, France
Carlos Gershenson	UNAM, Mexico
James Gleeson	University of Limerick, Ireland
Kwang-Il Goh	Korea University, South Korea
Jennifer Golbeck	University of Maryland, USA
Andreea Gorbatai	UC Berkeley, USA
Przemyslaw Grabowicz	Max Planck Institute for Software Systems, Germany
André Grow	KU Leuven, Belgium
Christophe Guéret	Accenture, Ireland
Scott Hale	University of Oxford, UK
Alex Hanna	University of Toronto, Canada
Tim Hannigan	University of Alberta, Canada
Mohammed Hasanuzzaman	ADAPT Centre, Dublin, Ireland
Takako Hashimoto	Chiba University of Commerce, Japan
Agnes Horvat	Northwestern University, USA
Yuheng Hu	University of Illinois at Chicago, USA
Baden Hughes	Glentworth Consulting, UK
Laurent Hébert-Dufresne	Santa Fe Institute, USA
Adam Jatowt	Kyoto University, Japan
Marco Alberto Javarone	University of Hertfordshire, UK
Mark Jelasity	University of Szeged, Hungary
Pablo Jensen	ENS Lyon, France
Hang-Hyun Jo	Pohang University of Science and Technology, South Korea
Andreas Kaltenbrunner	Eurecat - Technology Centre of Catalonia, Spain
Fariba Karimi	GESIS-Leibniz Institute for the Social Sciences, Germany
Kazuhiro Kazama	Wakayama University, Japan
Przemysław Kazienko	Wroclaw University of Technology, Poland

Pan-Jun Kim	Korea Advanced Institute of Science and Technology (KAIST), South Korea
Katharina Kinder-Kurlanda	GESIS Leibniz Institute for the Social Sciences, Germany
Mikko Kivela	Aalto University, Finland
Adam Kleinbaum	Tuck School of Business at Dartmouth, USA
Andreas Koch	University of Salzburg, Austria
Farshad Kooti	Facebook, USA
Renaud Lambiotte	University of Namur, Belgium
Walter Lamendola	University of Denver, USA
David Laniado	Eurecat, Spain
Georgios Lappas	Western Macedonia University of Applied Sciences, Greece
Deok-Sun Lee	Inha University, South Korea
Juyong Lee	National Institutes of Health, USA
Sang Hoon Lee	Korea Institute for Advanced Study, South Korea
Wonjae Lee	KAIST, South Korea
Sune Lehmann	Technical University of Denmark, Denmark
Akoglu Leman	CMU, USA
Zoran Levnajic	Faculty of Information Studies in Novo Mesto, Slovenia
Elisabeth Lex	Graz University of Technology, Austria
Vera Liao	University of Illinois at Urbana-Champaign, USA
David Liben-Nowell	Carleton College, USA
Ee-Peng Lim	Singapore Management University, Singapore
Yu-Ru Lin	University of Pittsburgh, USA
Huan Liu	Arizona State University, USA
Yabing Liu	Northeastern University, USA
Jiebo Luo	University of Rochester, USA
Mark Lutter	Max Planck Institute for the Study of Societies, Germany
Xiao Ma	Cornell Tech, USA
Matteo Magnani	Uppsala University, Sweden
Rosario Mantegna	Università di Palermo, Italy
Emanuele Massaro	EPFL, Switzerland
Naoki Masuda	University of Bristol, UK
Julian McAuley	UC San Diego, USA
Peter McMahan	University of Chicago, USA
Yelena Mejova	Qatar Computing Research Institute, Qatar
Rosa Meo	University of Turin, Italy
Stasa Milojevic	Indiana University, USA
Marija Mitrovic	Institute of Physics Belgrade, Serbia
Asako Miura	Kwansei Gakuin University, Japan
Hisashi Miyamori	Kyoto Sangyo University, Japan
Suzy Moat	University of Warwick, UK
John Mohr	University of California, Santa Barbara, USA

Mostafa Salehi   University of Tehran, Iran
Kazutoshi Sasahara   Nagoya University, Japan
Michael Schaub   Massachusetts Institute of Technology, USA
Maximilian Schich   The University of Texas at Dallas, USA
Rossano Schifanella   University of Turin, Italy
Harald Schoen   University of Mannheim, Germany
Ralph Schroeder   University of Oxford, UK
Frank Schweitzer   ETH Zurich, Switzerland
Amirhossein Shirazi   Shahid Beheshti University, Iran
Thanakorn Sornkaew   Ramkhamheang University, Thailand
Rok Sosic   Stanford University, USA
Viktoria Spaiser   University of Leeds, UK
Bogdan State   Stanford University, USA
Markus Strohmaier   University of Koblenz-Landau, Germany
Pål Sundsøy   Telenor ASA, Norway
Taro Takaguchi   National Institute of Information and Communications
                                    Technology, Japan
Katsumi Tanaka   Kyoto University, Japan
Maurizio Teli   Madeira Interactive Technologies Institute, Portugal
Xian Teng   University of Pittsburgh, USA
Rochelle Terman   UC Berkeley, USA
John Ternovski   Yale University, USA
Dimitrios Thilikos   National and Kapodistrian University of Athens,
                                    Greece
Bart Thomee   Google, USA
Michele Tizzoni   ISI Foundation, Italy
Klaus G. Troitzsch   University of Koblenz-Landau, Germany
Milena Tsvetkova   University of Oxford, UK
Lyle Ungar   University of Pennsylvania, USA
Carmen Vaca Ruiz   ESPOL, Ecuador
George Valkanas   University of Athens, Greece
Onur Varol   Northeastern University, USA
Julita Vassileva   University of Saskatchewan, Canada
Bertram Vidgen   University of Oxford, UK
Dani Villatoro   IIIA-csic, Spain
Daniele Vilone   National Research Council of Italy, Italy
Yana Volkovich   Appnexus, USA
Dylan Walker   Boston University, USA
Ning Wang   University of Oxford, UK
Wenbo Wang   GoDaddy Inc., USA
Ingmar Weber   Qatar Computing Research Institute, Qatar
Xidao Wen   University of Pittsburgh, USA
Tim Weninger   University of Notre Dame, USA
Adam Wierzbicki   Polish-Japanese Institute of Information Technology,
                                    Poland
Joss Wright   Oxford University, USA

Contents – Part I

Economics, Science of Success, and Education

Simple Acoustic-Prosodic Models of Confidence and Likability
are Associated with Long-Term Funding Outcomes for Entrepreneurs 3
   Natalie A. Carlson

ABCE: A Python Library for Economic Agent-Based Modeling 17
   Davoud Taghawi-Nejad, Rudy H. Tanin, R. Maria Del Rio Chanona,
   Adrián Carro, J. Doyne Farmer, Torsten Heinrich, Juan Sabuco,
   and Mika J. Straka

The Dynamics of Professional Prestige in Fashion Industries of Europe
and the US: Network Approach 31
   Margarita Kuleva and Daria Maglevanaya

Matching Graduate Applicants with Faculty Members 41
   Shibamouli Lahiri, Carmen Banea, and Rada Mihalcea

Network science

Why Groups Show Different Fairness Norms? The Interaction
Topology Might Explain 59
   Mohsen Mosleh and Babak Heydari

Constrained Community Detection in Multiplex Networks 75
   Koji Eguchi and Tsuyoshi Murata

News, Misinformation, and Collective Sensemaking

Seminar Users in the Arabic Twitter Sphere 91
   Kareem Darwish, Dimitar Alexandrov, Preslav Nakov,
   and Yelena Mejova

Exploiting Context for Rumour Detection in Social Media 109
   Arkaitz Zubiaga, Maria Liakata, and Rob Procter

Multidimensional Analysis of the News Consumption of Different
Demographic Groups on a Nationwide Scale 124
   Jisun An and Haewoon Kwak

Trump vs. Hillary: What Went Viral During the 2016
US Presidential Election.   143
   Kareem Darwish, Walid Magdy, and Tahar Zanouda

Understanding Online Political Networks: The Case of the Far-Right
and Far-Left in Greece.   162
   Pantelis Agathangelou, Ioannis Katakis, Lamprini Rori,
   Dimitrios Gunopulos, and Barry Richards

Polarization in Blogging About the Paris Meeting on Climate Change   178
   Dag Elgesem

Event Analysis on the 2016 U.S. Presidential Election Using Social Media . . .   201
   Tarrek A. Shaban, Lindsay Hexter, and Jinho D. Choi

Badly Evolved? Exploring Long-Surviving Suspicious Users on Twitter   218
   Majid Alfifi and James Caverlee

Opinions, Behavior, and Social Media Mining

Like at First Sight: Understanding User Engagement with the World
of Microvideos   237
   Sagar Joglekar, Nishanth Sastry, and Miriam Redi

Compression-Based Algorithms for Deception Detection   257
   Christina L. Ting, Andrew N. Fisher, and Travis L. Bauer

'Dark Germany': Hidden Patterns of Participation in Online Far-Right
Protests Against Refugee Housing.   277
   Sebastian Schelter and Jérôme Kunegis

An Analysis of UK Policing Engagement via Social Media   289
   Miriam Fernandez, Tom Dickinson, and Harith Alani

What Makes a Good Collaborative Knowledge Graph:
Group Composition and Quality in Wikidata   305
   Alessandro Piscopo, Chris Phethean, and Elena Simperl

Multimodal Analysis and Prediction of Latent User Dimensions   323
   Laura Wendlandt, Rada Mihalcea, Ryan L. Boyd,
   and James W. Pennebaker

Characterizing Videos, Audience and Advertising in Youtube Channels
for Kids.   341
   Camila Souza Araújo, Gabriel Magno, Wagner Meira Jr.,
   Virgilio Almeida, Pedro Hartung, and Danilo Doneda

Comparing Influencers: Activity vs. Connectivity Measures in Defining
Key Actors in Twitter *Ad Hoc* Discussions on Migrants in Germany
and Russia   360
  Svetlana S. Bodrunova, Anna A. Litvinenko, and Ivan S. Blekanov

The President on Twitter: A Characterization Study of @realDonaldTrump . . .   377
  Brooke Auxier and Jennifer Golbeck

Social Networking Sites Withdrawal   391
  Carlos Osorio, Rob Wilson, and Savvas Papagiannidis

When *Follow* is Just One Click Away: Understanding Twitter *Follow*
Behavior in the 2016 U.S. Presidential Election   409
  Yu Wang, Jiebo Luo, and Xiyang Zhang

Inferring Spread of Readers' Emotion Affected by Online News   426
  Agus Sulistya, Ferdian Thung, and David Lo

How Polarized Have We Become? A Multimodal Classification
of Trump Followers and Clinton Followers   440
  Yu Wang, Yang Feng, Zhe Hong, Ryan Berger, and Jiebo Luo

Can Cross-Lingual Information Cascades Be Predicted on Twitter?   457
  Hongshan Jin, Masashi Toyoda, and Naoki Yoshinaga

An Analysis of Individuals' Behavior Change in Online Groups   473
  David Jurgens, James McCorriston, and Derek Ruths

The Message or the Messenger? Inferring Virality and Diffusion
Structure from Online Petition Signature Data   499
  Chi Ling Chan, Justin Lai, Bryan Hooi, and Todd Davies

Proximity, Location, Mobility, and Urban Analytics

Measuring Ambient Population from Location-Based Social Networks
to Describe Urban Crime   521
  Cristina Kadar, Raquel Rosés Brüngger, and Irena Pletikosa

Robust Modeling of Human Contact Networks Across Different Scales
and Proximity-Sensing Techniques   536
  *Michele Starnini, Bruno Lepri, Andrea Baronchelli, Alain Barrat,
  Ciro Cattuto, and Romualdo Pastor-Satorras*

Personalized Recommendation of Points-of-Interest Based
on Multilayer Local Community Detection   552
  Roberto Interdonato and Andrea Tagarelli

Designing for Digital Inclusion: A Post-Hoc Evaluation
of a Civic Technology   572
   Claudia López and Rosta Farzan

Security, Privacy, and Trust

The Cognitive Heuristics Behind Disclosure Decisions.   591
   Vincent Marmion, Felicity Bishop, David E. Millard,
   and Sarah V. Stevenage

Tools and Methods

A Propagation-Based Method of Estimating Students'
Concept Understanding   611
   Rafael López-García, Makoto P. Kato, and Katsumi Tanaka

Seeds Buffering for Information Spreading Processes.   628
   Jarosław Jankowski, Piotr Bródka, Radosław Michalski,
   and Przemysław Kazienko

Author Index   643

Contents – Part II

Poster Papers: Economics, Science of Success, and Education

Mobile Social Media and Academic Performance 3
  Fausto Giunchiglia, Mattia Zeni, Elisa Gobbi, Enrico Bignotti,
  and Ivano Bison

Towards Real-Time Prediction of Unemployment and Profession 14
  Pål Sundsøy, Johannes Bjelland, Bjørn-Atle Reme, Eaman Jahani,
  Erik Wetter, and Linus Bengtsson

The Digital Flynn Effect: Complexity of Posts on Social Media
Increases over Time 24
  Ivan Smirnov

An Exploration of Wikipedia Data as a Measure of Regional
Knowledge Distribution 31
  Fabian Stephany and Fabian Braesemann

Differential Network Effects on Economic Outcomes:
A Structural Perspective 41
  Eaman Jahani, Guillaume Saint-Jacques, Pål Sundsøy,
  Johannes Bjelland, Esteban Moro, and Alex 'Sandy' Pentland

Poster Papers: Health and Behaviour

Stance Classification in Out-of-Domain Rumours: A Case Study
Around Mental Health Disorders 53
  Ahmet Aker, Arkaitz Zubiaga, Kalina Bontcheva, Anna Kolliakou,
  Rob Procter, and Maria Liakata

Predicting Multiple Risky Behaviors via Multimedia Content 65
  Yiheng Zhou, Jingyao Zhan, and Jiebo Luo

On the Role of Political Affiliation in Human Perception The Case
of Delhi OddEven Experiment 74
  Tahar Zanouda, Sofiane Abbar, Laure Berti-Equille, Kushal Shah,
  Abdelkader Baggag, Sanjay Chawla, and Jaideep Srivastava

Discovering the Typing Behaviour of Parkinson's Patients
Using Topic Models 89
  Antony Milne, Mihalis Nicolaou, and Katayoun Farrahi

Poster Papers: Network Science

Effects of Contact Network Models on Stochastic Epidemic Simulations   101
  Rehan Ahmad and Kevin S. Xu

From Relational Data to Graphs: Inferring Significant Links
Using Generalized Hypergeometric Ensembles   111
  *Giona Casiraghi, Vahan Nanumyan, Ingo Scholtes,
  and Frank Schweitzer*

DepthRank: Exploiting Temporality to Uncover Important Network Nodes. . .   121
  Nikolaos Bastas, Theodoros Semertzidis, and Petros Daras

Poster Papers: News, Misinformation, and Collective Sensemaking

On Early-Stage Debunking Rumors on Twitter: Leveraging
the Wisdom of Weak Learners   141
  Tu Ngoc Nguyen, Cheng Li, and Claudia Niederée

Convergence of Media Attention Across 129 Countries   159
  Jisun An, Hassan Aldarbesti, and Haewoon Kwak

Attention Please! Exploring Attention Management on Wikipedia
in the Context of the Ukrainian Crisis   169
  Jon Roozenbeek and Mariia Terentieva

I Read It on Reddit: Exploring the Role of Online Communities
in the 2016 US Elections News Cycle   192
  Jon Roozenbeek and Adrià Salvador Palau

How do eyewitness social media reports reflect socio-economic effects
of natural hazards?   221
  Nataliya Tkachenko, Rob Procter, and Stephen Jarvis

What Can Software Tell Us About Media Coverage and Public Opinion?
An Analysis of Political News Posts and Audience Comments
on Facebook by Computerised Method   230
  Yunya Song and Yin Zhang

Poster Papers: Opinions, Behavior, and Social Media Mining

GitHub and Stack Overflow: Analyzing Developer Interests Across
Multiple Social Collaborative Platforms   245
  Roy Ka-Wei Lee and David Lo

How Are Social Influencers Connected in Instagram?   257
  Seungbae Kim, Jinyoung Han, Seunghyun Yoo, and Mario Gerla

Affinity Groups: A Linguistic Analysis for Social Network
Groups Identification.. 265
  Jonathan Mendieta, Gabriela Baquerizo, Mónica Villavicencio,
  and Carmen Vaca

Deliberative Platform Design: The Case Study of the Online Discussions
in Decidim Barcelona 277
  Pablo Aragón, Andreas Kaltenbrunner, Antonio Calleja-López,
  Andrés Pereira, Arnau Monterde, Xabier E. Barandiaran,
  and Vicenç Gómez

Computational Controversy 288
  Benjamin Timmermans, Tobias Kuhn, Kaspar Beelen, and Lora Aroyo

Evaluative Patterns and Incentives in YouTube................. 301
  David Garcia, Adiya Abisheva, and Frank Schweitzer

Beyond the Culture Effect on Credibility Perception on Microblogs 316
  Suliman Aladhadh, Xiuzhen Zhang, and Mark Sanderson

Twigraph: Discovering and Visualizing Influential Words
Between Twitter Profiles 329
  Dhanasekar Sundararaman and Sudharshan Srinivasan

An Exploratory Study on the Influence of Guidelines
on Crowdfunding Projects in the Ethereum Blockchain Platform.......... 347
  Vanessa Bracamonte and Hitoshi Okada

Lost in Re-Election: A Tale of Two Spanish Online Campaigns 355
  Helena Gallego, David Laniado, Andreas Kaltenbrunner,
  Vicenç Gómez, and Pablo Aragón

Beyond Item Recommendation: Using Recommendations to Stimulate
Knowledge Sharing in Group Decisions........................ 368
  Müslüm Atas, Alexander Felfernig, Martin Stettinger,
  and Thi Ngoc Trang Tran

A Hierarchical Topic Modelling Approach for Tweet Clustering 378
  Bo Wang, Maria Liakata, Arkaitz Zubiaga, and Rob Procter

Combining Network and Language Indicators for Tracking
Conflict Intensity 391
  Anna Rumshisky, Mikhail Gronas, Peter Potash, Mikhail Dubov,
  Alexey Romanov, Saurabh Kulshreshtha, and Alex Gribov

Like Trainer, Like Bot? Inheritance of Bias in Algorithmic
Content Moderation.. 405
  Reuben Binns, Michael Veale, Max Van Kleek, and Nigel Shadbolt

Poster Papers: Proximity, Location, Mobility, and Urban Analytics

Modeling and Managing Airport Passenger Flow Under Uncertainty:
A Case of Fukuoka Airport in Japan   419
  Hiroaki Yamada, Kotaro Ohori, Tadashige Iwao, Akifumi Kira,
  Naoyuki Kamiyama, Hiroaki Yoshida, and Hirokazu Anai

When Internet Really Connects Across Space: Communities of Software
Developers in Vkontakte Social Networking Site   431
  Olessia Koltsova, Sergei Koltcov, and Yadviga Sinyavskaya

Inferring the Social-Connectedness of Locations from Mobility Data   443
  Tristan Brugman, Mitra Baratchi, Geert Heijenk, and Maarten van Steen

Towards Simulating Criminal Offender Movement Based on Insights
from Human Dynamics and Location-Based Social Networks   458
  Raquel Rosés Brüngger, Robin Bader, Cristina Kadar,
  and Irena Pletikosa

Poster Papers: Security, Privacy, and Trust

The Importance of Consent in User Comfort with Personalization   469
  Jennifer Golbeck

Nudging Nemo: Helping Users Control Linkability Across Social Networks . . .   477
  Rishabh Kaushal, Srishti Chandok, Paridhi Jain, Prateek Dewan,
  Nalin Gupta, and Ponnurangam Kumaraguru

Mediated Behavioural Change in Human-Machine Networks:
Exploring Network Characteristics, Trust and Motivation   491
  Paul Walland and J. Brian Pickering

Hunting Malicious Bots on Twitter: An Unsupervised Approach   501
  Zhouhan Chen, Rima S. Tanash, Richard Stoll,
  and Devika Subramanian

Poster Papers: Tools and Methods

Exploratory Analysis of Big Social Data Using MIC/MINE Statistics   513
  Piyawat Lertvittayakumjorn, Chao Wu, Yue Liu, Hong Mi, and Yike Guo

Exploring Emerging Topics in Social Informatics: An Online Real-Time
Tool for Keyword Co-Occurrence Analysis   527
  Florian Cech

Writer Profiling Without the Writer's Text   537
  David Jurgens, Yulia Tsvetkov, and Dan Jurafsky

Erratum to: Social Informatics E1
  Giovanni Luca Ciampaglia, Afra Mashhadi, and Taha Yasseri

Author Index   559

Economics, Science of Success, and Education

Simple Acoustic-Prosodic Models of Confidence and Likability are Associated with Long-Term Funding Outcomes for Entrepreneurs

Natalie A. Carlson[(✉)]

Columbia Business School, 3022 Broadway, New York, NY 10027, USA
ncarlson19@gsb.columbia.edu

Abstract. Entrepreneurship pitches are an increasingly common way for startup founders to attract the attention of potential investors, who may be swayed by style as well as content. This study examines whether vocal features can capture some of the perceived traits of entrepreneurs, and whether those perceptions are associated with long-term funding outcomes for the firm. Using 122 pitches from the TechCrunch Disrupt Startup Battlefield competition, I find that eventual funding amounts are significantly greater for those entrepreneurs who are perceived as more confident and less likable, and that these traits can be well modeled by features associated with the intensity (loudness) of their speech patterns.

Keywords: Speech · Paralinguistic analysis · Entrepreneurship · Perception

1 Introduction

In the increasingly glamorized world of technology entrepreneurship, much is made about the importance of the pitch: a short, pithy speech in which an aspiring entrepreneur attempts to sell his or her business to potential investors. While dramatized television shows such as *Shark Tank* may give the impression that pitching is not a fundamentally serious method of raising funds, pitch competitions remain a useful way for entrepreneurs to raise their profile and attract the attention of future investors. The 648 alumni of TechCrunch Disrupt's Startup Battlefield, for example, have to date raised an aggregate $6.9 billion in funding [17]. High-profile competitions like TechCrunch share pitch videos online, where they are preserved indefinitely and may ultimately be viewed by a much wider audience. This level of notoriety endows these short oral presentations with a significant level of pressure.

Prior research shows that even experienced investors are more influenced by presentational factors than they realize – relative to content – and that they tend to subsequently rationalize these decisions [4]. Because of this fact, elements of

N.A. Carlson—Many thanks to Michelle Levine, Sarah Ita Levitan, Bruce Kogut, Dan Wang, and Stephan Meier for their helpful comments on this manuscript.

G.L. Ciampaglia et al. (Eds.): SocInfo 2017, Part I, LNCS 10539, pp. 3–16, 2017.
DOI: 10.1007/978-3-319-67217-5_1

an entrepreneur's presentation style may be associated with long-term startup outcomes. This study investigates whether entrepreneurs' speaking style in pitch competitions, approximated by simple acoustic-prosodic features, can predict eventual funding outcomes for their companies.

1.1 Previous Research

This work is broadly related to the literature on the science of success and impression formation. Much of the prior work in this area focuses on facial appearance judgments. Gheorghiu et al. [6], for example, find that first impressions based on the appearance of scientists, and whether they match expectations of what "good scientists" look like, impact judgments of research quality. Similarly, Todorov et al. [16] show that one-second judgments of congressional candidates' competence from facial photographs are predictive of election outcomes. In a related and surprising finding, Castelli et al. [2] find that while perceived competence does predict election outcomes, perceived sociability as inferred from facial judgments is negatively associated with winning elections. Examining vocal impression formation, Surawski and Ossoff show that vocal attractiveness impacts perceptions of politicians' competence, trustworthiness and leadership ability [15].

Researchers have established that the process of evaluating an entrepreneur – even when the evaluator is knowledgeable and experienced – is not always as systematic as many would imagine. In Clark's study of business angels, he describes their decision-making as a "highly unsystematic, idiosyncratic, error-prone process", in stark contrast to the evidence-based system that investors would prefer [4]. As an extreme example, Pentland [9] showed that models based on observing the social skills of entrepreneurs at a party the night before a competition could predict the decisions made by judges the next day. About the pitches, Pentland noted: "they were listening to how excited the presenter was about the plan; they were not listening to the facts." For this reason, the body of work on assessing persuasiveness, charisma or likability from speech may be highly relevant to the context of pitch competitions.

Much of the literature on charisma, likability and persuasion blurs these constructs quite a bit. Signorello et al. [13] employ one of the more detailed theoretical models of charisma by breaking it down into several factors: pathos, ethos-benevolence, ethos-competence, ethos-dominance, and emotional induction. Using a 67-adjective charisma scale, they perform a factor analysis to discover that charisma actually appears to load onto three factors, which they term proactive-attracting, benevolent-competent, and authoritarian-threatening. They suggest that charismatic leaders will score highly on at least one of these factors.

Regardless of the difficulties entailed in definition and somewhat low inter-coder reliability, models attempting to automatically perceive charisma from text and speech perform reasonably well. Rosenberg and Hirschberg find that acoustic-prosodic features associated with charisma include standard measures of fundamental frequency – mean, standard deviation, max and min – as well as the speaking rate [11]. That is, those who speak faster, higher in their range, and with more variation in pitch are rated as more charismatic. This concurs with William Stolzman's "Elevator Rater" elevator pitch model, which finds that speaking rate explains a great deal of variation in the perceived persuasiveness of short pitches [14].

Closely related to charisma and persuasion is likability. There is a good amount of work attempting to classify likability based on speech, because this was a particular challenge introduced by INTERSPEECH in 2010. This proves to be a difficult problem, as once again human coders do not have especially high agreement on likability, but by treating it as a binary classification problem researchers are able to attain a reasonable level of accuracy [10]. Gonzalez and Anguera find they can achieve good performance with a model that uses only seven features, including speech active level, mean speech variance, and silent time per second [7].

There is also a body of literature on perceived passion, particularly with regard to entrepreneurship. Many investors have stated that they look for passion in entrepreneurs, and it is colloquially known as a driver of success [8]. It is not clear, however, that passion is necessarily that closely related to persuasiveness, charisma, or likability. In fact, several papers on perceived passion show that it is in fact not passion that predicts investors' decisions, but rather perceived preparedness on the part of the entrepreneur [1,3].

This study contributes to the literature by linking the problem of paralinguistic analysis – detecting personality and other traits from low-level vocal features – to real-world success outcomes. The results suggest a relationship between patterns of vocal intensity, perceptions of confidence and likability, and eventual funding amounts raised by entrepreneurs.

2   Data and Methods

The data consist of 122 pitches from five years of the TechCrunch Disrupt Startup Battlefield competition, including both New York and San Francisco editions. The format for the competition consists of a six-minute presentation followed by a question-and-answer session with the judges; this study examines only the pitch portion. Only solo-presented pitches were collected in order to isolate the impact of one particular speaker. Implicit is the assumption that person selected to give the pitch would continue to serve as the primary "face" of the company in any interactions with future investors.

Using public data sources such as Crunchbase, AngelList, and press releases, data was hand-collected on the number of funding rounds and total funding received as of February 2017. For 13 of the companies, there existed records of a funding round of undisclosed value. These unknown amounts are assumed to be relatively small, as larger funding rounds are typically announced so as to discourage investment in competing firms. Therefore, for the primary analysis, the value of these unknown funding rounds was imputed at the tenth percentile; however, the results are not sensitive to the level of imputation and persist when the unknown amounts are imputed as zero or at the median level of funding.

Using workers from Amazon's Mechanical Turk, the pitches were then assessed for a number of subjective traits. Workers were asked to rate on a one-to-five scale the extent to which they perceived the speaker as confident, likable, competent, physically attractive, and how viable they perceived the business to be. Each pitch was rated by an average of 10 to 11 workers, who were selected from an elite pool of Mechanical Turk workers to ensure high data quality. Inter-coder agreement was generally high, with an average standard deviation of less than one for each video-trait pair.

Finally, the audio was extracted from the videos and processed using OpenS-mile, an open-source feature extractor for audio files [5]. The loudness measures referenced in the tables refer to those specified in the 2010 INTERSPEECH Par-alinguistic Challenge; that is, "the loudness as the normalized intensity raised to a power of 0.3" [12]. The features are calculated using a smoothed mov-ing average. Due to the desire for interpretability and the concern for spurious correlations that might be present with such a small sample size, only a small selection of highly interpretable features were examined: fundamental frequency (pitch), loudness, speaking rate, and shimmer (an indicator of vocal roughness or hoarseness).

3   Results

Table 1 displays regressions of the log value of total funding to date on the per-ceived traits as evaluated by the workers on Mechanical Turk, controlling for gender, year and city of competition. Perceived confidence has a positive asso-ciation with eventual funding amount ($p = 0.06$), but this relationship becomes much stronger when perceived likability is added to the model. Because confi-dence and likability are positively correlated (with a Pearson coefficient of 0.55), it seems that once the common factor that explains both these traits is accounted for, those entrepreneurs who are perceived as more confident and less likable are significantly more successful in their eventual fundraising efforts. Interest-ingly, perceived competence, physical attractiveness, and the evaluations of the businesses' viability have no relationship with funding outcomes. These same patterns can be observed when modeling funding rounds to date, as shown in Appendix Table 6.

Further exploring the relationship between confidence and likability, Table 2 shows the funding outcomes regressed on the difference between these two values, and Fig. 1 plots the difference against the number of funding rounds raised by the entrepreneur to date. This simple confidence-likability difference, with most values falling between one and negative one, has a striking relationship with eventual funding outcomes. One possible explanation for the result is that those entrepreneurs who are perceived as relatively more confident and less likable are in fact more assertive, pushier, or more aggressive, which can be advantageous traits in the competitive world of venture financing, but this assertion is ripe for further exploration.

Table 1. Total funding to date regressed on perceived traits

	Dependent variable						
	Ln (total funding)						
	(1)	(2)	(3)	(4)	(5)	(6)	(7)
Confidence	1.84*					3.79***	3.76***
	(0.97)					(1.15)	(1.20)
Likability		−1.93				−5.28***	−5.39**
		(1.52)				(1.78)	(2.07)
Competence			0.63				1.30
			(1.48)				(1.65)
Attractiveness				−0.79			−0.50
				(0.89)			(0.97)
Business viability					0.20		−0.44
					(1.44)		(1.50)
Male	4.14***	4.20***	4.00***	3.73***	4.15***	4.20***	3.62**
	(1.28)	(1.29)	(1.36)	(1.39)	(1.31)	(1.24)	(1.43)
Constant	3.06	18.05***	7.99	13.33***	9.85*	15.69**	14.18*
	(4.58)	(6.35)	(6.47)	(3.91)	(5.47)	(6.14)	(7.68)
Year FE	Yes	Yes	Yes	Yes	Yes	Yes	Yes
Competition FE	Yes	Yes	Yes	Yes	Yes	Yes	Yes
Observations	122	122	122	122	122	122	122
R^2	0.19	0.18	0.17	0.17	0.16	0.25	0.26

Note: $^*p < 0.1$; $^{**}p < 0.05$; $^{***}p < 0.01$

Examining the relationship between these perceived traits and vocal features, the next part of the analysis regresses the confidence, likability, and confidence-likability difference scores on the set of acoustic-prosodic features extracted from the pitches. Appendix Table 7 displays the regressions with the full set of features, including speaking rate, shimmer, and fundamental frequency measures, but the most explanatory features for confidence and likability seem to be associated with vocal intensity, or loudness. Table 3 regresses the perceived traits on just two features, the mean and standard deviation of loudness, along with the standard set of controls. Those who are louder on average are perceived to be more confident *and* more likable, while those with higher *variation* in loudness are perceived to be significantly less likable. Greater variance in the loudness of the voice has the effect of a punchier, more energetic, more forceful sound, which may be driving this effect.

Table 4 regresses the total funding amount on the predicted values from Table 3, effectively employing the loudness measures as instrumental variables for perceived confidence and likability. Similar patterns can be observed for predicted confidence, predicted likability, and the predicted difference between the

Table 2. Funding outcomes regressed on confident-likable difference

	Dependent variable			
	Ln (total funding)		Funding rounds	
	OLS		*Poisson*	
	(1)	(2)	(3)	(4)
Confident - likable	3.30***	3.38***	0.48***	0.47***
	(1.20)	(1.24)	(0.18)	(0.18)
Competence		0.18		0.09
		(1.54)		(0.21)
Attractiveness		−0.94		−0.09
		(0.89)		(0.12)
Business viability		−0.31		0.03
		(1.45)		(0.19)
Male	4.06***	3.51**	0.51***	0.44**
	(1.26)	(1.46)	(0.19)	(0.21)
Constant	10.20***	13.88*	0.71**	0.54
	(2.25)	(7.66)	(0.28)	(1.03)
Year FE	Yes	Yes	Yes	Yes
Competition FE	Yes	Yes	Yes	Yes
Observations	122	122	122	122
R^2	0.22	0.23		
Akaike inf. crit.			415.51	420.91

Note: *p < 0.1; **p < 0.05; ***p < 0.01

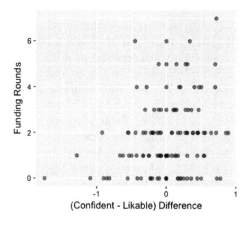

Fig. 1. Confident-likable difference and funding rounds

Table 3. First stage regressions modeling confidence and likability with loudness features

	Dependent variable		
	Confidence	Likability	Conf.-like. diff.
	(1)	(2)	(3)
Loudness std. dev.	−2.66	−4.44***	2.04
	(2.26)	(1.46)	(1.86)
Loudness mean	3.55**	3.44***	−0.40
	(1.54)	(1.00)	(1.27)
Male	0.02	0.04	0.02
	(0.12)	(0.08)	(0.10)
Constant	3.19***	3.79***	−0.49
	(0.39)	(0.25)	(0.32)
Year FE	Yes	Yes	Yes
Competition FE	Yes	Yes	Yes
Observations	122	122	122
R^2	0.13	0.12	0.10

Note: *p < 0.1; **p < 0.05; ***p < 0.01

two values, to those observed when modeling the perceived measures directly. These effects continue to hold when accounting for the other perceived traits (competence, attractiveness, business viability). The results suggest that confidence and likability may be reasonably well modeled by using these simple vocal features.

Notably, significant direct effects of the standard deviation in loudness can be observed on both funding outcomes. Table 5 shows the total funding and funding rounds regressed on the two loudness features along with controls (Appendix Table 8 displays the full set of acoustic-prosodic features). Controlling for average loudness, the variance in loudness has a strong positive relationship with funding raised. Figure 2 plots this relationship among the subset of entrepreneurs who received any funding amount. The magnitude of the funding effect is quite large. To illustrate, the median value for loudness standard deviation is 0.21; those below the median on this feature raised an eventual average of approximately $4.1 million, while those above the median eventually raised an average of $17.8 million.

Table 4. Second stage regressions with predicted values from acoustic-prosodic features

	Dependent variable							
	Ln (total funding)				Funding rounds			
	OLS				Poisson			
	(1)	(2)	(3)	(4)	(5)	(6)	(7)	(8)
Predicted confidence	11.01**	10.81**			0.98	1.11*		
	(4.63)	(4.76)			(0.62)	(0.63)		
Predicted likable	−19.11***	−19.33**			−2.29**	−2.63***		
	(7.23)	(7.50)			(0.90)	(0.95)		
Predicted (confident - likable)			13.97**	13.59**			1.34*	1.43*
			(5.88)	(6.04)			(0.78)	(0.80)
Competence		0.39		0.35		0.08		0.08
		(1.55)		(1.55)		(0.21)		(0.21)
Attractiveness		−0.66		−0.71		−0.05		−0.08
		(0.90)		(0.90)		(0.12)		(0.12)
Business viability		0.81		0.41		0.26		0.15
		(1.49)		(1.47)		(0.21)		(0.19)
Male	4.32***	3.76**	3.70***	3.17**	0.52***	0.45**	0.47**	0.40*
	(1.27)	(1.47)	(1.29)	(1.47)	(0.19)	(0.21)	(0.19)	(0.21)
Constant	40.15**	39.82**	9.11***	8.84	5.64**	5.37**	0.60**	0.01
	(18.83)	(19.64)	(2.35)	(7.59)	(2.30)	(2.39)	(0.30)	(1.03)
Year FE	Yes	Yes	Yes	Yes	Yes	Yes	Yes	Yes
Competition FE	Yes	Yes	Yes	Yes	Yes	Yes	Yes	Yes
Observations	122	122	122	122	122	122	122	122
R^2	0.22	0.22	0.20	0.21				
Akaike inf. crit.					418.22	422.16	419.85	424.70

Note: *p < 0.1; **p < 0.05; ***p < 0.01

A great deal of further exploration is required to explain the relationships observed in this data sample, but the results suggest that perceived traits of entrepreneurs as observed in oral pitches may explain a great deal of variation in future outcomes for those entrepreneurs' firms, and that these traits can be modeled well by using a simple set of acoustic-prosodic features extracted from the vocal audio.

Table 5. Funding outcomes regressed on loudness features

	Dependent variable:			
	Ln (total funding)		Funding rounds	
	OLS		Poisson	
	(1)	(2)	(3)	(4)
Loudness std. dev.	19.22**	55.63**	1.66	7.57**
	(8.89)	(24.25)	(1.19)	(2.95)
Loudness mean		−26.68		−4.40**
		(16.55)		(2.04)
Male	4.00***	3.82***	0.51***	0.46**
	(1.28)	(1.28)	(0.19)	(0.19)
Constant	2.88	2.93	0.08	0.10
	(4.21)	(4.18)	(0.57)	(0.57)
Year FE	Yes	Yes	Yes	Yes
Competition FE	Yes	Yes	Yes	Yes
Observations	122	122	122	122
R^2	0.20	0.22		
Akaike inf. crit.			420.83	418.22

Note: $^*p < 0.1$; $^{**}p < 0.05$; $^{***}p < 0.01$

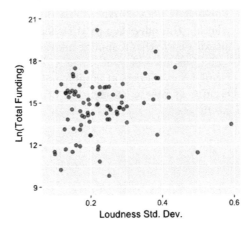

Fig. 2. Loudness std. dev. plotted against total funding for funded entrepreneurs

4   Conclusion and Future Work

It is impossible to draw causal conclusions from the associations discussed in this paper – for example, the perceived traits measured here might correspond to actual dispositional traits of the entrepreneurs, which are driving the effects observed on long-term outcomes, or they may simply relate to the way that entrepreneurs are perceived by investors. Similarly, the acoustic-prosodic features may be associated with other features – body language or facial expressions, for example – that are actually driving the trait perceptions, rather than necessarily being the direct cause. Furthermore, the quality of the business or idea itself is unobserved, and this may be associated with the confidence levels of the entrepreneur. However, the fact that these strong relationships exist and appear to be quite predictive of funding outcomes in this sample is notable, and worthy of further exploration.

It is also worth noting that it is difficult to talk about technology and entrepreneurship without making any reference to gender. An astute reader will have noted from the tables that the men in the sample raised significantly more funding than the women. The effects observed here on confidence, likability, and loudness appear to persist for both genders, but it is difficult to draw conclusions, as only 27 of the 122 entrepreneurs in the sample were female. Fortunately, the variance in loudness measure has no correlation with gender, unlike other vocal features such as pitch. Future work will hopefully further explore the way that these relationships interact with gender, particularly when it is so highly relevant to the context and is of acute interest to both academics and practitioners.

The interaction between perceived confidence and likability represents a puzzle that can hopefully be further explored in other relevant contexts. Given that being likable is nearly universally considered to be a positive trait, it would be interesting to examine whether this effect is a peculiar feature of this highly competitive, high-profile context, or whether a similar interaction can be observed in other entrepreneurship- and business-relevant settings. Ideally, the relationships displayed in this study can be examined in similar entrepreneurship competitions to TechCrunch Disrupt, as well as explored in other populations, such as among high-visibility executives.

Appendix

See Fig. 3.

Table 6. Funding rounds to date regressed on perceived traits

	Dependent variable						
	Funding rounds						
	(1)	(2)	(3)	(4)	(5)	(6)	(7)
Confidence	0.17					0.37**	0.37**
	(0.13)					(0.16)	(0.16)
Likability		−0.19				−0.50**	−0.59**
		(0.18)				(0.23)	(0.27)
Competence			0.09				0.26
			(0.20)				(0.23)
Attractiveness				−0.06			−0.05
				(0.11)			(0.13)
Business viability					0.10		
					(0.19)		
Male	0.53***	0.54***	0.51**	0.50**	0.52***	0.54***	0.44**
	(0.19)	(0.19)	(0.20)	(0.20)	(0.19)	(0.19)	(0.21)
Constant	0.10	1.51**	0.39	0.98**	0.43	1.23	0.52
	(0.61)	(0.77)	(0.87)	(0.49)	(0.71)	(0.79)	(0.96)
Year FE	Yes	Yes	Yes	Yes	Yes	Yes	Yes
Competition FE	Yes	Yes	Yes	Yes	Yes	Yes	No
Observations	122	122	122	122	122	122	122
Akaike inf. crit.	421.18	421.71	422.53	422.49	422.47	418.43	419.73

Note: *p $<$ 0.1; **p $<$ 0.05; ***p $<$ 0.01

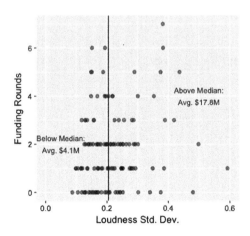

Fig. 3. Loudness std. dev. plotted against funding rounds

Table 7. Modeling confidence and likability with acoustic-prosodic features

	Dependent variable		
	Confidence	Likability	Conf.-like. diff.
	(1)	(2)	(3)
Loudness std. dev.	−3.74	−4.84***	1.27
	(2.35)	(1.53)	(1.95)
Loudness mean	4.35***	3.65***	0.32
	(1.59)	(1.03)	(1.31)
Speaking rate	0.03	−0.01	0.07
	(0.07)	(0.05)	(0.06)
Vocal shimmer mean	1.65	2.52	−1.57
	(3.07)	(1.99)	(2.54)
Pitch Mean	0.01	0.01*	−0.0000
	(0.005)	(0.003)	(0.004)
Pitch Std. Dev	0.99	0.45	0.54
	(1.03)	(0.67)	(0.85)
Pitch Mean x Male	0.01	0.0004	0.01**
	(0.01)	(0.005)	(0.01)
Pitch std. dev. x Male	−0.0004	−0.002	0.001
	(0.01)	(0.004)	(0.004)
Male	−0.01	0.002	−0.01
	(0.01)	(0.01)	(0.01)
Constant	0.64	2.32**	−1.52
	(1.49)	(0.97)	(1.23)
Year FE	Yes	Yes	Yes
Competition FE	Yes	Yes	Yes
Observations	122	122	122
R^2	0.20	0.18	0.16

Note: *p < 0.1; **p < 0.05; ***p < 0.01

Table 8. Full set of acoustic-prosodic features and funding outcomes

	Dependent variable	
	Ln (total funding)	Funding rounds
	OLS	*Poisson*
	(1)	(2)
Loudness std. dev.	67.15**	8.82***
	(25.69)	(3.26)
Loudness mean	−33.98*	−4.89**
	(17.32)	(2.19)
Speaking rate	−1.46*	−0.09
	(0.77)	(0.10)
Vocal shimmer mean	−1.02	4.88
	(33.49)	(4.30)
Pitch mean	0.01	0.02**
	(0.05)	(0.01)
Pitch std. dev.	16.24	5.12***
	(11.27)	(1.84)
Pitch mean × male	0.06	0.02
	(0.08)	(0.01)
Pitch std. dev. × male	−0.05	−0.02*
	(0.06)	(0.01)
Male	−0.04	−0.01
	(0.11)	(0.02)
Constant	4.50	−5.39**
	(16.26)	(2.39)
Year FE	Yes	Yes
Competition FE	Yes	Yes
Observations	122	122
R^2	0.25	
Akaike inf. crit.		419.71

Note: *p < 0.1; **p < 0.05; ***p < 0.01

References

1. Cardon, M.S., Sudek, R., Mitteness, C.: The impact of perceived entrepreneurial passion on angel investing. Front. Entrep. Res. **29**(2), 1 (2009)
2. Castelli, L., Carraro, L., Ghitti, C., Pastore, M.: The effects of perceived competence and sociability on electoral outcomes. J. Exp. Soc. Psychol. **45**(5), 1152–1155 (2009)
3. Chen, X.-P., Yao, X., Kotha, S.: Entrepreneur passion and preparedness in business plan presentations: a persuasion analysis of venture capitalists' funding decisions. Acad. Manag. J. **52**(1), 199–214 (2009)
4. Clark, C.: The impact of entrepreneurs' oral pitch presentation skills on business angels' initial screening investment decisions. Venture Cap. **10**(3), 257–279 (2008)
5. Eyben, F., Wollmer, M., Schuller, B.: Opensmile: the Munich versatile and fast open-source audio feature extractor. In: Proceedings of 18th ACM International Conference on Multimedia (2010)
6. Gheorghiu, A.I., Callan, M.J., Skylark, W.J.: Facial appearance affects science communication. In: Proceedings of National Academy of Sciences, 201620542 (2017)
7. Gonzalez, S., Anguera, X.: Perceptually inspired features for speaker likability classification. In: ICASSP (2013)
8. Jourdan Jr., L.F.: The relationship of investor decisions and entrepreneurs' dispositional and interpersonal factors. Entrep. Exec. **17**, 49 (2012)
9. Pentland, A.: We can measure the power of charisma. Harv. Bus. Rev. **88**, 34–35 (2009)
10. Pohjalainen, J., Rasanen, O., Kadioglu, S.: Feature selection methods and their combinations in high-dimensional classification of speaker likability, intelligibility and personality traits. Comput. Speech Lang. **29**, 145–171 (2015)
11. Rosenberg, A., Hirschberg, J.: Charisma perception from text and speech. Speech Commun. **51**, 640–655 (2009)
12. Schuller, B.W., Steidl, S., Batliner, A., Burkhardt, F., Devillers, L., Muller, C.A., Narayanan, S.S.: The INTERSPEECH 2010 paralinguistic challenge. In: INTERSPEECH (2010)
13. Signorello, R., D'Errico, F., Poggi, I., Demolin, D.: A multidimensional approach. In: Privacy, Security, Risk and Trust (PASSAT), 2012 International Conference on and 2012 International Conference on Social Computing (SocialCom) (2012)
14. Stolzman, W.T.: Toward a social signaling framework: activity and emphasis in speech. Dissertation, Massachusetts Institute of Technology (2006)
15. Surawski, M.K., Ossoff, E.P.: The effects of physical and vocal attractiveness on impression formation of politicians. Curr. Psychol. **25**(1), 15–27 (2006)
16. Todorov, A., Mandisodza, A.N., Goren, A., Hall, C.C.: Inferences of competence from faces predict election outcomes. Science **308**(5728), 1623–1626 (2005)
17. TechCrunch: About Startup Battlefield (2017). https://techcrunch.com/startup-battlefield/about/

ABCE: A Python Library for Economic Agent-Based Modeling

Davoud Taghawi-Nejad[1,2]([⊠]), Rudy H. Tanin[4,5], R. Maria Del Rio Chanona[1,2], Adrián Carro[1,2], J. Doyne Farmer[1,2,3], Torsten Heinrich[1,2], Juan Sabuco[1,2], and Mika J. Straka[1,6]

[1] Institute for New Economic Thinking at the Oxford Martin School, University of Oxford, Oxford OX2 6ED, UK
davoud@taghawi-nejad.de, {davoud.taghawinejad,rita.delriochanona, adrian.carro,doyne.farmer,torsten.heinrich}@maths.ox.ac.uk
[2] Mathematical Institute, University of Oxford, Oxford OX1 3LP, UK
[3] Santa-Fe Institute, Santa Fe, NM 87501, USA
[4] Department of Physics, MIT, Cambridge 02139, USA
rht@mit.edu
[5] Independent Scholar, Tallinn, Estonia
[6] IMT School for Advanced Studies Lucca, 55100 Lucca, Italy
mika.straka@imtlucca.it

Abstract. The rise of computational power makes agent-based modelling a viable option for models capturing the complex nature of an economy. However, the coding implementation can be tedious. Because of this, we introduce ABCE, the Agent-Based Computational Economics library. ABCE is an agent-based modeling library for Python that is specifically tailored for economic phenomena. With ABCE the modeler specifies the decision logic of the agents, the order of actions, the goods and their physical transformation (the production and the consumption functions). Then, ABCE automatically handles the actions, such as production and consumption, trade and agent interaction. The result is a program where the source code consists of only economically meaningful commands (e.g. decisions, buy, sell, produce, consume, contract, etc.). ABCE scales on multi-core computers, without the intervention of the modeler. The model can be packaged into a nice web application or run in a Jupyter notebook.

Keywords: Agent-based models · Agent-based macroeconomics · Python · Economic simulation · Computational economics · Computational techniques · Simulation modeling

1 Introduction

An economy is a complex system where the interaction of heterogeneous agents plays a crucial role. However, current economic models used by academics, the

D. Taghawi-Nejad—This author gratefully acknowledge the financial support from MS AMLIN plc, London.

G.L. Ciampaglia et al. (Eds.): SocInfo 2017, Part I, LNCS 10539, pp. 17–30, 2017.
DOI: 10.1007/978-3-319-67217-5_2

central banks and policy makers fail to acknowledge its complexity and are either based on empirical statistical models fitted to past data (econometrics) or assume a perfect world (DSGE) and by their very nature rule out crisis [4]. Agent-based models (ABM) can take into account of this complexity since they are expressive computer simulations of heterogeneous agents which interact across different spatial and temporal scales according to predefined rules. When modeling an economy, agents represent firms, households, banks and other important entities that define the systems dynamic.

In social sciences and in particular in economics where designing replicable experiments is usually impossible, agent-based models present an opportunity for policy testing. To give true insights on economic phenomena, a large number of heterogeneous agents and often stock-flow consistency[1] are crucial. Here we introduce the Agent-Based Computational Economics library (ABCE) a Python library with the computational efficiency needed for state of the art ABM's. ABCE has been continuously been updated and extended for 6 years after its conceptual framework was unveiled in Taghawi-Nejad (2013) [13].

While Taghawi-Nejad (2013) [13] discusses the theory that agent-based modeling is a language to express economic phenomena as dynamical processes, this paper gives a practical overview over how and why to use ABCE. It also incorporates the many updates that have been introduced in ABCE.

ABCE[2] is a Python-based modeling platform for economic simulations and part of the Economic Simulation Library[3]. For simulations of trade, production and consumption, ABCE comes with standard functions that implement these kinds of interactions and actions. The modeler only implements the decision logic of an agent, then ABCE takes care of all exchange of goods and production and consumption. Furthermore it can also handle contracts and even generate balance sheets.

One feature of ABCE is that goods have the physical properties of goods in reality. That means that, if agent A gives a good to agent B, then - unlike information - agent B receives the good and agent B does not have the good anymore. The library handles trade production and consumption of goods according to the decision of the agents.

The audience of ABCE are economists, computer scientists, mathematicians, scientists conducting interdisciplinary research, and people of similar areas that want to create agent-based models involving trade, production or contracts. Simulations can be similar to standard economic models such as general or partial equilibrium models, but allow the assumptions to be relaxed to the extent of removing equilibrium. Current development efforts will make it possible to automatically handle contracts, contractual obligations and balance-sheets. ABCE uses Python - a language that is especially beginner friendly, but also easy to learn for people who know object oriented programming languages such as Java,

---

[1] Meaning that goods and money are not created "out of thin air". ABCE is stock flow consistent, if the stock-flow consistency is not explicitly broken.

[2] https://abce.readthedocs.io.

[3] https://economicsl.github.io.

C++ or MATLAB. Syntactically, Python code looks like executable pseudo code [11]. Moreover, in science, code is meant to be read, verified, and reused by other scientists, so we decide to cut down the development time and the time required to comprehend our code rather than execution time. Where speed is relevant, ABCE's back-end is written in C via Cython.

2   Design

ABCE's main design goal is that code can be rapidly written to enable a modeler to quickly write down code and quickly explore different alternatives of a model. In Python, variables do not have to be declared, garbage does not have to be collected and classes have no boiler-plate code. Another advantage of Python that facilitates rapid coding is its rich environment of libraries. For example, Mesa enables representation of agents in a spatial world. Installation of packages is much simpler in Python than in Java, C, or C++.

Execution speed is a secondary concern to the goal of rapid development. Execution speed is increased by making use of multiple-cores/processors and using C (via Cython) for backend tasks. For the user, the library is a pure python library, with the C back-end completely hidden from the user. Although Python is slower than Java or C in terms of execution speed, this disadvantage can be largely overcome by using various optimized packages for numerical calculations, such as NumPy [15] and SciPy [5], which make use of back-end implementations in C. ABCE allows to parallelize the code and gain significant speed advantage over single-threaded code.

Thirdly the design is giving full modelling liberty to the programmer. This is done by not implementing any economic assumptions in the simulation engine of the library. Depending on the use case, a user may decide to not use the pre-defined agents in the library, and may instead define new agents from scratch without restrictions. While ABCE provides stock methods such as trade, consume and produce, it does not force specific economic assumptions.

There are predefined agents (Agent, Firm or Household) which are Python classes that can be inherited from. This will allow the modeler to concentrate on defining the behaviour of the agents and the specification of goods, production/consumption functions. ABCE automatically handles the communication, trade and consumption of goods.

ABCE agents are ordinary Python objects, but they can be run parallel on a multi-core/processor computer without further configuration or intervention. The parallel execution of agents is the only non-standard feature of ABCE, which bypasses Pythons global interpreter lock (GIL). The speed advantages of the parallelization are observed when running simulations involving 10000 agents or more.

A simulation run in ABCE is a sequence of rounds, with sub-rounds in which agents execute actions in parallel. Each agent executes these actions possibly using some of the built-in functions, such as messaging, trade, production and consumption of ABCE. As agents communicate only between sub-rounds, all actions within one sub-round are executed as if they were executed in parallel. It is also possible to run a simulation as a discrete event simulation, where events are scheduled at particular times.

2.1 Physical Goods

Physical goods are at the heart of most economic models. The core feature and main difference to other ABM platforms is the implementation of physical goods. In contrast to information or messages, sharing a good means having less of it. If agent A transfers a good to agent B then agent A does not have this good anymore. One of the major strength of ABCE is that this is automatically handled.

In ABCE goods can be created, destroyed, traded, given or changed through production and consumption. All these functions are implemented in ABCE and can be inherited by an agent. These functions are automatically handled by ABCE upon decision from the modeler.

Every agent in ABCE must inherit from the abce.Agent class. This gives the agent a couple of stock methods: create, destroy, trade, and give. Create and destroy create or destroy a good immediately. Because trade and give involve a form of interaction between the agents, they are run over several sub-rounds. Selling of a good for example works as follow:

– subround 1: the first agent offers the goods
  post-subround ABCE handler: the good is automatically subtracted from the agents possessions, to avoid double selling
– subround 2: the counter agent receives the offer. The agent can
  • accept: the goods are added to the counter parts possessions. Money is subtracted
  • reject (or equivalently ignore): nothing happens in this sub-round
  • partially accept the offer: the partial amount of goods is added to the counter parts possessions. Money is subtracted
– subround 3: in case of
  • acceptance, the money is credited
  • rejection the original good is re-credited
  • partial acceptance the money is credited and the unsold part of the good is re-credited

Objects have a special stance in agent-based modeling:

– objects can be recovered (resources)
– exchanged (trade)
– transformed (production)
– consumed
– destroyed and depreciate over time

ABCE takes care of trade, production/transformation and consumption of goods automatically. Good categories can also be made to perish or yield another good. E.g. a field can grow crops and an oilfield oil. The modeler has only to decide on the when and how.

2.2   Services or Labor

We can model services and labor as goods that perish and that are replenished every round. This would amount to a worker that can sell one unit of labor every round, that disappears if not used.

Let us assume for the sake of the argument that we want to simulate actions that happen in real life in parallel, but we can only run agents sequentially in the simulation. Since these actions happen in parallel we know they (a) start with the same information set and (b) cannot affect each other. This has two implications: they must start with the same information set and the effects on the other agents must happen after they have all finished, i.e. the information set can only be updated after all agents actions have been executed.

Generally speaking, multithreading and parallel execution have to cope with the problem that actions do not necessarily finish at the same time, which has to be considered when updating the information set.

To address this issue, in ABCE time is discrete and actions happen in lock-step. Temporal events consist of rounds and sub-rounds. Rounds correspond to real-time intervals, e.g. days. In each subround all agents execute the same action. So for example in overnight-loans:

– subround 1: banks send a request for overnight loans
  post-subround ABCE handler: messages are delivered
– subround 2: banks receive requests and process them
  post-subround ABCE handler: messages and payments are delivered
– subround 3: money has arrived, banks can make new requests if they still need money
– ...

In conclusion, time in ABCE is discrete and actions that happen in the same subround do not causally affect each other. Communication happens only between the sub-rounds simulating simultaneity of the actions in one subround.

For example, a sales transaction is handled in the following way:

The transfer of goods between agents and its consistency is handled by ABCE. In other words, if a good is sent, it gets subtracted from one agent and added to the other. However, ABCE also ensures that objects cannot be transferred twice: if an agent gives an object to another agent it is immediately taken from his possessions and credited only in the next round. In case of a sale offer, or analogously a purchase offer, the good gets committed to the sale as soon as the offer is made.

The game tree is as follows

– subround 1: Agent A offers the good:
    self . sell ('receiver', receiver_id, 'good', quantity, price)
    post-subround ABCE handler: the quantity of the good is subtracted from his possessions immediately
– either of

- subround 2a: Agent B accepts self . accept (offer)
      post-subround ABCE handler: the money is subtracted immediately,
      then the good is added immediately
- subround 3a: (pre-subround ABCE handler) the money is added to Agent
  A's possessions
- ...

or

- subround 2b: Agent B rejects self . reject (offer)

- subround 3b: (pre-round ABCE handler) the good is refunded
- ...

2.3   Closed Economy

Imposing that goods can only be transformed, but neither created nor destroyed, amounts to modeling a physically closed economy, which is stock and flow consistent. In ABCE this can be achieved by calling the respective creation/destruction functions for goods, money, etc. only in the initialization phase.

3   Difference to Other Agent-Based Modeling Frameworks

We identified several survey articles as well as a quite complete overview of agent-based modeling software on Wikipedia [1,7,10,12,14,16]. The articles Tools of the Trade by Madey and Nikolai [7] and Survey of Agent Based Modelling and Simulation Tools by Allan [1] attempt to give a complete overview of agent-based modelling platforms/frameworks. The Madey and Nikolai paper categorizes the ABM-platforms according to several categories (Programming Language, Type of License, Operating System and Domain). According to this article, there is only one software platform which aims at the specific domain of economics: JASA. JASA aims specifically at auctions. Wikipedia [16] lists JAMEL as an economic platform JAMEL is closed source and an non-programming platform. The Survey of Agent Based Modelling and Simulation Tools by Allan [1] draws our attention to LSD, which follows a dynamical systems approach rather than an agent-based modeling platform.

While the formerly mentioned papers on modeling platforms aim to give a complete overview, Evaluation of free Java - libraries for social scientific agent based simulation by Tobias and Hoffman [14] chooses to concentrate on a smaller number of simulation packages. Tobias and Hoffman analyze: RePast, Swarm, Quicksilver, and VSEit. We will follow this approach and concentrate on a subset of ABM models. First as economics is a subset of social science we dismiss all platforms that are not explicitly targeted at social science. The list of social science platforms according to [7] Madey and Nikolai is: AgentSheets, LSD, FAMOJA, MAML, MAS-SOC, MIMOSE, NetLogo, Repast SimBioSys, StarLogo, StarLogoT, StarLogo TNG, Sugarscape, VSEit NetLogo and Moduleco.

We dismiss some of these frameworks/platforms from our analysis: AgentSheets, because it is closed source and not programmable. LSD, because it uses dynamical systems approach rather than an agent-based modeling environment. MAML, because it does not use a standard programming language, but it is its own. MAS-SOC, because we could not find it in the internet and its documentation according to [1] is sparse. MIMOSE, an interesting language, but we will not analyze as it is based on a completely different programming paradigm, i.e., functional programming, as opposed to object-oriented programming. SimBioSys, because it has, according to Allan [1] and our research, a sparse documentation. StarLogo, StarLogoT, StarLogo TNG, because they have been superseded by NetLogo Moduleco, because it has, according to Allan [1] and our research, a sparse documentation. Furthermore, it has not been updated since roughly 2001.

We will concentrate on the most widely used ABM frameworks/platforms: MASON, NetLogo, Repast.

4   General Differences to Other Agent-Based Modeling Platforms

First of all ABCE is specifically designed for economic problems. It provides the basic functions such as production, consumption, trade and communication as fully automated stock methods. Because any kind of agent interaction (communication and exchange of goods) is handled automatically by ABCE, it can run the agents (virtually) parallel and run simulations on multi-core/processor systems without any intervention by the modeler.

The second biggest difference between ABCE and other platforms is that ABCE introduces the physical good as an ontological object in the simulation. Goods can be exchanged and transformed. ABCE handles these processes automatically, so that for the model a physical good behaves like a physical good and not like a message.

Thirdly, ABCE is just a scheduler that schedules the actions of the agents and a Python class that enables the agent to produce, consume, trade and communicate. A model written in ABCE, is therefore standard Python code and the modeler can make use of the complete Python language and the Python language environment.

Fourthly, many frameworks such as FLAME, NetLogo, StarLogo, Ascape and SugarScape and, in a more limited sense, Repast are designed with spatial representation in mind. For ABCE, a spatial representation is possible, but not a design goal. Since agents in ABCE are ordinary Python objects, they can use Python modules such as Mesa and therefore gain a spatial representation much like NetLogo. This does not mean that ABCE could not be a good choice for a problem where the spatial position plays a role. Particularly if the model has different transport costs or other properties according to the geographical position of the agents, but the agents do not move or the movement does not have to be represented graphically, ABCE could still be a good choice.

5   Comparison to Other Agent-Based Modeling Platforms

5.1   MASON

MASON is a single-threaded discrete event platform that is intended for simulations of social, biological and economical systems. [6]. Mason is a platform that was explicitly designed with the goal of running it on large platforms. MASON distributes a large number of single threaded simulations over different computers or processors. ABCE on the other hand is multi-threaded it allows to run agents in parallel. A single run of a simulation in MASON is therefore not faster on a computing cluster than on a potent single-processor computer. ABCE on the other hand uses the full capacity of multi-core/processor systems for a single simulation run. The fast execution of a model in ABCE allows a different software development process, modelers can 'try their models while they are developing and adjust the code until it works as desired. The different nature of both platforms make it necessary to implement a different event scheduling system. MASON is a discrete event platform. Events can be scheduled by the agents. ABCE on the other hand is scheduled - it has global list of sub-rounds that establish the sequence of actions in every round. Each of these sub-rounds lets a number of agents execute the same actions in parallel. However ABCE also supports discrete event scheduling. MASON, like Repast Java is based on Java, while ABCE is based on Python.

5.2   NetLogo

Netlogo is a multi-agent special purpose programming language that integrates with Java. It can, if required, be supplemented with Java code and is run in a Java VM. First released in 1999, NetLogo dates back to the early days of agent-based modeling and is widely advertised for its ease of use and appeal to scholars without prior programming experience. This, however, comes at a price: As Netlogo is an interpreted language running on top of a Java implementation, performance and speed of NetLogo simulations are impeded. Further, NetLogo is heavily centered on visualization and spatial structure, even if the spatial structure does not have a useful interpretation for the use case at hand.

In contrast to Netlogo, ABCE is not a special purpose language but a library that can directly be included from programs written in the general purpose language Python. It also places much fewer restrictions on the modelers modelling decisions and will, for instance, not enforce the use of spatial (or any other) structures. That said, NetLogo-style spatial simulations can be implemented in an ABCE simulation by using Mesa.

5.3   Repast

Repast is a modeling environment for social science. It was originally conceived as a Java rewrite of SWARM. [3,8] Repast has API in several flavors: Java, .Net, and a Python-like language. Repast has been superseded by Repast Simphony which maintains all functionality, but is limited to Java. Repast Simphony has a point and click interface for simple models. :raw-tex:citeNORTH2005a Repast supports static and dynamic scheduling. [3] Repast is vast, which contains 210 classes in 9 packages :raw-tex'citeCollier'. ABCE, thanks to its limited scope and Python, has only 8 classes visible to the modeler in a single package.

5.4   JABM, JMAB and Special Purpose ABM Tools

Recent years have seen the emergence of a variety of other ABM platforms and tools. One of them is the Java Macro Agent-Based (JMAB) toolkit, which is explicitly designed for building stock-flow consistent Macroeconomic ABM [2]. As such, it limits the modelers possibilities by design, precluding for instance micro-level models that do not presume to fully represent the entirety of an economy, but also inter-disciplinary approaches that place their focus on a field other than economics. The JMAB toolkit is, in turn, based on the Java Agent-Based Modelling (JABM) toolkit, another ABM library. Both JMAB and JABM run on Java and concentrate significant parts of their design on dependency injection: Experiments can be defined by the modeler in a configuration file and run without having to touch any Java code. [9] This creates desirable properties in terms of controlling consistency across experiments but may impede the flexibility of the modeler.

5.5   Mesa

Mesa is a modular ABM framework, with a goal to be Python 3-based alternative to NetLogo, Repast, or MASON. Its specific strength is the spatial representation of agent positions. Which is the same as in Netlogo. ABCE, on the other hand, is specifically built for economic modelling, has core components written in Cython, and has been optimized for parallel execution.

6   How to Write an Agent-Based Model in ABCE

The first step to make an ABM is to define the agents. ABCE provides the programmer with a predetermined set of benchmark agents and functions. However the main advantage of ABCE is that gives total flexibility for the modeler to define its own agents. Therefore we explain how an agent class must be defined.

The agent classes must inherit the base agent (abce.Agent) and possibly the firm (abce.Firm) or the household class (abce.Household). The base class gives agents the ability to interact with other agents. That includes amongst others the ability to send messages and trade. The firm and household classes give agents the ability to produce and consume. For firm and household agents the modeler has to specify the functional form of the production or consumption function in the __init__ method. Below we show an example where a firm is created with a money budget of 10 and produces "GOOD" with a Cobb-Douglas production function.

```
import abce

class Firm(abce.Agent, abce.Firm):
    def init(self, simulation_params, agent_params):
        """
        1. Gets an initial amount of money
        2. create a cobb_douglas function:
        GOOD = 1 * labor ** 1.
        """
        self.create('money', 10)
        self.set_cobb_douglas("GOOD", 1, {"labor": 1})
```

The simulation_parameters and agent_parameters must be given when the simulation is called, as we will explain further down below.

The modeler must also specify the agents decision logic. For every method of the agent class the modeler has to decide under which conditions agents, interact, trade, produce, consume, etc. or do other things. Its is instructive to consider the following code snippet: look on code for this:

```
# Agent 1
def sell_cookies(self):
    self.sell(buyer, 2, 'cookies', price=1, quantity=2.5)


# Agent 2
def buy_cookies(self):
    offers = self.get_offers('cookies')
    for offer in offers:
        if offer.price < 0.5:
            try:
                self.accept(offer)
            except NotEnoughGoods:
                self.accept(offer,
                           (self.possession('money') /
                           offer.price))
```

Amongst others agent 1 sends an offer of cookies to agent 2. The agent receives all offers of cookies. She can iterate over all offers and decide, which offers to accept and which not. Note that the interesting thing here is that the modeler only implements the decision logic, but the transactions are handled by ABCE in the background.

Once the agents have been defined, the simulation must be run in a start file. Here the simulation class is instantiated, which then builds the agents from the agent classes already defined as explained above. It is in this part that the simulation parameters and agent parameters are defined as shown in the code snipet below. The order of execution of agents action has to be specified, as well as goods and their properties, such as services or perishable, respectively.

Finally, we need to define which observables should be measured throughout the simulation.

```
parameters = {'name': '2x2',
              'random_seed': None,
              'rounds': 10}

@gui(parameters)
def main(parameters):
    w = Simulation(rounds=parameters['rounds'])
    w.declare_round_endowment(resource='adult', units=1,
            product='labor')
    w.declare_perishable(good='labor')

    w.panel('household', possessions=['money', 'GOOD'],
            variables=['current_utiliy'])
    w.panel('firm', possessions=['money', 'GOOD'])

    firms = w.build_agents(Firm, 'firm', 1)
    households = w.build_agents(Household, 'household', 1)
    for r in w.next_round():
        households.do('sell_labor')
        firms.do('buy_labor')
        firms.do('production')
        firms.do('panel')
        firms.do('sell_goods')
        households.do('buy_goods')
        households.do('panel')
        households.do('consumption')

if __name__ == '__main__':
    main(parameters)
```

The fact that ABCE is designed to be a library means that the same start.py file can use other Python libraries. For example we can use a calibration tool and a statistical package that runs the simulation repeatedly with different parameters to achieve a certain fit, read from a relational database to calibrate the agents, frame the agents to move around and gather resources in a 2D/3D mesh or a graph.

7   GUI and Database

ABCE has several ways of collecting data. For example, agents can log data directly to the database or the simulation can monitor variables and possessions of agents and log them collectively to the database. The database is used to generate graphs and can be used for further processing.

All data that has been collected can be automatically displayed on an interactive webpage. What is more the whole simulation can be packaged into a web-app. In this case, a menu can be displayed in the browser, from which simulation parameters can be chosen. A user can set the parameters, run the simulation, and observe the results directly in the browser. Past simulations remain accessible in the menu. Examples of simulations written in ABCE with interactive web interface can be accessed in https://www.taghawi-nejad.de/portfolio (Figs. 1 and 2).

Fig. 1. An interactive web interface for the simulation

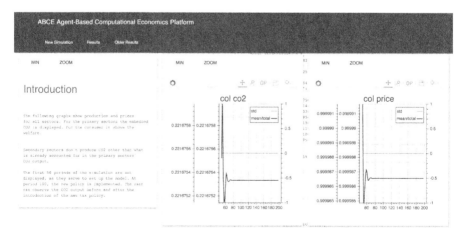

Fig. 2. A screenshot of an interactive exploration of the simulation as reflected in the graphs

8   Conclusion

ABCE is a modeling library that allows economic modelers to write agent-based models in a concise fashion. The modeler can concentrate on the decision logic of the model and does not have to deal with transactions between the agents or physical consistency. ABCE accelerates simulations from vanilla Python by providing core libraries in Cython and parallelizing computations on multi-core PCs. Moreover, ABCE collects statistics on observables defined by the user and makes them accessible in a nice web app interface, which provides an immediate representation of results. ABCE's documentation can be accessed in http://abce. readthedocs.io.

ABCE has been developed and used internally for the past 6 years. It is now our intention to open up the development to the community. For this purpose ABCE's source code is available at: https://github.com/DavoudTaghawiNejad/ abce. ABCE is licensed under the Apache License, Version 2.0, and can thus be used permissively for academic and commercial purposes.

References

1. Allan, R.: Survey of agent based modelling and simulation tools. Technical report, October 2010. http://purl.org/net/epubs/work/50398
2. Caiani, A., Godin, A., Caverzasi, E., Gallegati, M., Kinsella, S., Stiglitz, J.E.: Agent based-stock flow consistent macroeconomics: towards a benchmark model. J. Econ. Dyn. Control **69**, 375–408 (2016). http://dx.doi.org/10.1016/j.jedc.2016. 06.001
3. Collier, N.: RePast: an extensible framework for agent simulation (2003)
4. Farmer, J.D., Foley, D.: The economy needs agent-based modelling. Nature **460**(7256), 685–686 (2009). https://www.nature.com/nature/journal/v460/ n7256/full/460685a.html
5. Jones, E., Oliphant, T., Peterson, P., et al.: SciPy: open source scientific tools for Python (2001). http://www.scipy.org/. Accessed 10 June 2017
6. Luke, S., Cioffi-Revilla, C., Panait, L., Sullivan, K., Balan, G.: Mason: a multiagent simulation environment. Simulation **81**(7), 517–527 (2015). http://dx.doi.org/10. 1177/0037549705058073
7. Nikolai, C., Madey, G.: Tools of the trade: a survey of various agent based modeling platforms. J. Artif. Soc. Soc. **12**(2), 2 (2009). http://jasss.soc.surrey.ac.uk/12/2/ 2.html
8. North, M., Howe, T., Collier, N., Vos, J.: The repast simphony runtime system. In: Proceedings of Agent 2005 Conference on Generative Social Processes, Models, and Mechanisms, p. 151 (2005)
9. Phelps, S.: Applying dependency injection to agent-based modeling: the JABM toolkit. Technical report WP056-12, Centre for Computational Finance and Economic Agents (CCFEA) (2012). http://www.bracil.net/ccfea/WorkingPapers/ 2012/CCFEA-Wpp.056-12-r2.pdf
10. Railsback, S.F., Lytinen, S.L., Jackson, S.K.: Agent-based simulation platforms: review and development recommendations. Simulation **82**(9), 609–623 (2006). http://dx.doi.org/10.1177/0037549706073695

11. Rossum, G.V.: Glue it all together with Python. In: Position Paper for OMG-DARPA-MCC Workshop on Compositional Software Architecture (1998). https://www.python.org/doc/essays/omg-darpa-mcc-position/

12. Serenko, A., Detlor, B.: Agent toolkits: a general overview of the market and an assessment of instructor satisfaction with utilizing toolkits in the classroom (2002). http://hdl.handle.net/11375/5601

13. Taghawi-Nejad, D.: Modelling the economy as an agent-based process: ABCE, a modelling platform and formal language for ACE. J. Artif. Soc. Soc. Simul. (2013). http://jasss.soc.surrey.ac.uk/16/3/1.html

14. Tobias, R., Hofmann, C.: Evaluation of free Java-libraries for social-scientific agent based simulation. J. Artif. Soc. Soc. Simul. 7(1) (2004). http://jasss.soc.surrey.ac.uk/7/1/6.html

15. Walt, S.V.D., Colbert, S.C., Varoquaux, G.: The NumPy array: a structure for efficient numerical computation. Comput. Sci. Eng. **13**(2), 22–30 (2011)

16. Wikipedia: Comparison of agent-based modeling software – Wikipedia, the free encyclopedia (2017). https://en.wikipedia.org/w/index.php?title=Comparison_of_agent-based_modeling_software&oldid=783176104. Accessed 14 June 2017

The Dynamics of Professional Prestige in Fashion Industries of Europe and the US: Network Approach

Margarita Kuleva[1,2(✉)] and Daria Maglevanaya[1]

[1] National Research University Higher School of Economics, Saint Petersburg, Russia
mkuleva@hse.ru, dvmaglevanaya@edu.hse.ru
[2] Centre for German and European Studies, SPBSU – Bielefeld University, Saint Petersburg, Russia

Abstract. Career trajectories of fashion models have different outcomes and depend on every project (photoshoot, catwalk etc.) where they do participate. In this field, it is common practice that there are choices between salary and symbolic capital as recognition and new connections in the world of fashion and art which they can acquire after collaboration with brands or journals. From this, it follows that present affiliation influences their future career path, so they exchange among themselves their level of prestige. In this paper we use longitudinal data on cover photoshoots in fashion and lifestyle magazines from 1975 to 2016 to see, how journals and fashion models occupy positions in this field and how their prestige transforms at different time periods according to cultural and economic mechanisms.

Keywords: Sociology of fashion · Social network analysis · Media · Prestige · Fashion models · Symbolic capital

1 Introduction

The field of fashion is represented by different institutions and organizations which are closely linked to each other and have their own agents who perform as gatekeepers. This system functions as an analogue of the hierarchized art world, where agent's position is based on his/her own prestige and on the status of his/her affiliation [2,4,5,18]. Moreover, Bourdieu talking about trajectories that are supported by recognition in cultural production field structures.

There are different approaches in the studies of creative career trajectories, but most of them look at a very restricted number of creative laborers: writers or artists who are publishing in magazines or participating in gallery exhibitions [9,11]. The main idea of this paper was to see how organizations and the creatives exchanging their symbolic capital through the working process and then acquire different levels of prestige because every future career step depends on the previous one. Also, there is a comparison with the process of mountain climbing while creative agents trying to reach upper positions [12] and there we

G.L. Ciampaglia et al. (Eds.): SocInfo 2017, Part I, LNCS 10539, pp. 31–40, 2017.
DOI: 10.1007/978-3-319-67217-5_3

come across with collective action and rules by which this field is organized. And conventions which are common in creative production also spread on roles and positions of actors [1,3].

A lot of research was conducted in the field of fashion modeling, but most of them pay attention to "bodily capital", recognition of the beauty and gatekeepers whose mission is controlling standards of the body [10,14,15]. But instead of the body features, there are a lot of conventions and characteristics of the market which define trajectories of the art business [8,16,17]. In the paper we follow the network analysis strand in these studies. The main assumption here is that the modelling labor is divided into 2 parts, which are concentrated on a maximization of two different axes - with symbolic capital or with economic, which are spoken by the researchers of the cultural industry. In this paper, we want to test whether this is happening in the labor market, which is adjacent to the media, culture, fashion and the manipulation of bodily capital.

2 Methodology and Sample

To explore dynamics of prestige in models affiliations we decided to track their career movements through their collaborations with fashion and "lifestyle" magazines, on which covers they have shot on. Data was taken from web site models.com, where model agencies store portfolios of their models and their projects. In result, we have information about 13961 covers of 106 magazines in the period from the 1975 year to January 2017. At this stage, it is worth to mention that it was decided to combine the same magazines under the publishing of different countries (for example, VOGUE Italy and VOGUE Russia were considered as VOGUE) and to accept for one agent. Such an association can be accomplished within the framework of the same structure of intercountry issues, topics of their content and the status of the "name" of the magazine as a brand [13]. Then we separate this massive on 6 time periods for next network analysis and model creation.

Drawing on the methodological framework of De Nooy [9], who measured the status hierarchies of the printed editions of artists and the circulation of authors between them, an equation of prestige of two types was derived: primary (for the first time cut, excluding agents that passed through the magazine) and in dynamics (taking into account the parameter of the models who stayed at previous magazines). This methodological framework allows to assign agents a level of prestige, based on their parametric characteristics and Weights. As a result, one variable is created from several criteria. After that, we need to create indexes which can help to measure prestige. Following Wouter de Nooy steps with assignment characteristics of magazine production, we similarly took static parameters of each magazine: year of the first issue, price of the print version in Euro, circulation (quantity of copies in each issue) and quantity of countries, where the magazine is distributed.

Next, we use an Exploratory Factor Analysis to create static prestige factor and to extract weights of each variable. We did two types of factors for the first point and for the next time slices. There were some transformations with the value of the year of the first issue into the years between first issue and this cover shoot and factors were done with the varimax rotation.

For the first time period (1975–1999) we took the following formula of fashion magazines prestige:

Prestige = (0.8 * circulation + 0.7 * countries + 0.6 * years since first issue + 1 * magazine price)/4.

And for the other five periods of time we took next formula:

Prestige = (0.9 * circulation + 0.7 * countries + 0.6 * years since first issue + 1 * magazine price + 0.4 * quantity of models which are stay from the previous wave)/5.

These coefficients can help to see the differentiation between fashion magazine market and its labors.

Also, to compare dynamics of prestige in different time intervals with changes of the whole network structure we use Siena model and CONCOR method of networks clustering. For this analysis we use Visone software application [6], UCINET and RStudio.

3   Model and Results

The number of covers grew with the years, the volume of labour force involved in the production of their products and journal products increased, including the arrival of new models in this market and the connection of interactions between agents (Fig. 1).

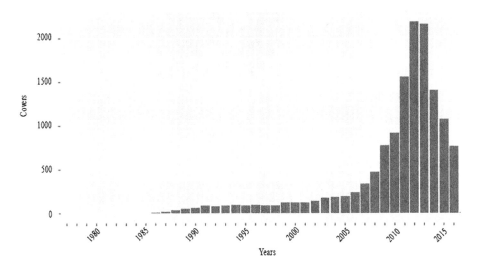

Fig. 1. Fashion models affiliations

Since the task was to look at the formation of communities in the space of the professional market of models and magazines, first we should pay attention to the general structure of agents' connections through a network of model and magazine collaborations. Figure 2 shows a two-mode network with a nuclear peripheral structure, at the core of which are journals that connect most of the workforce of the labor market to models, and on the periphery, there are journals that have collaborated with fewer more disparate models [7]. It can also be observed that there is a group of some models that have cooperated for the most part with magazines from the periphery, and some of them have done this multiple times. Here we see that the magazines are divided into 2 types: cooperating with the majority and cooperating with a diverse minority.

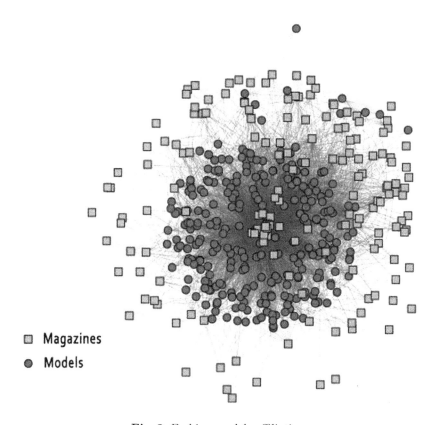

Fig. 2. Fashion models affiliations

Next, it is necessary to see, how links between magazines are being created through the time (Fig. 3). With each new period, the number of agents involved in the production system is increasing, and the number of common intersections in the models participating in this labour market is also growing and creating more work opportunities as we see on the next networks, but moving to the fourth wave we can pay attention to the graph structure, which has not got clusters and boundaries between magazine differentiation are smoothed. This tendency is inherent to the beginning of 2010s that most of the journals are covered by the same fashion model, however, some years further we can observe recession between work flows of different magazines, so density becomes weakly. The same picture we can observe by density of graphs, which parameter becomes higher and then falls sharply (Table 1).

Through the following model of Siena dynamic networks (Table 2), we see how the parameter for the formation of new bonds grows from the coefficient next to 2 (from the first time slice to the second) to 37 (in the transition from the 4 time period to 5), but then the growth rate of the new ties formation is reduced to parameter equal to 30. This also confirms the growth of the industry in the field of modeling work resources [14] and the institutionalization of this field.

Table 1. Density of networks by wave

Wave	Density
Wave 1	0.00916442
Wave 2	0.007726864
Wave 3	0.05336927
Wave 4	0.1297394
Wave 5	0.1265049
Wave 6	0.02120395

Table 2. Siena model specification of constant network rate by time periods

Effect name	Parameter value
Constant network rate (period 1)	2.746
Constant network rate (period 2)	11.583
Constant network rate (period 3)	31.427
Constant network rate (period 4)	37.026
Constant network rate (period 5)	30.855
Degree (density)	−1.086

On the Fig. 4 criteria for a formalized status indicator were used to assign weights to journals in order to measure their formalized prestige in the space of the fashion industry. And here we have the following results.

Here we see that there are no groups with features of large or small weight. At the same time, each graph has one main component, and the weights of the magazines are distributed between agents in the network approximately the same, which we see by the size of the nodes.

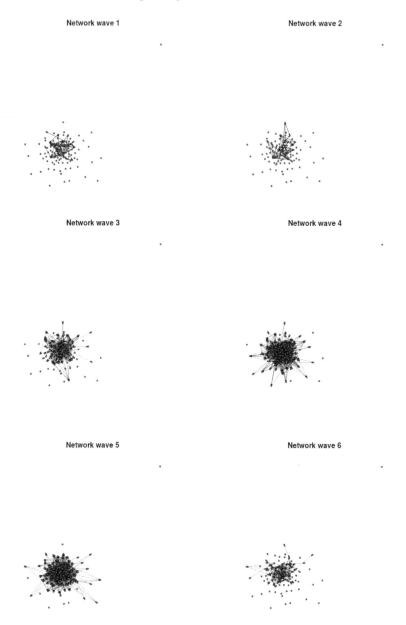

Fig. 3. Fashion models affiliations

Since the main assumption was that the work field of the journals is segmented relatively to working relationships and models that are "prescribed" for collaborative projects, and this works through homophily and interaction between agents with equal status, a number of some procedures were carried out.

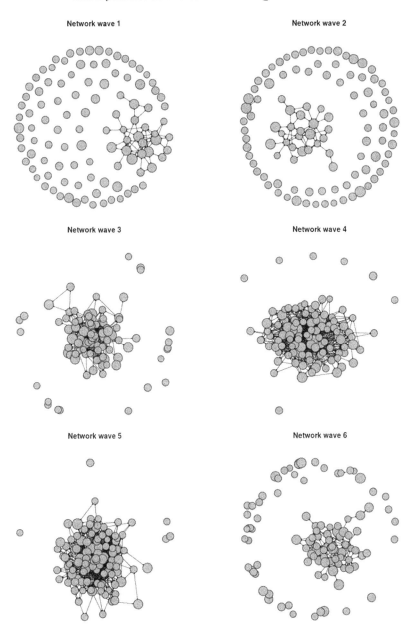

Fig. 4. Weighted prestige in log scale

In order to see how the groups are divided theoretically into 2 radical communities (with high economic capital, after collaboration with which the model's career is declining, or magazines with high symbolic capital that serve as the model status assignment, which allows occupying position of the legitimate actor in the fashion industry), the method of structural equivalence of the network and the CONCOR algorithm were applied. It makes it possible to calculate the similarity between agents regarding the equality of their social positions in the network, excluding their mutual connections, but taking into account similar patterns of interaction with other participants similar to them. The similarity between agents was calculated on the basis of Euclidean distances along the matrix of connections between agents.

For each of the periods, the value of the division into 2 groups was set to the maximum, and the significance of independence between the agents' relationships relative to these groups was calculated (Table 3):

Table 3. Subgroup independence

Wave	R2
1	.162
2	.116
3	.052
4	.003
5	.013
6	.061

To see the characteristics by which the groups in waves 3, 4 and 5 differ, the ANOVA test was used (Tables 4, 5 and 6). It shows the distinction between subgroups in waves.

A single parameter that would distinguish groups in all networks was not found, however, for this segmentation, the parameters of the number of journal links between each other were important. We saw such a separation first through a close core and periphery, and proximity to the network when in one of the groups the journals have a larger number of shortest paths to the rest of the network. That is, they have more binding models. And here we can say about the existence of two groups of journals, which confirms the hypothesis. Those logs with the largest number of links in the core of the network come from the fact that models move from magazine to magazine according to their status, while logs on the periphery had fewer links and with a "scattered" range of models that In a consequence, they could finish their careers and not receive proposals.

Another important differentiating parameter was the magazine's launch year, which could also be due to the winning of legitimate positions, due to the time of journal activity and the receipt of status positions through exchanges with other actors in the field of the fashion industry.

Table 4. Differentiation by groups. Wave 3

	Df	Sum Sq	Mean Sq	F value	Pr (>F)
Countries	1	1.33	1.33	6.61	0.0117
Closeness	1	1.25	1.25	6.22	0.0144
Residuals	96	19.38	0.20		

Table 5. Differentiation by groups. Wave 4

	Df	Sum Sq	Mean Sq	F value	Pr (>F)
Year start	1	2.25	2.25	10.83	.0014
Circulation	1	0.94	0.94	4.53	.0359
Degree	1	2.35	2.35	11.34	.0011
Residuals	96	19.92	0.21		

Table 6. Differentiation by groups. Wave 5

	Df	Sum Sq	Mean Sq	F value	Pr (>F)
Year start	1	1.43	1.43	6.96	.0097
Degree	1	1.06	1.06	5.16	.0253
Closeness	1	2.78	2.78	13.54	.0004
Residuals	97	19.93	0.21		

4   Discussion

In this paper, the formation of status groups in the fashion industry through professional collaboration of models and journals was studied. Despite the rapid growth of this part of the fashion industry and the specifics of interchange, when the trajectories of one of the agent types do not depend on institutionalized incorporated capital, but depend on its connections with other agents in the network and their status in the field of fashionable production, a number of things have been revealed that affect the positions occupied in the space of this professional field.

Status markers that distinguish polar groups have become patterns of formation of connections between agents. In this case, it is reproduced by where they move from one magazine to another model, suggesting a choice of homophily of agents. We also considered a number of countries publishing a certain magazine as an economic parameter which has an impact on the professional community.

This research is an ongoing project and as further trajectories, we are planning to supplement the network of such cooperation with attribute data of models: regular photo shoots in magazines - not from covers, but also data on podium cooperation with clothing brands, as these agents also exchange their status characteristics when interacting. This will complement the picture of the mutual exchange of symbolic capital by agents between each other. Moreover, it will be meaningful to join approaches of cultural sociology and fashion management to reproduce social status model of this field.

References

1. Aspers, P.: Markets in Fashion: A Phenomenological Approach. Routledge, Abingdon (2012)
2. Bakker, G., Caves, R.E., May, L.: Creative Industries: Contracts Between Art and Commerce (2001)
3. Becker, H.S.: Art worlds. Arch. Rat. Mech. Anal. **78**, 315–333 (1982)
4. Blumer, H.: Fashion: from class differentiation to collective selection. Sociol. Q. **10**, 275–291 (1969)
5. Bourdieu, P.: The field of cultural production, or: the economic world reversed. Poetics **12**, 311–356 (1983)
6. Brandes, U., Wagner, D.: Analysis and visualization of social networks. In: Jünger, M., Mutzel, P. (eds.) Graph Drawing Software, pp. 321–340. Springer, Heidelberg (2004). doi:10.1007/978-3-642-18638-7_15
7. Cattani, G., Ferriani, S.: A core/periphery perspective on individual creative performance: social networks and cinematic achievements in the hollywood film industry. J. Manag. Stud. **39**, 123–146 (2008)
8. Caves, R.E.: Creative Industries: Contracts Between Art and Commerce. Harvard University Press, Cambridge (2000)
9. De Nooy, W.: The dynamics of artistic prestige. Poetics **30**(3), 147–167 (2002)
10. Entwistle, J., Wissinger, E.: Keeping up appearances: aesthetic labour in the fashion modelling industries of London and New York. Sociol. Rev. **54**(4), 774–794 (2006)
11. Faulkner, R.R., Anderson, A.B.: Short-term projects and emergent careers: evidence from Hollywood. Am. J. Sociol. **92**, 879–909 (1987)
12. Giuffre, K.A.: Webs of opportunity: success in the art world. Soc. Forces **77**, 815–832 (1999)
13. McCracken, E.: Decoding Women's Magazines: From Mademoiselle to Ms. Springer. Palgrave Macmillan, London (1992)
14. Mears, A.: Pricing Beauty: The Making of a Fashion Model. University of California Press, Berkeley (2011)
15. Mora, E.: Collective production of creativity in the Italian fashion system. Poetics **34**, 334–353 (2006)
16. O'Mahony, S., Bechky, B.A.: Stretchwork: managing the career progression paradox in external labor markets. Acad. Manag. J. **49**, 918–941 (2006)
17. Tams, S., Arthur, M.B.: New directions for boundaryless careers: agency and interdependence in a changing world. J. Organ. Behav. **31**, 629–646 (2010)
18. Uzzi, B., Spiro, J.: Collaboration and creativity: the small world problem. Am. J. Sociol. **111**, 447–504 (2005)

Matching Graduate Applicants with Faculty Members

Shibamouli Lahiri[✉], Carmen Banea, and Rada Mihalcea

University of Michigan, Ann Arbor, MI 48109, USA
{lahiri,carmennb,mihalcea}@umich.edu

Abstract. Every year, millions of students apply to universities for admission to graduate programs (Master's and Ph.D.). The applications are individually evaluated and forwarded to appropriate faculty members. Considering human subjectivity and processing latency, this is a highly tedious and time-consuming job that has to be performed every year. In this paper, we propose several information retrieval models aimed at partially or fully automating the task. Applicants are represented by their statements of purpose (SOP), and faculty members are represented by the papers they authored. We extract keywords from papers and SOPs using a state-of-the-art keyword extractor. A detailed exploratory analysis of keywords yields several insights into the contents of SOPs and papers. We report results on several information retrieval models employing keywords and bag-of-words content modeling, with the former offering significantly better results. While we are able to correctly retrieve research areas for a given statement of purpose (F-score of 57.7% at rank 2 and 61.8% at rank 3), the task of matching applicants and faculty members is more difficult, and we are able to achieve an F-measure of 21% at rank 2 and 24% at rank 3, when making a selection among 73 faculty members.

Keywords: Graduate application · Statement of purpose · Keyword extraction · Information retrieval

1 Introduction

Every year, millions of students worldwide apply for graduate education in the United States. In Fall 2012 alone, US universities received 1.98 million graduate applications, and more than 461,000 students enrolled in graduate studies for the first time between Fall 2011 and Fall 2012.[1] With such a high number of students applying to US universities for graduate studies, and that number increasing over the years,[2] the problem of processing this voluminous amount of applicant data into a more manageable and more automated pipeline assumes paramount importance.

---

[1] https://www.cgsnet.org/us-graduate-schools-report-slight-growth-new-students-fall -2012.

[2] http://www.cgsnet.org/ckfinder/userfiles/files/R_IntlApps12_I.pdf.

© Springer International Publishing AG 2017
G.L. Ciampaglia et al. (Eds.): SocInfo 2017, Part I, LNCS 10539, pp. 41–55, 2017.
DOI: 10.1007/978-3-319-67217-5_4

Ph.D. applicants in particular pose a greater challenge because they need to be screened for funding offers and matched with potential advisors. While some applicants do specify the group or the professor with whom they would like to work with, many do not provide a selection. The problem is somewhat alleviated by having a separate survey in online application forms that allows applicants to mention which faculty members they would like to work with, and rank those faculty members in order of preference. Still, it largely remains the university's and ultimately the departments' responsibility to ensure Ph.D. applicants are matched with appropriate faculty members. Departments typically employ a faculty subgroup or separate staff members to read through graduate applications, forward them to appropriate faculty members, and create online "profiles" of applicants so that they could be matched more easily with faculty members. The problem, however, is that not all faculty members toward whom an applicant shows interest can offer financial support or have a matching interest in the applicant.

Our goal in this project is to *automate the process of matching applicants with faculty members*. In particular, we want to leverage the free text available as part of the applications to aid us in the decision process. To showcase our approach, we use the applicant data from the Computer Science and Engineering department at a large Midwestern university that had over 1,100 graduate applications in Fall 2014. Manual matching of Ph.D. applicants with appropriate faculty members was also available. We designed several information retrieval systems that would:

1. Match applicants and research areas:
   (a) given an applicant, retrieve the most likely research areas the applicant would match;
   (b) given a research area, retrieve from the pool of available applicants those most likely to be a good match;
2. Match applicants and faculty:
   (a) given an applicant, retrieve those faculty members with similar research interests;
   (b) given a faculty member, retrieve the most likely applicants to possess similar research interests;
   (c) given an applicant, retrieve the most likely research areas the applicant would match, and then from those, select faculty members with similar research interests.

The rest of the article is organized as follows. We outline related studies in Sect. 2, followed by a description of our dataset in Sect. 3. Section 4 presents exploratory analysis of the keywords extracted from faculty published work and applicants' statement of purpose, setting the stage for Sect. 5, where we describe information retrieval systems and the importance of keywords in constructing them. Section 6 concludes the paper, outlining future research directions.

2   Related Work

The problem of matching graduate students with faculty members has three close analogs in natural language processing: authorship attribution, author profiling, and author-topic modeling.

In authorship attribution, the goal is to predict who authored a particular document. The problem is usually cast as a classification task, where we have a large set of training documents with known authors, and a smaller set of test documents with unknown authors. Machine learning models are trained on the training documents, and then deployed on test documents to predict the unknown authors. For details on authorship attribution, please see the surveys by Juola [1], Stamatatos [10], and Koppel et al. [3]. In some flavors of authorship attribution, test documents are used as search queries against training documents, and the author of the top-ranked (training) document is considered predicted label [10]. In our study, we consider papers written by faculty members as "training documents", and statements of purpose written by students as "test documents". Performance on the test set is judged based on the ground truth faculty-applicant pairing we have. A potential limitation of this approach comes from the fact that in authorship attribution, we would like to uncover the *writing style* of an author, whereas in this case, we are interested in the *content match* between a paper written by a faculty member, and a statement of purpose authored by an applicant. We resolve this issue by using keywords (cf. Sects. 4 and 5).

Author profiling is very similar to authorship attribution, except that the goal here is to build a "stylistic profile" of an author instead of predicting a class label. The profile is usually a vector of words and/or phrases frequently used by the author, and may also include grammatical constructs and parse tree fragments. An author is represented by several vectors that are built on documents written by him/her. These vectors can be used to identify the author's unique writing style (*fingerprint*) and to extract other useful properties such as gender, age, education, and personality traits. Author profiling has been discussed in depth in the survey by Stamatatos [10]. In our case, author profiling could serve as a fundamental building block where papers written by faculty members are used to create their authorship profiles, and then a statement of purpose that is most similar to a faculty member's profile, is assigned the corresponding faculty member. This approach, albeit sound in principle, has the same important drawback as authorship attribution; it focuses on *stylistic* rather than content information, and is therefore not very useful.

Content information of authors can be explicitly incorporated in a probabilistic setting, where documents are modeled as a collection of topics, and topics are modeled as a collection of words. Topic generation depends on authors represented as (observed) random variables in the model [8]. An unseen document can be assigned a probability distribution over authors and topics, thereby helping find out which authors are the most likely to have written that document. In our case, we could use the set of papers written by faculty members to train an author-topic model, and then the statements of purpose could be "folded in" the model to extract their most representative author and topic probability distributions.

While all the above ideas are good, we did not find an approach that closely matches our purpose. The only similar study we found comes from IBM India Research Lab [9]. They designed a system called "PROSPECT" to screen candidates for recruitment. Their system combines elements from recommender systems, information retrieval, and author profiling to come up with a software and graphical user interface that improves candidate ranking by 30% and provides faceted search functionality to conduct fine-grained analyses such as highest degree of the candidate, relevant and total work experience, skills, and his/her city of residence. Since companies like IBM receive thousands of job applications for many job postings, it becomes crucial to augment the slow and cumbersome manual candidate-screening process with an automated decision-making tool such as PROSPECT. Our use case is also very similar, in that we want to screen hundreds of graduate applicants and match them with potential advisors. In our case, faculty members serve the same purpose as human resources staff screening job postings, and graduate applicants are similar to job candidates. Inspired by PROSPECT, we pursued five keyword-based approaches to tackle this problem. All approaches use information retrieval techniques, and stand to benefit from *learning to rank*, given enough data [5].

3   Data Description

Since our problem formulation involves the ranking of *faculty members* against *applicants* (and vice versa), we need a convenient textual representation for both. We opt to represent applicants by their *statements of purpose* (SOP), and faculty members by the papers they have (co-)authored in the prior 12 years (between 2004 and 2015). Anonymized statements of purpose are available for all applicants in the Fall 2014 cohort at the Computer Science and Engineering department at the university in question. Note that SOPs usually talk about what the applicant has achieved in the *past*, what (s)he is doing at *present*, what (s)he would like to do/be in the *future*, and how all these *connect* with the particular department and its faculty.

Papers were collected for 73 faculty members from their Google Scholar Citations[3] and DBLP[4] profiles. We collected 4,534 papers authored between 2004 and 2015, and converted their PDFs into text using UNIX *pdftotext* utility. Sometimes multiple faculty members collaborate on a single paper; we counted those papers multiple times, once for each participating faculty. Authorship statistics of the 5 most prolific authors are shown in Table 1. Note that a few of the most prolific authors wrote over 200 papers between 2004–2015, or almost 17 papers a year. This data follows a power-law distribution with exponent $\alpha = 3.45$ (statistically significant with p-value $= 0.999$).

We also obtained a pairing of Ph.D. applicants (Fall 2014 cohort) with faculty members, constructed manually by a small group of faculty. Note that each applicant is identified by a numeric ID and may be matched with multiple faculty members. On the other hand, a faculty member is represented by his/her

---

[3] http://scholar.google.com/.

[4] http://www.informatik.uni-trier.de/~ley/db/.

Table 1. Number of papers (co-)written by several faculty members (anonymized) between 2004 and 2015.

Faculty member	Number of papers
Tommy M. Rosenbalm	331
Thomas M. Burns	300
Ali H. Salgado	212
Richard G. Meza	146
Nicole L. Thompson	140

username, and may be matched with (or express interest in) several different applicants. There were 1107 applicants in total, of which 304 were matched with a faculty member. Different faculty members received a different number of applications. Faculty members receiving the highest number of applications in Fall 2014 cohort are shown in Table 2.

Table 2. Number of applicants assigned to several faculty members (anonymized).

Faculty member	Number of applicants
Richard C. Hardy	45
George E. Ford	45
Robert S. Peters	42
Jeff L. Jurgens	41
Dennis R. Salisbury	38

Table 3. Research areas at the Computer Science and Engineering department at a large Midwestern university. Highest value in each column is boldfaced. Applicants are from Fall 2014 pool.

Research area	Number of faculty	Applicant of faculty ratio	% of applicants in area
Artificial intelligence	**29**	7.03	**67.11**
Chip design, architecture, and emerging devices	22	3.41	24.67
Databases and data mining	6	**16.00**	31.58
Embedded and mobile systems	12	6.67	26.32
Human-computer interaction	8	6.63	17.43
Languages, compilers, and runtime systems	13	3.54	15.13
Networking, operating systems, and distributed systems	16	4.56	24.01
Robotics in CSE	7	11.71	26.97
Secure, trustworthy, and reliable systems	22	4.32	31.25
Theory of computation	10	5.4	17.76
Warehouse-scale and parallel systems	19	4.16	25.99

The faculty conducts research in 11 different areas, as shown in Table 3. The areas vary in terms of number of faculty, percentage of applicants, and applicant-to-faculty ratio. Artificial Intelligence (AI), for example, has the highest number of faculty members and the highest percentage of applicants. Databases and Data Mining, on the other hand, comprises the lowest number of faculty and the second highest percentage of applicants, which leads to the highest applicant-to-faculty ratio across all research areas. These observations could be helpful in identifying areas where additional faculty members need to be recruited.

4   Exploratory Analysis of Keywords

To represent the SOPs and papers by their *content* rather than *style*, we use an automatic system to extract keywords. We employ a state-of-the-art system previously used in the email domain [4]. Keyword statistics are provided in Table 4; note that we also include the counts for filtered keywords using Wikipedia article titles to obtain a more salient listing of keywords.

Table 4. Keyword statistics.

Keyword type	SOPs keyword count	Papers keyword count
All keywords	53,166	123,171
Multi-word keywords	44,473	98,470
All keywords after filtering	13,472	27,563
Multi-word keywords after filtering	6,022	10,170

Table 5. Top multi-word keywords from SOPs, ranked by *tf.idf*.

Machine learning	1166.78
Computer vision	713.66
Computer science and engineering	706.06
Artificial intelligence	679.31
Computer architecture	651.95
Data mining	562.43
Electrical engineering	516.14
Natural language	493.75

We first want to see *what students talk about most* in their SOPs in terms of keywords. Table 5 shows that the most salient keywords in SOPs are general and trendy terms such as "machine learning," "artificial intelligence," "data mining," and "computer vision." Other terms are even more generic, such as "computer science and engineering," and "electrical engineering". These keywords indicate that students are indeed familiar with the trendy terms and buzzwords in Computer Science and Engineering, and most students want to go to those areas. In comparison, when we look at *what the faculty talk about most* in their papers (cf. Table 6), we observe highly technical terms and domain-specific keywords such as "nash equilibrium" and "episodic memory." This observation leads support to the fact that students are usually not sufficiently aware of the publication records of different faculty members (*information gap*), and students usually apply to "hot" areas rather than established areas (where there are more papers), perhaps because of increased media attention to those areas. This information gap further shows that our problem is complex, as we need to match texts from students and texts from faculty containing disparate sets of keywords.

Table 6. Most important keywords from papers published in different years. Importance was measured by *tf.idf*. Top keywords that are unique to each year are shown in boldface.

2004	2005	2006	2007
Test set	File system	File system	Natural language
Ubiquitous computing	Sensor network	Natural language	File system
Power management	Error rate	Data set	Data race
Computer science	Virtual machine	Error rate	Ad hoc
Lower bound	Power management	Ad hoc	Energy consumption
2008	**2009**	**2010**	**2011**
File system	**Network virtualization**	Power consumption	Data race
Control logic	Control logic	File system	Shared memory
Power consumption	Power consumption	**Reward function**	**Episodic memory**
Energy consumption	Data set	Computer science	Error rate
Computer science	Virtual machine	Signal processing	**Medical device**
2012	**2013**	**2014**	**2015**
Energy consumption	Electrical engineering	**Social media**	**Homomorphic encryption**
Energy efficiency	**Data center**	Anomaly detection	Data mining
Nash equilibrium	Computer science	Power consumption	Anomaly detection
Computer science	Natural language	Data mining	**Data science**
Electrical engineering	Energy efficiency	**Computational linguistics**	**Reinforcement learning**

An intriguing question at this point is to explore *how the keywords change over the years*. We analyzed the publications of all faculty members by year and ranked the keywords used by *tf.idf*. Table 6 shows that there is a distinct *trend* in the top-ranked keywords, in the sense that each year seems to focus on some particular problems (perhaps at the expense of others), and each year has some *new problems* that were not salient before. Year 2014, for example, introduces "social media" as a salient keyword, whereas year 2015 introduces "data science." It is important to note that graduate applicants are often not aware of such subtle variations and trends going on in the research community and thus cannot prepare accordingly.

We next explore *how the faculty members rank according to their diversity and focus* of research topics, as related to applicants. While diversity is usually defined as the opposite of similarity in Information Retrieval [7], we measured

Table 7. Ranking of faculty members (anonymized). Top faculty members that are unique to a particular ranking are shown in boldface.

Diversity	Focus	Content density
Nicole L. Thompson	**Stephen M. Evans**	Jack J. Santoro
Francis G. Okelley	**Richard C. Hardy**	Rodolfo C. Hayes
John L. Wheatley	**Kevin D. Llanes**	Nicole L. Thompson
Tommy M. Rosenbalm	**George E. Ford**	James C. Rhinehart
Ali H. Salgado	Michael M. Lewis	Francis G. Okelley

diversity in the context of keywords by Jaccard Similarity[5] between all keywords of a faculty and keywords from all applicants, whereas *focus* was measured by Jaccard Similarity between all keywords of a faculty and keywords from applicants assigned to him/her. Table 7 shows that these two rankings are substantially different. Furthermore, looking at *content density* (total number of keywords as a fraction of total number of words – averaged over papers), we see that the ranking changes again. It is important to note such subtle differences, because they help applicants make an informed decision.

Intriguingly, we find *focus* to be highly positively correlated with *popularity* (Spearman's $\rho = 0.8$), where the latter is measured by *how many students are assigned to a faculty* (cf. Table 2). *Diversity* and *popularity* are only moderately correlated (Spearman's $\rho = 0.28$), whereas the correlation between *diversity* and *focus* is even lower ($\rho = 0.12$). Very low correlation is observed between *content density* and *focus* ($\rho = 0.04$). Similarly low values are obtained for correlations between *content density* and *popularity*.

5   Information Retrieval Models

The objective of our study is to help academic departments *match applicants with faculty members*. We cast this problem as an *information retrieval*-like task, where given an applicant as query, our system retrieves research areas and faculty members. The system is also able to retrieve applicants with respect to faculty members as queries. We consider the following use cases:

1. match applicants and research areas
   (a) consider an applicant's statement of purpose as a query, while all publications in a given research area form a single document, and retrieve the most similar of these documents; retrieval is done among 11 research areas. We will call this variation *SOP as query, research areas as documents*.
   (b) consider all publications in a research area as a query for which we seek to retrieve the strongest matching statement of purpose pertaining to the applicants; retrieval is done among 304 applicants. We will refer to this variation as *research area as query, SOP as documents*.

---

[5] https://en.wikipedia.org/wiki/Jaccard_index.

2. match applicants and faculty
   (a) consider an applicant's statement of purpose as a query, while all publications pertaining to a given faculty as a single document; the retrieval is done for the most similar documents. This variation is represented as *applicant as query, faculty members as documents*; retrieval is done among 73 faculty members.
   (b) consider the cumulative publications of a faculty member as query, while each applicant is represented through his/her statement of purpose. This variation is referred to as *faculty as query, applicants as documents*. Retrieval is performed among 304 applicants.
   (c) consider an applicant's statement of purpose as a query. Retrieval of the most relevant faculty members is performed hierarchically, first with respect to the best matching research groups (represented through the totality of articles published by faculty in that group), and then with respect to the best matching faculty members from within the top groups. We will refer to this variation as *applicant as query, faculty members as documents – hierarchical*; retrieval is first performed against the 11 research areas, and then against the faculty members in the top research areas.

While applicant publications and/or data gathered from application forms could potentially be used to match applicants with faculty, we considered such an approach to be problematic because of the difficulty in gathering data, lack of prior publications (esp. for Master's applicants), and penalizing applicants that mostly have industry experience.

5.1 Vector Generation

For each one of the approaches mentioned above, vectors are generated for different feature types, filtering, and weighting options.

Feature Types. Two types of vectors are derived to represent a query or a document: using the vocabulary of single words encountered in the text (*unigrams*), or using the keywords encountered in the same text (*mwe*[6]). While the first technique is straightforward, for the second technique we extract keywords from applicant statements of purpose (SOPs) using a state-of-the-art supervised keyword extractor [4] trained on two keyphrase extraction corpora. The first corpus consists of a set of 211 academic papers with keyword annotations [6], while the second corpus was released as part of the SEMEVAL 2010 Keyphrase Extraction Task [2] and also encompasses a set of 184 academic papers annotated for keywords. The extractor uses noun phrases and named entities as candidates, as well as surface, frequency, phraseness, and graph-based features; it performs shallow post-processing after extraction to remove punctuation.

---

[6] "mwe" stands for multi-word expressions.

Filtering. The unigrams and the keywords mentioned above are referred to in the ensuing experiments as *all*, since they do not undergo filtering. A second instance of these features is derived, based on whether they are associated with a Wikipedia article[7]; this list is referred to as *filtered*, and retains fewer, higher quality and more salient entries.

We should emphasize that all the vectors are constructed on keywords/unigrams extracted from SOPs rather than those appearing in the published articles. The SOP-derived keyword list/vocabulary tends to be more generic and concise, as applicants do not yet have an in-depth grasp of various research areas and their SOP is shorter than an article, thus allowing the vectorial space to model applicants more closely while also being more efficient.

Weighting Options. The above feature types are weighted using three common weighting schemes: *binary*, term frequency (*tf*), and term frequency inverse document frequency (*tf.idf*).

Information Retrieval Framework. Using a query vector, document vectors are ranked with respect to their cosine similarity computed against the query vector, and the top k are retrieved by the system. The system predictions are evaluated against ground truth faculty-applicant pairings that were manually derived by a small group of faculty members. Performance was measured using standard precision, recall, and F-score at different ranks (k).

Overall, we construct 12 vector space models encompassing all the combination of parameters detailed above. The most robust results are obtained using: keywords and unigrams (for vocabulary), tf.idf (for feature weighting), and all and filtered (for filtering). As such, in the subsequent discussions we will focus on these variations. The baseline is represented through the combination *unigram all tf.idf*, namely using all the vocabulary encountered in the SOPs as unigrams with tf.idf weighting.

5.2 Matching Applicants and Research Areas

Our first use case scenario matches applicants and research areas. This scenario allows departmental faculty or staff to be provided with the best research areas for a given candidate, and then manually assign candidates to faculty in those areas, thereby simplifying the matching process. We explore two venues:

1. Applicant as query, research areas as documents.
2. Research area as query, applicants as documents.

Figure 1a shows the interpolated precision-recall curve for the first approach (SOP query, area documents), while Fig. 1b shows the same metrics for the second approach (area query, SOP documents) all of these derived for rank $k = 5$.

---

[7] Listing of article titles retrieved from https://dumps.wikimedia.org/.

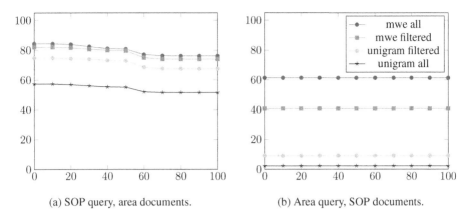

(a) SOP query, area documents.   (b) Area query, SOP documents.

Fig. 1. Interpolated precision-recall curves (at $k = 5$) showing two approaches for matching applicants and research areas, each with four variations. X-axis shows the recall level (%), while Y-axis shows the interpolated precision level (%).

We note that the first approach performs significantly better, achieving an interpolated precision level of over 80%, compared to the best performing variation falling under the second approach, which achieves an interpolated precision level of approximately 60%. Focusing on the first approach, the best performing variation is *mwe all tf.idf*, but is closely followed by *mwe filtered tf.idf*. Given that the former uses approximately 44 thousand dimensions, while the latter uses only 6,022 dimensions, we can conclude that (1) modeling via multi-word keywords is significantly better than accounting for the entire vocabulary, and (2) filtering these keywords for saliency achieves a more compact and efficient model, without a meaningful drop in performance.

Figure 2 shows the corresponding F-score curve for the two approaches, this time for different ranks. We notice that the best F-score of 61.8% occurs at rank 3 (21.2% higher than the corresponding baseline), while the second best F-score of 59.9% is encountered at rank 4 (where the baseline F-score is the highest, yet the prediction still surpasses it by 17.5%). A higher F-score is to be expected in this scenario compared to results achievable for matching students and faculty, since here we are limiting our match to 11 research areas.[8] We should stress that the optimal usability outcome for this task is represented through high performance at low ranks, i.e. the system should *correctly* retrieve a few matching research groups for a given SOP; as shown, the system achieves very high performance for ranks 2 through 4. This should accurately guide the process of assigning professors from those top retrieved groups and reduce the amount of manual work involved.

---

[8] The random baseline in this scenario is 9.1%.

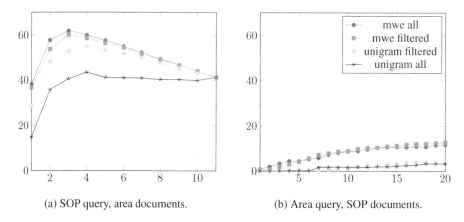

(a) SOP query, area documents.   (b) Area query, SOP documents.

Fig. 2. F-score curves for two approaches for matching applicants and research areas, each with four variations. X-axis shows the Rank, while Y-axis shows the F-score (%).

5.3   Matching Applicants and Faculty

The second and more desirable scenario consists of matching applicants and faculty. This allows the entire task to be automated, and therefore provides most savings in terms of financial and human resources for a department. We identify three venues:

1. applicant as query, faculty members as documents
2. faculty member as query, applicants as documents
3. applicant as query, faculty members as documents – hierarchical

The first two are similar to those proposed in the previous section, but this time the match is done directly with the faculty member, while the third consists of a hierarchical approach, where the match is first performed in regards to the best matching research group, and then the faculty is retrieved from within that group.

Probing further into the behavior of our system and baseline, we plotted the *interpolated precision-recall curve*, averaged over all search queries at a rank $k = 5$. The resulting graphs are shown in Fig. 3. We observe that similarly to the equivalent variations in Sect. 5.2, the SOP (applicant) query-based retrieval outperforms faculty query-based retrieval under all variations (see Figs. 3a and b). This is to be expected, since in the first scenario the retrieval is made among 73 faculty members, while in the second scenario, it is made among 304 applicants. Enacting a hierarchical based approach which generates an intermediary mapping to research areas and then retrieves the strongest matching faculty candidates from within the returned areas, achieves a similar performance to the first approach directly mapping to faculty (see Fig. 3c). As in the previous subsection, the best variation remains *mwe all tf.idf*, with a performance of approximately 40% interpolated precision level, 35% higher than the *unigram all tf.idf* baseline achieving slightly below 5% interpolated precision level. This

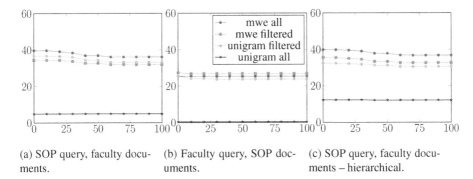

(a) SOP query, faculty documents.

(b) Faculty query, SOP documents.

(c) SOP query, faculty documents – hierarchical.

Fig. 3. Interpolated precision-recall curves (at $k = 5$) showing three approaches for matching applicants and faculty, each with four variations. X-axis shows the recall level (%), while Y-axis shows the interpolated precision level (%).

shows that keywords rather than vocabulary offer a lot more plasticity and bring more value for this task.

Figure 4 showcases the performance of the three approaches matching applicants to faculty at different ranks. Here as well, the *SOP query, faculty documents* represents the highest performing use case, retaining its high performance at low k values by achieving a F-score higher than 19% for ranks 2 through 10 using the best performing *mwe all tf.idf* variation, and reaching a maximum of 24.4% for rank 3. The hierarchical system displays a similar performance, as it is able to attain an F-measure above 19% starting at rank 2 as well, but since it is a two step system, it is too inefficient compared to a one step system to motivate its usage. The random baseline accuracy for matching an applicant to a faculty member is 1.4%.

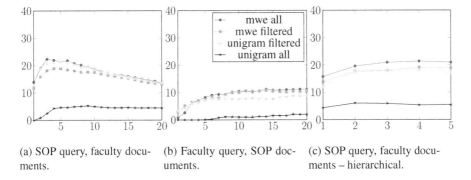

(a) SOP query, faculty documents.

(b) Faculty query, SOP documents.

(c) SOP query, faculty documents – hierarchical.

Fig. 4. F-score curves showing three approaches for matching applicants and faculty, each with four variations. X-axis shows the Rank, while Y-axis shows the F-score (%).

Considering all the use cases, however, we can say that we are able to successfully retrieve research areas and faculty members against SOP queries. Our system always surpasses the baseline by a wide margin, and using the *mwe all tf.idf* variation consistently achieves the best results. This is a great boon for the faculty members and staff members, because instead of manually sifting through hundreds of applications, they can now use our system to screen applicants before starting the laborious manual checking process. Anecdotal evidence from faculty members in our department showed that this was indeed the case, and they were happy with the search results produced by our system.

6 Conclusion

In this paper, we introduced a new task – matching graduate applicants with faculty members using text-based features. The problem is complex, given that there are no standard annotated datasets, not much relevant related work, and *content disparity* between the textual materials authored by applicants and those authored by faculty members. We created our own dataset comprising 4,534 papers authored by 73 different faculty members at the Computer Science and Engineering department of a large Midwestern university. We further considered an in-house set of 1,107 statements of purpose, and a set of 788 faculty-applicant pairings constructed manually. Keywords were extracted from papers and SOPs, and a detailed exploratory analysis was performed leading to insights regarding the content depth and subtlety of documents. We obtained encouraging results using standard information retrieval techniques using five different use cases, concluding that keywords offer a significantly better representation (more efficient and better results) compared to bag-of-words variations. Overall, we are able to match students to research groups with an F-score of 62%, while for the more difficult task of matching students to faculty, we are able to achieve a 24% F-score. Our future work includes obtaining more data (especially applicant data), more reliable faculty-applicant annotations, and more sophisticated models that take into account the sparsity of the task.

Acknowledgements. We are grateful to Lauren Molley and Joseph Zimmer for their help with the implementation of some system components. We also want to thank the reviewers for their valuable feedback. This material is based in part upon work supported by the Michigan Institute for Data Science, by the National Science Foundation (grant #1344257), and by the John Templeton Foundation (grant #48503). Any opinions, findings, and conclusions or recommendations expressed in this material are those of the author and do not necessarily reflect the views of the Michigan Institute for Data Science, the National Science Foundation, or the John Templeton Foundation.

References

1. Juola, P.: Authorship attribution. Found. Trends Inf. Retr. **1**(3), 233–334 (2006)
2. Kim, S.N., Medelyan, O., Kan, M.-Y., Baldwin, T.: SemEval-2010 task 5: automatic keyphrase extraction from scientific articles. In: Proceedings of 5th International Workshop on Semantic Evaluation, SemEval 2010, Stroudsburg, PA, USA, pp. 21–26. Association for Computational Linguistics (2010)
3. Koppel, M., Schler, J., Argamon, S.: Computational methods in authorship attribution. J. Am. Soc. Inf. Sci. Technol. **60**(1), 9–26 (2009)
4. Lahiri, S., Mihalcea, R., Lai, P.-H.: Keyword extraction from emails. Nat. Lang. Eng. **23**(2), 295–317 (2017)
5. Li, H.: A short introduction to learning to rank. IEICE Trans. **94–D**(10), 1854–1862 (2011)
6. Nguyen, T.D., Kan, M.-Y.: Keyphrase extraction in scientific publications. In: Goh, D.H.-L., Cao, T.H., Sølvberg, I.T., Rasmussen, E. (eds.) ICADL 2007. LNCS, vol. 4822, pp. 317–326. Springer, Heidelberg (2007). doi:10.1007/978-3-540-77094-7_41
7. Smyth, B., McClave, P.: Similarity vs. diversity. In: Aha, D.W., Watson, I. (eds.) ICCBR 2001. LNCS (LNAI), vol. 2080, pp. 347–361. Springer, Heidelberg (2001). doi:10.1007/3-540-44593-5_25
8. Rosen-Zvi, M., Griffiths, T., Steyvers, M., Smyth, P.: The author-topic model for authors and documents. In: Proceedings of 20th Conference on Uncertainty in Artificial Intelligence, UAI 2004, Arlington, Virginia, USA, pp. 487–494. AUAI Press (2004)
9. Singh, A., Rose, C., Visweswariah, K., Chenthamarakshan, V., Kambhatla, N.: PROSPECT: a system for screening candidates for recruitment. In: Proceedings of 19th ACM International Conference on Information and Knowledge Management, CIKM 2010, New York, NY, USA, pp. 659–668. ACM (2010)
10. Stamatatos, E.: A survey of modern authorship attribution methods. J. Am. Soc. Inf. Sci. Technol. **60**(3), 538–556 (2009)

Network science

Why Groups Show Different Fairness Norms? The Interaction Topology Might Explain

Mohsen Mosleh[(✉)] and Babak Heydari[(✉)]

Stevens Institute of Technology, Hoboken, NJ 07093, USA
{mmosleh,bheydari}@stevens.edu
http://web.stevens.edu/cens/

Abstract. Computational models of prosocial norms are becoming important from the perspective of theoretical social sciences as well as engineering of autonomous systems, who also need to show prosocial behavior in their social interactions. Fairness, as one of the strongest prosocial norms has long been argued to govern human behavior in a wide range of social, economic, and organizational activities. The sense of fairness, although universal, varies across different societies. In this study, using a computational model based on evolutionary games on graphs, we demonstrate emergence of fair behavior in structured interaction of rational agents and test the hypothesis that the network structure of social interaction can causally explain some of the cross-societal variations in fairness norms, as previously reported by empirical studies. We show that two network parameters, community structure, as measured by the modularity index, and network *hubiness*, represented by the skewness of degree distribution, have the most significant impact on emergence of fairness norms. These two parameters can explain much of the variations in fairness norms across societies and can also be linked to hypotheses suggested by earlier empirical work. We devised a multi-layered model that combines local agent interactions with social learning, thus enables both strategic behavior as well as diffusion of successful strategies. We also discuss some generalizable methods that are used in the selection of network structures and convergence criteria used in simulations for work. By applying multivariate statistics on the results, we obtain the relation between network structural features and the collective fair behavior.

Keywords: Social norms · Fairness · Social network · Ultimatum game

1 Introduction

Computational models for emergence and evolution of social norms are of interest to computational social scientists, not only because of the inherent centrality of norms and conventions in social sciences, but more importantly because of their importance in engineering of future autonomous systems. Autonomous systems are finding an inevitable and strong role in many domains of our social life, such as transportation, disaster response, trading or allocation of energy, bandwidth

© Springer International Publishing AG 2017
G.L. Ciampaglia et al. (Eds.): SocInfo 2017, Part I, LNCS 10539, pp. 59–74, 2017.
DOI: 10.1007/978-3-319-67217-5_5

or information resources. In most such cases, decisions that autonomous systems make are not limited to single-agent planning or optimization, but are made in *social* interaction with people, other autonomous agents, or in many cases both.

Such social contexts can differ from typical autonomous agent problems at least in two aspects: One aspect concerns how autonomous decisions can be reconciled with human sense of morality; as has been argued in the context of self-driving cars by the famous trolley problem [1,2] or autonomous two sided matching algorithms in organ transplant [3]. The other aspect, which is a motivation to this paper, deals with strategic decisions that are solutions of strategic games that the autonomous agent plays with a combination of people and other agents. How should autonomous agents play in such strategic situations? There are many evidences that in most strategic decisions humans on average behave more *pro-social* and are more fair and more cooperative than what is expected by textbook-based game theoretic solutions. Empirical evidences of such deviation have been reported for a number of canonical games such as the Prisoners' Dilemma, public goods game, the dictator game, and the Ultimatum Game (See [4,5] for overview of such models).

In human societies, many social norms are collectively protected via various forms of punishments by other people, in the case of norm deviation [6]. As a result, in many contexts we want the autonomous agents to follow such pro-social strategies not just because of moral concerns, but due to utilitarian considerations; since deviation from pro-social behavior might result in punishments from others and hamper the payoff of the agent. But how a group of rational, autonomous agents can evolve pro-social norms? What are the factors that affect emergence of these norms, and their variations across different groups and societies? Such questions that have been formerly in the domain of social sciences, are becoming also of interest in social computing, multi-agent systems and computational social sciences.

In this paper, we use a computational method based on evolutionary games on networks to study the evolution of fairness norms in a group of strategic learning agents that interact by playing pairwise ultimatum games as a resource allocation scheme that captures fairness and includes the possibility of punishment. We focus on the role of interaction network structure on evolution of fairness, and cross-society variations of such norms. Our model offers two main contributions: (1) It indicates a causal relationship between changes of structural characteristics of social network and variation of fairness norms. (2) It identifies structural features that are aligned with the findings of empirical studies of inter-societal variations of fairness norms and sheds some light on role of social structure as one of key determinants in explaining the variation of fairness across societies. Concurring with previous computational studies [7,8], the results of our study show that structures that are close to all-inclusive interactions (full-graph) exhibit less fairness. Our study, however, identifies two other structural drivers that have been missing in the literature: community structure, represented by network modularity index, and network *hubiness*, represented by skewness of degree distribution of the network. The latter two network parameters also help to further clarify some of the empirical findings that relate social institution parameters to fairness norms. A more comprehensive discussion on the methods and results of this study can be found in the journal publication of the authors [9] that look at the problem from a slightly different perspective.

2   Fairness Models and Empirical Evidences

Human's deep presuppositions of fairness and inequality are proven in a wide range of contexts, such as the relationship between relative income and reported job satisfaction [10], happiness [11], health and longevity [12], and reward-related brain activity [13]. These attitudes towards fairness play an important role in governing human behavior in social, economic, and organizational activities [14–16].

Earlier studies on fairness norms that were largely restricted to industrial societies showed relatively small fairness variation among different populations, suggesting that fairness norms were mostly the result of universal behavior patterns. This was later challenged by the seminal work of [17] and a number of other studies that show significant variations in fairness attitudes across different societies [18,19] and organizations [20–22]. These studies hypothesize the role of certain social and institutional factors on the scale and intensity of fairness norms [17,23–25]. However, a systematic explanation of variation in fairness norms across different human societies has remained an open question that motivates our paper. Here, we hypothesize that the overall structure of social interactions, as captured by the network topology, can causally influence fairness norms and can also be linked to the hypothesized factors that have been suggested by earlier empirical studies. We take a computational approach to investigate the role of macro-level structural features of social networks in explaining the inter-societal variation of fairness norms.

The variations of fairness across societies have been largely attributed to cultural differences, yet interpretations have been mixed [24,26,27]. Cross-country results of experimental studies using canonical economic games under different conditions of the balance of power between two parties suggest that difference in the national culture results in differing beliefs about fairness [28].

Studies that attempted to attribute variations of these beliefs to country-level *cultural variables* [29,30] show a relationship between the behavior of individuals and *the scale of respect for authority* [25]. Moreover, recent experimental studies tentatively suggest religion as one of the influential factors affecting individuals' fair behavior [31]. As a canonical paradigm to investigate fairness, the majority of these studies use the Ultimatum Game.

The Ultimatum Game (UG hereafter) has been the bedrock of a large number of studies that investigate the systematic deviation of human altruistic behavior from theoretical models that are based on the *homo economicus* assumption [15,32,33]. In the UG, two players are supposed to decide about sharing a fixed amount of money; one player acts as the *Proposer* and the other plays the role of the *Responder*. The proposer offers a split of the amount and the responder accepts or rejects. No bargaining is allowed. If the responder accepts, both players receive their amount based on the split; otherwise neither player receives anything. A rational responder, seeking to maximize her utility, would accept even the smallest positive offer. Being aware of the rationality of his partner, a rational proposer would therefore claim almost the entire amount. However, the results of a large number of experimental studies using the UG contradict with the prediction of pure rational models; most proposers offer a fair share and most responders reject low (but nonzero) offers [34–36]. The division of the money in the UG represents a measure for fairness norms. Experimental studies based on the Ultimatum Game have reported significant cross-societal variations in average size of the offers by the proposers and the rejection rates by the responders. Table 1 shows the results of a number of key empirical studies of variation of fairness norms across different societies together with attributed institutional factors. The variation has particularly been bolder when experiments are conducted in non-industrial societies. In [17] for example, the UG was played in 15 small-scale societies; the mean offer varied between 0.26 to 0.58 (as a proportion) and the rejection rate for low offers (offers of 0.2 or less) had a range between 0 to 0.8. Later studies conducted in other non-industrial societies have shown comparable large variations [23]. What social and institutional factors cause such variations? One potential key determinant is the macro-level structure of social networks. Experimental studies have previously shown that network structure of social interaction has a significant impact on evolution of collective behavior related to cooperation and competition [37], inequality [38], and exploration/exploitation [39]. Moreover, empirical studies based on experimental UG suggest factors that can be related to social structure. A series of studies that explored the motivation for fairness in anonymous interactions across dramatically diverse population show that fairness co-varies with *Payoffs to Cooperation* (PC) and *Market Integration* (MI) where PC represents the size of a group's payoff from cooperation in economic production, and MI represents how much people rely on market exchange in their daily lives as opposed to rely on home-grown or hunted [17].

Table 1. Empirical studies of variation of fairness norms using the Ultimatum Game and attributed social/institutional factors.

Empirical study	Mean offers	Rejection rates	Attributed institutional factors (as mentioned in each study)
[17]	0.26–0.58	0–0.8[2]	*Payoffs to Cooperation, Market Integration*
[23]	0.15–0.61	0–0.4[3]	*Hierarchy of Chiefdom System, Scale of Cooperative Units*
[25]	0.26–0.58	0–0.4	Cultural difference (*Respect for Authority*)
[24]	0.42–0.46	0.07–0.20[1]	Cultural difference (no specific factor is identified)

3 Model

To study the effect of structure on agents' strategies playing the UG, we developed a computational agent-based model based on evolutionary game theory on networks [5]. Each agent has a strategy vector containing the offer value and the acceptance threshold, each varies between 0 and 1; where higher values represent stronger fairness norms. In each evolutionary round, agents interact based on a pairwise UG while using the same strategy vector against all partners and collect payoffs (Eq. 1). Once all agents have completed one round of the UG with all of their partners, game scores are calculated (Eq. 2).

An evolutionary process based on the agents' game scores (Eq. 3) represents learning and strategy adoption by agents. That is, agents stochastically adopt the strategy of their neighbors with higher game scores where the probability of adoption is an increasing function of the difference between the two agents' scores. The evolutionary process represents cultural evolution through social learning but it can also represent genetic evolution, both of which have been linked to the emergence of fairness in the UG [40]. In the context of cultural evolution, an individual tends to imitate the strategy of another individual with a higher payoff and mutation denotes either exploring a new strategy or incorrectly imitating the strategies used by other individuals. In the context of genetic evolution, individuals are born and die, and mutation creates variation into the gene pool.

We adopt the multi-layered computational model developed by [41] that captures the effect of structure of interaction between individual agents on the formation and evolution of social norms. We model interaction between individual agents by one-shot ultimatum game, use a stochastic update rule to evolve strategies and use networks to model the structure of interactions. Finally, we do multivariate statical analysis on the agents' strategy at the equilibrium and network structural features to find which features play the most important role in promoting fair behavior. Our model has the following layers (Fig. 1).

(a) **Strategy space.** The strategy of each agent $i \in \{1, .., N\}$ is characterized by $s_i = (p_i, q_i)$, where $p_i \in [0, 1]$ is the amount that i offers when she acts as the proposer and $q_i \in [0, 1]$ is the acceptance threshold when she plays the role of the responder in the UG (without loss of generality we assumed the amount to be divided is one unit).

(b) **One-shot ultimatum game.** Every agent i plays the UG with all agents j in her neighborhood with a fixed strategy and equal probability of being the proposer or the responder i.e., in each interaction between two given agents, one of the agents is randomly and with equal chance selected as the proposer and the other agent is assigned as the responder (in some alternative models the chance of being the proposer/responder can be a function of the agent's degree or the outcome of its previous interactions [42]). The payoff of an agent i in interaction with agent j is calculated according to Eq. 1. For each agent i the accumulated payoff is normalized by the agent's degree (k_i) in the network and is used as the game score, $\Pi_i^{k_i}$ (Eq. 2).

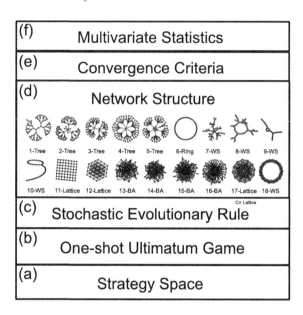

Fig. 1. Multi-layered agent-based computational model.

$$\Pi_{i \leftarrow j} = \begin{cases} 1 - p_i & \text{if } i \text{ acts as the proposer and } p_i \geq q_j \\ 0 & \text{if } i \text{ acts as the proposer and } p_i < q_j \\ p_j & \text{if } j \text{ acts as the proposer and } p_j \geq q_i \\ 0 & \text{if } j \text{ is the proposer and } p_j < q_i \end{cases} \tag{1}$$

$$\Pi_i^{k_i} = \frac{1}{k_i} \sum_{j \in N(i)} \Pi_{i \leftarrow j} \tag{2}$$

(c) **Stochastic update rule.** Agents' strategies evolve based on a social learning rule. The implicit assumption of this model is the ability of the agents to assess and learn from their peers—as opposed to adaptive models, in which agents learn from their previous interactions [43]. The evolutionary strategy update process is as follows. Every agent i randomly selects an agent j in the neighborhood, if the score of j is greater than the score of i then i adopts the strategy of j with a probability $W(s_i \rightarrow s_j)$. The probability of the strategy adoption is given by the Fermi rule in Eq. 3 in which β is the selection intensity.

$$W(s_i \rightarrow s_j) = [1 + exp(\beta(\Pi_i - \Pi_j))]^{-1} \tag{3}$$

In order to account for innovation in each strategy update, a small perturbation is introduced in the value of the strategy vector. That is, if agent i adopts the strategy of j then $(p_i, q_i) = (p_j + \delta_1, q_j + \delta_2)$ with δ_1 and δ_2 being randomly and independently picked from a small interval $[-\delta, \delta]$. Once the strategy update is completed, payoffs are reset to zero for the next evolutionary round.

(d) **Network structure.** The interaction structure of agents is determined by the topology of the network where agents are represented as nodes and only interact with their immediate neighbors in the network. To make simulations computationally efficient, we make the search space of network structures sparse based on key structural features that represent characteristics of social structure.

The structural features that we selected for this study are network average degree, girth and average shortest path that represent compactness of the society, and transitivity that represents dyadic closures in the population. We use the network modularity index to measure the strength of community structure. Modualrity is an emergent structural feature of many evolving networks [44] and has also been found to have a significant impact on the emergence of prosocial behavior [41,45]. To capture the role of hierarchy and relative power structure, we measure the degree of *hubiness* of the network calculated based on the degree distribution. Hubiness is a structural feature of a wide range of real networks, such as co-authorship networks [46], the World Wide Web [47], and the dependency network of natural language [48,49], that are formed through the mechanisms of growth and preferential attachment where new nodes prefer to link to the more connected nodes [50,51]. Huby structures are argued to result in economic efficiency for a certain range of network parameters [52,53]. In such network structures, the higher tendency to link to highly connected nodes results in higher skewness of degree distribution since several nodes are directly connected to a few central nodes (*hubs*).

To find a set of networks that represent the interaction structure between agents in our model we need to balance the trade-off between generating the variation of structural features and the computational efficiency. We carefully selected 26 structures by changing the parameters of network formation models to sufficiently capture variations of structural features in this study. The structures selected for this study are as follows. Four Barabási-Albert networks, four Watts-Strogatz networks, five Tree structures, four Erdős-Rényi networks, and four networks based on Watts-Strogatz model to generate required variation of average path length. The other network structures are a 2D-Lattice, 3D-Lattice, Circular Lattice, Ring, and a fully connected graph. Additionally, we selected the size of the networks to keep the model computationally efficient while the effect of structure remains significant in the evolution of agent's strategies (Fig. 2). The size of most networks used in this study is 100 nodes with two exceptions for circular lattice and 3D lattice which have 125 ($5 \times 5 \times 5$) nodes. We also verified that the results are not sensitive to the deviation of 100–125 nodes in the network size.

(e) **Convergence criteria.** Unlike similar computational models where the value at the equilibrium is calculated by averaging strategies over a certain number of generations after a transient stage with a fixed and large number of generations, we used an adaptive convergence criteria. As suggested by

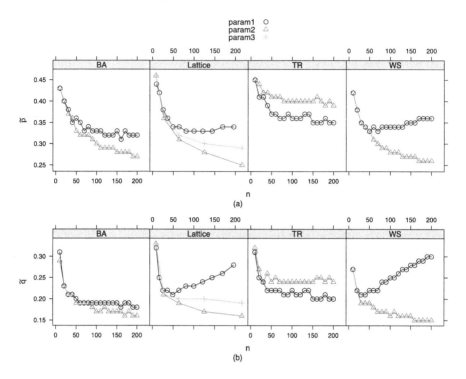

Fig. 2. Average strategy versus network size for different network models and the network models' parameters. Each panel represents one network model and shows the value of average strategy (i.e., (a) offer value, and (b) acceptance threshold) at the equilibrium versus network size for two (three) network model parameters.

[41], in our model the evolutionary process continued over a number of generations until no more than one agent updates its strategy for a consecutive window of 100 generations. To enhance convergence, we considered a noise threshold of $\epsilon = 0.05$ for strategies below which agents do not adopt a new strategy. This approach (1) ensures that evolutionary process continues until strategies of all agents stabilize in the population and (2) is more computationally efficient as the number of generations for the convergence becomes a function of the network structure as well as the initialization.

(f) **Simulation Data Analysis.** In order to find the relationship between network structural features and agents' average strategy at equilibrium, we use Principal Component Analysis (PCA) on the simulation data. PCA helps us to represent the variations of structural features and strategy vectors based on fewer number of linearly uncorrelated components and determine variations of which variables are related.

4   Results

In each simulation initialization, we populated the network with agents for each structure and draw a random value for p_i and q_i independently from a uniform distribution $U(0, H)$ for each agent where $H \in \{0.5, 1\}$. We determined the number of initializations so that the average value over all runs for each network structure is reasonably robust. We used 1024 initializations for each network structure and calculated the average value of strategies for each network. This ensures less than 1% variation in the average strategy at the equilibrium for our case. We used $\beta = 0.1$ in the Fermi rule (Eq. 3) for the selection intensity and $\delta = 0.005$ for perturbation in strategy adoption. All runs converged for these simulation parameters across all network structures selected for this study.

The simulation took approximately 40 min for all network structures on a 256-core cluster. The results of the simulation was aggregated in a data table, in which rows represent network structures and columns represent average values of strategies at the equilibrium as we as the structural features. We measured the skewness of degree distribution (g_1) for each network structure using $g_1 = \frac{m_3}{m_2^{3/2}}$ where m_2 and m_3 are, respectively, the second and the third moments of the degree distribution. Larger values (in magnitude) of g_1 indicate more skewness in the distribution [54]. To measure the strength of the community structure (Q), we first used the algorithm suggested in [55] to partition the network into communities of densely connected nodes, with the nodes belonging to different communities being only sparsely connected. Next, we measured modularity index using $Q = \frac{1}{2m} \sum_{i,j} [A_{ij} - \frac{k_i k_j}{2m}] \delta(c_i, c_j)$ where, for an unweighted graph, A_{ij} represents an edge between i and j, k_i is the degree of vertex i, c_i is the community to which vertex i is assigned, function $\delta(u, v)$ is 1 if $u = v$ and 0 otherwise, and m is the number of edges in the graph [56].

In order to find the key structural features that drive fairness in the population of agents, we used Principal Component Analysis (PCA) on the simulation data [41]. The variables in the PCA include network characteristics (i.e., average degree, average path length, transitivity, modularity, and hubiness) and average strategy vector (i.e., $\tilde{p}$: average offer and $\tilde{q}$: average acceptance threshold) of all runs for a network at the equilibrium. We used modularity index, a scalar value that represents the number of links within communities compared to links between communities [56], as a measure for community structure. We used the heuristic method in [55] for calculating the modularity of network structures. To measure *hubiness* of the structures, represented by the lack of symmetry in the degree distribution, we used the coefficient of skewness from [54] (Methods 3).

Figure 3 shows the results of the PCA on the correlation matrix constructed from the simulation data. We used the first two components that cumulatively account for 80% of the total variance in the whole data set. Figure 3b shows the *biplot* for the first two components and their correlations with network characteristics and average strategies at the equilibrium. In the biplot, average offer has an opposite direction to the average degree and is approximately orthogonal to the average path length and girth. However, the average offer value is

	PC1	PC2
Average offer ($\tilde{p}$)	**0.815**	**0.437**
Average acceptance threshold ($\tilde{q}$)	0.913	-0.048
Degree	**-0.837**	-0.258
Girth	0.487	-0.755
Modularity	**0.896**	-0.100
Path	0.667	-0.713
Hubiness	0.268	**0.792**
Transivity	-0.802	-0.240

(a)

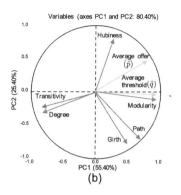

(b)

Fig. 3. (a) Correlations between the initial variables and the independent principal components. (b) Principal Component Analysis results summary.

more aligned with modularity and hubiness, suggesting a significant effect of these two structural features. The correlations between network structural features together with average strategies and principal components are provided in Fig. 3a. Average offer is significantly loaded on PC1 and PC2 while modularity is only highly loaded on PC1 and hubiness is highly loaded on PC2. Average degree is negatively loaded on PC1.

Panel (a) in Fig. 4 shows the level of fairness, measured by average offer value, versus skewness of degree distribution (hubiness). The lowest level of fairness belongs to the Full and Erdős-Rényi networks, and the highest is attributed to Tree structures. The results show that an increase in hubiness led to higher fairness. Variation of hubiness is mainly generated by varying the power of preferential attachment in the Barabási-Albert scale free and the number of children in Tree networks. However, average offers are higher in Tree structures than those in the Barabási-Albert networks. Not only do tree structures have skewed degree distribution but they also have stronger community structure. The rest

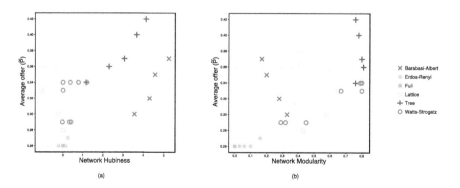

Fig. 4. Fairness versus network topology parameters. (a) Average offer value vs. network hubiness. (b) Average offer value vs. network modularity.

of the networks with lower hubiness are located along the y-axis; however, the level of fairness varies among these structures. This indicates that hubiness is not the only structural feature affecting the level of fairness. Panel (b) in Fig. 4 depicts the level of fairness versus modularity index and shows that an increase in network modularity results in an increase in the level of fairness. Variation of modularity index has been generated by different lattice structures and Watts-Strogatz network model, in which modularity index varies by changing the probability of rewiring. These structures have similar hubiness and are located along the y-axis in Panel (a). The difference of modularity index and the level of fairness between Tree structures and the Barabási-Albert networks are evident in Panel (b) i.e., Barabási-Albert and Tree structures do not have much variation in modularity index, yet Tree structures have stronger community and exhibit higher level of fairness.

5   Discussion

Our results identify three key structural features of social networks to explain the variation of fairness across different populations: average degree, community structure, and hubiness. Average degree of a network with a fixed number of nodes represents the density of interactions among a population. The results of our model show that populations with a large number of social interactions per individual exhibit lower levels of fairness. This is consistent with previous findings [7,8,57] and is due to the fact that the increase in the density of social interactions leads to a well-mixed population and weakens the effect of structure, thus reduces overall level of fairness.

The intuition behind the role of community structure, captured by network modularity, in variations of fairness is as follows. When the interaction between agents follows a network structure, the success of a strategy S_1 invading a population with strategy S_2 not only depends on the payoff that is obtained from the encounter with the vast majority (i.e., $E\{S_2, S_1\}$ and $E\{S_1, S_2\}$) but also on local interactions of the invaders (i.e., $E\{S_2, S_2\}$ and $E\{S_1, S_2\}$) [7]. When initial strategies are randomly distributed, a subset of agents will have a fair strategy. A strong community structure would help formation of clusters around agents with similar fair strategies and increases the chance of the fair strategy to take over the population. This concurs with an earlier study that investigates the level of fairness in a range of networks sorted according to a measure of *order* that shows that the level of fairness decreases as the community structure weakens [58].

Another structural feature that promote fairness in our model is *hubiness*, which is measured by the skewness of degree distribution. Prior studies have shown the significant role of huby structures (structures dynamically generated through the mechanisms of growth and preferential attachment) in the evolutionary dynamics of formation of social norms [59–61]. Our results suggest societies in which few individuals play the role of hubs, which are connected to large number of low-degree individuals, exhibit higher levels of fair behavior in the

UG. The intuition is similar to how average degree affects fairness, as explained earlier. Given that higher number of interactions decreases fairness (as the structure becomes closer to a well-mixed population), for a fixed average degree, the structure in which degree of a larger number of nodes is smaller exhibit a higher fairness. That is, the connections are shifted from a majority of nodes to a few hubs while total average degree is constant which results in skewed degree distribution.

Empirical data that directly supports the effect of social network structure on fairness is often difficult to gather. On the one hand, isolating the effect of social structure from other factors in field experiments is often hard. On the other hand, lab experiments that simultaneously accommodate sufficiently large number of subjects on various network structures is challenging. Despite these limitations, we can attribute some of the factors that are empirically hypothesized to explain fairness in cross-country and cross-organization to social network parameters. Here, we first compare our findings to the results of two empirical studies that demonstrate significant cross societal differences in playing the UG. The first one is a series of papers [17,31] led by Henrich based on playing a number of fairness related games, including the UG, in 15 diverse small-scale societies that suggest that societies in which the size of a group's payoff from cooperation in economic production (*Payoffs to Cooperation*) is higher, and those in which people rely on the market for their daily life (*Market Integration*) have higher levels of fairness. The second study [23] is based on results of playing the UG in two multi-village Tanzanian ethnic groups (Pimbwe and Sukuma) which are embedded in similar environments and political systems, yet have drastically different social institutions. The significantly higher levels of fairness among Sukuma members are attributed to two important institutional factors between the two groups: Firstly, unlike Pimbwe whose loosely linked clans are controlled by a single chief in a central village, the Sukuma (the original inhabitants of the area) live in multiple chiefdom system with a high level of cooperation among chiefdoms. Secondly, Pimbwe has smaller scale cooperative units, mostly limited to family and friends within each village, whereas in Sukuma there are larger scale cooperative units at the village level that go beyond family boundaries. The average within-village (between village) offers in the UG for the Sukuma is reported 42% (4 times) higher than the Pimbwe.

Our results are in agreement with key hypotheses of these empirical findings. The determining role of *Payoffs to Cooperation* in the Henrich study and the impact of the scale of cooperative units on fairness in ethnic groups in the Tanzania study can be explained by the significant role of network modularity in increasing fairness norms. That is, in a society with a stronger community structure, there are more interactions within each group as opposed to between groups, hence people are more likely to be involved in group cooperation for an economic production. The role of *Market Integration* in the first study and governance structure (single chiefdom versus multiple interacting chiefdoms) can further be supported by our result which points to the impact of network hubiness on fairness norms. Clearly, the multi-chiefdom governance of the Sukuma suggests a social structure with higher level of hubiness compared to Pimbwe. We also expect societies with high market integration to include entities with which a large number of people have social interactions (as opposed to relying on home-grown products which results in a flat structure).

Additionally, cross-organizational studies of fairness suggest structural parameters that are related to hubiness. Cross-organizational study of fairness shows that the more connections there are from employees to managers, the higher the perception to fairness is [22]. In organizations with such structure, managers play the role of the hub and the more connections to the hub results in a more skewed distribution of number of interactions of individuals. Another study that investigates fairness across organizations shows that for a given number of workers, the lower the organization complexity (defined by the number of levels of hierarchy), the higher the perception of fairness is [20]. That is, for a fixed number of individuals, the decrease in the number of organizational levels results in having few individuals with a larger number of interactions and a more skewed degree distribution in the network of social interactions.

6 Conclusion

Our model determines structural features whose variations cause changes in the collective fair behavior. However, even the most similar results from empirical studies imply that fairness co-varies with the structural changes of social network. A future direction is to experimentally evaluate the causality between structural features of social network and variations of fairness, and create setups comparing similar *societies* side by side where the only difference is the connectivity structure of individuals' social interactions. Results of this work can provide engineering insights into designing network environments that would result in fairness in autonomous agents. It can also help with future directions of empirical research in fairness norms: So far, the variations in fairness norms have been mostly observed in non-industrial societies with drastically different institutional structures. Our results can be used to design better cross-societal studies within industrial countries by targeting sub-groups whose social interactions vary according to the findings of this research.

Acknowledgement. This work is in part supported by the National Science Foundation (NSF) under Grant No. CMMI-1548521. Authors are grateful to David Gianetto for the insightful comments on the computational framework.

References

1. Lin, P.: Why ethics matters for autonomous cars. In: Maurer, M., Gerdes, J., Lenz, B., Winner, H. (eds.) Autonomous Driving, pp. 69–85. Springer, Heidelberg (2016). doi:10.1007/978-3-662-45854-9_4
2. Goodall, N.J.: Can you program ethics into a self-driving car? IEEE Spectr. **53**(6), 28–58 (2016)

3. Roth, A.E., Sönmez, T., Ünver, M.U.: Kidney exchange. Q. J. Econ. **119**(2), 457–488 (2004)
4. Sigmund, K.: The Calculus of Selfishness. Princeton University Press, Princeton (2010)
5. Szabó, G., Fath, G.: Evolutionary games on graphs. Phys. Rep. **446**(4), 97–216 (2007)
6. Fehr, E., Fischbacher, U.: Third-party punishment and social norms. Evol. Hum. Behav. **25**(2), 63–87 (2004)
7. Page, K.M., Nowak, M.A., Sigmund, K.: The spatial ultimatum game. Proc. R. Soc. Lond. B: Biol. Sci. **267**(1458), 2177–2182 (2000)
8. Killingback, T., Studer, E.: Spatial ultimatum games, collaborations and the evolution of fairness. Proc. R. Soc. Lond. B: Biol. Sci. **268**(1478), 1797–1801 (2001)
9. Mosleh, M., Heydari, B.: Fair topologies: community structures and network hubs drive emergence of fairness norms. Sci. Rep. **7** (2017). doi:10.1038/s41598-017-01876-0
10. Clark, A.E., Oswald, A.J.: Satisfaction and comparison income. J. Public Econ. **61**(3), 359–381 (1996)
11. Luttmer, E.F.P.: Neighbors as negatives: relative earnings and well-being. Q. J. Econ. **120**(3), 963–1002 (2005)
12. Marmot, M.: Status syndrome. Significance **1**(4), 150–154 (2004)
13. Fliessbach, K., Weber, B., Trautner, P., Dohmen, T., Sunde, U., Elger, C.E., Falk, A.: Social comparison affects reward-related brain activity in the human ventral striatum. Science **318**(5854), 1305–1308 (2007)
14. Kahneman, D., Knetsch, J.L., Thaler, R.H.: Fairness and the assumptions of economics. J. Bus. **59**, S285–S300 (1986)
15. Thaler, R.H.: Anomalies: the ultimatum game. J. Econ. Perspect. **2**(4), 195–206 (1988)
16. Rabin, M.: Incorporating fairness into game theory and economics. Am. Econ. Rev. **83**, 1281–1302 (1993)
17. Henrich, J., Boyd, R., Bowles, S., Camerer, C., Fehr, E., Gintis, H., McElreath, R.: In search of homo economicus: behavioral experiments in 15 small-scale societies. Am. Econ. Rev. **91**(2), 73–78 (2001)
18. Blake, P.R., McAuliffe, K., Corbit, J., Callaghan, T.C., Barry, O., Bowie, A., Kleutsch, L., Kramer, K.L., Ross, E., Vongsachang, H., et al.: The ontogeny of fairness in seven societies. Nature **528**, 258–261 (2015)
19. Lamba, S., Mace, R.: The evolution of fairness: explaining variation in bargaining behaviour. Proc. R. Soc. Lond. B: Biol. Sci. **280**(1750), 20122028 (2013)
20. Schminke, M., Cropanzano, R., Rupp, D.E.: Organization structure and fairness perceptions: the moderating effects of organizational level. Organ. Behav. Hum. Decis. Process. **89**(1), 881–905 (2002)
21. Schminke, M., Ambrose, M.L., Cropanzano, R.S.: The effect of organizational structure on perceptions of procedural fairness. J. Appl. Psychol. **85**(2), 294 (2000)
22. Lamertz, K.: The social construction of fairness: social influence and sense making in organizations. J. Organ. Behav. **23**(1), 19–37 (2002)
23. Paciotti, B., Hadley, C.: The ultimatum game in southwestern tanzania: ethnic variation and institutional scope 1. Curr. Anthropol. **44**(3), 427–432 (2003)
24. Chuah, S.-H., Hoffmann, R., Jones, M., Williams, G.: Do cultures clash? Evidence from cross-national ultimatum game experiments. J. Econ. Behav. Organ. **64**(1), 35–48 (2007)
25. Oosterbeek, H., Sloof, R., Van De Kuilen, G.: Cultural differences in ultimatum game experiments: evidence from a meta-analysis. Exp. Econ. **7**(2), 171–188 (2004)

26. Roth, A.E., Prasnikar, V., Okuno-Fujiwara, M., Zamir, S.: Bargaining and market behavior in Jerusalem, Ljubljana, Pittsburgh, and Tokyo: an experimental study. Am. Econ. Rev. **81**, 1068–1095 (1991)
27. Roth, A.E.: Bargening experiments (chapter 4). In: Kagel, J.H., Roth, A.E. (eds.) The Handbook of Experimental Economics, pp. 253–348. Princeton University Press, Princeton (1995)
28. Buchan, N.R., Croson, R.T.A., Johnson, E.J.: When do fair beliefs influence bargaining behavior? Experimental bargaining in Japan and the United States. J. Consum. Res. **31**(1), 181–190 (2004)
29. Inglehart, R.: Culture and democracy. In: Culture Matters: How Values Shape Human Progress, pp. 80–97 (2000)
30. Hofstede, G.: Cultures and Organizations: Software of the Mind, vol. 1. McGraw-Hill, New York (1991)
31. Henrich, J., Ensminger, J., McElreath, R., Barr, A., Clark, B., Bolyanatz, A., Cardenas, J.C., Gurven, M., Gwako, E., Henrich, N., et al.: Markets, religion, community size, and the evolution of fairness and punishment. Science **327**(5972), 1480–1484 (2010)
32. van Damme, E., Binmore, K.G., Roth, A.E., Samuelson, L., Winter, E., Bolton, G.E., Ockenfels, A., Dufwenberg, M., Kirchsteiger, G., Gneezy, U., et al.: How Werner Güth's ultimatum game shaped our understanding of social behavior. J. Econ. Behav. Organ. **108**, 292–318 (2014)
33. Skyrms, B.: Evolution of the Social Contract. Cambridge University Press, Cambridge (2014)
34. Henrich, J., McElreath, R., Barr, A., Ensminger, J., Clark, B., Bolyanatz, A., Cardenas, J.C., Gurven, M., Gwako, E., Henrich, N., et al.: Costly punishment across human societies. Science **312**(5781), 1767–1770 (2006)
35. Güth, W., Kocher, M.G.: More than thirty years of ultimatum bargaining experiments: motives, variations, and a survey of the recent literature. J. Econ. Behav. Organ. **108**, 396–409 (2014)
36. Straub, P.G., Murnighan, J.K.: An experimental investigation of ultimatum games: information, fairness, expectations, and lowest acceptable offers. J. Econ. Behav. Organ. **27**(3), 345–364 (1995)
37. Rand, D.G., Nowak, M.A., Fowler, J.H., Christakis, N.A.: Static network structure can stabilize human cooperation. Proc. Natl. Acad. Sci. **111**(48), 17093–17098 (2014)
38. Nishi, A., Shirado, H., Rand, D.G., Christakis, N.A.: Inequality and visibility of wealth in experimental social networks. Nature **526**(7573), 426–429 (2015)
39. Mason, W., Watts, D.J.: Collaborative learning in networks. Proc. Natl. Acad. Sci. **109**(3), 764–769 (2012)
40. Rand, D.G., Tarnita, C.E., Ohtsuki, H., Nowak, M.A.: Evolution of fairness in the one-shot anonymous ultimatum game. Proc. Natl. Acad. Sci. **110**(7), 2581–2586 (2013)
41. Gianetto, D.A., Heydari, B.: Network modularity is essential for evolution of cooperation under uncertainty. Sci. Rep. **5**, 9340 (2015)
42. Wu, T., Fu, F., Zhang, Y., Wang, L.: Adaptive role switching promotes fairness in networked ultimatum game. Sci. Rep. **3**, 1550 (2013)
43. Duan, W.-Q., Stanley, H.E.: Fairness emergence from zero-intelligence agents. Phys. Rev. E **81**(2), 026104 (2010)
44. Heydari, B., Dalili, K.: Emergence of modularity in system of systems: complex networks in heterogeneous environments. IEEE Syst. J. **9**(1), 223–231 (2015)

45. Gianetto, D.A., Heydari, B.: Sparse cliques trump scale-free networks in coordination and competition. Sci. Rep. **6**, 21870 (2016)
46. Wagner, C.S., Leydesdorff, L.: Network structure, self-organization, and the growth of international collaboration in science. Res. Policy **34**(10), 1608–1618 (2005)
47. Barabási, A.-L., Albert, R.: Emergence of scaling in random networks. Science **286**(5439), 509–512 (1999)
48. Qian, L., Chunshan, X., Liu, H.: Can chunking reduce syntactic complexity of natural languages? Complexity **21**(S2), 33–41 (2016)
49. Cancho, R.F.-i.: Hubiness, length, crossings and their relationships in dependency trees. arXiv preprint arXiv:1304.4086 (2013)
50. Kunegis, J., Blattner, M., Moser, C.: Preferential attachment in online networks: measurement and explanations. In: Proceedings of the 5th Annual ACM Web Science Conference, pp. 205–214. ACM (2013)
51. Barabási, A.-L.: Network science (2016)
52. Heydari, B., Mosleh, M., Dalili, K.: Efficient network structures with separable heterogeneous connection costs. Econ. Lett. **134**, 82–85 (2015)
53. Heydari, P., Mosleh, M., Heydari, B.: Efficient integration in multi-community networks. In: Working Paper (2017). SSRN https://ssrn.com/abstract=2990086
54. Zwillinger, D., Kokoska, S.: CRC Standard Probability and Statistics Tables and Formulae. CRC Press, Boca Raton (1999)
55. Blondel, V.D., Guillaume, J.-L., Lambiotte, R., Lefebvre, E.: Fast unfolding of communities in large networks. J. Stat. Mech: Theory Exp. **2008**(10), P10008 (2008)
56. Newman, M.E.J.: Modularity and community structure in networks. Proc. Natl. Acad. Sci. **103**(23), 8577–8582 (2006)
57. Sinatra, R., Iranzo, J., Gomez-Gardenes, J., Floria, L.M., Latora, V., Moreno, Y.: The ultimatum game in complex networks. J. Stat. Mech: Theory Exp. **2009**(09), P09012 (2009)
58. Kuperman, M.N., Risau-Gusman, S.: The effect of the topology on the spatial ultimatum game. Eur. Phys. J. B **62**(2), 233–238 (2008)
59. Santos, F.C., Rodrigues, J.F., Pacheco, J.M.: Graph topology plays a determinant role in the evolution of cooperation. Proc. R. Soc. Lond. B: Biol. Sci. **273**(1582), 51–55 (2006)
60. Santos, F.C., Pacheco, J.M.: Scale-free networks provide a unifying framework for the emergence of cooperation. Phys. Rev. Lett. **95**(9), 098104 (2005)
61. Gómez-Gardenes, J., Campillo, M., Floría, L.M., Moreno, Y.: Dynamical organization of cooperation in complex topologies. Phys. Rev. Lett. **98**(10), 108103 (2007)

Constrained Community Detection in Multiplex Networks

Koji Eguchi and Tsuyoshi Murata[✉]

Department of Computer Science, School of Computing,
Tokyo Institute of Technology, W8-59 2-12-1 Ookayama,
Meguro, Tokyo 152-8552, Japan
eguchi@net.c.titech.ac.jp, murata@c.titech.ac.jp
http://www.net.c.titech.ac.jp/

Abstract. Constrained community detection is a kind of community detection taking given constraints into account to improve the accuracy of community detection. Optimizing constrained Hamiltonian is one of the methods for constrained community detection. Constrained Hamiltonian consists of Hamiltonian which is generalized modularity and constrained term which takes given constraints into account. Nakata proposed a method for constrained community detection in monoplex networks based on the optimization of constrained Hamiltonian by extended Louvain method.

In this paper, we propose a new method for constrained community detection in multiplex networks. Multiplex networks are the combinations of multiple individual networks. They can represent temporal networks or networks with several types of edges. While optimizing modularity proposed by Mucha et al. is popular for community detection in multiplex networks, our method optimizes the constrained Hamiltonian which we extend for multiplex networks. By using our proposed method, we successfully detect communities taking constraints into account. We also successfully improve the accuracy of community detection by using our method iteratively. Our method enables us to carry out constrained community detection interactively in multiplex networks.

Keywords: Multiplex networks · Constrained community detection · Gen Louvain method · Constrained Hamiltonian

1 Introduction

Methods for detecting dense subnetworks in given networks (community detection) are useful for understanding, visualizing and compressing the networks. We focus on community detection in multiplex networks [7]. Multiplex networks are the combinations of multiple networks by connecting same nodes in different networks with edges.

Optimization of modularity [10] is often used in conventional community detection. Modularity is a function to evaluate the quality of communities based

© Springer International Publishing AG 2017
G.L. Ciampaglia et al. (Eds.): SocInfo 2017, Part I, LNCS 10539, pp. 75–87, 2017.
DOI: 10.1007/978-3-319-67217-5_6

on the deviation from random partitioning. Louvain method [1] is one of the popular greedy methods for modularity optimization. Gen Louvain [5] is the method for optimizing modularity in multiplex networks proposed by Mucha et al. [8]. The method is an extension of Louvain method, and is often used for multiplex community detection.

Constrained community detection reflects prior knowledge or feedbacks from users when we detect communities. We expect to detect community structure which is more accurate by taking given constraints into account. One of the methods for constrained community detection is optimizing constrained Hamiltonian [4]. The constrained Hamiltonian consists of constrained term and Hamiltonian [12] which is a generalization of modularity. It is often optimized by simulated annealing [6]. However, there seems to be no research on constrained community detection in multiplex networks.

In this paper, we extend Hamiltonian for multiplex networks, construct constrained Hamiltonian with constrained term, and optimize by Gen Louvain method for constrained community detection in multiplex networks. Based on our proposed method, we successfully detect communities taking given constraints into account. We also successfully improve the accuracy of community detection by giving constraints incrementally. Our method enables us to carry out constrained community detection interactively in multiplex networks.

2   Related Works

2.1   Multiplex Networks

Multiplex networks [7] consist of multiple networks connected with each other by edges. Each component network is called a 'layer'. All the layers have the same sets of nodes, and inter-layer edges connect only between the same nodes in different layers. Inter-layer edges are called 'couplings'. Ordinal coupling connects the same nodes in adjacent layers and categorical coupling connects the same nodes in all the layers.

2.2   Modularity for Multiplex Networks

A modularity for multiplex networks proposed by Mucha et al. [8] is represented as the following formula:

$$Q_{\text{multi}} = \frac{1}{2\mu} \sum_{ijsr} \left[\left(A_{ijs} - \gamma_s \frac{k_{is}k_{js}}{2m_s} \right) \delta_{sr} + \delta_{ij} C_{jsr} \right] \delta(g_{is}, g_{jr}), \qquad (1)$$

where μ is the total number of edges, A_{ijs} is the element (i, j) of an adjacency matrix A in layer s, γ_s is resolution parameter, k_{is} is the degree of node i in layer s, m_s is the number of edges in layer s, g_{is} is the index of community which node i belongs to in layer s, respectively. δ is the Kronecker's delta. C_{jsr} is ω if an edge exists between node j in layer s and r, and is 0 otherwise. ω is the weight of inter-layer edges.

2.3 Hamiltonian

Hamiltonian [12] is one of the objective functions for community detection proposed by Reichardt and Bornholdt. Hamiltonian $\mathcal{H}$ is shown as the following formula:

$$\mathcal{H} = -\sum_{i \neq j} a_{ij} A_{ij} \delta(g_i, g_j) + \sum_{i \neq j} b_{ij}(1 - A_{ij})\delta(g_i, g_j)$$
$$+ \sum_{i \neq j} c_{ij} A_{ij}(1 - \delta(g_i, g_j)) - \sum_{i \neq j} d_{ij}(1 - A_{ij})(1 - \delta(g_i, g_j)). \tag{2}$$

The formula (2) gives rewards when intra-community edges are present or inter-community edges are absent, and gives penalties when intra-community edges are absent or inter-community edges are present. A_{ij} represents the element (i, j) of an adjacency matrix A. a_{ij} and d_{ij} are parameters of the weights of reward, and b_{ij} and c_{ij} are parameters of the weights of penalty. g_i is the index of the community which node i belongs to.

Formula (2) can be transformed to formula (3) by setting $a_{ij} = c_{ij} = 1 - \gamma k_i k_j / 2m$, $b_{ij} = d_{ij} = \gamma k_i k_j / 2m$:

$$\mathcal{H} = -2 \sum_{i \neq j} \left(A_{ij} - \gamma \frac{k_i k_j}{2m} \right) \delta(g_i, g_j) + \sum_{i \neq j} \left(A_{ij} - \gamma \frac{k_i k_j}{2m} \right), \tag{3}$$

where k_i is the degree of node i and γ is a resolution parameter. We can ignore the second term of formula (3) because it does not depend on the result of community detection. The formula of modularity is obtained by adjusting the first degree coefficient. Therefore, we can conclude Hamiltonian is a generalization of modularity.

2.4 Constrained Community Detection

Community detection with prior knowledge or feedbacks from users is called constrained community detection. Constrained Hamiltonian [4], which is the objective function of constrained community detection, consists of Hamiltonian and constrained term. Constrained term U is shown as the following formula:

$$U = \sum_{i \neq j} \left(u_{ij}(1 - \delta(g_i, g_j)) + \bar{u}_{ij} \delta(g_i, g_j) \right). \tag{4}$$

Label l_i represents i's community, and the label is given for each node as the constraints. Label $l_i = -1$ is formally given for nodes having no labels. u_{ij} and $\bar{u}_{ij}$ are defined as follows using the label:

$$u_{ij} = \begin{cases} 1 & (\text{when } l_i = l_j \neq -1) \\ 0 & (\text{otherwise}) \end{cases} \tag{5}$$

$$\bar{u}_{ij} = \begin{cases} 1 & (\text{when } l_i \neq l_j \wedge l_i \neq -1 \wedge l_j \neq -1) \\ 0 & (\text{otherwise}) \end{cases} \tag{6}$$

Constrained Hamiltonian $\mathcal{H}'$ consists of Hamiltonian and constrained term which is weighted by parameter μ. It is shown as the following formula which is composed of the Hamiltonian in formula (2) and constrained term in formula (4):

$$\mathcal{H}' = \mathcal{H} + \mu U$$
$$= -2 \sum_{i \neq j} (A_{ij} - \gamma P_{ij} + \mu \Delta U_{ij}) \delta(g_i, g_j) + K, \tag{7}$$

where μ is a parameter to adjust the balance between Hamiltonian and constrained term, $P_{ij} = k_i k_j / 2m$, $\Delta U_{ij} = (u_{ij} - \bar{u}_{ij})/2$, $K = \sum_{i \neq j}(A_{ij} - \gamma P_{ij}) + \mu \sum_{i \neq j} u_{ij}$, respectively. K is the constant which does not depend on the result of community detection. Simulated annealing [6] has been often used to optimize constrained Hamiltonian in formula (7). Nakata proposed a method for detecting constrained communities based on the optimization of constrained Hamiltonian by extended Louvain method [9]. The method enables us to detect communities with higher speed without decreasing the accuracy.

2.5 Gen Louvain Method

Gen Louvain method [5] is often used as the optimization method of modularity for community detection in multiplex networks. This is a greedy algorithm which is a generalization of Louvain method [1]. Figure 1 is the schematic diagram of Louvain method described in [1]. Louvain method is for monoplex networks, but the algorithm is almost the same. In Gen Louvain method, we just apply this algorithm to multiple layers. In this method, we assume that each of the nodes belongs to different communities in the initial state. In other words, the number

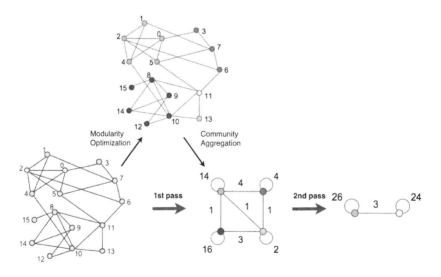

Fig. 1. Schematic diagram of Louvain method (cited from [1])

of communities is the same as that of nodes in the initial state. The following two phases are iteratively repeated afterwards:

1. Community membership of a selected node is moved to its all adjacent communities and calculate the value of modularity in each case. The community structure which takes maximum increase of the value of modularity is adopted. Iterating this process for all the nodes until the value of modularity does not increase.
2. A new network is constructed by assuming each community as a node. Go back to phase 1 if the network is not converged.

The community structure with the maximum value of modularity in a multiplex network can be obtained by iterating these phases until the community structure does not change further more. That community structure is hierarchical.

3 Proposed Method

3.1 Hamiltonian in Multiplex Networks

In order to extend Hamiltonian for multiplex networks, all we have to consider is inter-layer edges because presence or absence of inter-layer edges is shown as value 0 or ω. We define Hamiltonian in multiplex networks $\mathcal{H}_{\text{multi}}$ as in formula (8):

$$
\begin{aligned}
\mathcal{H}_{\text{multi}} = &-\sum_{ijsr} a_{ijs} A_{ijs}\delta(g_{is}, g_{js})\delta_{sr} + \sum_{ijsr} b_{ijs}(1 - A_{ijs})\delta(g_{is}, g_{js})\delta_{sr} \\
&+ \sum_{ijsr} c_{ijs} A_{ijs}(1 - \delta(g_{is}, g_{js}))\delta_{sr} - \sum_{ijsr} d_{ijs}(1 - A_{ijs})(1 - \delta(g_{is}, g_{js}))\delta_{sr} \quad (8) \\
&- \sum_{ijsr} e_{jsr} C_{jsr}\delta(g_{js}, g_{jr})\delta_{ij} + \sum_{ijsr} f_{jsr} C_{jsr}(1 - \delta(g_{js}, g_{jr}))\delta_{ij},
\end{aligned}
$$

where $a_{ijs}, d_{ijs}, e_{jsr}$ are the parameters for reward weights, and $b_{ijs}, c_{ijs}, f_{jsr}$ are those for penalty weights. The first four terms in formula (8), which are for intra-layer edges, are the same as Hamiltonian in formula (2), and the fifth and the sixth terms are for inter-layer edges. When inter-layer edges are present between two nodes, reward is given when the nodes belong to the same community and penalty is given when the nodes belong to different communities.

When we set the parameters of $\mathcal{H}_{\text{multi}}$ as $a_{ijs} = c_{ijs} = 1 - \gamma_s k_{is} k_{js}/2m_s$, $b_{ijs} = d_{ijs} = \gamma_s k_{is} k_{js}/2m_s$, $e_{jsr} = f_{jsr} = 1$, the following formula is obtained:

$$
\begin{aligned}
\mathcal{H}_{\text{multi}} = &-2 \sum_{ijsr} \left[\left(A_{ijs} - \gamma_s \frac{k_{is} k_{js}}{2m_s} \right) \delta_{sr} + \delta_{ij} C_{jsr} \right] \delta(g_{is}, g_{jr}) \\
&+ \sum_{ijsr} \left[\left(A_{ijs} - \gamma_s \frac{k_{is} k_{js}}{2m_s} \right) \delta_{sr} + \delta_{ij} C_{jsr} \right],
\end{aligned} \quad (9)
$$

where γ_s is a resolution parameter in layer s as in formula (1). The formula equivalent to formula (1) is achieved when the second term (constant) in formula (9) is ignored and the coefficient is adjusted. We can say that Hamiltonian which we constructed is a generalization of modularity in multiplex networks.

3.2   Constrained Hamiltonian in Multiplex Networks

Constrained Hamiltonian is constructed by adding constrained term to Hamiltonian in multiplex networks. In the case of monoplex networks, we give labels representing the community for each node as the constraints. In general, communities in multiplex networks contain nodes in different layers, and it is very difficult to consider relations between nodes in different layers and in the same layer at the same time. If we give labels for nodes as the constraints, the labels are effective only within the same layer or between layers and it might be impossible to detect intended communities composed of nodes in different layers. Therefore we give constraints for pairs of nodes, not for each node as a label. We propose constrained term to Hamiltonian in multiplex networks by giving constraints that a pair of nodes should belong to the same community (must-link constraint) or they should belong to the different communities (cannot-link constraint). Constraints to the pairs of nodes in different layers are given for only the same nodes. Constrained term in multiplex networks U_{multi} is shown in formula (10):

$$
\begin{aligned}
U_{\text{multi}} = &\sum_{ijsr} \left(u_{ijs} \left(1 - \delta(g_{is}, g_{js}) \right) + \bar{u}_{ijs} \delta(g_{is}, g_{js}) \right) \delta_{sr} \\
&+ \sum_{ijsr} \left(v_{jsr} \left(1 - \delta(g_{js}, g_{jr}) \right) + \bar{v}_{jsr} \delta(g_{js}, g_{jr}) \right) \delta_{ij},
\end{aligned}
\tag{10}
$$

where $u_{ijs} \bar{u}_{ijs} v_{jsr} \bar{v}_{jsr}$ are shown in formulas (11) through (14) respectively:

$$
u_{ijs} = \begin{cases} 1 & \text{(when node } i \text{ and } j \text{ in layer } s \text{ have must-link constraint)} \\ 0 & \text{(otherwise)} \end{cases}
\tag{11}
$$

$$
\bar{u}_{ijs} = \begin{cases} 1 & \text{(when node } i \text{ and } j \text{ in layer } s \text{ have cannot-link constraint)} \\ 0 & \text{(otherwise)} \end{cases}
\tag{12}
$$

$$
v_{jsr} = \begin{cases} 1 & \text{(when node } j \text{ in layer } s \text{ and } r \text{ have must-link constraint)} \\ 0 & \text{(otherwise)} \end{cases}
\tag{13}
$$

$$
\bar{v}_{jsr} = \begin{cases} 1 & \text{(when node } j \text{ in layer } s \text{ and } r \text{ have cannot-link constraint)} \\ 0 & \text{(otherwise)} \end{cases}
\tag{14}
$$

Constrained Hamiltonian in multiplex networks $\mathcal{H}'_{\text{multi}}$ is defined in formula (15) with Hamiltonian in formulas (9) and (10):

$$
\begin{aligned}
\mathcal{H}'_{\text{multi}} = &\mathcal{H}_{\text{multi}} + \mu U_{\text{multi}} \\
= &-2 \sum_{ijsr} \left(A_{ijs} - \gamma_s \frac{k_{is} k_{js}}{2m_s} + \mu \Delta U_{ijs} \right) \delta(g_{is}, g_{js}) \delta_{sr} \\
&- 2 \sum_{ijsr} \left(C_{jsr} + \mu \Delta V_{jsr} \right) \delta(g_{js}, g_{jr}) \delta_{ij} \\
&+ \sum_{ijsr} \left(A_{ijs} - \gamma_s \frac{k_{is} k_{js}}{2m_s} + \mu u_{ijs} \right) \delta_{sr} + \sum_{ijsr} (C_{jsr} + \mu v_{jsr}) \delta_{ij},
\end{aligned}
\tag{15}
$$

where $\Delta U_{ijs} = (u_{ijs} - \bar{u}_{ijs})/2$, and $\Delta V_{jsr} = (v_{jsr} - \bar{v}_{jsr})/2$. The third term and the fourth term in formula (15) are constants and do not depend on the result of community detection. We call constrained Hamiltonian in formula (15) as "proposed Hamiltonian" from here in this paper. We use proposed Hamiltonian as the objective function and propose optimizing it by Gen Louvain method for constrained community detection in multiplex networks.

4 Experiments

4.1 Effectiveness of Constrained Term

The difference of the results of community detection with or without constraints is discussed in this section. "Padgett Florentine families" [11] is used for the dataset. This network consists of 16 nodes, 35 unweighted edges and 2 layers. $\omega = 1, \gamma_s = 1$ is used and $\mu = 0$ in community detection without constraints and $\mu = 2$ in constrained community detection is used as in the previous study [9]. We checked the effect of constraints appears in the result when μ value exceeds 2 in the preliminary experiment.

The community structure as the result of experiments under various conditions is compared and visualized by MuxViz [3] in this experiment. The community structure obtained by community detection without constraints is shown in Fig. 2. In the figure, each color of nodes indicates the community which the node belongs to and the nodes whose degree is 0 are not shown.

From here, we show the results of constrained community detection in the same network, "Padgett Florentine families". We cannot choose the pair of nodes which are given a constraint based on the reliable information because this network has no ground truth. Therefore we choose the pair of nodes which is near the boundary of communities and in both layers in common.

We have detected communities with must-link constraint for node 4 and node 11 in layer 1. The community structure as the result is shown in Fig. 3. We can find that node 4 and node 11 originally belong to different communities but they belong to the same community when must-link constraint is given by comparing Fig. 3 with Fig. 2. Node 4 and node 11 in layer 2 also belong to the same community and the number of the communities as a whole changes from 4 to 2.

Constrained community detection was carried out giving cannot-link constraint for node 5 and node 11 in layer 1 of Fig. 2. The community structure of this result is shown in Fig. 4. We can find that node 5 and node 11 in layer 2 also belong to the different communities by comparing this result with Fig. 2. Node 3, 5, 11 and 15 belong to the same community in layer 1 in Fig. 2, but node 4, 7, 8, 11 and 15 belong to the same community in Fig. 4.

Constrained community detection was carried out giving cannot-link constraint for node 6 in layer 1 and layer 2 of Fig. 2. The community structure of this result is shown in Fig. 5. We can find that node 6 in layer 1 and layer 2 of the same community belong to the different communities and node 6 in layer 1 constitutes a community with node 2, 4, 7 and 8 and node 6 in layer 2 constitutes a community with node 3, 5 and 11, respectively by comparing this result with Fig. 2.

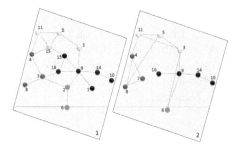

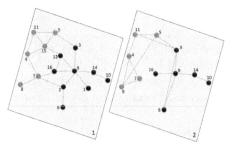

Fig. 2. Community detection without constraints ("Padgett Florentine families") (Color figure online)

Fig. 3. Constrained community detection with a positive constraint between node 4 and 11 in layer 1 ("Padgett Florentine families")

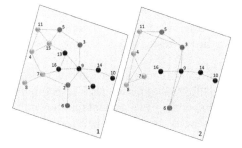

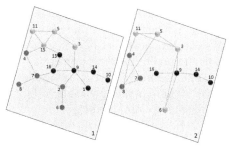

Fig. 4. Constrained community detection with a negative constraint for node 5 and 11 in layer 1 ("Padgett Florentine families")

Fig. 5. Constrained community detection with a negative constraint for node 6 in layer 1 and 2 ("Padgett Florentine families")

We can say proposed method takes the constraints into account because the community structure changes by giving constraints. In addition to the nodes with the constraints, those without the constraints also move to other communities. When the nodes without constraints move to other communities, both the nodes in the same layer which constrained node belongs to and those in the different layer are affected. The same nodes in different layers are connected by inter-layer edges. If a node is given a constraint, the same nodes in different layers are affected based on the value of ω (the weight of the inter-layer edges) and the community structure is changed. The proposed method is expected to detect appropriate communities with constraints.

4.2 Experiments of Constrained Community Detection Giving Incremental Constraints

The result of this experiment shows how the result of constrained community detection changes by giving incremental constraints. There are two possible ways to give constraints when we detect communities with constraints in the networks whose ground truth is unknown. One is the method for updating the result of community detection by giving constraints one by one and the other is giving all constraints at once. We adopt the former because it is more realistic than the latter. We assume this experiment as the case of community detection which users give feedbacks based on the result. This experiment is based on the one in monoplex networks [9]. Synthetic benchmark by De Domenico [2] is used to evaluate the accuracy of community detection. NMI in multiplex networks [2] is used to measure the accuracy. The experiment of community detection giving incremental constraints was carried out as follows:

1. No constraint is given to any nodes in the initial state.
2. Proposed Hamiltonian is optimized by Gen Louvain method for constrained community detection.
3. Compute the accuracy of the result of community detection with NMI. Finish the experiment when NMI=1.
4. Count the number of adjacent communities of each node.
5. Give constraints for the pairs of nodes selected based on the strategies mentioned below.
6. Go back to 2.

   The first experiment is to verify which node should be given constraints (Experiment A). The variation of the accuracy after community detection was studied in this experiment with three strategies to give constraints: boundary strategy (we call 'boundary' for short) giving constraints preferentially for nodes with more adjacent communities, hub strategy ('hub') giving constraints preferentially for nodes with more degree and random strategy ('random') giving constraints for nodes at random. The network "Sample1-3" shown later in Table 1 was used for this experiment. Each parameter is set as $\omega = 1$, $\gamma_s = 1$ and $\mu = 2$. The result is shown in Fig. 6. The accuracy is not very high in the case of random. Convergence speed is almost same in the case of hub and boundary, but boundary keeps a little higher accuracy than hub. Similar experiments in monoplex networks show that boundary is outstanding in [9]. We can say it is confirmed that boundary is a useful strategy also in multiplex networks.

   We explain the intuitive reason why boundary is a useful strategy. The number of adjacent communities of certain nodes means the number of possible community which the node may belong to, in which case it becomes difficult to decide which community the node should belong to. Giving constraints preferentially to such nodes makes it easy to decide the community which the node belongs to. It is expected that the community structure of the whole network will be easily decided.

   The variation of the accuracy in community detection was studied by increasing the number of constraints in each case: when multiplex networks with the same number of nodes and different number of layers are used (Experiment B) and when multiplex networks with the same number of layers and different number of nodes are used (Experiment C). The details of benchmark used in Experiment B and C are shown in Tables 1 and 2.

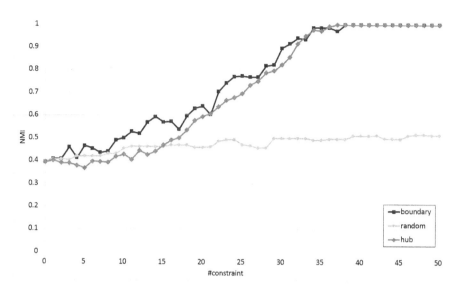

Fig. 6. Experiment A (Horizontal axis: the number of constraints, vertical axis: NMI)

Table 1. The benchmarks used in Experiment B

Benchmark	#Nodes	#Edges	#Layers
Sample1-1	10	11	3
Sample1-2	20	36	3
Sample1-3	30	54	3
Sample1-4	40	67	3
Sample1-5	50	78	3

Table 2. The benchmarks used in Experiment C

Benchmark	#Nodes	#Edges	#Layers
Sample2-1	30	55	2
Sample2-2	30	54	3
Sample2-3	30	57	4
Sample2-4	30	55	5

Boundary is used in this experiment as the strategy to give constraints. The parameter is defined as $\omega = 1$, $\gamma_s = 1$, $\mu = 2$. The results of Experiment B and C are shown in Figs. 7 and 8. We can find that the accuracy of community detection becomes higher by iterating constrained community detection giving incremental constraints from the result of this experiment. Therefore it is likely that we can detect desirable community structure by taking the feedbacks from users interactively in the networks without ground truth.

The accuracy of community detection varies rapidly when the number of nodes is less and mildly when the number of nodes is more. It is explained because the ratio that one node contributes to the whole networks is different when the number of nodes in the whole networks is different. On the other hand, the variation of the number of layers does not influence the variation of the accuracy. The influence by

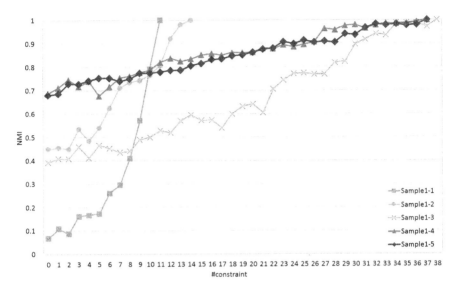

Fig. 7. Experiment B (Horizontal axis: the number of constraints, vertical axis: NMI)

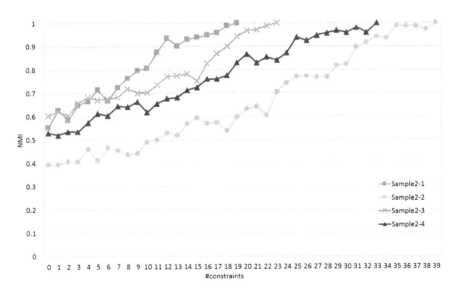

Fig. 8. Experiment C (Horizontal axis: the number of constraints, vertical axis: NMI)

the increase in the number of layers is small because the same nodes in different layers belong to the same community in the benchmark.

5 Conclusion

We have extended Hamiltonian for multiplex networks and constructed constrained Hamiltonian adding constrained terms in this paper. We also proposed a method which optimizes the proposed Hamiltonian by Gen Louvain method for constrained community detection in multiplex networks.

The experiment confirms that the proposed method is eligible for constrained community detection in multiplex networks. The accuracy of community detection becomes higher by iterating constrained community detection adding incremental constraints in synthetic benchmark. This confirms that interactive constrained community detection in multiplex networks is possible. The accuracy of community detection does not increase easily with more nodes, and the number of layers does not influence as much on the accuracy.

Our future work is to improve the algorithm of community detection to reduce the burden of users and to give less number of constraints. Another issue which is left is to run experiments in various networks where constraints are given automatically for the proposed method to be applied for various networks, such as large-scale networks and directed networks. In particular, we think that applying our proposed method to large-scale networks is important because real world networks are often large and complicated. If we can detect communities with constraints in real world networks, we can analyze social networks such as human relation, SNS, transportation and so on. Giving constraints automatically is necessary to do that. We would like to solve these issues and aim for less burden for users and the improvement of the quality of the proposed method.

Acknowledgement. This work was supported by Tokyo Tech - Fuji Xerox Cooperative Research (Project Code KY260195), JSPS Grant-in-Aid for Scientific Research(B) (Grant Number 17H01785) and JST CREST (Grant Number JPMJCR1687).

References

1. Blondel, V.D., Guillaume, J.L., Lambiotte, R., Lefebvre, E.: Fast unfolding of communities in large networks. J. Stat. Mech.: Theory Exp. **2008**(10), P10008 (2008). doi:10.1088/1742-5468/2008/10/P10008
2. De Domenico, M., Lancichinetti, A., Arenas, A., Rosvall, M.: Identifying modular flows on multilayer networks reveals highly overlapping organization in social systems. Phys. Rev. X **5**, 011027 (2015). doi:10.1103/PhysRevX.5.011027
3. De Domenico, M., Porter, M.A., Arenas, A.: MuxViz: a tool for multilayer analysis and visualization of networks. J. Complex Netw. **3**(2), 159–176 (2015). doi:10.1093/comnet/cnu038
4. Eaton, E., Mansbach, R.: A spin-glass model for semi-supervised community detection. In: Proceedings of the Twenty-Sixth AAAI Conference on Artificial Intelligence (AAAI-2012), pp. 900–906 (2012)

5. Jutla, I.S., Jeub, L.G.S., Mucha, P.J.: A generalized Louvain method for community detection implemented in matlab (2011–2014). http://netwiki.amath.unc.edu/GenLouvain
6. Kirkpatrick, S., Gelatt, C.D., Vecchi, M.P.: Optimization by simulated annealing. Science **220**(4598), 671–680 (1983). doi:10.1126/science.220.4598.671
7. Kivelä, M., Arenas, A., Barthelemy, M., Gleeson, J.P., Moreno, Y., Porter, M.A.: Multilayer networks. J. Complex Netw. **2**(3), 203–271 (2014). doi:10.1093/comnet/cnu016
8. Mucha, P.J., Richardson, T., Macon, K., Porter, M.A., Onnela, J.P.: Community structure in time-dependent, multiscale, and multiplex networks. Science **328**(5980), 876–878 (2010). doi:10.1126/science.1184819
9. Nakata, K., Murata, T.: Fast optimization of hamiltonian for constrained community detection. In: Mangioni, G., Simini, F., Uzzo, S.M., Wang, D. (eds.) Complex Networks VI. SCI, vol. 597, pp. 79–89. Springer, Cham (2015). doi:10.1007/978-3-319-16112-9_8
10. Newman, M.E.J., Girvan, M.: Finding and evaluating community structure in networks. Phys. Rev. E **69**, 026113 (2004). doi:10.1103/PhysRevE.69.026113
11. Padgett, J.F., Ansell, C.K.: Robust action and the rise of the medici, 1400–1434. Am. J. Sociol. **98**(6), 1259–1319 (1993). doi:10.1086/230190
12. Reichardt, J., Bornholdt, S.: Statistical mechanics of community detection. Phys. Rev. E **74**, 016110 (2006). doi:10.1103/PhysRevE.74.016110

News, Misinformation, and Collective Sensemaking

Seminar Users in the Arabic Twitter Sphere

Kareem Darwish[1](✉), Dimitar Alexandrov[2], Preslav Nakov[1],
and Yelena Mejova[1]

[1] Qatar Computing Research Institute, HBKU, Doha, Qatar
{KDarwish,PNakov,YMejova}@hbku.edu.qa
[2] Sofia University, Sofia, Bulgaria
Dimityr.Alexandrov@gmail.com

Abstract. We introduce the notion of "seminar users", who are social media users engaged in propaganda in support of a political entity. We develop a framework that can identify such users with 84.4% precision and 76.1% recall. While our dataset is from the Arab region, omitting language-specific features has only a minor impact on classification performance, and thus, our approach could work for detecting seminar users in other parts of the world and in other languages. We further explored a controversial political topic to observe the prevalence and potential potency of such users. In our case study, we found that 25% of the users engaged in the topic are in fact seminar users and their tweets make nearly a third of the on-topic tweets. Moreover, they are often successful in affecting mainstream discourse with coordinated hashtag campaigns.

Keywords: Seminar users · Astroturfing · Politics · Propaganda · Malicious users · Social media · Twitter · Social bots

1 Introduction

What is the connection between a fishing exhibition in Abu Dhabi and ISIS rhetoric? We encountered this puzzle while analyzing ISIS supporters and opponents on Twitter in 2014 [34], finding, to our surprise, the hashtag *#Abu-DhabiFishingExhibition*[1] to be one of the most discriminating features. Tracing the accounts that used this hashtag, we found that they had an abnormally high overlap between the tweets they retweeted and the hashtags they used, suggesting they were colluding in some way. However, these accounts did not seem to be political bots [19], which display "interests" in multiple subjects, such as the above-mentioned ones. Neither were they trolls. While their political messages were spirited, they were not provoking others into conflict [24]. They were not selling products or phishing with fake URLs, as spammers would do [5]. However, they were consistent in supporting and promoting the actions of a particular political entity. The closest notion of this behavior in the literature is *astroturfing*, in which users try to give the impression that a grassroots movement is taking place [46]. Unlike most astroturfing efforts, these users did not mask their identity, and had a persistent political stance over months or years.

---

[1] We translate all tweets and hashtags from Arabic to English to ease readability.

© Springer International Publishing AG 2017
G.L. Ciampaglia et al. (Eds.): SocInfo 2017, Part I, LNCS 10539, pp. 91–108, 2017.
DOI: 10.1007/978-3-319-67217-5_7

In order to describe users who appear to be real people with persistent political orientation, yet who engage in a coordinated political speech, we use a term originally referring to callers to radio stations who espouse strong political sentiment, namely a "seminar caller."[2] The term signifies a specific type of person, who receives instructions in a "seminar" on how to deliver talking points on a live talk show effectively, as if sitting in a "seminar" instructing them. Similarly, Twitter *seminar users* typically attempt to appear like normal individuals, while using specific talking points to promote specific agendas, to manipulate public opinion, and to give the impression of grassroots support. The operating definition that we use for *seminar users* in this work is the following: "A politically oriented account acting alone or in a group that is dedicated to the consistent support of a specific entity (government, political party, etc.) or its agenda; the account must not be an official account of the entity." A seminar user could be a paid employee of an entity that (s)he actively promotes and could be part of a group of such employees. Incidentally, given our interest in this work is the Arabic Twitter sphere, the term *seminar user* is closely related to the coined Arabic term for such users namely لجان إلكترونية (*lijan electroniyya*), which literally translates as "electronic committees".

Increasingly in the Arab world, seminar users are being employed by governments and opposition parties as a propaganda tool to promote specific agendas, to influence public opinion, or to push policies or future directions. For example, on April 13, 2016, General Sisi of Egypt said he could sway social media agenda using *electronic brigades*.[3] The activities of such organized users are potentially harmful in a number of ways. From a data processing perspective, they pollute social media streams, and skew measurements of public opinion. From a political and social perspective, they may give the impression of grassroots support for questionable or illegal activities such as physically harming opponents. Here are some examples of such activity:

- Pro-Sisi seminar users promoted the hashtag *#HoldingOnToSisi* in the days leading up to the fifth anniversary of the 2011 Egyptian uprising that overthrew Hosny Mubarak. A sample tweet in this campaign states (translation): "#HoldingOnToSisi #IAmAnElectronicCommitteeForSisi we are proud electronic committees for our country, our president, our military, and our police."
- Anti-Sisi seminar users promoted the hashtag *#ThePeopleTellSisiWeStronglyReject(you)* between December 13–16, 2015. A sample tweet states: "demonstrate and tell injustice to go away, demonstrate and tell Sisi we strongly reject (you) #ThePeopleTellSisiWeStronglyReject."

Although the phenomenon of *seminar users* is similar to other phenomena in the field of online political speech, we find no existing definitions that capture this notion in a satisfactory way: these users are not trolls, neither are they astroturfers or bots. In fact, below we will show that state-of-the-art bot detection tools fail to discern these accounts.

---

[2] http://en.wikipedia.org/wiki/Seminar_caller.
[3] http://albedaiah.com/news/2016/04/13/111001 *(in Arabic)*.

Thus, the contributions of this work are as follows:

– We present a method for the automatic detection of seminar users that engage in political discourse in the Arab world. We manually label users who are engaged in political discourse related to Egypt, United Arab Emirates, Saudi Arabia, and Yemen. Using these identified seminar users, we build a classification model using a variety of content-based and network features.
– As a case study, we use the classifier to identify and study pro- and anti-Sisi seminar users. Specifically, we examine (i) how much influence such users have on normal users, (ii) whether seminar users are colluding, and (iii) whether there is any interaction between seminar users from opposing sides.

The remainder of this paper is organized as follows. First, we discuss some related work. Then, we present our experiments in finding seminar users. This is followed by a case study of pro- and anti-Sisi seminar users. Finally, we conclude with a general discussion and possible directions for future work.

2   Related Work

The behavior of *seminar users* is closely related to other manipulative and potentially disruptive practices in social media, including discussion trolling, political astroturfing, sockpuppeting, and use of Internet water army, which we outline below. We further discuss some recent work that analyzes political speech in Arabic.

The promise of social media to democratize content creation [27] has also been accompanied by many malicious attempts to spread misleading information over this new medium. News community forums in particular saw the rise and proliferation of fake news [25], aggressiveness [40], and trolling [13]. The latter often is understood to concern malicious online behavior that is intended to disrupt interactions, to aggravate interacting partners, and to lure them into fruitless argumentation in order to disrupt online interactions and communication [11]. Thus, Twitter has taken measures to suspend users who are recognized to be malicious [60]. Nevertheless, more sophisticated malicious profiles such as opinion manipulation *trolls* (paid [38] or just perceived [37]), *sockpuppets* [7,28,31,35], and *Internet water army* [11] are still barely detectable.

Sockpuppets are people who assume a false identity in an Internet community and then speak to/about themselves while pretending to be another person. The term has also been used to refer to opinion manipulation, e.g., in Wikipedia [53]. Sockpuppets have been identified using authorship-identification techniques and link analysis [7]. It has been also shown that sockpuppets differ from ordinary users in their posting behavior, linguistic traits, and social network structure; moreover, sockpuppets tend to start fewer discussions, write shorter posts, use more personal pronouns such as "I", and have more clustered ego-networks [28]. Furthermore, gangs of sockpuppets controlled by a single person can be identified by the similarity of sentiment orientation toward topics based on their posted comments [31]. Unlike *sockpuppets, seminar users* do not try to hide their identity.

Internet Water Army is a literal translation of the Chinese term *wangluo shuijun*, which is a metaphor for a large number of people who are well organized to flood the Internet with purposeful comments and articles. Internet water army is allegedly used in China by the government (known also as *50 Cent Party* as people involved in the campaign were allegedly paid about 50 cents per post) as well as by private organizations. Chen et al. [11] used semantic analysis and some non-semantic features such as percentage of replies among the posts, average time between posts, number of active days, and number of news posts a user has commented on. Unlike *Internet water army* users, *seminar users* could act alone and are consistent in their support for a given entity over a long period of time.

Trolling Behavior is present in all kinds of online media: online magazines [6], social networking sites [13], online computer games [56], online encyclopedia [51], government e-petition pages [58], online newspapers [47], etc. Trolling can be dangerous, as it can increase the risk of suicidal behavior and self-harm amongst targeted users [52]. *Troll detection* has been addressed using semantic analysis [9], domain-adapted sentiment analysis [49], various lexico-syntactic features about user writing style and structure [12], as well as graph-based approaches over signed social networks [45]. There have been also studies on general troll behavior [8] and cyber-bullying [48], as well as on linking fake troll profiles to real users [21]. The term *troll* is often used in popular culture to designate users who engage in opinion manipulation in social media and Web forums; it has been also shown that users who have been called a *troll* by several different people have common characteristics with paid opinion manipulators [39]. Although similar in their ability to influence discourse, seminar users do not employ as disruptive language as trolls. Instead, they push a consistent political message, which is more closely aligned to *astroturfing*, and more precisely a kind of an *Internet water army* [11].

Astroturfing. Named after a brand of fake plastic grass, astroturfing is an effort to simulate a fake political grassroots movement. Recent preoccupation with it has been motivated by strong interest from political science, and research methods driven by the presence of massive streams of microblogging data, largely centering around the Twitter accounts involved. Since Ratkiewicz et al. proposed a system to detect astroturfing called Truthy [46], studies have shown that people can be poor judges of a tweet's credibility [41]. Subsequently, tools to automatically assess the credibility of tweets and their origins spanned both political news [10] and disaster response [23], as well as for the related tasks of stance classification [62] and contradiction detection in rumors [29]. Finally, Lukasik et al. [32] and Ma et al. [33] used temporal patterns to detect rumors, and Zubiaga et al. [63] focused on conversational threads.

Identification of Malicious Accounts in social networks reaches beyond fake political grassroots movements, and includes detecting spam accounts [4,36], fake accounts [14], compromised accounts and phishing accounts [2]. Fake profile detection has also been studied in the context of cyber-bullying [22].

Web Spam Detection is another related problem, which has been addressed as a text classification problem [50], e.g., using spam keyword spotting [17], lexical affinity of arbitrary words to spam content [26], frequency of punctuation and word co-occurrence [30]. Yet another related problem is that of detecting racist/radicalized posts, e.g., on the Tumblr micro-blogging website [3].

Predicting Online Extremism is a topic, which involves fighting with a special type of malicious users, very similar to the seminar users group. The goal in [20] is to find Twitter accounts used by ISIS members and to report them to Twitter. After the manual annotation of some ISIS supporters, the authors used a classifier (based on logistic regression and random forests) to predict whether a regular user would retweet a message posted by an ISIS account [20].

Social Bot Detection involves detecting accounts that are programmatically controlled to produce content and to interact with other users. Social bots may spread messages, ads, or propaganda while trying to mimic human behavior [57]. Varol et al. [57] detected bots using profile, friends, network, temporal, content, and sentiment features. For detecting seminar users, we use features such as lexical diversity and sentiment, which overlap with their features. For social bots in the Arab world, Morstatter et al. [42] looked for keywords that relate to the Arab Spring in Libya. They used several features such as retweet and URL sharing frequencies, tweet length, time between tweets, and topic distribution. Abokhodair et al. [1] looked at the behavior of a social botnet related to the ongoing civil war in Syria and the propensity of the botnet in influencing the mainstream discourse.

Unlike the work above, here we focus on a particular kind of malicious users, i.e., *seminar users*, which show dedicated support to a particular political entity, acting alone or as part of an organized group.

3   Identifying Seminar Users

3.1   Data

We collected Arabic tweets between December 1, 2015 and January 25, 2016. This period is interesting as it constitutes the days leading up to the fifth anniversary of the January 25, 2011 uprising in Egypt, which is part of the Arab Spring and led to the ouster of Hosny Mubarak from power. Though the dates are unlikely to affect the first part of the work concerning the automated detection of seminar users, it would likely make subsequent analysis of specific pro- and anti-Sisi seminar users more interesting. We collected the tweets using the Twitter4j Java interface for the Twitter streaming API, where we searched using the query "lang:ar" to get Arabic tweets. Eventually, we accumulated 417 million tweets with an average of 7.4 million tweets per day over 56 days. We manually labeled 150 users as seminar users vs. non-seminar users. To label them, we picked users who discussed potentially politically polarizing issues about Egypt, United Arab Emirates (UAE), Yemen, and the Kingdom of Saudi Arabia (KSA).

Specifically, we randomly picked 2,000 users (500 for each country) who mentioned General Sisi of Egypt, Mohamed bin Zayed (vice president of UAE), Yemen, and Saudi Arabia in their tweets. Next, an annotator who is privy to the politics of the Middle East manually examined the tweets of the 2,000 users in random order until he tagged 150 users as fitting our definition of seminar users or not. In the interest of data cleanliness, the annotator labeled users who were clearly seminar users or were clearly not, and he excluded borderline (ambiguous) users where he could not make a clear-cut decision. The annotator was asked to keep the dataset balanced with a comparable number of seminar and non-seminar users. Of the 150 users, 71 were seminar users and 79 were not. To ensure the quality of the annotation, another annotator was asked to independently tag a subset of the tagged users containing 35 users and both annotators agreed on 32 users (91.4% agreement, with a Cohen's Kappa of 0.83).

Tagging users as seminar users is quite different from tagging them as bots. To demonstrate the difference, we automatically tagged all seminar users from our dataset using BotOrNot,[4] which gives a score between 0 and 100 to each user, with 100 signifying the most extreme bot-like behavior [18]. Figure 1 shows the scores for the seminar users (after excluding 16 accounts that were deleted, protected, or suspended). As the figure shows, BotOrNot reckoned that most of the accounts were not bot-like, with only one user getting the highest score of 61 for any user in our dataset. This may indicate that the accounts are being managed by humans. However, this does not preclude the possibility that some user might manage more than one account.

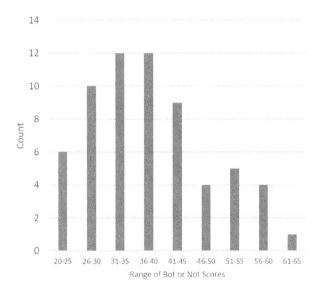

Fig. 1. Distribution of BotOrNot scores for seminar users in our dataset

---

[4] http://truthy.indiana.edu/botornot/.

3.2   Detecting Seminar Users

Methodology. Given our set of 150 users that were tagged as seminar users or not, we trained an SVM classifier with a radial basis function kernel[5] using a variety of features:

- (Interaction features) The relative use of tweet interaction elements. Specifically, the percentage of tweets containing retweets, URLs, hashtags, mentions, and embedded images. The rationale for these features is that seminar users may engage heavily in the promotion of hashtags or memes. (5 features)
- (Diversity features) The diversity of content, where seminar users may concentrate on specific topics and use a smaller vocabulary. We measured
    - the percentage of tweets containing the top n retweeted accounts or mentioned accounts, where n was set to 1, 3, 10, and 20 (8 features);
    - the percentage of tweets containing the top n used hashtags for each user, where n was set to 5 and 15 (2 features);
    - the percentage of tweets containing the top n used words (excluding stopwords) for each user, where n was set to 10, 30, and 50. We performed basic Arabic letter normalization [16] and English case folding. (3 features)
- (Style features) The style of language, where seminar users are more likely to praise the party they support and malign opponents. We used the following:
    - The percentage of tweets containing sentiment words. We used the sentiment lexicon of 3,982 words described in [44]. (1 feature)
    - The percentage of tweets containing vulgar or combative words. We used a word list containing Arabic vulgar and obscene words containing 3,840 words and phrases such as "son of a dog" and "filthy" [43]. (1 feature)

We avoided using user similarity features, as such features are computationally expensive. The advantage of our proposed features is that each user can be classified in isolation, without considering the other users, which makes classification computationally efficient. Also, since many users subscribe to services that post mostly religious tweets on their behalf, we assembled a list of the most popular such services and filtered out all tweets that they generate. The services we excluded are du3a.org, ghared.com, 7asnat.com, mezani.net, d3waapp.org, zad-muslim.com, and rtw8.com. We also excluded tweets containing the hashtags #quran and #hadith, or that were retweeted from specific accounts that specifically indicate religious content.

Evaluation. Due to the limited number of examples in our dataset, we used leave-one-out cross-validation for training and testing, where we held each of the users in our set out for testing and trained on the remaining users. We experimented with using the Interaction, Diversity, and Style features separately and in combination.

---

[5] We used the SVM^{Light} implementation available from http://svmlight.joachims.org/.

Table 1 reports the classification results using precision (P), recall (R), and F1-measure (F1). We can see that the interaction features are the most important ones. While the combination of all feature types yields the best results, using a combination of interaction and diversity features only, which are language-independent, slightly degrades the performance. This gives us hope that the classifier may work effectively for users in other regions without the need for language-specific resources. Overall, the results show that we can identify seminar users with relatively high precision and recall.

Table 1. Classification results for seminar users and normal (non-seminar) users including precision (P), recall (R), F1-measure (F1), and Macro F1-measure.

Features	Seminar			Normal			Macro
	P	R	F1	P	R	F1	F1
Interaction	77.2	62.0	68.8	71.0	83.5	76.7	72.8
Diversity	73.2	57.7	64.6	68.1	81.0	74.0	69.3
Style	0.0	0.0	0.0	52.7	**100.0**	69.0	34.5
Interaction + Diversity	83.9	73.2	78.2	78.4	87.3	82.6	80.4
All	**84.4**	**76.1**	**80.0**	**80.2**	87.2	**83.6**	**80.9**

4   Pro- and Anti-Sisi Seminar Users: Case Study

4.1   Data

For the second part of the study, we focus on the behavior of pro- and anti-Sisi seminar users. On July 3, 2013, General Sisi used the military to overthrow the democratically elected government that transpired after January 25, 2011 Egyptian uprising. He was named president a year later. Sisi is a divisive figure in Egyptian politics. We identified 9,506 users who mentioned Sisi ten or more times in our aforementioned dataset containing tweets that are collected between December 1, 2015 and January 25, 2016. To label users as pro- or anti-Sisi, we used label propagation. We manually tagged an initial set of 100 users. Then, we automatically tagged all the tweets mentioning Sisi for those 100 users using their user tags. For example, all tweets mentioning Sisi and posted by pro-Sisi users would be tagged as pro-Sisi. It is not unreasonable to do so as people's opinions generally remain stable over extended periods of time. In particular, we assumed that the overwhelming majority of users would not change their opinion over the span of 56 days. We further assumed that unlabeled users who retweeted consistently pro-Sisi tweets should be pro-Sisi, and likewise those who consistently retweeted anti-Sisi tweets should be anti-Sisi. Thus, we were able to tag 2,743 more users. We repeated this process for three iterations, which ultimately yielded 7,427 tagged users. To check the reliability of label propagation on our data, we took a random sample of 100 users and we labeled them for stance manually and also automatically, obtaining the same label for 99 users.

We applied our seminar user detector on the 7,427 users that we identified as pro- and anti-Sisi. As a result, we identified 1,839 users as seminar users, including 492 who were pro-Sisi and 1,347 who were anti-Sisi. In order to verify the efficacy of the classifier on the new data, we randomly sampled 50 users from the set of 7,427 users, and we asked our annotator to manually and independently label them as seminar users or not. The annotator labeled 20 users as seminar users, 29 as normal users, and 1 as a spammer. Our classifier labeled 14 (out of the 50) users as seminar users, of which 11 were in fact seminar users (Precision = 0.78; Recall = 0.55). Unlike the training data, not all users were clearly discernible as seminar users or not. The annotator labeled all ambiguous users (8 users) using his best guess. This likely contributed to lower results over the sample compared to the aforementioned classification results.

Table 2 summarizes the number of users for each group and other basic statistics about them. The summary shows that the ratio of seminar users to normal users is 1:1.7 and 1:3.5 for pro- and anti-Sisi users, respectively. It is noteworthy that pro-Sisi seminar users authored more tweets than pro-Sisi non-seminar users. Conversely, normal anti-Sisi users produced more than twice as many tweets as anti-Sisi seminar users. Seminar users produced on average 60% more tweets per user, and they tweeted more on average about Sisi.

Table 2. Stats of pro- and anti-Sisi users and tweets.

	Seminar users		Normal users	
Stance	Pro-Sisi	Anti-Sisi	Pro-Sisi	Anti-Sisi
Users	492	1,347	846	4,748
Tweets	860,085	4,200,619	847,383	9,057,758
Avg tweets/user	1,748	3,118	1,001	1,908
Tweets mentioning Sisi	22,932	65,478	34,026	146,762
Avg tweets mentioning Sisi/user	46.6	48.6	40.2	30.9

4.2 Characteristics of Pro- and Anti-Sisi Seminar Users

Figure 2 shows the top-5 self-declared user locations producing the highest number of pro- and anti-Sisi tweets. We can see that most users did not declare their location. Moreover, even though there were far fewer pro-Sisi users from UAE compared to Egypt, they produced five times as many tweets. Similarly for anti-Sisi users, there were nearly six times as many users from Egypt than from KSA, but the number of tweets from Egypt were only 19% more than those from KSA. This may indicate that Egyptian seminar users are less active than non-Egyptian ones. Table 3 lists the top retweeted accounts by both groups. As the table shows, for both groups, the majority of these accounts were not from Egypt, and UAE and KSA users account for most pro-Sisi seminar users.

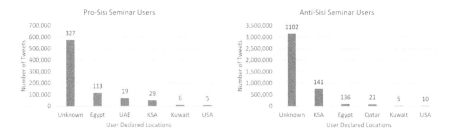

Fig. 2. Top-5 self-declared user locations of pro- and anti-Sisi seminar users. Values at the top of the bars indicate the number of users.

Table 3. Top retweeted accounts for pro- and anti-Sisi seminar users.

Pro-Sisi			Anti-Sisi		
User	Description	Count	User	Description	Count
Forsan_UAE	UAE user	33,229	ALAMAWI	Syrian pro-Arab Spring media	58,203
Henry Kesnger	Unknown	10,452	almokhtsar	News aggregator	29,968
fdeet_alnssr	KSA	7,817	raawnq	Suspended	26,117
meshaluk	KSA user in London	5,840	EHSANFAQEH	Jordanian author	23,005
alkhaldi_ksa	Suspended	4,578	Wesal_TV	KSA (anti-Iran media)	19,767
Dhahi_Khalfan	UAE user	4,258	S7K00	Suspended	19,403
bestwalid92	Egypt	3,778	AJArabic	Aljazeera (media)	18,212
amirelghareb	Egypt user	3,696	kasimf	Aljazeera presenter	15,492
a_e5552000	Suspended	3,627	AboShla5Libraly	KSA user	14,389
shereen_hussen	Egypt user	3,502	YZaatreh	Palestinian author	13,639

Seminar users typically engage in campaigns to promote specific messages typically with associated hashtags. We identified such campaigns by identifying hashtags that combine both high volume and high standard deviation (σ) from day to day. Thus, we scored hashtags by combining volume and standard deviation:

$$score = \frac{\sigma}{\sum daily\_counts} \tag{1}$$

We only considered hashtags that were used more than 100 and 300 times for pro- and anti-Sisi groups, respectively, and we ranked them using scoring formula (1). We picked different thresholds for the two groups in order to account for the difference in volume. Figure 3 shows the top-15 hashtag campaigns for both groups. We can see that the campaigns typically lasted for one or two days and then died out. The pro-Sisi group was involved in continuous campaigns, while the anti-Sisi group campaigns started at the end of December as the anniversary of the 2011 Egyptian uprising drew closer. For the pro-Sisi group, 3 out of 15 of the top hashtags were related to Egypt and 7 were related to UAE. In contrast, 14 out of 15 hashtags were related to Egypt in the anti-Sisi group.

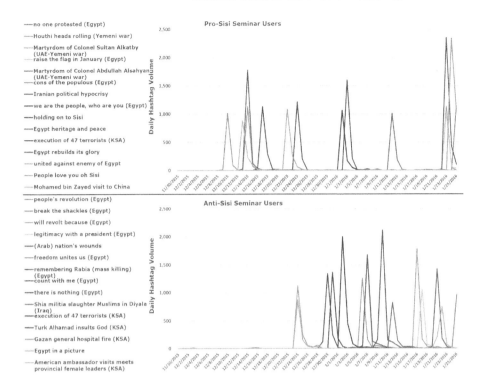

Fig. 3. Top hashtag campaigns for pro- and anti-Sisi seminar users.

4.3   Effectiveness, Cohesiveness, and Interactions Between Seminar Users

We set out to answer three research questions aimed to assess the effectiveness and the cohesiveness of seminar users, and the extent to which they interact with each other. Our first question is the following: how successful are seminar users in penetrating the mainstream? To answer this question, we considered the 5,618 pro- and anti-Sisi users that our classifier deemed as non-seminar users.

We considered the top-100 most used hashtags with a score greater than 0.02, using formula (1). Then, we compared the top-100 hashtags for the pro- and anti-Sisi seminar groups to the top hashtags for non-seminar users, focusing on the following statistics: (i) percentage of hashtags that made the list from non-seminar users, (ii) average rank of hashtags in the list, and (iii) volume magnification factor, which is the volume of hashtags from non-seminar users divided by the volume generated by seminar users. Table 4 reports on these three statistics for the pro- and anti-Sisi seminar users. We can see that anti-Sisi seminar users were more successful than pro-Sisi ones in penetrating the mainstream with 29% (compared to 10%) of their top-100 hashtags appearing in the top hashtags for non-seminar users with an average rank of 22.6 (vs. 46.1). However, volume magnification for pro-Sisi users is much higher (9.0 vs. 1.6).

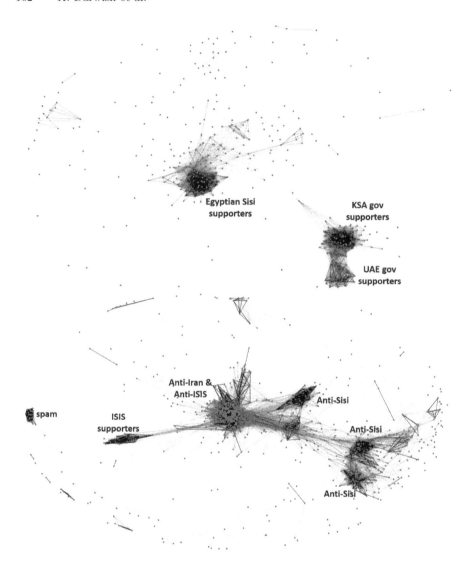

Fig. 4. Pro- and anti-Sisi user network graph (top and bottom, respectively). We indicate cosine similarity greater than 0.8 as black edges, between 0.6 and 0.8 as green edges, and less than 0.6 as light yellow edges. We further show text labels for the main strongly-connected cliques. (Color figure online)

Three caveats need to be taken into account when reading these results: (*i*) anti-Sisi seminar users outnumber pro-Sisi ones by a factor 2.7 to 1, (*ii*) pro-Sisi seminar users do not concentrate on Egypt-related issues, and (*iii*) seminar users may adopt an existing hashtag, instead of introducing a new one.

Our second research question we study is the following: how similar are seminar users in each camp? To answer this question, we computed the cosine similarity between pro- and anti-Sisi seminar users using the frequency of the hashtags that they used as features. Next, we drew the network of users shown in Fig. 4 using NetworkX,[6] which uses Fruchterman-Reingold force-directed algorithm to space out the nodes. As the network graphs show, the seminar users are not homogeneous, but rather they are groups of strongly-connected cliques. We labeled the major cliques in the graphs based on sample users from each clique. We can see that pro-Sisi seminar users are composed of three major cliques from Egypt, KSA, and UAE. Given the apparent skew toward UAE-related topics, it seems that the pro-UAE group is most productive in terms of volume. For the anti-Sisi seminar users, there is a large anti-Iran group, which is also pro-Syrian revolutionaries, there are three different Egyptian anti-Sisi groups, one pro-Islamic State (ISIS) group, and one group of spammers. All of these groups are supportive of the Arab Spring uprisings in one way or another. Prior work has discussed the relationship between support for ISIS and the Arab Spring [34].

Our third research question is the following: how much do the two groups of seminar users interact? To answer this question, we measured whether the two camps used the same hashtags. In essence, we wanted to detect hashtag hijacking. We found that the two camps shared only nine of the top 100 most frequent hashtags, and the rest were used exclusively by one of them. This included seven shared hashtags of broad interest such as #KSACutsDiplomaticTiesWithIran and #DubaiFire. The other two hashtags were #PeopleWantToOverthrowRegime (used 96% of the time by the anti-Sisi camp) and #KnowThePerpetrator (used 65% of the time by the pro-Sisi camp). The results suggest that both pro- and anti-Sisi seminar users operate fairly independently and with limited interaction.

Table 4. Penetration of pro- and anti-Sisi seminar users into the mainstream.

	% of appearance	Avg. rank	Vol. magnification
pro-Sisi	10%	46.1	9.0x
anti-Sisi	29%	22.6	1.6x

5   Discussion and Conclusions

We have introduced the so-called "seminar users", as users who engage in political propaganda. The existence of such users can distort social media analysis and can be socially and politically troubling. Thus, we have presented a robust method for automatically detecting such users by looking at their interactions, their tweet content diversity, and their tendency to use sentiment-bearing and offensive words. Note that we did not use user similarity features as mining the user graph of interactions is computationally expensive.

---

[6] http://networkx.readthedocs.io/en/networkx-1.10/.

Our seminar vs. regular user classifier achieved precision of 84.4% and recall of 76.1% on our dataset, which is a very strong result. We have further demonstrated that seminar users are quite different from bots. Complementary to recent research that has shown that it is possible to distinguish automatically real human Twitter accounts from bots [55], our work points to a need for detecting networks of colluding Twitter users, beyond the detection of ephemeral bot accounts.

We further applied our classifier on Twitter users who discuss a politically controversial topic, namely attitude toward General Sisi of Egypt. Our classifier labeled 25% of these users as seminar users, but we suspect that the actual percentage should be even higher. Moreover, our analysis shows that seminar users produce more tweets on average compared to normal users, e.g., more than half of the pro-Sisi and about a third of the anti-Sisi tweets in our dataset were posted by seminar users. We further found that seminar users are often successful in affecting the mainstream discourse, which is evident by the hashtags that they popularize. The prevalence of seminar users in the Arabic Twitter-sphere and the large volume of tweets that they produce complicate Twitter-based studies, particularly for controversial or political issues. The success of seminar users in affecting the mainstream has the potential of promoting human rights abuses, or making such abuses sound like a normal thing. Thus, the ability to detect such users can help analysis in two major ways, namely (*i*) filtering out such users can help focus analysis on normal users, and (*ii*) focusing exclusively on seminar users can help elucidate what political actors are promoting aside from what they say officially.

We have shown that seminar users with similar stances on specific issues may actually belong to wildly different or even opposing groups of Twitter users, and that they may even come from different countries altogether. In particular, for anti-Sisi seminar users, we can clearly see a group that supports ISIS and another larger group that opposes ISIS. In the example of pro-Sisi seminar users, we have seen such users from UAE and KSA, who work across borders to support Sisi and to oppose his adversaries. Moreover, we have shown that groups of seminar users may or may not engage with the hashtags of opposing groups, e.g., in the form of hashtag hijacking. Overall, in our case study, we have found very limited evidence for this kind of cross-group engagement. We suspect that the seminar users phenomenon is not unique to the Arab region, but exists in different regions of the world with varying potency. We plan to test whether our seminar vs. normal users classifier can generalize to other regions of the world, and whether seminar users behave similarly across regions and whether they share some universal characteristics.

Last but not least, by focusing our study on the political issues in the Arab world, we contribute to a growing literature examining the role of social media in political communication around the world. Although studies about United States are most prominent (e.g., those on the Presidential elections [61]), there is also recent work focusing on Latin America [59], China [54], Europe [15], and the Middle East [34]. We hope that the present work would enable further research on the role and use of social media in Arab politics.

References

1. Abokhodair, N., Yoo, D., McDonald, D.W.: Dissecting a social botnet: growth, content and influence in Twitter. In: Proceedings of the 18th ACM Conference on Computer Supported Cooperative Work and Social Computing, CSCW 2015, Vancouver, British Columbia, Canada, pp. 839–851 (2015)
2. Adewole, K.S., Anuar, N.B., Kamsin, A., Varathan, K.D., Razak, S.A.: Malicious accounts: dark of the social networks. J. Netw. Comput. Appl. **79**, 41–67 (2017)
3. Agarwal, S., Sureka, A.: Characterizing linguistic attributes for automatic classification of intent based racist/radicalized posts on Tumblr micro-blogging website. arXiv preprint arXiv:1701.04931 (2017)
4. Almaatouq, A., Shmueli, E., Nouh, M., Alabdulkareem, A., Singh, V.K., Alsaleh, M., Alarifi, A., Alfaris, A., et al.: If it looks like a spammer and behaves like a spammer, it must be a spammer: analysis and detection of microblogging spam accounts. Int. J. Inf. Secur. **15**(5), 475–491 (2016)
5. Benevenuto, F., Magno, G., Rodrigues, T., Almeida, V.: Detecting spammers on Twitter. In: Proceedings of the Conference on Collaboration, Electronic Messaging, Anti-abuse and Spam, CEAS 2010, Redmond, Washington, USA, vol. 6, p. 12 (2010)
6. Binns, A.: DON'T FEED THE TROLLS! Managing troublemakers in magazines online communities. Journal. Pract. **6**(4), 547–562 (2012)
7. Bu, Z., Xia, Z., Wang, J.: A sock puppet detection algorithm on virtual spaces. Know.-Based Syst. **37**, 366–377 (2013)
8. Buckels, E.E., Trapnell, P.D., Paulhus, D.L.: Trolls just want to have fun. Pers. Individ. Differ. **67**, 97–102 (2014)
9. Cambria, E., Chandra, P., Sharma, A., Hussain, A.: Do not feel the trolls. In: Proceedings of the 3rd International Workshop on Social Data on the Web, SDoW 2010, Shanghai, China (2010)
10. Castillo, C., Mendoza, M., Poblete, B.: Predicting information credibility in time-sensitive social media. Internet Res. **23**(5), 560–588 (2013)
11. Chen, C., Wu, K., Srinivasan, V., Zhang, X.: Battling the internet water army: detection of hidden paid posters. In: Proceedings of the 2013 IEEE/ACM International Conference on Advances in Social Networks Analysis and Mining, ASONAM 2013, Niagara, Ontario, Canada, pp. 116–120 (2013)
12. Chen, Y., Zhou, Y., Zhu, S., Xu, H.: Detecting offensive language in social media to protect adolescent online safety. In: Proceedings of the 2012 International Conference on Privacy, Security, Risk and Trust and of the 2012 International Conference on Social Computing, PASSAT/SocialCom 2012, Amsterdam, Netherlands, pp. 71–80 (2012)
13. Cole, K.K.: "It's like she's eager to be verbally abused": Twitter, trolls, and (en) gendering disciplinary rhetoric. Feminist Media Stud. **15**(2), 356–358 (2015)
14. Cresci, S., Di Pietro, R., Petrocchi, M., Spognardi, A., Tesconi, M.: Fame for sale: efficient detection of fake Twitter followers. Decis. Support Syst. **80**, 56–71 (2015)
15. Cross, J.P., Greene, D., Belford, M.: Tweeting Europe: a text-analytic approach to unveiling the content of political actors' Twitter activities in the European parliament. In: Proceedings of 6th Annual General Conference of the European Political Science Association, EPSA 2016, Brussels, Belgium (2016)
16. Darwish, K., Magdy, W., Mourad, A.: Language processing for Arabic microblog retrieval. In: Proceedings of the 21st ACM International Conference on Information and Knowledge Management. CIKM 2012, Maui, Hawaii, USA, pp. 2427–2430 (2012)

17. Dave, K., Lawrence, S., Pennock, D.M.: Mining the peanut gallery: opinion extraction and semantic classification of product reviews. In: Proceedings of the 12th International World Wide Web Conference, WWW 2003, Budapest, Hungary, pp. 519–528 (2003)

18. Davis, C.A., Varol, O., Ferrara, E., Flammini, A., Menczer, F.: BotOrNot: a system to evaluate social bots. In: Proceedings of the 25th International Conference Companion on World Wide Web, WWW 2016, Montréal, Québec, Canada, pp. 273–274 (2016)

19. Ferrara, E., Varol, O., Davis, C., Menczer, F., Flammini, A.: The rise of social bots. Commun. ACM **59**(7), 96–104 (2016)

20. Ferrara, E., Wang, W.-Q., Varol, O., Flammini, A., Galstyan, A.: Predicting online extremism, content adopters, and interaction reciprocity. In: Spiro, E., Ahn, Y.-Y. (eds.) SocInfo 2016. LNCS, vol. 10047, pp. 22–39. Springer, Cham (2016). doi:10. 1007/978-3-319-47874-6_3

21. Galán-García, P., De La Puerta, J.G., Gómez, C.L., Santos, I., Bringas, P.G.: Supervised machine learning for the detection of troll profiles in Twitter social network: application to a real case of cyberbullying. Logic J. IGPL **24**, 42–53 (2015)

22. Galán-García, P., de la Puerta, J.G., Gómez, C.L., Santos, I., Bringas, P.G.: Supervised machine learning for the detection of troll profiles in Twitter social network: application to a real case of cyberbullying. In: Proceedings of the International Joint Conference SOCO 2013-CISIS 2013-ICEUTE 2013, pp. 419–428. Advances in Intelligent Systems and Computing (2014)

23. Gupta, A., Lamba, H., Kumaraguru, P., Joshi, A.: Faking sandy: characterizing and identifying fake images on Twitter during hurricane Sandy. In: Proceedings of the 22nd International Conference on World Wide Web, WWW 2013, pp. 729–736 (2013)

24. Hardaker, C.: Trolling in asynchronous computer-mediated communication: from user discussions to theoretical concepts. J. Politeness Res. **6**(2), 215–242 (2010)

25. Hardalov, M., Koychev, I., Nakov, P.: In search of credible news. In: Dichev, C., Agre, G. (eds.) AIMSA 2016. LNCS (LNAI), vol. 9883, pp. 172–180. Springer, Cham (2016). doi:10.1007/978-3-319-44748-3_17

26. Hu, M., Liu, B.: Mining and summarizing customer reviews. In: Proceedings of the 10th ACM SIGKDD International Conference on Knowledge Discovery and Data Mining, KDD 2004, Seattle, Washington, USA, pp. 168–177 (2004)

27. Kaplan, A.M., Haenlein, M.: Users of the world, unite! The challenges and opportunities of social media. Bus. Horiz. **53**(1), 59–68 (2010)

28. Kumar, S., Cheng, J., Leskovec, J., Subrahmanian, V.: An army of me: sockpuppets in online discussion communities. In: Proceedings of the 26th International Conference on World Wide Web, WWW 2017, Perth, Australia, pp. 857–866 (2017)

29. Lendvai, P., Reichel, U.D.: Contradiction detection for rumorous claims. arXiv preprint arXiv:1611.02588 (2016)

30. Li, W., Zhong, N., Liu, C.: Combining multiple email filters based on multivariate statistical analysis. In: Esposito, F., Raś, Z.W., Malerba, D., Semeraro, G. (eds.) ISMIS 2006. LNCS (LNAI), vol. 4203, pp. 729–738. Springer, Heidelberg (2006). doi:10.1007/11875604_81

31. Liu, D., Wu, Q., Han, W., Zhou, B.: Sockpuppet gang detection on social media sites. Front. Comput. Sci. **10**(1), 124–135 (2016)

32. Lukasik, M., Cohn, T., Bontcheva, K.: Point process modelling of rumour dynamics in social media. In: Proceedings of the 53rd Annual Meeting of the Association for Computational Linguistics and the 7th International Joint Conference on Natural Language Processing, Beijing, China, pp. 518–523 (2015)

33. Ma, J., Gao, W., Wei, Z., Lu, Y., Wong, K.F.: Detect rumors using time series of social context information on microblogging websites. In: Proceedings of the 24th ACM International on Conference on Information and Knowledge Management, CIKM 2015, Melbourne, Australia, pp. 1751–1754 (2015)
34. Magdy, W., Darwish, K., Weber, I.: #FailedRevolutions: using Twitter to study the antecedents of ISIS support. First Monday **21**(2) (2016). doi:10.5210/fm.v21i2. 6372
35. Maity, S.K., Chakraborty, A., Goyal, P., Mukherjee, A.: Detection of sockpuppets in social media. In: Proceedings of the 2017 ACM Conference on Computer Supported Cooperative Work and Social Computing, CSCW 2017, Portland, Oregon, USA, pp. 243–246 (2017)
36. McCord, M., Chuah, M.: Spam detection on twitter using traditional classifiers. In: Calero, J.M.A., Yang, L.T., Mármol, F.G., García Villalba, L.J., Li, A.X., Wang, Y. (eds.) ATC 2011. LNCS, vol. 6906, pp. 175–186. Springer, Heidelberg (2011). doi:10.1007/978-3-642-23496-5_13
37. Mihaylov, T., Georgiev, G., Nakov, P.: Finding opinion manipulation trolls in news community forums. In: Proceedings of the Nineteenth Conference on Computational Natural Language Learning, CoNLL 2015, Beijing, China, pp. 310–314 (2015)
38. Mihaylov, T., Koychev, I., Georgiev, G., Nakov, P.: Exposing paid opinion manipulation trolls. In: Proceedings of the International Conference Recent Advances in Natural Language Processing, RANLP 2015, Hissar, Bulgaria, pp. 443–450 (2015)
39. Mihaylov, T., Nakov, P.: Hunting for troll comments in news community forums. In: Proceedings of the 54th Annual Meeting of the Association for Computational Linguistics, ACL 2016, Berlin, Germany, pp. 399–405 (2016)
40. Moore, M.J., Nakano, T., Enomoto, A., Suda, T.: Anonymity and roles associated with aggressive posts in an online forum. Comput. Hum. Behav. **28**(3), 861–867 (2012)
41. Morris, M.R., Counts, S., Roseway, A., Hoff, A., Schwarz, J.: Tweeting is believing?: understanding microblog credibility perceptions. In: Proceedings of the ACM 2012 Conference on Computer Supported Cooperative Work, CSCW 2012, Seattle, Washington, USA, pp. 441–450 (2012)
42. Morstatter, F., Wu, L., Nazer, T., Carley, K., Liu, H.: A new approach to bot detection: striking the balance between precision and recall, ASONAM 2016, San Francisco, California, USA, pp. 533–540 (2016)
43. Mubarak, H., Darwish, K., Magdy, W.: Abusive language detection on Arabic social media. In: Proceedings of the Workshop on Abusive Language Online, ALW 2017, Vancouver, British Columbia, Canada (2017)
44. Muhammad, A., Kübler, S., Diab, M.: Samar: a system for subjectivity and sentiment analysis of Arabic social media. In: Proceedings of the 3rd Workshop in Computational Approaches to Subjectivity and Sentiment Analysis, WASSA 2012, Copenhagen, Denmark, pp. 19–28 (2012)
45. Ortega, F.J., Troyano, J.A., Cruz, F.L., Vallejo, C.G., Enriquez, F.: Propagation of trust and distrust for the detection of trolls in a social network. Comput. Netw. **56**(12), 2884–2895 (2012)
46. Ratkiewicz, J., Conover, M., Meiss, M., Gonçalves, B., Patil, S., Flammini, A., Menczer, F.: Truthy: mapping the spread of astroturf in microblog streams. In: Proceedings of the 20th International Conference on World Wide Web, WWW 2011, Hyderabad, India, pp. 249–252 (2011)

47. Ruiz, C., Domingo, D., Micó, J.L., Díaz-Noci, J., Meso, K., Masip, P.: Public sphere 2.0? The democratic qualities of citizen debates in online newspapers. Int. J. Press/Polit. **16**(4), 463–487 (2011)
48. Sarna, G., Bhatia, M.: Content based approach to find the credibility of user in social networks: an application of cyberbullying. Int. J. Mach. Learn. Cybern. **8**(2), 677–689 (2017)
49. Seah, C.W., Chieu, H.L., Chai, K.M.A., Teow, L.N., Yeong, L.W.: Troll detection by domain-adapting sentiment analysis. In: Proceedings of the 18th International Conference on Information Fusion, FUSION 2015, Washington, D.C., USA, pp. 792–799 (2015)
50. Sebastiani, F.: Machine learning in automated text categorization. ACM Comput. Surv. (CSUR) **34**(1), 1–47 (2002)
51. Shachaf, P., Hara, N.: Beyond vandalism: Wikipedia trolls. J. Inf. Sci. **36**(3), 357–370 (2010)
52. Slee, P.T., Skrzypiec, G.: School bullying, victimization and pro-social behaviour. Well-Being, Positive Peer Relations and Bullying in School Settings. PE, pp. 109–133. Springer, Cham (2016). doi:10.1007/978-3-319-43039-3_6
53. Solorio, T., Hasan, R., Mizan, M.: Sockpuppet detection in Wikipedia: a corpus of real-world deceptive writing for linking identities. In: Proceedings of the Ninth International Conference on Language Resources and Evaluation, LREC 2014, Reykjavik, Iceland, pp. 1355–1358 (2014)
54. Song, Y., Dai, X.Y., Wang, J.: Not all emotions are created equal: expressive behavior of the networked public on China's social media site. Comput. Hum. Behav. **60**, 525–533 (2016)
55. Stieglitz, S., Brachten, F., Berthelé, D., Schlaus, M., Venetopoulou, C., Veutgen, D.: Do social bots (still) act different to humans? - comparing metrics of social bots with those of humans. In: Meiselwitz, G. (ed.) SCSM 2017, HCI 2017. LNCS, vol. 10282, pp. 379–395. Springer, Cham (2017). doi:10.1007/978-3-319-58559-8_30
56. Thacker, S., Griffiths, M.D.: An exploratory study of trolling in online video gaming. Int. J. Cyber Behav. Psychol. Learn. (IJCBPL) **2**(4), 17–33 (2012)
57. Varol, O., Ferrara, E., Davis, C.A., Menczer, F., Flammini, A.: Online human-bot interactions: detection, estimation, and characterization. arXiv preprint arXiv:1703.03107 (2017)
58. Virkar, S.: Trolls just want to have fun: electronic aggression within the context of e-participation and other online political behaviour in the United Kingdom. Int. J. E-Polit. **5**(4), 21–51 (2014)
59. Waisbord, S., Amado, A.: Populist communication by digital means: presidential Twitter in Latin America. Inf. Commun. Soc. **20**(9), 1330–1346 (2017). Populist Online Communication
60. Wei, W., Joseph, K., Liu, H., Carley, K.M.: The fragility of Twitter social networks against suspended users. In: Proceedings of the 2015 IEEE/ACM International Conference on Advances in Social Networks Analysis and Mining 2015, ASONAM 2015, Paris, France, pp. 9–16 (2015)
61. Wells, C., Shah, D.V., Pevehouse, J.C., Yang, J., Pelled, A., Boehm, F., Lukito, J., Ghosh, S., Schmidt, J.L.: How Trump drove coverage to the nomination: hybrid media campaigning. Polit. Commun. **33**(4), 669–676 (2016)
62. Zubiaga, A., Kochkina, E., Liakata, M., Procter, R., Lukasik, M.: Stance classification in rumours as a sequential task exploiting the tree structure of social media conversations. arXiv preprint arXiv:1609.09028 (2016)
63. Zubiaga, A., Liakata, M., Procter, R., Wong Sak Hoi, G., Tolmie, P.: Analysing how people orient to and spread rumours in social media by looking at conversational threads. PLoS ONE **11**(3), 1–29 (2016)

Exploiting Context for Rumour Detection in Social Media

Arkaitz Zubiaga[1(✉)], Maria Liakata[1,2], and Rob Procter[1,2]

[1] University of Warwick, Coventry, UK
a.zubiaga@warwick.ac.uk
[2] Alan Turing Institute, London, UK

Abstract. Tools that are able to detect unverified information posted on social media during a news event can help to avoid the spread of rumours that turn out to be false. In this paper we compare a novel approach using Conditional Random Fields that learns from the sequential dynamics of social media posts with the current state-of-the-art rumour detection system, as well as other baselines. In contrast to existing work, our classifier does not need to observe tweets querying the stance of a post to deem it a rumour but, instead, exploits context learned during the event. Our classifier has improved precision and recall over the state-of-the-art classifier that relies on querying tweets, as well as outperforming our best baseline. Moreover, the results provide evidence for the generalisability of our classifier.

Keywords: Social media · Rumour detection · Breaking news · Journalism

1 Introduction

Social media platforms such as Twitter are increasingly being used by people to follow newsworthy events [25] and by journalists for news gathering [37]. However, the speed at which news unfolds on social media means that much of the information posted in the early stages of an event is unverified [22], which makes it more difficult for the public to distinguish verified information from rumours and covering the news becomes more challenging for journalists [29].

We set out to develop a rumour detection system that enables distinguishing between verified and unverified posts. This can be useful to limit the diffusion of information that might turn out subsequently to be false and so reduce the risk of harm to individuals, communities and society [32]. Research in rumour detection is scarce in the scientific literature, [35] being the only published work to date that addresses this issue. They introduced an approach that looks for 'enquiring' tweets, i.e., tweets that query or challenge the credibility of a previous posting to determine whether it is rumourous; a tweet is deemed to be enquiring if it matches one of a number of manually curated, regular expressions. While this is an ingenious approach, it has some important limitations: it is reliant on there

© Springer International Publishing AG 2017
G.L. Ciampaglia et al. (Eds.): SocInfo 2017, Part I, LNCS 10539, pp. 109–123, 2017.
DOI: 10.1007/978-3-319-67217-5_8

being a human in the loop to regularly revise the list of regular expressions as these may not generalise well to new datasets; it assumes that enquiring posts will arise, though this may lead to low recall as not all rumourous posts will necessarily provoke queries; and it takes no account of the context surrounding the post, which we believe can be exploited to gain insight into the way it emerges. Other work has dealt with "rumour detection" with what we argue is a questionable definition and which conflicts with definitions established in the literature [1,8]. These studies understand rumours as false pieces of information, and therefore misdefine the rumour detection task as consisting of distinguishing true and false stories. In our study we adhere to the established definition that understands a rumour as information circulating while its veracity is yet to be confirmed [1,8]. Consequently, we define the goal of the rumour detection task as that of identifying posts that are yet to be verified, distinguishing them from non-rumours [40].

To the best of our knowledge, our work is the first to attempt rumour detection without having to observe enquiring tweets. Instead, we introduce a sequential approach based on Linear-Chain Conditional Random Fields (CRF) to learn the dynamics of posts, which enables us to classify a post as a rumour or non-rumour while relying on the content of a tweet, in conjunction with context learnt from earlier posts associated with the same event, to determine if it is rumourous. We investigate the performance of CRF as a sequential classifier on five Twitter datasets associated with breaking news to detect tweets that constitute rumours. The performance of CRF is compared with its non-sequential equivalent, a Maximum Entropy classifier, as well as the state-of-the-art rumour detection approach by [35] and other baseline classifiers. Our experiments show substantial improvements and these improvements are consistent across the different events in our dataset.

2   Related Work

Despite increasing interest in rumours in social media [23,26,28,31,39,40], there has been very little work in automatic rumour detection [36]. Much of what work that has been done on rumour detection [10,11,24] has been limited to finding rumours known *a priori*. A classifier is fed with a set of predefined rumours (e.g., *Obama is muslim*), which then classifies new tweets containing a set of relevant keywords (e.g., *Obama* and *muslim*) as being related to one of the known rumours or not (e.g., *I think Obama is not muslim* would be about the rumour, while *Obama was talking to a group of Muslims* would not). An approach like this can be useful for long-standing rumours, where one wants to identify relevant tweets to track the rumours that have already been identified; one may also refer to this task as *rumour tracking* rather than *rumour detection*, given that the rumour is known *a priori*. However, this would not work for contexts such as breaking news, where previously unseen rumours emerge and *a priori* the specific keywords linked to the rumour are not yet known. In such cases, a classifier has to determine if each new update is yet to be verified and hence constitutes a rumour. To deal with such situations, a classifier would need to learn generalisable patterns that will help identify new rumours during breaking stories.

To the best of our knowledge, the only work to tackle the detection of new rumours is that by [35]. Their approach builds on the assumption that rumours will provoke tweets from skeptical users who question or enquire about their veracity; the fact that a post has a number of enquiring tweets associated with it would then imply it is rumourous. The authors created a manually curated list of five regular expressions (e.g., "is (that | this | it) true"), which are used to identify querying tweets. These enquiring tweets are then clustered by similarity, each cluster being ultimately deemed a candidate rumour. Their best approach achieved 52% and 28% precision for two datasets. While this work builds on a sensible hypothesis and presents a clever approach to the rumour detection task, there are three potential limitations: (1) being based on manually curated regular expressions the approach may not generalise well; (2) the hypothesis might not always apply and hence lead to low recall as, for example, certain rumours reported by reputable media are not always questioned by the general public [40]; (3) it takes no account of the context that precedes the rumour, which can give additional insights into what is going on and how a post can be rumourous in that context (e.g., the rumour that *a gunman is on the loose*, when the police have not yet confirmed it, is easier to be deemed a rumour if we put it into the context of preceding events, such as posts that the identity of the gunman is unknown).

While not strictly doing rumour detection, other researchers have worked on related tasks. For instance, there is an increasing body of work [10,11,15,17,24, 34] looking into stance classification of tweets discussing rumours, categorising tweets as supporting, denying or questioning the rumour. The approach has been to train a classifier from a labelled set of tweets to categorise the stance observed in new tweets discussing rumours; however, these authors do not deal with non-rumours, assuming instead that the input to the classifier is already cleaned up to include only tweets related to rumours. There is also work on veracity classification both in the context of rumours and beyond [4,12,14,15,18,19,33]. Work on stance and veracity classification can be seen as complementary to our objectives; one could use the set of rumours detected by a rumour detection system as input to a classifier that determines stance of tweets in those rumours and/or veracity of those rumours [36].

3   Dataset

We collected a diverse set of stories that would not necessarily be known *a priori* and which would include both rumours and non-rumours. We did this by emulating the scenario in which a journalist is following reports associated with breaking news. Seeing a timeline of tweets about the breaking news, a user would then annotate each of the tweets as being a rumour or a non-rumour.

Tweets were collected from the Twitter streaming API relating to news-worthy events that could potentially prompt the initiation and propagation of rumours. As soon as our journalist collaborators informed us about a newsworthy event, we set up the data collection process, tracking the main hashtags and keywords pertaining to the event as a whole. Note that while launching the collection slightly after the start of the event means that we may have missed the very early tweets, we kept collecting subsequent retweets of those early tweets, making it much more likely that we would retrieve the most retweeted tweets from the very first minutes. Once we had the collection of tweets for a newsworthy event, we sampled the timeline to enable manual annotation (signaled by highly retweeted tweets associated with newsworthy current events). Afterwards, the journalists read through the timeline to mark each of the tweets as being a rumour or not, making sure that the identification of rumours was in line with the established criteria [39]. A tweet was annotated as a rumour when there was no evidence or no authoritative source had confirmed it. Note that the annotation of a tweet as a rumour does not imply that the underlying story was later found to be true or false, but instead it reflects that the story was unconfirmed at the time of posting.

We followed the process above for five different newsworthy events, all of which attracted substantial interest in the media and were rife with rumours:

- Ferguson unrest: citizens of Ferguson in Missouri, USA, protested after the fatal shooting of an 18-year-old African American, Michael Brown, by a white police officer on August 9, 2014.
- Ottawa shooting: shootings occurred on Ottawa's Parliament Hill, resulting in the death of a Canadian soldier on October 22, 2014.
- Sydney siege: a gunman held hostage ten customers and eight employees of a Lindt chocolate cafe located at Martin Place in Sydney on December 15, 2014.
- Charlie Hebdo shooting: two brothers forced their way into the offices of the French satirical weekly newspaper Charlie Hebdo, killing 11 people and wounding 11 more, on January 7, 2015.
- Germanwings plane crash: a passenger plane from Barcelona to Düsseldorf crashed in the French Alps on March 24, 2015, killing all passengers and crew. The plane was ultimately found to have been deliberately crashed by the co-pilot.

Given the large volume of tweets in the datasets, we sampled them by picking tweets that provoked a high number of retweets. The retweet threshold was set to 100, selected based on the size of the resulting dataset. For each of these tweets in the sampled subset, we also collected all tweets that replied to them. While Twitter does not provide an API endpoint to retrieve 'conversational threads' [30] provoked by tweets, it is possible to collect them by scraping tweets through the web client interface. We developed a script that enabled us to collect and store complete threads for all the rumourous source tweets[1]. We used replying tweets for two purposes: (1) for manual annotation work, where replies to each

---

[1] Collection script available at https://github.com/azubiaga/pheme-twitter-conversation-collection.

tweet can provide useful context for the annotator to decide if a tweet is a rumour where the tweet itself does not provide sufficient details; (2) we to reproduce one of our baselines classifiers, i.e. the classifier introduced by [35]. However, our approach ignores replying tweets, relying only on the source tweet itself.

The sampled subsets of tweets were visualised in a separate timeline per day and sorted by time. Using these timelines, the journalists were asked to use their knowledge of the events to identify rumours and non-rumours. Along with each tweet, journalists could optionally click on the bubble next to the tweet to visualise replying tweets. The annotation work led to the manual categorisation of each tweet as being a rumour or not. As the journalists progressed along the timeline, new tweets reporting repeated stories were assigned the same annotation as in the previous instance.

The final dataset comprised 5,802 annotated tweets, of which 1,972 were classified as rumours and 3,830 as non-rumours. These annotations are distributed differently across the five events, as shown in Table 1. While slightly over 50% of the tweets were rumours for the Germanwings Crash and the Ottawa Shooting, less than 25% were so for Charlie Hebdo and Ferguson. The Sydney Siege had an intermediate rumour ratio of (42.8%).

Table 1. Distribution of annotations of rumours and non-rumours for the five events.

Event	Rumours	Non-rumours	Total
Charlie Hebdo	458 (22.0%)	1,621 (78.0%)	2,079
Ferguson	284 (24.8%)	859 (75.2%)	1,143
Germanwings Crash	238 (50.7%)	231 (49.3%)	469
Ottawa Shooting	470 (52.8%)	420 (47.2%)	890
Sydney Siege	522 (42.8%)	699 (57.2%)	1,221
Total	1,972 (34.0%)	3,830 (66.0%)	5,802

4   The Rumour Detection Task

We define the rumour detection task as that in which, given a timeline of tweets, the system has to determine which tweets are reporting rumours and hence spreading information that is yet to be verified. Note that the fact that a tweet constitutes a rumour does not imply that it will later be deemed true or false, but that it is unverified at the time of posting. The identification of rumours within a timeline is ultimately meant to warn users that the information has not been confirmed and, while it may later be confirmed, it may also turn out to be false.

Formally, the task takes an evolving timeline of tweets $TL = \{t_1, \ldots, t_{|TL|}\}$ as input, and the classifier has to determine whether each of these tweets, t_i, is a rumour or a non-rumour by assigning a label from $Y = \{R, NR\}$. Hence, we formulate the task as a binary classification problem, whose performance is evaluated by computing the precision, recall and F1 scores for the target category, i.e., rumours.

5 Exploiting Context for Rumour Detection

5.1 Hypothesis

In our dataset there were examples where the tweet alone provided sufficient evidence for classifying it as a rumour. For example, in *"the name of the police officer who fatally shot the kid would be reportedly announced by the police later in the day"* the use of "reportedly" expresses uncertainty and so we may conclude that the post is not confirmed. In contrast, posts such as *"the kid was involved in a robbery before being shot"* may not be as easily classified from the tweet alone. Hence, this argues for the need to leverage additional information in the form of context that may help the classifier distinguish between rumours and non-rumours.

One source of tweet context is how others react to it [35]. For example, the tweet *"the kid was involved in a robbery before being shot"* provoked the response *"is that true?"*. However, close examination of rumours in our dataset revealed that this cannot be relied upon. For example, *"the kid was shot 10 times by the police"* provoked no querying response, though it was subsequently revealed to be untrue. Hence, while reactions may be indicative of a posting being unverified, we conclude that relying on this will lead to a classifier with low recall and that the classifier needs to be aware of how the event is unfolding, drawing on the posts that constitute it before the current post. The tweet to be classified as rumour or non-rumour should therefore leverage earlier posts, both rumours and non-rumours, that make up a 'thread' in which th e current tweet fits. For example, a tweet reporting the rumour that *"the police officer who shot the kid has left the town"* may be easier to classify given previous reports related to the police officer and the killing. Based on this, we hypothesise that *aggregating rumourous and non-rumourous posts preceding the tweet being classified will improve performance of the rumour detection system.* We operationalise this by using a sequential classifier that learns from the dynamics of reports observed preceding the current tweet.

5.2 Classifiers

In order to test our hypothesis, we used Conditional Random Fields (CRF) as a sequential classifier that enables aggregation of tweets as a thread of individual posts. We used a Maximum Entropy classifier as the non-sequential equivalent of CRF to test the validity of the hypothesis and also use additional baseline classifiers for further comparison. Moreover, we also reproduced a baseline [35] to compare the performance of our approach with that of a state-of-the-art method.

Conditional Random Fields (CRF). We modeled the twitter thread as a linear chain or graph as a sequence of rumours and non-rumours. In contrast to classifiers that choose a label for each input unit (e.g., a tweet), CRF also considers the neighbours of each unit, learning the probabilities of transitions of label pairs. The input for CRF is a graph $G = (V, E)$, where in our case each of the vertices V is a tweet and the edges E are relations of tweets, i.e., a link between a tweet and its preceding tweet in the event. Hence, having a data sequence X as input, CRF outputs a sequence of labels Y [13], where the output of each element y_i will not only depend on its features, but also on the probabilities of other labels surrounding it. The generalisable conditional distribution of CRF is shown in Eq. 1 [27][2].

$$p(y|x) = \frac{1}{Z(x)} \prod_{a=1}^{A} \Psi_a(y_a, x_a) \qquad (1)$$

where $Z(x)$ is the normalisation constant and Ψ_a is the set of factors in the graph G.

Hence, for rumour detection, CRF exploits the sequence of rumours and non-rumours leading up to the current tweet to determine whether it is a rumour. It is important to note that with CRF the sequence of rumours and non-rumours preceding the tweet being classified will be based on the predictions of the classifier itself and will not use any ground truth annotations. Errors in early tweets in the sequence may then increase errors in subsequent tweets.

Maximum Entropy Classifier (MaxEnt). As the non-sequential equivalent of CRF, we used a Maximum Entropy (or logistic regression) classifier, which operates at the tweet level. This enabled us to compare directly the extent to which treating the tweets posted during an event as a sequence can boost the performance of the classifier.

Enquiry-Based Approach [35]. We reproduced this approach, classifying a tweet as a rumour if at least one of the replying tweets matched one of the following regular expressions: (1) is (that | this | it) true, (2) wh[a]*t[?!][?1]*, (3) (real? | really? | unconfirmed), (4) (rumor | debunk), (5) (that | this | it) is not true.

Additional Baselines. We also compared three more non-sequential classifiers[3]: Naive Bayes (NB), Support Vector Machines (SVM) and Random Forests (RF).

We performed the experiments in a 5-fold cross-validation setting, having in each case four of the events for training and the remainder event for testing. This enabled us to simulate a realistic scenario where an event is completely unknown to the classifier and it has to identify rumours from the knowledge garnered from events in the training set. For evaluation purposes, we aggregated the output of all five runs as the micro-averaged evaluation across runs.

---

[2] We use the PyStruct package to implement CRF [21].
[3] We used the scikit-learn Python package for these baselines.

5.3   Features

We used two types of features: content-based features and social features, testing them individually as well as combined. These two types of features are intended to capture the role that both textual content and user behaviour play in the detection of rumours. Features are limited to those that can be obtained in a real-time scenario, hence we do not consider some features like number of retweets or number of favourites, which are zero at the very beginning and takes time for them to increase as people react.

Content-Based Features. We use seven different features extracted from the content of the tweets:

- **Word Vectors:** to create vectors representing the words in each tweet, we built word vector representations using Word2Vec [20]. We trained five different Word2Vec model with 300 dimensions, one for each of the five folds, training the model in each case from the collection of tweets pertaining to the four events in the training set, so that the event (and the vocabulary) in the test set was unknown.
- **Part-of-speech Tags:** we built a vector of part-of-speech (POS) tags with each feature in the vector representing the number of occurrences of a certain POS tag in the tweet. We used Twitie [3] to parse the tweets for POS tags, an information extraction package that is part of GATE [5].
- **Capital Ratio:** the ratio of capital letters among all alphabetic characters in the tweet. Use of capitalisation tends to reflect emphasis, among other attributes.
- **Word Count:** the number of words in the tweet, counted as the number of space-separated tokens.
- **Use of Question Mark:** a binary feature representing if the tweet had a question mark in it. Question marks may be indicative of uncertainty.
- **Use of Exclamation Mark:** a binary feature representing if the tweet had an exclamation mark in it. Exclamation marks may be indicative of emphasis or surprise.
- **Use of Period:** a binary feature representing if the tweet contained a period. Punctuation may be indicative of good writing and hence careful reporting.

Social Features. We used five social features, all of which can be inferred from the metadata associated with the author of the tweet and which is embedded as part of a tweet object retrieved from the Twitter API. We defined a set of social features that are indicative of a user's experience and reputation:

- **Tweet Count:** we inferred this feature from the number of tweets a user had posted on Twitter. As numbers can vary substantially across users, we normalised them by rounding up the 10-base logarithm of the tweet count: $\lceil \log_{10}(statusescount) \rceil$.

- **Listed Count:** this feature was computed by normalising the number of lists a user belongs to, i.e., the number of times other users decided to add them to a list: $\lceil \log_{10}(\text{listedcount}) \rceil$.
- **Follow Ratio:** we looked at the reputation of a user as reflected by their number of followers. However, the number of followers might occasionally be rigged, e.g., by users who simply follow many others to attract more followers. To control for this, we defined the follow ratio as the logarithmically scaled ratio of followers over followees: $\lfloor \log_{10}(\#\text{followers}/\#\text{following}) \rceil$.
- **Age:** we computed the age of a user as the rounded number of years that the user has spent on Twitter, i.e., from the day the account was set up to the day of the current tweet.
- **Verified:** a binary feature representing if the user had been verified by Twitter or not, i.e., those whose identity Twitter has validated, and tend to be reputable people.

6   Results

6.1   Comparison of Classifiers

Table 2 shows the results for different classifiers using either or both content-based and social features, as well as the results for the state-of-the-art classifier [35]. Performance using content-based features suggests a remarkable improvement for CRF over the other classifiers. This is especially true when we look at precision, where CRF performs substantially better than the rest. Only the Naive Bayes classifier performs better in terms of recall, however, it performs poorly in terms of precision. CRF clearly balances precision and recall better, outperforming all the other classifiers in terms of the F1 score.

The results are not as clear when we look at social features. CRF still performs best in terms of precision, but recall performance drops, where most of

Table 2. Classifier performance.

Classifier	Content			Social			Cont + Social		
	P	R	F1	P	R	F1	P	R	F1
SVM	0.355	0.445	0.395	0.337	**0.524**	**0.410**	0.337	0.483	0.397
Random Forest	0.271	0.087	0.131	0.343	0.433	0.382	0.275	0.099	0.145
Naive Bayes	0.309	**0.723**	0.433	0.294	0.010	0.020	0.310	**0.723**	0.434
MaxEnt	0.329	0.425	0.371	0.336	0.476	0.394	0.338	0.442	0.383
CRF	**0.683**	0.545	**0.606**	**0.462**	0.268	0.339	**0.667**	0.556	**0.607**

State-of-the-art Baseline			
Classifier	P	R	F1
Zhao et al. [35]	0.410	0.065	0.113

the classifiers perform better than CRF, with SVM being the best. The F1 score shows that SVM best exploits social features, however, performance results using social features are significantly worse than those using content-based features, suggesting social features alone are not sufficient.

When both content-based features and social features are combined, we see that the results resemble that of the use of content-based features alone. CRF outperforms all the rest in terms of precision, while Naive Bayes is good only in terms of recall. The aggregation of features also leads to CRF being the best classifier in terms of F1 score, with CRF giving an improvement of 39.9% over Naive Bayes, the second best classifier. If we compare the results of CRF with the use of content-based features alone or combining both types of features, we notice that all F1 scores for combined features are superior to their counterparts using content-based features alone, among which CRF performs best.

Comparison with respect to the baseline approach [35] supports our conjecture that a manually curated list of regular expressions may lead to low recall. This approach gets a relatively good precision score but it performs substantially worse than CRF. Expanding and/or adapting the list of regular expressions to our specific set of events might improve performance but requires significant manual effort and may still not guarantee better performance in the general case.

6.2   Evaluation by Event

We now examine classifier performance broken down by event so that we can analyse the extent to which the CRF classifier performs well across datasets (see Table 3). The results are mostly consistent across events and in line with the

Table 3. Classifier performance broken down by event.

Classifier	Germanwings			Charlie Hebdo			Ottawa Shooting		
	P	R	F1	P	R	F1	P	R	F1
SVM	0.463	0.504	0.483	0.239	0.546	0.332	0.496	0.428	0.459
Random Forest	0.438	0.029	0.055	0.215	0.203	0.209	0.556	0.053	0.097
Naive Bayes	0.506	**0.882**	0.643	0.223	**0.961**	0.361	0.436	0.087	0.145
MaxEnt	0.475	0.441	0.458	0.239	0.535	0.330	0.512	0.409	0.454
Zhao et al. [35]	0.636	0.059	0.108	0.268	0.057	0.094	0.651	0.060	0.109
CRF	**0.743**	0.668	**0.704**	**0.545**	0.762	**0.636**	**0.841**	**0.585**	**0.690**

Classifier	Sydney Siege			Ferguson		
	P	R	F1	P	R	F1
SVM	0.435	0.485	0.458	0.240	0.451	0.313
Random Forest	0.466	0.065	0.114	0.254	0.127	0.169
Naive Bayes	0.426	**0.962**	**0.590**	0.248	**0.820**	0.381
MaxEnt	0.425	0.429	0.427	0.245	0.370	0.295
Zhao et al. [35]	0.429	0.075	0.127	0.355	0.077	0.127
CRF	**0.764**	0.385	0.512	**0.566**	0.394	**0.465**

overall performance scores. The Naive Bayes classifier performs best in terms of recall in most cases, however, this is due to it being skewed towards determining that tweets are rumours, as seen in the low precision scores. The CRF classifier achieves the highest precision scores consistently for all the datasets. Moreover, it also achieves the best balance of precision and recall. These results reaffirm the CRF classifier's superiority with respect to the range of classifiers under study, confirming also that exploiting context learned during the event as a sequential set of postings leads to substantially improved performance.

These results also show that while the baseline classifier [35] is among the best in terms of precision, and is often only outperformed by the CRF classifier, it nevertheless performs poorly in terms of recall.

7   Discussion

The aim of a social media rumour detection system is to identify posts whose content have yet to be verified. One application would be alerting users that a report is yet to be verified and so should be treated with caution. Another would be as input to classifiers that determine stance of tweets towards rumours [16,38] or classifiers that determine the veracity of rumours [9]. A rumour detection system can in fact be the first component of a system that deals with rumours [36]: (1) rumour detection; (2) rumour tracking; (3) rumour stance classification, and (4) rumour veracity classification.

Our rumour detection experiments on five datasets, each associated with a breaking news story, show that a classifier that sequentially exploits context from earlier tweets achieves significant improvements over non-sequential classifiers. Our CRF classifier substantially outperforms its non-sequential counterpart, a Maximum Entropy classifier, as well as other non-sequential classifiers. Moreover, our approach is better than the state-of-the-art baseline [35] that uses regular expressions to classify as rumours. The latter fails to achieve a competitive recall score, which we believe is for two main reasons: (1) rumours will not always provoke enquiring reactions; and (2) regular expressions may have limited generalisability and require regular manual updates. In contrast, our automated sequential classifiers can classify a tweet as a rumour or non-rumour from its own content and context from earlier tweets, without having to wait for any reactions.

While we are confident that our approach covers a diverse range of rumours and non-rumours, one caveat is that our experiments have been limited to tweets retweeted at least 100 times. While this is consistent with one of the key characteristics of rumours, i.e., that they have to attract a substantial interest to be deemed rumours, it is necessary to wait until a tweet gets retweeted a number of times before it can be considered a candidate for input to the classifier. The development of a classifier that identifies these highly retweeted tweets promptly would enable earlier detection of rumours. Likewise, experimentation with a dataset that includes tweets annotated as rumour or non-rumour which has not been filtered by retweet count would be useful to extend our work and validate with an entire timeline of tweets. The latter has not been possible in our case owing to the cost associated with such large-scale annotation of tweets.

8 Conclusion

We have introduced a novel approach to rumour detection in social media by leveraging the context preceding a tweet with a sequential classifier. Experimenting over five news datasets collected from Twitter and annotated for rumours and non-rumours by journalists, we have shown that this can substantially boost rumour detection performance. Our approach has also proven to outperform the state-of-the-art rumour detection system [35] that relies on finding querying posts that match a set of manually curated list of regular expressions. Their approach performs well in terms of precision but fails in terms of recall, suggesting that regular manual input is needed to revise the regular expressions. Our fully automated approach instead achieves superior performance that is better balanced for both precision and recall.

Social media and user-generated content (UGC) are increasingly important in a number of different ways for the work of not only journalists but also government agencies such as the police and civil protection agencies [22]. However, their use presents major challenges, not least because information posted on social media is not always reliable and its veracity needs to be checked before it can be considered as fit for use in the reporting of news, or decision-making in the case of responses to civil emergencies [22] or natural disasters [2]. Hence, it is vital that tools be developed that can aid: (a) the detection of rumours; (b) determination of their likely veracity. In the Pheme project [7], we have been developing tools that address the need for the latter [6,16,40]. However, for tools for rumour veracity determination to be effective, they need to be applied in combination with the former and progress so far has been limited. In this paper, we present a novel approach whose performance suggests it has the potential to address this problem.

Finally, we have made the annotated datasets publicly available to promote further research.[4]

Acknowledgments. This work has been supported by the PHEME FP7 project (grant No. 611233). Maria Liakata and Rob Procter were also supported by the Alan Turing Institute. We would also like to thank Queen Mary University of London for the use of its MidPlus computational facilities, which was supported by QMUL Research-IT and funded by EPSRC grant EP/K000128/1.

References

1. Allport, G.W., Postman, L.: An analysis of rumor. Publ. Opin. Q. **10**(4), 501–517 (1946)

---

[4] https://figshare.com/articles/PHEME_dataset_of_rumours_and_non-rumours/4010619.

2. Bazerli, G., Bean, T., Crandall, A., Coutin, M., Kasindi, L., Procter, R.N., Rodger, S., Saber, D., Slachmuijlder, L., Trewinnard, T.: Humanitarianism 2.0. Glob. Policy J. (2015). http://www.globalpolicyjournal.com/projects/global-policy-responses/humanitarianism-20

3. Bontcheva, K., Derczynski, L., Funk, A., Greenwood, M.A., Maynard, D., Aswani, N.: TwitIE: an open-source information extraction pipeline for microblog text. In: Proceedings of the International Conference on Recent Advances in Natural Language Processing. Association for Computational Linguistics (2013)

4. Cai, G., Wu, H., Lv, R.: Rumors detection in Chinese via crowd responses. In: IEEE/ACM International Conference on Advances in Social Networks Analysis and Mining (ASONAM), pp. 912–917. IEEE (2014)

5. Cunningham, H., Maynard, D., Bontcheva, K.: Text Processing with Gate. Gateway Press CA, Murphys (2011)

6. Derczynski, L., Bontcheva, K., Liakata, M., Procter, R., Wong Sak Hoi, G., Zubiaga, A.: SemEval-2017 task 8: RumourEval: determining rumour veracity and support for rumours. In: Proceedings of the 11th International Workshop on Semantic Evaluation (SemEval-2017), pp. 69–76. Association for Computational Linguistics, Vancouver (2017)

7. Derczynski, L., Bontcheva, K., Lukasik, M., Declerck, T., Scharl, A., Georgiev, G., Osenova, P., Lobo, T.P., Kolliakou, A., Stewart, R., et al.: PHEME: computing veracity - the fourth challenge of big social data. In: Proceedings of the Extended Semantic Web Conference EU Project Networking session (ESCW-PN) (2015)

8. DiFonzo, N., Bordia, P.: Rumor, gossip and urban legends. Diogenes **54**(1), 19–35 (2007)

9. Giasemidis, G., Singleton, C., Agrafiotis, I., Nurse, J.R.C., Pilgrim, A., Willis, C., Greetham, D.V.: Determining the veracity of rumours on Twitter. In: Spiro, E., Ahn, Y.-Y. (eds.) SocInfo 2016. LNCS, vol. 10046, pp. 185–205. Springer, Cham (2016). doi:10.1007/978-3-319-47880-7_12

10. Hamidian, S., Diab, M.T.: Rumor detection and classification for Twitter data. In: Proceedings of the Fifth International Conference on Social Media Technologies, Communication, and Informatics (SOTICS), pp. 71–77 (2015)

11. Hamidian, S., Diab, M.T.: Rumor identification and belief investigation on Twitter. In: Proceedings of NAACL-HLT, pp. 3–8 (2016)

12. Jin, Z., Cao, J., Zhang, Y., Luo, J.: News verification by exploiting conflicting social viewpoints in microblogs. In: Thirtieth AAAI Conference on Artificial Intelligence, pp. 2972–2978 (2016)

13. Lafferty, J., McCallum, A., Pereira, F.: Conditional random fields: probabilistic models for segmenting and labeling sequence data. In: Proceedings of the Eighteenth International Conference on Machine Learning, ICML, vol. 1, pp. 282–289 (2001)

14. Liang, G., He, W., Xu, C., Chen, L., Zeng, J.: Rumor identification in microblogging systems based on users' behavior. IEEE Trans. Comput. Soc. Syst. **2**(3), 99–108 (2015)

15. Liu, X., Nourbakhsh, A., Li, Q., Fang, R., Shah, S.: Real-time rumor debunking on Twitter. In: Proceedings of the 24th ACM International on Conference on Information and Knowledge Management, pp. 1867–1870. ACM (2015)

16. Lukasik, M., Bontcheva, K., Cohn, T., Zubiaga, A., Liakata, M., Procter, R.: Using Gaussian processes for rumour stance classification in social media. arXiv preprint arXiv:1609.01962 (2016)

17. Lukasik, M., Cohn, T., Bontcheva, K.: Classifying tweet level judgements of rumours in social media. In: Proceedings of the 2015 Conference on Empirical Methods in Natural Language Processing (EMNLP), pp. 2590–2595 (2015)
18. Ma, J., Gao, W., Mitra, P., Kwon, S., Jansen, B.J., Wong, K.F., Cha, M.: Detecting rumors from microblogs with recurrent neural networks. In: Proceedings of the International Joint Conference on Artificial Intelligence (IJCAI), pp. 3818–3824 (2016)
19. Ma, J., Gao, W., Wei, Z., Lu, Y., Wong, K.F.: Detect rumors using time series of social context information on microblogging websites. In: Proceedings of the 24th ACM International on Conference on Information and Knowledge Management, pp. 1751–1754. ACM (2015)
20. Mikolov, T., Sutskever, I., Chen, K., Corrado, G.S., Dean, J.: Distributed representations of words and phrases and their compositionality. In: Advances in Neural Information Processing Systems, pp. 3111–3119 (2013)
21. Müller, A.C., Behnke, S.: PyStruct: learning structured prediction in python. The J. Mach. Learn. Res. **15**(1), 2055–2060 (2014)
22. Procter, R., Crump, J., Karstedt, S., Voss, A., Cantijoch, M.: Reading the riots: what were the police doing on Twitter? Polic. Soc. **23**(4), 413–436 (2013)
23. Procter, R., Vis, F., Voss, A.: Reading the riots on Twitter: methodological innovation for the analysis of big data. Int. J. Soc. Res. Methodol. **16**(3), 197–214 (2013)
24. Qazvinian, V., Rosengren, E., Radev, D.R., Mei, Q.: Rumor has it: identifying misinformation in microblogs. In: Proceedings of the 2011 Conference on Empirical Methods in Natural Language Processing (EMNLP), pp. 1589–1599 (2011)
25. Sankaranarayanan, J., Samet, H., Teitler, B.E., Lieberman, M.D., Sperling, J.: Twitterstand: news in tweets. In: Proceedings of the 17th ACM SIGSPATIAL International Conference on Advances in Geographic Information Systems, pp. 42–51. ACM (2009)
26. Starbird, K., Maddock, J., Orand, M., Achterman, P., Mason, R.M.: Rumors, false flags, and digital vigilantes: misinformation on Twitter after the 2013 Boston marathon bombing. In: Proceedings of iConference 2014 (2014)
27. Sutton, C., McCallum, A.: An introduction to conditional random fields. Mach. Learn. **4**(4), 267–373 (2011)
28. Takayasu, M., Sato, K., Sano, Y., Yamada, K., Miura, W., Takayasu, H.: Rumor diffusion and convergence during the 3.11 earthquake: a Twitter case study. PLoS ONE **10**(4), e0121443 (2015)
29. Tolmie, P., Procter, R., Randall, D.W., Rouncefield, M., Burger, C., Wong Sak Hoi, G., Zubiaga, A., Liakata, M.: Supporting the use of user generated content in journalistic practice. In: Proceedings of the 2017 CHI Conference on Human Factors in Computing Systems, pp. 3632–3644. ACM (2017)
30. Tolmie, P., Procter, R., Rouncefield, M., Liakata, M., Zubiaga, A.: Microblog analysis as a programme of work. arXiv preprint arXiv:1511.03193 (2015)
31. Tolosi, L., Tagarev, A., Georgiev, G.: An analysis of event-agnostic features for rumour classification in Twitter. In: ICWSM Workshop on Social Media in the Newsroom, pp. 151–158 (2016)
32. Webb, H., Burnap, P., Procter, R., Rana, O., Stahl, B., Williams, M., Housley, W., Edwards, A., Jirotka, M.: Digital wildfires: propagation, verification, regulation, and responsible innovation. ACM Trans. Inf. Syst. **34**(3), 15:1–15:23 (2016)
33. Wu, K., Yang, S., Zhu, K.Q.: False rumors detection on sina weibo by propagation structures. In: 2015 IEEE 31st International Conference on Data Engineering, pp. 651–662. IEEE (2015)

34. Zeng, L., Starbird, K., Spiro, E.S.: # unconfirmed: classifying rumor stance in crisis-related social media messages. In: Tenth International AAAI Conference on Web and Social Media, pp. 747–750 (2016)
35. Zhao, Z., Resnick, P., Mei, Q.: Enquiring minds: early detection of rumors in social media from enquiry posts. In: Proceedings of the 24th International Conference on World Wide Web, pp. 1395–1405. ACM (2015)
36. Zubiaga, A., Aker, A., Bontcheva, K., Liakata, M., Procter, R.: Detection and resolution of rumours in social media: a survey. arXiv preprint arXiv:1704.00656 (2017)
37. Zubiaga, A., Ji, H., Knight, K.: Curating and contextualizing twitter stories to assist with social newsgathering. In: Proceedings of the 2013 International Conference on Intelligent User Interfaces, pp. 213–224. ACM (2013)
38. Zubiaga, A., Kochkina, E., Liakata, M., Procter, R., Lukasik, M.: Stance classification in rumours as a sequential task exploiting the tree structure of social media conversations. In: Proceedings of the International Conference on Computational Linguistics (COLING). Association for Natural Language Processing (ANLP) (2016)
39. Zubiaga, A., Liakata, M., Procter, R., Bontcheva, K., Tolmie, P.: Crowdsourcing the annotation of rumourous conversations in social media. In: Proceedings of the 24th International Conference on World Wide Web Companion, pp. 347–353. International World Wide Web Conferences Steering Committee (2015)
40. Zubiaga, A., Liakata, M., Procter, R., Wong Sak Hoi, G., Tolmie, P.: Analysing how people orient to and spread rumours in social media by looking at conversational threads. PLoS ONE **11**(3), 1–29 (2016). http://dx.doi.org/10.1371%2Fjournal.pone.0150989

Multidimensional Analysis of the News Consumption of Different Demographic Groups on a Nationwide Scale

Jisun An[(⊠)] and Haewoon Kwak

Qatar Computing Research Institute, Hamad Bin Khalifa University, Doha, Qatar
{jisun.an,haewoon}@acm.org

Abstract. Examining 103,133 news articles that are the most popular for different demographic groups in Daum News (the second most popular news portal in South Korea) during the whole year of 2015, we provided multi-level analyses of gender and age differences in news consumption. We measured such differences in four different levels: (1) by actual news items, (2) by section, (3) by topic, and (4) by subtopic. We characterized the news items at the four levels by using the computational techniques, which are topic modeling and the vector representation of words and news items. We found that differences in news reading behavior across different demographic groups are the most noticeable in subtopic level but neither section nor topic levels.

Keywords: News consumption · Online news · News media · News topic · Daum · News portal · Demographics · Gender differences · Age differences

1 Introduction

Demographics play an important role in news consumption. What women in their fifties read is very different from that of men in their twenties. Understanding such differences in news consumption can potentially help journalists to pitch news articles better, help editors to decide which ones to put on the front page, and help computer scientists design new algorithms for recommending articles. That is the reason why news consumption of demographic groups has been actively studied in both the domains of journalism study and computer science [14,18,24,31,39,40].

The previous literature regarding news consumption in the study of journalism has mainly focused on the gender differences in the consumption of news genres [18,24,40] primarily due to the lack of other detailed data. On the other hand, in computer science, previous studies have mainly focused on developing models for predicting clicks and for news recommendations at an individual level with large-scale data [14,31,39].

© Springer International Publishing AG 2017
G.L. Ciampaglia et al. (Eds.): SocInfo 2017, Part I, LNCS 10539, pp. 124–142, 2017.
DOI: 10.1007/978-3-319-67217-5_9

In this study, we attempt to bridge these two worlds and uncover the differences in news consumption across demographic groups by large-scale news consumption data. Specifically, we aim to quantify such differences in four dimensions: actual news items, sections, topics, and subtopics. While the existence of the "differences" is expected, our multidimensional analysis shows how such differences can be differently captured in each dimension.

For this study, we collected and analyzed the daily top 30 news items for each gender (male and female) and age group (10s, 20s, 30s, 40s, and 50s) in Daum News, the second most popular news portal service in South Korea, for the entire year of 2015. The number of the unique news items collected is 103,133. Daum News can have the accurate, not self-reported, information on the user's age and gender based on one's social security number. This practice is not common in the Western web services. In South Korea, to join a website, it is mandatory for identity verification to provide the social security number that contains your birth year and gender. Also, Daum News has a strong user base that reads news with a logged-in status mainly because Daum News offers a wide range of services, which include e-mail, Internet community, or messenger, for example, based on the logged-in status.

2 Related Work

2.1 Sex-Typed Media Preference

Sex-typed media preference has long been investigated for various types of media. Regarding movie and TV genres, studies have found that women are more likely to watch tragedies, soaps, dramas, medical serials, and romances; men, on the other hand, tend to prefer horror, sports, and action and adventure content [21,37,38,41,42]. Psychological research suggests that such sex-typed media selections might well be rooted in societal gender stereotypes – men are expected to achieve more, and women are expected to interact more [16].

Scholars of the study of journalism have examined how demographics, such as sex or age, relate to news-seeking behavior and news preferences [15]. When attending to news, the sexes typically pursue remarkably different interests – in terms of topics, men tend to follow news on politics, sports, and business and finance, whereas women turn to news about community and health issues [18,40]. Also, women read more about social/interpersonal issues than men, and men read more about achievement/performance than women [24]. Scholars suggested that the origin of gender difference in news consumption is not considered from biological differences but from the psychological traits led by the sex-typed socialization [33].

While news preferences have been extensively studied for the news section, little is known about the topic or subtopic preferences of different demographic groups' news consumption. The key reason for this oversight is mainly due to a lack of data. Most of the previous work is based on surveys or experiments in the laboratory setting [18,24,40]. By contrast, our work relies on the longitudinal data collection where a huge number of Korean Internet news readers are unobtrusively monitored.

2.2 News Related Research with Large-Scale Data

Since news sites have been publishing online, we now have access to large-scale data of individual news consumption with detailed personal profiles. Computer scientists have addressed news-related questions but with different interests and approaches from scholars in journalism or communication studies. News-related research by computer scientists has predominantly focused on modeling news sharing behavior [3–5], news diffusion [1,7,17,19,26,29,36,44,49], and modeling the relative prominence of items or topics [2,6,8,13,25,28].

Computer scientists also have exploited news consumption patterns of individuals mainly for building a better news recommendation system to give readers a personalized experience when reading the news. Systems that make recommendations according to demographic classes were initially introduced [39]. More recently, the demographic information has often been used as a feature of those models [14,31]. However, the demographic differences in news consumption have not been fully uncovered, particularly in different dimensions of news such as topic or subtopic.

3 Data

3.1 News Consumption in South Korea

Online news consumption in South Korea has increased drastically. About 86% of South Korean people access news online at least once a week[1]. Given the 92% Internet and 85% smartphone penetrations, such a drastic increase makes sense. Web portal sites such as Naver and Daum are especially popular digital news platforms. Due to the extreme popularity of these portals, news providers in South Korea have been eager to publish their content via portals for years. In 2015, Naver and Daum formed the Committee for the Evaluation of News Partnership, complete with a set of ethical standards to help decide which providers should be eligible to supply news to portals. As a result, we can reasonably say that news providers and the news readers of Daum News are representative of the general South Korean news media and population, respectively.

3.2 Data Collection

Daum is the second largest web portal in South Korea, followed by Naver. Daum plays a significant role in providing a place for accessing online news to South Korea; 41% of South Koreans (24.6 M users) access Daum news on a weekly basis. Daum News provides different ways to explore news articles, for example, by its

---

[1] http://www.digitalnewsreport.org/.

recency, by current issues, by regions, or by popularity based on the number of views or the number of comments. A unique feature of Daum News is that it provides the top 30 most popular news articles on a particular day for each gender and age group, which are [male or female] and [10s, 20s, 30s, 40s, and 50s and above]. We note that Naver does not provide a ranked list of news articles by different demographic groups, and thus, we focus on Daum News data even though it is the second largest news portal in South Korea.

We crawled the top 30 most popular articles for different age and gender groups of each day for a one-year period (01/01/2015−31/12/2015). We carefully designed our crawlers not to degrade the performance of Daum's web servers. In our data set, we have 103,133 listed news items with 54,274 unique news titles. For each news item, we have its unique item ID, demographic group, rank in the group, title, summary, news source, and published date. We note that news articles about entertainment and sports are not included in the lists due to Daum News's policies.

4 Methodology

We need to determine the section, topic, and subtopic of the news items we collected. Next, we will briefly describe the methodology that we adopt for the analysis.

4.1 Four Dimensions of News

Defining the operational coding scheme for news has been a central issue for communication studies. In this study, we introduce four dimensions of news (sections, topics, subtopics, and individual news items) by which we investigate news consumption patterns. The diagram of the four dimensions of news is illustrated in Fig. 1. The first dimension is the news section (e.g., society, politics, etc.), which is a category of news often adopted in newsrooms and which has been popularly used for sex-typed news preference studies. Next, a news topic refers to a specific happening (e.g., a MERS outbreak in South Korea or child abuse case in a daycare center). Within a topic, we further explore subtopics by distinguishing different aspects of a topic. Finally, there is a dimension where

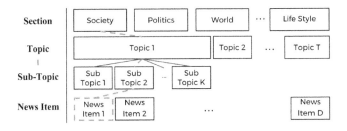

Fig. 1. Four dimensions of news.

all individual news items are aligned. We then can characterize the entire news collection (e.g., a news collection of South Korea in 2015) according to the four dimensions.

4.2 Categorizing News: Section

The most common way of categorizing news is perhaps to use a news section as defined by the news media. Especially for online news, which news section a news article belongs to can be inferred from the meta information embedded in the news URLs. For example, the URL http://media.daum.net/society/labor/newsview?newsid=20160709180100906l is categorized as "Society." We parsed all of the collected URLs and extracted the section information.

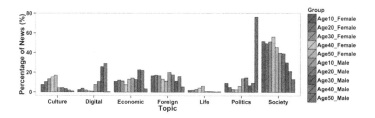

Fig. 2. Group distribution by section.

Figure 2 shows the proportion of news items for each demographic group for each news section. In our dataset, Daum News has seven different news sections, which are Culture, Digital, Economic, Foreign, Life, Politics, and Society. We note that the Entertainment and Sports sections are not included in the dataset. We observe that female groups are more alike than male groups in terms of news section preference. For female groups, Society and Culture were the two most popular news sections. For Age10_Male and Age20_Male groups, Society, Foreign, and Politics were more popular than the others. Then, for the Age30_Male and Age40_Male groups, their interests were Digital (i.e., technology news), Economics, and Politics. We also find one noticeable behavior of the Age50_Male group: 78% of their top 30 most popular news items over a year are about Politics. These news section preferences align well with previous work on sex-typed news consumption observed internationally [18,40].

4.3 Categorizing News: Topic

The news section category provided by Daum News abstractly captures the high-level topic of a news item. In this study, we go beyond a mere news section preference and examine whether the gender- or age-specific topic or subtopic preferences exist. To do that, we need to understand the semantic content of the news articles. For example, news about "Violence at daycare" and "A killer of his family" are both categorized under Society, but they are two different *topics*.

We automatically discover a topic-specific categorical structure from a set of titles and classify each news article based on it. Topic modeling techniques such as probabilistic Latent Semantic Indexing (pLSI) [23], Latent Dirichlet Allocation (LDA) [11], and Hierarchical Dirichlet Processes (HDP) [46] can be employed to induce topics from the set of news titles. We manually compare the three methods in terms of the interpretability of the induced topics and the quality of the clustered news titles for each of the included topics. For two slices of subsets, May and October 2015, we examined the top 20 topics resulting from the three methods with their top 30 words. For our dataset, pLSI's top topics were mapped more clearly with news events in the corresponding month than LDA's and HDP's topics were. One possible reason is that LDA and HDP were penalized more for modeling topics with short titles than pLSI was. Thus, we use pLSI to detect candidate topics. There are also specialized topic models for short texts, such as a biterm topic model (BTM) [48], and we leave it as a future work to improve our topic categorization method.

One problem with these topic modeling techniques is that they are not time-sensitive. The following two news titles, "Anyang Killer – a man killed his family" and "Wife killer – a man killed his wife but did not show any grief," are likely to be categorized as the same topic even though one event happened in January 2015, and the other happened in October 2015. To handle this problem, we first split our dataset by month, and then we build a pLSI model for each of the monthly datasets. Each pLSI model induces 100 topics, giving us 1,200 candidate topics in total. Each topic is represented by word distributions. We then aggregate similar candidate topics by examining the representative keywords for topics (words with the highest probabilities). In our case, we aggregate topics if they share more than three top words. After this, we classify each news title as one of these candidate topics based on the score given by the pLSI model. Finally, we split every candidate topic further into multiple topics by considering the publication times of news items. Only news items published for days in a row are tagged as the same topic, resulting in 2,122 topics. News titles without any matching candidate topic are considered stand-alone topics. Altogether, we have 41,452 topics.

Across all topics, the most popular news event is the Middle East Respiratory Syndrome (MERS) outbreak in South Korea. We find 2,756 matching news items regarding MERS. The most frequent words are MERS, a vice prime minister, confirmed patients, infected, hospital, Daejeon, tourists, etc.

Validation of Topic Categorization. For the purpose of validation, we cross-matched the set of news items extracted by the topic-model-based clustering method with the set of news items extracted by a keyword-based method. We focus on one particular news topic, MERS outbreak in South Korea. The outbreak lasted for a month and a half starting on May 20th. A total of 186 cases occurred during the outbreak, with a death toll of 36. Due to the outbreak, 2,208 schools were temporarily closed, and 16,693 people were quarantined. MERS was the most sensational news event in South Korea in 2015. We extract news items whose title contained the word "MERS", which results in 961 news items. By including more keywords, we may be able to extract more news items. However, we use a single word to be sure that all the retrieved news items are relevant to the news event. We find that 97% of news items about the MERS outbreak (929 out of 961 news items) overlap with those by the topic modeling based method. Then, to examine the relevance of those articles without the word "MERS," we randomly select 100 articles that do not explicitly include the word "MERS" and examine what they are about. We find that all are relevant to the MERS. This indicates that our method can extract news items even when the title of news does not include a key topic word. However, a set of topic words (not one word) will also be able to retrieve all relevant news items.

4.4   Categorizing News: Subtopic

Once we have a set of news articles on a certain topic, we further need to group them by subtopic. To this end, we train our data to represent each news item on a vector space and then cluster news items. Semantic vector space models of language represent each word with a real-valued vector. Firstly introduced by Hinton [22], the methods have been extended using neural network [9,45] and applied for the practical uses. In recent years, Milkolvo's skip-gram and distributed bag-of-word (DBOW) models [34] are popularly used for learning vector representation of words and documents due to its computational efficiency. In the skip-gram model, the objective is to predict a word's context given the word itself, whereas the objective in the DBOW model is to predict a word given its context.

More recently, the concept of embeddings has been extended beyond words to a number of text segments, including phrases [35], sentences and paragraphs [27], and documents. Adopting the document representation method, we learn distributed representations of news items in our Daum news collection. Each of news items is represented as low-dimensional vectors and are jointly learned with distributed vector representations of words using a DBOW model explained in [27]. In this vector space, two news items of semantically similar meaning are located nearby.

In our news embeddings (henceforth *News2Vec*), every news item is mapped to a unique vector in a matrix that represents news items, and every word is mapped to a unique vector in a matrix that represents words. We denote by **N2V** the $s \times f$ matrix of s which is the sum of n news items ($N_1, N_2, \ldots, N_n$) and f dimensions ($F_1, F_2, \ldots, F_f$). A great advantage of learning distributed representation vectors for news in this way is that the algorithm is not sensitive to news item length and does not require specific tuning for word weights. The row of the matrix **N2V**, $\mathbf{N_i}$, is a vector of f dimensions representing the i-th news item. The dimension of vector f is set to 200, and the model is trained with 40 epochs.

Once we have News2Vec, we apply the hierarchical clustering method using Ward's method [43] to this resulting matrix to cluster news items of the same subtopic. The hierarchical clustering method builds a dendrogram among entities. Then, one can cluster entities based on the dendrogram. Its main advantage is that the dendrogram is computed only once regardless of the number of clusters of interest. Once the dendrogram is built, we can simply choose the number of clusters (k) of our interest.

Validation for Subtopic Categorization. To evaluate the News2Vec based subtopic clustering method, we prepared a corpus in which each news item is labeled by two authors. We used 961 news items about MERS extracted by the keyword-matching method. Then, we manually classify news items by subtopics. We conduct a qualitative content analysis to develop a taxonomy of subtopics for MERS news.

Following an open-coding method [47], we identify the subtopics of MERS news in a two-phase process. We first read titles and descriptions of 100 news items to develop an initial coding scheme and then used an affinity diagramming technique [10] to iteratively develop a classification scheme for subtopics until a new subtopic did not emerge. Table 1 lists the resulting 10 subtopics. The individual authors manually classified all news items into one of the subtopic categories. Using the Delphi method [30], after each researcher independently coded the titles, we then iteratively compared and recoded the news items as necessary until we came to an agreement.

The ten subtopics regarding the MERS with the number of corresponding news items are listed in Table 1. ST1 "Reporting new cases" was the most popular subtopic with 254 news articles in our data set, followed by ST7 "Responsibility of Government" with 153 news items and ST9 "Economical Consequences" with 106 news items.

We then use this labeled data for the evaluation of our subtopic categorization method. We first learn News2Vec using entire Daum News data. Then, we cluster

Table 1. Ten subtopics regarding the MERS outbreak in South Korea in 2015. The total number of news items is 961.

	Subtopic	# Items
ST1	Reporting new cases	254
ST2	Track the path of outbreak	67
ST3	Schools closing down	34
ST4	Factual information	54
ST5	Verification of rumors	24
ST6	Problem of medical systems	71
ST7	Responsibility of government	153
ST8	Government' solution	103
ST9	Economical consequences	106
ST10	Societal problems	95

those 961 news items into ten groups ($k = 10$) using vectors from the resulting News2Vec. We evaluate the resulting subsets of news items with manually tagged clusters. For each detected subset, we find the best matched manual cluster based on the proportion of matching news items. Across ten subsets, our News2Vec subtopic classification achieved an 82.2% matching rate on average where the maximum matching rate is 92.8% and the minimum is 77.2%.

In our method, selecting the k is challenging. Here, we propose one possible solution to assist in the k selection procedure. The idea is that the average similarity scores for all pairs of news items within the same subtopic (S_{within}) should be smaller than across the subtopics (S_{across}). When news items are in vector representation, one can use any distance measures, such as Euclidean distance or cosine similarity, to measure the similarity score between two news items. Those two values, once found empirically, can play a role as thresholds for selecting the k for different topics. In our evaluation data set, S_{within} is 0.02 and S_{across} is 0.15 when using cosine similarity.

For further evaluation, we use these two values to find the subtopics of another topic, "Daycare child abuse." For 342 news items regarding the topic, we find k equals five. The manual inspection reveals the following five subtopics emerged: (1) What the teacher did to a child; (2) How cruel the teacher is; (3) Investigation and prosecution; (4) A new regulation on CCTV installation at daycare centers; and (5) Other cases of child abuse.

5   Group Differences in News Consumption

We now quantify differences in news consumption across demographic groups in four dimensions: (1) by actual news item, (2) by section, (3) by topic, and (4) by subtopic.

5.1   By News Item

As a first attempt to compare the news consumption of different groups, we look at actual news items. We measure the similarity among groups based on commonly consumed news items (by their unique news IDs) among the top 30 articles consumed by each group over a one-year period. We use Jaccard Similarity to compute group similarity. For the two sets, A and B, the Jaccard Similarity is given by: $J(A, B) = \frac{|A \cap B|}{|A \cup B|}$. In our case, let A and B be sets of news items corresponding to the two groups to be compared. Strictly, $|A \cap B|$ would translate to the count of the news items matched across the sets of A and B. Figure 3(a) shows the Jaccard similarity among groups as a heatmap. For example, the pair of Age10_Female and Age20_Female has a Jaccard score of 0.15. This means that, among the union set of all their consumed news items, 15% are common. The higher the similarity score is, the more news items are viewed in common between the two groups.

We find that within same-sex groups, the similarity generally increases as the age difference decreases, with female groups have a stronger tendency of it than male groups (the average similarity score among all pairs of female groups is 0.217 while that of male groups is 0.071). However, we observe two exceptions, Age10_Female and Age10_Male. They are more similar to the Age30 or Age40 than the Age20 same-sex groups. In Fig. 2, we can see that the Age10 groups have more Politics and Foreign news items in the top lists, indicating their similarity to older groups.

We then find strikingly low similarity scores between different sex groups. Age40_Male and Age50_Male have almost no news items in common with the female groups, and the same happens for the Age40_Female and Age50_Female groups. With these results, we can conclude that the set of popular news items that females consume is very different from what males read.

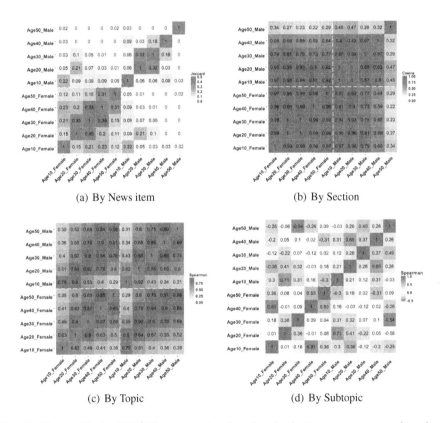

(a) By News item

(b) By Section

(c) By Topic

(d) By Subtopic

Fig. 3. [Zoom-able in PDF] Heatmap showing the similarity across groups based on comparison of (a) news items – Jaccard similarity scores, (b) sections – Cosine similarity between section vectors, (c) topics – Spearman's rank correlation test of two lists of news topics ranked by their lifespans, and (d) subtopics – Spearman's rank correlation test of two lists of subtopics ranked by their number of news articles about the MERS outbreak.

5.2   By Section

We have shown that there is a striking difference between the popular news items for the male groups and those of the female groups. Now, we will examine the news consumption of those groups in terms of sectional interests. This analysis will tell us whether the existing framework of news consumption based on sex or age is also found in Korea.

For each group g, we created a vector $S_g = (w_{1,g}, w_{2,g}, \ldots, w_{s,g})$ in which each dimension corresponded to a predefined section from Daum News where $s = 7$ in our case (see 7 sections in Fig. 2). The weight $w_{s,g}$ was computed by the proportion of the news items in the section s for the group g. We then computed the cosine similarity between two vectors to compare the sectional interests of two groups. The results are shown in Fig. 3(b) as a heatmap.

For female groups, we find high similarity scores between all pairs (>0.97), showing that the proportion of news items in each section is similar in each group. A similar pattern is also observed for male groups but to a lesser extent, and with one exception, Age50_Male, which shows a very different sectional interest. The reason is that they exclusively read political news – 83% of the top 30 news items for a one-year period are about politics (see Fig. 2).

Male groups are further split into two groups, as Age10_Male and Age20_Male are more similar to female groups, but Age30_Male and Age40_Male have sectional interests distinct from those of female groups. This partly supports the traditional sex-typed news consumption theory – our data set also shows different sectional preferences in different gender groups. However, we find such differences are driven more by Age30_Male and Age40_Male and less by Age10_Male and Age20_Male.

In summary, the sectional interests seem to be alike across all groups except Age50_Male. Considering that news consumption largely depends on current, local issues, this could make sense. However, given the striking differences in common news items, the fact that groups largely share sectional interests is still surprising. We now move onto the similarities in the topics that different groups consume.

5.3   By Topic

Given that sectional interests are similar among groups, but not the actual news items, it is intuitive to think that even if two groups are visiting the same news section, such as Society, they might consume different topics – older people might read more about "Baby killer" while young people read more about "Violence at school."

To investigate such topic-specific differences in news consumption, we map each news item to a specific topic. The topics are identified by the method we described in Sect. 4.3. Then, we quantify the importance or the level of attention to a specific topic for a group by computing the lifespan. We define the lifespan of a topic as the longest period of time when that topic appeared on the top 30 list for each group.

We then measure the similarities between groups based on the importance of the different topics. We select topics that are consumed by at least two groups, resulting in 36,134 topics and compute each topic's lifespan for each group. This gives us a ranked list of topics for each group, and we use Spearman's rank correlation coefficient (ρ) to compare the two ranked lists. Figure 3(c) shows the results as a heatmap. All pairs of rankings are statistically significantly different ($p < 0.05$).

In this heatmap, we compare pairs of values. For example, a value of 0.9 between Age40_Female and Age40_Male is hard to interpret by itself. Comparing one similarity score to other entries, one observes that this value is higher to that for the 'Age40_Male' – 'Age30_Male' pair or 'Age40_Male' – 'Age50_Male' pair. Simply put, one could claim that gender differences lead to more strongly pronounced news consumption than 10 years of age difference.

By comparing pairs of values, we observe that age differences play important roles in news consumption – a similar pattern was also found when looking at common news items in Sect. 5.1. Given that a pair of different sex groups have few common news items consumed, the high similarity between two ranked list of topics ($\rho > 0.8$) is striking. This means that all users of Daum News are interested in similar topics, but what they read is different; less than 10% of news items on average were in common for those pairs of different sex groups while the average ρ is 0.65 for these pairs. We also find that two groups, Age10_Male and Age10_Female, are generally more different from other groups, confirming the existence of an age gap between 10-year-olds and others. We also note that while the Age50_Male group has very different sectional interests, it has similar topic preferences to those of other groups.

5.4   By Subtopic

We firstly observed that demographic groups show such different news consumption patterns at news item level. Then, the high similarity scores at section and topic levels tell us that the overall news consumption is largely driven by current issues. However, groups still have distinct news consumption patterns. This suggests that news consumption even for one particular topic may be very different across groups.

For this analysis, we use our evaluation data set and focus on the subtopic consumption regarding the MERS outbreak. The MERS outbreak was a deviant event, and all ten demographic groups have at least one news item about MERS. However, the volume of news items about MERS is different across groups. News items about MERS are more popular in female groups than in male groups–on average, the female group has 427.4 popular news items about MERS while that of the male group is 123.8.

We then quantify the differences in MERS news consumption in terms of the content between two groups. To do this, for each group, we rank the subtopics of MERS outbreak in Table 1 by the number of news items. Then, we test the similarity between two groups by computing the Spearman's ranking correlation coefficient. This will tell us which two groups have the most similar consumption of subtopics about MERS. Figure 3(d) shows the results as a heatmap. All pairs of rankings are statistically significantly different ($p < 0.05$).

From the heatmap, we observe that (1) the popular news is more similar within the same sex groups than within the different sex groups; (2) female groups are more similar to each group than male groups are; and (3) age differences matter, except in the Age10_Male and Age10_Female groups. Interestingly, all three of these observations are also found in our previous analysis that compares actual news items in Sect. 5.1. All these results lead us to conclude that all groups are generally interested in similar news sections or topics; however, for the same topic, they are attracted to different subtopics, leading to the big differences in popular news among groups.

To gain insights into how popular news items about MERS differ between different demographic groups, we extract the most discriminative words in news titles for each group. We focus on the group-specific words of news titles, specifically on those with a high *phi* score, the Chi-square test statistics [12], for discriminating between one group and others (e.g., Age10_Female vs. Non-Age10_Female (all other groups)). Table 2 shows the top 20 words ranked by *phi*. Two authors of this work translated Korean words to English words. Some interesting differences were observed. Overall, female groups are likely to check the status of the MERS outbreak, such as how many people are infected (the number of patients, death, this week), the symptoms of MERS (high fever, cytokine storm), and the protection against MERS (mask, gloves). The Age30_Female group showed an interest in news about pregnant women who had been diagnosed with MERS and other women's cases. The Age40_Female group, in particular, was more interested in the status of closed schools and other education-related topics. On the other hand, the male groups were more interested in the political issues surrounding the MERS outbreak, the accusations towards the government's response to the MERS outbreak (e.g., ruling and opposition parties, the lack of a proper response, misreporting, false propaganda), and the responsibility of politicians.

News2Vec offers an opportunity to visualize each news item in the vector space by applying t-SNE, a widely-used dimensionality reduction based on manifold learning [32]. Figure 4 shows where each news item (colored circle) consumed by each gender (Fig. 4(a)) or age (Fig. 4(b)) group is located in the vector space. In the figure, closed circles are that news items have similar representations in the vector space and thus fall in similar subtopics. For the clarity of the visualization, we focus on the news items consumed by a single demographic gender or age group. Figure 4(a) shows a better clustered structure than Fig. 4(b), meaning that gender difference is well aligned with the difference of vector representation of news items than age difference. In Fig. 4(b), we can also see some clustered structures, such as groups of green circles (news on patients' deaths read by 30s), blue circles (news on Choongbuk-Daejeon regions read by 10s), red circles (news on the closing of schools read by 40s), and purple circles (news on the prime minister read by 50s) from the top to the bottom, while colored circles

Table 2. Most discriminative words in news title about MERS outbreak across demographic groups, ranked by *phi*

Group	Distinctive words
Age10_Female	80s, Manpower, Everyone, Driven by, Increased, Died, Death, Self-quarantine, Getting on, Face the crossroads, Defenseless, Government, 19 people, Investigation, Virus, Heat wave, Still, 9 people
Age20_Female	Jeju island, Cases, Positive test result, Seoul, Possibility, Refuser, Wild ticks, Cytokine storm, Contact, Female, A patient, Virus, Trot, Condition
Age30_Female	Pregnant women, Occur, A patient, High fever, 2 people, Adding, Mask, Entrance, Gloves, Local hospitals, Close contact, Increased, 180 people, Cured, The number of patients, A public servant, Male
Age40_Female	Student, Infection, School, A patient, Son, On leaves, Elementary school students, Medical team, False charge, Grandmother, Visited, Guardian, Closed down, 100 places, Hospital, Kindergarten, Children, Teaching
Age50_Female	Samsung Seoul Hospital, Partially closed down, Infection, Gandong Sungsim Hospital, Large hospitals, Working, Epicenter, Concentration, 9 days, This week, Stable situation, Mystery, Diagnosis, Keep the principle, Remaining, Ambush, Close-packed, Go through, Jongdo Lim
Age10_Male	Believable, Diverse, A MERS map by a programmer, Imported cars, Fall down, Early next week, The executives, Hongik University, Confirmed infected patients, Removed, Jonlo, How far, For taking metro, Mockery flyers
Age20_Male	President, Won-soon Park (The mayor of Seoul), Jae-myeung Lee (The mayor of Sungnam), On leaves, Announcement, 35 times, WHO, SARS, Direct, Misreport, Doctors, Hyungpyo Moon, Entrance, Troll, Soldiers, Qatar, Stigma
Age30_Male	Won-soon Park, Samsung Seoul hospital, Mu-sung Kim (Floor leader of ruling party), SARS, The mayor of Sungnam, President, WHO, Trot, Troll, Problem, Exterminator, Standard procedure, Responsibility, Our nation, 35 times
Age40_Male	President Park, False propaganda, A boy, Over-reaction, Firmly, Shepherd, Make, Should not do it, Rumor, Damage, Response, Provided, Separate, Many people, Marine Police, Step on, Last year, President, Disgust, Medical schools
Age50_Male	Replacement, Lacks proper response, Vice minister, Sorry, Lowering, Kyo-ahn Hwang (Prime minister), Delayed, Ruling and opposition parties, Shaking hands, Response, Briefing, 41 people, Presidential candidate, Political issue

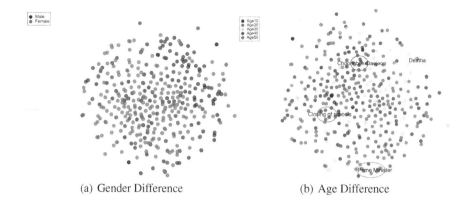

(a) Gender Difference   (b) Age Difference

Fig. 4. t-SNE visualization of news items colored by gender (a) and age (b) (Color figure online)

are mostly dispersed over the space mostly. This is another evidence that gender difference is more noticeable than age difference at the subtopic level.

6   Discussion and Conclusion

To the best of our knowledge, this is the first study to conduct a multidimensional analysis of the news consumption of different demographic groups on a nationwide scale. Differences in news consumption between different demographic groups exist among South Koreans. We look into news consumption at different levels and find that section and topic preferences are similar across groups, but subtopic preferences are not. This means that only the behavioral differences in the subtopic level can explain the strikingly low numbers of common news items across different demographic groups, whereas the differences in the news section or topic levels cannot. In summary, while different demographic groups are interested in similar topics, they read news articles belonging to different subtopics, indicating that subtopics make the news consumption of the different groups different. For the following studies, our work suggests that the differences between demographic groups should be examined at the appropriate level.

One potential limitation is that we analyze a single news portal service, even though it is an extremely popular service in South Korea. To the best of our knowledge, Daum is the only data source where (1) the user-registered demographic information is credible, and (2) the user base spans all generations and parties. We are willing to extend our approach to new data sources that satisfy above two conditions so that we can find demographic differences in news consumption.

We note that all the users are exposed to the same layout and the same items if they visit the website at the same time. Thus, the ways to show news, such as news clustering or adaptive layout, cannot selectively influence on a certain user segment.

While the differences in news consumption between demographic groups can be explained partly by different interests on subtopics, there could be other latent factors such as sentiments or frames of news. For instance, Grabe and Kamhawi found that men recognize and respond more to negatively framed messages, while women are more aroused by and engaged with positively framed messages [20]. By adding another dimension to our news dimensions, we can understand human behavior on consuming news in depth. In this work, we examined the most critical aspects of news, which are section, topic, and subtopic, and saved the other dimensions for the future work.

Our results also bring the practical implications for news organizations. Our characterization of user behavior allows them (1) to gain a better understanding of what people consume and (2) to produce more relevant and engaging content for different demographic groups. Such demographic-based profiling can help tackle the cold-start problem for new users. By simply knowing the gender and age of a new user, one can provide a better user experience when reading online news. The opposite direction of the inference can also be useful. Given the first few sets of news articles, one can infer the demographics of the reader. This will be particularly useful if the demographics of users are not readily available on news sites.

References

1. Adar, E., Adamic, L.A.: Tracking information epidemics in blogspace. In: Proceedings of the 2005 IEEE/WIC/ACM International Conference on Web Intelligence, pp. 207–214. IEEE Computer Society, Washington, D.C. (2005)
2. Ahmed, M., Spagna, S., Huici, F., Niccolini, S.: A peek into the future: predicting the evolution of popularity in user generated content. In: Proceedings of the Sixth ACM International Conference on Web Search and Data Mining, pp. 607–616. ACM (2013)
3. An, J., Cha, M., Gummadi, K., Crowcroft, J.: Media landscape in Twitter: a world of new conventions and political diversity. In: ICWSM 2011: Proceedings of the 5th International AAAI Conference on Weblogs and Social Media, pp. 18–25 (2011)
4. An, J., Quercia, D., Cha, M., Gummadi, K., Crowcroft, J.: Sharing political news: the balancing act of intimacy and socialization in selective exposure. EPJ Data Sci. **3**(1), 12 (2014)
5. An, J., Quercia, D., Crowcroft, J.: Partisan sharing: Facebook evidence and societal consequences. In: CoSN 2014: Proceedings of the 2nd ACM Conference on Online Social Networks, pp. 13–24. ACM (2014)
6. Asur, S., Huberman, B.A., Szabo, G., Wang, C.: Trends in social media: persistence and decay. In: ICWSM 2011: Proceedings of the 5th International AAAI Conference on Weblogs and Social Media, pp. 434–437. Association for the Advancement of Artificial Intelligence (AAAI), Menlo Park (2011)
7. Bakshy, E., Rosenn, I., Marlow, C., Adamic, L.A.: The role of social networks in information diffusion. In: WWW 2012: Proceedings of the 21st International Conference on World Wide Web. ACM, New York (2012)

8. Bandari, R., Asur, S., Huberman, B.A.: The pulse of news in social media: forecasting popularity. In: ICWSM 2012: Proceedings of the 6th International AAAI Conference on Weblogs and Social Media, pp. 26–33. Association for the Advancement of Artificial Intelligence (AAAI), Menlo Park (2012)
9. Bengio, Y., Ducharme, R., Vincent, P., Janvin, C.: A neural probabilistic language model. J. Mach. Learn. Res. **3**, 1137–1155 (2003)
10. Beyer, H., Holtzblatt, K.: Contextual Design: Defining Customer-Centered Systems. Elsevier, Amsterdam (1997)
11. Blei, D.M., Ng, A.Y., Jordan, M.I.: Latent dirichlet allocation. J. Mach. Learn. Res. **3**, 993–1022 (2003)
12. Casella, G., Berger, R.L.: Statistical Inference, vol. 2. Duxbury, Pacific Grove (2002)
13. Cheng, J., Adamic, L.A., Dow, P.A., Kleinberg, J., Leskovec, J.: Can cascades be predicted? In: WWW 2014: Proceedings of the 23th international conference on World Wide Web, pp. 925–936. ACM, New York (2014)
14. Chu, W., Park, S.T.: Personalized recommendation on dynamic content using predictive bilinear models. In: WWW 2009: Proceedings of the 18th International Conference on World Wide Web, pp. 691–700. ACM (2009)
15. Chyi, H.I., Lee, A.M.: Online news consumption: a structural model linking preference, use, and paying intent. Digit. Journal. **1**(2), 194–211 (2013)
16. Cross, S.E., Madson, L.: Models of the self: self-construals and gender. Psychol. Bull. **122**(1), 5 (1997)
17. Dow, P.A., Adamic, L.A., Friggeri, A.: The anatomy of large Facebook cascades. In: ICWSM 2013: Proceedings of the 7th International AAAI Conference on Weblogs and Social Media, pp. 145–154. Association for the Advancement of Artificial Intelligence (AAAI), Menlo Park (2013)
18. d'Haenens, L., Jankowski, N., Heuvelman, A.: News in online and print newspapers: differences in reader consumption and recall. New Media Soc. **6**(3), 363–382 (2004)
19. Goel, S., Anderson, A., Hofman, J., Watts, D.J.: The structural virality of online diffusion. Manag. Sci. **62**(1), 180–196 (2016)
20. Grabe, M.E., Kamhawi, R.: Hard wired for negative news? Gender differences in processing broadcast news. Commun. Res. **33**(5), 346–369 (2006)
21. Hansen, C.H., Hansen, R.D.: Music and music videos. In: Media Entertainment: The Psychology of its Appeal, pp. 175–196 (2000)
22. Hinton, G.E., McClelland, J.L., Rumelhart, D.E.: Distributed representations. In: Rumelhart, D.E., McClelland, J.L., PDP Research Group CORPORATE (eds.) Parallel Distributed Processing: Explorations in the Microstructure of Cognition, vol. 1, pp. 77–109. MIT Press, Cambridge (1986). ISBN 0-262-68053-X. http://dl. acm.org/citation.cfm?id=104279.104287
23. Hofmann, T.: Probabilistic latent semantic indexing. In: Proceedings of the 22nd Annual International ACM SIGIR Conference on Research and Development in Information Retrieval, pp. 50–57. ACM (1999)
24. Knobloch-Westerwick, S., Alter, S.: The gender news use divide: Americans' sex-typed selective exposure to online news topics. J. Commun. **57**(4), 739–758 (2007)
25. Kupavskii, A., Ostroumova, L., Umnov, A., Usachev, S., Serdyukov, P., Gusev, G., Kustarev, A.: Prediction of retweet cascade size over time. In: CIKM 2012: Proceedings of the 21st ACM International Conference on Information and Knowledge Management, pp. 2335–2338. ACM, New York (2012)
26. Kwak, H., Lee, C., Park, H., Moon, S.: What is Twitter, a social network or a news media? In: WWW 2010: Proceedings of the 19th International Conference on the World Wide Web, pp. 591–600. ACM, New York (2010)

27. Le, Q., Mikolov, T.: Distributed representations of sentences and documents. In: ICML 2014: Proceedings of the 31st International Conference on Machine Learning, pp. 1188–1196. PMLR (2014)

28. Lerman, K., Hogg, T.: Using a model of social dynamics to predict popularity of news. In: WWW 2010: Proceedings of the 19th International Conference on World Wide Web, pp. 621–630. ACM (2010)

29. Leskovec, J., Backstrom, L., Kleinberg, J.: Meme-tracking and the dynamics of the news cycle. In: KDD 2009: Proceedings of the 15th ACM SIGKDD International Conference on Knowledge Discovery and Data Mining, pp. 497–506. ACM, New York (2009)

30. Linstone, H.A., Turoff, M., et al.: The Delphi Method: Techniques and Applications, vol. 29. Addison-Wesley, Reading (1975)

31. Liu, J., Dolan, P., Pedersen, E.R.: Personalized news recommendation based on click behavior. In: IUI 2010: Proceedings of the 15th International Conference on Intelligent User Interfaces, pp. 31–40. ACM (2010)

32. Maaten, L.V.D., Hinton, G.: Visualizing data using t-SNE. J. Mach. Learn. Res. 9(Nov), 2579–2605 (2008)

33. Maccoby, E.E.: Gender as a social category. Dev. Psychol. 24(6), 755 (1988)

34. Mikolov, T., Chen, K., Corrado, G., Dean, J.: Efficient estimation of word representations in vector space. arXiv preprint arXiv:1301.3781 (2013)

35. Mikolov, T., Sutskever, I., Chen, K., Corrado, G.S., Dean, J.: Distributed representations of words and phrases and their compositionality. In: Advances in Neural Information Processing Systems, pp. 3111–3119 (2013)

36. Myers, S., Zhu, C., Leskovec, J.: Information diffusion and external influence in networks. In: Yang, Q., Agarwal, D., Pei, J. (eds.) KDD 2012: Proceedings of the 18th ACM SIGKDD International Conference on Knowledge Discovery and Data Mining, pp. 33–41. ACM, New York (2012)

37. Oliver, M.B.: Exploring the paradox of the enjoyment of sad films. Hum. Commun. Res. 19(3), 315–342 (1993)

38. Oliver, M.B.: The respondent gender gap. In: Media Entertainment: The Psychology of its Appeal, pp. 215–234 (2000)

39. Pazzani, M.J.: A framework for collaborative, content-based and demographic filtering. Artif. Intell. Rev. 13(5–6), 393–408 (1999)

40. Pew Research Center for the People, the Press: News audiences increasingly politicized-Online news audience larger, more diverse: Biennial media consumption 2004 (2004). http://www.people-press.org/2004/06/08/news-audiences-increasingly-politicized/. Accessed 20 July 2017

41. Potts, R., Dedmon, A., Halford, J.: Sensation seeking, television viewing motives, and home television viewing patterns. Pers. Individ. Differ. 21(6), 1081–1084 (1996)

42. Preston, J.M., Clair, S.A.: Selective viewing: cognition, personality and television genres. Br. J. Soc. Psychol. 33(3), 273–288 (1994)

43. Rokach, L., Maimon, O.: Clustering Methods. Springer, Boston (2005)

44. Romero, D.M., Meeder, B., Kleinberg, J.: Differences in the mechanics of information diffusion across topics: idioms, political hashtags, and complex contagion on Twitter. In: WWW 2011: Proceedings of the 20th International Conference on World Wide Web, pp. 695–704. ACM, New York (2011)

45. Schwenk, H.: Continuous space language models. Comput. Speech Lang. 21(3), 492–518 (2007)

46. Teh, Y.W., Jordan, M.I., Beal, M.J., Blei, D.M.: Sharing clusters among related groups: hierarchical dirichlet processes. In: Advances in Neural Information Processing Systems, pp. 1385–1392 (2005)
47. Tesch, R.: Qualitative Research: Analysis Types and Software Tools. Psychology Press, Hove (1990)
48. Yan, X., Guo, J., Lan, Y., Cheng, X.: A biterm topic model for short texts. In: WWW 2013: Proceedings of the 22nd International Conference on World Wide Web, pp. 1445–1456. ACM (2013)
49. Yang, J., Leskovec, J.: Modeling information diffusion in implicit networks. In: ICDM 2010: Proceedings of the 2010 IEEE International Conference on Data Mining, pp. 599–608. IEEE Computer Society, Washington, D.C. (2010)

Trump vs. Hillary: What Went Viral During the 2016 US Presidential Election

Kareem Darwish[1]([✉]), Walid Magdy[2], and Tahar Zanouda[1]

[1] Qatar Computing Research Institute, HBKU, Doha, Qatar
{kdarwish,tzanouda}@hbku.edu.qa
[2] School of Informatics, The University of Edinburgh, Edinburgh, Scotland
wmagdy@inf.ed.ac.uk

Abstract. In this paper, we present quantitative and qualitative analysis of the top retweeted tweets (viral tweets) pertaining to the US presidential elections from September 1, 2016 to Election Day on November 8, 2016. For everyday, we tagged the top 50 most retweeted tweets as supporting or attacking either candidate or as neutral/irrelevant. Then we analyzed the tweets in each class for: general trends and statistics; the most frequently used hashtags, terms, and locations; the most retweeted accounts and tweets; and the most shared news and links. In all we analyzed the 3,450 most viral tweets that grabbed the most attention during the US election and were retweeted in total 26.3 million times accounting over 40% of the total tweet volume pertaining to the US election in the aforementioned period. Our analysis of the tweets highlights some of the differences between the social media strategies of both candidates, the penetration of their messages, and the potential effect of attacks on both.

Keywords: US elections · Quantitative analysis · Qualitative analysis · Computational social science

1 Introduction

Social media is an important platform for political discourse and political campaigns [27,32]. Political candidates have been increasingly using social media platforms to promote themselves and their policies and to attack their opponents and their policies. Consequently, some political campaigns have their own social media advisers and strategists, whose success can be pivotal to the success of the campaign as a whole. The 2016 US presidential election is no exception, in which the Republican candidate Donald Trump won over his main rival Hilary Clinton.

In this work, we showcase some of the Twitter trends pertaining to the US presidential election by analyzing the most retweeted tweets in the sixty eight days leading to the election and election day itself. In particular, we try to answer the following research questions:

© Springer International Publishing AG 2017
G.L. Ciampaglia et al. (Eds.): SocInfo 2017, Part I, LNCS 10539, pp. 143–161, 2017.
DOI: 10.1007/978-3-319-67217-5_10

(1) Which candidate was more popular in the viral tweets on Twitter? What proportion of viral tweets in terms of number and volume were supporting or attacking either candidate?
(2) Which election related events, topics, and issues pertaining to each candidate elicited the most user reaction, and what were their effect on each candidate? Which accounts were the most influential?
(3) How credible were the links and news that were shared in viral tweets?

To answer these questions, we analyze the most retweeted (viral) 50 tweets per day starting from September 1, 2016 and ending on Election Day on November 8, 2016. The total number of unique tweets that we analyze is 3,450, whose retweet volume of 26.3 million retweets accounts for over 40% of the total tweets/retweets volume concerning the US election during that period. We have manually tagged all the tweets in our collection as supporting or attacking either candidate, or neutral (or irrelevant). For the different classes, we analyze retweet volume trends, top hashtags, most frequently used words, most retweeted accounts and tweets, and most shared news and links. Our analysis of the tweets shows some clear differences between the social media strategies of each candidate and subsequent user responses. For example, our observations show that the Trump campaign seems to be more effective than the Clinton campaign in achieving better penetration and reach for: the campaign's slogans, attacks against his rival, and promotion of campaign activities in different US states. We also noticed that the prominent vulnerabilities for each candidate were Trump's views towards women and Clinton's email leaks and scandal. In addition, our analysis shows that the majority of tweets benefiting Clinton were actually more about attacking Trump rather than supporting Clinton, while for Trump, tweets in his favor had more balance between supporting him and attacking Clinton. By analyzing the links in the viral tweets, the tweets attacking Clinton had the most number of links (accounting for 58% of the volume of shared links), where approximately half were to highly credible sites and the remaining were to sites of mixed credibility. We hope that our observations and analysis would aid political and social scientists in understanding some of the factors that may have led to the eventual outcome of the election.

2   Background

Social media is a fertile ground for developing tools and algorithms that can capture the opinions of the general population at a large scale [13]. Much work has studied the potential possibility of predicting the outcome of political elections from social data. Yet, there is no unified approach for tackling this problem. While Bollen et al. [4] analyzed people's emotions (not sentiment) towards the US 2008 Presidential campaign, the authors used both US 2008 Presidential campaign and election of Obama as a case study. Sentiment typically signifies preconceived positions towards an issue, while emotions, such as happiness or sadness, are temporary responses to external stimulus. Though the authors mentioned the feasibility of using such data to predict election results, they did not offer supporting results. Using the same approach, O'Connor et al. [23] discussed the feasibility of using Twitter data to replace polls. Tumasjan et al. [28] provided one of the earliest attempts for using this kind of data to estimate election results. They have used twitter data to forecast the national German federal election, and investigated whether online interactions on Twitter validly mirrored offline political sentiment. The study was criticized for being contingent on arbitrary experimental variables [9,10,14,21]. Metaxas et al. [21] argued that the predictive power of Twitter is exaggerated and it cannot be accurate unless we are able to identify unbiased representative sample of voters. However, these early papers kicked off a new wave of research initiatives that focus on studying the political discourse on Twitter, and how this social platform can be used as a proxy for understanding people's opinions [22]. On the other hand, many studies have questioned the accuracy, and not just the feasibility, of using social data to predict and forecast [9,10]. Without combining the contextual information, together with social interactions, the results might lead to biased findings. One of the main problems of studying political social phenomena on Twitter is that users tend to interact with like-minded people, forming so-called "echo chambers" [1,6,18]. Thus, the social structure of their interactions will limit their ability to interact in a genuinely open political space. Though the literature on the predictive power of twitter is undoubtedly relevant, the focus of this work is on performing post-election analysis to better understand the potential strengths and weaknesses of the social media strategies of political campaigns and how they might have contributed to eventual electoral outcomes.

A step closer to our politically motivated work, we find some studies that focused on studying the US presidential election. For the 2012 US presidential election, Shi et al. [26] analyzed millions of tweets to predict the public opinion towards the Republican presidential primaries. The authors trained a linear regression model and showed good results compared to pre-electoral polls during the early stages of the campaign. In addition, the Obama campaign data analytics system[1], a decision-making tool that harnesses different kind of data ranging from social media to news, was developed to help the Obama team sense the pulse of public opinion and strategically manage the campaign. With an attempt to study the recent US presidential election, early studies have showed promising results. For example, Wang et al. [30] studied the growth pattern of Donald Trump's followers at a very early stage. They characterized individuals who ceased to support Hillary Clinton and Donald Trump, by focusing on three dimensions of social demographics: social status, gender, and age. They also analyzed Twitter profile images to reveal the demographics of both Donald Trump and Hillary followers. Wang et al. [31] studied the frequency of 'likes' for every tweet that Trump published. More recently, Bovet et al. [5] developed an analytical tool to study the opinion of Twitter users, in regards to their structural and social interactions, to infer their political affiliation. Authors showed that the resulting Twitter trends follow the New York Times National Polling Average.

---

[1] edition.cnn.com/2012/11/07/tech/web/obama-campaign-tech-team/index.html.

Concerning disseminating information, recent research has focused on how candidates engaged in spreading fake news and in amplifying their message via the use of social bots, which are programmatically controlled accounts that produce content and automatically interact with other users [7,15]. Bessi and Ferrara [3] investigated how the presence of social media bots affected political discussion around the 2016 U.S. presidential election. Authors suggest that the presence of social media bots can negatively affect democratic political discussion rather than improving it, which in turn can potentially alter public opinion and endanger the integrity of the presidential election. In the same context, Giglietto et al. [11] studied the role played by "fake-news" circulating on social media during the 2016 US Presidential election. In this study, we provide a quantitative and qualitative analysis of tweets related to the 2016 US presidential election. By tapping into the wealth of Twitter data, we focus on analyzing and understanding the possible factors underlying the success and failure of candidates. Our work builds upon the aforementioned research in social and computer sciences to study and measure the volume and diversity of support for the two main candidates for the 2016 US presidential elections, Donald Trump and Hillary Clinton.

3   Data Collection and Labeling

To acquire the tweets that are relevant to the US presidential election, we obtained the tweets that were collected by *TweetElect.com* from September 1, 2016 to November 8, 2016 (Election Day). TweetElect is a public website that aggregates tweets that are relevant to the 2016 US presidential election. It shows the most retweeted content on Twitter including text tweets, images, videos, and links. The site uses state-of-the-art adaptive filtering methods for detecting relevant tweets on broad and dynamic topics, such as politics and elections [19,20]. TweetElect used an initial set of 38 keywords related to the US elections for streaming relevant tweets. Consequently, adaptive filtering continuously enriches the set of keywords with additional terms that emerge over time [20]. The 38 seeding keywords included all candidate names and common keywords (including hashtags) about the elections and participating parties. During the period of interest, the total number of aggregated tweets per day (including retweets) related to the US elections typically ranged between 200 K and 600 K. This number increased dramatically after specific events or revelations, such as after the presidential debates and Election Day, when the number of tweets exceeded 3.5 million tweets. The total number of unique tweets collected by TweetElect between September 1 and November 8 was 6.8 million, while the full volume of tweets including retweets was 65.8 million.

In this work, we are interested in analyzing the most "viral" tweets pertain to the US presidential elections, as they typically express the topics that garnered the most attention on Twitter [17]. Specifically, we constructed a set of the most retweeted 50 tweets for everyday in the period of interest. Thus, our collection contained 3,450 unique tweets that were retweeted 26.6 million times, representing more than 40% of the total volume of tweets during that period. Out of the 3,450 tweets in our collection, 700 were authored by the official account of Donald Trump, accounting for 8.7 million retweets, and 698 were authored by Clinton's official account, accounting for 4.7 million retweets. Figure 1 shows the distribution of the number of tweets collected by TweetElect in the US elections in the period of study. The number of unique tweets, retweets volume, and retweets volume of the top viral daily tweets are displayed. As shown, the volume of tweets increased as election day approached. The biggest four peaks in the graph represent the days following the presidential debates and the election day. As it is shown, the retweet volume of the top 50 daily viral tweets correlates well with the full retweet volume, with a Pearson correlation of 0.92, which indicates nearly identical trend.

We calculated the daily coverage C_{daily} of the top 50 daily viral tweets to the full tweet volume. The daily coverage ranged between 23% and 66%, with the majority of the days having C_{daily} over 40%. This indicates that the top 50 viral daily tweets may offer good coverage and reasonable indicators for public interaction with the US election on Twitter.

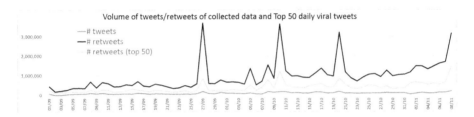

Fig. 1. Volume of retweets the top 50 daily viral tweets on the US collection compared to the full volume of tweets and retweets.

All tweets were labeled with one of five class labels, namely: "support Trump", "attack Trump", "support Clinton", "attack Clinton", or "neutral/irrelevant", with tweets being allowed to have multiple labels if applicable. Support for a candidate included praising or defending the candidate, his/her supporters, or staff, spreading positive news about the candidate, asking people to vote for the candidate, mentioning favorable polls where the candidate is ahead, promoting the candidate's agenda, or advertising appearances such as TV interviews or rallies. Attacking a candidate included maligning and name calling targeted at the candidate, his/her supporters, or staff, spreading negative news about the candidate, mentioning polls where the candidates is behind, or attacking the candidate's agenda. Other tweets were labeled as neutral/irrelevant. Tweets were allowed to have more than one label such as "support Trump, attack Clinton". The labeling was done by an annotator with strong knowledge of US politics. The annotator was instructed to check the content of tweets carefully including any images, videos, or external links to obtain accurate annotations. In addition, we advised the annotator to check the profile of tweet authors to better understand their position towards the candidates if needed. One of the authors took a random sample of 50 tweets to verify the correctness of the annotation. In all, both agreed fully on 90% of the sample, partially agreed on 8%, and disagreed on the remaining 2%. The agreement between the annotator and the author, as measured using Cohen's Kappa, is 0.87, meaning nearly perfect agreement. Table 1 shows few sample labeled tweets.

Table 1. Example annotations

Label	Tweet
Attack Trump, support Clinton	Donald Trump is unfit for the office of president. Fortunately, there's an exceptionally qualified candidate @HillaryClinton
Attack Trump, attack Clinton	Donald Trump looks like what Hillary Clinton smells like
Attack Clinton	A rough night for Hillary Clinton ABC News
Attack Trump	Trump to Matt Lauer on Iraq: I was totally against the war. Here's proof Trump is lying: https://t.co/6ZhgJMUhs3
Neutral	It s official: the US has joined the #ParisAgreement https://t.co/qYN1iRzSJk

4   Tweet Analysis

We analyze tweets in every class from different perspectives. Specifically, we look at: user engagement with class over time, most viral events during election, most discussed topics, most shared links and news, and most influential accounts supporting them.

Popularity of Candidates on Twitter. Table 2 shows the number of tweets and their retweet volume for each label. For further analysis, we ignore tweets that are labeled as neutral/irrelevant as they are not interesting to this work. Figure 2 shows a break down for each label across all days. Table 2 shows that the majority of the tweets and retweets volume were in favor of Trump (61.9%

Table 2. Number of tweets and retweet volume per class.

Class	No. of tweets	% of tweets	No. of retweets	% of retweets
Support Clinton	506	13.6%	3,205,303	11.5%
Attack Trump	712	19.1%	6,373,549	22.8%
Support Trump	848	22.8%	6,896,940	24.7%
Attack Clinton	1,458	39.2%	9,441,921	33.8%
Neutral/irrelevant	199	5.3%	1,978,784	7.1%

of tweets, 58.6% of retweet volume), either by supporting him or attacking Clinton, while those in favor of Clinton represent only (32.7% of tweets, 34.3% of retweet volume) of the total, either supporting her or attacking Trump. It can be observed that the retweet volume of tweets attacking Clinton outnumbered the retweet volume of tweets supporting her by nearly a 3-to-1 margin, while for Trump those supporting and attacking him were almost evenly matched. Figure 2(a) shows the distribution of support/attack of each candidate over the period of study. Figure 2(b) shows the relative per day retweet volume for tweets supporting/attacking each candidate. As expected, large spikes in volume happen in conjunction with major events such the presidential and vice presidential debates, Election Day, the release of Trump's lewd Access Hollywood tape, and the FBI announcement concerning the reopening of the investigation of Clinton. An interesting observation from Fig. 2(b) is that tweets in favor of Trump (either supporting him or attacking Clinton) were retweeted more than tweets in favor of Clinton for 85% of the days, with the exception of a few days, especially the day following the first presidential debate and following the release of Trump's lewd tape. This observation might be different to the trends in normal media, where large number of articles were more negative towards Trump [29].

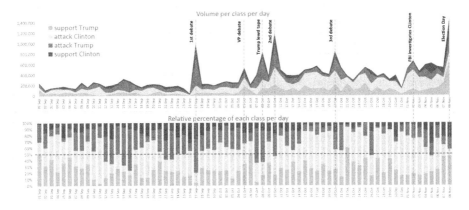

Fig. 2. (a) Retweet volume for each label per day, and (b) Percentage of labels per day.

Table 3 lists the three days for every class when each class had the largest percentage of tweet volume along with the leading topic. As can be seen, the "support Clinton" class not only had the lowest average overall, but it also never exceed 33% on any given day. All other classes had days when their volume exceeded 60% of the total retweet volume, with the "attack Clinton" class reaching nearly 73%. The relative volume of "support Clinton" retweets peaked after public appearances (promotional video, debate, and TV interview). The "attack Clinton" class peaked when her health came into question and after WikiLeaks leaks questioned her integrity. For the "support Trump" class, it peaked after

Table 3. Top 3 days when relative volume for each class peaked with leading topic and percentage.

Date	Leading topic	%
Support Clinton		
11/5	Release of a video promoting Clinton	32.9%
9/26	After first presidential debate	32.2%
9/22	Interview w/ comedy program (two Ferns)	28.2%
Attack Clinton		
9/11	Clinton faints at 9/11 memorial	72.9%
10/31	WikiLeaks: Clinton got gifts from foreign governments	69.4%
10/19	WikiLeaks: Clinton got gift from Qatar	62.9%
Support Trump		
10/22	Trump leads in 3 national polls	60.2%
10/6	Trump leads in Virginia poll	50.7%
9/1	Trump says to build wall with Mexico	50.1%
Attack Trump		
9/16	Sanders attacks Trump on immigration	66.4%
9/15	Trump quoted: "pregnancy very inconvenient for business"	60.2%
10/7	Trump lewd tape released	55.5%

polls showed he was ahead and after he announced the building of a wall with Mexico. The "attack Trump" class peaked due positions on immigration and women. The most frequent hashtags and terms reflect similar trends.

Most Frequent Hashtags. In order to understand the most discussed topics in the viral tweets, Table 4 shows the top hashtags that are used in attacking or supporting either candidate divided into categories along with the volume in each category. The top used hashtags for the different labels reveal some stark contrasts between the two candidates. These include:

(i) The top most frequently appearing hashtags favoring Clinton were those praising her debate performances and attacking Trump. On the Trump side, the most frequently appearing hashtags were those iterating his campaign slogans, encouraging people to vote, and spreading campaign news.
(i) Hashtags of Trump's campaign slogans appeared nearly 200 times more than Clinton's campaign slogan (#IAmWithHer). In fact, Trump's campaign slogans category has the most frequently appearing hashtags.
(ii) Hashtags indicating "Get out of the vote" were 4 times more voluminous for Trump than Clinton. Trump and his campaign were more effective in promoting their activities (ex. #ICYMI – in case you missed it, #TrumpRally).
(iii) Hashtags pertaining to the presidential debate appeared for every class. The support to attack hashtag volume ratio was roughly 3-to-2 for Clinton and

Table 4. Top hashtags attacking or supporting both candidates with their categories.

Category	#tag Freq.	Hashtags
Support Clinton		
Debate performance	486,402	#DebateNight #Debate #SheWon #VPDebate #Debates2016 #NBCNewsForum
Attacking Trump	114,614	#TrumpTapes #ImVotingBecause #TangerineNightmare #InterrogateTrump #ImWithTacos #AlSmithDinner
Get out the vote	86,297	#ElectionDay #Election2016 #Voting #OHVotesEarly #Vote #Elections2016
Campaign issues	15,055	#NationalComingOutDay #LatinaEqualPay
Campaign slogan	10,084	#ImWithHer
Attack Clinton		
Corruption/lying	842,892	#DrainTheSwamp #CrookedHillary #BigLeagueTruth #GoldmanSach #FollowTheMoney #PayToPlay
Wikileaks releases	640,330	#PodestaEmails #Wikileaks #PodestaEmails{8,31,28,26,15} #SpiritCooking #Podesta #DNCLeak #DNCLeak2 #FreeJulian #AnthonyWeiner
Debate performance	348,749	#Debates2016 #Debate #DebateNight #VPDebate #Debates
Health care	113,318	#ObamaCare #ObamaCareFail #ObamaCareInThreeWords
Tension w/Sanders supporters	86,333	#FeelTheBern #BasementDwellers
Media/Election Bias	78,511	#VoterFraud #RiggedSystem
Ben Ghazi attack	46,725	#BenGhazi
Clinton's health	30,747	#HillarysHealth
Support Trump		
Campaign slogans	2,089,162	#MAGA (Make America Great Again) #DrainTheSwamp #AmericaFirst #MakeAmericaGreatAgain #ImWithYou #TrumpTrain #TrumpPence16
Get out the vote	349,078	#VoteTrumpPence16 #ElectionDay #VoteTrump #Vote #IVoted #ElectionNight #TheHoodForTrump #Vote2016 #EarlyVote
Campaign news	183,031	#ICYMI (in case you missed it) #TrumpRally #Gettysburg (public speech)
Debate performance	74,808	#VPDebate #DebateNight #Debates #Debates2016
Attacking Clinton	66,318	#FollowTheMoney #DNCLeak #ObamaCareFailed #BigLeagueTruth
Attack Trump		
Debate performance	776,956	#DebateNight #Debate #VPDebate #Debates #NBCNewsForum
Sexual misconduct	78,043	#TrumpTapes #NatashaStoynoff
General attacks and insults	44,100	#ImVotingBecause #TangerineNightmare #Lunatic #DangerousMan #Unfit #Deceit #InterrogateTrump
Comedy attacks	26,980	#ACloserLook (segment on Seth Meyer comedy show) #AlSmithDinner (charity dinner)
Attacking Trump's speech	21,117	#LoveTrumpsHate #NastyWoman

1-to-9 for Trump. Further, the debates were the number one category for the "support Clinton" and the "attack Trump" classes. It seems that most users thought that she did better in the debates than him.

(iv) Attacks against Clinton focus on her character and on the WikiLeaks leaks, which cover Clinton's relationship with Wall Street (ex. #GoldmanSachs), alleged impropriety in the Clinton Foundation (ex. #FollowTheMoney, #PayTo-Play), mishandling of the Ben Ghazi attack in Libya, Democratic Party primary race against senator Sanders (ex. #BasementDewellers), the FBI investigation of Clinton (#AnthonyWeiner), and accusation of witchcraft (#SpiritCooking).

(v) Attacks against Trump were dominated by his debate performance. The frequency of hashtags for the next category pertaining to accusations of sexual misconduct (ex. #TrumpTapes) is one order of magnitude lower than the frequency of those about the debate. This suggests that accusations of sexual misconduct against Trump were not the primary of focus of users.

(vi) Policy issues such as health care (ex. #ObamaCare, #LatinaEqualPay) were eclipsed by issues pertaining to the personalities of the candidates and insults (ex. #CrookedHillary, #TangerineNightmare).

Most Frequent Terms. We look at the most frequent terms in the tweets to better understand the most popular topics being discussed. Figure 3 shows tag-clouds of the most frequent terms for the different classes, which exhibit similar trends to those in the most frequent hashtags. For example, top terms in the "attack Clinton" class include "crooked", "emails", "FBI", "WikiLeaks", and "#DrainTheSwamp". Similarly, "#DebateNight" was prominent in the "support Clinton" and "attack Trump" classes. One interesting word in the "support Trump" class is the word "thank", which typically appears in Trump authored tweets in conjunction with polls showing Trump ahead (ex. "Great poll out of Nevada- thank you!"), after rallies (ex. "Great evening in Canton Ohio-thank you!"), or in response to endorsements (ex. "Thank you Rep. @MarshaBlack-burn!"). Words of thanks appeared in 167 "support Trump" tweets that were retweeted more than 1.5 million times compared to 15 "support Clinton" tweets that were retweeted 75 thousand times only. Another set of words that do not show in the hashtags are "pregnancy" and "inconvenient" that come from two tweets that mention that "Trump said pregnancy is very inconvenient for businesses". One of these tweets is the most retweeted in the "attack Trump" class.

Mentions of States. One of the top terms that appeared in tweets supporting Trump is "Florida", Fig. 3(c). This motivated us to analyze mentions of states in the tweets of each class. The frequency of state mentions may indicate states of interest to candidates and Twitter users. Figure 4 lists the number of times each of the 15 most frequently mentioned states. To obtain the counts, we tagged all tweets using a named entity recognizer that is tuned for tweets [25]. We automatically filtered entities to obtain geolocations, and then we manually filtered locations to retain state names and city and town names within states. Then, we mapped city and town names to states (ex. "Grand Rapids" → "Iowa"). As

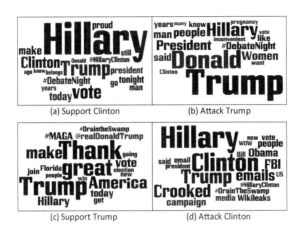

Fig. 3. Tag-cloud of top frequent terms in each class support/attack Clinton/Trump.

expected, so-called "swing states", which are states that could vote Republican or Democrat in any given election[2], dominated the list. The only non-swing states on the list are New York, Washington, and Texas. Interestingly, the number of mentions in "support Trump" tweets far surpasses the counts for all other classes. Most of the mentions of swing states were in tweets authored by Trump indicating Trump rallies being held in these states. This suggests that the Trump campaign effectively highlighted their efforts in these states, and there was significant interest from Twitter users as indicated by the number of retweets. Of the swing states in the figure, Trump won the first six, namely Florida, Ohio, North Carolina, Pennsylvania, Michigan, and Arizona, along with Iowa and Wisconsin.

Most Shared Links. An important debate that surfaced after the US elections was whether fake news affected the election results or not [11, 16]. Thus, we analyze the credibility of the websites that were most linked to in the tweets for each class. Our analysis shows that 29% of the viral tweets (21% of the full retweet volume) contained external links. Table 5 shows the top 10 web domains that were linked to in the tweets dataset along with ideological leaning and credibility rating. Aside from the official websites of the campaigns (ex. HillaryClinton.com, Democrats.org, and DonaldJTrump.com), the remaining links were to news websites (ex. CNN and NYTimes) and social media sites (ex. Facebook, Instagram, and YouTube). As Table 5 shows, the candidates' official websites received the most links. However, it is interesting to note the large difference in focus between both. Clinton's website attacked Trump than it supported Clinton, while Trump's website did the exact opposite. This again shows the differences in strategies and trends between both candidates and their supporters. We checked the leaning and credibility of the news websites on mediabiasfactcheck.com, a fact checking website which rates news sites anywhere between "Extreme Left" to "Extreme Right"

---

[2] https://projects.fivethirtyeight.com/2016-election-forecast/.

Table 5. Top shared links per class – support/attack Clinton/Trump – with ideological leaning (-5 extreme left to 5 extreme right) and credibility (high or mixed) according to https://mediabiasfactcheck.com/

Link	Count	Volume	Leaning	Credibility	Link	Count	Volume	Leaning	Credibility
Support Clinton					*Attack Trump*				
Hillaryclinton.com	63	363,153	Left	–	Hillaryclinton.com	65	236,126	Left	–
Democrats.org	8	120,026	Left	–	WashingtonPost.com	23	102,179	−2	High
IWillVote.com	26	101,996	Left	–	IWillVote.com	11	95,126	Left	–
SnappyTV.com	14	58,926	N/A	Mixed	SnappyTV.com	14	86,100	N/A	Mixed
CNN.com	6	43,355	−3	High	Democrats.org	3	67,843	Left	–
WashingtonPost.com	10	27,264	−2	High	Newsweek.com	11	55,663	−3	High
Medium.com	8	27,187	−2	Mixed	NYTimes.com	9	37,993	−2	High
BusinessInsider.com	4	16,010	−2	High	CNN.com	6	27,275	−3	High
NYTimes.com	6	15,886	−2	High	Vox.com	4	13,992	−4	High
YouTube.com	2	11,564	N/A	Mixed	Facebook.com	2	11,973	N/A	Mixed
Support Trump					*Attack Clinton*				
DonaldJTrump.com	77	503,375	right		WikiLeaks.org	47	406,607	2	High
Facebook.com	25	164,995	N/A	Mixed	DailyCaller.com	22	195,695	4	Mixed
WashingtonPost.com	7	56,855	−2	Hight	FoxNews.com	28	146,571	4	Mixed
Lifezette.com	3	49,132	4	Mixed	YouTube.com	29	107,915	N/A	Mixed
SnappyTV.com	4	36,663	N/A	Mixed	Breitbart.com	17	102,949	5	Mixed
Instagram.com	5	36,132	N/A	Mixed	Politico.com	11	93,165	−2	High
DailyCaller.com	3	35,474	4	Mixed	NYPost.com	14	92,147	3	Mixed
NYPost.com	4	34,930	3	Mixed	CNN.com	11	78,797	Right	
Periscope.tv	3	22,596	N/A	Mixed	Vox.com	16	77,340	3	High
YouTube.com	5	20,046	N/A	Mixed	Facebook.com	9	63,896	3	High

and their credibility between "Very Low" and "Very High" with "Mixed" being the middle point. We assumed social media sites to have no ideological leaning with a credibility of "Mixed". We opted for assigning credibility to websites as opposed to individual stories, because investigating the truthfulness of individual stories is rather tricky and is beyond the scope of this work. Though some stories are easily debunked, such as the Breitbart story claiming that "Hillary gave an award to a terrorist's wife[3,4]", other mix some truth with opinion, stretched truth, and potential lies, such as the Breitbart story that the "FBI is seething at the botched investigation of Clinton".

Figure 4 aggregates all the number of retweets for each category for the websites with credibility of "High" and "Mixed" – none of the sites had credibility of "Very High", "Low", or "Very Low". The aggregate number of links for all categories to "High" and "Mixed" credibility websites was 1.04 million and 1.18 million respectively. The figure shows that a significantly higher proportion of highly credible websites were linked to for the "support Clinton" and "attack Trump" categories compared to mixed credibility sites. The opposite was true for the "support Trump" category, where the majority of links used to support Trump was from mixed creditability websites. This may indicate that Trump supporters were more susceptible to share less credible sources compared

---

[3] http://bit.ly/2d99lWD/.
[4] http://bit.ly/2tEUxVw.

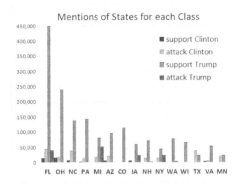

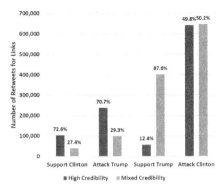

Fig. 4. Mentions of states for each class.

Fig. 5. Credibility of websites that are linked to from each category

to Clinton supporters. High and mixed credibility sites were evenly matched for the "attack Clinton" category. WikiLeaks was the foremost shared site for attacking Clinton, which has high credibility. This again highlights the role of WikiLeaks in steering public opinion against Clinton. It worth mentioning that "The Podesta Emails[5]" was the most popular link. Thus, though lower credibility links were used to attack Clinton, high credibility links featured prominently. For ideological orientation, left leaning sources featured prominently in the "support Clinton" and "attack Trump" classes, and right leaning sources featured prominently for the two other classes. The only left leaning sources appearing on the "support Trump" and "attack Clinton" lists were Washington Post and Politico (Fig. 5).

Most Retweeted Tweets. Table 6 lists the top 5 most retweeted[6] tweets for each class. They illustrate the trends to those exhibited in our previous analysis, namely: "support Clinton" tweets are led by talk about debates and attacks against Trump; the most retweeted "attack Clinton" tweets are from WikiLeaks; Trump campaign slogans appear atop of "support Trump" tweets; and the most retweeted attack Trump" tweets cover demeaning statements against women and minorities and mockery of Trump. An interesting observation is that the most retweeted tweet attacking Trump came from a Nigerian account with screen name "Ozzyonce" who had less than 2,000 followers at the time when she posted the tweet. Nonetheless, this tweet received over 150 K retweets in one day.

Most Retweeted Accounts. Table 7 lists the most retweeted accounts for each class. As expected, the most retweeted accounts for "support" and "attack" classes were those of the candidates themselves and their rivals respectively. Notably:

(*i*) Clinton authored 10% more "attack Trump" tweets (with 35% more volume) than "support Clinton". In contrast, Trump authored 81% more "support

---

[5] https://wikileaks.org/podesta-emails/.

[6] The number of retweets in the table are taken in November 2016.

Trump" tweets (with 38% more volume) than "attack Clinton" tweets. This suggests that Clinton expended more energy attacking her opponent than promoting herself, while Trump did the exact opposite. Trump campaign staffers and accounts, such as Kellyanne Conway, Dan Scavino Jr., and Official Team Trump, were slightly more active in the "attack Clinton" class than the "support Trump" class.

(*ii*) Trump Campaign accounts featured prominently in "support Trump" and "attack Clinton" classes, capturing 7 out of 10 and 4 out of 10 top spots for both classes respectively. In contrast, Clinton campaign account captured 2 out of 10 and 1 out of 10 top spots for "support Clinton" and "attack Trump" classes respectively. Top Clinton aides like Huma Abedin and John Podesta were absent from the top list, suggesting a more concerted Trump campaign Twitter strategy.

(*iii*) Though Clinton authored 48% more tweets attacking her rival than tweets Trump authored attacking her, his attack tweets led to 34% more retweet volume. This suggests that his attacks were more effective than her attacks. Trump tweets were more retweeted on average than Clinton's tweets with an average of 11,195 and 6,120 retweets per tweet for both respectively. Highlighting WikiLeaks' role in the election, WikiLeaks was the second most retweeted account attacking Clinton and had four times as much retweet volume than the next account.

5   Discussion

Our analysis contrasts differences in support for either candidate, namely:

Popularity: While Trump received more negative coverage than Clinton in mainstream media [24], Trump benefited from many more tweets that are either supporting him or attacking his rival. In fact, 63% of the volume of viral content on US election were in his favor compared to only 37% in favor of Clinton. Similarly, on 85% of the days in the last two months preceding the election, Trump had more tweets favoring him than Clinton. This observation shows the gap between the trends of social media and traditional news media.

Positive vs Negative Attention: The volume of tweets attacking and supporting Trump were evenly matched, while the volume of tweets attacking Clinton outnumbered tweets praising her by a 3-to-1 margin. Given the importance of social media in elections, this may have been particularly damaging.

Support Points: Trump campaign accounts featured more prominently in the top retweeted accounts supporting their candidate. Support came in the form of promoting his slogans, urging supporters to vote, and featuring positive polls and campaign news. Conversely, Clinton support came mostly in the form of contrasting her to her rival, praise for her debate performance against Trump, and praise for her attacks on Trump. In fact, viral tweets from her campaign account were attacking Trump more than promoting her. Unfortunately for her, she was framed in reference to her rival, and research has

Table 6. Top retweeted tweets for each class – support/attack Clinton/Trump.

Date	Author	Text	Count
Support Clinton			
9/27	Jerry Springer	Hillary Clinton belongs in the White House. Donald Trump belongs on my show	78,872
9/27	Hillary Clinton	RT this if you re proud to be standing with Hillary tonight. #debatenight https://t.co/91tBmKxVMs	72,443
10/10	Erin Ruberry	Hillary is proof a woman can work hard rise to the top of her field still have to compete against a less qualified man for the same job	72,167
10/20	Hillary Clinton	RT if you're proud of Hillary tonight. #DebateNight #SheWon https://t.co/H7CJep7APX	72,150
10/8	Richard Hine	Trump: Don t judge me on the man I was 10 years ago. But please judge Hillary on the man her husband was 20 years ago #TrumpTapes	66,817
Attack Clinton			
11/1	WikiLeaks	No link between Trump Russia No link between Assange Russia But Podesta Clinton involved in selling 20% of US uranium to Russia	51,311
10/14	WikiLeaks	Democrats prepared fake Trump grope under the meeting table Craigslist employment advertisement in May 2016 https://t.co/JM9JMeLYet	45,348
10/3	WikiLeaks	Hillary Clinton on Assange Can t we just drone this guy – report https://t.co/S7tPrl2QCZ https://t.co/qy2EQBa48y	45,233
11/4	Donald J. Trump	If Obama worked as hard on straightening out our country as he has trying to protect and elect Hillary we would all be much better off!	42,331
11/8	Cloyd Rivers	To everyone who wants to vote for Hillary just to keep Trump from becomin President watch this... https://t.co/TuUpD7Qgcg	41,047
Support Trump			
11/8	Donald J. Trump	TODAY WE MAKE AMERICA GREAT AGAIN!	352,140
11/5	Donald J. Trump	MAKE AMERICA GREAT AGAIN!	60,718
10/8	Donald J. Trump	Here is my statement. https://t.co/WAZiGoQqMQ	52,887
11/7	Immigrants4Trump	If you make this go viral Trump will win. It s about 2 min that makes the choice in this election crystal clear https://t.co/CqMY4CSJbp	43,627
10/10	Mike Pence	Congrats to my running mate @realDonaldTrump on a big debate win! Proud to stand with you as we #MAGA	42,178
Attack Trump			
9/15	Ozzyonce	Donald Trump said pregnancy is very inconvenient for businesses like his mother s pregnancy hasn't been inconvenient for the whole world	152,756
10/26	Bailey Disler	Good morning everyone especially the person who destroyed Donald Trump s walk of fame star https://t.co/IcBthxMPd9	124,322
10/21	Stephen King	My newest horror story: Once upon a time there was a man named Donald Trump and he ran for president. Some people wanted him to win	121,635
10/10	Kat Combs	Trump writing a term paper: Sources Cited: 1. You Know It 2. I know It 3. Everybody Knows It	105,118
10/8	Es un racista	Anna for you to sit here call Trump a racist is outrageous Anna: OH?! Well lemme do it again in 2 languages! https://t.co/nq4DO7bN7J	102,063

Table 7. Top retweeted accounts per class – support/attack Clinton/Trump. Accounts of candidates and campaign affiliates are italicized.

Account	Count	Volume	Account	Count	Volume
Support Clinton			*Attack Trump*		
Hillary Clinton	331	2,025,821	*Hillary Clinton*	363	2,698,209
President Obama	4	122,947	Bernie Sanders	11	304,860
Senator Tim Kaine	15	84,245	Ozzyonce	1	152,756
Jerry Springer	1	78,872	Bailey Disler	1	124,322
Erin Ruberry	1	72,167	Stephen King	2	121,635
Richard Hine	1	66,817	Kat Combs	1	105,118
Bernie Sanders	7	46,180	Es un racista	1	102,063
CNN	6	41,983	Rob Fee	1	99,401
Funny Or Die	1	27,909	Jerry Springer	1	78,872
Channel 4 News	1	27,409	Master of None	1	67,690
Support Trump			*Attack Clinton*		
Donald J. Trump	446	4,992,845	*Donald J. Trump*	246	3,613,025
Kellyanne Conway	51	199,511	WikiLeaks	141	1,454,903
Mike Pence	36	195,824	*Kellyanne Conway*	92	349,025
Dan Scavino Jr.	40	181,601	Paul Joseph Watson	78	297,273
Official Team Trump	14	141,289	*Official Team Trump*	23	150,932
Donald Trump Jr.	20	112,835	*Donald Trump Jr.*	34	126,744
Eric Trump	8	79,387	Jared Wyand	19	85,742
Immigrants4Trump	4	52,256	Cloyd Rivers	7	84,063
Cloyd Rivers	2	45,493	Juanita Broaddrick	4	83,903
Paul Joseph Watson	10	38,474	James Woods	16	78,719

shown that debates have a dwindling effect election outcomes as the election day draws closer [2,8,12]. Consequently, her post-debate surges in volume of attacks against Trump eclipsed surges of support for her.

Attack Points: Both candidates were attacked on different things. Trump was mainly attacked on his debate performance, eclipsing attacks related to his scandals, such as the lewd Access Hollywood tape. Luckily for him, debates have a diminishing effect on voters as election day draws near [2,8,12]. Conversely for Clinton, persistent allegations of corruption and wrongdoing triggered by WikiLeaks and the FBI investigation of her emails dominated attacks against her. These attacks may have led to her eventual loss, with polls suggesting that "email define(d) Clinton"[7].

Message Penetration: Trump's slogan, "Make America Great Again", had a far greater reach than that of his rival, "Stronger Together". Similarly, his

---

[7] gallup.com/poll/185486/email-defines-clinton-immigration-defines-trump.aspx.

policy positions and agenda items, such as the proposal to build a wall with Mexico, attracted significantly more attention than those of Clinton, where her proposed policy positions received very little mention.

Geographical Focus: Trump and his supporters effectively promoted his campaign's efforts in swing state, with frequent mentions of rallies and polls from these states along with messages of thanks for people turning-out for his rallies. The volume of tweets mentioning swing states and supporting Trump were typically two orders of magnitude larger than similar tweets supporting Clinton. This might have contributed to the narrow victory he achieved in many of them.

Low Credibility Links: Trump supporters were more likely to share links from websites of questionable credibility than Clinton supporters. However, WikiLeaks, which has high credibility, was the most prominent source attacking Clinton.

To better understand the presented results, a few limitations that need to be considered. First, the top 50 viral tweets do not have to be representative of the whole collection. Nonetheless, they still represent over 40% of the tweets volume on the US elections during the period of the study. Second, the results are based on tweets collected from TweetElect. Although it is highly robust, the site uses automatic filtering methods that are not perfect [19]. Therefore, there might be other relevant viral tweets that were not captured by the filtering method. Lastly, measuring support for a candidate using viral tweets does not have to represent actual support on the ground for many reasons. Some of these reasons include the fact that demographics of Twitter users may not match the general public, more popular accounts have a better chance of having their tweets go viral, or either campaign may engage in astroturfing, in which dedicated groups or bots may methodically tweet or retweet pro-candidate messages [3].

6   Conclusion

In this paper, we presented quantitative and qualitative analysis of the top retweeted tweets pertaining to the US presidential elections from September 1, 2016 to election day on November 8, 2016. For everyday, we tagged the top 50 most retweeted tweets as supporting/attacking either candidate or as neutral/irrelevant. Then we analyzed the tweets in each class from the perspective of: general trends and statistics; most frequent hashtags, terms, and locations; and most retweeted accounts and tweets. Our analysis highlights some of the differences between the social media strategies of both candidates, the effectiveness of both in pushing their messages, and the potential effect of attacks on both. We show that compared to the Clinton campaign, the Trump campaign seems more effective in: promoting Trump's messages and slogans, attacking and framing Clinton, and promoting campaign activities in "swing" states. For future work, we would like to study the users who retweeted the viral tweets in our study to ascertain such things as political leanings and geolocations. This can help map the political dynamics underlying the support and opposition of both candidates.

References

1. Barberá, P., Jost, J.T., Nagler, J., Tucker, J.A., Bonneau, R.: Tweeting from left to right is online political communication more than an echo chamber? Psychol. Sci. **26**(10), 1531–1542 (2015)

2. Benoit, W.L., Hansen, G.J., Verser, R.M.: A meta-analysis of the effects of viewing us presidential debates. Commun. Monogr. **70**(4), 335–350 (2003)

3. Bessi, A., Ferrara, E.: Social bots distort the 2016 us presidential election online discussion. First Monday **21**(11) (2016)

4. Bollen, J., Mao, H., Pepe, A.: Modeling public mood and emotion: Twitter sentiment and socio-economic phenomena. ICWSM **11**, 450–453 (2011)

5. Bovet, A., Morone, F., Makse, H.A.: Predicting election trends with twitter: Hillary Clinton versus Donald Trump. arXiv preprint (2016). arXiv:1610.01587

6. Colleoni, E., Rozza, A., Arvidsson, A.: Echo chamber or public sphere? Predicting political orientation and measuring political homophily in Twitter using big data. J. Commun. **64**(2), 317–332 (2014)

7. Davis, C.A., Varol, O., Ferrara, E., Flammini, A., Menczer, F.: Botornot: A system to evaluate social bots. In: Proceedings of the 25th International Conference Companion on World Wide Web, pp. 273–274. International World Wide Web Conferences Steering Committee (2016)

8. Erikson, R.S., Wlezien, C.: The Timeline of Presidential Elections: How Campaigns do (and do not) Matter. University of Chicago Press, Chicago (2012)

9. Gayo-Avello, D.: Don't turn social media into another 'literary digest' poll. Commun. ACM **54**(10), 121–128 (2011)

10. Gayo Avello, D., Metaxas, P.T., Mustafaraj, E.: Limits of electoral predictions using Twitter. In: Proceedings of the Fifth International AAAI Conference on Weblogs and Social Media. Association for the Advancement of Artificial Intelligence (2011)

11. Giglietto, F., Iannelli, L., Rossi, L., Valeriani, A.: Fakes, news and the election: a new taxonomy for the study of misleading information within the hybrid media system (2016)

12. Hillygus, D.S., Jackman, S.: Voter decision making in election 2000: campaign effects, partisan activation, and the clinton legacy. Am. J. Polit. Sci. **47**(4), 583–596 (2003)

13. Jungherr, A.: Analyzing Political Communication with Digital Trace Data. Springer, Cham (2015)

14. Jungherr, A., Jürgens, P., Schoen, H.: Why the pirate party won the german election of 2009 or the trouble with predictions: a response to tumasjan, a., sprenger, to, sander, pg, & welpe, im "predicting elections with twitter: what 140 characters reveal about political sentimen". Soc. Sci. Comput. Rev. **30**(2), 229–234 (2012)

15. Kollanyi, B., Howard, P.N., Woolley, S.C.: Bots and automation over Twitter during the first us presidential debate. Comprop Data Memo (2016)

16. Kucharski, A.: Post-truth: study epidemiology of fake news. Nature **540**(7634), 525–525 (2016)

17. Magdy, W., Darwish, K.: Trump vs. Hillary analyzing viral tweets during us presidential elections 2016. arXiv preprint arXiv:1610.01655 (2016)

18. Magdy, W., Darwish, K., Abokhodair, N., Rahimi, A., Baldwin, T.: # isisisnotislam or# deportallmuslims?: predicting unspoken views. In: Proceedings of the 8th ACM Conference on Web Science, pp. 95–106. ACM (2016)

19. Magdy, W., Elsayed, T.: Adaptive method for following dynamic topics on Twitter. In: ICWSM (2014)

20. Magdy, W., Elsayed, T.: Unsupervised adaptive microblog filtering for broad dynamic topics. Inf. Process. Manag. **52**(4), 513–528 (2016)

21. Metaxas, P.T., Mustafaraj, E., Gayo-Avello, D.: How (not) to predict elections. In: 2011 IEEE Third International Conference on Privacy, Security, Risk and Trust (PASSAT) and 2011 IEEE Third International Conference on Social Computing (SocialCom), pp. 165–171. IEEE (2011)

22. Mislove, A., Lehmann, S., Ahn, Y.Y., Onnela, J.P., Rosenquist, J.N.: Understanding the demographics of Twitter users. In: 5th ICWSM 2011 (2011)

23. O'Connor, B., Balasubramanyan, R., Routledge, B.R., Smith, N.A.: From tweets to polls: linking text sentiment to public opinion time series. ICWSM **11**(122–129), 1–2 (2010)

24. Patterson, T.E.: News coverage of the 2016 national conventions: negative news, lacking context (2016)

25. Ritter, A., Clark, S., Etzioni, O., et al.: Named entity recognition in tweets: an experimental study. In: Proceedings of the Conference on Empirical Methods in Natural Language Processing, pp. 1524–1534. Association for Computational Linguistics (2011)

26. Shi, L., Agarwal, N., Agrawal, A., Garg, R., Spoelstra, J.: Predicting us primary elections with Twitter. (2012) http://snap.stanford.edu/social2012/papers/shi.pdf

27. Shirky, C.: The political power of social media: technology, the public sphere, and political change. Foreign Aff. **90**(1), 28–41 (2011)

28. Tumasjan, A., Sprenger, T.O., Sandner, P.G., Welpe, I.M.: Predicting elections with Twitter: what 140 characters reveal about political sentiment. ICWSM **10**, 178–185 (2010)

29. Van Aelst, P., Van Erkel, P., DâĂŽheer, E., Harder, R.A.: Who is leading the campaign charts? Comparing individual popularity on old and new media. Inf. Commun. Soc. **20**(5), 715–732 (2017)

30. Wang, Y., Li, Y., Luo, J.: Deciphering the 2016 us presidential campaign in the Twitter sphere: a comparison of the trumpists and clintonists. arXiv preprint arXiv:1603.03097 (2016)

31. Wang, Y., Luo, J., Niemi, R., Li, Y., Hu, T.: Catching fire via "likes": inferring topic preferences of trump followers on Twitter. arXiv preprint arXiv:1603.03099 (2016)

32. West, D.M.: Air Wars: Television Advertising and Social Media in Election Campaigns, 1952–2012. Sage, Thousand Oaks (2013)

Understanding Online Political Networks: The Case of the Far-Right and Far-Left in Greece

Pantelis Agathangelou[1], Ioannis Katakis[1(✉)], Lamprini Rori[2],
Dimitrios Gunopulos[1], and Barry Richards[2]

[1] University of Athens, Athens, Greece
pandelisagathangelou@gmail.com, {katak,dg}@di.uoa.gr
[2] Bournemouth University, Poole, UK
{lrori,brichards}@bournemouth.ac.uk

Abstract. This paper examines the connectivity among political networks on Twitter. We explore dynamics inside and between the far right and the far left, as well as the relation between the structure of the network and sentiment. The 2015 Greek political context offers a unique opportunity to investigate political communication in times of political intensity and crisis. We explore interactions inside and between political networks on Twitter in the run up to the elections of three different ballots: the parliamentary election of 25 January, the bailout referendum of 5 July, the snap election of 20 September; we, then, compare political action during campaigns with that during routinized politics.

1 Introduction

According to the 'echo chamber' thesis, political networks on the internet are fragmented and limiting. Online political communication basically preaches to the converted with little or no possibility to influence opinions, spread new ideas, or ensure a plurality of views. If this is the case, exposure on the web is constrained to reinforcement inside more or less ideologically homogeneous communities, and to silence or polarization towards politically divergent networks. However, constant expansion in the use of social media platforms and fluidity in voter choices oblige us to re-examine the dynamics of political networks, particularly in contexts of extreme uncertainty and polarization. Moreover, the popularity of the echo chamber claim has neglected important functions and dynamics of online political networks such as the relation between network structure and discourse. Whereas, furthermore, we have investigated the types of political structures formed in social media, we know little about the online communication of the ideological edges in the political system. Psycho-social theories and political research on radicalism show that inter-group polarity and opposition are vital for solidifying intra-group identity and trust. Political and community conflict can be exacerbated by the behaviour of antagonistic parties even when this behaviour does not constitute an attempt to affect the outcome of the conflict by gaining advantage in influence or material position.

© Springer International Publishing AG 2017
G.L. Ciampaglia et al. (Eds.): SocInfo 2017, Part I, LNCS 10539, pp. 162–177, 2017.
DOI: 10.1007/978-3-319-67217-5_11

The Case of Greece. We examine a series of innovative hypotheses, by focusing on the case of Greece during the period of the great crisis which started in 2010, under the light of the wealth of possibilities that the new media revolution has opened for political action and communication. Greece has been the country firstly and most severely hit by the recent financial crisis in the EU. It received immense international financial aid, which has been followed by acute austerity measures. As a result, big parts of the Greek society radicalized, which was often reflected on a dense protest cycle, violent and anti-systemic. Polarization and electoral volatility prevailed throughout a period of political instability, consecutive elections and negotiations with the bailout partners. The evolution of the party competition signaled a passage from an until 2009 centripetal democracy, to a centrifugal democracy formed by the earthquake elections of May 2012 to a polarized multi-party system, which has been established ever since. The dominant parties of the two-party system which existed since the 1980s collapsed; whereas the country experienced since then the meteoric rise of old minor or marginal political actors (SYRIZA, HA), as well as the emergence of a series of splinter parties, mainly radical (ANEL, LAE). We consider Greece as a unique product of the financial crisis, in the sense that since 2012 the third party in parliament is a neo-Nazi party, whereas the government in place since 2015, is a coalition of the far left and the far right. Greece, hence, brings topical phenomena and trends of European politics to their limits.

The contributions of this paper can be summarized in the following points:

- We study the online blueprint of radicalization in times of crises; how the emergence of new cleavages is reflected in the online political world and what dynamics it produces between different political spaces.
- We bring into discussion the online polarization in multi-party systems, which covers an existing lacuna stemming from the fact that most relevant studies focus on the US two-party system.
- We propose and utilize a novel method for advocate identification. An algorithm that assigns citizens to political spaces based to their activity in social media.
- We collect two large sets of twitter messages that we break into three time windows relevant to our research. Our method permits to capture variation of political networks over time, as well as change in individual stances.
- We test our hypotheses by measures of political cohesion, communication density and network visualizations.

2   Related Work

In this section we overview theoretical discussions relevant to our research questions and hypotheses.

Communication, Information and Influence. In contemporary democratic environments, citizens receive information mainly through interpersonal communication, mass media and digital media. Despite tendency of interpersonal communication to reinforce confirmed beliefs and relations with like-minded people, disagreement perseveres, mainly in low-density networks, that leave room for relatively distanced acquaintances. Mass media are more likely to expose individuals to diverse information in comparison with face-to-face discussions [14]. Nonetheless, the public is not passive when exposed to the media. Selective exposure research has pointed that individuals are driven in media channels or information, which match their beliefs [2], whilst secluding others with which they disagree. Because of their choice-enhancing capacities and the algorithms which define suggestions on who to follow [5], social media are said to be more conducive to ideological self-segregation.

Political Homophily in Social Media. Political discussions on social media are said to take place inside 'echo chambers' [4], which correspond to political sub-groups characterized by a broad ideological homogeneity. Among a series of parameters, ideological stances affect the levels of individual and group fragmentation. The echo chamber thesis is not, however, uncontested. Holbert, Garrett and Gleason argued that the fact that digital political communication increases individual exposure to like-minded ideas and sources of information, this does not mean that the same individuals avoid [9] or can totally filter out contrary or different viewpoints. Social media facilitate contact with diverse and heterogeneous political opinions unintentionally, when individuals use them for non-political reasons [22], since information circulates across networks on various, different occasions [3]. A recent strand of research brings in discussion the importance of the nexus between online and offline political discussions, as well as elements stemming from political psychology theories, like the level of openness of an individual and the level of political interest [20].

Polarization and Political Extremism. Ideology is the driving force in echo chambers formation. In a systematic large scale comparative research of fragmentation on Twitter between individuals, groups and group-dyads, [20] finds that political parties networks which are distanced in ideological terms, interact less and that echo chambers are mostly likely formed by users and groupings positioned at the extreme ends of the ideological scale. Under certain circumstances, like in periods of financial crises and political tensions, individuals facing relative deprivation or grievances of various kinds can radicalize towards political extremism. Ideology, emotions [6], as well as trigger events and socialization environments can play a role in embracing extremist views or actions. Extremist and terrorist groups use the internet for a myriad of purposes, including the dissemination of propaganda, the recruitment of members and the development of operational planning. While right-wing extremist communities have had an online presence for years through dedicated websites, there has been an increased activity on social media in recent years. Nevertheless, the extent to which the Internet affects radicalization into violence is contested.

The Decline of the Left-Right Ideological Distinction and the Rise of New Cleavages. Since the outbreak of the financial crisis, the collapse of the old twopartyism and the rise of radical and extreme parties, a new, more polarized bipolar system has restructured political conflicts and expressed emerging issues [7]. Hence, from 2010 until the summer of 2015, in a context of unprecedented polarization, parties of the centre-right and the centre-left have supported bailout policies, the European currency and stay in the EU, whereas parties of the far right and the far left shared anti-bailout stances, populism and Euroscepticism, which for some amongst them turned to fierce hostility towards the EU and the desire of adopting the national currency. A paradoxical political alliance has been the coalition government which was formed in January 2015 between the radical left party of SYRIZA (Coalition of the Radical Left) and the far right party of ANEL (Independent Greeks) [18]. Research on polarization in social media cannot neglect those important shifts in party competition and political alliances. Measures of fragmentation should take into account at the same time the old Left-Right divide and the new bailout-anti-bailout conflict, and hence examine the frequency and nature of interactions of political networks formed alongside those lines of divisions.

Study of Discussions in Social Media. [12] study on-line discussions in order to identify patterns in how German politicians acted in social media during the 2013 elections. Their main data source is the Twitter network. [17] present a study of Twitter during the Brazilian protests of 2013. Similar to our work, sentiment analysis and user activity is the tool for exploring the data. The authors observed that activity and sentiment peaks coincide with the days of the protests. [21] infer the political signature of the Twitter users by applying a walking algorithm over the social graph. The output of the method is the estimated distribution of political preference over the eight Flemish political parties. A case study on the 2014 national elections is presented. [4] discuss the way Twitter reacts on major political and non-political events. Their main conclusion is that polarization in social media is limited in comparison with what has been observed by previous work.

Identifying Advocates. In [16] the authors build a framework for identifying advocates for political campaigns in social media. The framework models message strategies, propagation strategies and community structure. These three elements comprise the features that are utilized as input in data classification algorithms like Linear Discriminant Analysis. The authors observe that the proposed frame-work outperforms a set of baseline methods (random assignment, total number of tweets as a feature, bag-of-words) in identifying advocates. Experiments include two use cases utilizing Twitter data. The first regards elections in India while the second is about gun rights in the United States. [8] investigate the possibility of automatically identifying peoples voting intentions for the Scottish Independence Referendum by analyzing their Tweets.

Opinion Mining and Sentiment Analysis. In recent years, many research studies focus on the problem of sentiment lexicon construction. Most of them utilize some opinion seed words and word similarities to construct the sentiment lexicon. According to the way in which the word similarities are obtained, these studies can be categorized into three types of approaches: (a) the semantic thesaurus based approaches [10,11] (b) the corpus based approaches

[13,19], and (c) the pattern based approaches [15]. In this paper we will utilize a tool developed by our research team that falls into the third category [1].

3 Data Collection and Advocate Identification

3.1 Data Collection

In order to test the hypotheses under study, we collected **three** large sets of twitter datasets that were relevant to our research. What is necessary for our data collection is a pool of **leaders** (representatives of each space) that will aid in identifying the political networks (i.e. the advocates of each political space).

Time Periods. In order to capture variation over time and between periods of different political intensity, we introduced two 3-month periods of political campaigns and different kinds of elections and one period of routinized politics.

- *First Period:* The important political events of the first period (01.11.2014–30.01.2015) are the presidential election in parliaments which led to a stalemate and provoked an early parliamentary election; the victory of SYRIZA in the January 2015 election and the coalition government with ANEL.
- *Second Period:* The second period (21.06.2015–21.09.2015) is the most polarized among the three, dominated by the referendum for the bailout agreement, the enduring negotiations of the Greek government with the European partners, intense and consecutive parliamentary procedures and the snap parliamentary election of September 2015.
- *Third Period:* In the third period (01.03.2016–30.05.2016) the main events where the refugee crisis and the new austerity measures. Given the fact that no elections took place between the 2nd and the 3rd period, neither during the third, the political networks are formed by the same initial set of political candidates.

A set of statistics regarding the three periods can be seen in Tables 3 and 1 (tweets sent by users through their complete timelines) and Table 2 (tweets sent by users through the specific time windows).

Party Candidates (Leaders). We utilized the set of official political candidates running for the parliamentary elections in our different periods of study who had a Twitter account. Some statistics related to the political candidates can be found in Table 3. Note that we manually identified the twitter accounts

Table 1. Total number of tweets (unfiltered) collected from the timelines of the candidates and confirmed advocates discovered in each period.

Period	KKE	ANTARSIA	LAE	SYRIZA	PASOK	POTAMI	ND	HA	ANEL	Total
1st	0.04M	0.16M	-	1.22M	0.89M	0.88M	1.55M	0.13M	0.66M	**5.51M**
2nd–3rd	0.05M	1.07M	0.41M	0.63M	1.20M	0.71M	1.84M	0.14M	0.56M	**6.60M**

Table 2. Number of tweets sent by users sent during the specific time periods.

Period	KKE	ANTARSIA	LAE	SYRIZA	PASOK	POTAMI	ND	HA	ANEL	Total
1st	.004K	3.3K	-	28.54K	11.31K	10.47K	14.23K	.95K	14.77K	**83.57K**
2nd	.79K	7.22K	9.82K	30.12K	26.07K	28.09K	32.93K	5.48K	20.8K	**161.32K**
3rd	3.14K	9.68K	13.78K	31.21K	40.68K	29.26K	59.1K	6.56K	22.45K	**215.84K**

Table 3. Political candidates with Twitter accounts, and confirmed advocates extracted for each party

Party	1st Period				2nd, 3rd Periods			
	Candidates	Accounts	Percentage	Confirmed Advocates	Candidates	Accounts	Percentage	Confirmed Advocates
1 KKE	413	6	1.45%	41	482	8	1.66%	48
2 ANTARSIA	366	42	11.48%	158	341	39	11.44%	1119
3 LAE	-	-	-	-	698	61	8.74%	420
4 SYRIZA	433	180	41.57%	1485	424	136	32.08%	866
5 PASOK	399	108	27.07%	680	406	126	31.03%	842
6 POTAMI	405	113	27.90%	1087	406	103	25.37%	1003
7 ND	425	242	56.94%	1514	423	241	56.97%	1845
8 HA	388	65	16.75%	130	320	56	17.50%	142
9 ANEL	407	92	22.60%	695	404	78	19.31%	560

of the candidates since such list does not exist. Due to space limitation, we do not present the names of the candidates and their respective twitter accounts.

Definition of Political Spaces. Here we present the Greek political parties that we organized in three political spaces (Far Right, Center, Far left). The abbreviations below are used throughout the paper.

- *Far Right:* ▶ ANEL (Independent Greeks): Splinter part of ND (New Democracy), founded in 2012. Populist, conspirationanist, nationalist, anti-bailout and anti-european, anti-semitic. ▶ HA (Golden Dawn): Marginally exists since 1980s. Extremist, ultra-nationalist, racist, nazi-friendly, violent, welfare chavinism, anti-establishment.
- *Far Left:* For the definition of the far Left political space in Greece we selected the following parties. ▶ SYRIZA (Coalition of Radical Left): Party of the radical left, since 2004 Ethno-populist, eurosceptic, anti-bailout, conspirationist. ▶ KKE (Communist Party of Greece): Orthodox Communist Party, since 1920s. ▶ LAE (Popular Unity): Splinter party of SYRIZA, since September 2015. Anti-Euroepan, pro-national currency, anti-German, pro-Russian. ▶ ANTARSIA (Anticapitalist Left Cooperation for the Overthrow): Stalinst and violent, left radicals, anarchists, antifascist, leftists.
- *Center:* We have grouped as political parties belonging to the center: ▶ PASOK (Panhellenic Socialist Movement): Party of the centre-left, existing since the 1974 transition to democracy, pro-European, pro-bailout. ▶ POTAMI (River): Social-liberal party of the centre, founded in 2014, pro-European, pro-bailout. ▶ NEA DEMOCRATIA (New Democracy): Centre-right party, founded in 1974, pro-European, pro-bailout.

3.2 Advocate Identification

In order to illustrate and analyze the political network we identify users that advocate one or more of the political spaces defined. To do this, we use the retweets as an indication of endorsement. Based on this assumption we followed the steps below:

- Initially, we identify a pool of 'Potential Advocates' (PA). These are the users that have been retweeted by the Political Candidates (PC - see previous section), at least once.
- If the Potential Advocates have *retweeted back* the Political Candidates (Leaders) then we consider them as 'Confirmed Advocates' (CAs) (this means that we are confident that these are members of the same political space as the one they have been endorsed through the re-tweet).
- In order to find more Confirmed Advocates we follow the same process in an iterative fashion. After the first iteration, we seek to see if a Potential Advocate has been re-tweeted by a Political Candidate or a Confirmed Advocate. When we find new Confirmed Advocates we add them to the pool, and so forth. The process stops when no new Confirmed Advocates are found.

An illustration of these steps can be seen in Fig. 1. From our experimental evaluation we observed that the process stops after two or three iterations. The accuracy of the above algorithm has been assessed by manually investigation and we confirmed that it accurately extracts advocates of all political spaces.

Collected Data. Data collection was operated with the following algorithm:

1. Identify the Twitter accounts of the political candidates (leaders).
2. Collect messages from their timelines (up to 2000 messages)
3. Collect the twitter followers that leaders have ReTweeted at least once (PAs).
4. Collect the timelines of the PAs (up to 2000 messages).
5. Based on the full timelines of leaders and PAs, scan for ReTweets and apply the Advocate Identification algorithm (see Fig. 1) in order to extract the list of confirmed advocates.

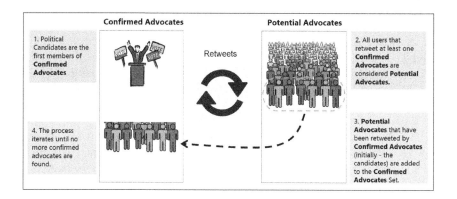

Fig. 1. Advocate identification

6. The confirmed advocates are the users that we utilize to illustrate the interactions among the political spaces. We filter out all messages not belonging
to the three periods under study.

In Tables 1, 2 and 3 we present details about the collected data. Interestingly, there
is a significant variation in the number of candidates who owned a twitter account
(ranging from 1–60%) among different political parties. The number of advocates
per network is changing over time, which means that networks are dynamic and
not static, reflecting the off-line political fluidity of the context under study.

4 Hypotheses Under Investigation

In this paper, we will investigate the following hypotheses:

- H1. In line with findings which show that individuals and groupings which
  sit at the extreme ends of the ideological scale are particularly likely to form
  echo chambers, we expect to find strong levels of cohesion on the edges of the
  political systems (echo chambers' hypothesis).
- H2. Given the level of polarization that emerged over the financial crisis, we
  expect to find levels of interaction of radical actors which do not only reflect
  traditional ideological proximity, but also coalitions formed around emerging
  divides (hypothesis on convergence over new divisions).
- H3. Given the ideological differences regarding hierarchy between the extreme
  edges of the party system, we expect that far right networks will display higher
  level of internal cohesion but lower levels of internal interaction than far left
  communities. (intra-group hierarchy hypothesis).
- H4. We expect to find intensity of sentiment to be stronger in extremist and
  radical political networks. (differences in sentiment).

4.1   (H1) Echo Chambers

We introduce the metric of *internal cohesion*, in order to calculate the level
of interaction in the three periods under study. By internal cohesion we define
the proportion of interaction which targets the members of the same political
network. More specifically, the internal cohesion of party i is defined as follows:
Given a set of political parties $P = \{p_1 \cup \ldots \cup p_N\}$ where N is the total number
of parties, and U a set of users belonging to all political parties:

$$\text{Internal Cohesion}_i = \frac{\text{Interactions of all users } u_j \in p_i \text{ with users } u_k \in p_i}{\text{Interactions of all users } u_k \in P \text{ with users } u_j \in p_i} \quad (1)$$

This metric counts cohesion on a relative scale and can, thus, account for
'echo chamberness' by comparing levels of cohesion between political networks.
In order to explore the kinds of interactions, we examined separately the cohesion of communication by replies and retweets. We consider replies to denote
discussions or exchanges of opinions, whereas retweets to manifest agreement or
endorsement of ideas.

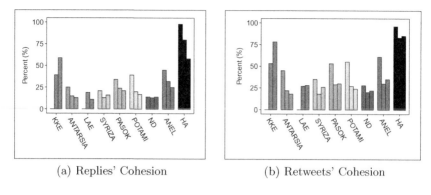

(a) Replies' Cohesion   (b) Retweets' Cohesion

Fig. 2. Evolution of internal cohesion - 1st, 2nd, 3rd period for each party.

As Fig. 2 depicts, retweets display higher levels of cohesion than replies, for all political networks. This finding testifies the different use that advocates attribute to those two modes of communication and is in line with our assumption on the matter. Networks at the edges of the party system are more cohesive than parties at the centre. HA and ANEL on the far right and KKE and ANTARSIA are the most cohesive political networks in the three periods under study. The right-wing extremist party (HA) is the one which mostly resembles to an echo chamber, followed by the orthodox communist (KKE). We can thus tentatively validate our first hypothesis. Nonetheless, interestingly the overall trend for cohesion is to decrease over time for all parties except from KKE, which means that political networks are not static; they develop particular dynamics and in our case study, they tend to lose degrees of 'echo chamberness', especially from the first to the second period, that political intensity and polarization increased. Hence, polarization can reduce cohesion of the most introvert political networks.

4.2 (H2) Alliances over New Divisions

In Fig. 3 we observe the retweet networks (i.e. who retweeted whom) in the three periods under study. Nodes represent the advocates of each space and the edges are the retweets. Different colours in the nodes illustrate the different political parties. The size of the nodes shows the level of degree (indegree and outdegree interactions). In other words the size is indicative of how active the advocate is in terms of retweets. In order to analyze these results, we defined the measures of *density* and *interactivity* of a network (see Equations below). The first one illustrates how active the users are as a network and the second calculates the degree in which the main communication is channeled from a small number of users (active) to their followers (inactive users).

$$\text{density} = \frac{\text{number of messages}}{\text{total number of users}} \tag{2}$$

$$\text{interactivity} = \frac{\text{number of users sending messages}}{\text{total number of users}} \tag{3}$$

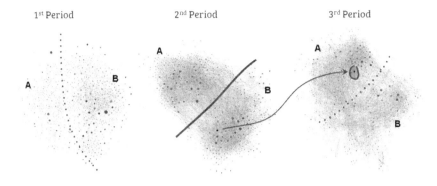

1st Period   2nd Period   3rd Period

Fig. 3. Retweets' political network

Table 4. Density and interactivity of the political network of Fig. 3

Period	Messages	Senders	Recipients	Density	Interactivity
1st	24588	732	1957	9.14	0.27
2nd	104922	939	3787	22.20	0.20
3rd	117972	1389	4221	21.03	0.25

Density of communication increases considerably from the first period to the second: from 9.14 messages per user to 22.20, whereas it remains almost equally dense in the third. Interactivity is nonetheless low in the three periods under study, reaching its lowest point during the second, when 20% of users in the networks retweet others. Overall, polarization increased density of discussions but did not foster interactivity between users (Table 4).

During the first period, we can observe two sub-areas. Sub-area A is more mixed than B and portrays retweets of advocates of PASOK, POTAMI and ND. All three are pro-bailout or pro-EU parties. In sub-area B we can observe parties of the far-right and the far-left, which are closer than with parties of sub-area A, but distinct party spaces. In the second and the third period, the network is denser and the communication polarized. During the second period, we can distinguish a fragmented network in two distanced clusters. The first cluster still contains the pro-bailout parties, the connectivity of which is much bigger, whereas the second cluster pertains the anti-bailout or anti-EU parties (HA, ANEL, SYRIZA, LAE, KKE, ANTARSIA), which have now merged. As a result, we can no longer see distinct party spaces. During the third period, the network is still divided and clustered, the main difference with the second period being the position of the right-wing extremist HA, which has moved away from the pro-bailout camp. This is due to the fact that during the third period, the agenda was largely dominated by the refugee crisis, which is an issue of division between the far-right and the far-left. Overall, the visualization of the network following their retweets' traces shows us that there are changes in the structure of the network

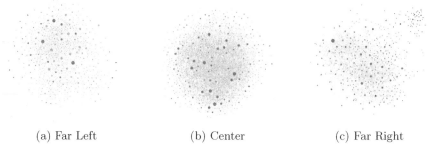

(a) Far Left   (b) Center   (c) Far Right

Fig. 4. Interaction among political extreme groups for the 2nd period.

depending on the political context. As polarization increased from the first to the second and the third period, communication became more fragmented, with its structure moving from party-oriented to issue-oriented. Polarization facilitated convergence between ideological divergent spaces and reinforced the merging of the extremes of the party networks (Fig. 4).

What we generally observe is that party advocates not only retweet the usual suspects their ideological neighbours following the Left-Right axis but also that they retweet their allies inside the pro-bailout or the anti-bailout camp.

4.3   (H3) Intra-group Hierarchy

The different levels of internal cohesion are portrayed in Fig. 2. Strong levels of cohesion have been found on networks belonging to the edges of the party systems. HA displays the highest internal cohesion among all party networks, followed by KKE. Even though the far-right ANEL also presents relatively higher cohesion than parties of the far-left or the centre, the differences are small. Hence, higher levels of internal cohesion seem to relate with spaces associated with totalitarian ideologies. In order to compare how communication is diffused inside the edges of the political system online, we divided the network in three ideological spaces: the far left, the centre and the far right. For each space, we portray the internal architecture, the structure of the network, as it is formed by the replies and the retweets of users targeting advocates of the same ideological space. Figure 5 depicts the visualization of the diffusion of communications flows inside each space. At first sight, the shape of the networks on the far right and the far left is fragmented, whereas connectivity seems homogeneously distributed for the political centre. On the far right, the right-wing extremist component (HA) seems hardly connected to the populist, radical one (ANEL), only via a few users-bridges. Fragmentation appears also on the far left, even though its different components do not figure so distanced as on the far right. In the centre, we can discern certain parts of the networks being more populated by distinct colours, which manifests conversations at the party-level, developed around prominent figures. Nonetheless, the political centre portrays a better connected and densely populated online network. Hence, ideology seems to correlate with the internal communication structure of neighbouring political networks.

Table 5. Density and interactivity for the politically extreme groups

Period	Political group	Messages	Senders	Recipients	Density	Interactivity
1st	Far Left	6269	600	473	5.84	0.56
	Center	8329	352	994	6.19	0.26
	Far Right	4121	99	232	12.45	0.30
2nd	Far Left	23514	316	1309	14.47	0.19
	Center	52045	519	2121	19.71	0.20
	Far Right	7150	145	316	15.51	0.31
3rd	Far Left	24173	411	1326	13.92	0.24
	Center	66694	805	2456	20.45	0.25
	Far Right	6737	194	364	12.07	0.35

By calculating the density and interactivity for each ideological space, we can compare the nature of communication inside each ideological space. Table 5 depicts the evolution of the two measures over time. Communication is denser among the far right in the first period and among the center in the second and the third. The intensity of discussions is dropping for the far left in the third period, most probably due to the capitulation of the government over the bailout agreement and the splinter inside the family of the far left. Overall polarization increased density of communications inside the three political spaces. Interactivity in the far left is the highest during the first period among the three political spaces, despite its low levels of density. The trend is reversed in the next two periods: the far right displays the highest levels of interactivity among the three political spaces. Our hypothesis is thus rejected. This means that polarization increased interactivity of the far right spectrum and communication is not hierarchical as we would expect, following the organizational norms of the far right party family.

4.4   (H4) Differences Between Far Right and Far Left Sentiment

To investigate this hypothesis we conducted sentiment analysis on the within network discussions. More specifically, we applied our opinion mining algorithms [1] to the messages sent (as replies) between users of the same political space. Our tool, DidaxTo [1], is able to extract the opinion words (terms like 'beautiful' or 'convenient') for any domain in an unsupervised fasinon. Opinion words can be positive or negative. Examples of opinion words discovered by DidaxTo for the given set of tweets are: 'charismatic', 'responsibility', 'solidarity' and 'unsustainability', 'overthrow', 'unconstitutional'.

Based on these, we calculated the sentiment of an individual tweet by subtracting the number of negative words from the number of positive words. If, for example, a tweet contains more positive words it is considered positive. Then we calculated the sentiment of each day by subtracting the negative tweets at that day from the positive ones. In Figs. 5a, b and c we expose the sentiment

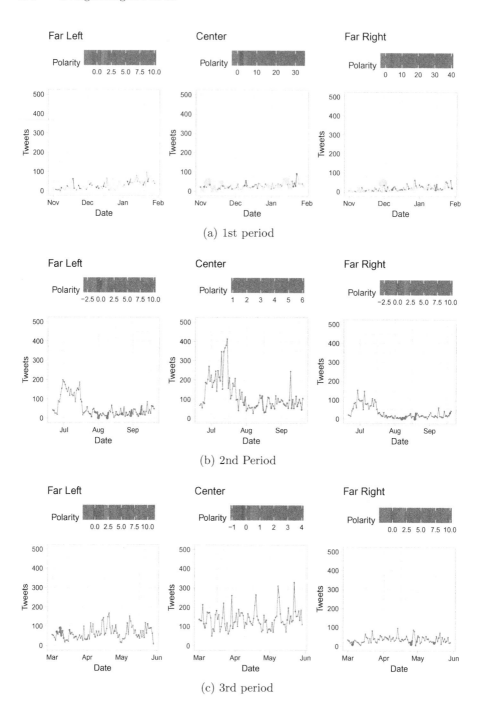

Fig. 5. Sentiment intensity (Color) and tweets volume (y axis) in the replies within a political space for all periods (Color figure online)

plots for each period and political space. The 'y' axes expresses the number of tweets per day and the color represents negative/positive sentiment; the size of the dot represents the absolute value of the sentiment. In the first period we recorded more 'extreme' days in terms of sentiment comparing to the other two periods since sentiment reaches values like +30 or +40. In the second period we see that there is high activity during July in all political spaces, which was the most polarized period, due to the referendum and the enduring negotiations of the government with the EU. The most negative sentiment is expressed during that period. Overall, the sentiment is positive most of the time in all periods and spaces. However, the volume of negative sentiment is higher in the far left and the far right. This finding validates our hypothesis and is associated to the radical nature of those ideological spaces and the way this is reflected in their discourse.

5   Conclusions

Times of crises are also times of political reshuffling and realignment. In this study, we have shown that in periods of crises, online political networks are porous. Contrary to previous findings which considered political discussions taking place only inside echo chambers, we showed that political networks are not static neither solid, as political actors consider turbulence and volatility as structures of political opportunity in order to gain visibility, leverage and issue-ownership. This finding is particularly interesting for the radical and extremist actors: even through we have shown that their introvertness is higher compared to moderate networks, they tend to lose levels of cohesion when polarization increases. By focusing on the great Greek crisis at periods of different political intensity, we showed how emerging divisions related to the crisis affected the structure of the networks and facilitated convergence between the edges of political networks. Political networks evolved from party-oriented to issue-oriented. We showed that when electoral competition is not driven by the left-right divide, the online world absorbs the new cleavage. When delving into the structure of the network and the sentiment within the far right and the far left, no significant differences were found. Further research needs to be done in order to explore the impact of the agenda on the structure of political networks.

Acknowledgement. This work received funding from the European Union Horizon 2020 Programme (Horizon2020/2014–2020), under grant agreement 688380.

References

1. Agathangelou, P., Katakis, I., Koutoulakis, I., Kokkoras, F., Gunopulos, D.: Learning patterns for discovering domain-oriented opinion words. Knowl. Inf. Syst. 1–33 (2017)
2. Ball-Rokeach, S., DeFleur, M.: A dependency model of mass-media effects. Commun. Res. **3**(1), 3–21 (1976)

3. Barberá, P.: Birds of the same feather tweet together: Bayesian ideal point estimation using Twitter data. Polit. Anal. **23**(1), 76–91 (2015)
4. Barberá, P., Jost, J.T., Nagler, J., Tucker, J.A., Bonneau, R.: Tweeting from left to right is online political communication more than an echo chamber? Psychol. Sci. **26**(10), 1531–1542 (2015)
5. Bucher, T.: The friendship assemblage. Telev. New Media **14**(6), 479–493 (2013)
6. Davou, B., Demertzis, N.: Feeling the greek financial crisis. In: Demertzis, N. (ed.) Emotions in Politics. PSPP, pp. 93–123. Palgrave Macmillan UK, London (2013). doi:10.1057/9781137025661_6
7. Dinas, E., Rori, L.: The 2012 Greek parliamentary elections: fear and loathing in the polls. West Eur. Polit. **36**(1), 270–282 (2013)
8. Fang, P., Liu, M., Xue, Y., Yao, J., Zhang, Y., Shen, H., Yang, P.: Controlling non-specific trypsin cleavages in LC-MS/MS-based shotgun proteomics using optimized experimental conditions. Analyst **140**, 7613–7621 (2015)
9. Holbert, R.L., Garrett, R.K., Gleason, L.S.: A new era of minimal effects? A response to Bennett and Iyengar. J. Commun. **60**(1), 15–34 (2010)
10. Hu, M., Liu, B.: Mining and summarizing customer reviews. In: Proceedings of the Tenth ACM SIGKDD International Conference on Knowledge Discovery and Data Mining, KDD 2004, pp. 168–177. ACM, New York (2004). http://doi.acm.org/10.1145/1014052.1014073
11. Kamps, J., Marx, M., Mokken, R.J., De Rijke, M., et al.: Using wordnet to measure semantic orientations of adjectives. In: LREC, vol. 4, pp. 1115–1118 (2004)
12. Lietz, H., Wagner, C., Bleier, A., Strohmaier, M.: When politicians talk: assessing online conversational practices of political parties on twitter. arXiv preprint arXiv:1405.6824 (2014)
13. Lim, K.W., Buntine, W.: Twitter opinion topic model: extracting product opinions from tweets by leveraging hashtags and sentiment lexicon. In: Proceedings of the 23rd ACM International Conference on Conference on Information and Knowledge Management (CIKM), pp. 1319–1328. ACM (2014)
14. Mutz, D.C.: Facilitating communication across lines of political difference: the role of mass media. Am. Polit. Sci. Rev. **95**(1), 97114 (2001)
15. Qiu, G., Liu, B., Bu, J., Chen, C.: Expanding domain sentiment lexicon through double propagation. In: Proceedings of the 21st International Joint Conference on Artifical Intelligence, IJCAI 2009, pp. 1199–1204. Morgan Kaufmann Publishers Inc., San Francisco (2009). http://dl.acm.org/citation.cfm?id=1661445.1661637
16. Ranganath, S., Hu, X., Tang, J., Liu, H.: Understanding and identifying advocates for political campaigns on social media. In: Proceedings of the Ninth ACM International Conference on Web Search and Data Mining, WSDM 2016, pp. 43–52 (2016). http://doi.acm.org/10.1145/2835776.2835807
17. dos Reis Costa, J.M., Murnane, E.L., Rotabi, R., Choudhury, T.: It is not only about grievances: emotional dynamics in social media during the Brazilian protests. In: Proceedings of the Ninth International Conference on Web and Social Media, ICWSM 2015, University of Oxford, Oxford, UK, 26–29 May 2015, pp. 594–597 (2015)
18. Rori, L.: The 2015 Greek parliamentary elections: from great expectations to no expectations. West Eur. Polit. **39**(6), 1323–1343 (2016). doi:10.1080/01402382.2016.1171577
19. Turney, P.D.: Thumbs up or thumbs down?: semantic orientation applied to unsupervised classification of reviews. In: Proceedings of the 40th Annual Meeting

on Association for Computational Linguistics, ACL 2002, pp. 417–424. Association for Computational Linguistics, Stroudsburg (2002). http://dx.doi.org/10.3115/1073083.1073153

20. Vaccari, C., Valeriani, A., Barber, P., Jost, J.T., Nagler, J., Tucker, J.A.: Of echo chambers and contrarian clubs: exposure to political disagreement among German and Italian users of Twitter. Soc. Media+ Soc. **2**(3), 2056305116664221 (2016). doi:10.1177/2056305116664221

21. Van Gysel, C., Goethals, B., de Rijke, M.: Determining the presence of political parties in social circles. In: ICWSM, vol. 2015, pp. 690–693 (2015)

22. de Ziga, H.G., Valenzuela, S.: The mediating path to a stronger citizenship: online and offline networks, weak ties, and civic engagement. Commun. Res. **38**(3), 397–421 (2011)

Polarization in Blogging About the Paris Meeting on Climate Change

Dag Elgesem[(⊠)]

University of Bergen, 5020 Bergen, Norway
dag.elgesem@uib.no

Abstract. To what extent was the blogging about the recent Paris meeting on climate change polarized? This paper addresses this question by way of a series of analyses of a comprehensive corpus of English language blog posts about the negotiations to reach an agreement to mitigate climate change. We identify two groups of bloggers, the engaged bloggers and the contrarian bloggers and use the contents of their blog posts and the patterns in their linking to sources to characterize and compare the two groups. The paper combines computational methods and manual analyses and uses co-citation networks in an innovative way to characterize and compare the contexts of the linking in the two groups. We address challenges that using computational methods to study polarization in blogs raises. We argue that the ideological profiles of the sources the blogs link to are clear signals of polarization.

Keywords: Polarization · Blogs · Climate change · Citation networks

1 Introduction

1.1 Blogging About Climate Change

Blogs play an important role in the public discourse on climate change, perhaps the most pressing social issue today. Blogs are important both because the number of blogs discussing different aspect of climate change is known to be very large [7, 18] and also because blogs are the main outlet for those that hold the contrarian view on climate change–i.e. those that are rejecting the consensus view on anthropogenic global warming (AGW). Because the AGW-skeptical viewpoints get relatively less attention in the mainstream media than the blogs have instead been the main outlets for the contrarians. There have however been few studies of the blogging on climate change and we know little about the structure of the climate change "blogosphere". In this paper, we present an analysis of the English language blogging before, during and after the meeting in Paris in December 2015 (COP21). In the Paris meeting, leaders and representatives from the international community met to negotiate a framework for how to meet the challenge of climate change [5]. The meeting ended up with an agreement on how to reduce emission to meet the goal of keeping the rise in global warming below 2°. The negotiations and the meeting did of course get enormous attention in both mainstream, niche and social media. Here we will look specifically at the discussion of the meeting in the blogs:

© Springer International Publishing AG 2017
G.L. Ciampaglia et al. (Eds.): SocInfo 2017, Part I, LNCS 10539, pp. 178–200, 2017.
DOI: 10.1007/978-3-319-67217-5_12

- To what extent was the blogging about the Paris meeting polarized?

In the general discussion, the relationship between those that accept the consensus on AGW and those that reject this consensus is more like confrontation than dialogue [6, 12, 16, 21]. The aim here is to explore how this deep disagreement manifests itself in the blogs in the context of the Paris meeting. For this, we use computational methods for the analysis of the texts of the blog posts and their networks of hyperlinks. In particular, we make innovative use of co-citation networks to give a rich characterization of the patterns of in-flow of information from linked sources to the blogs.

1.2 Polarization

Investigating polarization among blogs with computational methods raises a series of challenges. One challenge relates to the concept of polarization. In the literature, polarization refers to a *process* where people change to a more extreme variant of their original position as the result of deliberation. In particular, Sunstein [19] have argued that polarization frequently happens with discussions online:

> The term "group polarization "refers to something simple: after deliberation, people are more likely to move toward a more extreme point in the direction to which the group's members were originally inclined. With respect to the Internet and social media, the implication is that groups of like-minded people, engaged in discussion with each other, will typically end up thinking the same thing that they thought before-but in a more extreme form [18]. (p. 67).

This fragmentation of the online public sphere is a serious problem for democratic processes, Sunstein argues, and it is thus important to try to get a better understanding of polarization online. However, in most cases, like in the present case of blogging about climate change, we only have access to information about the *state* of a system of communication, and not to the whole process that created that state. In particular, we do not have access to measurements of how extreme people's opinions were at different points of time. Furthermore, to study processes of polarization rigorously one needs a laboratory setting where one can control with whom the participants discuss and what arguments they get to read or hear. We lack this kind of control in most real world setting. Still it makes sense to study the state of a system of communication from the perspective of polarization: we can meaningfully ask if polarization is a plausible explanation of the properties of the system that we can observe. We will follow this strategy in this paper.

There are different explanations for polarization as observed in the laboratory. One explanation is that, in the course of discussions in a group of people who more or less agree on the issue at hand there will come up mostly arguments and information in support of the favored position. People in the group are thus exposed to a limited pool of persuasive arguments that support one side of the issue and as a result are becoming even more attached to that view. Polarization happens, according to this theory, because people get more entrenched in their own views and therefore have a tendency to be moved in the more extreme direction [8, 9, 19].

On a second theory polarization is more likely to happen in groups where the issue at hand is important for defining their identity as a group.

With respect to polarization, perception of identity and group membership are important, both for communications in general and social media in particular. Group polarization will significantly increase if people think of themselves as part of a group having a shared identity and a degree of solidarity. If they think of themselves in this way, group polarization is both more likely and more extreme. [19], (p. 75).

On this theory, polarization is more likely to happen in a group where people see themselves as having a shared identity in virtue of having a common cause. Adopting the more extreme view tend to strengthen group identity and at the same time sharpen their opposition to other points of view [9, 19, 20].

A third explanation is that polarization happens when people are exposed to viewpoints that challenge their own. On this account, polarization happens because people, when they encounter challenging arguments, start to activate counter-argument to defeat the challenging arguments. By rehearsing counter-arguments, people tend to get more entrenched in their own views, and thereby move themselves towards a more extreme version of their position [13].

These explanations are not competing as the different mechanisms can be operative at the same time. We will argue in the discussion below that all of these explanations of polarization are relevant to the understanding of the situation among the bloggers on the Paris meeting.

The study presented below uses pattern in hyperlinks in blog posts as evidence of polarization. This idea is not new, of course, and patterns in hyperlinks was used to characterize the fragmentation in the American, political blogosphere already by Adamic and Glance [2]. In contrast to [2], the present study does not focus primarily on the links between the blogs, but analyzes extensively the patterns in the ideological profiles of the sources to which the blogs link. Thus, like other studies of polarization in social media, we use patterns in the sharing of sources as data [3, 10, 22]. We also share with these other studies the view that polarization cannot be studied by analyzing the ideological profiles of linked sources alone but that the content of the posts also have to be taken into consideration. There are several reasons for this. First, as convincingly argued by Guera et al. [10] the fact that two groups systematically link to different types of sources does not show that they have opposing views – the simpler explanation could be that they are not aware of the views of the other group. Because polarization involves conflicting viewpoints we therefore also have to check what the targets of the arguments of the posts are. Second, the meaning of a link cannot be inferred form the type of the source alone [1]: a blogger can link to a source with a particular profile, either because she endorses that view or because she is criticizing the view presented by the source. Again, it is necessary to check the content of the post to determine the intention behind the link. However, as argued below, with a polarized topic like with the debate on climate change, bloggers will be less likely to link to a source created by the other camp – because, presumably, they do not want to drive traffic in the "wrong" direction.

1.3   Blogs as Data

While computational methods make it possible to analyze blog networks on a large scale there are also challenges related to the use of such methods for researching blogs. The first is that no precise definition of blogs that it is straightforward to implement does not exist. The "definition" of a blog cited in Wikipedia is standard: "a discussion or informational website published on the World Wide Web consisting of discrete, often informal diary-style text entries ("posts"). Posts are typically displayed in reverse chronological order, so that the most recent post appears first, at the top of the web page". How to implement this is not straightforward and the company that have indexed the blogs we use for this study, Twingly (twingly.com), has developed through trial error over many years a method for classifying a website as a blog that gives results that seem to be compatible with their user's concepts of what a blog is. We do not believe a "correct" or better definition of a blog is available and have also found the items in Twingly's output to be intuitively acceptable as blogs. Twingly keeps the details of the algorithm secret.

The second challenge is that, because the texts of blog posts are not written following any standard and are often much less focused than newspaper articles, for example, the classification of texts using text mining software has to be supplemented with manual analysis of the texts. We have done this to some extent, as explained below.

A third challenge is the definition of the borders of the network of blogs. For one thing, there no such thing as "the blogosphere" because, as we will also see in this study, the blogs are tightly integrated with other sources on the web, in particular mainstream and social media sites. The interaction between the blogs and other online sources is explored extensively in the present study.

There are two strategies for sampling blogs: either one can crawl out-links from a set of seed blogs to get a network of connected blogs, or one can select blogs through search for blog posts that match some search criterion [17]. We have followed second strategy. This way, we can get a comprehensive set of blog posts that write about the topic of interest. We also get a network consisting of the blog posts and their links to sources, some of which will be other blogs in our sample. We will however not get information about the full network of our selected blogs and those to which they connect. The network we get is a *citation network* and not a social network. As we will see below, the internal linking between the blogs in our samples are quite sparse.

1.4   Topically Defined Blog Networks

Our research on the blogging about the Paris meeting starts with the topic – the Paris meeting – and proceeds to identify the blogs that are the most engaged with the development of the negotiations. We then go on to identify the contrarian bloggers to see how they relate to the meeting and compare them with the blogs in the engaged group. In particular, we investigate in some depth patterns in their sharing of sources to characterize the differences in their respective informational environments of the engaged group and the group of contrarians. We argue that polarization is a plausible explanation of the patterns that we see.

Two hypotheses guide our approach:

1. A contrarian who rejects the consensus of AGW will also necessarily reject the premise of the Paris meeting and therefor have little motivation to engage actively with the day-to-day development of the negotiations. We therefore hypothesize that there will be few contrarians in the engaged group.
2. A link to a source makes the source visible to the readers of the blog and is an amplification of the source. In blogging about an ideologically charged issue like climate change, we hypothesize that bloggers will tend not link to sources, which advocate the opposing view.

2 Data Collection

We collected the blog data via the API of the company Twingly (twningly.com). The company specializes in the indexing of blogs and offers paid access to blogs in a range of different languages, including English. For the collection, we used a very wide search criterion, "paris" & "climate", to make sure we got as good a coverage as possible of the discussion of the Paris meeting at the outset. We later filtered the data to capture the most relevant blog posts, as explained below. The period from which we selected post was from November 1st to December 31st, 2015. The meeting took place from November 30 to December 12 so we wanted to capture the blogging that took place in the weeks before the meeting, during the meeting, and immediately after the meeting. Given Twingly's broad definition of blogs and thus extensive coverage of the blogosphere we believe this wide search criterion gave us a set of blog posts that included most of the important posts – both contrarian and non-skeptical – published in English during the selected period.

The search gave us an initial set of 11.620 English blog posts. For each blog post, we have the following data: date of publication, blog URL, the title of the post, text of the post, URL of the post, and out-links from the post. The posts were published by 5.567 different blogs and there the total number of out-links from the blog posts was 101.101.

Most of the links from the posts were targeting other sources than blogs, like mainstream media sites. Moreover, while none of the links from the posts targeted other blog posts in the data set, 6.738 links from blog posts were to other blogs in our data. There are thus very few internal links between the blogs and the density of the network of blogs is very low (0.00021). Furthermore, the network of blogs did not have much by way of structure, like larger communities or clusters.

A manual analysis of a selection of posts revealed that many of them were not concerned with the discussion of climate change or the COP21 meeting. For example, several blog posts from November 2015 discussed the terrorist attacks that took place in Paris on November 13. We thus had to narrow our selection to get the blog posts that were concerned with the negotiations in the Paris meeting.

3   Analysis

3.1   Topic Modeling

We did several rounds of topic modeling using the Mallet-package in R [15], of the 11.620 texts from the blog posts, using different numbers (15, 20, 25, 30, and 40) of topics, to identify the posts most relevant to the discussion of the Paris negotiations. Three topics of particular relevance came up in several rounds and we chose to use these for further analysis the results of the topic modeling with 20 topics. Based on the set of the most probable words generated by the topic modeling for each topic, and the reading of a selection of 25 of the "top" documents from each topic, i.e. documents where the topic was present to a high degree (>0.80), we labelled the three most interesting topics like this:

(a) *Climate science* (The 10 most probable words from the topic analysis: 'climate', 'change', global', 'warming', 'world', 'sea, 'water', 'scientists', 'temperatures', 'weather'.

(b) *Local COP21-events* (The 10 most probable words from the topic analysis: 'climate', 'change', 'paris', 'world', 'leaders', 'global', 'obama', meeting', 'cop', 'people'.

(c) *Paris meeting* (The 10 most probable words from the topic analysis: 'climate', 'countries', 'agreement', emissions', 'paris', 'developing', 'nations', 'change', 'cop', 'carbon'.

To validate the topic modelling further we used Wordsmith [15], a tool for corpus analysis, to measure the key-ness of the texts of the posts from each of the three topics. This analysis identifies salient words in the text by comparing frequencies of words in the text to frequencies of words in the billion-word British National Corpus [4]. This helped us identify the characteristic differences of the language used in the posts in the three topics. For this analysis, we took for each topic the texts with a topic prevalence higher than 0.3. From topic (a), 810 documents had a score above 0.3 and topic (b) had 874 documents with a score above 0.3. The topic (c), "Paris meeting", had 2.399 documents with a score above 0.3 and was thus the largest group by far. Top of the results of the key-ness analysis of topic (c) is in the Appendix (Table 7).

Through these analyses, we found that topic (b) was mostly about announcements and reports from local events around the world related to the Paris meeting, and contained little by way of discussions of the negotiations in the meeting. We therefore chose to discard this topic. The analysis of topic (a) showed that many of the posts with a topic score higher than 0.3 discussed the science of climate change as in relation to the Paris negotiations. We will use this topic to characterize the difference between the two groups.

We found that topic (c) was clearly the most relevant one to our interest in charting the discussion of the negotiations that took place in Paris. In the discussion below we will focus on the documents which has a topic score higher than 0.3 and their links.

The 2.399 blog posts focusing on topic (c), "Paris meeting", were published by 1.458 different blogs. The average productivity of each blog was 1.65 and the distribution of the blogs over time showed the clearest peak around the time of the publication of the agreement (around December 12, 2015). There were 12.265 out-links from the blog posts, targeting 1.931 unique sources. The top 15 targets of the blog posts in this group were as follows (Table 1):

Table 1. The 15 most linked sources from blog posts with a focus on the topic "Paris meeting"

	Linked sources	Number of links	%
1	unfccc.int	1066	8.7
2	theguardian.com	660	5.4
3	twitter.com	452	3.7
4	nytimes.com	356	2.9
5	en.wikipedia.org	289	2.4
6	climatecentral.org	182	1.5
7	bbc.co.uk	153	1.3
8	theconversation.com	132	1.1
9	news.google.com	128	1.0
10	cop21.gouv.fr	114	0.9
11	facebook.com	111	0.9
12	motherjones.com	107	0.8
13	topics.nytimes.com	104	0.8
14	whitehouse.gov	96	0.8
15	youtube.com	90	0.7

The top 15 sources, which are also the sources that have more than 90 links from different blog posts, are of four types. The first type are sources related to the conference (1, 10), the second group consists of important mainstream media sites (2, 4, 7, 13), the third type are news sites that supported the ambition of the Paris meeting (6, 8, 12, 14), and the fourth are social media sites (3, 5, 11, 15).

The strong presences of the topic "Paris meeting" in the posts thus seem to be a reasonably good signal of engagement with the negotiations. However, we also observed that some blog posts were in fact about the negotiations without having this topic so strongly. We therefore choose not to rely only on the topic modelling for the selection of the engaged blogs. Indeed, it would be naïve to think that we could define a single criterion that will give us all and only blogs actively engaging with the Paris negotiations. Instead, for the identification of relevant blog posts we will proceed as follows. First, we select the blogs that link to the website of the organizers, unfccc.int. It is reasonable to assume that most of these blog posts actively attended to what was going on in the negotiations. Second, we compare and find that most, but not all, of the blogs in this group have a high score on the topic "Paris meeting" and that they frequently link to the same external sources as the blog posts with a high score on the topic "Paris meeting". Third, we manually check the focus and ideological tone of the blog posts that link to the unfccc website. We find that most of the blogs in the group attend to the negotiations. We do not claim to have captured all of the blogs that attend to the negotiations but argue that the one we have identified is *one* important and interesting group of bloggers that actively engage with the negotiations. Below, we first characterize the blog posts and linking patterns of the group of blogs linking to the unfccc and then compare them with a group of skeptical blogs.

3.2   Blogs Linking to the unfccc

We found that 789 blog posts from 568 blogs linked to the unfccc-website. We chose to include in our analysis all posts published by these 568 blogs. There were 11.113 out-links from these blog posts to 1.916 different (unique) sources. However, only 561 of these links targeted another blog in our data set. The density of the resulting network of blogs connected by out-links from other blogs, was higher than for the network of blogs with posts that focus on topic (c), but still very low (0.0017).

The set of blogs that links to the unfccc-website have several similarities with the blog post that focus the most on topic (c), "Paris negotiations", discussed above. These are the 15 most linked sources from the blog posts in this group (Table 2):

Table 2. The 15 most linked sources from blog posts linking to unfccc.int

	Linked sources	Number of links	%
1	unfccc.int	1570	15.0
2	theguardian.com	413	4.0
3	twitter.com	367	3.5
4	en.wikipedia.org	294	2.8
5	nytimes.com	197	1.9
6	climatecentral.org	165	1.5
7	conditions.healthgrove.com	157	1.5
8	theconversation.com	133	1.3
9	slate.com	96	0.9
10	un.org	83	0.8
11	washingtonpost.com	81	0.8
12	facebook.com	79	0.8
13	youtube.com	74	0.7
14	www.cop21.gouv.fr	73	0.7
15	flickr.com	71	0.6

We see that 9 of the 15 most cites sources in this group are also among the 15 most cited sources by the blogs that focus on the topic (c), "Paris meeting", discussed above, and that the 5 most cited sources are the same with both groups. There is a large overlap between the most linked sources of the two groups, as 68 sources are among the 100 most cited sources in both. All of the top 15 sources for the "Paris meeting"-group are among the top 100 sources of the group that links to the unfccc website. We also observe that, among the 100 most cited sources of the unfccc-blogs there are only one sources that is clearly contrarian: corbettreport.com (rank 35).

Furthermore, the two groups of blog posts also to a large extent overlap, as 456 of the 789 blog posts that link to the unfccc-website are also in the set of blog posts that focus on the topic "Paris meeting". Third, and related to this, the mean score for the topic "Paris meeting" is 0.37 for the posts published by the group of blogs that link to the unfccc-website, which is high, and this topic is the most prevalent one in these blog posts. The similarities of the group of unfccc bloggers to the larger groups of blogs that focus on the topic "Paris meeting" support our assumption that the blogs in the former group actively attend to the negotiations: they not only link to the unfccc-website, the "Paris meeting"-topic is also the most characteristic of their posts.

We have manually checked a sample consisting of 30% of the posts in the unfccc-group for their attitude to the Paris negotiations. We found that only 5% of the posts in this group reject the very idea of the Paris negotiations, i.e. most blog posts in this group do not question the rationale for the event. Some posts just describe the events neutrally, while others provide interpretations of the events as they develop. Some blog posts offer critical perspectives on the negotiations or the agreement without questioning the rationale for the negotiations, typically criticizing the agreement for not being strong enough to meet the 2C-degree target. The titles of the rejecting 39 blog posts, which in most cases signal clearly the attitude of the post, are listed in the Appendix (Table 8). We take this result as partial confirmation of our hypothesis that bloggers that engage actively with the negotiations tend not to reject the rationale for them.

3.3   Skeptical Bloggers

We have seen that the group of bloggers that engage actively with the negotiations are predominantly supportive of the rationale of the negotiations. But as we know (see [7, 18]) that there are a number of very active and visible bloggers on the skeptical side, we would expect to find more blog posts that reject the rationale of the negotiations than we have seen so far. One would indeed expect that blogger that reject the idea of anthropogenic global warming (AGW) would also reject as pointless a meeting devoted to the fight against AGW. We therefore selected blogs that linked to the 10 skeptical blogs found to have the highest centrality by [18]:

- wattsupwiththat.com
- climateaudit.org
- joannenova.com.au
- bishophill.squarespace.com
- www.junkscience.com
- www.desmogblog.com
- www.judithcurry.com
- www.drroyspencer.com
- motls.blogspot.no
- climatedepot.com

In addition, we included three contrarian sources that the contrarian blogs in the unfccc group cited frequently:

- cfact.org
- heartland.org
- dailysignal.com

Using links to these 13 sites as our selection criteria we found 139 blog posts in our corpus, published by 116 different blogs, had a link to one or more of these sources. We manually checked a random sample of 25 of these blog posts and found that 24 are skeptical of the rationale of the Paris meeting. The titles of these blog posts are listed in the Appendix (Table 9).

The blog posts from the AGW-skeptical blogs have 2.239 links to 653 different (unique) sources. Like in the previous cases, the internal linking between the blogs is very sparse, as only 38 links goes from one blog in our date set to another. The density of the network of blogs based on out-links from the blog posts is even lower than that of the unfccc-blogs (0.0028) and the network is highly fragmented.

This set of skeptical blog posts differ from those of the blog posts in the unfccc-group. First, there are only 21 blog posts in intersection of the two groups. The manual check of the documents in this overlap showed that 15 were rejecting the rationale for the negotiations and six were not. Again, the list of the titles of the posts are in the Appendix (Table 10). Second, the topic profile of the skeptical group is different from that of the unfccc-blogs as the mean topic score of the "Paris meeting"-topic is 0.17 (as compared to 0.37 in the unfccc-group) and the mean score on the topic "Climate science" is 0.24 (as compared to 0.09 in the unfccc-group). The topical foci of the blogging in the two groups are therefore quite different. Third, the blogs in the skeptical group link to different sources than the two others. The 15 most linked sources in the skeptical group are:

We see that, one mainstream media site is among the most cites sources as with the unfccc-group (theguardian.com) and that the unfccc-site (10) is also cited relatively frequently, as are some social media sites (8, 9). However, the rest of the sources (1, 2, 3, 4, 5, 6, 11, 12, 13, 14, and 15) are contrarian sources that were strongly critical of the Paris negotiations. The overlap of sources linked by the two groups is generally low, as only 35 sources are in the intersections of the two group's 100 most cited sources. All of those are mainstream media or social media sites. There are no sites or blogs dedicated to the AGW side of the issue among the 100 most cited sources by the contrarian group.

The relatively high proportion of links from the contrarian blogs to theguardian.com is interesting as this newspaper is known for its clear position in support of the efforts to mitigate anthropogenic climate change. Looking at the 32 posts that link to this website we find that the contexts of the links to theguardian.com in these posts are of four types. (1) Contrarian blog posts that are critical of the Paris meeting and that cite an article in theguardian.com in support of their criticism. (2) Contrarian blog posts that cite an article in theguardian.com in order to criticize its view on climate change. (3) One non-skeptical blog post cites articles in theguardian.com in support of his criticism of the contrarians - and also linking also to wattsupwiththat.com. (4) Six identical posts published by a non-skeptic that link to theguardian.com in support of an argument for climate change mitigation (also with a link also to wattsupwiththat.com.) While the majority (25) of the posts promote a contrarian viewpoint we see that a link to theguardian.com from a blog that also links to one of the contrarian sources does not necessarily imply a criticism of the view of theguardian.com on climate change.

Some might think it is problematic that we first use a set of linked sources to select the contrarian blog posts and then characterize the profile of the blogs by analyzing their sources. This would have been a fair criticism if our aim was to capture all contrarian posts in the corpus. But since our aim is more modestly to identify the posts of a central group of contrarians, but not necessarily all contrarian blog posts, this is a valid procedure. First, we undertook a manual check of the selected posts that strongly indicated that they were dismissive of the Paris event. Second, the procedure did generate new information about which the sources the contrarian blog posts linked to, as illustrated by the fact that only three of the sites on the list we used to make the selection (wattsupwiththat.com and cfact.org, heartland.org) are among the 15 most cited sources. In particular the most cited source, breibart.com, was not among the sites used for the selection, and some of the sources on the initial list are ranked low among the 100 most cited sources by the contrarians. For example, the central Australian, skeptic joannenova.com.au is only the 40th most linked source with the contrarian bloggers. Furthermore, we expanded the set of blog post to include all posts published by the blogs we identified initially thereby expanding he set of linked sources to include all of the sources linked from these blogs.

4 Co-citation Networks

4.1 Co-citation Graphs

To explore further the flow of information from sources into the blogs in the different groups we constructed the co-citation (or co-link) networks for the sources. In these networks, the vertices are the sources and there is an edge between two sources if there is a link to both sources from the same blog post. This gives a complete different network. To illustrate the difference, we found that, while there are 11.113 links from unfccc blog posts to different sources, there are 280.320 co-citation links between these sources. The network conveys information about which sources are linked to together and thus about the context of the linking. The co-citation graphs therefore give us additional information about the pattern of the in-flow from the sources to the blogs than to what we get from the list of the most frequently linked sources alone. The edges in the co-citation graph have weights, which represents how often the same blog post targets two (linked) sources. The weight on an edge represent therefore the conditional probability of a link between the two linked sources. This means that, while the probability of a link to a certain source can be high, the conditional probability that one of these links connects to a particular co-linked source can be low. The co-citation network of the 15 most cited sources listed in Table 3 is visualized in Fig. 1 below. Note that the size of the nodes in the graph depicts the number of links from blog posts to that source, and not the total number of times the source is co-cited with another source. The width of the edges do represent how relatively often that pairs of sources in the graph are co-cited.

Table 3. The 15 most linked sources from contrarian blogs

	Linked sources	Number of links	%
1	breitbart.com	128	5.7
2	wattsupwiththat.com	117	5.2
3	climatedepot.com	62	2.8
4	polarbearscience.com	36	1.6
5	corbettreport.com	35	1.6
6	patriotpost.us	32	1.4
7	theguardian.com	32	1.4
8	youtube.com om	31	1.4
9	en.wikipedia.org	30	1.3
10	unfccc.int	30	1.3
11	cfact.org	27	1.2
12	zerohedge.com	26	1.2
13	click.icptrack.com	25	1.1
14	heartland.org	25	1.1
15	freedomforce.com	23	1.0

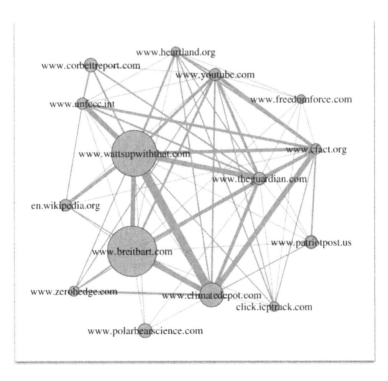

Fig. 1. The co-citation network of the 15 sources linked most frequently by contrarian blogs. (Created with the iGraph package [21] in R.)

We see that, for example, that posts that link to wattsupwiththat.com frequently also link to climatedepot.com. And while breitbart.com is the most frequently linked source by the contrarian bloggers none of its edges are as thick as that between watsupwiththat.com and climatedepot.com. This means that the blog posts that link breitbart.com tend to co-cite it with a broader range of different other sources and that than do the posts that link to wattsupwiththat.com. And, to mention another example, theguardian.com has fewer in-links than some of the other sources, but when it is linked, it is frequently co-cited with wattsupwiththat.com. In general, the graph shows that the blogs that give attention to contrarian sources most frequently do that in the context of amplifying other contrarian sources, and less frequently in the context of sources with the opposing view. This illustrates how the co-citation graph provides information about the patterns in the in-flow form the sources to the blogs by depicting the contexts of the linking.

Compare the picture above to the visualization of the co-citation graph of the sources that the unfccc-blogs link to, depicted in Fig. 2 below. Again the nodes are the 15 most cited sources by the unfccc blogs and the size of the nodes represent the number of times the sources have been linked by the blog posts (and not how the number of times the sources are co-cited in a blog post). The width of the links represent the relative frequency of co-linking of pairs of sources.

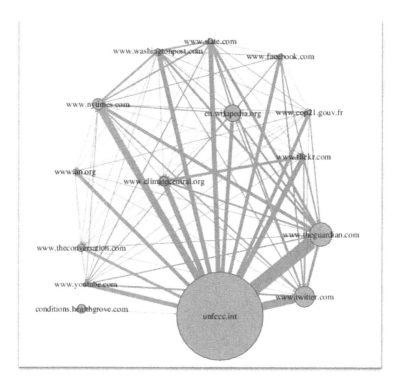

Fig. 2. The co-citation network of the 15 sources linked most frequently by the unfccc blogs. (Created with the iGraph package [21] in R)

We again see that the co-citation provides more information about the context of the linking and thus of the patterns of the in-flow of sources to the blogs. For example, frequently cited together are also the three most frequently linked sources (unfccc.int, theguardian.com and twitter.com). The site healthgrove.com, on the other hand, while it is among the 15 most cited sources by unfccc blog posts it is seldom cited together with the other, frequently linked sources. This suggests that there is a special group of blogs that creates most of the links to that site (the co-links to which are not shown in the visualization). We also see that nytimes.com, which is linked less frequently than some of the other media sites, when is it linked it is usually together with unfccc.int and theguardian.com. Again, the point is to illustrate how the co-citation networks gives information about the patterns of linking to sources that adds to what we get from looking at which sources get the most links.

4.2   Analyzing the Co-citation Graphs

The co-citation graphs can be used to explore and compare more systematically the probabilities of links between sources that are central to the two groups. To illustrate, Table 4 below show the 20 most probable links in the co-citation graphs of the contrarian and unffc blogs, respectively.

Table 4. The 20 most frequent links between sources by, respectively, the unfccc group and the contrarian group.

Top contrarian co-citations (%)	Top unfcc co-citations (%)
wattsupwiththat.com - climatedepot.com (0.1)	unfccc.int - theguardian.com (0.5)
wattsupwiththat.com - theguardian.com (0.09)	unfccc.int - twitter.com (0.3)
climatedepot.com - breitbart.com (0.08)	unfccc.int - nytimes.com (0.3)
wattsupwiththat.com - nytimes.com (0.08)	unfccc.int - flickr.com (0.2)
wattsupwiththat.com - unfccc.int (0.08)	unfccc.int - climatecentral.org (0.2)
wattsupwiththat.com-onlinelibrary.wiley.com (0.08)	unfccc.int - slate.com (0.2)
wattsupwiththat.com - breitbart.com (0.07)	unfccc.int-climatechangenews.com (0.2)
wattsupwiththat.com - wsj.com (0.07)	unfccc.int - ipcc.ch (0.2)
wattsupwiththat.com - joannenova.com.au (0.07)	unfccc.int - washingtonpost.com (0.2)
wattsupwiththat.com - www.amazon.com (0.07)	nfccc.int - carbonbrief.org (0.1)
climatedepot.com - wsj.com (0.07)	unfccc.int - climateactiontracker.org (0.1)
climatedepot.com - cfact.org (0.07)	unfccc.int - youtube.com (0.1)
wsj.com - cfact.org (0.07)	unfccc.int - un.org (0.1)
telegraph.co.uk - cfact.org (0.07)	unfccc.int - en.wikipedia.org (0.1)
theguardian.com - wsj.com (0.05)	unfccc.int - facebook.com (0.1)
theguardian.com - twitter.com (0.05)	**theguardian.com - nytimes.com** (0.1)
theguardian.com - nytimes.com (0.05)	cop21.gouv.fr - unfccc.int (0.1)
wattsupwiththat.com - en.wikipedia.org (0.05)	unfccc.int - bbc.com (0.1)
climatedepot.com - telegraph.co.uk (0.05)	unfccc.int - whitehouse.gov (0.1)
wsj.com - telegraph.co.uk (0.05)	**theguardian.com - twitter.com** (0.1)

We see that only two co-citation links (theguardian.com-nytimes.com and the-guardian.com-twitter.com) appear on both lists. We also see that, while the link (wattsupwiththat.com - unfccc.int) appears among the top skeptical co-citation links the skeptical blog wattsupwiththat.com is not among the most frequently co-cited sites in the unfccc-group. Furthermore, all the co-linked sources on the unfccc-side are non-skeptical, while half of the co-cited sources on the contrarian side support an anti-AGW position (wattsupwiththat.com, climatedepot.com, breitbart.com, joannenova.com.au, cfact.org, telegraph.co.uk).

To explore further the differences and similarities between the two co-citation graphs we selected three central nodes from each of the graphs (see Figs. 1 and 2 above). From the contrarian co-citation graph we selected wattsupwiththat.com, breitbart.com, climatedepot.com and from the co-citation graph induced by the blogs that link to the unfccc.int we selected unfccc.int, theguardian.com and climatecentral.org. In Table 5 below we have computed the proportion of links between these six sources in the two co-citation graphs. Remember that the links are undirected. The upper-right part of the table gives the proportion of links between the sources in the co-citation graph induced by the unfccc-blogs while the lower-left part of the table gives the proportion of links between the six sources in the co-citation graph induced by the contrarian blogs.

Table 5. Proportion of links in the co-citation graphs for six important sources

	unfccc	guardian	climatecentral	wuwt	breitbart	climatedepot
unfccc		0.5	0.2	0.01	0.005	0.002
guardian	0.03		0.06	0.003	0.001	0
climatecentral	0.01	0.005		0	0	0
wuwt	0.08	0.09	0		0.001	0
breitbart	0.02	0.03	0	0.07		0
climatedepot	0.01	0.05	0	0.1	0.08	

Let us focus, first, on the two blogs climatecentral.org and climatedepot.org, which are advocate sites on the non-skeptical and skeptical side, respectively. We see that, among the contrarian blogs, there are no co-links between the three contrarian blogs and climatecentral.org and, on the unfccc-side, there are almost no co-citations of climatedepot.org with any sources. Thus, bloggers in both groups seldom link to these two advocates in the same post.

A striking difference is the high probability of a co-citation in the unfccc group of the unfccc.int-website with theguardian.com and climaecentral.org as compared to the contrarian side. It is also noteworthy that, while a co-link between wattsupwiththat.com and unfccc.int has a low probability in the engaged group it has a substantially higher probability in the skeptical group. Worth mentioning is also the difference between the co-citation of theguardian.com and breitbart.com in, respectively, the contrarian and the unfccc-groups. Again, the co-citation analysis gives a different but complementary and richer picture of the linking patterns of the two sides, as compared to what we get from only considering the most frequently sited sources.

We mentioned that, in the graphs above, the sizes of the nodes represents the total number of links from blog posts to those sources, not how often they are co-linked by all other sources, but that the width of the edge between two nodes represented how often, relatively speaking, the two nodes are co-linked. Let us now turn to the pure co-citation graph where both the vertices and the edges are weighted by the number of co-citation. In Table 6 below the sources of two groups graph are ranked by, respectively, their degree centrality and between-ness centrality.

Table 6. The 25 sources with the highest degree centrality and the betweenness centrality in the co-citation network of, respectively, the contrarian group and the unfccc group

Contrarian co-citation graph		unfccc co-citation graph	
Degree centrality	Betweenness centrality	Degree centrality	Betweenness centrality
wattsupwiththat.com	wattsupwiththat.com	unfccc.int	unfccc.int
theguardian.com	climatedepot.com	theguardian.com	theguardian.com
wsj.com	theguardian.com	nytimes.com	twitter.com
breitbart.com	desmogblog.com	twitter.com	nytimes.com
youtube.com	joannenova.com.au	carbonbrief.org	carbonbrief.org
telegraph.co.uk	wsj.com	washingtonpost.com	facebook.com
climatedepot.com	breitbart.com	bbc.com	en.wikipedia.org
joannenova.com.au	youtube.com	en.wikipedia.org	bbc.com
reuters.com	nytimes.com	whitehouse.gov	ipcc.ch
twitter.com	twitter.com	ipcc.ch	youtube.com
facebook.com	reuters.com	facebook.com	whitehouse.gov
cfact.org	cfact.org	reuters.com	washingtonpost.com
thehill.com	washingtonpost.com	youtube.com	cop21.gouv.fr
politico.com	unfccc.int	nature.com	nature.com
washington-examiner.co	facebook.com	slate.com	reuters.com
independent.co.uk	zerohedge.com	climatechangenews.com	cop21.paris.org
desmogblog.com	thehill.com	cop21.gouv.fr	un.org
nature.com	telegraph.co.uk	huffingtonpost.com	flicr.com
washingtonpost.com	en.wikipedia.org	wri.com	climatechangenews.com
zerohedge.com	washingtonexaminer.com	thinkprogress.org	huffingtonpost.com
mercurynews.com	news.investors.com	flickr.com	wri.org
nationalreview.com	dailycaller.com	cop21.paris.org	climate-actiontracker.org
dailycaller.com	politico.com	350.org	slate.com
amazon.com	independent.co.uk	climate-actiontracker.org	350.org
shoutout.wix.com	dailymail.co.uk	climatecentral.org	worldbank.org

The co-citation networks provide a different but complementary picture on the influence of different sources. We see, first, that there are some differences in the ideological profiles of the sources on each side, like with the most frequently linked sources: the partisan sites wattsupwiththat.com, bretibart.com, joannenovava.co.au, cfact.org, desmogblog.com, zerohedge.com and dailycaller.com, are central in the contrarian co-citation network, while carbonbrief.org, climateactiontracker.org, climateactiontracker.org, and 350.org are central sources in the co-citation network of the unfccc-bloggers. Second, some of the contrarian sites that were among the 15 most cited sources are not central in this network, and some sources that were not among the most frequently linked ones are found to be central in the co-citation network. For example, joannenova.com.au that was the 40th most cited sources among the contrarian bloggers, is central in the co-citation network on both measures (rank 8 and 5, respectively). This means that the relatively few blog posts that link to this source, also link to a large number of other sources at the same time. The position of the unfccc.int-website is also noteworthy. While it is the 10th most linked source of the skeptics it is not among the 25 most co-linked sources (as measured by degree centrality) still it has a relatively high between-ness centrality. In general, the ideological profiles of the co-citation networks appear as quite distinct.

5   Discussion and Conclusion

Two hypotheses guided our approach:

1. A contrarian who rejects the consensus of AGW will necessarily also reject the premise of the Paris meeting and therefor have little motivation to engage actively with the day-to-day development of the negotiations. We therefore hypothesize that there will be few contrarians in the engaged group.
2. A link to a source makes the source visible to the readers of the blog and is an amplification of the source. In blogging about an ideologically charged issue like climate change, we hypothesize that bloggers will tend not link to sources, which advocate the opposing view.

We defined as the engaged group the blogs with a link to unfccc.int, the website of the organizers of the Paris meeting. We take the fact that only 5% of the blog posts that linked to the unfccc-website were contrarian as evidence in support of the first hypothesis. Despite the fact that a minority of contrarians actually did link to a source of which they are very critical, this absence of links from most contrarian blogs to the site of the event of they criticize is a symptom of a polarized sphere of communication.

We also find support in our data for the second hypothesis. We saw in particular that there is little by way of linking across the ideological divide to the very partisan sources, such as climatecentral.org and climatedepo.com and that few links go from the engaged group to the most linked skeptical source, breitbart.com. These patterns suggest polarization but, on the other hand, we also saw that there are a number of common sources and some similarities of co-citations on both sides and thus that there are sources of information that are shared by the two groups.

Our research question was:

• To what extent was the blogging about the Paris meeting polarized?

Polarization means that people are moving to a more extreme position as the result of deliberation with like-minded people. As argued above, while we cannot say whether the bloggers got more extreme in the course of the period we observe, we can meaningful ask whether some of the preconditions for polarization are present. We will argue that this is the case.

Above we sketched three explanations for polarization. The first explanation was that polarization happen because people who discuss with like-minded people mostly read or hear arguments that they find persuasive from their own standpoint, and information that support their own view. This is to a large extent true of the bloggers if we look at the sources to which the two sides link and which sources the two groups most frequently co-cite. It is true that the links and co-links from both groups involving mainstream media sources–theguardian.com in particular - suggests that the two groups at least to some extent share some of the same sources of information. But apart from the linking to some mainstream media sources, the linking and the co-linking by the two groups clearly reflect their different ideological positions. It is thus plausible to say that, the preconditions for polarization is present to some extent. Of course, bloggers get information from many sources they do not link to, but these clear patterns in the differences in the sharing of sources do suggest informational preferences and therefore polarization.

The second explanation of why polarization happens is that people tend to get more extreme when an issue is central to the identity of the group to which the person belong. Here it is an interesting difference between the contrarian and the non-contrarian groups. The contrarian position is defined by the very rejection of the consensus view on anthropogenic global warming and the contrarians for this reason also see themselves very much as a group in opposition to the mainstream majority. In contrast, the majority of people that share the consensus on AGW, while they do reject the skeptical view on climate change, they do not identify themselves through this rejection of the skeptics. It is symptomatic that we could find only one single blog post in the engaged group that criticized the skeptics, while all of the skeptical blog posts criticized the people on the other side. In this sense, the situation for the contrarian group and the engaged group is different: there is an asymmetric polarization where the skeptics hold an extreme position in relation to the broad consensus on anthropogenic global warming. We see this in the blogging about the Paris meeting. There are a number of different positions on the negotiations among those that accept that joint international efforts are necessary to meet that challenges of climate change. Some people argue, for example, that the agreement is not sufficient to meet the target of reducing the rise in global temperature. But this is a less extreme position than one that rejects the negotiations as necessary. We find evidence of this asymmetric polarization in the fact that the contrarians link and co-cite partisan sources much more than does the other side. Again, one of the pre-conditions for polarization – for the contrarian bloggers–seems to be present.

The third explanation of polarization was that, when people encounter views that challenge their own they typically try to avoid changing their beliefs and start to mobilize counter-arguments. In the analysis above, we saw that the skeptics also linked to mainstream sources like theguardian.com, reuters.com, washingtonpost.com, and wsj.com, which of course was reporting on the Paris negotiations and some – theguardian.com - took a clear stance in support of the effort to reach an international agreement to mitigate climate change. These linking behaviors clearly show that the contrarian blogs did engage with views and information from the other side and, furthermore, the views of the other side are the target of almost all their writing. We can see already from the titles of the skeptical blog posts cited in the Table 10 in the Appendix that they are heavily engaged in the production of counter-arguments to the claims made by the consensus side. It therefore seems that also this third precondition for polarization is present.

Appendix

See Tables 7, 8, 9 and 10.

Table 7. Key-ness analysis of topic "Paris meeting"

1	PARIS
2	CLIMATE
3	BINDING
4	GLOBAL
5	LEGALLY
6	DRAFT
7	AMBITIOUS
8	AGREEMENT
9	UNIVERSAL
10	CHANGE
11	HISTORIC
12	EMISSIONS
13	TEXT
14	NATIONS
15	FINAL
16	GOAL
17	REACH
18	INTERNATIONAL
19	WARMING
20	REACHED
21	KYOTO
22	GREENHOUSE
23	ADOPTED
24	CARBON
25	PARTIES
26	OBAMA
27	STRONG
28	COP
29	NEGOTIATIONS
30	COMMITMENTS
31	ESTABLISHES
32	ADOPTION
33	CALLS
34	AMBITION
35	FRAMEWORK

Table 8. Titles of contrarian blog posts that link to the unfccc.int-website

Title of rejecting posts	n
"United Nations Plans Tribunal for Climate Justice"	1
"U N PLANNING COURT TO JUDGE U S FOR CLIMATE JUSTICE"	2
"U N PLANNING COURT TO JUDGE U S FOR CLIMATE JUSTICE"	3
"U N PLANNING COURT TO JUDGE U S FOR CLIMATE JUSTICE"	4
"U N PLANNING COURT TO JUDGE U S FOR CLIMATE JUSTICE"	5
"Global warming it's all about centralized power"	6
"UN Creating An International Tribunal of Climate Justice To Bypass US Congress"	7
"Another Day Another Reason to Get Out of the U N"	8
"UN planning court for climate justice"	9
"The Court of AGW"	10
"Climate Conference Just In Time For The Liberals"	11
"The Corbett Report: NASA Admits Antarctica Gaining Land Ice"	12
"The Corbett Report: NASA Admits Antarctica Gaining Land Ice"	13
"UN Planning Court For Climate Justice"	14
"AL Gore Warmist Pride No Debate in Paris on the Science Al Gore"	15
"50 Years After Warning No Debate in Paris on the Science"	16
"NASA Admits Antarctica Gaining Land Ice"	17
"A Question For Veterans Are you Fighting for Sovereignty"	18
"We need more CO2"	19
"We need more CO2"	20
"THE CLIMATE TERRORISTS CONVERGE ON PARIS"	21
"A story of the climate change debate How it ran why it failed"	22
"What is So Bad About CO2"	23
"Already sinking Climate talks hit negotiating iceberg"	24
"Already sinking Climate talks hit negotiating iceberg"	25
"The unreadable Paris climate draft"	26
"The Ozone Scare Was A Dry Run For The Global Warming Scare"	27
"Stream Climate Circus Climate Clowns at COP21"	28
"Failing Grade"	29
"This El Ni o is not Godzilla What can we learn from the 2"	30
"World Leaders Approve Global Climate Change Tax In Fulfillment Of Luke 2"	31
"Stunning scientific illiteracy behind the Paris 2C target"	32
"Governmental Hysterical Myths about Global Warming"	33
"A closer look at scenario RCP8 5"	34
"World Leaders Approve Global Climate Change Tax In Fullfillment Of Luke 2"	35
"Climate change as dissociation"	36
"Massive End Times Prophecy Explodes Before Our Eyes What Just Happened Will Leave You"	37
"Climate change deal Five reasons to be glad five to be gloomy"	38
"The Great Climate Propaganda Fail"	39

Table 9. Titles of 25 randomly selected posts from the skeptical group. 24 blog posts are rejecting the negotiations, one is not.

Post titles	Rejecting negotiations
"U.N. PLANNING COURT TO JUDGE U.S. FOR 'CLIMATE JUSTCE"	Y
"Cult Of Climastrology Ramping Up The Catastrophe Warming ahead of	Y
"Paris Climate Change Conference Washup"	Y
"Japan pays off the global high priests of the "climate change"	Y
"UN planning court for 'climate justice'"	Y
«The Court of AGW»	Y
"Paris, Religion, Money and Temperature"	Y
"Report: NASA Admits Antarctica Gaining Land Ice"	Y
"NASA Admits Antarctica Gaining Land Ice"	Y
"Paris Conference: be aware of the greenwashing"	Y
«A Prayer for Paris»	NO
"Global Scientists Define Next Great Challenge"	Y
"Schoolboy sniggers at COP21 and conspiracy theories"	Y
"What's So Bad About CO2?"	Y
"A story of the climate change debate"	Y
"Paris Conference Leaders Want You to Think the Planet Is Facing a Climate Change Crisis. That's Not True"	Y
"Claim: France Terror Attacks Improved Chances of a Climate Deal"	Y
"Paris Global Warming conference this week is "last chance to save the world, and this time we really, really mean it"	Y
"COP21 Talks Delayed – US Threatens To Walk Out of Paris Deal If Financial Obligations Made Legally Bining"	Y
"Twelve Reasons Why The Paris Climate Talks Are A Total Waste"	Y
"The (Watered Down?) COP21 Agreement explained"	Y
"Welcome to a new geologic era – the Idiocene"	Y
"Bringing Climate Realism to Paris at COP-21"	Y
"THE CLIMATE TERRORISTS CONVERGE ON PARIS"	Y
"Vladimir Putin; Climate and Political Realist?"	Y
"Polar Bears Are In Pole Position"	Y
«That's $5 trillion Australian»	Y

Table 10. Titles of the 21 blog posts in the overlap between the contrarian group and the engaged group. Fifteen posts reject the rationale of the negotiations, six do not.

Post titles	Rejecting negotiations
"UN Planning Court For Climate Justice"	Y
"UN Planning Court For Climate Justice"	Y
"United Nations Plans Tribunal for Climate Justice"	Y
"Another Day, Another Reason to Get Out of the U.N."	Y
UN planning court for 'climate justice'	Y
The Court of AGW	Y
"The Corbett Report: NASA Admits Antarctica Gaining Land Ice"	Y
"Report: NASA Admits Antarctica Gaining Land Ice"	Y
"NASA Admits Antarctica Gaining Land Ice"	Y
"Paris Conference: be aware of the greenwashing"	Y
"THE CLIMATE TERRORISTS CONVERGE ON PARIS"	Y
"A story of the climate change debate"	Y
"Schoolboy sniggers at COP21 and conspiracy theories"	NO
"What's So Bad About CO2?"	Y
"COP21 Week 2 - and open thread"	NO
"The Ozone Scare Was A Dry Run For The Global War"	Y
"Stunning scientific illiteracy behind the Paris 2°C target"	Y
"Real test of Paris climate agreement"	NO
"Real test of Paris climate agreement"	NO
"A closer look at scenario RCP8.5"	NO
"Here's what you need to know about the new Paris climate agreement"	NO

References

1. Adamic, L.: The social link. In: Turow, J., Tsui, L. (eds.) The Hyperlinked Society, pp. 227–248. University of Michigan Press, Ann Arbor (2008)
2. Adamic, L., Glance, N.: The political blogosphere and the 2004 election: divided they blog. In: Proceedings of the 3rd International Workshop on Link Discovery, KDD 2005, pp. 36–43 (2005)
3. Bakshy, E., Messing, E., Adamic, L., et al.: Exposure to ideologically diverse news and opinion on facebook. Science **348**, 1130–1132 (2015)
4. British National Corpus homepage. http://www.natcorp.ox.ac.uk/
5. COP21, Wikipepedia article. https://en.wikipedia.org/wiki/2015_United_Nations_Climate_Change_Conference

6. Dunlap, R.E., McCright, M.J.: Organized climate change denial. In: Dryzek, J.S., Norgaard, R.B., Schlosberg, D. (eds.) The Oxford Handbook of Climate Change and Society. Oxford University Press, New York (2011)

7. Elgesem, D., Steskal, L., Diakopoulos, N.: Structure and content of the discourse on climate change in the blogosphere: the big picture. Environ. Commun. 9(2), 169–188 (2015)

8. Isenberg, D.J.: Group polarization: a critical review and meta-analysis. J. Pers. Soc. Psychol. 50, 1141–1151 (1986)

9. Fiske, S.T., Taylor, S.E.: Social Cognition – from Brains to Culture. SAGE, Los Angeles (2013)

10. Guera, P.H.C., et al.: A measure of polarization on social media networks based on community boundaries. In: Proceedings of the Seventh International AAAI Conference on Weblogs and Social Media (2013)

11. Himelboim, I., et al.: Birds of a feather tweet together: integrating network and content analyses to examine cross-ideology exposure on Twitter. J. Comput. Mediat. Commun. 18 (2), 40–60 (2013)

12. Hulme, M.: Why We Disagree About Climate Change. Cambridge University Press, Cambridge (2009)

13. Lodge, M., Taber, C.S.: Motivated political reasoning. In: The Rationalizing Voter. Cambridge University Press, Cambridge (2013). (Chapter 7)

14. iGraph (2017). http://igraph.org/r/

15. Mallet (2017).https://cran.r-project.org/web/packages/mallet/mallet.pdf

16. Mann, M.E.: The Hockey Stick and the Climate Wars. Columbia University Press, New York (2012)

17. Salway, A., Elgesem, D., Hofland, K., Reigem, Ø., Steskal, L.: Topically-focused blog corpora for multiple languages. In: Proceedings of the 10th Web as Corpus Workshop (WAC-X) (2016)

18. Sharman, A.: Mapping the climate sceptical blogosphere. Glob. Environ. Change 26, 159–170 (2014)

19. Sunstein, C.: #republic. Princeton University Press, Princeton (2017)

20. Turner, J.C., et al.: Rediscovering the Social Group: A Self-Categorization Theory. Basil Blackwell, New York (1987)

21. Washingthon, H., Cook, J.: Climate Change Denial. Earthscan, London (2011)

22. Wordsmith homepage. http://www.lexically.net/wordsmith/

23. Yardi, S., Boyd, D.: Dynamic debates: an analysis of group polarization over time on Twitter. Bull. Sci. Technol. Soc. 30(5), 316–327 (2010)

Event Analysis on the 2016 U.S. Presidential Election Using Social Media

Tarrek A. Shaban$^{(\boxtimes)}$, Lindsay Hexter, and Jinho D. Choi

Emory University, Atlanta, GA 30322, USA
tshaban@alumni.emory.edu, {lindsay.hexter,jinho.choi}@emory.edu

Abstract. It is not surprising that social media have played an important role in shaping the political debate during the 2016 presidential election. The dynamics of social media provide a unique opportunity to detect and interpret the pivotal events and scandals of the candidates quantitatively. This paper examines several text-based analysis to determine which topics have a lasting impact on the election for the two main candidates, Clinton and Trump. About 135.5 million tweets are collected over the six weeks prior to the election. From these tweets, topic clustering, keyword extraction, and tweeter analysis are performed to better understand the impact of the events occurred during this period. Our analysis builds upon a social science foundation to provide another avenue for scholars to use in discerning how events detected from social media show the impacts of campaigns as well as campaign the election.

Keywords: Presidential election · Topic clustering · Keyword extraction · Twitter analysis · Social media

1 Introduction

It has been shown that among many events occurring during a campaign, relatively few of them change the course of the election [1]. Scholars these days can accurately predict the two-party national vote even months before the election happens [2,3]. The 2016 U.S. presidential election was not an exception; although Hillary Clinton and Donald Trump each faced an onslaught of potentially debilitating scandals; the popular vote was still predicted accurately before these events transpired [2]. Yet, political pundits endlessly pontificated on how each development would have transformed the campaign.

As discussed, most of the events did not change the fundamental dynamics of the election. This opens the question: Which events, if any, did make changes? We address this by applying natural language processing and information retrieval techniques to a dataset of over 135.5 million tweets collected during the election campaign. To that end, several notable events are interpreted, providing quantitative analysis to a practice which has been primarily qualitative. The assumption underlying this approach is that there is meaningful political discourse occurring on social media. Donald Trump's efficacious use of the platform shows pivotal in his bid for the White House; indeed, Trump's victory over

© Springer International Publishing AG 2017
G.L. Ciampaglia et al. (Eds.): SocInfo 2017, Part I, LNCS 10539, pp. 201–217, 2017.
DOI: 10.1007/978-3-319-67217-5_13

Clinton has cemented his legacy as the first Twitter president. Moreover, social media allow anyone, anywhere to engage in conversations and debates of the sort which could have been reserved for the dinner tables, water-coolers, or other intimate social events. Because of this, social scientists, journalists and businesses alike view social media as measurable conduits of public opinion [4].

In this paper, news articles published during the election are first clustered using vector space models and keywords are extracted from each of the resulting clusters (Sect. 3.2). Additional keywords are extracted from our Twitter corpus to represent the topics of discussions on social media using a novel variation of TF-IDF (Sect. 3.3). Event keywords are then used to identify which tweets are good representatives of those discussions. Both the quantitative and qualitative analyses on the trends and topics of the election by this work (Sect. 3.4) provide a foundation for future exploratory work. Our datasets are publicly available for further research: http://nlp.mathcs.emory.edu/election-2016.

2   Background

2.1   Election Prediction

Election models fall into two broad categories: historical-fundamentals and opinion polling [5]. Historical-fundamental models, often created by social scientists, are statistical models built around a theoretically and historically based presupposition of how the electorate behaves [2]. The best of such models are able to predict the outcome of an election months beforehand [6–10]; in fact, the median model included in *PS*'s symposium perfectly predicted Hillary Clinton's share of the popular vote for the 2016 election [2]. On the other hand, models based on opinion polls will be updated as new survey results are available [11]. Such models do not give weight to anything but the results of polls–which often are conducted by a plethora of organizations [12,13]. Polling is costly [14], but these models are similarly accurate to historical-fundamentals approaches [12].

2.2   Campaigns and Polling

There is ample evidence to suggest that historical-fundamentals models can accurately predict an election months beforehand [2]. Yet, there is a large public demand for daily polls [15,16]. Though there are various explanations for this demand [17,18], our focus is on the utility of polling to campaigns. Since Kennedy's bid for the White House [19], polls have had a profound impact on the way elections are won [20,21]; they allow candidates to make decisions based upon how the public feels. Campaigns now can act upon polls as a source of public sentiment when purposing policies or deciding how to handle an event [21]. Such benefits are available to the victor of the election when they begin to govern [22]. However, this poses an implicit contradiction: how can social scientists accurately predict the outcome of an election so far ahead of time if a candidate's strategy, decided in part using the information provided by polls, can change the course of an election?

Gelman and King [23] resolve this by suggesting that a campaign's primary function is to enlighten voters to their candidate and policy preferences. Scholars, using historical-fundamental approaches, predict what the electorate's preferences ought to be while the candidates work to enlighten voters to these preferences before election day [23,24]. One critical assumption made by Gelman and King [23] is that both campaigns operate in a balanced environment, with similar resources and staff talents. Thus, neither candidate is able to gain a perceivable advantage in voter influence that would drastically change the political scientists' early models [23]. Assuming that two candidates are running balanced campaigns, only an event with a sizable impact on the electorate can cause a break from the election's deterministic outcome (i.e., the historical-fundamentals models predictions) [23,25].

2.3 Event Detection

As Twitter has matured over the past ten years, so have the algorithms used for automatic event detection [26]. There are ample situations when more efficient or reliable event detection would provide a competitive advantage [26–28]. The presidential election, however, is not one. Campaigns, by design, control much of the national attention. Hundreds of news outlets around the country are manually identifying events. To this point, previous studies of event identification have found that events are often associated with a burst in news coverage [29]. In essence, the activity of news media builds a corpus to work with when analyzing tweets surrounding these events.

Once an event is detected, it then becomes necessary to extract indicative information from the tweets. This task, often referred to as document summarization, can be approached in many different ways [30–32]. See [33] for a survey of approaches to text summarization. Often the goal of multi-tweet summarization algorithms is to determine a representative tweet [34]. However, identifying such a tweet does not lend itself as well to accomplishing this papers objective: understanding the prevalence of discussion surrounding campaign events. For this reason, we turn to keyword extraction algorithms; the most famous of which is TF-IDF [35–37]. Section 3.3 discusses issues with TF-IDF as applied to the dataset described in Sect. 3.1.

3 Event Analysis

In order to analyze which events mattered during the election, we collect both tweets and news articles (Sect. 3.1). For the purpose of extracting keywords to describe the topics that those events represent, we then cluster the articles (Sect. 3.2). These keywords allow us to match relevant tweets to the above mentioned clusters. Additionally, we extract a separate set of keywords from tweeter themselves to analyze the discussions happening online (Sect. 3.3). We then use raw count, win and loss terms, and sentiment to provide a lens through which we will discuss the utility of Twitter in understanding a presidential campaign (Sect. 3.4).

3.1 Data Collection

About 135.5 million tweets were collected from Sep. 25th to Nov. 8th, 2016. This number was derived at by feeding Twitter streaming API eight keywords to watch for: {hillary, clinton, @hillaryclinton, donald, trump, @realdonaldtrump, election, and debate}.[1] Upon the collection of each tweet, relaxed string matching was used to determine if the tweet referenced Clinton, Trump, both Clinton and Trump, or neither Clinton nor Trump. Only those which reliably referred to a single candidate were included in our final dataset; 35.7 million tweets discussed Clinton (26.4%), 51.9 million tweets discussed Trump (38.3%), 28.6 million tweets discussed both (21.1%), and the rest did not discuss either of those candidates (14.2%).

To assist with the identification of important events during the campaign, *The New York Times'* (NYT) API was used to build a news dataset.[2] The idea being that these articles could be considered the ground truth for event occurrence. Using the API, we gathered the headline and the lead paragraph for every article published by NYT from Sep. 25th to Nov. 8th, 2016. Only articles which appeared in the news section and politics subsection were included. In total, 760 articles composed our news dataset.

3.2 Event Clustering on the News Dataset

Events in the news dataset are rarely one time occurrences, particularly important ones. Instead, stories regarding any given event are published over time. Thus, a hurdle to understanding events during a political campaign is tracking how and when these stories are discussed over time. Complicating things, is that a relatively small vocabulary is used repeatedly in all of the articles in the news dataset; across the 760 articles, only 6,037 unique words are occurred. This causes a concern as two articles including the same topic words may discuss entirely different events. As an example, take the following two stories from the news dataset, with both articles using topic words *Email* or *F.B.I.* although they talk about two separate events:

> *Emails Warrant No New Action Against Hillary Clinton, F.B.I. Director Says*
> *F.B.I.'s Email Disclosure Broke a Pattern Followed Even This Summer*

In order to counter this issue, a word embedding model, trained by FastText [38] on our Twitter dataset, is used. The word embeddings from this model allows us to represent and compare these articles using the average vectors [39]. To further increase the effectivness of clustering these vectors, we intelligently prune unnecessary words from each article before finding the average vector. We utilize a variant of TF-IDF, term frequency - *probabilistic* inverse document frequency [40], to accomplish this. TF-pIDF was used beacuse, in our tests, TF-IDF was not producing desireable results. In accordance with this, a TF-pIDF score

---

[1] Twitter Streaming API: https://dev.twitter.com/streaming/overview.
[2] New York Times API: https://developer.nytimes.com/archive_api.json.

Table 1. Results of the event clustering on our news dataset. The topics are qualitatively analyzed and the top-3 most frequent words are selected from each cluster. The total column shows the number articles in each cluster, and the purity column shows the number of the articles discussing about the indicated topics over the total (in %).

ID	Topics	Top-3 words	Total	Purity
C1	Debates	*debate, presidential, first*	64	95.31
C2	FBI and emails	*emails, campaign, fbi*	81	87.65
C3	Policies	*tax, obama, bill*	107	91.59
C4	Supreme court	*court, supreme, justices*	33	87.88
C5	Campaigning	*campaign, obama, presidential*	124	85.48
C6	Voting and polls	*voters, states, polls*	80	47.50
C7	Congress	*senate, republicans, house*	81	88.89
C8	Women	*says, debate, women*	70	60.00
C9	Election	*presidential, campaign, women*	120	98.33

was calculated for every word in every article and only those terms under a certain threshold are used to generate the embedding to represent the article. These average vectors were then clustered into nine groups using k-means++ [41]. Note that we also experimented with the agglomerative clustering algorithm; nonetheless, k-means++ consistently produced more reliable results. Table 1 details the nine clusters produced by this algorithm and the top-3 most frequent terms in each cluster:

We manually labeled the topic for each cluster by looking at the top terms extracted from the cluster and the articles which comprise it. When it could be determined that multiple sub-topics are present in a cluster, the broadest topic label is chosen. For example, C_8 includes, among others, articles discussing "Trump's interactions with women", "Accusations about Trump by women," and "Bill Clinton's affairs." Thus, "women" was chosen to be the topic label. The quality of these clusters were also manually evaluated; our attempt at clustering yields the total purity score of 83.55%, which is very promising. It is clear, upon review of the clustering results, that smaller clusters, generally more precise, focus on single events. This observation matches what is suggested by calculating a gap statistic for the dataset: 23. Yet, the results when clustering into a higher number of clusters are varied. Some of the resulting clusters are more precise, but often they tend to cluster based upon one word or a phrase.

Figure 1 shows a broad overview of the topics in each cluster over the time period. For example, C_1 appears only within the days proximate to the presidential and vice-presidential debates. Further, there are peaks in activity the day after each debate. This makes sense as the debates are at night and one would expect a flood of news coverage the following day. As expected, clusters broader in scope are clearly less indicative of particular events occurrence. C_7 demonstrates this. Articles discussing "congress" and "congressional elections" are scattered. On the other hand, C_4 about the "Supreme Court" is highly indicative of important events, which are shown in the very specific dates.

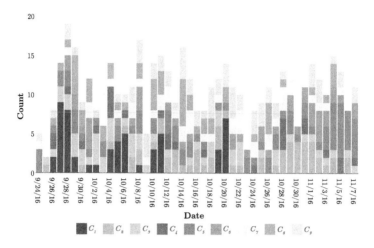

Fig. 1. The number of articles per day for each of the clusters detailed by Table 1. (Color figure online)

3.3 Keyword Extraction on the Twitter Dataset

Using the keywords (top-3 most frequent words) extracted from the news dataset alone to determine which events matter on a given day fall short. The domain from which these keywords have been extracted is one, particularly at the highest levels such as NYT, where word choices matter. The vernacular of journalists reflects this. Moreover, there are many events which occur that a reputable news source simply would not report on (e.g., fake news) [42]. Therefore, another source of keywords is required in order to reflect the events occurring in the discussions on social media.

The traditional approach to quantify the importance of words is TF-IDF [37]. However, this approach fails here due to the unique composition of the Twitter dataset. Specifically, many words in this dataset, like "hillary," appear with such a high frequency that the inverse document frequency (IDF) fails at normalizing their scores. In order to demonstrate this issue, Fig. 2 shows the TF-IDF scores for "hillary" and "fbi." As is apparent, the scores for "hillary" dominates those for "fbi," even on the Oct. 28th when it was revealed that the FBI director had sent a letter to Congress. There was a near unanimous consensus that this event was remarkably important as it threw Clinton's bid for the White House into disarray. Because our goal is for words to only spike on days they are uniquely important, another measurement is needed to draw clearer trends.

We propose a new weighting scheme based on TF. This scheme, weighted logarithmic term frequency (wTF), works as it normalizes the count of each term t by aTF$_t$ the average frequency of the term t across all D days. wTF is calculated for each term t on each day d as follows:

$$w\text{TF}_{t,d} = \log_2 \frac{\text{TF}_{t,d}}{a\text{TF}_t} \qquad \text{where} \qquad a\text{TF}_t = \frac{\sum_{n=1}^{D} \text{TF}_{t,d_n}}{D} \qquad (1)$$

Figure 2(b) demonstrates the advantage of wTF to calculate the keyword scores over TF-IDF; "hillary" shows no clear trend whereas "fbi" shows clear spikes on certain days. This new scoring mechanism allows useful keywords to be selected from tweets each day.

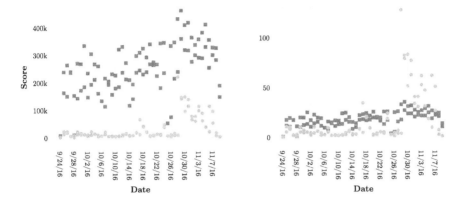

Fig. 2. (a) TF-IDF scores for the terms "hillary" (blue squares) and "fbi" (green circles). (b) The same graph but with measured with wTF. (Color figure online)

However, an additional component is required before the selected keywords are meaningful. Because wTF treats the growth as a scalar, a term that is used, on average, 10 times a day and is mentioned 10^3 times suddenly would have a similar wTF as a term which, on average, is used 10^3 times a day seeing a spike to 10^5 times. With this in mind, a filter is required before running wTF to remove words with a low count. This hyperparameter allows one to tune the algorithm in terms of sensitivity to outside noise. The tweets are divided into separate documents by date, and the top-10 keywords based upon their wTF scores are selected from each day. Stop words, variations on the candidates' names, and any word which appears more than 80% and less than the max term each day are excluded from the keyword selection. Our qualitative review of the extracted keywords indicates that they are meaningful and aligned with the events.

3.4   Overview of Twitter Trends

With the sucessful extraction of keywords from the Twitter dataset (Sect. 3.3) we turn our attention to associating tweets with topics generated when clustering the news dataset. To achieve this, the keywords extracted from each day are mapped to the news articles published that day. We perform this mapping with the normalized Damerau-Levenshtein distance between the keyword and each word in the article [43,44] and the cosine similarity between them using the FastText model discussed a priori. If either measurement provides an approximate match, the tweet is mapped to the article. Thus, each tweet can be linked to a topic as long that it matches to an article.

Table 2. Examples of the mapping between the twitter keywords and the news articles.

Date	Tweet keywords	News articles
10/12	catholics, leaked, camp, wikileaks, campaign	WikiLeaks emails appear to show Clinton spokes-woman joking about Catholics and evangelicals
10/29	weiner, comey, huma, investigation, fbi, emails	FBI director Comey faces fury for cryptic letter about Clinton email inquiry
10/08	apology, trumptapes, lewd, comments, billy, statement	Donald Trump apology caps day of outrage over lewd tape
10/13	allegations, michelle, assault, sexual, women, obama	Michelle Obama's speech on Donald Trump's alleged treatment of women

The implicit assumption to our approach is that if a tweet uses similar vocabulary to an article, it is likely to discuss the same topic. More than just linking tweets to topics, the key to this paper's contribution is performing several natural language processing and information retrieval techniques to classify and analyze these tweets. Following the example set by [45–47], the raw count of tweets and sentiment analysis are used to understand opinion on Twitter; Projects like Viz 2016 have provided a platform to visualize live tweet statistics during the election [48]. This paper extends such approaches by pairing them with keyword extraction and event clustering to understand how the events impacted the 2016 election cycle.

Daily Volume of Tweets. Previous scholarship has indicated that the volume of activity on Twitter is a good indicator of polling and event detection [49]. Figure 3 displays the quantity of tweets discussing each canidate over time. There are two clear spikes when looking at Clinton's count: Oct. 12th and Oct. 29th. We can look to the keywords extracted in Sect. 3.3 to determine what events of importance occured those days. Table 2 lists the top keywords for Clinton on Oct. 12th and Oct. 29th. These make it clear that on Oct. 12th attention was on the WikiLeaks' dumps of Clinton's emails. Similarly, on Oct. 29th, the keywords extracted are all related to the new of Comey sending a letter to Congress, which occured the previous day. Looking back at the campaign, these events were two of the most recognizable and discussed scandals regarding Clinton.

Trump's count shows a similarly convincing match to what an astute observer of politics would expect. Looking at Fig. 3 two largest spikes in volume for Trump are on Oct. 8th and on Oct. 13th. The first of these was, by far, the largest single day increase in tweet count for either canidate during the period of collection. Keywords extracted that day point to the lewd tapes published by the Washington Post as the motivating event. The spike in tweets on Oct. 13th points to a different event of the same type: Trump's behavior with women. In particular, the keywords indicate that it was Michelle Obama's speech that day at a Clinton campaign rally which captured Twitter's attention.

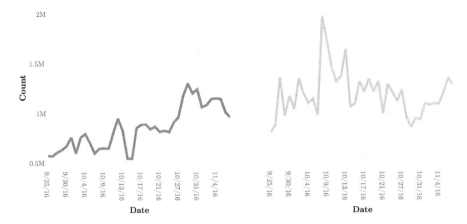

Fig. 3. Raw counts of tweets for Clinton (left) and Trump (right) in our dataset.

Sentiment Classification of Tweets. To perform sentiment analysis on the tweets, a convolutional neural network model with lexicon embeddings by Shin et al. was utilized, which has shown the state-of-the-art accuracy on tweets [50].

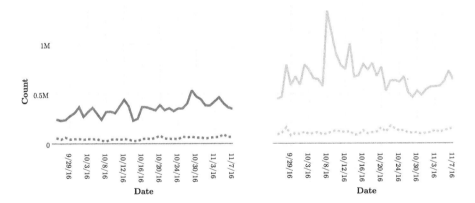

Fig. 4. The volume of negative tweets (solid line) and positive tweets (dashed line) discussing Clinton (left) and Trump (right) during the collection period.

Using this model, all of the 135.5 million tweets are classified as positive, neutral, or negative. Starting with Clinton's sentiment in Fig. 4, there is a conspicuous closeness between the negative sentiment and volume of tweets. In fact, there is a 91.3% Pearson correlation between Clinton's negative sentiment and raw tweet counts. Trump's correlation is 96.1%. The implication of this is intuitive: When a canidate is being talked about on Twitter, it is likly due to a negative event. To put it another way, people focus on the negative.

However, when examined closely, it becomes clear this may not be the case. The correlation between normalized negative sentiment of either canidate and the volume of tweets about them is less than 50% for both Clinton and Trump. One would expect that this would have yielded results similar to the straight correlation between the voume of tweets and volume of negative tweets. During the end of the campaign season, Clinton saw her highest volume of tweets. Moreover, she also saw the highest percentage of objective tweets as well during this time period. We examined this relationship and found a 71.9% correlation between normalized objective count and total tweet count for Clinton. Yet, this did not hold up when applied to Trump's counts, resulting in a correlation of -37.5%.

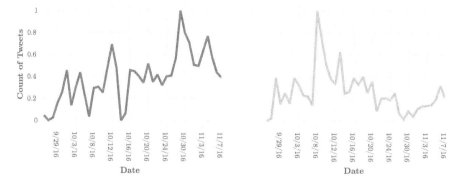

Fig. 5. Normalized volume of negative tweets for Clinton (left) and Trump (right)

To investigate this irregularity, we look to Fig. 5 which shows the normalized negative sentiment without including objective tweets. This shows significently diffrent results, ones more in line with expectations, than the previous correlations suggested. It is clear that when there is a peak in tweet count, there is generally an accompanying peak in negative sentiment which follows it. For example, compare the max negative sentiment for Clinton in Fig. 5 with that observed in Fig. 3. They both appear on October 29th. One possible explaination for the rise in objective tweets on days of high volume (*e.g.* potentially important events) is that the type of tweet's which appear those days–shared news articles and the like–might use words that are more likly to be objective.

Though neither sentiment nor volume alone can give the full picture of an event's importance, taken together they provide a good approximation. We now can apply these measures of conversation to the event clusters through the tweet linking described above; Fig. 6 allows us to explore the results of this application for two clusters: C_1 and C_2. Both of which suggest promising results for those clusters with clear, focused topics and will be discussed in Sect. 4.

Yet, we have not yet addressed an assumption underlying this discussion: The increase in negative sentiment on Twitter a major event is a reliable indicator

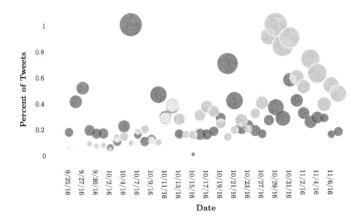

Fig. 6. The percentage of tweets identified as a member of the clusters C_1 (blue) and C_2 (orange) from Table 1. The size of each point is proportional to the normalized count of tweets that are classified as negative. (Color figure online)

of how individuals are responding to the event. Admittedly, it is not possible to refute this point entirely within the parameters of the current study. This being said, there are a few indications that this is not the case. The most convincing of which is that the increases in negative sentiment are logical. When discussion keywords which indicate a scandal that plagued one of the candidates surface, there is generally a corresponding rise in negative sentiment. Moreover, the jumps in sentiment are compartmentalized among the article clusters. When the tweets matched with C_1's keywords indicate a jump in negative sentiment on Oct. 5th, C_2's sentiment did not follow.

Analysis of Win and Loss Terms. Election rhetoric often focuses around which candidate is winning or losing. For this reason, it only feels natural to also count how many tweets include words similar to "win" and "lose". This concept is inspired by the use of emoji for determining the sentiment of a tweet [51]. To better account for variations in terminology, a set of win/loss words is extracted from the WordNet synsets [52]. Each tweet is then matched against this set to count how many tweets per candidate include win/loss terms.

Neither Clinton nor Trump's win/loss counts in Fig. 7 indicate the same connection to volume as sentiment does. Nevertheless, this does not discount the value of win and loss counts for event analysis. In certain situations, the increase of win or loss count is a signal to an important shift in discussions.

Let us compare Clinton's small spike in loss counts on Oct. 4th with Trump's spike on Oct. 8th. In the case of Clinton's loss increase, there is no clear event that caused this spike. A few event which the keywords point to that day use the loss terms prominently, but does not seem indicative of widespread discussions about a Clinton's loss. However, the Oct. 8th event, as previously discussed, is

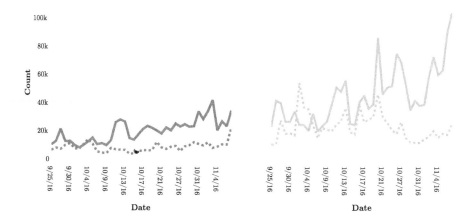

Fig. 7. The usage volume of *win* terms (solid lines) and *loss* terms (dotted lines) for Clinton (left) and Trump (right).

accompanied by a tremendous increase in both raw count and negative sentiment regarding Trump. Additionally, a qualitative understanding of the event would indicate that there was speculation by both Democratic and Republican leaders that Trump might lose after the scandal. Based upon this, it is reasonable to believe that this spike is meaningful in understanding the publics discussions surrounding Trump at the time.

4   Discussion

There are many theories as to why Clinton lost the election to Trump. She was seen as the front-runner by many leading into the final strech of the election. Because of this, we beleive the events and scandals surrounding Clinton are more important to investigate than those surrounding Trump. Therefore, this section will discuss two of the major events that followed the Democratic standard bearer during the 2016 election.

4.1   Presidential Election Debates

It is only natural to begin our discussion around the 2016 election with the presidential debates. Following the first debate, Clinton's poll numbers steadily increased. This was not by chance; by all accounts, Clinton handily bested Trump on stage at Hofstra University while 84 million Americans watched at home.[3] The following are three headlines from the news dataset published by NYT about the first presidential debate:

---

[3] See sielsen's ratings: http://www.nielsen.com/us/en/insights/news/2016/first-presi dential-debate-of-2016-draws-84-million-viewers.html.

Debate Takeaways: Hillary Clinton Digs In and Prevails
Suburban Women Find Little to Like in Donald Trumps Debate Performance
After a Disappointing Debate, Donald Trump Goes on the Attack

Clinton's clear victory, along with her coresponding rise in opinion polling, might indicate that the debate caused some voters to revaluate their support for Trump in favor of Clinton. Such an outcome would conform to Gelman and King's [23] enlightenment model of campaigns discussed in Sect. 2.

Now, let us turn our attention to the data collected from Twitter. Figure 8 shows the normalized volume of positive tweets discussing Clinton over time. In addition, Fig. 8 also includes annotations to mark debate dates to help with our analysis. Notice that Clinton recieves a bump in positive sentiment, as expected, following the first debate. Moreover, the positive discussion of Clinton on Twitter spikes after each of the three debates. This phenomina is not unexpected as Clinton performed well in all three presidential debates.

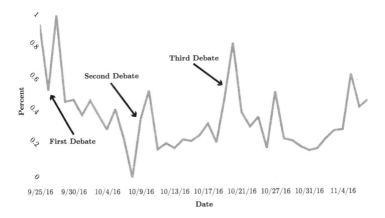

Fig. 8. The normalized volume of positive tweets discussing clinton annotated with debate dates

Seeing that a discernable pattern in conversation on Twitter can be seen in Fig. 8 surrounding the debates, we thusly turn our attention to understanding the importance of each debate. First we can look to the duration of the conversation on Twitter surrounding each debate. In other words, compare how long debate-related terms were continued to be extracted as keywords. Following the first debate, related keywords appeared for three nights: 9/26, 9/27, 9/28. This measure was fell to one night for both the second and third debates.

Consquently, this provides evidence to support the theory that the first debate was the focus of conversation on Twitter longer than either of the other two debates and, thus, more important. What is more, Silver's polling model [12] highlights that both the second and third debate had substaintily less impact on the Clinton's standing in the race. To demonstrate this, compare the increase in Clinton's two-party support between the first debate and the second debate (2.63%) and the second debate and the third debate (0.99%) [12]. All things considered, it is clear that the first debate was far more impactful on the election than either of the other debates.

4.2 Clinton's Email Related Scandals

During the 2016 election campaign, Clinton faced two email related scandals: the Wikileaks' email dumps about her campaign, and the FBI investigation into her use of a private email server as Secretary of State. As discussed in Sect. 3.2 news stories about both scandals were generally clustered into C_2. Wikileaks, as the first of these, is a constant source of conversation on Twitter about Clinton. In fact, on more than 50% of the days where tweets were collected, a Wikileaks related term was one of the top-6 keywords extracted using wTF. Yet, based upon a review of NYT, only three articles referred to Wikileaks by name, and only a handful more reported on the events connected to said keywords. One way to explain this is by looking at NYT reporting bias [53]. NYT tends to both not report on unverifiable events (*i.e.* fake news) and favor the liberal position in its coverage [42,53]. Many of the events indicated by the Wikileaks related keywords are examples of fake news and are, without exception, negative for Clinton [42]. Under these circumstances, it is both understandable and expected that NYT did not publish more stories regarding the Wikileaks events. We raise this point to highlight the need for multiple sources to serve as refrence data for studies into events discussed on social media.

Regardless of the fact that many of these events were fake news, let us examine the Twitter trends to understand how the conversations might reflect the importance of events. Identifying the leaks which were most harmful to clinton may be accomplished by examining the days when the negative sentiment surrounding Clinton reaches a peak and a Wikileaks related keyword is extracted from the twitter corpus. The challenge to this methodology is the potential for false positives. However, the scores for the subset of Tweets which relates to C_2 provide an indication of importance. Leading up to Comeys letter sent to Congress the morning of October 28th, there were three distinct peaks: October 12th, October 17th, and October 27th. Interestingly enough, the Wikileaks related events on these three days were veridical news. Moreover, these stories were wildly reported on by mainstream media outlets instead of the fringe sites which comment on the fake news amid the Wikileaks dumps. This resulted in these stories being discussed more on Twitter, as seen in Fig. 3.

The largest spike in Fig. 6 occurred on October 28th. This coincided with Jim Comey's letter to Congress regarding the Clinton email investigation. Based upon the results in Fig. 6, this was likely the most important event in this cluster. Referencing Fig. 3, it is also clear that this event propagated the most conversation about Clinton –another indicator to the significance of the event. Additionally, the sentiment seen in Fig. 5 contiunes this trend; the day after Comey sent his letter had the highest normalized negative sentiment. What seems likley, looking at the reaction on Twitter to this event and the polling information from Silver's model, is that Comey's letter caused Clinton to lose much of the additional support gained through the debates.

5   Conclusion

In this paper, we give a through event analysis using news and social media. For our experiments, we create two datasets by collecting news articles and tweets. Our event clustering gives groups of articles associated with certain topics, which show the trendlines of these topics over time. Our keyword extraction technique using weighted log frequency shows extrodinary promise to capture topic words among tweets given any day during the election. Analyses of the data captured from Twitter showed that the first debate seemed to be more important than either of the others, and gave Clinton a lead in the polls. A lead which she shed in the fallout of Comey's letter to Congress. Without a doubt, there are many questions still yet to answer regarding the final weeks of the 2016 election, and on the whole, this research indicates that Twitter can provide vital clues to answering these questions.

References

1. Shaw, D.R.: A study of presidential campaign event effects from 1952 to 1992. J. Polit. **61**(2), 387–422 (1999)
2. Campbell, J.E., Norpoth, H., Abramowitz, A.I., Lewis-Beck, M.S., Tien, C., Erikson, R.S., Wlezien, C., Lockerbie, B., Holbrook, T.M., Jerôme, B., Jerôme-Speziari, V., Graefe, A., Armstrong, J.S., Jones, R.J., Cuzán, A.G.: Recap of the 2016 election forecasts. PS: Polit. Sci. Polit. **50**(2), 331–338 (2017)
3. Lewis-Beck, M.S., Stegmaier, M.: US presidential election forecasting. PS: Polit. Sci. Polit. **47**(2), 284–288 (2014)
4. Clark, T.S., Staton, J.K., Wang, Y., Agichtein, E.: Using Twitter to study public discourse in the wake of judicial decisions: public reactions to the supreme court's same-sex marriage cases (2014)
5. Leigh, A., Wolfers, J.: Competing approaches to forecasting elections: economic models, opinion polling and prediction markets. Econ. Rec. **82**(258), 325–340 (2006)
6. Abramowitz, A.I.: An improved model for predicting presidential election outcomes. PS: Polit. Sci. Polit. **21**(4), 843–847 (1988)
7. Campbell, J.E., Wink, K.A.: Trial-heat forecasts of the presidential vote. Am. Polit. Q. **18**(3), 251–269 (1990)
8. Campbell, J.E., Cherry, L.L., Wink, K.A.: The convention bump. Am. Polit. Q. **20**(3), 287–307 (1992)
9. Norpoth, H., Bednarczuk, M.: History and primary: the Obama re-election. In: APSA 2012 Annual Meeting Paper, September 2012
10. Abramowitz, A.: Forecasting in a polarized era: the time for change model and the 2012 presidential election. PS: Polit. Sci. Polit. **45**(4), 618–619 (2012)
11. Hillygus, D.S.: The evolution of election polling in the united states. Public Opin. Q. **75**(5), 962–981 (2011)
12. Silver, N.: Who will win the presidency? (2016)

13. Gollin, A.E.: Polling and the news media. Public Opin. Q. **51**(part 2: Supplement: 50th Anniversary Issue), S86 (1987)
14. Tenpas, K.D., McCann, J.A.: Testing the permanence of the permanent campaign: an analysis of presidential polling expenditures, 1977–2002. Public Opin. Q. **71**(3), 349–366 (2007)
15. Iyengar, S., Norpoth, H., Hahn, K.S.: Consumer demand for election news: the horserace sells. J. Polit. **66**(1), 157–175 (2004)
16. Rosenstiel, T.: Political polling and the new media culture: a case of more being less. Public Opin. Q. **69**(5), 698–715 (2005)
17. Miller, P.R., Conover, P.J.: Red and blue states of mind. Polit. Res. Q. **68**(2), 225–239 (2015)
18. Harris, L.: Election polling and research. Public Opin. Q. **21**(1, Anniversary Issue Devoted to Twenty Years of Public Opinion Research), 108 (1957)
19. Jacobs, L.R., Shapiro, R.Y.: Issues, candidate image, and priming: the use of private polls in Kennedy's 1960 presidential campaign. Am. Polit. Sci. Rev. **88**(3), 527–540 (1994)
20. King, R., Schnitzer, M.: Contemporary use of private political polling. Public Opin. Q. **32**(3), 431 (1968)
21. Jacobs, L.R.: Polling politics, media, and election campaigns. Public Opin. Q. **69**(5), 635–641 (2005)
22. Jacobs, L.R., Shapiro, R.Y.: The rise of presidential polling: the nixon white house in historical perspective. Public Opin. Q. **59**(2), 163 (1995)
23. Gelman, A., King, G.: Why are American presidential election campaign polls so variable when votes are so predictable? Br. J. Polit. Sci. **23**(4), 409 (1993)
24. Arceneaux, K.: Do campaigns help voters learn? A cross-national analysis. Br. J. Polit. Sci. **36**(1), 159 (2005)
25. Wlezien, C., Erikson, R.S.: The timeline of presidential election campaigns. J. Polit. **64**(4), 969–993 (2002)
26. Atefeh, F., Khreich, W.: A survey of techniques for event detection in Twitter. Comput. Intell. **31**(1), 132–164 (2013)
27. Ivan, C., Moldovan, A.: Twitrends: a real time trending topics detection system for Twitter social network. Int. J. Comput. Appl. **152**(4), 16–25 (2016)
28. Becker, H., Naaman, M., Gravano, L.: Beyond trending topics: real-world event identification on Twitter. In: ICWSM, vol. 11, pp. 438–441 (2011)
29. Yang, Y., Pierce, T., Carbonell, J.: A study of retrospective and on-line event detection. In: Proceedings of the 21st Annual International ACM SIGIR Conference on Research and Development in Information Retrieval - SIGIR 1998. ACM Press (1998)
30. Conroy, J.M., O'leary, D.P.: Text summarization via hidden Markov models. In: Proceedings of the 24th Annual International ACM SIGIR Conference on Research and Development in Information Retrieval - SIGIR 2001. ACM Press (2001)
31. Becker, H., Naaman, M., Gravano, L.: Selecting quality Twitter content for events. In: ICWSM 2011 (2011)
32. Yajuan, D., Zhimin, C., Furu, W., Ming, Z., Shum, H.Y.: Twitter topic summarization by ranking tweets using social influence and content quality. In: Proceedings of the 24th International Conference on Computational Linguistics, pp. 763–780 (2012)
33. Nenkova, A., McKeown, K.: A survey of text summarization techniques. In: Aggarwal, C., Zhai, C. (eds.) Mining Text Data, pp. 43–76. Springer, Boston (2012). doi:10.1007/978-1-4614-3223-4_3

34. Xu, W., Grishman, R., Meyers, A., Ritter, A.: A preliminary study of tweet summarization using information extraction. In: NAACL 2013, p. 20 (2013)
35. Matsuo, Y., Ishizuka, M.: Keyword extraction from a single document using word co-occurrence statistical information. Int. J. Artif. Intell. Tools **13**(1), 157–169 (2004)
36. Mishra, A., Vishwakarma, S.: Analysis of TF-IDF model and its variant for document retrieval. In: 2015 International Conference on Computational Intelligence and Communication Networks (CICN). IEEE, December 2015
37. Ramos, J.: Using TF-IDF to determine word relevance in document queries. In: Proceedings of the First Instructional Conference on Machine Learning (2003)
38. Bojanowski, P., Grave, E., Joulin, A., Mikolov, T.: Enriching word vectors with subword information. arXiv preprint arXiv:1607.04606 (2016)
39. Campr, M., Ježek, K.: Comparing semantic models for evaluating automatic document summarization. In: Král, P., Matoušek, V. (eds.) TSD 2015. LNCS, vol. 9302, pp. 252–260. Springer, Cham (2015). doi:10.1007/978-3-319-24033-6_29
40. Polettini, N.: The vector space model in information retrieval-term weighting problem. Entropy 1–9 (2004)
41. Arthur, D., Vassilvitskii, S.: k-means++: the advantages of careful seeding. In: Proceedings of the Eighteenth Annual ACM-SIAM Symposium on Discrete Algorithms, pp. 1027–1035. Society for Industrial and Applied Mathematics (2007)
42. Allcott, H.: Social Media and Fake News in the 2016 Election (2017)
43. Levenshtein, V.I.: Binary codes capable of correcting deletions, insertions and reversals. In: Soviet Physics Doklady, vol. 10 (1966)
44. Damerau, F.J.: A technique for computer detection and correction of spelling errors. Commun. ACM **7**(3), 171–176 (1964)
45. Bermingham, A., Smeaton, A.F.: On using Twitter to Monitor Political Sentiment and Predict Election Results (2011)
46. O'Connor, B., Balasubramanyan, R., Routledge, B.R., Smith, N.A.: From tweets to polls: linking text sentiment to public opinion time series. In: ICWSM 2011, pp. 122–129 (2010)
47. Marchetti-Bowick, M., Chambers, N.: Learning for microblogs with distant supervision: political forecasting with Twitter. In: Proceedings of the 13th Conference of the European Chapter of the Association for Computational Linguistics, pp. 603–612. Association for Computational Linguistics (2012)
48. Viz 2016 (2015)
49. Tumasjan, A., Sprenger, T.O., Sandner, P.G., Welpe, I.M.: Predicting elections with twitter: what 140 characters reveal about political sentiment. ICWSM **10**(1), 178–185 (2010)
50. Shin, B., Lee, T., Choi, J.D.: Lexicon integrated CNN models with attention for sentiment analysis. In: Proceedings of the EMNLP Workshop on Computational Approaches to Subjectivity, Sentiment and Social Media Analysis, WASSA 2017 (2017)
51. Novak, P.K., Smailović, J., Sluban, B., Mozetič, I.: Sentiment of emojis. PLoS ONE **10**(12), e0144296 (2015)
52. Kilgarriff, A., Fellbaum, C.: WordNet: An Electronic Lexical Database, vol. 76. JSTOR, September 2000
53. Xiang, Y., Sarvary, M.: News consumption and media bias. Mark. Sci. **26**(5), 611–628 (2007)

Badly Evolved? Exploring Long-Surviving Suspicious Users on Twitter

Majid Alfifi[(⊠)] and James Caverlee

Department of Computer Science and Engineering, Texas A&M University,
College Station, TX, USA
{alfifi,caverlee}@tamu.edu

Abstract. We study the behavior of long-lived eventually suspended accounts in social media through a comprehensive investigation of Arabic Twitter. With a threefold study of (i) the content these accounts post; (ii) the evolution of their linguistic patterns; and (iii) their activity evolution, we compare long-lived users versus short-lived, legitimate, and pro-ISIS users. We find that these long-lived accounts – though trying to appear normal – do exhibit significantly different behaviors from both normal and other suspended users. We additionally identify temporal changes and assess their value in supporting discovery of these accounts and find out that most accounts have actually being "hiding in plain sight" and are detectable early in their lifetime. Finally, we successfully apply our findings to address a series of classification tasks, most notably to determine whether a given account is a long-surviving account.

1 Introduction

Social media enables an unprecedented shift in how we communicate to others and how we consume content. And yet, this change has also enabled innovative new methods to manipulate at scale: examples include spreading propaganda and misinformation [18,19], polluting information streams with spam [1,10], and strategically distracting populations by fabricating social media posts [13,23]. For example, [6] found that politically motivated individuals provoked interaction by injecting partisan content into information streams whose primary audience consists of ideologically-opposed users.

While these suspicious efforts can affect social media users worldwide, of special importance is their impact in Arabic social media. The past few years have seen social media as an effective tool for facilitating uprisings and enticing dissent in the Middle East [2,16,21]. The embrace of social media in the region has made it a battle ground for ISIS and similar groups and existing regimes, all spreading propaganda, recruiting sympathizers, and even undermining rivals [2]. Of these different movements, what do they post? How do they evolve? Do they engage in particular strategies to evade detection?

Towards tackling these questions, we focus in this paper on an initial investigation into the behaviors of a special type of users in Arabic social media – long-surviving content polluters who engage in pro-terrorism, spam, and other negative behaviors. Specifically, we analyze all of Arabic Twitter from 2015 (Fig. 1)

© Springer International Publishing AG 2017
G.L. Ciampaglia et al. (Eds.): SocInfo 2017, Part I, LNCS 10539, pp. 218–233, 2017.
DOI: 10.1007/978-3-319-67217-5_14

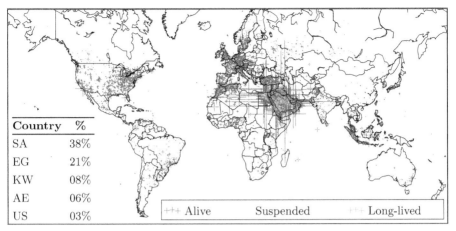

Dataset	Size
Tweets	9,285,246,636
Accounts	26,711,275
Tweets from Suspended Accounts	1,960,160,536
Suspended Accounts	6,175,113

Fig. 1. Arabic tweets in 2015. 21% of the tweets were generated by eventually suspended accounts which represent 23% of all active accounts in 2015.

to identify the complete set of active[1] long-surviving content polluters, totaling 17,909 accounts and 42,630,795 tweets. A previous work [15] manually identified 816 spam accounts on Twitter, monitored them until later suspended, and then explored effective features for detecting such long-surviving accounts. Our work takes a different approach as we already have at our disposal all Arabic tweets generated in 2015, including those of suspended accounts, and therefore can look back at long-surviving accounts in retrospect, enabling us to study long-surviving accounts at a much larger scale taking into considerations different types of accounts.

In contrast to many efforts that have focused on short-lived accounts engaging in "extreme" (and easily detectable behavior) [10,11,20,24], our interest is on the activities and behaviors of long-lived accounts. Do these accounts always engage in bad behaviors over time? Or do they begin as somewhat legitimate accounts before evolving into bad ones? Is the rate of change gradual? Or do we observe abrupt changes?

Hence, we conduct a threefold study of these long-lived accounts to complement existing studies of traditional anti-spam efforts [14,24,26]: (i) first, we study the content of what these accounts post, finding multiple classes of account types including traditional spammers, pro-ISIS groups, and other politically-motivated

---

[1] We consider an account to be active and long-surviving if it had tweeted at least once on at least six different months in 2015.

groups; (ii) second, we analyze the evolution of linguistic patterns of these accounts – including an examination of their self-similarity and cross-entropy versus the rest of Arabic Twitter; (iii) third, we examine the activity evolution of these users, to explore their differences with legitimate and short-lived accounts. Finally, we apply our findings to address several classification tasks about the different groups most notably determining if an account is a long-surviving account.

2   Data and Preliminary Analysis

We obtain a large dataset of 9.3 billion tweets (Fig. 1) representing all tweets generated in the Arabic language in 2015 through a private full access to the Twitter Firehose. Of these 9.3 billion tweets, about 2 billion were from suspended accounts. Using all the geotagged tweets in our dataset as a proxy to estimate the level of contribution from different regions in the world, we see in Fig. 1 that most tweets were generated from the Middle East and Africa, but with a global footprint. We find that only 50% of the accounts are suspended after their first tweet (Fig. 2a), with many accounts posting 100s and even 1000s of tweets. This stands in contrast to previous studies [24], reported in 2011, finding 77% of Twitter spam accounts being suspended within a day of their first tweet. Spammers might have developed more sophisticated methods over time or maybe Twitter spam control isn't as efficient on Arabic Twitter although we notice a dramatic improvement over time in fighting spam (Fig. 3).

Moreover, we find that while 90% of spam accounts are suspended within 40 days of their creation (Fig. 2b), a large group of accounts live much longer, in some cases for years.

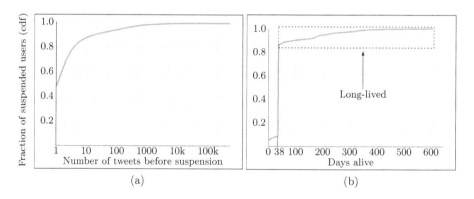

Fig. 2. Lifespan of suspended accounts. (a) 50% of accounts are suspended after their first tweet, but many accounts post 100s and even 1000s of tweets. While most accounts get suspended within 38 days of creation (b), 10% of accounts live for more than 40 days with some for years.

To support our study of the characteristics of such long-lived (but ultimately suspended) accounts, we focus on four types of users extracted from this large dataset:

Suspended Long-Lived Accounts (Long-Lived): We first identify our base set of accounts who lived for at least six months, were active, and were ultimately suspended. We focus on accounts that were created in 2015 and tweeted in at least six different months. In total, we identify 17,909 long-lived accounts who created 42,630,795 tweets.

Suspended Short-Lived Accounts (Short-Lived): To complement this collection of long-lived accounts, we identify an equal-size randomly sampled set of 17,909 short-lived accounts. We consider a short-lived account to be one that lived for 30 days or less in 2015 before being suspended. In total, these randomly sampled accounts generated 14,129,870 tweets.

Legitimate Accounts (Legit): In contrast to these two collections of suspended accounts, we identify a set of legitimate accounts as a point of comparison. We randomly sample 17,909 accounts from all legitimate accounts that were created in 2015 and were still active in November 2016. We further require these accounts to have stopped tweeting the last two months in our dataset as a potential end-of-life signal. This latter restriction is useful when we later compare the evolution of different groups from birth to death. These legitimate accounts posted 9,772,176 tweets.

ISIS-Related Accounts (ISIS): Finally, we identify a collection of ISIS accounts, based on the Anonymous group initiative called LuckyTroll: this effort originally identified more than 25,000 ISIS sympathizers and supporters through crowdsourced reporting[2]. We only use accounts that have actually been suspended by Twitter, indicating multiple users have reported those accounts. Similar to other groups, we consider ISIS accounts that were born in 2015 and were suspended before 2016. This leaves us with 17,518 ISIS accounts responsible for 11,849,065 tweets[3]. We find only 7 common accounts between this ISIS dataset and long-surviving accounts mainly because we use all ISIS accounts without further filtering by level of activity and length of life. A previous work [9] used this same ISIS users dataset but, due to Twitter limitations, they were only able to recover 10% of their tweets through the Truthy project at Indiana University [8]. By contrast, in this work we were able to recover 100% of the content they generated in 2015 with our private full access to the Twitter Firehose.

Having considered all active long-lived accounts we decided to sample same-size sets of the much larger sets of legit and short-lived accounts for manageability and to avoid class imbalance when we later explore automatic detection of long-lived accounts.

---

[2] The website hosting this dataset has been taken offline but we were able to recover accounts from http://archive.is/A6f3L.

[3] Contact the first author for access to the ISIS dataset.

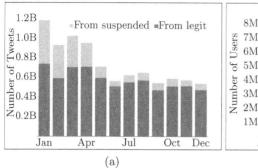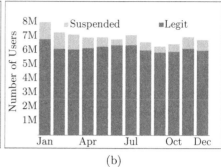

(a)   (b)

Fig. 3. Twitter cracks down on spam in 2015 resulting in 50% reduction in content (a) while roughly maintaining the same number of monthly active users (b).

3   Investigation

Given these four distinct user groups, we focus here on the behaviors of long-lived suspended accounts.

3.1   What Do Long-Lived Accounts Post?

We begin by examining the types of long-lived accounts through an application of LDA [3] over all the tweets posted by these accounts. With the help of a native Arabic speaker on the team, we identify six popular account types among these long-lived accounts, as illustrated in Table 1. We additionally highlight the potential violation of Twitter rules after inspecting accounts in each group[4]. We see that the most popular group is dominated by ostensibly legitimate topics like sports and news, while also inserting low-quality spam URLs. Similarly, the fourth group (e.g., Muhammed, Prophet) posts innocuous religious posts while also inserting spam URLs. The second group of accounts focuses on account manipulation, by posting offers for buying retweets and followers. In an interesting direction, we do find multiple groups of accounts engaged in potentially politically motivated posts: the third group (e.g., ISIS, Syria, Aleppo) is pro-ISIS; from inspection these accounts appear to have been suspended for promoting terrorism. The sixth group (e.g., Saudi, support, Yemen) posts about the Saudi-Yemen war from a pro-Saudi perspective. Finally, we find the fifth group (e.g., retweet, clips, bypass) posts mainly adult content. These findings indicate that long-lived accounts are diverse, with many different goals.

We further apply LDA to each month's tweets posted by these accounts. We find consistent recurring topics over the months giving a first hint that long-lived accounts exhibit the same behavior throughout their lifetime but have managed to evade detection. This finding suggests that these accounts have not engaged in legitimate behavior for most of their lives before engaging in some "extreme" behavior (and being suspended).

---

[4] https://support.twitter.com/articles/18311-the-twitter-rules.

Table 1. LDA topics for long-lived suspended accounts.

#	Keywords	English Translation	Potential Violation	%
1	شاهد، الخبر، مدريد، الهلال مباراة، ريال، الاتحاد، برشلونة	watch, News, Real Madrid, Al-Hilal, match, Ittihad, Barcelona	Spam	37%
2	للبيع، الف، تبادل، للطلب رتويت، واتس، اليوم، الرياض	For sale, thousand, exchange, orders, retweet, WhatsApp, today, Riyadh	Selling or purchasing account interactions	19%
3	الدولة، جبهة، الشيخ، النصرة سوريا، حلب، داعش، الشام	State, Front, Sheikh, Nusrah Syria, Aleppo, Daesh(ISIS), Levant	Promoting terrorism	12%
4	وسلم، صلى، محمد، النبي قروب، البخاري، مسلم، رسول	Peace, pray, Muhammed, Prophet, group, Bukhari, Muslim, Messenger	Spam	11%
5	محارم، افلام، الحجب، للمشاهده خاص، تتناك، بنت، عرض	Incest, clips, blocked, watch private, fucked, girl, show	Graphic content	11%
6	السعودية، دعم، اليمن، ايران الداخلية، الرياض، الحوثيين، الجنوب	Saudi, support, Yemen, Iran, Interior, Riyadh, Houthis, south	Spam	10%

3.2 How Do Long-Lived Accounts Evolve?

In this section, we investigate the evolution of each of our four user groups from three perspectives: self-similarity, linguistic evolution, and behavioral evolution.

User Lifecycles. To compare the lifecycle of different accounts and since they all may land on different set of months, we split the lifespan of each user into 10 stages and distribute their activities over these stages [7]. A life-stage of 1% corresponds to birth and a life-stage of 100% corresponds to death (either getting suspended for the case of suspended users, or never tweeting for more than 2 months for legit users). We then can compare how different users evolved by comparing their corresponding life-stages regardless of the actual months they were active in and regardless of the real length of their lifetime.

Self-similarity. We first measure how much accounts mimic their own previous tweets. We expect legitimate normal accounts to be more innovative in their use of language while accounts of spammy nature may repeat themselves more often since they usually have a specific agenda or target to achieve. For this purpose we measure the lexical overlap between the set of words used in each tweet and the previous 10 tweets produced by the same account using Jaccard similarity. For example, given a tweet (t) after the tenth tweet and the previous 10 tweets t_j ($1 \leq j \leq 10$), the self-similarity SS at t is calculated as follows:

$$SS = \frac{1}{10} \sum_{j=1}^{10} \frac{|t \cap t_j|}{|t \cup t_j|}$$

Then, we average the calculated self-similarities at each stage in a user lifespan.

Figure 4a shows that short-lived accounts repeat themselves the most; these users clearly engage in the most copy-paste "extreme" behavior, indicating why

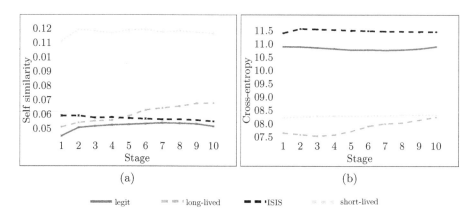

Fig. 4. Self-similarity and cross-entropy: long-lived accounts tend to repeat themselves more at their last stages (a) and also increasingly deviate more from the community (b), hinting that they may have been used as a "sleeper-cell" accounts. The usually extreme content of ISIS pushes them the furthest on the linguistic cross-entropy scale (b). Throughout this paper, error bars indicate the standard error of the mean.

they may have been detected so quickly. In contrast, the legitimate, long-lived, and ISIS accounts engage in much less self-similarity. The ISIS accounts behave most similarly to the legitimate accounts, suggesting that these pro-ISIS posters are mostly real users and not bots. And notice the uptick in self-similarity for the long-lived accounts; this finding offers evidence that these accounts engage in more repeated posting later in the lifespans. Perhaps they are "sleeper cells", who have behaved in a legitimate-like way for much of their lifespan before becoming "activated" and behaving in a more extreme (hence detectable) fashion.

Linguistic Evolution. The examination of self-similarity gives some hints that long-lived accounts are fundamentally different than our other user groups. Here, we extend this investigation to study how these four groups differ from the overall Twitter community over their lifetime. Do these accounts reflect the overall evolution of the Twitter community? Or is there a sign of "sleeper cell" behavior where accounts keep generating some common text and at some point start to post on a different topic? For this purpose we build a series of bigram language models [7] with Katz back-off smoothing [12] one for each month in 2015 that represents the overall background language used by all accounts in that month. Then we quantify how the language of an individual tweet (t) differs from the background language model (BLM) of the month (m) it was produced in by calculating the cross entropy between t and BLM_m:

$$H_t(t, \text{BLM}_m) = -\frac{1}{N} \sum_i \log P_{\text{BLM}_m}(b_i)$$

where b_i are the bigrams of t and $P_{\text{BLM}_m}(b_i)$ is the probability of b_i based on the corresponding month's language model. Cross entropy captures how surprising a

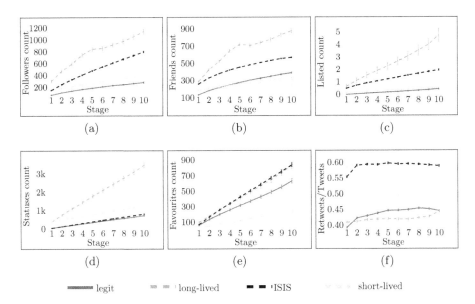

(a)   (b)   (c)

(d)   (e)   (f)

━━━ legit   ⁓ ⁓ long-lived   ■ ■ ʼISIS   ⁓ ⁓ short-lived

Fig. 5. Evolution of user features. Overall, long-lived accounts tend to be more <u>active</u>. On average, they have more followers (a), more friends (b), manage to get listed more (c), generate more tweets (d), favorite more tweets (along with ISIS accounts) (e), but they might have reduced their retweeting ratio to evade detection (f).

tweet t is with respect to the language used by the rest of the Twitter community: higher values indicate that a tweet differs more. We then calculate the average tweet cross entropy of a user (u) at each stage (i):

$$H_u(u, S_i) = \frac{1}{|S_i|} \sum_{t \in S_i} H_t(t, \mathrm{BLM}_m)$$

where S_i is the set of all tweets generated by a user u at a stage i. Note that a stage may span multiple months but the cross-entropy for each tweet is calculated based on the month the tweet was posted in irrespective of the <u>latent</u> stage it ends up on.

Figure 4b shows that different groups start off at a certain distance from the overall community that basically defines their <u>social character</u> for the rest of their lifetime. We observe that ISIS accounts and legitimate accounts are linguistically the most innovative (high values of cross-entropy compared to the background language model). Reinforcing our finding that ISIS accounts engage in little self-similarity, these two findings suggest that ISIS accounts are managed by a sophisticated human-in-the-loop command-and-control with fundamentally different posting tactics than traditional spam accounts. We may also attribute the high cross-entropy for ISIS accounts to their unique extreme messaging which may be rejected by the majority of other users (the background language model) making them appear more "surprising" and therefore furthest

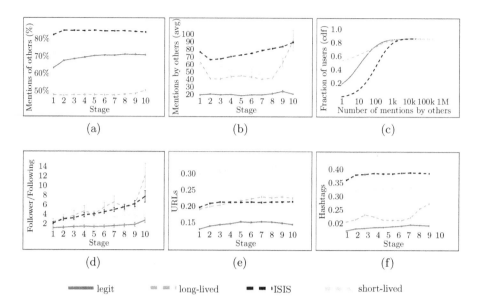

Fig. 6. Evolution of user features cont'd. (a) ISIS accounts are mainly used for interacting with others with 85% of their tweets having at least one mention; long-lived are less interactive. (b) Long-surviving accounts get activated and exposed to the Twitter community in the last stages of their life resulting in their suspension. (c) ISIS accounts do a good job getting high fraction of their accounts mentioned by the community; about 60% of long-lived and short-lived accounts are never mentioned at all. (d) Over time, ISIS accounts improve their follow-back ratio as opposed to long-lived accounts who greatly fluctuates over time - a sign of manipulation. Short-lived accounts spread more URLs (e) and hashtags (f) than other groups. Long-lived accounts engage in increased hashtag sharing (f) in the last stages of their lives.

from the Twitter community. Both long-lived and short-lived accounts are linguistically the least innovative, giving some counter-evidence to our suspicion that long-lived accounts are engaging in a "sleeper cell" behavior. Indeed, the long-lived accounts are the least innovative throughout their lifetimes. This indicates that these accounts, though surviving for a long time, may reveal clear signals that could be used for early detection.

Activity Evolution. Finally, we study the activity signals, other than text, over the lifetime of these four different groups. How sharply does a group gain (or lose) followers? does the community lose (or gain) interest in a group more than others over time? Overall, as shown in Fig. 5, we find that long-lived accounts tend to be more <u>active</u> compared to the other groups in our study. For example, they have more followers, more friends, get listed more often, and generate more tweets. However, long-surviving accounts avoid excessive retweeting possibly a detection evading strategy. In addition, Fig. 6d shows that the followers/following ratio of long-lived and ISIS accounts tend to increase over time indicating that they succeed in getting more users to follow them back. However, the followers/following ratio of long-surviving accounts fluctuates hinting at a potential use of fake accounts pool constantly suspended by Twitter in bulk and hence the sudden decrease. ISIS accounts show a much stable curve another sign that those accounts are managed differently. We also notice a sudden interest by the Twitter community in the long-lived accounts towards the end of their life (Fig. 6b) indicating that those accounts were <u>activated</u> and also exposed to detection and hence got suspended. Figure 6c shows that the ratio of ISIS accounts that get mentioned by other users is higher than any other group indicating a better outreach compared to long-lived accounts where 60% of their accounts never get mentioned.

Turning to the activity patterns of the tweets themselves, we see that on average short-lived accounts use more URLs than any other group, indicating a common theme of using the platform to spread external content (Fig. 6e). In contrast, ISIS accounts use more hashtags (Fig. 6f) than any other group and make more use of mentions (Fig. 6a) showing a preference of interacting directly with others rather than communicating one-way, potentially an effort to spread agenda or seek support and sympathy from the community.

4   Automatic Long-Survivors Detection

This initial investigation has highlighted several dimensions in which long-lived content polluters differ from traditional (short-lived) spammers, legitimate users, and even highly-focused pro-ISIS users. We are now in a position to apply these findings by building machine-learned classifiers to automate some important decisions revolving around these suspicious accounts. We consider the following questions about long-surviving and pro-terrorism accounts:

1. Is an account a long-surviving suspicious account?
2. Is an account pro-terrorism?
3. Is a long-surviving account also pro-terrorism?
4. Are long-surviving and pro-terrorism accounts sleeper cells?

Features. Previous studies have evaluated different features and their effectiveness in detecting overall spam accounts on Twitter [1,5,10,14,22,25,27]. We consider the following three types of features (See Table 2 for more details):

– **Language features:** Our results have shown that cross-entropy of the language of an account against the overall Twitter community and self-similarity of an account are two powerful differentiators of the different types making them first candidate to use for our classification tasks.
– **Behavior:** We have also seen that mentions by others is a good discriminator so we use it in addition to the follow-back ratio.
– **Content:** We noticed how long-surviving accounts use hashtags less and more URLs so we add these two features for comparison purposes.

Table 2. Classification features

Feature	Group	Source	Description
Cross-entropy	Language	Ours	How surprising is the language of an account?
Self-similarity	Language	Ours	How much does an account repeat itself?
Interaction (self)	Behavior	[25]	Tweets with mentions/all tweets
Interaction (community)	Behavior	ours	Mentions by user/mentions of user by others
Follow-back ratio	Behavior	[14]	Followers/following
Hashtags ratio	Content	[25]	Tweets with hashtags/all tweets
URLs ratio	Content	[14]	Tweets with URLs/all tweets

Classification Algorithm. We experimented with a variety of classification algorithms available in the Apache Spark machine learning package [17,28] - logistic regression, decision trees, naive Bayes, and random forests - and found the latter to work best. Hence all results reported here were obtained using random forests [4] implementation available in Apache Spark.

We use balanced training and test sets containing equal numbers of positive and negative examples, so random guessing results in an accuracy and area under the receiver operating characteristic (ROC) curve (AUC) of 50%. We performed all classification experiments using 10-fold cross validation.

4.1 Classification Tasks

We answer the above questions with the following specific three tasks along with a fourth orthogonal task that evaluates tasks performances as accounts evolved throughout their lifetime.

Task 1: Is an Account a Long-Surviving Account? Here the objective is to detect if a given Twitter account is currently running under the radar and should be suspended. Is it possible to distinguish a long-surviving account from other suspicious groups and also from normal users?

Here the set of positive examples consists of all 17,909 long-surviving accounts and the negatives examples are the 17,909 legit active accounts randomly sampled from the much larger set of legitimate accounts.

Task 2: Is an Account Pro-extremism? This is similar to Task 1 but here we would like to find out if accounts such as ISIS supporters are different from normal accounts.

Here the positive examples are the 17,518 community reported ISIS accounts and the negative examples are 17,518 randomly sampled legitimate accounts.

Task 3: Is a Long-Surviving Account also Pro-terrorism? This should give some insight on how ISIS operates its social networking campaigns. Do they hire the same teams that might be operating other long-surviving accounts? Or do they have their own methods?

Similarly to Task 2, we use our set of 17,518 ISIS accounts as the positive examples but we now sample 17,518 long-surviving accounts from the 17,909 long-surviving accounts.

How Early Can We Classify Accounts? Finally, we add an orthogonal task to the above three tasks that considers the evolution of accounts over their lifetime. Does detection accuracy improve as accounts progress in their lifespan? i.e. has an account always be suspicious or was there a moment when it turned bad and hence got suspended? Did an ISIS account exist for the purpose of supporting terrorism or was it recruited after being a normal account for some time.

Here we use the same sets of positive and negative examples set up for each of the first three tasks but we now train a series of classifiers, one for each stage of the accounts' lifespan. Does classifier performance improve as we learn more about the accounts?

4.2 Results

Table 3 reports the performance on our first three tasks when using all the features. Surprisingly distinguishing ISIS accounts from other long-surviving accounts (Task 3) is the easiest task, with an accuracy (AUC) of 88% (94%), easier than distinguishing them from legitimate users (Task 2), yet another indicator that ISIS supporters are being operated at a different level and are slightly more successful at appearing normal. Distinguishing long-surviving accounts (Task 1) and ISIS supporters (Task 2) from legitimate accounts is equally challenging to our classifier with accuracy of 85% (93%) and 86% (92%) respectively.

Table 3. Classification results for all tasks.

Task	Accuracy	AUC
Is a Twitter account a long-surviving account?	85%	93%
Is a Twitter account pro-extremism?	86%	92%
Are ISIS accounts different from other long-surviving accounts?	88%	94%

Figure 7 shows performance results for all tasks by considering the whole lifetime of accounts. We notice that all tasks can be answered with an accuracy of 82% or more by only knowing the first few weeks (10% of lifespan) of an account. Interestingly we also see that there are no signs of recruitment of ISIS supporters (i.e. most ISIS accounts existed for that purpose from the beginning). This is evident in the classifier's ability to detect ISIS supporters early in the accounts lifetime. It's also interesting to see that except for Task 1 the classifier didn't improve by knowing more historical information about long-surviving accounts strongly suggesting that most of those accounts have been hiding in plain sight!

Feature Importance. In order to understand which features are important for which task, we evaluate smaller models that consist of only one of the three feature groups (Table 2). We used feature forward selection strategy to order

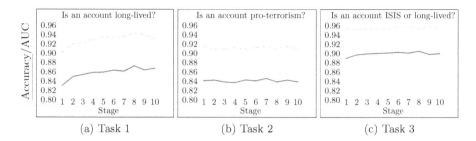

(a) Task 1   (b) Task 2   (c) Task 3

Fig. 7. Tasks performance over accounts lifetime. All classification tasks achieved 82% or better from even at the first few weeks of accounts creation strongly suggesting such accounts have always been suspicious. Distinguishing long-lived accounts from legit accounts slightly improves over accounts lifetime (a) while other tasks remain almost the same. (c) Better classification performance hints that long-surviving ISIS accounts are very different from other long-surviving accounts.

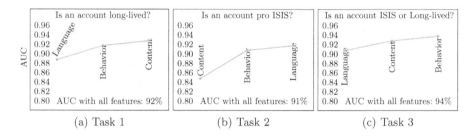

(a) Task 1   (b) Task 2   (c) Task 3

Fig. 8. Results of forward feature selection for first three tasks. Different feature groups contribute their share with language group being the most discriminative most of the time.

feature groups by importance. Figure 8 shows the results for the three tasks. The conclusion is that all feature groups contribute their share, but with diminishing returns and that the discriminating power of different feature groups changes based on the task with language being the most discriminative most of the time.

5   Conclusion

We have explored a unique subset of content polluters on social networks, namely long-surviving suspicious accounts on Twitter. We utilized large-scale private access to all Arabic tweets generated in 2015 to study this group, comparing it to normal Twitter users, pro-terrorism users, and the prevalent short-lived spam. We found that the majority of these long-lived accounts have been successfully evading detection for long time mainly by avoiding behaviors that lead to detection such as mainly posting URLs or participating in many trending hashtags. We uncovered characteristic differences in terms of linguistic character, self-similarity, and other behavioral signals.

We have also exploited a labeled dataset of more than 25k ISIS accounts to further investigate the role of those long-surviving accounts in terrorism. We found that ISIS users are quite different from other long-surviving content polluters and that they are hungry for interaction with the Twitter community rather than a one-way communication style adopted by other spam accounts, giving insight into ISIS's sophisticated use of social media. However, we similarly find that most of these accounts have been ISIS supporters for the majority of their life and are hence detectable early in their lifetime.

We relied on our findings to build an automatic classification system to determine whether an account is a long-surviving or a pro-terrorism. By combining features from the language these accounts use, the content they post, and their behavioral signals we were able to classify users with an accuracy of 84% or more and AUC/ROC of 91% or more. Furthermore, knowing only the first 10% of an account lifetime, we were able to classify an account with 82% accuracy and 90% AUC/ROC strongly suggesting many of these accounts could have been detected earlier.

We are eager to extend this work to explore the community structure underlying these long-lived users – do we find tight clusters of inter-connected users with similar patterns of linguistic evolution? Although we have found that the majority of accounts are created for a purpose that doesn't change, we are still exploring methods to identify "change points" in the lifespan of a small fraction of users that have shown signs of bad evolution to identify users whose behaviors are shifting (e.g., to find ISIS sympathizing accounts).

In this work, we only focused on Arabic Twitter and we only considered the Twitter platform utilizing our access to all Arabic tweets in 2015. However, we are yet to find if our results will transfer to different platforms and different demographics.

Acknowledgments. This work was supported in part by AFOSR grant FA9550-15-1-0149. Majid Alfifi is partially funded by a scholarship from King Fahd University of Petroleum and Minerals. Any opinions, findings and conclusions or recommendations expressed in this material are the author(s) and do not necessarily reflect those of the sponsors. We'd like to also thank the anonymous reviewers for their helpful feedback.

References

1. Benevenuto, F., Magno, G., Rodrigues, T., Almeida, V.: Detecting spammers on Twitter. In: Collaboration, Electronic Messaging, Anti-abuse and Spam Conference (CEAS), vol. 6, p. 12 (2010)
2. Berger, J.M., Morgan, J.: The ISIS Twitter census: defining and describing the population of ISIS supporters on twitter. In: The Brookings Project on US Relations with the Islamic World, vol. 3, no. 20 (2015)
3. Blei, D.M., Ng, A.Y., Jordan, M.I.: Latent dirichlet allocation. J. Mach. Learn. Res. **3**(Jan), 993–1022 (2003)
4. Breiman, L.: Random forests. Mach. Learn. **45**(1), 5–32 (2001)

5. Castillo, C., Mendoza, M., Poblete, B.: Information credibility on Twitter. In: Proceedings of the 20th International Conference on World Wide Web, pp. 675–684. ACM (2011)
6. Conover, M., Ratkiewicz, J., Francisco, M.R., Gonçalves, B., Menczer, F., Flammini, A.: Political polarization on Twitter. ICWSM **133**, 89–96 (2011)
7. Danescu-Niculescu-Mizil, C., West, R., Jurafsky, D., Leskovec, J., Potts, C.: No country for old members: user lifecycle and linguistic change in online communities. In: Proceedings of the 22nd International Conference on World Wide Web, pp. 307–318. International World Wide Web Conferences Steering Committee (2013)
8. Davis, C.A., Varol, O., Ferrara, E., Flammini, A., Menczer, F.: Botornot: a system to evaluate social bots. In: Proceedings of the 25th International Conference Companion on World Wide Web, pp. 273–274. International World Wide Web Conferences Steering Committee (2016)
9. Ferrara, E., Wang, W.-Q., Varol, O., Flammini, A., Galstyan, A.: Predicting online extremism, content adopters, and interaction reciprocity. In: Spiro, E., Ahn, Y.-Y. (eds.) SocInfo 2016. LNCS, vol. 10047, pp. 22–39. Springer, Cham (2016). doi:10.1007/978-3-319-47874-6_3
10. Grier, C., Thomas, K., Paxson, V., Zhang, M.: @ spam: the underground on 140 characters or less. In: Proceedings of the 17th ACM Conference on Computer and Communications Security, pp. 27–37. ACM (2010)
11. Hu, X., Tang, J., Zhang, Y., Liu, H.: Social spammer detection in microblogging. In: Twenty-Third International Joint Conference on Artificial Intelligence (2013)
12. Katz, S.: Estimation of probabilities from sparse data for the language model component of a speech recognizer. IEEE Trans. Acoust. Speech Sig. Process. **35**(3), 400–401 (1987)
13. King, G., Pan, J., Roberts, M.E.: How the Chinese government fabricates social media posts for strategic distraction, not engaged argument. Harvard University (2016)
14. Lee, K., Caverlee, J., Webb, S.: Uncovering social spammers: social honeypots+ machine learning. In: Proceedings of the 33rd International ACM SIGIR Conference on Research and Development in Information Retrieval, pp. 435–442. ACM (2010)
15. Lin, P.C., Huang, P.M.: A study of effective features for detecting long-surviving twitter spam accounts. In: 2013 15th International Conference on Advanced Communication Technology (ICACT), pp. 841–846. IEEE (2013)
16. Lotan, G., Graeff, E., Ananny, M., Gaffney, D., Pearce, I., et al.: The Arab spring— the revolutions were tweeted: information flows during the 2011 Tunisian and Egyptian revolutions. Int. J. Commun. **5**, 31 (2011)
17. Meng, X., Bradley, J., Yavuz, B., Sparks, E., Venkataraman, S., Liu, D., Freeman, J., Tsai, D., Amde, M., Owen, S., et al.: Mllib: machine learning in apache spark. J. Mach. Learn. Res. **17**(34), 1–7 (2016)
18. Mustafaraj, E., Metaxas, P.T.: From obscurity to prominence in minutes: political speech and real-time search. In: Proceedings of the WebSci10: Extending the Frontiers of Society On-Line (2010)
19. Ratkiewicz, J., Conover, M., Meiss, M.R., Gonçalves, B., Flammini, A., Menczer, F.: Detecting and tracking political abuse in social media. ICWSM **11**, 297–304 (2011)
20. Song, J., Lee, S., Kim, J.: Spam filtering in Twitter using sender-receiver relationship. In: Sommer, R., Balzarotti, D., Maier, G. (eds.) RAID 2011. LNCS, vol. 6961, pp. 301–317. Springer, Heidelberg (2011). doi:10.1007/978-3-642-23644-0_16

21. Starbird, K., Palen, L.: (How) will the revolution be retweeted?: information diffusion and the 2011 Egyptian uprising. In: Proceedings of the ACM 2012 Conference on Computer Supported Cooperative Work, pp. 7–16. ACM (2012)
22. Stringhini, G., Kruegel, C., Vigna, G.: Detecting spammers on social networks. In: Proceedings of the 26th Annual Computer Security Applications Conference, pp. 1–9. ACM (2010)
23. Thomas, K., Grier, C., Paxson, V.: Adapting social spam infrastructure for political censorship. In: LEET (2012)
24. Thomas, K., Grier, C., Song, D., Paxson, V.: Suspended accounts in retrospect: an analysis of Twitter spam. In: Proceedings of the 2011 ACM SIGCOMM Conference on Internet Measurement Conference, pp. 243–258. ACM (2011)
25. Wang, A.H.: Don't follow me: spam detection in Twitter. In: Proceedings of the 2010 International Conference on Security and Cryptography (SECRYPT), pp. 1–10. IEEE (2010)
26. Wei, W., Joseph, K., Liu, H., Carley, K.M.: The fragility of Twitter social networks against suspended users. In: Proceedings of the 2015 IEEE/ACM International Conference on Advances in Social Networks Analysis and Mining 2015, pp. 9–16. ACM (2015)
27. Yang, C., Harkreader, R.C., Gu, G.: Die free or live hard? Empirical evaluation and new design for fighting evolving Twitter spammers. In: Sommer, R., Balzarotti, D., Maier, G. (eds.) RAID 2011. LNCS, vol. 6961, pp. 318–337. Springer, Heidelberg (2011). doi:10.1007/978-3-642-23644-0_17
28. Zaharia, M., Chowdhury, M., Das, T., Dave, A., Ma, J., McCauley, M., Franklin, M.J., Shenker, S., Stoica, I.: Resilient distributed datasets: a fault-tolerant abstraction for in-memory cluster computing. In: Proceedings of the 9th USENIX Conference on Networked Systems Design and Implementation, p. 2. USENIX Association (2012)

Opinions, Behavior, and Social Media Mining

Like at First Sight: Understanding User Engagement with the World of Microvideos

Sagar Joglekar[1]([✉]), Nishanth Sastry[1], and Miriam Redi[2]

[1] Kings College, London, UK
sagar.joglekar@kcl.ac.uk
[2] Bell Labs, Cambridge, UK

Abstract. Several content-driven platforms have adopted the 'micro video' format, a new form of short video that is constrained in duration, typically at most 5–10 s long. Micro videos are typically viewed through mobile apps, and are presented to viewers as a long list of videos that can be scrolled through. How should micro video creators capture viewers' attention in the short attention span? Does quality of content matter? Or do social effects predominate, giving content from users with large numbers of followers a greater chance of becoming popular? To the extent that quality matters, what aspect of the video – aesthetics or affect – is critical to ensuring user engagement?

We examine these questions using a snapshot of nearly all ($>120,000$) videos uploaded to globally accessible channels on the micro video platform Vine over an 8 week period. We find that although social factors do affect engagement, content quality becomes equally important at the top end of the engagement scale. Furthermore, using the temporal aspects of video, we verify that decisions are made quickly, and that first impressions matter more, with the first seconds of the video typically being of higher quality and having a large effect on overall user engagement. We verify these data-driven insights with a user study from 115 respondents, confirming that users tend to engage with micro videos based on "first sight", and that users see this format as a more immediate and less professional medium than traditional user-generated video (e.g., YouTube) or user-generated images (e.g., Flickr).

1 Introduction

In the last few years, we have seen the introduction of a new form of user-generated video, where severe restrictions are placed on the duration of the content. High profile examples include Vine, which allowed users to create videos up to 6.5 s long; Instagram, which introduced videos up to 15 s duration; and Snapchat, whose videos are officially limited to 10 s and are deleted after 24 h. Although most user-generated video platforms have placed some form of limit on the duration or size of videos (e.g., YouTube had a 10 min limit, which has since been softened to a 'default' limit of 15 min[1]), the extremely short duration

---

[1] https://techcrunch.com/2010/12/09/youtube-time-limit-2/.

G.L. Ciampaglia et al. (Eds.): SocInfo 2017, Part I, LNCS 10539, pp. 237–256, 2017.
DOI: 10.1007/978-3-319-67217-5_15

time limits of Vine etc. has led to the coining of a new term: *micro videos*. Some media commentators have argued that the restrictions imposed by the micro video format could fundamentally change the way we communicate [7]. Indeed, it has been argued that Vine has had a significant cultural impact far beyond its user base, generating several widely shared memes in its short lifetime[2].

At the same time, as the format is still very new, virtually all major micro video platforms are experimenting with the format, making significant changes in the last year. For instance, Instagram extended the limit from 15 s to 1 min[3]. Vine is undergoing a major overhaul – Twitter recently said it would close down the Vine website and community. The new version of the Vine app retains the 6.5 s video format, but the videos will be published directly on Twitter's feed and thus more closely integrated with its social network[4].

This paper aims to examine how crucial changes such as social network integration and time limit expansion might affect user engagement with this new format. To better understand these issues, we formulate the following research questions:

RQ1 What are the relative roles of social and content quality factors in driving engagement and popularity in micro-videos?

RQ2 How does the strict time limit impact video quality, and user engagement (both as creators and consumers) with such videos?

We answer these questions from an empirical perspective, using a dataset of nearly all ($\approx 120,000$) Vine videos that were uploaded to one of the 18 globally available channels on Vine during an 8 week period. We complement these with other datasets including a curated dataset (*POP12K*) of 12,000 popular Vine videos, as well as samples from other micro-video platforms such as Instagram[5].

To address **RQ1**, we take the three metrics of popularity we collect – counts of loops, reposts and likes – as quantification of the *collective* user engagement of the consumers of a video, and ask to what extent the content- and social network-related features affect these metrics. To answer this question, we adopt a novel methodology. We train a random forest classifier that, given a threshold for a metric of popularity, is able to able to distinguish items on either side of the threshold into popular and unpopular classes with high accuracy, precision and recall, using the features we have identified. The relative importance of different features then gives an indication of the extent to which those features affect the metric under consideration. We progressively consider higher and higher threshold values for videos to qualify as popular or engaging, and thereby identify trends and changes of relative importance of different features. Interestingly, we find that as the threshold for popularity becomes more and more stringent,

---

[2] http://www.theverge.com/2016/10/28/13456208/why-vine-died-twitter-shutdown.

[3] http://www.theverge.com/tech/2016/3/29/11325294/instagram-video-60-seconds.

[4] http://www.theverge.com/2017/1/5/14175670/vine-shutting-down-rebrand-downlo ad-archive.

[5] On acceptance, our newly crawled data will also be shared for non commercial research.

features that represent quality of the content become collectively as important as social features such as the number of followers. Echoing an effect also observed in Instagram photos [1], we find that presence of faces in vine videos significantly increases engagement, and is the most important content-related factor.

Next, to explore **RQ2** we look at how the quality of the video varies over time in micro-videos, and discover a *primacy of the first second* phenomenon: the best or most salient parts of the video, whether in the aesthetic space or affect (sentiment) space, are more prevalent in the initial seconds of the micro video, suggesting that the authors are consciously or subconsciously treating micro-videos similar to images – in the initial part, the video is composed with aesthetics and affective quality in mind, resulting in a higher quality level; but quality declines as the video plays over time. Furthermore, echoing the primacy of the first second phenomenon, we find that the quality of the first seconds of the video are as effective as the quality of the whole video in predicting popularity/engagement. Figure 1 shows examples of these effects through two videos in our dataset of popular videos. In both videos, we observe content quality deteriorate over time, illustrating the primacy of the first seconds.

Fig. 1. Vine samples from first, second and thirds one thirds of the video. Images (a), (b) and (c) show a progressive drop in brightness and sharpness due to shaky camera. Images (d), (e) and (f) shows a progressive drop in contrast.

We confirm these computationally acquired findings with real user impressions by designing a survey which was answered by 115 respondents: Over 66% of users react to (like/comment on) content from their friends, making social interaction a significant part of content consumption; and 44% of users form opinions about videos in the first few seconds, validating the observed primacy of first seconds effect. Our survey also suggests that platforms such as Vine are seen as less professional and more immediate formats than, say Flickr images or YouTube videos, providing support to David Pogue's position that micro videos are a new kind of user-generated content [25], and therefore should be treated differently when it comes to user engagement.

2 Related Work

Our paper closely relates to those works in machine vision that infer intangible properties of images and videos. While computer vision frameworks typically focus on analysing image semantics using deep neural networks [13], researchers have started exploring concepts beyond semantics, such as image memorability [9], emotions [19], and, more broadly, pictorial aesthetics [4,5,18]. This work specifically focuses on-line visual content collected from social media. Researchers have shown that, by leveraging social media data in combination with vision techniques, systems can estimate visual creativity [26], sentiment [10,32] and sarcasm [28].

More specifically, our work closely relates to research that combines social media studies and computer vision to analyse popularity and diffusion for social media posts: for example, Zhong et al. were able to predict the number of post "re-pins" given the visual preferences of a Pinterest user [35]; recent work [20] has also used multimodal features to predict the popularity of brand-related social media posts. Different from these works which focus on prediction, this paper looks at understanding user engagement.

Media popularity prediction studies generally focus on non-visual features. For example, [33] used textual annotations to predict various popularity metrics of social photos. Social metrics such as early views [24] or latent social factors [22] have also been used to effectively estimate video popularity. However, the fact that many popular media items may not depend on the social network [2] suggests that intrinsic media quality is an important factor for diffusion, engagement and popularity, which we explore in this paper.

Recent work in the field has explored the importance of visual content in analysing popularity: [30] analysed the visual attributes impacting image diffusion, and [27] studied relations between image quality and popularity in on-line photo sharing platforms. Bakhshi et al. [1] showed that pictures with faces tend to be more popular than others. Similar to our paper, researchers have used computer vision techniques to estimate image popularity in Flickr [12]. Moreover, a work done by Fontanini et al. [6] explores the relevance of perceptual sentiments to popularity of a video. Unlike these works, we explore content features to fully understand user engagement and popularity in micro videos, a new form of expression radically different from both the photo medium and the video medium.

Micro videos are relatively new, so work specifically on micro video analysis has been limited. Redi et al. [26] quantify and build on the notion of creativity in micro-videos. A large dataset of 200K Vine videos was collected by Nguyen et al. [21], focusing on analysis of tags. Closest to our work is Chen et al. [3] who use multimodal features to predict popularity in micro videos. However, although we use popularity prediction as an intermediate tool, our focus is on understanding impact and importance of different features in determining popularity or engagement. To this end, we introduce a novel methodology that allows understanding up to which point social features are prominent over content features. Additionally, we demonstrate the "immediacy" of engagement with micro videos by showing that the content from the first two seconds of the video is just as good at predicting popularity as the entire content. Collectively, these results allow us to characterise Vine as a new medium of expression, different from previous work.

3 Introduction to Datasets

Micro videos were pioneered and popularised by Vine[6], which was launched in 2012. Vine videos are constrained to a maximum length of 6.5 s. Videos are typically created using the mobile app and posted on user's profile which can be followed and shared by other users within the app or the website. We stress most of our work on videos sampled from Vine, complemented by Instagram data, which will be introduced as appropriate. The rest of this section gives details about the Vine datasets.

3.1 Dataset Description

The data used in this paper is summarised in Table 1, and was collected in two phases as described below:

Popular Videos Dataset. First, we collected ≈12,000 videos which have been marked by Vine as 'popular', by tracking the 'popular-now' channel[7] over a three week period in Dec 2015, and downloading all videos and associated metadata once every six hours, and removing any overlapping videos from the previous visit. The crawling period was chosen to ensure that consecutive crawls have an overlap of several videos, and this sufficed for all visits made to the website during the data collection period; thus the dataset we collected is a complete collection of all 'popular-now' vines during the 21 days under consideration.

Table 1. Summary characteristics of datasets used

Dataset	Posts (total)	Loops/Views (median)	Reposts (median)	Likes (median)
POP12K	11448	318566	2173	7544
ALL120K	122327	80	0	2

Vine does not disclose the algorithm used to mark a Vine as popular; yet we observe (see Table 1) orders of magnitude more loops, reposts and likes in the popular-now dataset than in the non-popular dataset. Thus we believe that the algorithm used by Vine to select vines for the 'popular-now' channel is strongly affected by the numbers of loops/revines/likes. Note that the numbers of loops etc. were collected at the time of crawl, within a maximum of six hours of being

---

[6] http://vine.co.
[7] https://vine.co/popular-now.

posted on the 'popular-now' channel, which limits the possibility that the counts increased *as a result* of being featured on the popular-now channel. In the rest of the paper, we use the counts in the popular-now dataset to calibrate the definition of 'high engagement'. While there is a possibility that this is a biased proxy for global engagement, it nevertheless provides a baseline against which to compare all videos.

All Channel Videos Dataset. In the second phase, we collected videos accessible from each of the 18 global Vine channels or categories over a period of 8 weeks from Aug 16 to Oct 12 2016. Again, a crawling period of six hours was chosen for consecutive visits to the same channel, and the 100 most recent vines were fetched with each visit. The number 100 was a result of an API limit from Vine. Our dataset captures nearly all videos uploaded to Vine and assigned to a channel. The only exception is the extremely popular comedy channel, for which we nearly always find more than 100 new videos (we only download the 100 most recent videos for the comedy channel). In total, this results in a dataset of ≈120,000 videos. We track loop, revine and like counts over time, periodically updating each video's counts every three days until the end of data collection. At the last tracking cycle, we have metadata for each post for 3 weeks after initial upload.

Note that while we obtain nearly all videos across the channels, our dataset does *not* capture *all* videos uploaded to Vine – Vine creators do not need to assign a video to a channel. However, due to the Vine platform structure, vines that are not in channels have near-zero probability to get seen by other users apart from the followers. We use channels to restrict ourselves to vines which have a chance to get exposed to a reasonably global audience of those interested in a topic category, and therefore to vines that have a higher potential for garnering high engagement.

3.2   Feature Descriptions

In order to fully understand how micro-videos engage users, we characterize the content of videos using computer vision and computational aesthetics techniques and extract a number of features (Table 3 in Appendix), which can be divided into the following categories:

Image Quality Features. These features are mostly taken from computational aesthetics literature, and have been recognized as heuristics for good photography. Prior work [35] has identified a set of image quality features that robustly predict user interest in images. We adapt these to videos by computing the features on images taken at regular intervals from the video under consideration, and use the values to understand intrinsic quality of Vine videos. We use a combination of low-level features such as contrast, colourfulness, hue saturation, L-R balance, brightness and sharp pixel proportion, together with higher level features such as simplicity, naturalness of the image, and adherence to the "rule of thirds" heuristic.

Audio Features. Following previous work on micro videos [26], we use audio features known to have an impact on emotion and reception. Using open source tools [14,15], we measure *loudness* (overall volume of the sound track), the *mode* (major or minor key), *roughness* (dissonance in the sound track), and *rhythmical* features describing abrupt rhythmical changes in the audio signal.

Higher Level Features. Affect (emotions experienced) is well known to strongly impact on user engagement [16,23]. To understand the sentiment conveyed by the video frames, we use the Multi Lingual Sentiment Ontology detectors [10] which express visual sentiment of video frames on a scale of 1 (negative) to 5 (positive). We sample frames at regular intervals and compute the affect evoked by these frames using this 5-point scale. Another higher level feature we consider is the presence of faces, which has previously been shown to have a strong influence on likes and comments in image-based social media [1]. We therefore adapt it to the video context by computing the *fraction of frames with faces*. Finally *Number of past posts* by the creator of the video under consideration is also included to reflect user experience and activity on the social media network.

Social Features. We consider the *number of followers* of the author of a content as a direct feature to reflect the user's social network capital.

A more detailed description of all the features can be seen in Table 3.

4   User Engagement in Micro Videos

We begin our analysis by devising a novel methodology to analyze how the previously defined features impact user engagement in micro videos (**RQ1**). Our results indicate the importance of social features for highly engaging videos, and that the presence of faces is a strong content-related feature that positively impacts user engagement.

4.1   Metrics and Methodology

To understand which aspects or features are important for user engagement, we need to: (*i*) define a metric for engagement, and (*ii*) develop a methodology to study how the metric is influenced by different features.

Defining a Metric for User Engagement: In this paper, we use *number of loops* of a micro video as a proxy for user engagement towards it[8]. Although user engagement is a broadly used term, and other metrics may well be used to represent user engagement, our choice is in line with previous related social media studies (e.g. [1]) that have used social attention metrics such as likes and

---

[8] We obtained similar trends using number of reposts, but only report results with loops. Note that the loop counts of videos are highly correlated with reposts and likes. For example for videos in POP12K, $corr(Loops, Likes) = 0.80$, $corr(Likes, Reposts) = 0.91$, $corr(Reposts, Loops) = 0.74$.

comments to study user engagement. Video hosting platforms like Youtube also use the number of views (similar to number of loops on Vine) as a core metric for their user engagement API[9]. In the rest of the paper, we will use popularity and engagement interchangeably.

Motivating the Methodology: Given a set of features, if we can build a machine learning model that uses the features to predict which content items are highly engaging, the relative importance of the different features in making the prediction can tell us about the relationship between the features and engagement. However, our results will only be as 'good' as the model is in predicting loop counts. Since predicting popularity with exact numbers such as loop counts is a hard problem, we turn to a simpler one: We define an arbitrary threshold count for loops, and categorize micro videos as popular or unpopular depending on whether the loop count is over or under the threshold. We then design a classifier that predicts whether a micro videos is popular or unpopular (alternately, as engaging or not) based on our set of 28 features (Table 3). As discussed next, a simple random forest classifier can be trained to make this prediction with high precision and accuracy. The relative importance of different features then tells us about how the features affects user engagement.

This method has one major limitation: its dependence on the arbitrarily defined loop count threshold. Therefore, we conduct a sensitivity analysis by training a series of binary classifiers for different loop count thresholds. This also allows us to study shifts in relative importance, as we move up the scale towards more popular and engaging objects, by defining increasingly higher numbers of loop counts as the threshold for categorizing a video as popular (or engaging).

4.2   Model Details

Setup. We sample 12,000 videos from our dataset, out of which 6,000 are popular videos from POP12K, and 6,000 randomly sampled from the ALL120K dataset, thus representing the entire spectrum of engagement levels. In each video, we sample the video track for individual frames at every second, and extract the audio track as well as meta-data related to the video and its author. Using these, we then compute the 28 dimensional vector of all the features in Table 3 and train a random forest classifier to distinguish popular and unpopular videos for different thresholds of popularity. We used the implementation from the *SKLearn* package with $\sqrt{n_{features}}$ split and 500 estimators, which provided the best trade-off between speed and prediction performance.

Performance Results. Different classifiers are trained using the above method for different engagement/popularity thresholds, using an 80-20 split for training and validation. Figure 2c shows how these perform as we vary the threshold of "engagement" (popularity) from 80 loops (the median for ALL120K) to ≈500,000 loops (1.5 times the median of the popular videos i.e., POP12K). At each training iteration with a changed "engagement" threshold, we re-balance the dataset by

---

[9] https://developers.google.com/youtube/analytics/v1/dimsmets/mets

choosing equal number of samples which fall in either classes. We take care that we are training on at-least 20% of the complete dataset by the end of the process, and stop increasing the threshold beyond that point to avoid over-fitting. The classifiers gave consistently high performance on the validation dataset (see lines labeled 6 s), never dropping below 90% for accuracy, and 80% F-1 score, validating our next results about the importance of different features.

4.3 Feature Analysis and Implications

The impact of individual features on user engagement is calculated using Gini importance [17], and combined into social- and content-related (i.e., audio and video-related) features as described before (Sect. 3.2). Figure 2a shows the trends in feature importance as a function of engagement threshold used (see lines labeled 6 s). We observe that at lower thresholds of popularity, social features are much more important than content-related features, but at higher thresholds, content-related features increase in importance to become just as important as social features, suggesting that *content quality is important for user engagement at the top end of engagement.* This facet of users' engagement with Vine might legitimize Twitter's decision to more closely integrate the Vine platform with its social network: since a large part of micro-video popularity can be explained with social factors, a better social network might further foster engagement with this unique form of expression.

We drill down further in Fig. 2b, and examine the importance of different kinds of content-related features. For each class of content-related features, we plot the mean of the feature set of the class. We observe that in terms of effective importance of different feature tracks, sentiment is the weakest influencer in the classifier decision process. We conjecture that the relative lack of importance of sentiments may partly be due to the extremely short nature of micro videos, which does not let emotional 'story arcs' and plots (e.g., drama) to develop as strongly as in longer videos.

Further, we observe that the presence of faces in a frame strongly outweighs all other content-related features in predicting popularity. We confirm this in Fig. 3 by comparing the percentage of faces in popular POP12K videos with the corresponding percentage in ALL120K videos (which contain a large number of unpopular videos as well as a few popular ones). These results indicate that popular videos tend to have more faces, i.e., *"faces engage us"*. This is in alignment with similar results on other platforms, which also indicate that faces greatly enhance popularity related metrics such as likes and comments [1].

5   Primacy of the First Seconds

Next, we try to understand these findings further by examining the quality of the individual frames of the videos: One way to think about videos is as a sequence of images. With micro videos, this sequence is of course much shorter than in other videos, and we investigate whether this has impact on video quality

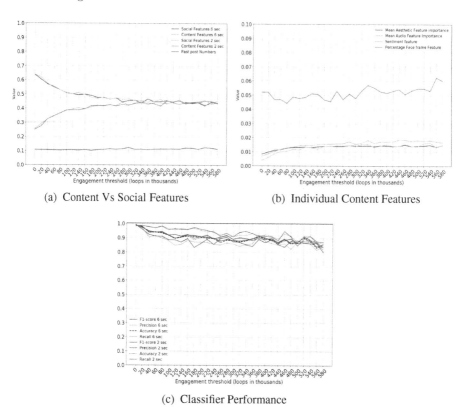

(a) Content Vs Social Features   (b) Individual Content Features

(c) Classifier Performance

Fig. 2. Understanding engagement for different thresholds (min. number of loops considered as engaging). Two different classifiers are used, one using quality of the entire micro video (labeled 6 s), the second measuring quality from only the first two seconds (labeled 2 s). (a) As threshold becomes higher, content-related factors become as important as social factors (both classifiers). Note that unlike content quality computed from the first 2 s ('Content features 2 s') rather than the entire 6 s of the video ('Content features 6 s'), 'social features 6 s' uses the same feature values as social features 2 s', but the two are plotted separately to show the relative importance of social features in the 6 s vs 2 s classifier. (b) Amongst content features alone, presence of faces in the video is the single most dominant feature, across all threshold levels (6 s classifier) (c) Both 2 s and 6 s classifiers perform similarly across all metrics such as Precision, Recall and F1-score. Performance is high across all engagement thresholds: all metrics are consistently over 0.8 or 0.9.

(**RQ2**). Our results show a "primacy of the first seconds" effect, with quality deteriorating over time and the quality at the beginning is as good a predictor of engagement as quality of the entire video.

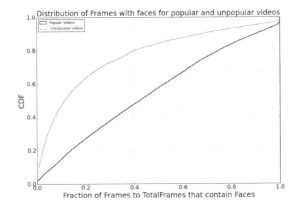

Fig. 3. CDF for popular and unpopular videos. The CDF signifies the cumulative distribution of percentages of frames containing faces in a vine video. The observation here is popular videos tend to have higher face percentage than unpopular videos

5.1   Image Quality Deteriorates over Time

Vine videos can be at most 6.5 s long. We sample the videos twice every second and represent the whole video as a series of 12–13 static frames. This sampling rate is not too low to miss any considerable frame transitions, neither is it too high to include a lot of mid transition frames. For each sampled frame, we calculate the feature under consideration – sentiment, percentage of faces, and aesthetic score. To compute the aesthetic score, we extract the 18 aesthetic features described in Table 3 for each frame. To find an aggregate overall aesthetic score of each frame, we use a weighted sum of all the features (This is possible because all the features are on the same scale), where the weights are calculated to be proportional to the importance of each feature in the classifier designed in the previous section.

For each video and each feature, we then compute when in the video the feature reached its maximum value. We then divide the videos into two second intervals, essentially dividing the video into its first third, second third and third. We then ask what proportion of videos had the maximum value of a feature in the first (respectively second and third) third. This procedure tells us when we are likely to find the 'best' part of the video.

Figure 4 shows the result for each major category of content-related feature, plotted over both our datasets (ALL120K and POP12K). We observe a general trend where the first third has the maximum (best) value for all features considered. For instance, the best aesthetic score is to be found in the first two seconds. Similarly, the proportion of faces, an important predictor of engagement (Fig. 3), is also maximum in the first third.

Note that for sentiment values, the minimum value is just as valid and valuable as the maximum, representing a sad or emotionally dark segment of the movie with negative sentiment, in contrast to a happy segment of the movie with positive sentiment. Therefore, we calculate which third of the movie we

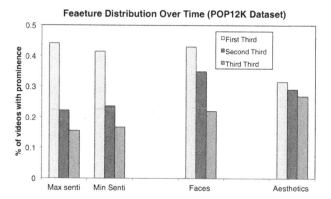

Fig. 4. Evolution of Feature magnitude: The graph shows sharp trend in prevalence of strongest component of a feature in the first one third of the video. The strength decreases progressively for the successive thirds. (Results shown for POP12K dataset. Similar results obtained for ALL120K.)

find the maximum and minimum sentiment values and plot these separately. In both cases, we find yet again that the first third of the video has the maximum (minimum) sentiment value for the majority of videos.

5.2 Loops and Likes are Obtained on First Sight: Initial Seconds Predict Engagement

Collectively, the results above paint a picture where the first seconds of the micro video are highly important in engaging the user. We conjecture that this might be because of the mobile-first nature of Vine: the primary user interface is the Vine app, where users select which videos to watch by scrolling over it. The vine only plays when the user retains focus over the video, and hence the first seconds are likely critical for grabbing user attention and engaging them.

We next take this result to its logical conclusion, and ask how the classifier developed in the previous section for predicting engagement would work if using only content-related features from the first third of the video rather than from the whole micro video. Following the same methodology as described in the previous sub-section, we develop a series of classifiers for different popularity thresholds, training this time on image content-related features drawn from the first two seconds of the video rather than from across the whole video. The same set of hyper parameters were used as in the previous setting. As shown in Fig. 2c, the resulting classifiers (labeled 2 s) perform very similarly to the classifiers developed before (labeled 6 s). Further, Fig. 2a shows that the relative importance of different features is also nearly identical to the previous results. It should be emphasized that although these results were obtained using loop counts as the metric for user engagement, similar results have also been obtained using reposts (re-vines).

These results point to a *primacy of the first seconds* effect, whereby the first seconds of a micro video matter as much as the whole video, suggesting that they behave almost like still images in terms of user engagement.

6   User Study

To complement the data analysis and gain deeper insight into what drives user actions and engagement, we designed an anonymous user study which captures user behavior when engaging with micro-videos.

6.1   Survey Methodology

We initially recruited undergraduate students, obtaining about 33 responses. Subsequently, we tweeted the survey out to the Official Vine Twitter account and to the accounts of Vine and Instagram users, in order to gain further exposure amongst users of these platforms. In all, 115 users responded to our survey. Table 2 summarizes the respondents' demography and usage preferences. Most questions asked were to be answered either on a 5-point Likert scale (Strongly agree to Strongly Disagree), and or in a semantic differential format, with three options to choose from.

Table 2. Summary of survey responses

Attribute	Value
Male respondents (%)	44.2
Female respondents (%)	55.8
Age Demography (%)	
18–24	43.4
25–31	34.5
32–40	14.2
40+	8

6.2   Validation of Data-Driven Results

To understand engagement with micro-videos and validate the findings that emerged from our analysis of **RQ1** and **RQ2**, the survey asked the following 5 questions to be answered on a 5 level Likert scale (strongly agree - strongly disagree):

A I tend to like/comment on videos from friends rather than from strangers
B I always form an opinion of a video in the initial few seconds, once the video starts playing

C I rarely watch short videos (Snapchats, stories), all the way to the end
D I prefer to watch short videos of humans on these platforms. E.g. I like to see a person talking/expressing rather than outdoor scenery, or Cats.

Almost 66% users agreed to question **A**, which reaffirms the tendency of socially embedded users being able to get high engagement scores. 44% of users agreed to question **B** (and further ≈30% users were neutral) and 38% users agreed with statement **C**, supporting the observed the "primacy of the first seconds" effect. Contrary to our findings regarding faces, only 34% users agreed with statement **D** (although a further 39% remained neutral; thus only a minority 27% of users disagreed or disagreed strongly). Such result might suggest that for many users, our attraction towards face shapes is innate [29] and people do not consciously engage more with faces.

6.3   Understanding What Matters to Users

The next part of the survey went beyond confirming the data-driven analysis by asking the respondents how their behavior changed when it comes to *acting* on a video they engaged with, i.e., when do they like/forward, comment or stop playing the video? 44% like, comment or share videos only after finishing watching it, and but a sizable 56% agreed that they do so in the middle of watching the video itself, or right at the beginning (19% share at the beginning. 37% somewhere in the middle); again pointing to the need for capturing users in the initial parts of the video.

Interestingly, a majority of 55% of respondents agreed (on a 5 point Likert scale) to the statement: "I don't really care about the quality of the micro-video or stories, as long as I like the content". This result, together with the previous answers seems to imply that the fall off in content quality in the latter parts of micro videos does not negatively impact user engagement. However, users do see a difference between micro videos and "traditional" (and older) user generated content platforms such as YouTube: an overwhelming 75% of respondents rate the production quality of YouTube videos quality as more professional than micro videos.

7   Discussion and Conclusions

In this paper, we took a first look at user engagement with micro videos. Defining engagement in terms of social attention metrics such as likes, revines (reposts) and loop counts, we find that content quality-related features have as strong an influence as social network-based exposure in driving these metrics. Furthermore, the quality of the first couple of seconds is higher than the quality of subsequent seconds, and can predict whether a micro video will be engaging or not, just as well as looking at the quality of the entire video. We further conduct a user study to understand ground-truth user behavior when it comes to micro-videos. The study suggests that users tend to make quick opinions regarding micro-videos and engage with them almost in an image-like fashion, where they may begin but not finish watching the short 5–10 s long video.

These aspects of micro video user engagement has important implications and bearing on future work:

1. Advertisements on the Web are driven by social attention metrics. Therefore advertisers need to know and adjust their strategies based on the insight that user attention is driven to a large extent by the initial seconds. Although video ads do not appear to be common in today's micro videos, how to place ads that grab user attention within a short duration of time will be a problem that is interesting both from a research and a business perspective.
2. A possible reason for the deterioration of image quality is that it may be difficult to maintain image composition, focus etc. using a mobile phone camera with moving subjects. Novel UI and multimedia techniques that can help correct for such quality deterioration could greatly help micro video creators – and also represent a second promising direction for further study.
3. Recently, several micro video platforms have started extending the duration of micro videos. Although the wisdom of longer micro videos without appropriate editing tools has been questioned[10], from a research perspective it would be interesting to study how user behavior and engagement changes as longer micro videos become more common place. Interestingly, we find that in a small sample of about 6000 Instagram videos (where the maximum permitted duration is 60 s), users continue to prefer shorter videos, with 70% of videos less than 20 s long, and the median duration at just under 15 s. Such user preferences can and should be considered as the micro video format evolves further on different platforms.

More generally, in this work we considered user engagement as a single dimension. However, we acknowledge that user engagement is a very subjective notion, impacted by different factors including user location, habits, gender, visual preferences. In future work, we plan to explore how such different user sub-cultures perceive and engage with micro videos, following recent works from the Multimedia community studying the impact of culture in subjective image perception [10]. A second dimension to explore in our future work is generalising the above findings to other micro video platforms – our preliminary studies indicate that key results such as the Primacy of the first seconds effect, are robust across platforms, applying to Instagram videos as well. However, more work is required in this direction.

---

[10] http://www.theverge.com/2013/6/20/4448906/video-on-instagram-hands-on-photos-and-video.

A   Appendix: Feature Table

Table 3. Dimensionality and description of features used to describe Vine videos

Features	Dim	Description
Visual quality features		
RMS contrast	1	RMS contrast is calculated as standard deviation across all the pixels relative to mean intensity
Weber Contrast	1	Weber contrast is calculated as $$F_{weber} = \sum_{x=width} \sum_{y=height} \frac{I(x,y) - I_{average}}{I_{average}}$$
Gray Contrast	1	Gray contrast is calculated in similar to RMS contrast in HSL colour space for the L value of pixels
Simplicity	2	Simplicity of composition of a photograph is a distinguishable factor that directly correlates with professionalism of the creator [11]. We calculate Image simplicity by two methods: Yeh simplicity [34] and Luo simplicity [18]
Naturalness	1	How much does the image colors and objects match the real human perception? To compute image naturalness we convert the image into the HSV color space and then identify pixels corresponding to natural objects like skin, grass, sky, water etc. This is done by considering pixels which an average brightness $V \in [20, 80]$ and saturation $S > 0.1$. The final naturalness score is calculated by finding the weighted average of all the groups of pixels. [35]
Colourfulness	1	A measure of colourfulness that describes the deviation from a pure gray image. It is calculated in RGB colour space as $\sqrt{\sigma_{rg}^2 + \sigma_{yb}^2} + 0.3\sqrt{\mu_{rg}^2 + \mu_{yb}^2}$ where $rg = R - G$ and $yb = \frac{R+G}{2}$ and μ and σ represent mean and standard deviation respectively
Hue Stats	2	Hue mean and variance which signifies the range of pure colours present in the image. It is directly derived from the HSL colour space
LR balance	1	Difference in intensity of pixels between two sections of an image is also a good measure of aesthetic quality. In non-ideal lighting conditions, images and videos tend to be over exposed in one part and correctly exposed in other. This is generally a sign of amateur creator. To capture this we compare the distribution of intensities of pixels in the left and right side of the image. The distance between the two distributions is measured using Chi-squared distance

(continued)

Table 3. (*continued*)

Features	Dim	Description
Rule of Thirds	1	This feature deals with compositional aspects of a photograph. This feature basically calculates if the object of interest is placed in one of the imaginary intersection of lines drawn at approximate one third of the horizontal and vertical positions. This is a well known aesthetic guideline for photographers
ROI proportion	1	Measure of prominence given to salient objects. This measure detects the salient object in an image and then measures proportion of pixels its relative to the image
Image brightness	3	Features signify brightness of the image. Includes average brightness, saturation and saturation variance
Image Sharpness	1	A measure of the clarity and level of detail of an image. Sharpness can be determined as a function of its Laplacian normalized by the local average luminance in the surroundings of each pixel, i.e. $\sum_{x,y} \frac{L(x,y)}{\mu_{xy}}$, with $L(x,y) = \frac{\partial^2 I}{\partial x^2} + \frac{\partial^2 I}{\partial y^2}$ where $\mu_x y$ denotes the average luminance around pixel (x, y)
Sharp Pixel Proportion	1	Out of focus or blurry photographs are generally not considered aesthetically pleasing. In this feature we measure the proportion of sharp pixels compared to total pixels. We compute sharp pixels by converting the image in the frequency domain and then looking at the pixel corresponding to the regions of highest frequency [34], using the OpenIMAJ [8] tool
Higher level features		
Face Percentage	1	Percentage of frames in a video, which have been tested positive for at-least one face. Faces detected using Viola Jones Detector [31]
Frame sentiment	1	Median frame sentiment of all the sampled frames from a micro video. The sentiment was calculated using the Multilingual Visual Sentiment Ontology detector [10]
Past post count	1	Number of past posts user has uploaded prior to current one. This is a good measure of user's experience with the platform and activity
Audio features		
Zero Crossing rate	1	Zero crossing rate measures the rhythmic component an audio track [15]. It ends up detecting percussion instruments like Drums in the track
Loudness	2	This feature expresses overall perceived loudness as two components. Overall energy and average short time energy [14]

(*continued*)

Table 3. (*continued*)

Features	Dim	Description
Mode	1	This feature estimates the musical mode of the audio tract (major or minor). In western music theory, major modes give a perception of happiness and minor modes of sadness. [15]
Dissonance	1	Consonance and dissonance in an audio track has been shown to be relevant for emotional perception [15]. The values of dissonance are a calculate by measuring space between peaks in the frequency spectrum of the audio track. Consonant frequency peaks tend to be spaced evenly where as dissonant frequency peaks are not
Onset Rate	1	This measures the the Rhythmical perception. Onsets are peaks in the amplitude envelop of a track. Onset rate is measured by counting such events in a second. This typically gives a sense of speed to the track
Social features		
Followers	1	Number of followers that the user posting a video has. This is the prime social feature available from the user meta-data. The number of followers directly represent the audience which are highly probably to engage with the video on upload

References

1. Bakhshi, S., et al.: Faces engage us: photos with faces attract more likes and comments on instagram. In: Proceedings of the 32nd Annual ACM Conference on Human Factors in Computing Systems, pp. 965–974. ACM (2014)
2. Cha, M., et al.: A measurement-driven analysis of information propagation in the flickr social network. In: Proceedings of the 18th WWW, WWW 2009, pp. 721–730. ACM, New York (2009)
3. Chen, J., et al.: Micro tells macro: predicting the popularity of micro-videos via a transductive model. In: Proceedings of the 2016 ACM on Multimedia Conference, MM 2016, pp. 898–907. ACM, New York (2016). http://doi.acm.org/10.1145/2964284.2964314
4. Datta, R., et al.: Algorithmic inferencing of aesthetics and emotion in natural images: an exposition. In: 2008 15th IEEE ICIP, pp. 105–108. IEEE (2008)
5. Kalayeh, M.M., et al.: How to take a good selfie? In: Proceedings of the 23rd ACM International Conference on Multimedia, MM 2015, pp. 923–926. ACM, New York (2015). http://doi.acm.org/10.1145/2733373.2806365
6. Fontanini, G., et al.: Web video popularity prediction using sentiment and content visual features. In: Proceedings of the 2016 ACM on ICMR, pp. 289–292. ACM (2016)
7. Grossman, D.: Can micro video change how we communicate? BBC Newsnight, September 2013

8. Hare, J.S., et al.: Openimaj and imageterrier: Java libraries and tools for scalable multimedia analysis and indexing of images. In: Proceedings of the 19th ACM MM 2011, pp. 691–694. ACM, New York (2011). http://doi.acm.org/10.1145/2072298.2072421

9. Isola, P., Xiao, J., Torralba, A., Oliva, A.: What makes an image memorable? In: 2011 IEEE Conference on CVPR, pp. 145–152. IEEE (2011)

10. Jou, B., et al.: Visual affect around the world: a large-scale multilingual visual sentiment ontology. In: Proceedings of the 23rd ACM MM, pp. 159–168. ACM (2015)

11. Ke, Y., Tang, X., Jing, F.: The design of high-level features for photo quality assessment. In: 2006 IEEE CVPR 2006, vol. 1, pp. 419–426. IEEE (2006)

12. Khosla, A., et al.: What makes an image popular? In: Proceedings of the 23rd International Conference on World Wide Web, WWW 2014, New York, NY, USA (2014). http://doi.acm.org/10.1145/2566486.2567996

13. Krizhevsky, A., et al.: Imagenet classification with deep convolutional neural networks. In: NIPS, pp. 1097–1105 (2012)

14. Lartillot, O., Toivianinen, P.: A matlab toolbox for musical feature extraction from audio. In: International Conference on Digital Audio Effects, pp. 237–244 (2007)

15. Laurier, C., Lartillot, O., Eerola, T., Toiviainen, P.: Exploring relationships between audio features and emotion in music (2009)

16. Leung, L.: User-generated content on the internet: an examination of gratifications, civic engagement and psychological empowerment. New Media Soc. **11**(8), 1327–1347 (2009)

17. Louppe, G., et al.: Understanding variable importances in forests of randomized trees. In: NIPS, pp. 431–439 (2013)

18. Luo, Y., Tang, X.: Photo and video quality evaluation: focusing on the subject. In: Forsyth, D., Torr, P., Zisserman, A. (eds.) ECCV 2008. LNCS, vol. 5304, pp. 386–399. Springer, Heidelberg (2008). doi:10.1007/978-3-540-88690-7_29

19. Machajdik, J., Hanbury, A.: Affective image classification using features inspired by psychology and art theory. In: Proceedings of the 18th ACM MM, MM 2010. ACM, New York (2010). http://doi.acm.org/10.1145/1873951.1873965

20. Mazloom, et al.: Multimodal popularity prediction of brand-related social media posts. In: Proceedings of the 2016 ACM on Multimedia Conference, MM 2016, New York, NY, USA (2016). http://doi.acm.org/10.1145/2964284.2967210

21. Nguyen, P.X., Rogez, G., Fowlkes, C., Ramamnan, D.: The open world of micro-videos. arXiv preprint arXiv:1603.09439 (2016)

22. Nwana, A.O., et al.: A latent social approach to Youtube popularity prediction. In: 2013 IEEE (GLOBECOM), pp. 3138–3144. IEEE (2013)

23. O'Brien, H.L., Toms, E.G.: What is user engagement? A conceptual framework for defining user engagement with technology. J. Am. Soc. Inform. Sci. Technol. **59**(6), 938–955 (2008)

24. Pinto, H., et al.: Using early view patterns to predict the popularity of Youtube videos. In: Proceedings of the sixth ACM ICWSM, pp. 365–374. ACM (2013)

25. Pogue, D.: Why are micro movies so popular these days? Sci. Am. (2013)

26. Redi, M., et al.: 6 seconds of sound and vision: creativity in micro-videos. In: Proceedings of the IEEE CVPR, pp. 4272–4279 (2014)

27. Schifanella, R., et al.: An image is worth more than a thousand favorites: surfacing the hidden beauty of flickr pictures. In: Proceedings of THE 9TH ICWSM 2015 (2015)

28. Schifanella, R., et al.: Detecting sarcasm in multimodal social platforms. In: Proceedings of the 2016 ACM MM, pp. 1136–1145. ACM (2016)

29. Slater, A., Kirby, R.: Innate and learned perceptual abilities in the newborn infant. Exp. Brain Res. **123**(1–2), 90–94 (1998)
30. Totti, L.C., et al.: The impact of visual attributes on online image diffusion. In: Proceedings of the 2014 ACM Conference on Web Science, WebSci 2014. ACM, New York (2014)
31. Viola, P., Jones, M.J.: Robust real-time face detection. Int. J. Comput. Vis. **57**(2), 137–154 (2004)
32. Wang, Y., et al.: Inferring sentiment from web images with joint inference on visual and social cues: a regulated matrix factorization approach. In: Ninth ICWSM (2015)
33. Yamasaki, T., et al.: Social popularity score: predicting numbers of views, comments, and favorites of social photos using only annotations. In: Proceedings of the First International Workshop on Internet-Scale Multimedia Management, WISMM 2014. ACM, New York (2014)
34. Yeh, C.H., et al.: Personalized photograph ranking and selection system. In: Proceedings of the 18th ACM MM, pp. 211–220. ACM (2010)
35. Zhong, C., et al.: Predicting pinterest: automating a distributed human computation. In: Proceedings of the 24th WWW, WWW 2015. ACM, New York (2015)

Compression-Based Algorithms for Deception Detection

Christina L. Ting$^{(\boxtimes)}$, Andrew N. Fisher, and Travis L. Bauer

Sandia National Laboratories, Albuquerque, NM 87123, USA
{clting,anfishe,tlbauer}@sandia.gov

Abstract. In this work we extend compression-based algorithms for deception detection in text. In contrast to approaches that rely on theories for deception to identify feature sets, compression automatically identifies the most significant features. We consider two datasets that allow us to explore deception in opinion (content) and deception in identity (stylometry). Our first approach is to use unsupervised clustering based on a normalized compression distance (NCD) between documents. Our second approach is to use Prediction by Partial Matching (PPM) to train a classifier with conditional probabilities from labeled documents, followed by arithmetic coding (AC) to classify an unknown document based on which label gives the best compression. We find a significant dependence of the classifier on the *relative* volume of training data used to build the conditional probability distributions of the different labels. Methods are demonstrated to overcome the data size-dependence when analytics, not information transfer, is the goal. Our results indicate that deceptive text contains structure statistically distinct from truthful text, and that this structure can be automatically detected using compression-based algorithms.

1 Introduction

Deception, whether in content or style, is a common element across all forms of communication. However, human judgement performs roughly at chance at identifying deception [5]. Furthermore, with the massive amounts of textual information produced online, analysts need an automatic method for identifying features that are indicative of deception.

Previous work in deception detection has primarily relied on manual feature selection based on, for example, psycholinguistic theories of deception and/or computational linguistics, followed by supervised machine learning to build a classifier [1,6,18,22,23,28]. In this work, we explore an alternative to explicit feature selection based on compression. In particular, we use compression to automatically identify the most significant structural and statistical elements common among deceptive documents in order to distinguish them from truthful documents. The approach can be generalized to other applications in which the goal is to identify similarities among common entities, *e.g.* authorship detection or user categorization.

© Springer International Publishing AG 2017
G.L. Ciampaglia et al. (Eds.): SocInfo 2017, Part I, LNCS 10539, pp. 257–276, 2017.
DOI: 10.1007/978-3-319-67217-5_16

In Sect. 2, we review related work on deception detection. In Sect. 3 we briefly discuss the two compression methods used to identify deceptive text; additional details can be found in the Appendix. In Sect. 4, we present results on two separate datasets for deception: a hotel dataset [21,22] containing truthful and deceptive hotel reviews (deception in opinion), and the *(Extended) Brennan-Greenstadt* [6] corpus on authentic, obfuscated, and imitated writing samples (deception in identity). We also discuss modifications to improve the performance of PPM/AC on unbalanced training data when the lossless information transfer component of compression does not need to be preserved. Finally, in Sect. 5, we conclude with the main findings of this work.

2   Related Work

2.1   Deception Detection

As discussed in the Introduction, most work on deception detection in text has focused on identifying features that are indicative of deception. In this section, we provide a brief review of these studies, followed by an alternative, statistical-based approach to motivate our current work.

Newman et al. [18] approached deception detection by developing a linguistic profile of deception based on the notion that *how* people express themselves may be more informative than *what* they express. The authors were able to apply their Linguistic Inquiry and Word Count (LIWC) text analysis program [24] to correctly identify deception at a rate of 67% when given a singular topic and 61% overall. Their results indicate liars show lower cognitive complexity, fewer self-references and other-references, and more negative emotion words. Building off Pennebaker's earlier work, Ott *et al.* [22] viewed the problem of deception detection in three ways: a standard text categorization task based on n-gram classifiers; an application of psychological effects of lying emerging in text based on LIWC; and an example of genre identification based on distributions of part-of-speech tags [4,25], where deceptive and truthful writing fit into sub-genres of imaginative and informative writing, respectively. The authors found that the n-gram classifier outperforms both the psycholinguistically-motivated features and genre identification, but that a combined classifier is able to achieve nearly 90% accuracy on their dataset of truthful and deceptive hotel reviews.

In a similar approach to the above two groups, Afroz *et al.* [1,6] proposed to look for subtle changes in human behavior due to the additional cognitive effort required for deception. According to the authors, these subtle changes are manifested in stylistic differences between truthful and deceptive text. The authors explored three feature sets: a *Writeprints feature set* containing lexical, syntactic, and content specific features [26]; a *lying-detection feature set* containing features of lying in computer mediated communications and typed documents [8,13]; and a *9-feature set* containing features from the neural network experiments by Brennan and Greenstadt [7]. As with Pennebaker, the authors found that non-specific features (*e.g.*, function words) are as effective as content-specific features for identifying deception.

In addition to the dictionary bag-of-words and parts-of-speech features discussed above, Probabilistic Context Free Grammars (PCFGs) have been applied to extract deeper syntactic stylometry features with improved results [11]. Finally, a statistical language modeling (SLM) approach has also been used for deception detection [27]. In their work, Zhou *et al.* were motivated by a general technique that does not require explicit feature selection or extraction. Their SLM approach captures dependecies between words in n-grams and considers all words as potential features. Similarly, compression algorithms for text have been developed to automatically identify the most significant structural and statistical features in a document, and have found previous success in authorship identification and classification in general [2, 9, 12, 15, 19].

3   Methods

Compression algorithms for text attempt to take a document and reduce the number of bits used to encode the document. The reason it is possible to reduce the number of required bits for a document is that similar structures in a document allow one to assign fewer bits for more common characters. For example, if one sees a q in a document, the likelihood that the next character is a u is so high that it is almost not necessary to include the u. Compression exploits these types of facts by using fewer bits to represent qu than to represent something like q-. Thus, if a document has a lot of similar structure, then usually a compression algorithm can compress it into fewer bits.

The basic assumption behind our use of compression algorithms for classifying truthful versus deceptive writings is that truthful documents should share a similar structure and deceptive documents should share a similar structure distinct from truthful documents. This structure can then be automatically detected by using a compression algorithm resulting in a compression to a fewer number of bits. The two methods that we use exploit this feature of compression in two different ways. With NCD [14], compression is used as a method of determining the similarity between two documents; with PPM/AC [10], compression is used to determine how similar a document is to a training set. Details of the two methods are provided in the Appendix; here we focus our discussion on modifications made to the standard implementation of PPM.

3.1   Modifications to PPM

As mentioned in the beginning of Sect. 3 and in the Appendix, we want to use PPM to create models for truthful and deceptive documents. When applying PPM for compression, the algorithm builds a set of tables that predicts the probability for the next character, given a finite set of previous characters. The finite set of previous characters is called the context. The model for truthful and deceptive documents is then the final state of the PPM tables after processing every document in the training set. Once we have the PPM tables for the truthful and deceptive models, we can use PPM with AC to compress a test document and classify the document according to which model compresses the test document best (i.e. with the fewest number of bits). For this compression, we use a modified, *static* version of the PPM algorithm. In particular, we use the PPM tables after building the models, and do not update the PPM tables while compressing the test document. We avoid the updating step to avoid biasing the models with information from the test document.

The modifications described above are enough to adapt the PPM algorithm to a classifier scheme. However, we also explore the inclusion or exclusion of two non-character symbols: the *eof* and the *esc*. In the implementation of the PPM algorithm that we use, both the *eof* and the *esc* are given a static count of 1 in *every* PPM table, while the characters are given a count equal to the number of times that they have been seen for a given context. The prediction for a character in a table is then given by the ratio of its count to the total counts in the table; see Appendix for details. So, if the total counts in a given table are large, then the additional count of 1 for the *eof* and 1 for the *esc* is negligible. However, if the total counts in a given table are small, then including *eof* and *esc* significantly changes the prediction for all the characters in that table.

In addition to modifying the prediction of the characters, the rational for excluding the *eof* and the *esc* is further motivated by the following. The purpose of the *eof* is to mark the end of the file; unless some particular regular structure is expected at the end of the document, the *eof* is not likely to provide much information. The purpose for the *esc* symbol in the usual implementation of the PPM compression scheme is to signal to the decompression algorithm that the current table does not provide a prediction for the next character, and that the next table will be considered; see Appendix for details. Since we are using compression only as a means for comparing similarity, we do not need to decompress the documents. Hence, we do not need to include symbols, such as the *esc*, that are necessary only for decompression. In what follows, we explore the effects of including or excluding the *eof* and the *esc*.

4   Results

4.1   Data

We present results on two datasets. The first dataset is the *Brennan-Greenstadt* (*BG*) corpus of truthful and deceptive writing samples from 12 authors. The truthful writing samples are pre-existing samples written for an academic or business purpose. Each author provided 7–10 samples, for a total of approximately 5000 words per author. The deceptive writing samples are written for the purpose of two types of adversarial attacks: obfuscation and imitation. For the obfuscated samples, authors are asked to write a 500-word article describing their neighborhood while hiding their identity. For the imitated samples, authors are asked to write a 500-word article describing a day in their life in the third person in the style of Cormac McCarthy's "The Road". An extended version of the *BG* corpus [6] was collected from Amazon Mechanical Turk (AMT), where

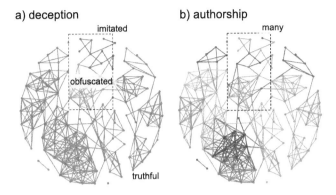

Fig. 1. Graphs showing the lowest 5% of the NCD scores for the BG dataset. (Color figure online)

the participants were asked to adhere to a set of submission guidelines. Out of 100 submissions, 45 were accepted.

The second dataset consists of truthful and deceptive hotel reviews collected by Ott et al. in separate studies on positive [22] and negative [21] opinion spam. The authors mined various online travel review communities for truthful reviews. Although not a *gold standard* for truthful, recent studies suggest that deception rates in these online travel review communities is small [16,20]. Deceptive reviews were then obtained through AMT, where each participant was given 30 min to complete the review and only one review per participant was allowed. 400 of each of the following categories were collected: truthful positive, truthful negative, deceptive positive, and deceptive negative.

4.2   NCD

We begin by computing the NCD between all pairs of documents within the BG corpus and visualizing the result as a graph, where the edge connecting documents d_i and d_j is assigned a weight corresponding to $NCD(d_i, d_j)$. To identify clusters with higher intracluster similarity, our approach is to remove edges above a maximum $NCD_{\max}$, where smaller values correspond to higher similarity. In Fig. 1, we visualize [3] the result of this approach using the Fruchterman-Reingold layout, where nodes correspond to documents and we keep only the lowest 5% of the NCD scores (*i.e.* the top 5% in terms of similarity). The two graphs are color-coded according to: (a) deception and (b) authorship. From the deception graph, it is apparent that the NCD score is able to correctly distinguish truthful documents (pink) from deceptive documents, where the latter can be further separated into "imitation" (blue) and "obfuscation" (green) categories. Within the truthful region of the deception graph, there appears to be several different clusters, which can be attributed from the authorship graph as belonging to different authors. In contrast, the two deception clusters, which are highlighted by the dashed box, can be seen to contain several different color nodes, indicating

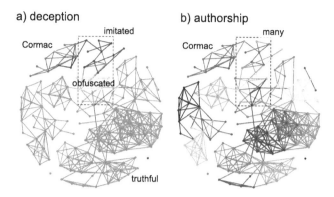

Fig. 2. Graphs showing the lowest 5% NCD scores for the *modified BG* dataset, where we have removed the word "neighborhood" from obfuscated text, and added authentic writing samples from Cormac McCarthy. (Color figure online)

documents from several different authors. This result suggests that deceptive documents contain features distinct from truthful documents and automatically discernible without global state.

Recall that deceptive documents in the *BG* corpus are collected by asking the authors to provide text that imitates Cormac McCarthy, and text that describes a neighborhood while obscuring the author's identity. One could then propose that the compression algorithm is picking up on these two features, rather than features of deception. To test this hypothesis, we have modified the BG corpus in two ways. First, to test whether NCD identifies Cormac McCarthy rather than imitation, we added writing samples of Cormac McCarthy taken from "The Road", "Blood Meridian", and "All the Pretty Horses". Second, to test whether NCD identifies "neighborhood" rather than obfuscation, we removed this word from the corpus. In Fig. 2 we show results for our *modified BG* corpus. Even without the "neighborhood" feature, the NCD algorithm is still able to correctly identify obfuscated (green) from truthful (pink) documents. In addition, there is a new cluster corresponding to the authentic Cormac McCarthy (purple) that is separate from imitated Cormac McCarthy (blue). These results suggests that, while it is possible to hide one's identity (*i.e.* separate from your own authorship cluster), it is less easy to imitate another's identity (*i.e.* participate in an authorship cluster not your own). Furthermore, we have identified two ways to "obscure" identity: intentional obfuscation and attempting to imitate another identity.

We also applied the NCD algorithm to the corpus of truthful and deceptive hotel reviews. In this case, we are unable to identify an NCD_{max} that separates truthful from deceptive documents. We hypothesize that the failure to identify deception in the hotel corpus as opposed to the *BG* corpus may be due to the difference in "deception" defined in the two datasets. For the hotel reviews, "deception" is in terms of lying about content; for the *BG* writing samples, "deception" is in terms of lying about identity. The results here suggest that

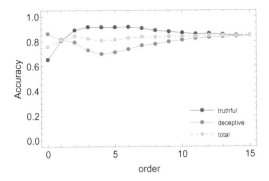

Fig. 3. PPMA/AC on hotel dataset: accuracy as a function of context order for classifying truthful (blue), deceptive (red), and total (green) documents. (Color figure online)

lying about content is more difficult to identify using the NCD compression algorithm. We have also tested whether the NCD algorithm is identifying hotels rather than deception, and were unable to obtain clusters of reviews written about the same hotel.

4.3 PPMA/AC

Here we present results using PPMA, followed by AC to build a classifier from a background collection of labeled documents. The category that compresses the unknown document with fewer bits is selected as the category. For categories, we consider "truthful" (T) and "deceptive" (D).

We begin with the hotel dataset, for which the NCD algorithm was unable to identify truthful and deceptive clusters. Figure 3 shows accuracy as a function of context order d, averaged across a 4-fold cross validation scheme when a test document is compressed to a set of static PPMA tables. When looking at the entire dataset, it can be seen that the accuracy quickly reaches a maximum of 0.85 at order 2, without significant gains at higher orders. We note that an optimal accuracy at order 2 is somewhat unexpected since the best compression for the English language (and verified in this dataset) is usually around order 4 [10]. However, this result suggests that, in contrast to NCD, PPMA/AC successfully distinguishes deceptive from truthful hotel reviews. Furthermore, Table 4 in the Appendix shows that PPMA/AC outperforms standard machine learning with stylometry features on the same dataset by at least 20%. Similar stylometry features have been applied for deception detection, where it has been proposed that deceptive text contains simpler words and shorter sentences than truthful text [8].

Although we could already be satisfied with the high accuracies obtained in our classification of truthful and deceptive hotel reviews using PPMA/AC, it is still useful to understand why the algorithm achieves such high accuracy so that we can understand how to modify the algorithm when this is not the case.

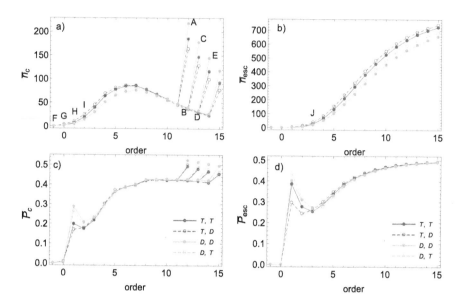

Fig. 4. PPMA/AC on hotel dataset: expected values for the counts $\bar{n}$ and probabilities $\bar{P}$ as a function of context order for max orders $d_{\max} \geq 12$. Panels (a) and (c) are for observed characters; (b) and (d) are for escapes. Figure label indicates test and model category, respectively. (Color figure online)

Therefore, we take a closer look at the statistics of the PPMA/AC algorithm on the hotel dataset. In Fig. 4, we show expected values for different statistics as a function of order for different max orders. Note that *max order* here refers to the same *order* used in Fig. 3. We need to distinguish max order here because each time the max order context has not been observed by the model, the PPMA algorithm emits an escape and drops to lower order contexts; see the Appendix for details. Thus, for a given $d_{\max}$ there will be relevant statistics for all context orders $d \leq d_{\max}$. Note that each curve corresponds to a different test-to-model pairing, where correct test-to-model pairings (T, T and D, D) are indicated by the solid curves and incorrect test-to-model pairings (T, D and D, T) are indicated by the dashed curves.

We begin with Fig. 4a, which shows the expected value for the observed character counts $\bar{n}_c(d; d_{\max})$ as a function of the context order and maximum allowed order for different max orders $d_{\max}$. For clarity, we show only $d_{\max} > 12$, but note that results can be generalized to all $d_{\max}$. In terms of the implications of $\bar{n}_c(d; d_{\max})$ to the accuracy of a classifier, it can be seen that for both truthful (blue) and deceptive (red) documents, the correct test-to-model pairings (solid) have higher expected values for higher orders (including $d_{\max}$) than the incorrect test-to-model pairings (dashed), where the latter also have higher expected values at the lower orders. In other words, a given test document is able to match higher order contexts of its correct model, which is intuitively what we would expect. Furthermore, Fig. 4c shows that the expected probabilities of

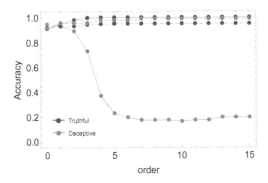

Fig. 5. PPMA/AC on *extended BG* dataset: accuracy as a function of context order for classifying truthful (blue) and deceptive (red) documents using PPMA for the *extended BG* dataset (solid) and for the *normalized BG* dataset (dashed). (Color figure online)

the observed contexts $\bar{P}_c(d; d_{\max})$ decrease as the context order decreases (except for order 1). Since lower probabilities require more bits to encode, the incorrect model will compress the test document worse than the correct model. These are precisely the desired properties for a compression algorithm used as a classifier.

Interestingly, the average counts per order overlap for all max orders except for $\bar{n}_c(d_{\max}; d_{\max})$. In fact, $\bar{n}_c(d_{\max}; d_{\max})$ can be shown to be the sum of all higher order counts from larger $d_{\max}$. This is equivalent to saying that anything observed at contexts larger than the maximum that is requested by $d_{\max}$ gets lumped into $\bar{n}_c(d_{\max}; d_{\max})$. In the figure, this fact is demonstrated by the following combinations: $A = C + B$, $C = E + D$, and $A = E + B + D$.

In addition to accounting for contexts previously observed in the model, PPM is required to account for unobserved contexts by emitting escapes. In Fig. 4b we plot the expected value for the number of escapes $\bar{n}_{\mathrm{esc}}(d)$ as a function of context order d. Note that the results for different $\bar{n}_{\mathrm{esc}}(d)$ are independent of $d_{\max}$, so that we only show $d_{\max} = 15$. It can be seen that for both truthful (blue) and deceptive (red) test documents, the incorrect model (dashed) emits more escapes across all orders than the corresponding correct model (solid). Therefore, for all context orders the test document more often misses the tables of the incorrect model, emits an escape, and drops to a lower order table. This is shown directly in Fig. 4 by noting that the number of escapes at any given order is directly related to the sum of the number of characters emitted by all the lower order tables: $J = F + G + H + I$. Thus, the more escapes emitted at a given order, the more characters must also be emitted at lower order contexts. This has two effects. First, the cost of emitting an escape and its corresponding probability (see Fig. 4d) are accounted for. Second, as discussed above, the cost of dropping to lower orders is accounted for through lower probabilities, on average, of the lower order contexts (see Fig. 4c). These are the two primary reasons why the PPMA/AC algorithm is able to correctly classify deceptive and truthful documents in the hotel dataset with such high accuracy.

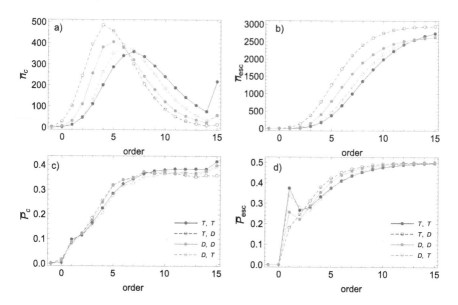

Fig. 6. PPMA/AC on *extended BG* dataset: expected values for the counts $\bar{n}$ and probabilities $\bar{P}$ as a function of context order for max order $d_{\mathrm{max}} = 15$. Panels (a) and (c) are for characters; (b) and (d) are for escapes. Figure label indicates test and model category, respectively. (Color figure online)

Next, we apply the PPMA/AC algorithm to the *extended BG* corpus. Figure 5 shows the accuracy of the truthful (blue solid) and deceptive (red solid) documents, where all deceptive (obfuscated and imitated) documents are grouped together. It can be seen that, while the truthful category reaches an accuracy near 1.0 by order 3, the deceptive category drops to 0.2 after order 5. We hypothesize that this result is due to an imbalance in training data. In particular, because the *extended BG* dataset contains nearly an order of magnitude more samples of truthful than deceptive documents, we obtain significantly more examples of truthful than deceptive contexts, which significantly alters the expected values of $\bar{n}_c(d; d_{\mathrm{max}})$ and $\bar{n}_{\mathrm{esc}}(d)$ to favor the truthful model. To test this hypothesis, we investigate the output of the PPMA/AC algorithm applied to the *extended BG* corpus; see Fig. 6.

There are some notable differences between Figs. 4 and 6 that explain the low accuracy of the deceptive documents of the *extended BG* dataset, compared to the hotel dataset. First, recall that accurate classification by the PPMA/AC algorithm requires the expected value of the character count $\bar{n}_c(d; d_{\mathrm{max}})$ to peak at higher orders for the correct model (solid) than for the incorrect model (dashed). This is expected, since the test document should, on average, match longer strings of the correct model. Whereas the truthful tests (blue) show this pattern, the deceptive tests (red) do not; see Fig. 6a. Second, an accurate classifier requires the correct model (solid) to emit fewer escapes $\bar{n}_{\mathrm{esc}}(d)$ than the incorrect model (dashed). The truthful test documents (blue) show this property across all

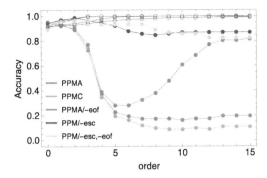

Fig. 7. Modified PPM on *extended BG* dataset: accuracy as a function of context order for classifying truthful and deceptive documents. Different colors correspond to different modifications to the PPM algorithm, where accuracy for all truthful documents are indicated by the empty circles. (Color figure online)

context orders d, whereas the deceptive test documents (red) do not; see Fig. 6b. Taken together, the truthful model compresses *both* the truthful and deceptive test documents with fewer bits by matching higher order contexts and emitting fewer escapes. These results are consistent with our hypothesis that because there are so many more examples of observed contexts in the training data for the truthful model, a given test (truthful or deceptive) will match higher order contexts of the truthful model. Therefore, we obtain low accuracies for deceptive documents in Fig. 5. Based on these observations, two modifications to improve the accuracy are proposed: (1) a modification of the PPMA/AC algorithm to ignore the *esc* and (2) a normalization of the size of the training data, followed by a voting scheme to select the best model. We note that in reality, situations where there are far more examples of "regular" than "anomalous" training data is normal, and so it is important to modify the compression algorithms to handle these situations.

4.4   Modifications to the Implementation of PPM

In Fig. 7 we show the accuracy of truthful and deceptive documents from the *extended BG* dataset, where different colors correspond to accuracies of the deceptive documents with different modifications to the PPMA/AC algorithm (see Sect. 3.1 for a discussion). However, we still show results for the accuracy of the truthful documents (empty markers) to demonstrate that none of the modifications we have considered reduce the accuracy of the truthful documents. The accuracy of identifying deceptive documents using PPMA is reproduced from Fig. 5 in red. It can be seen that ignoring the *esc* symbol (purple) increases the accuracy of the deceptive documents to nearly 100% for order 2, before dropping off again for higher orders. Interestingly, ignoring the *eof* symbol (magenta) eventually achieves an accuracy comparable to ignoring the *esc* symbol, but requires higher context orders: $d_{\max} > 12$. The combination of ignoring both the

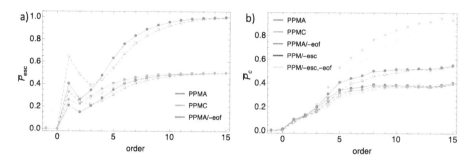

Fig. 8. Modified PPM on *extended BG* dataset: expected values for (a) the escape probabilities and (b) the character probabilities, for max order $d_{\max} = 15$. Different colors correspond to different PPM algorithms; D, D and D, T are given by solid and dashed lines, respectively. (Color figure online)

esc and the *eof* symbols significantly improves the accuracy across all contexts in a similar manner as ignoring only the *esc* symbol. In contrast to ignoring the *esc* and/or the *eof*, PPMC (green) decreases the accuracy. To understand how these modifications affect the accuracy, in Fig. 8(a) we take a closer look at the expected values for the escape probabilities $\bar{P}_{esc}(d)$. Here, the curves are distinguished by color according to the modification made to the PPMA/AC algorithm in Fig. 7 and we focus on deceptive test documents, where solid corresponds to D, D and dashed corresponds to D, T. The trivial result of ignoring the *esc* symbol is not shown.

PPMC (green) slightly increases $\bar{P}_{esc}(d)$, relative to PPMA, particularly at the lower context orders. This result can be expected by recalling that the PPMC algorithm assigns the escape a count equivalent to the number of distinct entries in a given table at a given context; see Appendix. PPMA, in contrast, assigns all escapes a count of 1. Both PPMA and PPMC converge to $\bar{P}_{esc}(d = 15) = 0.5$, since these higher order contexts have never been seen before and contain only the *eof* and the *esc* symbols, each with probability $1/2$. In contrast, PPMA without the *eof* symbol (magenta) significantly increases $\bar{P}_{esc}(d)$ across all orders, before eventually converging to $\bar{P}_{esc}(d = 15) = 1.0$. In other words, by ignoring the *eof*, the higher order tables now contain only a single symbol: the *esc*. Because a probability of 1.0 requires zero bits to encode, the *esc* symbol is essentially ignored for the higher order contexts, which are where the vast majority of the escapes are actually issued; recall Fig. 6(b). Therefore, ignoring the *eof* symbol has a very similar effect as ignoring the higher order escapes.

In cases where the expected value of escapes $\bar{n}_{esc}(d)$ is primarily determined by differences in training data size and are therefore meaningless, these results suggest that ignoring the *esc* symbol altogether is a successful method for recovering accuracy of the classifier. Instead, it is possible to use the structural information held in the context probabilities $\bar{P}_c(d; d_{\max})$. In particular, Fig. 8(b) shows that for all versions of PPM/AC, the probabilities $\bar{P}_c(d; d_{\max})$ of the deceptive test to the deceptive model (solid) are higher than the deceptive test to the truthful model (dashed). This is sufficient for better compression by the deceptive model once the escapes are removed. Note, however, that once the escapes are ignored, we no longer have an algorithm that can decompress. For analytic purposes, this is not our concern, and so we have the ability to modify our algorithm to optimize the output of compression for optimal classification.

4.5   Normalizing the Training Data

Finally, we consider a different approach to improving the low accuracies observed for the deceptive documents in the *extended BG* dataset. In particular, we propose to treat the discrepancy in the size of truthful versus deceptive training data head on: by dividing the truthful training data into subsets containing roughly the same number of documents as the deceptive training data. We then apply PPMA/AC to each subset of the truthful model, together with the full deceptive model, and assign a category using a voting scheme across all subsets, *i.e.* the final resulting category is the category that is selected most often while comparing a test document to a model of a subset of truthful training documents with a model of the full deceptive training documents. Results from this approach are shown in Fig. 5, where it can be seen that our normalization voting scheme (dashed) recovers high accuracy of the deceptive documents without significantly sacrificing the accuracy of the truthful documents.

Once again, we can compute the statistics of the counts and probabilities of characters and escapes, in order to better understand the accuracy of the algorithm. In Fig. 9 it can be seen that our normalization scheme produces statistics with similar trends to the hotel dataset. This result is not surprising since the hotel dataset was "normalized" to begin with. In particular, $\bar{n}_c(d; d_{\max})$ for the correct model (solid) now peaks at higher orders than the incorrect model (dashed) for both the truthful (blue) and the deceptive (red) test documents; and the incorrect model (dashed) emits more escapes on average $\bar{P}_{\mathrm{esc}}(d)$ across all orders than the correct model (solid) for both truthful (blue) and deceptive (red) test documents. Together these results suggest that indeed the low accuracy of classifying the deceptive documents is due to the discrepancy in the training data size, and that the normalization scheme discussed here is able to produce a classifier that recovers high accuracies for all categories.

5   Conclusion

In this work we extend compression-based algorithms for deception detection in text. The basic motivation for this work is that deceptive text contains structure statistically distinct from truthful text, and that this structure can be automatically detected using compression-based algorithms. We consider two approaches: one based on normalized compression distance (NCD) and one based on using Prediction by Partial Matching (PPM).

For our first approach, we use an unsupervised clustering based on the NCD between pairs of documents whereby we identify clusters by selecting a threshold for allowed distances. We found that NCD does well at identifying identity deception, where individuals are attempting to imitate another's style or obfuscate their own identity. Moreover, we found that these types of deceptions themselves were distinguishable. We also found that this technique was not as successful for detecting deception in terms of false opinions.

For our second approach, we use Prediction by Partial Matching (PPM) to train a classifier with conditional probabilities from labeled documents, followed by arithmetic coding (AC) to classify an unknown document based on which class gives the best compression. We found that this approach is able to fill the gap left by our NCD approach in that this approach was able to discern false opinions from truthful ones. However, in attempting to identify deception in identity, we found a significant dependence of the classifier on the *relative* volume of training data used to build the conditional probability distributions of the different classes. We show that by modifying the PPM/AC algorithm we are able to overcome the data size-dependence when compression is used as a means of measuring similarity. The most successful modifications are the removal of the *esc* and the introduction of a voting scheme that attempts to balance the training data for both categories of truthful and deceptive.

Acknowledgements. The authors acknowledge funding support from the U.S. Department of Energy. Sandia National Laboratories is a multimission laboratory managed and operated by National Technology and Engineering Solutions of Sandia, LLC., a wholly owned subsidiary of Honeywell International, Inc., for the U.S. Department of Energy's National Nuclear Security Administration under contract DE-NA0003525. SAND NO. SAND2017-7685 C.

A1   Appendix

A1.1   Normalized Compression Distance

Our first method of distinguishing between truthful and deceptive documents is to use a type of similarity measure called the *normalized compression distance* (NCD) [14]. NCD attempts to determine how similar two strings are to each other while also taking their size into account. Rather than providing an absolute distance, NCD is normalized in the sense that a pair of small strings should not be considered closer to one another than a pair of large strings simply because they are smaller. NCD is defined by:

$$\text{NCD}(x, y) = \frac{C(xy) - \min\{C(x), C(y)\}}{\max\{C(x), C(y)\}},$$

where $C(x)$ is a compression algorithm applied to a string x and xy denotes the concatenation of two strings x and y. We use LZMA as the compression algorithm.

To use the NCD in a clustering scheme, we compute the pairwise NCD between every pair of documents. We then use a threshold on the size of the distance in order to identify clusters.

A1.2   Prediction by Partial Matching and Arithmetic Coding

PPM using AC is a powerful method for compression and was used as the benchmark for compression algorithms for a number of years. The two algorithms complement each other in that PPM provides a model for predicting the next character in a document while AC takes a prediction model and uses the provided probabilities for each character to produce an encoded binary output. When the probability for a particular character or symbol is provided to AC we say that it is *emitted*. This terminology is helpful since PPM does not always provide the probability for the next character, but instead emits a sequence of other symbols called *escapes* to encode the fact that the PPM model is changing its internal state. These escapes, in turn, are used by a decoder so that the decoder can make the same changes.

The complementary nature of PPM and AC allows us to use them as part of a supervised learning scheme. We can use PPM to create models for truthful documents, called the *truthful model*, and for deceptive documents, called the *deceptive model*. We can then classify a document by using each predictive model together with AC and assigning the document to the class whose model produces the fewest number of bits for the compressed output.

For this scheme to work, it is possible to use a standard implementation of AC and the details are not necessary for understanding our method or results. There are only two facts that one needs to know. The first is that only non-zero probabilities are allowed and the second is that the higher the probability assigned to the next character the fewer the eventual bits needed for the compressed output. Saying the second fact another way, the better the predictor is at predicting the next character, the fewer the bits that are required.

Unlike AC, our way of using PPM is not the standard method. Moreover, in Sect. 4 we use two variants of PPM, known as PPMA and PPMC, and we make additional modifications to the PPM algorithm. To understand these changes, it is necessary to give a detailed overview of PPM, which we do next.

In general, PPM uses a set of tables of predictors of the next character that are conditioned on previous characters. The previous characters used are called the *context*, where the number of characters in the context, d, is called the *order*. Each table is representative of all the prediction of a given context within a given order, and is called an order-d table. Note that since there are multiple contexts that have the same order, there are several order-d tables for each order $d \geq 1$. For example, if one has the characters $abab$ as the context, then the prediction for the next character to be an a given $abab$ is contained in a table of order-4 with context $abab$. Thus, an order-d table for context $c_0 c_1 \ldots c_{d-1}$ is really the collection of conditional probabilities $P(c|c_0 c_1 \ldots c_{d-1})$ providing the probability of seeing a token c given that $c_0 c_1 \ldots c_{d-1}$ are the preceding characters. The special case when the order is 0 is $P(c)$, which is just the probability of c occurring.

For the versions of PPM that we consider (PPMA and PPMC), the orders that are allowed are bounded by a user–specified maximum order $d_{\max}$. When predicting the next character c, PPM first considers the previous $d = d_{\max}$ characters $c_0 c_1 \ldots c_{d-1}$ as the context, where c_{d-1} is the character directly preceding c. If $P(c|c_0c_1 \ldots c_{d-1})$ is non-zero, then this probability is provided to AC. However, it may be the case that $P(c|c_0c_1 \ldots c_{d-1}) = 0$, which is not an allowable probability for AC. When this event occurs, we say that the table does not contain c and PPM issues a probability for a special symbol called an *escape* to indicate that the character was not found. Then, PPM changes state and attempts to provide the probability of the next smaller context $P(c|c_1 \ldots c_{d-1})$. If $P(c|c_1 \ldots c_{d-1}) = 0$, then $P(c|c_2 \ldots c_{d-1})$ is considered, etc. If the character is not found with any context, then $P(c)$ is considered. Finally, if PPM has no prediction for $P(c)$, then a default uniform distribution is assumed for all characters. The table for this distribution is considered to have order -1. In addition to the characters, every table of order $d > -1$ has two additional symbols: an end-of-file symbol *eof* and an escape symbol *esc*. These symbols are present even if the probability for the characters may be zero.

PPM uses an adaptive strategy for generating the tables. Instead of keeping track of the probabilities for a given context directly, a character count is maintained for each character seen with the given context up to context order d_{max}. For example, consider the string *rowrowrow* and a max context order of $d_{max} = 2$. After receiving the first character r, the count r is incremented by one in the order-0 table. When o is received, the count for o is incremented by one in the order-1 table with context r, and the order-0 table. When w is received, the count of w is incremented by one in the order-2 table with context ro, in the order-1 table with context o, and in the order-0 table. When the next r is received, the count of r is incremented by one in the order-2 table with context ow, the order-1 table with context w, and the order-0 table. This process continues until all characters are received. The resulting character counts for this example are shown in Table 1. Note that this process is the exact process used for PPMA and the process we use for PPMC, though technically a pure implementation of PPMC updates the tables differently. In our results, it is the escapes that seem particularly influential on the number of output bits, so we chose to focus on the change that PPMC does for the escapes and not the change PPMC does for tables. More details on the pure implementation of PPMC are in [17].

Table 1. Resulting characters counts for the PPM tables after receiving the character string *rowrowrow*.

Order	Context	Character count			Total
		r	o	w	
2	*ro*			3	3
2	*ow*	2			2
2	*wr*		2		2
1	*r*		3		3
1	*o*			3	3
1	*w*	2			2
0		3	3	3	9

Table 2. Resulting symbol counts for PPMA and PPMC tables after receiving the character string *rowrowrow*.

Order	Context	Symbol count		
		eof	esc$_A$	esc$_C$
2	*ro*	1	1	1
2	*ow*	1	1	1
2	*wr*	1	1	1
1	*r*	1	1	1
1	*o*	1	1	1
1	*w*	1	1	1
0		1	1	3

Table 3. Resulting probabilities for the characters and symbols provided by PPMA and PPMC.

PPMA

Order	Context	Probability				
		r	o	w	eof	esc$_A$
2	*ro*			$\frac{3}{5}$	$\frac{1}{5}$	$\frac{1}{5}$
2	*ow*	$\frac{2}{4}$			$\frac{1}{4}$	$\frac{1}{4}$
2	*wr*		$\frac{2}{4}$		$\frac{1}{4}$	$\frac{1}{4}$
1	*r*		$\frac{3}{5}$		$\frac{1}{5}$	$\frac{1}{5}$
1	*o*			$\frac{3}{5}$	$\frac{1}{5}$	$\frac{1}{5}$
1	*w*	$\frac{2}{4}$			$\frac{1}{4}$	$\frac{1}{5}$
0		$\frac{3}{13}$	$\frac{3}{13}$	$\frac{3}{13}$	$\frac{1}{13}$	$\frac{3}{13}$

PPMC

Order	Context	Probability				
		r	o	w	eof	esc$_A$
2	*ro*			$\frac{3}{5}$	$\frac{1}{5}$	$\frac{1}{5}$
2	*ow*	$\frac{2}{4}$			$\frac{1}{4}$	$\frac{1}{4}$
2	*wr*		$\frac{2}{4}$		$\frac{1}{4}$	$\frac{1}{4}$
1	*r*		$\frac{3}{5}$		$\frac{1}{5}$	$\frac{1}{5}$
1	*o*			$\frac{3}{5}$	$\frac{1}{5}$	$\frac{1}{5}$
1	*w*	$\frac{2}{4}$			$\frac{1}{4}$	$\frac{1}{5}$
0		$\frac{3}{13}$	$\frac{3}{13}$	$\frac{3}{13}$	$\frac{1}{13}$	$\frac{3}{13}$

As mentioned above, it is not only the characters that are contained in the table, but also two symbols: *eof* and *esc*. The end-of-file symbol, *eof*, is always allocated a count of one. The count associated with the *esc* is different depending on whether we are using PPMA or PPMC. In fact, the difference in escape

Table 4. Machine learning on the hotel corpus.

Machine learning algorithm	Accuracy
Random forest	0.59
Gradient boosted forest	0.61
Linear support vector machine	0.63
Support vector machine	0.65
Stylometry features	
Number of line endings	
Number of punctuations	
Number of multiple punctuations	
Longest multiple punctuation	
Number of capital letters	
Number of words	
Average word length	
Average sentence length	
Average paragraph length	

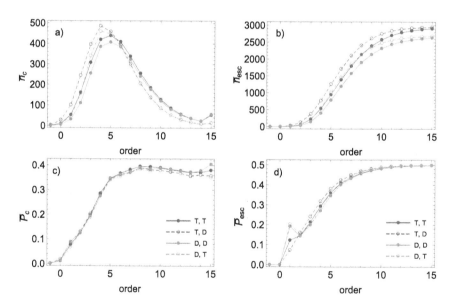

Fig. 9. Normalizing the *extended BG* dataset: expected values for the counts $\bar{n}$ and probabilities $\bar{P}$ as a function of context order for max order $d_{\max} = 15$. Panels (a) and (c) are for characters; (b) and (d) are for escapes. Figure label indicates test and model category, respectively.

counts is the only difference between PPMA and PPMC that we use in our implementation. For PPMA, the *esc* symbol is allocated a single count while for PPMC, the escape is given a count equal to the number of non-zero character entries in the table, or 1 if no non-zero character entries are present. Thus, for the order-0 table in Table 1 the corresponding count for the *esc* according to PPMC is 3 while for any of the order-1 tables, the count is 1. The symbol counts for both methods are shown in Table 2.

To get the probabilities that are sent to AC, PPM just normalizes the entries in the tables. For example, for PPMA $P(r|ow) = \frac{2}{4}$ since r has a character count of 2, *eof* has a count of 1, and *esc* has a count of 1. So, the total count is 4, which is the normalization factor. The rest of the probabilities for PPMA and PPMC are shown in Table 3. Note that each row in this table is really a full PPM table for a given context of a given order-d, as defined in the beginning of this section.

References

1. Afroz, S., Brennan, M., Greenstadt, R.: Detecting hoaxes, frauds, and deception in writing style online. In: Proceedings of the 2012 IEEE Symposium on Security and Privacy, pp. 461–475 (2012)
2. Amitay, E., Yogev, S., Yom-Tov, E.: Serial sharers: detecting split identities of web authors. In: ACM SIGIR 2007 Amsterdam. Workshop on Plagiarism Analysis, Authorship Identification, and Near-Duplicate Detection (2007)
3. Bastian, M., Heymann, S., Jacomy, M.: Gephi: an open source software for exploring and manipulating networks (2009). http://www.aaai.org/ocs/index.php/ICWSM/09/paper/view/154
4. Biber, D., Johansson, S., Leech, G., Conrad, S., Finegan, E., Quirk, R.: Longman Grammar of Spoken and Written English, vol. 2. MIT Press, Cambridge (1999)
5. Bond, C.F., DePaulo, B.M.: Accuracy of deception judgments. Pers. Soc. Psychol. Rev. **10**, 214–234 (2006)
6. Brennan, M., Afroz, S., Greenstadt, R.: Adversarial stylometry: circumventing authorship recognition to preserve privacy and anonymity. ACM Trans. Inf. Syst. Secur. **15**, 12:1–12:22 (2012)
7. Brennan, M., Greenstadt, R.: Practical attacks against authorship recognition techniques. In: Proceedings of the Twenty-First Conference on Innovative Applications of Artificial Intelligence (IAAI), Pasadena, CA (2009)
8. Burgoon, J.K., Blair, J.P., Qin, T., Nunamaker, J.F.: Detecting deception through linguistic analysis. In: Chen, H., Miranda, R., Zeng, D.D., Demchak, C., Schroeder, J., Madhusudan, T. (eds.) ISI 2003. LNCS, vol. 2665, pp. 91–101. Springer, Heidelberg (2003). doi:10.1007/3-540-44853-5_7
9. Cilibrasi, R., Vitányi, P.M.B., de Wolf, R.: Algorithmic clustering of music based on string compression. Comput. Music J. **28**, 49–67 (2004)
10. Cleary, J.G., Whitten, I.H.: Data compression using adaptive coding and partial string matching. IEEE Trans. Commun. **32**, 396–402 (1984)
11. Feng, S., Banerjee, R., Choi, Y.: Syntactic stylometry for deception detection. In: Proceedings of the 50th Annual Meeting of the Association for Computational Linguistics, pp. 171–175 (2012)
12. Frank, E., Chui, C., Whitten, I.H.: Text categorization using compression models. In: Proceedings of Data Compression Conference, DCC 2000 (2000)

13. Hancock, J.T., Curry, L.E., Goorha, S., Woodworth, M.: On lying and being lied to: a linguistic analysis of deception in computer-mediated communiation. Discourse Process. **57**, 1–23 (2006)
14. Li, M., Chen, X., Li, X., Ma, B., Vitányi, P.M.B.: The similarity metric. IEEE Trans. Inf. Theory **50**, 3250–3264 (2004)
15. Marton, Y., Wu, N., Hellerstein, L.: On compression-based text classification. In: Losada, D.E., Fernández-Luna, J.M. (eds.) ECIR 2005. LNCS, vol. 3408, pp. 300–314. Springer, Heidelberg (2005). doi:10.1007/978-3-540-31865-1_22
16. Mayzlin, D., Dover, Y., Chevalier, J.: Promotional reviews: an empirical investigation of online review manipulation. Am. Econ. Rev. **104**(8), 2421–2455 (2012). doi:10.1257/aer.104.8.2421
17. Moffat, A.: Implementing the PPM data compression scheme. IEEE Trans. Commun. **38**, 1917–1921 (1990)
18. Newman, M.L., Pennebaker, J.W., Berry, D.S., Richards, J.M.: Lying words: predicting deception from linguistic styles. Pers. Soc. Psychol. Bull. **29**, 665–675 (2003)
19. Nishida, K., Banno, R., Fujimura, K., Hoshide, T.: Tweet classification by data compression. In: Proceedings of the 2011 International Workshop on Detecting and Exploiting Cultural Diversity on the Social Web, pp. 29–34 (2011)
20. Ott, M., Cardie, C., Hancock, J.T.: Estimating the prevalence of deception in online review communities. In: Proceedings of the 21st International Conference on the World Wide Web, pp. 201–210 (2012)
21. Ott, M., Cardie, C., Hancock, J.T.: Negative deception opinion spam. In: Proceedings of the 2013 Conference of the North American Chapter of the Association for Computational Linguistics: Human Language Technologies, pp. 497–501 (2013)
22. Ott, M., Choi, Y., Cardie, C., Hancock, J.T.: Finding deceptive opinion spam by any stretch of the imagination. In: Proceedings of the 49th Annual Meeting of the Association for Computational Linguistics: Human Language Technologies, pp. 309–319 (2011)
23. Pennebaker, J.W., Chung, C.K., Ireland, M., Gonzales, A., Booth, R.J.: The development and psychometric properties of LIWC 2007. In: Austin, TX, LIWC. Net (2007)
24. Pennebaker, J.W., Frances, M.E., Booth, R.J.: Linguistic Inquiry and Word Count: LIWC 2001. Lawrence Erlbaum, Mahwah (2001)
25. Rayson, P., Wilson, A., Leech, G.: Grammatical word class variation within the British National Corpus sampler. Lang. Comput. **36**, 295–306 (2001)
26. Zheng, R., Li, J., Chen, H., Huang, Z.: A framework of authorship identification for online messages: writing style features and classification techniques. J. Am. Soc. Inf. Sci. Technol. **57**, 378–393 (2006)
27. Zhou, L., Shi, Y., Zhang, D.: A statistical language modeling approach to online deception detection. IEEE Trans. Knowl. Data Eng. **20**, 1077–1081 (2008)
28. Zhou, L., Twitchell, D.P., Qin, T., Burgoon, J.K., Nunamaker, J.F.: An exploratory study into deception detection in text-based computer mediated communication. In: Proceedings of the 36th Hawaii International Conference on System Sciences (2003)

'Dark Germany': Hidden Patterns of Participation in Online Far-Right Protests Against Refugee Housing

Sebastian Schelter[✉] and Jérôme Kunegis

University of Namur, Namur, Belgium
ssc.open@googlemail.com

Abstract. The political discourse in Western European countries such as Germany has recently seen a resurgence of the topic of refugees, fueled by an influx of refugees from various Middle Eastern and African countries. Even though the topic of refugees evidently plays a large role in online and offline politics of the affected countries, the fact that protests against refugees stem from the right-wight political spectrum has lead to corresponding media to be shared in a decentralized fashion, making an analysis of the underlying social and mediatic networks difficult. In order to contribute to the analysis of these processes, we present a quantitative study of the social media activities of a contemporary nationwide protest movement against local refugee housing in Germany, which organizes itself via dedicated Facebook pages per city. We analyse data from 136 such protest pages in 2015, containing more than 46,000 posts and more than one million interactions by more than 200,000 users. In order to learn about the patterns of communication and interaction among users of far-right social media sites and pages, we investigate the temporal characteristics of the social media activities of this protest movement, as well as the connectedness of the interactions of its participants. We find several activity metrics such as the number of posts issued, discussion volume about crime and housing costs, negative polarity in comments, and user engagement to peak in late 2015, coinciding with chancellor Angela Merkel's much criticized decision of September 2015 to temporarily admit the entry of Syrian refugees to Germany. Furthermore, our evidence suggests a low degree of direct connectedness of participants in this movement, (i.a., indicated by a lack of geographical collaboration patterns), yet we encounter a strong affiliation of the pages' user base with far-right political parties.

1 Introduction

In recent years, Europe has experienced a massive influx of refugees from Middle Eastern and African regions, mainly due to civil wars and economic stagnation in these areas. In Germany, this influx peaked in 2015 with 890,000 people seeking asylum [5], an order of magnitude more than the average number in the preceding ten years; in early September of 2015, chancellor Angela Merkel decided

© Springer International Publishing AG 2017
G.L. Ciampaglia et al. (Eds.): SocInfo 2017, Part I, LNCS 10539, pp. 277–288, 2017.
DOI: 10.1007/978-3-319-67217-5_17

to admit the entry of Syrian refugees stuck in South-East European countries. These developments have been accompanied by a steep rise in popularity of German right-wing organizations, especially in the form of the political party *AfD – Alternative für Deutschland*, ("Alternative for Germany") [2], which managed to enter the European parliament as well as multiple German state parliaments since its inception in 2012. The AfD and other right-wing organizations successfully leverage social media to communicate with their followers; recent research shows that their gains in popularity are highly correlated with growing interaction rates and user engagement on Facebook [14].

The refugees in Germany have been registered and temporarily placed in hastily implemented shelters distributed all over Germany. As a reaction to these refugee shelters (or mere plans to set up refugee housing), a large number of local protest movements have formed against their placement in the corresponding towns. Also, refugee shelters and refugees have become targets of a series of more than a thousand crimes in 2015 [1], including arsony of buildings designated for refugees as well as attacks with explosives against inhabitated shelters. Reports indicate that the communication within anti-refugee housing movements happens via dedicated Facebook pages, often titled "Nein zum Heim" ("No to the shelter") or "*X* wehrt sich" ("*X* fights back", where *X* usually stands for the name of a city). Many of these pages promote racist, xenophobic and islamophobic views. Moreover, setting up such Facebook pages to organize protests is explicitly recommended in guidelines published by radical right-wing organizations [7], and some of the pages openly advertise such organisations.[1] To this date, we are not aware of a comprehensive quantitative study of this phenomenon, even though the topic remains at the forefront of German politics as of 2017. To fill this gap, this paper presents a limited quantitative study on the scale of 136 protest pages in 2015, whose contents we have crawled, including more than one million interactions of more than 200,000 users with these pages. Given this data, we focus our efforts on two research questions:

RQ 1: What are the temporal characteristics of the social media activities of this protest movement?

RQ 2: What is the degree of connectedness and cooperation in this protest movement?

The goal of RQ 1 is to obtain insights into general activity patterns of this protest movement, therefore we analyze summary statistics of the activity on the social media pages. Our main aim is to gain insight into topics and the general keynote of the content posted on these pages, and to find hints on how these activities relate to external events. Our discovered topics closely resemble the topics found in a recent study of German right-wing activism on Twitter [12]. We observe that several activity metrics such as the number of posts issued, the negative polarity in comments as well as the attraction of new users peak in late 2015.

---

[1] e.g., https://facebook.com/nzh.koepenick/, https://facebook.com/Kein-Asylheim-in-der-Reinhardt-Kaserne-826300594067680/, https://facebook.com/Kein-Asylanten-Containerdorf-in-Falkenberg-1497894543825007/.

This peak coincides with chancellor Merkel's much criticized decision from early September to temporarily admit the entry of Syrian refugees to Germany [17].

For RQ 2, we focus on the connectedness of users of the protest pages in order to investigate the nature of cooperation between the participants in this protest movement. We investigate patterns of collaboration and connectedness of the users of protest pages on the level of direct interactions as well as on the level of interactions with the Facebook pages of political parties, which serve as an indicator for indirect connections between the users. Our data points at a low degree of direct connectedness: no regional collaboration patterns between users are apparent and their co-interaction network is highly disconnected. However, our data suggests that the user base of the protest pages is connected on a higher level, as we encounter a strong affiliation with far-right political parties. Interestingly, the affiliation pattern is very similar for both the extremist-right NPD party and the (self-proclaimed) non-extremist conservative AfD party.

The paper is structured as follows. We first describe the data acquisition methods and the dataset used in Sect. 2. In Sect. 3, we investigate the temporal characteristics of the movement, and in Sect. 4, we analyse its connectedness and cooperation patterns. Related work is reviewed in Sect. 5, and we conclude in Sect. 6. An extended abstract covering parts of this work has been previously published by the authors [15].

2   Data Acquisition

In order to gather a large number of protest pages for analysis, we consulted online articles listing pages and conducted several exhaustive searches on Facebook using the queries *"Nein zum Heim"* and *"wehrt sich"*, and manually inspected all search results. For the found protest pages, we crawled all publicly available posts with their corresponding likes and comments, restricted to the year 2015. Furthermore, we tagged each protest page with the geographical coordinates of the city it refers to. Thereby, we obtained 136 such pages, as depicted in Fig. 1. Our dataset comprises 46,880 posts and more than one million interactions (196,661 comments on posts, 791,072 likes on posts and 339,604 likes on comments) by 209,822 users. We do not have access to shared posts, page-level likes or profile information of users. Note that we only report aggregate statistics of the collected data, and do neither conduct analysis on the level of individual persons, nor re-distribute the data.

Fig. 1. Geographical mapping of the pages. The dot size is logarithmically proportional to the number of users of a page. A clustering of pages is apparent in the eastern part of Germany.

A first look into the data reveals some interesting patterns: As shown in Fig. 1 the vast majority (77%) of protest pages are located in the eastern part of Germany. This matches with the fact that, since the re-unification of Germany in 1990, far-right parties regularly score higher election results in this part of Germany compared to the western regions [20]. We find the distribution of per-page activity metrics (number of posts, users and comments) to be heavily skewed. For instance, the median number of users interacting with a page is 384, while the top 10% of pages attract more than 5,076 users each, up to a maximum of 30,346. Similarly, the median number of posts per page is 126, while the top 10% of pages issued more than 780 posts with a maximum of 5,643. The same also holds for comments, where the median is 213, the top 10% pages see more than 3,476 comments up to a maximum of 24,866.

3   RQ 1: Temporal Characteristics

As are any political and other movements, the anti-refugee protest movement is subject to temporal fluctuations – both due to internal and external changes. In order to understand such fluctuations in the community, we investigate a wide range of activities, such as posts and news articles issued by pages, the topics in these news articles, as well as the sentiment in user comments and general user engagement. We intend to gain insights into the general keynote of the content posted on the protest pages, and to find hints on how these activities relate to external events. Specifically, we investigate four aspects: (1) the general evolution over time of the volume of activity, (2) the change in the topics discussed and shared, (3) changes in the polarity of interactions, i.e., by positive and negative discourse, and (4) the ability of individual pages to attract a new audience over time.

3.1   Time Course of Page Posts

We analyze the time course of the number of published posts to gain insight into a general activity pattern of the pages. Figure 2 shows the weekly number of posts as issued by the pages and the corresponding number of posted news articles over time. We observe a peak in the end of the third quarter of 2015, which coincides with the aforementioned admission of Syrian refugees into Germany in September [17]. The same phenomenon has also been recognized in previous studies of far-right engagement on social media [14].

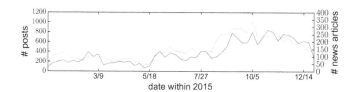

Fig. 2. Weekly aggregated time course of the number of posts and posted news articles on all protest pages in 2015. The peak in September/October follows the announcement of admission of Syrian refugees into Germany.

3.2   Topics over Time in Posted News Articles

Next, we analyze the contents of the posted news articles to gain insights into the conversation on the pages, as well as their time course. Therefore, we crawl the contents of news articles linked to in the posts on the protest pages. We clean the resulting textual data, and represent every news article as a bag-of-words of its nouns and named entity terms, extracted via a part-of-speech tagger [16]. The resulting dataset comprises 6,760 articles, 7,548,572 word tokens, and 17,402 distinct terms. In order to investigate the topics eminent in these articles, we conduct topic analysis via a variant of Latent Dirichlet Allocation (LDA) called *Topics over Time* [19] that not only captures the low-dimensional structure of post contents, but also how this structure changes over time. We select the number of topics via manual inspection of the resulting topic clusters, to maximize the interpretability of the model. Finally, we fit a model with ten clusters, employing the default hyperparameter settings of the implementation, which the authors report to be robust among several datasets.

For each topic, we report the five terms (translated from German) with highest likelihood of occurring in the topic, as well as the (translated) headlines of a set of news articles strongly associated with the topic. Analogously to [19], we illustrate the time course of the topics via a histogram of the document-topic assigment matrix learned by Latent Dirichlet Allocation, where the binning is based on the weeks of the articles' post date. Finally, we manually choose a label for each topic by inspecting the corresponding most likely terms and documents. We list data for four topics in Table 1.

The first topic we identify comprises discussions about housing capacities and costs, indicated by terms such as *city* and *housing*, and strongly associated news articles that talk about the rising costs for cities that set up housing for refugees. A second topic is concerned with sexual crimes, indicated by its most likely terms such as *man*, *perpetrator*, and *woman*, and by the headlines of strongly associated news articles concerning sexual violence offenses. These two topics seem to be general motives of the right-wing agenda, as both of these grow relatively constant with the volume of posted articles over time. A topic that peaks in September 2015 comprises discussions about the fact that the majority of European countries did not follow Germany's example in admitting the entry of large numbers of refugees, despite requests of the German government. This topic is indicated by terms such as *germany*, *hungary* and *eu*, and news articles that discuss that countries such as Hungary opposed German political demands for taking in refugees by closing their intra-European borders to Croatia in October 2015. Lastly, we encounter a topic that reflects the conflicts with leftist activists, indicated by terms such as *donation* or *support* and news articles that talk about militant action attributed to antifascist groups. The latter topics appear to be niche topics, which peak at special events, such as Hungary closing its borders or standoffs between right-wing and leftist activists in August 2015.

Table 1. Selection of topics from a time-sensitive topic model of news articles in posts on the protest pages. For each selected topic, we provide a manually chosen label, illustrate its time course via a histogram of the estimated document-topic matrix (binned weekly by posting dates of the articles), and list the five most likely terms, as well as headlines of a set of strongly associated news articles. Terms and headlines are translated from German.

Housing and Cost

refugees	0.01251
asylum seeker	0.00941
refugee	0.00736
city	0.00728
housing	0.00648

"Dresden invests 47.7 million euros for asylum seekers"	0.94
"County builds new shelters for refugees"	0.93
"Welcome to New-Aleppo, the refugee city"	0.91

Sexual Crime

man	0.01146
perpetrator	0.00881
years	0.00698
years old	0.00691
woman	0.00651

"29-year old woman sexually harassed by unknown man"	0.97
"Call for witnesses after rape in Dresden-Plauen"	0.95
"Another sexual attack on a young woman in Dresden"	0.94

Europe

refugees	0.00917
germany	0.00669
hungary	0.00604
eu	0.00572
humans	0.00556

"The ruins of asylum policy"	0.95
"Hungary closes route over the Balkans"	0.77
"Germany is Europe's refugee shelter"	0.73

Conflict with the Left

article	0.00857
donation	0.00718
support	0.00535
humans	0.00523
place	0.00501

"Federal police chief speculates about leftist perpetrators after arsony in Tröglitz"	0.90
"Antifacists scare off Saxony's minister of the interior"	0.84

3.3 Polarity in User Comments

Next, we place our focus on the users interacting with the pages and investigate the time course of overall sentiment in the user comments. For that, we employ a dictionary denoting the negative sentiment $\phi^-(t)$ and positive sentiment $\phi^+(t)$ of a German language term t when used in certain parts of speech [18]. We apply part-of-speech tagging to all comments in a given week w, which gives us all contained terms T_w. Next, we sum the contained polarity using the weights of the aforementioned dictionary and normalize the results by the number of terms in the comments per week to compute the normalized negative polarity p_{w^-} and normalized positive polarity p_{w^+} per week

$$p_{w^\pm} = \frac{1}{|T_w|} \sum_{t \in T_w} \phi^\pm(t).$$

Figure 3 shows the resulting time course of these polarities for all weeks in 2015. We observe that negative speech dominates the comments throughout the whole year. Furthermore, we encounter a peak in negative polarity, which again coincides with chancellor Merkel's decision from early September 2015 to admit the entry of Syrian refugees to Germany [17]. This finding confirms the general perception that Merkel's decision provoked widespread anger in the far-right political spectrum.

3.4   User Attraction

Finally, we analyze the pages' ability to attract users over time. For that, we compute the set of active users U_w for every week w, (users who comment on a post or like a post on at least one of the protest pages during that week). For every week w, we split these active users into two groups: *new* users

$$U_{w_{new}} = \{u \mid u \in U_w \wedge u \notin U_v \forall v \in 0, \ldots, w-1\},$$

which we encounter for the first time and *continuing* users $U_{w_{cont}} = U_w \setminus U_{w_{new}}$, whom we have already seen previously. The corresponding sizes of these users sets for all weeks in 2015 are shown in Fig. 4. We see a slight increase in both new and continuing users in the late second half of 2015. However, this increase starts to diminish again towards the end of the year. We find that the time

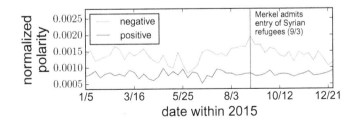

Fig. 3. Time course of normalized negative and positive polarity in user comments per week in 2015, computed from a sentiment dictionary. The vertical line marks chancellor Angela Merkel's decision to admit Syrian refugees.

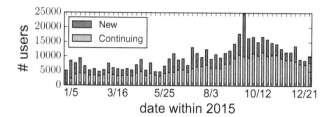

Fig. 4. Stacked bar plot of the time course of weekly active users on the protest pages in 2015. We distinguish between new users (active for the first time) and continuing users.

series of continuing users is very strongly correlated with the time series of posts $(0.91^{***})^2$ and comments (0.87^{***}) in the corresponding week. We observe a similarly directed but much weaker correlation between the time series of posts and new users (0.55^{***}) and posts and comments (0.56^{***}). Furthermore, we note that the number of mean weekly active users (9,935) is very small compared to the overall number of users. We encounter a strong correlation (0.87^{***}) of the number of continuing users with time index i, but cannot determine a similar significant correlation for new users. These findings suggest that the protest pages maintain a low constant growth of users, but fail at accelerating this growth.

4   RQ 2: Connectedness and Cooperation

The German anti-refugee movement is inherently decentralized – there is no dominating "no to refugees" or similar page that attracts the majority of likes, as is the case for a large number of non-controversial topics on Facebook. As a result, the likes are spread among a much larger number of pages, which ostensibly follow a geographical pattern, i.e., most such pages are, at least by name, specific to a single city or small region. In order to investigate to what extent the underlying social network itself exhibits collaboration patterns, we therefore shift our focus from the contents and time course of activities to the relationships between the participating users. In particular, we investigate patterns of collaboration and connectedness of the protest page users on two levels: We first investigate direct co-interactions between users on the social networking platform itself, and in a second step, we investigate their affiliation with the Facebook pages of political parties. This affiliation serves as an indicator for indirect connections between the users, in particular since individual friendship links are not made crawlable by Facebook. These investigations can act as input to future research on the longevity of the currently observed rise of far-right movements. In the following, we investigate (1) whether the geographical distance between two pages is reflected in the shared user base between the pages, (2) the presence of a giant

---

² *** indicates significance at the $p < 0.001$ level.

connected component in the co-like network, and (3) the degree of affiliation for Facebook pages of right-wing political pages.

4.1 Low Correlation Between Geographical Distance and Amount of Shared Users

In order to investigate geographical aspects of the data, we compute the geographical distance between the corresponding cities for each pair of pages, and compare this to the Jaccard similarity between their sets of users. We would expect to see a strong negative correlation if geographical closeness implicated co-operating user bases. However, the maximum Jaccard similarity is only 0.1428, and 4,727 page pairs exhibit non-zero similarity, leaving 3,916 page pairs with zero shared users. Even for pairs of pages with non-zero similarity, the correlation is low (-0.19^{***}), which suggests against a geographical collaboration pattern.

4.2 Absence of a Giant Connected Component in the User Co-like Network

Next, we construct the *user co-like network* as follows: users form the vertices of this network, and for every post, we introduce edges between all users that liked the post. The resulting network has 95,639,173 edges (co-likes among users). We study the connectivity of this network by computing the size of its largest connected component. This size amounts to 89,094 users, which account for only 57.5% of the overall user base. This is very atypical for real-world social networks, which typically exhibit a giant connected component containing nearly all users,[3] and gives a hint that the social media activities of the users on the pages might be highly separated. This is surprising in light of the fact that the users, as found in the previous experiment, were found to not follow a clustering into regions, hinting that another, non-geographic clustering of users is present in the data. The present dataset however does not allow us to identify the nature of this clustering.

4.3 Strong Affiliation with Far-Right Organizations

As we could not find evidence for collaboration patterns in the direct interactions between users, we investigate whether the users of the pages are connected on a higher level. Therefore, we analyse the affiliations of the users on these protest pages to political parties in Germany, with the aim to see whether these users are connected in that way. For that, we employ additional data about likes of posts on the parties' Facebook pages from our previous work [14]. Next, we compute the affiliation $\mathrm{aff}_{p,o}$ between a page p and a political party o as the ratio of users U interacting with the page that also liked posts on the party's page:

$$\mathrm{aff}_{p,o} = |U_{\mathrm{interact\text{-}with}(p)} \cap U_{\mathrm{like\text{-}post}(o)}| \, / \, |U_{\mathrm{interact\text{-}with}(p)}|$$

---

[3] See e.g. http://konect.uni-koblenz.de/statistics/coco.

In the resulting distributions, we observe that the median affiliation with the right-wing parties *AfD* (0.45) and *NPD* (0.41) is about one order of magnitude higher than the affiliation with parties from the remaining political spectrum, such as the christian-conservative *CDU* (0.04), the social-democratic *SPD* (0.04), the green party *Die Grünen* (0.03), and the socialist-left party *Die Linke* (0.02). While it is expected to see a strong affiliation with the *NPD*, which is commonly considered to be the voice of the extreme right and has repeatedly been the target of party-ban trials by the German state, it is suprising to see an even stronger affiliation with the *AfD*, as the latter party claims to locate itself in the conservative spectrum rather than the extremist-right spectrum.

5   Related Work

The social media usage of political movements is of interest to many studies, e.g., with a focus on the *Black Lives Matter* movement in the United States [6,11]. However, the German far-right has seen little attention so far, with current research mostly focusing on exploratory analysis of the social media activities of the AfD party on Facebook [14] and the topics discussed by the local anti-immigrant movement *Pegida* [12] on Twitter, as well as their corresponding news sources [13]. The concentration on social concerns with crime and housing cost, and the focus on European policies in topic clusters discovered by Puschmann et al. on Twitter closely resemble the topics we discovered in Sect. 3.

The rise of populist radical right parties in Europe has been extensively researched. While other countries, such as France, Denmark, Belgium, and Austria have experienced high levels of voting for populist radical right parties, for a long time Germany seemed to have been an exception with regard to the radical right in Western Europe [2]. With the rise of the AfD party, Germany now also becomes part of the "pathological normalcy" [9]. The term denotes that populist right-wing ideology is a radicalization of mainstream values, such as ethnic nationalism, anti-immigrant sentiment and authoritarian values. These attitudes have been present within a segment of the population even before the rise of the AfD, but have not been represented within mainstream party politics before. Scholarship on the conditions of radical right success have associated it with a convergence of the mainstream parties on the left and right, leaving a representational gap for the radical right to move in [3,4,8], while some are sceptical of this "convergence of the middle" thesis [10].

6   Conclusion

We studied the Facebook activities of a contemporary nationwide protest movement against refugee housing in Germany. We analysed data from 136 public Facebook pages, containing more than one million interactions by more than 200,000 users. We encountered peaks in several activity metrics that coincide with chancellor Merkel's decision to temporarily admit the entry of Syrian refugees to Germany, which suggests that this political move caused anger and outrage in far-right circles. However, despite the presumed mobilization effects stemming from Merkel's policies in 2015, our evidence suggests a low degree of user growth, connectedness and cooperation in this protest movement. From all German political parties, the *AfD* exhibited the strongest affiliation among the user base of the studied protest pages, which contradicts previous classifications of the *AfD* as not belonging to the far-right political spectrum [2]. Furthermore, while we can confirm that the Facebook pages of the anti-refugee movement in Germany are split into many small pages by geography, with no apparent regional collaboration patterns. A noteworthy limitation of our work is the lack of data on comparable movements on Facebook, which would allow for stronger conclusions about the specifity of the observed trends for the German radical right. In future work, we plan to conduct a deeper analysis of textual contents of user comments, in order to be able to measure controversy on the level of user interactions.

Acknowledgments. This research was partly funded by the European Regional Development Fund (ERDF/FEDER – IDEES).

References

1. Stiftung, A.A.: Chronik flüchtlingsfeindlicher Vorfälle (2015). https://www.mut-gegen-rechte-gewalt.de/service/chronik-vorfaelle?field_date_value[value][year]=2015
2. Arzheimer, K.: The AfD: finally a successful right-wing populist eurosceptic party for Germany. West Eur. Politics **38**, 535–556 (2015)
3. Arzheimer, K., Carter, E.: Political opportunity structures and right-wing extremist party success. Eur. J. Political Res. **45**(3), 419–443 (2006)
4. Van der Brug, W., Fennema, M., Tillie, J.: Why some anti-immigrant parties fail and others succeed: a two-step model of aggregate electoral support. Comp. Political Stud. **38**(5), 537–573 (2005)
5. Bundesministerium des Inneren: 890.000 Asylsuchende im Jahr 2015 (2016). https://goo.gl/bnG4UG, https://www.bmi.bund.de/SharedDocs/Pressemitteilungen/DE/2016/09/asylsuchende-2015.html
6. De Choudhury, M., Jhaver, S., Sugar, B., Weber, I.: Social media participation in an activist movement for racial equality. In: Proceedings of International Conference on Web and Social Media (2016)
7. Der Dritte Weg: Leitfaden: Kein Asylantenheim in meiner Nachbarschaft! (2015). https://www.bmi.bund.de/SharedDocs/Pressemitteilungen/DE/2016/09/asylsuchende-2015.html
8. Kitschelt, H., McGann, A.J.: The Radical Right in Western Europe: A Comparative Analysis. University of Michigan Press, Ann Arbor (1997)
9. Mudde, C.: The populist radical right: a pathological normalcy. West Eur. Politics **33**(6), 1167–1186 (2010)
10. Norris, P.: Radical Right: Voters and Parties in the Electoral Market. Cambridge University Press, Cambridge (2005)
11. Olteanu, A., Weber, I., Gatica-Perez, D.: Characterizing the demographics behind the #blacklivesmatter movement. In: AAAI Spring Symposium Series (2016)

12. Puschmann, C., Ausserhofer, J., Hametner, M., Maan, N.: What are the topics of populist anti-immigrant movements on Facebook?. In: Proc. Soc. Media and Soc. Conf vol. 13 (2016)

13. Puschmann, C., Ausserhofer, J., Maan, N., Hametner, M.: Information laundering, counter-publics: The news sources of islamophobic groups on Twitter. In: Proc. Soc. Media in the Newsroom Workshop at ICWSM (2016)

14. Schelter, S., Biessmann, F., Zobel, M., Teneva, N.: Structural patterns in the rise of Germany's new right on Facebook. Proc. Data Min. in Politics Workshop at ICDM (2016)

15. Schelter, S., Kunegis, J.: 'Dark Germany': Temporal characteristics and connectivity patterns in online far-right protests against refugee housing. In: Proc. ACM Web Sci. Conf. (2017)

16. Toutanova, K., Klein, D., Manning, C.D., Singer, Y.: Feature-rich part-of-speech tagging with a cyclic dependency network. In: Proc. Conf. Human Lang. and Technol. pp. 173–180 (2003)

17. Walker, M., Troianovski, A.: Behind Angela Merkel's open door for migrants, Wall Street Journal (2015) http://www.wsj.com/articles/behind-angela-merkels-open-door-for-migrants-1449712113

18. Waltinger, U.: GermanPolarityClues: A lexical resource for German sentiment analysis. In: Proc. Lang. Resour. and Evaluation (2010)

19. Wang, X., McCallum, A.: Topics over time: A non-Markov continuous-time model of topical trends. In: Proc. Int. Conf. on Knowl. Discov. and Data Min. pp. 424–433 (2006)

20. Wikipedia: Results of state elections in Germany (2017) https://de.wikipedia.org/wiki/rgebnisse_der_Landtagswahlen_in_der_Bundesrepublik_Deutschland

An Analysis of UK Policing Engagement via Social Media

Miriam Fernandez[(✉)], Tom Dickinson, and Harith Alani

Knowledge Media Institute, Open University, Milton Keynes, England
miriam.fs@gmail.com

Abstract. Police forces in the UK make use of social media to communicate and engage with the public. However, while guidance reports claim that social media can enhance the accessibility of policing organisations, research studies have shown that exchanges between the citizens and the police tend to be infrequent. Social media usually act as an extra channel for delivering messages, but not as a mean for enabling a deeper engagement with the public. This has led to a phenomena where police officers and staff started to use social media in a personal capacity in the aim of getting closer to the public. In this paper, we aim to understand what attracts citizens to engage with social media policing content, from corporate as well as from non-corporate accounts. Our approach combines learnings from existing theories and studies on user engagement as well as from the analysis of 1.5 Million posts from 48 corporate and 2,450 non-corporate Twitter police accounts. Our results provide police-specific guidelines on how to improve communication to increase public engagement and participation.

Keywords: Social media · Evidence-based policing · Engagement

1 Introduction

During the last decade, police forces all around the world have started to invest in the use of social media as a basis for engagement with the public, and guidelines have been created to train officers and to support this process.[1] However, while guidance reports claim that social media can enhance the reputation and accessibility of police staff to their communities,[2] research studies have shown that exchanges between the citizens and the police are infrequent. Social media often works as an extra channel for delivering messages but not as a mean for enabling a deeper engagement with the public [5].

Police organisations are generally very cautions when publishing in social media due to reputational risk [5]. Several research works, particularly those centred around US police, indicate that police organisations focus their efforts

---

[1] https://policemediablog.files.wordpress.com/2016/01/social-media-handbook-europ ol.pdf.

[2] http://connectedcops.net/wp-content/uploads/2010/04/engage.pdf.

© Springer International Publishing AG 2017
G.L. Ciampaglia et al. (Eds.): SocInfo 2017, Part I, LNCS 10539, pp. 289–304, 2017.
DOI: 10.1007/978-3-319-67217-5_18

on posting about crime and incident-related information, but lack responsiveness when it comes to establishing dialogues with the citizens [4,9,10].

As in the Netherlands [12], policing organisations in the UK are moving towards a more decentralised style of social media usage. This has led to a phenomena in which police officers and local teams have started to use social media in a personal capacity (creating non-corporate accounts) in the hope of getting closer to the public.

In this work we aim to study the landscape of UK policing engagement via social media by analysing both, corporate as well as non corporate Twitter accounts. Previous studies targeting citizen engagement towards police forces have been mainly focused on studying the different social media strategies that the police uses to interact with the public [4,6,10]; and on analysing the characteristics of police accounts' messages that are attracting higher attention levels [7,16]. Our work aims to advance these studies by combining learnings from existing theories on user engagement with the analysis of 1.5 Million posts from 48 corporate and 2,450 non-corporate UK Twitter police accounts. Our results provide specific guidelines on how to improve communication by the UK police to increase public engagement and participation. The contributions of this paper are as follows:

- Provide a deep state of the art analysis on social media engagement theories
- Explore engagement dynamics for both, corporate and non-corporate, UK Twitter police accounts
- Produce a set of guidelines to increase public engagement and participation based on a combination of the lessons learnt from the literature of social media engagement and from the results of our analysis

The rest of the paper is structured as follows. Section 2 presents our analysis of engagement theories, a summary of the works focused on police engagement, and an exploration of some of the key challenges faced by the police when engaging with the public via social media. Section 3 summarises our approach for analysing engagement dynamics across corporate and non-corporate accounts. Results are presented in Sect. 4 followed by a set of recommendations (Sect. 5) and a discussion on the implications and limitations of this work (Sect. 6). Conclusions are reported in Sect. 7.

2   Understanding Engagement

In this section, we first take a look at theoretical studies to better understand the communication strategies and methods that have been proposed to influence people's awareness and engagement via social media. We dissect the more general studies, and then explore studies focused on social media police engagement. We conclude this section by highlighting some of the key barriers faced by policing organisations when trying to promote awareness and increase engagement using social media as a medium.

2.1   Social Media Engagement

Social media engagement has been studied through multiple lenses including (e.g., marketing, economics, social sciences, psychology, etc.) and within multiple scenarios (product selling, elections, environmental campaigns, etc.). These studies, which are frequently based on the concept of 'social epidemics' (products, ideas, and behaviours diffuse through a population) aim to understand, among others, the following questions: how do we get people informed? How do we get people to talk (word of mouth)? How do we make people feel connected to a cause? How do we get people to act in new ways? Since our aim is to provide guidelines for the police on how to increase engagement, in this section we take a look to those works on engagement that take the perspective of the sender,[3] the one with a product to sell, and/or the information to give.[4]

The first important aspect to achieve engagement and impact is that the sender needs to have a clear message to tell with a very concrete action connected to it [1]. Policing organisations generally communicate many different stories (patrol or frontline policing activity, reports about incidents, missing persons, the development of partnerships with local authorities or emergency services, etc. [5]) and these stories can be connected to multiple types of actions from the public. Often it is unclear what people can do about these messages and how can they be involved. A user not only needs to be aware of the subject, she also needs to be aware of the various options to act.

The second important aspect of impact is the social transmission (word of mouth or social influence). Marketing professor at The Wharton School (University of Pennsylvania) Jonah Berger, lists three reasons why some products or ideas become more popular than others: quality, price and advertising. But he also claims that focussing solely on these properties will not make something catch on per se. Contrary to what a many media specialists say, Jonah Berger claims that virality is not born, it is made (i.e., there are many factors in a story that you can manipulate to enhance the possibility of something getting viral). Berger and his colleagues analysed many viral campaigns, messages, products and ideas, and extracted six principles of contagiousness or STEPPS [3]: *Social currency* (people share things that make them look good); *Triggers* (it is part of the users' everyday life, and on top of their minds); *Emotional resonance* (when users care about something, they share it with others); *Public* (the idea or product is built to show and built to grow); *Practical value* (people like to share practical or helpful information); and *Storytelling* (people tend to share stories, not information).

Vaynerchuk [17] emphasises the issue of differentiating each social medium when communicating a story, since different social media platforms are generally used for different needs and use different algorithms to promote content in the users' news feeds. A clear message is not enough. Senders also need to pay

---

[3] The term 'the sender' would cover all parties trying to 'sell' a product or idea. This would include a person, a company, an agency, etc.

[4] The term 'product' in this context is used as a placeholder for all things that you could 'sell' such as an idea, information, a story or an actual product.

attention to context (which platform is being used? what is happening in the world?), timing (what are the circumstances?) and audience (to whom is the message target? how are they called to action? etc.)

2.2 Social Media Police Engagement

Studies targeting citizen engagement towards police forces in social media have been mainly focused on studying the different social media strategies that police forces use to interact with the public. An example of such studies is the work of Denef and colleagues [6]. This work studied the tweeting practices of British police forces during the August 2011 riots by performing a qualitative analysis of 547 tweets as well as multiple workshops and interviews with the police. They distinguish between two types of approaches: an *instrumental approach*, in which the police aimed to remain in a controlled position and keep distance to the general public, and an *expressive approach*, in which the police actively decreased the distance to the citizens. The study concludes that, while an expressive approach requires high maintenance, it generally leads to a closer relation with the public and to an increase in the number of followers.

Mijer and Thaens [11] studied the differences of communication between North American police departments and identified three different types of social media strategies used by these departments: (i) the *push strategy*, in which social media is predominantly used to broadcast existing web content, (ii) the *push and pull strategy*, in which social media is used to provide citizens with information but also to get specific information from citizens, and (iii) the *networking strategy*, in which social media is used to build networks between individual police officers and citizens. Other works focused on US police departments [4,9,10] conclude that more social media interaction is needed. Police departments do not generally use social media to converse directly with members of the public, and they need to be more responsive in order to enhance engagement. They also highlight that police departments tend to focus their efforts on generating posts about crime, incidents, and public relations announcements, instead of using social media to mobilise citizens and enhance community engagement.

In addition to these works, Ruddell and Jones [15] have explored the type of audience that responds to the messages posted by the police, focusing their research on Canada. They conclude that social media consumers tend to be younger and better educated. Older citizens, by contrast, saw little value in the use of social media.

In the context of the composite project,[5] Bayerl investigated the acceptance of social media in European Police forces [2]. This study concludes that, while acceptance of social media among police officers is generally high, perceptions vary significantly depending on the country and task. For example, officers in community policing judge the usefulness of social media more positively than officers in emergency help.

---

[5] http://www.composite-project.eu/.

While all these works focus on understanding the different approaches of police communication, other works have focused on understanding what are they characteristics of those messages that get shared by the public (how are they written? when are they posted? which topics they talk about?).

Crump [5] conducted a study over UK policing accounts and investigated, among other aspects, the key categories of topics posted by the police: *patrol* (reports from police patrolling), *information* (police requesting information from the public), *partners* (messages associated with emergency services or local authorities) and *other* (messages that did not relate to any of the above categories). In a more focused study of the *@dorset* Twitter account, our previous work [7] shows that posts about missing persons, road problems or weather conditions are more likely to be retweeted, since by sharing these messages users feel they are helping others. On the other hand, posts about crime are less likely to be shared.

Focusing on different content and user characteristics, Mijer and colleagues performed a study over 1,000 Dutch policing Twitter accounts [16]. This study concluded that longer posts including URLs, mentions and hashtags, posted in the afternoon or evening are more likely to be retweeted. This study also analysed the authorship of the posts and observed that (a) having more followers is good but it reduces the effect of replies and mentions, (b) posting a lot reduces the chances of getting retweeted, and (c) older accounts have less chance of getting retweets, unless they have enough followers.

In line with these works, our purpose is to analyse engagement by observing the characteristics of those Twitter accounts and posts generating higher attention levels. Multiple key differences however can be highlighted. First, we aim to differentiate between corporate and non-corporate police accounts and observe the key differences in their engagement patterns. Secondly, we aim to complement our findings with existing theories of social media engagement and reflect on how these theories can be applied to police communication.

2.3   Barriers of Social Media Police Engagement

Different organisations face different challenges when it comes to engaging users via social media. In this section we summarise some of these challenges that we collected from the literature,[6] and from dialogues with members of the Centre for Policing Research and Learning.[7]

– *Reputational risk:* Reputation is a key element for multiple organisations, but particularly for the police. A post of an offending nature, such as the one from the Bordesley Green Police's official twitter account, where a female passenger was silence by a seatbelt,[8] can damage the reputation of the police and it is unclear if, and how, this reputation can be recovered.

---

[6] http://www.theiacp.org/Portals/0/documents/pdfs/2016-law-enforcement-use-of-s ocial-media-survey.pdf.

[7] centre-for-policing.open.ac.uk.

[8] http://www.birminghammail.co.uk/news/bordesley-green-police-twitter-cartoon-7 469583.

- *Official communication channels:* Events and questions reported to the police need to be registered via the official channels, such as 911 calls. Nowadays, the public is getting used to seeing companies and organisations using social media 24/7 as communication channels,[9] and have started to expect the same coverage and behaviour from the police. However, social media is not the main policing communication channel, and the police social media accounts are not active 24/7. There is therefore a mismatch between what the public expects, and what the police provides.
- *Surveillance*: Multiple studies have shown that an increase in the number of followers helps to increase engagement [14]. To gain more followers, one of the most common strategies is to pro-actively follow other accounts. This action however is easily misinterpreted, since some users may feel surveyed if a police account is following them.
- *Variety of topics*: Police communication messages span many different topics, such as traffic, crisis, public events, and crime prevention. However, different topics may require different types of communication [1]. It is therefore important to identify these different topics, understand their audiences, and shape the messages accordingly.
- *Legitimacy*: For the police to be effective in performing their duties they need the trust and confidence of the communities they serve [13]. Studies have shown that establishing a direct channel with citizens via social media and using it to communicate successes does help the police in strengthening their legitimacy, but only slightly and for a small group of interested citizens [8]. Random videos and images captured by the public about its actions can also help to enhance legitimacy (see for example this image of a police officer in the UK helping an old lady who lost her way[10]) as well as to decrease it (as it happened with the NYPD social media campaign in New York when people started posting images of police brutality.[11])
- *Budget*: For engagement as a subject, there are often no, or limited, budgets allocated. This limits the potential training of police staff as well as the organisation of concrete campaigns to engage the public more closely.

3   Engagement Analysis

In this section we present an overview of the data that have been collected for both, corporate and non-corporate police Twitter accounts and we present an overview of the methodology used to analyse these data.

---

[9] https://searchenginewatch.com/sew/study/2304492/brands-expected-to-respond-within-an-hour-on-twitter-study.
[10] https://twitter.com/CoastInspector/status/833665602850062336/photo/1.
[11] http://www.nbcnewyork.com/news/local/NYPD-Twitter-Backlash-myNYPD-Fail-Negative-Photos-Flood-Social-Media-256275661.html.

3.1   Data Collection

We collected a total of 154,679 posts from 48 different corporate Twitter accounts[12] and 1,300,070 posts from 2.450 non-corporate Twitter accounts.[13] These data was collected during January 2017 and goes back the maximum limit for each account, which Twitter establishes as the 3,200 of a user's most recent tweets. This is translated into tweets that went back to January 2014 in some cases. Twitter IDs for both, corporate and non-corporate accounts were extracted from the following Twitter lists generated by Nick Keane;[14] senior policy advisor on digital engagement and social media for UK policing.

3.2   Engagement Indicators

In the Twitter platform, retweeting, favouring and replying are actions that require an explicit interaction from a user towards another one. These actions have been repeatedly considered in the literature of social media as engagement indicators [14]. Note that when users retweet, they spread the message to their followers (as opposed to favouring or replying), leading to a potential stronger involvement and engagement. In this work we consider retweets as indicators of engagement for the rest of our analysis, leaving favourites and replies for our future lines of work. Tweets that have been retweeted at least once are considered seed-posts. Those tweets that have not been retweeted (i.e., have not obtained any direct engagement from the citizens) are considered non-seed posts.

All corporate accounts except two (@sussex_police and @ASPolice) have more than 60% of their tweets retweeted. Figure 1 displays the average number of retweets received, with most organisations receiving an average of 10 retweets per tweet. Among the top we find the Metropolitan police (MET), with more than 60 retweets per tweet, followed by Jersey, the National Crime Agency, West Midlands and Scotland. These organisations follow different strategies when it comes to achieving engagement. While some of them post original messages, others gather messages from relevant sources and retweet them. Figure 2 shows the top organisations in following this strategy. For example, more than 65.49% of the tweets posted by Northumbria are not original but gathered from other sources. A similar trend can be observed for Nottinghamshire, Jersey, Durham and North Yorkshire police. Note that most of the times these tweets are originated from a police-related Twitter account. The most retweeted account is Action Fraud (@actionfrauduk), retweeted 1,200 times between the 48 corporate accounts, followed by CEOP (@CEOPUK), GetSafeOnline.org (@GetSafeOnline), The National Crime Agency (@NCA_UK) and Prevent Tragedies (@PreventUK). The most retweeted non-corporate account is Stephen Martin (@ACC-MartinPSNI), assistant Chief Constable of the Police Service of Northern Ireland.

---

[12] https://twitter.com/nickkeane/lists/uk-police-force-twitters.

[13] https://twitter.com/nickkeane/lists/ukcops-who-tweet.

[14] https://twitter.com/nickkeane.

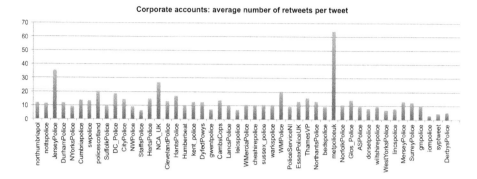

Fig. 1. Average number of retweets per tweet posted by corporate accounts

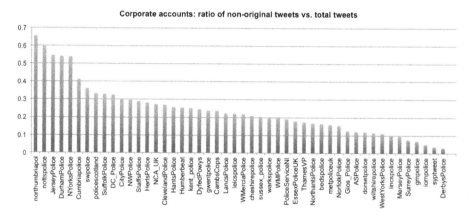

Fig. 2. Ratio of non-original tweets posted by corporate accounts

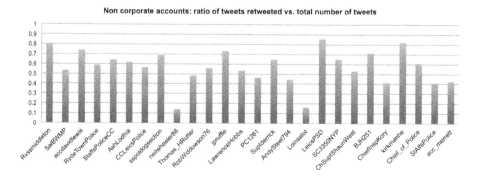

Fig. 3. Ratio of retweets retweeted per non-corporate accounts

A higher variance can be observed for non-corporate accounts, with 50% of them having more than 60% of their tweets retweeted. Figure 3 shows the top 47 non-corporate accounts, with some of them showing a ratio of retweets of more than 80%, and a much higher number of retweets on average (more than 150 for all of those 47 accounts). Note that not all tweets from these accounts are original. As for corporate accounts, non-corporate accounts also retweet heavily from other police accounts (either corporate or non-corporate), however, a wider

Table 1. Social and content features

Social features	Description
In-degree	Number of incoming connections to the user
Out-degree	Number of outgoing connections from the user
Post count	Number of posts that the user has made since being a Twitter member
User age	Length of time that the user has been a member of Twitter
Post rate	Number of posts made by the user per day
Content features	*Description*
Post length	Number of words in the post
Media	Indicates if the post contains a picture or a video
Complexity	Measures the cumulative entropy of terms within the post to gauge the concentration of language and its dispersion across different terms. Let n be the number of unique terms within the post p and f_i is the frequency of term t within p, therefore complexity is given by: $$\frac{1}{n} \sum_{i=1}^{n} f_i (\log n - \log f_i) \qquad (1)$$
Readability	Gunning fog index using average sentence length (ASL) and the percentage of complex words (PCW): $0.4 * (ASL + PCW)$ This feature gauges how hard the post is to parse by humans.[a]
Referral count	Count of the number of hyperlinks within the post
Time in the day	The number of minutes through the day that the post was made. This feature is used to identify key points within the day that are associated with seed or non-seed posts.
Informativeness	The novelty of the post's terms with respect to other posts. We derive this measure using the Term Frequency-Inverse Document Frequency (TF-IDF) measure: $$\sum_{t \in p} tf_{t,p} \times idf_t \qquad (2)$$
Polarity	Assesses the average polarity of the post using Sentistrength.[b] Our inclusion of this feature is to assess whether either positive or negative post polarity is associated with seeds or non-seeds, or whether subjective or objective posts also have an association

[a] https://en.wikipedia.org/wiki/Gunning_fog_index.
[b] http://sentistrength.wlv.ac.uk/.

range of sources (citizens, politicians, councils, and non policing organisations) can be observed among the authors from which non-corporate accounts retweet.

3.3   Engagement Dynamics

To analyse engagement dynamics for both, corporate and non-corporate accounts, we use a combination of qualitative and quantitative approaches. We first make use of our previously developed Machine Learning approach [14] to identify which factors correlate with engagement and how they differ across corporate and non-corporate accounts. We then explore a random set of 2,000 tweets from each group and perform a manual analysis to observe any additional differences. Identifying which factors correlate with engagement requires the examination of the impact of individual analysis features on the performance of our retweeting-prediction model, and then inspecting the effects of those features. The features used for our analysis are summarised in Table 1. Our approach consists of a two-stage process that functions as follows:

1. *Identify Seed Posts:* we first detect what are the most discriminative features that characterise seed posts - i.e. yield a retweet - vs. non-seed posts - i.e. posts are not retweeted. We implement this step by generating a Machine Learning (ML) classifier and performing feature selection over the model. Classifiers are created using balanced datasets. These datasets are balanced by performing random undersampling from the dominant class (seed or non-seed), resulting in a 50:50 split between seeds and non-seeds.
2. *Predict Activity Levels:* secondly we predict the level of activity that seed posts will generate - i.e. predicting a ranking based on the expected number of retweets that each post will yield. For performing this prediction we induce a logistic regression model and then inspect the coefficients of this model to see how a change in each feature is associated with the likelihood of engagement.

Table 2. Performance of the J48 classifier trained over different feature sets

Corporate	P	R	F1	MCC
Social	0.678	0.670	0.666	0.348
Content	0.819	0.816	0.815	0.635
Social+content	0.872	0.872	0.872	0.745
Non-corporate	P	R	F1	MCC
Social	0.948	0.946	0.946	0.894
Content	0.688	0.686	0.686	0.374
Social+content	0.958	0.957	0.957	0.915

4   Results

Table 3 shows a summary of the datasets used for this analysis, including the total number of posts and the total number of posts after filtering. Note that, in order to focus our analysis on those tweets generated by either corporate or non-corporate accounts we are eliminating from our dataset all of those posts that are retweeted, but not original, from these accounts. After filtering, we report the number of seeds (tweets that received an engagement action) vs. non-seeds.

We begin our analysis by examining the performance of different feature sets on predicting seed posts and how these feature sets differ between corporate and non-corporate accounts. Table 2 presents the performance of the J48 classification model when trained on isolated feature sets (social features, content features) and then all features together. Performance is computed using 10-fold cross validation and considering Precision, Recall, F-1, and the Matthew's correlation coefficient (MCC) as evaluation measures. We can observe for both, corporate and non-corporate accounts, that the combination of features exceeds the performance of using solitary feature sets. However, for corporate accounts content features perform better than social features, while the opposite happens for non-corporate accounts. This indicates that, *for non-corporate accounts the user that posts the message is key to generating engagement, while for corporate accounts the content of the tweet is more relevant*. When performing feature selection over the generated models (using subset selection with best first search) we observe that, for corporate accounts, the most discriminative features to differentiate seed vs. non-seed posts are: informativeness, media and in-degree, i.e., engaging posts from corporate accounts are informative, usually contain images or videos, and tend to originate from accounts with a high number of followers. Engaging posts from non-corporate accounts are also informative, usually contain URLs, images or videos and are posted by active accounts (i.e., accounts with a high post rate) but not necessarily popular accounts (i.e., accounts with a high number of followers).

Table 3. Statistics of the social media datasets used for these experiments

Dataset	Total	Filtering retweets	Seeds	Non-seeds
Corporate	154,679	118,220	91,758	26,463
Non-corporate	1,300,070	939,776	375,988	563,788

Figure 4 presents the plots of the feature coefficients in the logistic regression model. A positive value coefficient for a given feature (i.e., appearing above the x-axis) indicates that an increase in the magnitude of this feature has a positive bearing on the probability of a post initiating engagement. Conversely, a negative value (i.e., appearing below the x-axis) indicates that the feature has a negative effect on engagement probability, in essence the coefficients are log-odds ratios. Therefore by inspecting the coefficients of the model we can examine how engagement dynamics differ between corporate and non-corporate accounts and across the features. The logistic regression model also includes significance probabilities for each calculated coefficient.

Figure 4 indicates that there are similarities in engagement patterns between the examined groups (corporate vs. non-corporate). We can observe that for both type of accounts, tweets receiving higher engagement present the following patterns: they are longer, easy to read, have low complexity (i.e., avoid the use of complicated terms) and high informativeness (present new information). They have urls and media (pictures or videos) associated with them. Interestingly, mentions present a negative coefficient, indicating that the presence of mentions negatively impact engagement levels. Due to the nature of police communications, messages also tend to be more negative than positive (i.e., contain words associated with negative sentiment, such as crime, injury, accident). The key differences between the engagement patterns of these two groups can be observed in the social features. While tweets receiving high attention levels come from active corporate accounts that have been established for a longer time and have a high number of followers, for non-corporate accounts the authors of highly retweeted posts tend to have a high number of followers but they also follow many others.

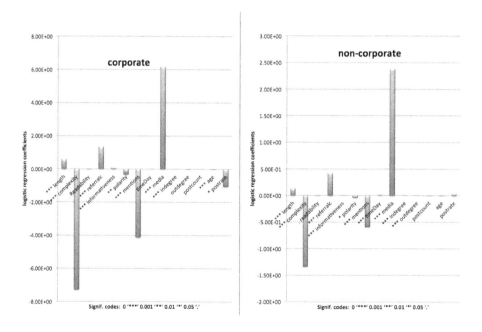

Fig. 4. Logistic regression coefficients

Regarding the discussed topics, by performing a frequency analysis of hashtags and manual analysis of 4,000 posts we observed that, for corporate accounts, tweets receiving higher engagement talk about roads and infrastructures, events, missing persons, and tend to mention locations. They also aim to raise awareness about important problems, such as domestic abuse, hate crime, or modern slavery. On the other hand, tweets receiving lower engagement talk about crime updates: such as burglary, assault or driving under the influence of alcohol, following requests (#ff) and advices to stay safe. In the case of non-corporate accounts, one of the key popular hashtags is #wearehereforyou. Seed posts tend to be those in which police officers communicate with the public to offer or ask for help, provide guidance, reassure safety, and advise on local issues. Non-seed posts, on the other hand, are also focused on crime reporting. From our manual analysis of content we have also observed that, while the tone tends to be more formal for corporate accounts and more friendly for non-corporate accounts, tweets receiving higher engagement levels for both, corporate and non-corporate are frequently humorous. See as example this tweet from Chester Police about parking problems outside the university,[15] or the following about a robbery posted by Northants police.[16]

5   Engagement Guidelines

Our analysis of content and literature have provided us with many useful insights that are summarised in the following guidelines:

- *Focus*: Police organisations deal daily with multiple different issues and may want to communicate with the public for a wide range of purposes (alert them about emergencies, advice them on strategies to prevent crime, request their help to find a missing person, establishing collaboration initiatives by local teams, etc.). When communicating to the public it is important to bare in mind, the key goal to achieve, the type of audience that needs to be engaged (general public, local communities, teenagers, etc.) and provide a clear message with a very concrete set of actions connected to it [1].
- *Be clear*: Complex messages full of police jargon are difficult to understand. Messages should be simple, informative and useful. Additional information such as URLs and images/videos also help to make the message more attractive. An emotional undertone and talking about concrete stories (e.g., success stories of community members and police staff) can also help to maximise the STEPPS criteria [3] and enhance dissemination. Respectful and sensitive humour can also make the message more engaging.
- *Interact*: Communication for corporate accounts generally functions as broadcasting, or a one-way communication, from the organisations to the public. One of the key elements that can be observed from our manual analysis of tweets is that non-corporate accounts are more interactive than the corporate ones. Another observation is that although non-corporate accounts may not have a large number of followers, they tend to have some key followers (e.g., local neighbours). They know their communities better and they manage to engage their community members by participating in discussions and

---

[15] https://twitter.com/PoliceChester/status/649264215455363072/photo/1.
[16] https://twitter.com/NorthantsPolice/status/788406138597441536.

providing direct feedback to users. Corporate accounts could benefit from identifying highly engaging police staff members and community leaders, and involve them more closely in their social media strategy.

- *Stay active*: Out analysis shows that having an account for a longer time may not be helpful if the account is not sufficiently active. Engagement should therefore be adopted as a long-term commitment.
- *Be respectful*: As we pointed out in Sect. 2.3, reputation and legitimacy are extremely important factors for the police. The content that is posed should be polite, safe, and respectful.

6   Discussion and Future Work

This paper presents an analysis of policing engagement via social media. The aim of the work is to understand the current landscape of UK police engagement via Twitter, particularly the key factors that differentiate engagement via corporate and non-corporate accounts, and to complement the lessons learnt from a data analysis perspective with insights derived from existing theories of engagement. In this section we highlight some limitations of this study and multiple directions for future work.

While multiple engagement indicators can be explored (particularly retweets, replies, and favourites), this work focused on retweets as a key indicator. When retweeting, the user is sharing content and making it her own, which can be interpreted as a stronger sign of engagement. However, it is part of our future work to capture replies and favourites to provide a more comprehensive overview of engagement. Our future work also aims to assess variances of engagement dynamics across disparate social media systems since our current study focuses only on Twitter.

A phenomenon that we have observed when conducting this study is that corporate and non-corporate accounts tend to heavily retweet from each other and from other police-related organisations. Our study therefore reflects not only what attracts citizens to social media policing content, but also what attracts other police accounts to this content. Our future work aims to differentiate among the engagement actions performed by citizen accounts, versus the engagement actions performed by police-related accounts.

While multiple relevant observations have been extracted from our data analysis approach and the manual assessment of posts, our work will strongly benefit from conducting a series of interviews with citizens to better understand their motivations to engage with the police via social media, and the factors that attract them to the policing content. Moreover, it is important to understand who is attracted to this type of content and communication medium and who is not. Is the police reaching a wide set of the general public or only particular subsets of users?

Police engagement via social media is a complex topic that can be studied from multiple different angles and perspectives. We hope that our analysis will

serve as a basis for future work within the social web and evidence-based policing communities and enable further research into the examination of policing
engagement dynamics.

7   Conclusions

Pursuing engagement with their communities, UK police department, officers
and staff are actively post via corporate as well as non-corporate social media
accounts. In this paper we study the landscape of UK police engagement in
Twitter by analysing nearly 1.5 Million posts from 48 corporate and 2,450 non-
corporate accounts. We complement the findings of our data analysis with the
lessons learnt from a deep state of the art investigation on the different theoretical
perspectives towards increasing engagement. Our results provide police-specific
guidelines on how to improve communication to increase public engagement and
participation.

References

1. Ariely, D.: Defining Key Behaviours (2014). http://irrationallabs.org/the-
   workbooks/#key-behaviors
2. Bayerl, P.S.: Social media study in European police forces: first results on usage
   and acceptance. COMPOSITE project (2012)
3. Berger, J.: Contagious: Why Things Catch on. Simon and Schuster, New York City
   (2016)
4. Brainard, L., Edlins, M.: Top 10 US municipal police departments and their social
   media usage. Am. Rev. Publ. Adm. **45**(6), 728–745 (2015)
5. Crump, J.: What are the police doing on Twitter? Social media, the police and
   the public. Policy Internet **3**(4), 1–27 (2011)
6. Denef, S., Bayerl, P.S., Kaptein, N.A.: Social media and the police: Tweeting practices of British police forces during the august 2011 riots. In: Proceedings of the
   SIGCHI Conference on Human Factors in Computing Systems, pp. 3471–3480.
   ACM (2013)
7. Fernandez, M., Cano, A.E., Alani, H.: Policing engagement via social media. In:
   Aiello, L.M., McFarland, D. (eds.) SocInfo 2014. LNCS, vol. 8852, pp. 18–26.
   Springer, Cham (2015). doi:10.1007/978-3-319-15168-7_3
8. Grimmelikhuijsen, S.G., Meijer, A.J.: Does twitter increase perceived police legitimacy? Publ. Adm. Rev. **75**(4), 598–607 (2015)
9. Heverin, T., Zach, L.: Twitter for city police department information sharing. Proc.
   Am. Soc. Inf. Sci. Technol. **47**(1), 1–7 (2010)
10. Lieberman, J.D., Koetzle, D., Sakiyama, M.: Police departments use of Facebook:
    patterns and policy issues. Police Q. **16**(4), 438–462 (2013)
11. Meijer, A., Thaens, M.: Social media strategies: understanding the differences
    between north american police departments. Gov. Inf. Q. **30**(4), 343–350 (2013)
12. Meijer, A.J., Torenvlied, R.: Social media and the new organization of government
    communications: an empirical analysis of Twitter usage by the Dutch police. Am.
    Rev. Publ. Adm. **46**(2), 143–161 (2016)

13. Rosenbaum, D.P., Lawrence, D.S., Hartnett, S.M., McDevitt, J., Posick, C.: Measuring procedural justice and legitimacy at the local level: the police-community interaction survey. J. Exp. Criminol. **11**(3), 335–366 (2015)
14. Rowe, M., Alani, H.: Mining and comparing engagement dynamics across multiple social media platforms. In: Proceedings of the 2014 ACM conference on Web science, pp. 229–238. ACM (2014)
15. Ruddell, R., Jones, N.: Social media and policing: matching the message to the audience. Safer Communities **12**(2), 64–70 (2013)
16. Van De Velde, B., Meijer, A., Homburg, V.: Police message diffusion on Twitter: analysing the reach of social media communications. Behav. Inf. Technol. **34**(1), 4–16 (2015)
17. Vaynerchuk, G.: Jab, Jab, Jab, Right Hook. Harper Collins, New York City (2013)

What Makes a Good Collaborative Knowledge Graph: Group Composition and Quality in Wikidata

Alessandro Piscopo[✉], Chris Phethean, and Elena Simperl

University of Southampton, Southampton, UK
{A.Piscopo,C.J.Phethean,E.Simperl}@soton.ac.uk

Abstract. Wikidata is a community-driven knowledge graph which has drawn much attention from researchers and practitioners since its inception in 2012. The large user pool behind this project has been able to produce information spanning over several domains, which is openly released and can be reused to feed any information-based application. Collaborative production processes in Wikidata have not yet been explored. Understanding them is key to prevent potentially harmful community dynamics and ensure the sustainability of the project in the long run. We performed a regression analysis to investigate how the contribution of different types of users, i.e. bots and human editors, registered or anonymous, influences outcome quality in Wikidata. Moreover, we looked at the effects of tenure and interest diversity among registered users. Our findings show that a balanced contribution of bots and human editors positively influence outcome quality, whereas higher numbers of anonymous edits may hinder performance. Tenure and interest diversity within groups also lead to higher quality. These results may be helpful to identify and address groups that are likely to underperform in Wikidata. Further work should analyse in detail the respective contributions of bots and registered users.

Keywords: Wikidata · Collaborative knowledge graphs · Group composition

1 Introduction

Peer production systems have been experimented with successfully in several fields. Wikipedia is probably the most well-known example, but the efforts of communities of users are behind diverse projects, including open source software (e.g. Apache or Linux), database management systems (e.g. PostgreSQL), or question-answer sites (e.g. Stack Overflow). Wikidata is a recent addition to this already large list. It is a community-driven knowledge graph started by the Wikimedia foundation in October 2012. Since its inception, it has gathered a user pool of around 100 thousand registered users, who are able to add facts about more than 24 million entities. Because of these and other features, Wikidata has drawn the attention of researchers and practitioners alike.

© Springer International Publishing AG 2017
G.L. Ciampaglia et al. (Eds.): SocInfo 2017, Part I, LNCS 10539, pp. 305–322, 2017.
DOI: 10.1007/978-3-319-67217-5_19

Knowledge Graphs (KGs) are large collections of structured data, encoded as terms describing entities and the relationships existing between them [26]. KGs are important as they provide data that can be processed by machines to create new, tailored information. For example, Wikidata was initially designed as a structured backbone for Wikipedia. Its primary aim was to offer an improved model to maintain the structured knowledge already contained in Wikipedia and make it available to other applications online. Besides, the use of a central store of knowledge and facts allows each localised version of Wikipedia to access the same data for each page or topic, improving coverage across the different languages of the site. Wikidata's aims go beyond the support of other Wikimedia projects. Its data is released under an open licence which grants free reuse and sharing. Hence, it can act as a source for any information-based application and, due to the large number of identifiers from and links to other resources, help integrate knowledge from several sources.

Wikidata is reliant on its community for adding and maintaining data. Its contributors can be divided into three types: bots (software programmed to perform edits and maintenance work) and registered and anonymous human editors. Bots carry out a large share of work in Wikidata [27]. However, although their activities have been analysed with regard to the type of tasks they perform on the overall KG [21], it is not yet clear to what extent they contribute to the quality of Wikidata.

Concerning human editors, the openness and versatility of the wiki model [32] allows users to collectively author structured information, with no official editorial oversight. People of different backgrounds, skills, and perspectives put their efforts together to build Wikidata's knowledge. An extensive body of literature analyses the effects of group composition and diversity, which we define as the distribution of members in a group with respect to a common feature [12]. Findings for off– and online contexts show that differences within a group may be a double-edged sword when it comes to performance. Analysing the effects of group demography on team outcomes, Ancona and Caldwell [2] show that diversity negatively influences performance, both directly and mediated by internal processes and communication. On the other hand, Jehn *et al.* [14] found that various types of diversity are positively related to perceived (social diversity) and actual group performance (informational diversity). Concerning online contexts, more heterogeneous groups are more likely to take better decisions [16] and, when the level of conflict is high, to create higher quality articles in Wikipedia [3]. To the best of our knowledge, no study has yet addressed the connections between group composition and diversity and the resulting outcome quality in Wikidata.

The current study aims to address the above mentioned gaps by investigating the 'right mix' of users that leads to good quality in Wikidata. First, it analyses the relationship between the share of contributions of bots, registered, and anonymous human users and outcome quality. Second, it investigates the effect of the distribution of two features within Wikidata groups: length of activity within the community and task knowledge, i.e. tenure and interest diversity.

These two variables were chosen due to the variations in activity across different levels of experience and different tasks reported by Wikidata editors in previous work [24].

Gaining insights about the relationship between group composition and performance is essential to improve the understanding of how Wikidata's knowledge is created and of the underpinning quality-related processes. It would enable one to recognise the community patterns that lead to good performance in the system, and possibly intervene on those which are likely to cause quality issues. Wikidata has been defined as a combination between a peer-production system and a collaborative ontology project [21]. Additionally, the size of its user pool has not been attained by previous analogue projects, such as Freebase [11]. These features set Wikidata apart from several online projects examined by the literature over group composition. Hence, this study extends previous observations about the effects of group diversity on the performance of online communities to collaborative KGs.

In the next section we present various aspects of Wikidata. Subsequently, we review a selection of works of relevance about group diversity and outline the research hypotheses tested in the current study. Following, we present methods and data employed. Finally, we provide results and discuss these and the limitations of our work.

2   Wikidata

Wikidata aims to create a general domain KG maintained by a community of users, openly shareable and reusable, and accessible by machines to perform reasoning and provide complex answers to queries. The next sections discuss its features in detail.

2.1   The Data Model of Wikidata

Knowledge in Wikidata is expressed through *items* and *properties*. Items refer to concrete things or characters (e.g. the Colosseum or William Shakespeare) or to abstract concepts and categories, e.g. humans or music. Properties define relationships between items and other items, or between items and literal values, and are used to state facts.

Language-independent URIs are used to refer to items and properties, and editors can add human-readable *labels*, *descriptions*, or *aliases* in up to 358 languages (see Fig. 1). This feature allows any user to edit each entity, regardless of his/her language. Structured data that goes beyond these simple labels and descriptions is represented using relationships in the form of property-value pairs named *claims*. These are the base of the data model of Wikidata. A claim may include an optional *reference*, (a link to its source) and/or a *qualifier* to provide additional contextual information for the claim, such as specifying the date that it refers to (Fig. 2(a)). Both items and properties are defined through statements, and a number of labels, aliases, and descriptions. Properties specify a permitted

Fig. 1. Multilingual labels, description, and aliases (under "Also known as") in a Wikidata Item. On the right, links to all Wikipedia language versions of the related article.

value datatype, e.g. a number (for a property such as 'population') or another Wikidata item (for a property such as 'spouse' — see Fig. 2). Additionally, they may include constraints, i.e. conditions that have to be met when the property is used. Constraints span from defining the domain and range to other characteristics of the property, e.g. requiring a symmetric property. However, constraints are not enforced in Wikidata's data model [9], and are used only for quality control purposes.

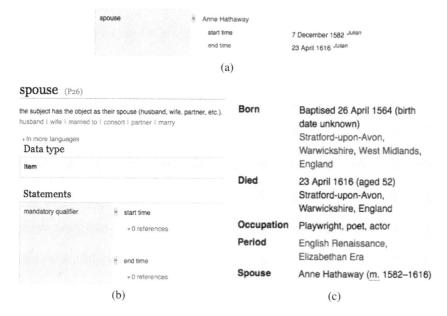

Fig. 2. Example Property for Shakespeare: 'Anne Hathaway' is another item, therefore the property in (a) states that Shakespeare (item) has a 'spouse' (property) which is 'Anne Hathaway' (another item). 'Spouse' (b) specifies qualifiers to provide additional details to the claim. On Wikipedia this relationship is displayed in an InfoBox (c).

2.2   Quality in Wikidata

The body of research around data quality in Wikidata has grown in recent years. Inconsistencies in Wikidata's taxonomy hierarchies are the focus of [7], which found many erroneous patterns deriving from misuse of properties such as *instance of* or *subclass*. Other research has compared the quality of data in Wikidata to other KGs. [29] studied Wikidata and DBpedia with respect to their fitness for open-domain question answering. Wikidata outperforms DBpedia in several of the domains tested. Faïrber *et al.* [10] evaluate Wikidata and four other KGs (DBpedia, Freebase, YAGO, and OpenCyc) along several data quality dimensions. Wikidata reaches quality levels comparable to the other KGs examined, if not higher in some cases, e.g. schema completeness.

The approaches mentioned above measured data quality over the whole KG or a subset of it. The current study focuses on the effects of group diversity on outcome quality, thus we sought a quality measure of elements identifiable as the result of the work of a group of editors. Items are the outcome of the cooperation of a set of users—a group—and are the building blocks of Wikidata's knowledge. For our analysis we used the single-grading scale quality labels in [33]. The advantages of this measure are twofold. First, it provides an overall score for item quality. This feature was appropriate for our aim to investigate how group diversity relates to performance in general, rather than to specific aspects of quality. Second, the item quality labels are based on criteria set up by the Wikidata community and are generated by the community itself. Hence, it is a meaningful measure of quality, as perception of information contributors is key to define quality in user-contributed systems [18]. We provide further details about this quality measure in Sect. 4.1.

2.3   Editing Wikidata

The community is responsible for adding and maintaining all the elements that constitute Wikidata. While the majority of these operations are very simple, requiring little skills or knowledge other than factual information, other tasks are more demanding and can potentially influence a larger part of the KG. These differences afford the classification of tasks into lightweight and heavyweight, according to the definition given in [13]. As an example of a lightweight task, if the claim about Shakespeare's place of birth was wrong, users could modify it, linking the *place of birth* property to the *Stratford-upon-Avon* item. The same applies to labels: if users want to include the Italian name for London, they only need to add it in the appropriate place. Adding and modifying claims and labels requires little specialised knowledge and is largely independent from other revisions; these tasks account for the vast majority of Wikidata edits and can be classified as lightweight contributions. Other less trivial tasks can be defined as heavyweight. Editing statements using the properties *instance of* or *subclass of* requires to be familiar enough with knowledge engineering concepts to understand the difference between the two and use them accordingly. The same skills are required to edit properties, whereby understanding their relationship with other properties, the constraints that may be applied to them, and their intended use is essential. The item-building process may thus be decomposed into several smaller tasks, which are loosely dependent from each other and include both light– and heavyweight tasks.

2.4 The Wikidata Community

Wikidata editors can be either bots or humans. Since the Wikidata philosophy allows anyone to contribute, human editors can either register or contribute anonymously.

Bots are developed by users and should be approved by the community before performing any operation[1]. Notwithstanding, several bots are functioning without a previous formal approval. Each bot is operated by a human user, who should maintain it and ensure that it does not cause any damage to the KG.

Although their number is small compared to human users (399 vs. around 17,000 monthly active users), bots do the lion's share of Wikidata edits (>95%) [27]. Almost 90% of bots' editing activities concerns the addition or modification of item statements (58%) or labels/descriptions/aliases (30%) [21]. According to the Wikidata policy about bots, these are required to include a reference with every new statement and to check if any revision they make violates any property constraints. Regarding the scope of bot edits, they often focus on a class or typology of items or statement. As an example, some bots add statements to items in the biomedical field, others focus on settlements of determined countries, and others map Wikidata items to their equivalent in other KGs, such as DBpedia. Human edits can override bot edits, and vice versa. No preference is granted to any user type over the other. Besides editing, bots perform a variety of maintenance tasks, which include checking property constraint violations, moving pages, or fixing wrong user names. Moreover, as Wikidata emerged, bots were created to move language links from Wikipedia over to Wikidata, in order to help build inter-language links connecting different language versions of Wikipedia pages [31].

Finally, human users can contribute anonymously. The revisions authored by these users are a small percentage of all Wikidata edits (0.5%), according to statistics we extracted about Wikidata editing activity. Anonymous users have been studied less since their activity is difficult to track over time. However, they contribute to properties in higher measure than bots.

3 Group Diversity and Outcome Quality

The effects of group diversity on outcome quality have been thoroughly investigated, both in offline and online contexts. Diversity appears to be both an

---

[1] The official Wikidata policy about bots is in https://www.wikidata.org/wiki/Wikidata:Bots, which is cited throughout this section. This was also the source for our list of bots and active users, together with https://www.wikidata.org/wiki/Category:Bots_without_botflag and https://www.wikidata.org/wiki/Special:Statistics.

opportunity as well as a challenge for work teams [19]. Differences among group members may generate a "creative abrasion" that positively affects performance [3]. On the other hand, diversity may hamper the identification of users within a group [19]. Researchers have tried to explain these mixed effects by categorising various types of diversity. In their review of studies about diversity in organisational groups, Milliken and Martins [19] distinguish observable and underlying attributes. Dissimilarity with regard to observable attributes, such as age, gender, or race, lead to higher turnover and lower integration [19]. Underlying attributes may refer to personality characteristics, values, skills and knowledge, and functional background, among others. Skills- or knowledge-related diversity affects positively performance in top-management and project teams, whereas the effects of other types of underlying attributes are less clear. In a similar fashion, Arazy et al. [3] identify surface- and deep-level diversity. Whereas the first encompasses demographic characteristics, the latter regards expertise, knowledge, and functional background. Deep-level diversity entails a higher variety of perspectives, which create better conditions for creativity and knowledge sharing. Other attempts to interpret different types of diversity see two contrasting viewpoints about its effects on group performance, the *social category* and the *information/decision making* perspectives [30]. The social category perspective focuses more on relational aspects. Homogeneous groups benefit from higher cohesion and member commitment, thus being able to produce a better output. The information/decision making perspective is shifted more towards job-related attributes and connected to less evident aspects of members, e.g. educational or functional background. Diversity also influences positively performance according to this perspective. In [30] these two perspectives are combined, by connecting them to the requirements and the elaboration of tasks. Diversity would lead to better performance in case of complex information-processing tasks, with respect to simple, repetitive ones.

A great deal of previous research has focused on demographic features of group members. [2] explored direct and indirect effects on performance by the distribution of organisation tenure and functional speciality in the team, with mixed results. Whereas both types of diversity have a direct negative effect on team- and managerial-rated performance, their indirect effects look more complex. More heterogeneous groups with regard to tenure, i.e. the length of activity within a team, are able to define better their goals and priorities. Higher functional diversity improves external communication. Both clarity of goals and priorities and improved external communication positively affect performance. These conflicting findings suggest a complex relationship between group diversity and outcomes, with effects that may change according to the context and the type of diversity studied. Pelled et al. in [23] draw similar conclusions about the complexity of the relationship between several types of diversity, conflict, and performance. Their study, carried out on corporation teams, finds a positive association between tenure and functional diversity and task conflict. In turn, this affects positively cognitive task performance, thus suggesting that differences in organisational tenure and functional background of group members may indirectly improve their outcome. Other variables, e.g. race and gender, do not seem to directly influence conflict.

With regard to online systems, [3, 8, 16] analyse how diversity affects outcome quality in Wikipedia, obtaining similar results. The relationship between cognitive diversity, task conflicts, and quality of Wikipedia articles is analysed in [3]. Cognitive diversity refers to the mental models and interests of the members of a group and positively influences outcome performance. The effects of tenure diversity on the quality of the decisions to delete Wikipedia articles are analysed in [16]. Whereas the presence of newcomers by itself appears detrimental for outcome quality, in agreement with previous literature on offline settings [20], a moderate tenure diversity is related to higher quality decisions. Chen *et al.* [8] study how interest and tenure diversity influence productivity and withdrawal in Wikipedia projects. Interest diversity is a concept close to cognitive and functional diversity. It refers to the variety of members' interests in a group. In collaborative projects such as Wikipedia or Wikidata, where users contribute voluntarily and generally choose which tasks to take on, an individual's interests may actually determine their activity and function within the project. According to [8], tenure diversity leads to higher productivity, but with diminishing results, while increasing member withdrawal, analogously to what noted in [16]. Interest diversity is linearly correlated to productivity, whereas no evidence is found about its influence on member withdrawal.

The current study focuses on tenure and interest diversity on Wikidata. Concerning tenure, previous work [24] has shown that Wikidata editors change the focus and scope of their activity as they gain experience within the system. This suggests that users with different levels of experience may bring complementary skills in building high-quality items. Editor activity may also vary along their edit scope [24]. Some users carry out similar tasks, i.e. adding references, on a broad spectrum of items, whereas others focus on a restricted number of items, specialising on a single domain. The contribution of these two types of users may thus be necessary to create good quality items.

3.1   Research Hypotheses

This section presents the hypotheses tested in this study. Hypotheses 1–3 concern the proportion of contributions by different user types. Hypotheses 4–5 regard tenure and interest diversity.

The importance of bot contributions for outcome quality has been noted already with regard to Wikipedia [22]. In Wikidata, the amount of bot editing activity and its scope means that their contribution is a crucial factor for outcome quality. Therefore, we formulate our first hypothesis:

Hypothesis 1: The percentage of bot edits is positively related to item quality.

Although the contribution of bots is important to set the basic structure of items—e.g. automatically adding Wikimedia links and labels in several languages—some tasks require human editors. These possess the knowledge and skills to add descriptions and aliases, and perform quality controls that are not routinely performed by bots. In their analysis of the emergence of user roles connected to the division of labour in Wikidata, Müller-Birn *et al.* observe that bots and humans perform similar tasks, however with a different distribution [21]. Bots' activities focus more on setting new statements, whereas human contributors primarily edit them and add references. Hence, bots and registered human editors may need to complement their effort in order to achieve high-quality items. On the other hand, users who edit anonymously may have lower levels of attachment and have shown to often generate spam and vandalism in other projects [1]. We refer to interaction between human and bot editors as the balance of the respective contributions to an item. Higher interaction means a more equal contribution from each of these two user types.

Hypothesis 2: High levels of interaction between human and bot users are positively related to quality.

Hypothesis 3: The percentage of anonymous human edits is negatively related to item quality.

As mentioned above, Wikidata editors take on different types of tasks along their evolution as part of the community [24]. Seasoned users focus on higher-level tasks, e.g. working on the conceptual structure of knowledge and on quality maintenance tasks, whereas newcomers tend to concentrate their efforts on adding and modifying statements. Items edited by users with various tenure levels may benefit from these different "specialisations". Additionally, more experienced users feel a sense of responsibility towards Wikidata. This might drive them to oversee the work done by other editors and help ensure quality.

Hypothesis 4: Tenure diversity is positively related to item quality.

A similar process may be at play with regard to interest diversity. Editors working on a broader range of items may lead to different perspectives to the creation of items. One of the peculiarities of KGs is that the entities they contain are linked, allowing machines to perform inferences and reason following these connections. Users with heterogeneous interests may facilitate the creation of internal links.

Hypothesis 5: Interest diversity is positively related to item quality.

4 Data and Methods

We describe in the following the approach employed to test our research hypotheses, including the variables examined, the analysis strategy, and the data used.

4.1 Dependent Variable

For the purpose of this study, we used a measure of quality generated by the authors of [33] in close-collaboration with the community of Wikidata. It is a single-grading scale which assigns labels to items from A (the highest) to E. The criteria on which the scale is based comprehend the completeness of the item, seen as the number of relevant statements; the plurality of the sources used to support the statements; labels and descriptions in an appropriate number of languages; links to other wiki projects; and possibly whether media files are attached[2]. Quality criteria were reviewed through discussions with the community, both on– and offline.

Item labels were collected for a sample of 5,000 Wikidata items, each evaluated by a Wikidata editor. A pilot campaign was previously run to verify and refine the quality of community-generated labels. The sample selection aimed to obtain a more balanced distribution of item quality classes, compared to the entirety of Wikidata, where the majority of items likely fall in classes C to E. Therefore, the authors of [33] over-represented classes A and B by selecting a certain number of items per size (in bytes), following the assumption that larger items would more likely have higher quality. Additionally, they included a number of 'special items', i.e. items whose ID has a particular meaning. The distribution of items per quality level is in Table 1.

Table 1. Distribution of quality levels.

Quality level	No. items	No. items (w/at least 1 human edit)
A	322	322
B	438	419
C	1773	1671
D	986	702
E	1468	1010

4.2   Independent Variables

We present here the independent variables included in our analysis. Diversity measures referred only to registered human users—to which we refer from now on as human users—because anonymous users often cannot be tracked across different edit sessions. Bot users were not included as well.

Tenure Diversity. This variable was computed for each item by using the coefficient of variation [4] calculated on the number of days between each human user's first edit and the last day in our dataset. This method has previously been applied to measure tenure diversity in [2,8].

Interest Diversity. The closeness of the editing patterns of users working on the same item has been used to estimate interest diversity, following the approach in [3]. To build this metric, we generated a two-dimensional matrix, in which all members of the group—all human users that performed at least one edit on the item considered—lie on one dimension and all items edited by anyone of them

---

[2] https://www.wikidata.org/wiki/Wikidata:Item_quality.

are on the other. Cells were assigned 0/1 values, according to whether a user had edited an item. The sparsity of the matrix—the ratio between the number zeros and the total number of cells—reflected how much the group members' editing patterns overlapped. The outcome values ranged from zero to one, with higher values indicating more diverse groups.

Proportion of Bot Edits. The proportion of edits made by bots over the total number of edits. This value was between 0 and 1.

Proportion of Anonymous Edits. The proportion of edits made by anonymous users over the total number of edits. This value was between 0 and 1.

Bot X Human Edits. This variable was included to test how the interaction between bot and human editors affect outcome quality. It was computed by multiplying the proportion of human edits by the proportion of bot edits. Considering the low amount of anonymous contributions, this variable has values distributed in an inverted U shape, with higher values reflecting more balanced contributions from bots and humans.

Control Variables. *Number of edits.* Items with a larger number of revisions are likely to have more statements and to have been reviewed and corrected more times.

Group Size. The literature reports diverse effects of group size on outcome quality. Larger groups may negatively affect performance, because they reduce the likelihood of collaboration and increase the chance of conflicts [17]. On the other hand, more members likely entail a broader range of information [28]. We included group size as a control variable to account for these possible effects. Group size was measured by computing the number of unique editors for each item.

Age of the Item. Older items have likely been seen, and reviewed, more times by editors. We used the number of days between the creation of an item and the last day in our dataset as a control variable.

4.3 Analysis Strategy

We performed an ordinal logistic regression (OLR) analysis to test the hypotheses. OLR takes into account the ordering of discrete response variables, such as the item quality labels used in this study, compared to other models which are either suitable to binary responses (standard logistic regression) or do not make any assumptions about the ordering of outcome discrete variables (multinomial logistic regression) [5]. OLR splits the distribution of the data corresponding to each rank in the response variable. It relies on the assumptions that independent variables have the same effect across different responses (*proportional odds* assumption) [6]. The ordering of these is modelled by considering cumulative probabilities for all different response categories, rather than by single category. As a consequence, the output of OLR provides an intercept value for each threshold between categories in the outcome variable.

We trained four models to predict item quality labels and verified the significance of the independent variables for prediction. The first model was the baseline and included only the control variables. Model 2 added variables related to the proportion of user type. Model 3 tested the influence of tenure and interest diversity, including only items that have ever been edited by humans in order to reduce sparsity of the data (tenure and diversity values were set to zero when no human users contributed to an item). Model 4 tested all the independent variables together, using all the items in our dataset.

4.4   Data

We accessed the complete dumps of Wikidata edit history[3], updated on 1st of April 2017, to provide data on every page in Wikidata at the time. We extracted from these dumps the completed revision history of each item in the labelled sample, including edit timestamp and user names. Only 4,987 items over 5,000 in the labelled sample were present in the dumps. Of these 4,124 were edited by human editors. Scripts and data generated for the analysis have been made openly available online[4].

5   Results

Table 2 reports descriptive statistics of and correlations among the variables used in the analysis. The items in the sample greatly vary in terms of number of edits, group size, and item age. The ratio between edit number and group size shows that each user in a group carried out on average four revisions. If we consider the median item age (around four years) and number of edits, items are seldom edited. The proportion of registered human edits was, not surprisingly, highly correlated to bot edits, therefore it was left out from the models. Regarding diversity, items are edited by a population of editors which is moderately heterogeneous in terms of tenure. On the other hand, interest diversity was very high, indicating that on average editors focus on different sets of items.

The baseline model (1, Table 3) shows a positive significant influence of item age, edit number, and group size on item quality. The increase in quality level is very low for all three variables though, with item age having the smallest effect. Model 2 adds variables related to the contribution of different types of users to an item. The proportion of bot edits has a positive significant interaction with the response variable, thus **supporting hypothesis 1**. The influence of bots on item quality increases when these interact with human editors, as shown in Table 3, which **supports hypothesis 2**. The proportion of anonymous users is significant for prediction as well and influences negatively item quality. This means that **hypothesis 3 was supported**.

Model 3 was trained on items with at least one human edit. The distribution of quality labels for this set of items was more skewed towards higher levels,

---

[3] https://dumps.wikimedia.org/wikidatawiki/20170401/.

[4] https://github.com/Aliossandro/WD-group_diversity.

Table 2. Descriptive statistics and correlations among independent variables. Item age is expressed in days since item creation.

	Mean	Median	Std	# Edits	p Bot edits	p Anonymous edits	p Human edits	Group size	Item age	Tenure div.
# Edits	135.4	28	239.19							
p Bot edits	.53	.50	.35	−.35						
p Anonymous edits	.01	0	0.03	.36	−.27					
p Human edits	.46	.50	.34	.32	−.99	.18				
Group size	36.32	7	57.48	.81	−.47	.49	.43			
Item age	1,182	1,507	557.16	.30	−.15	0.22	.13	.47		
Tenure diversity	.47	.38	.48	.40	−.49	.27	.48	.56	.62	
Interest diversity	.89	.98	.19	.11	.01	.12	−.02	.25	.16	−.12

compared to the full dataset (Table 1). The results of model 3 show a significant positive interaction of tenure diversity with item quality (Table 4), thus **supporting hypothesis 4**. Interest diversity was as well a significant predictor, albeit with a lower positive influence on quality. Hence, **hypothesis 5 was supported**. Finally, model 4 included all the dependent variables. Significant interactions did not change, with the exception of the proportion of anonymous edits, which ceased to be a predictor of quality. The effect of group size decreases, compared with model 2. Moreover, tenure diversity had a stronger positive influence on quality, whereas the effect of the interaction between bots and humans decreases.

Table 3. Ordinal logistic regression of number of edits and group size, editor types, and diversity measures. Note: *** p < .001, ** p < .01.

	Model 1			Model 2		
	Coef.	SE	P	Coef.	SE	P
Label>= D	−.0715	.0609		−1.3024	.1037	***
Label>= C	−1.2553	.0642	***	−2.5499	.1081	***
Label>= B	−4.4452	.1028	***	−5.7677	.1361	***
Label>= A	−6.2173	.1320	***	−7.6024	.1628	***
Item age	.0003	.0001	***	.0001	.0001	
Group size	.0279	.0014	***	.0330	.0015	***
# Edits	.0029	.0003	***	.0033	.0003	***
p Bot edits				1.4005	.1029	***
Bot X Human				4.6909	.3377	***
p Anonymous edits				−3.8258	1.2218	**

Table 4. Ordinal logistic regression of number of edits and group size, editor types, and diversity measures, trained on items with at least one human edit. Note: *** $p < .001$, ** $p < .01$. Model 3 has been trained on the set of items with at least one registered human edit.

	Model 3			Model 4		
	Coef.	SE	P	Coef.	SE	P
Label>= D	−1.1739	.1779	***	−2.6487	.2125	***
Label>= C	−2.3874	.1815	***	−4.1062	.2175	***
Label>= B	−5.8900	.2145	***	−7.5732	.2450	***
Label>= A	−7.4843	.2262	***	−9.2759	.2573	***
Item age	.0002	.0001		−.0008	.0001	***
Group size	.0152	.0015	***	.0248	.0016	***
# Edits	.0039	.0003	***	.0040	.0003	***
p Bot edits				2.4695	.1237	***
Bot X Human				3.7688	.3618	***
p Anonymous edits				−3.6628	1.2403	
Tenure diversity	1.5502	.1104	***	2.8043	.1166	***
Interest diversity	1.0104	.1972	***	1.1004	.1999	

6 Discussion

This paper has analysed the influence of group composition on outcome quality in Wikidata. First, we looked at how different proportions of bots, registered and anonymous human users affect quality. Second, we studied the effects of the distribution of two variables within groups of registered human users, tenure and members' interests.

The interaction between human editors and bots seems essential for the quality of Wikidata. It appears that the intertwinement of human and algorithmic contributions that led Niederer and van Dijck to define Wikipedia as a socio-technical system [22] is also key for Wikidata quality. The division of work outlined in [21] may explain the strong positive effect of bot–human interaction on item quality. Each type of user contributes to Wikidata by carrying out the tasks in which they are specialised and require each other, in order to achieve good quality. Future work should investigate in detail this interaction at item level, focusing on which share of light– and heavy-weight tasks need to take on each user type, in order to successfully build an item. Fewer than half of the items in our datasets were ever edited by anonymous users. Although this reflects the overall edit distribution in Wikidata, this suggests that caution should be taken in interpreting results related to hypothesis 3 and that a more in-depth study should be conduct to draw clearer statements about that.

Heterogeneous groups in terms of tenure of their members are more likely to produce higher quality items. This contradicts prior studies around tenure diversity in an offline context, such as [2,23]. On the contrary, it agrees with the observations around Wikipedia in [16]. An explanation may be that in online contexts the importance of the relational aspect, which sees homogeneous groups perform better due to increased cohesion, decreases. More diverse groups would benefit from the different perspectives brought by their members, according to the information/decision making perspective [30]. This would apply specifically to Wikidata, where contrasting statements can coexist and editors do not need to discuss on talk pages to reach consensus, in contrast to Wikipedia, in which discussion pages are used to settle disputes. Another likely cause for the positive influence of tenure diversity on quality is the diversification of tasks carried out by users at different times of their activity within Wikidata [24]. The contributions of editors with various tenure levels may thus be complementary.

Our models show a significant interaction between interest diversity and quality. This finding is in agreement with previous research, which noted a linear correlation between this type of diversity and productivity [8] and between cognitive diversity and quality of decisions in Wikipedia [16]. Varied editor interests may imply that these are more active over the whole KG and know its mechanisms better. Furthermore, group editors that are active over a wider portion of Wikidata may have increased chances to link an item to others in the KG through statements. The interest diversity measure used does not take into account how conceptually distant the items edited by members of a group are. For instance, two users may engage in adding content related to British musicians, while still working on different items. Future work may rely on semantic similarity measures such as that presented in [25] in order to address this limitation.

Finally, the current study aims to shed light on the 'right mix' of users that leads to higher quality in Wikidata. According to the models trained, groups with higher levels of cooperation between bot and human editors (where tasks are more equally shared among these) are able to achieve better performance. 'Ideal' groups also benefit from including members with different tenure, which may address various quality issues. Group size has only a limited positive influence on performance, which partially contradicts previous observations around Wikipedia [15,16]. The presence of anonymous users in these groups seems marginal and does not have any significant effect.

7   Conclusions

This is the first research to address the relationship between group composition and outcome quality in Wikidata. Users of this system can be human, anonymous or registered, or bots. This investigation analysed how the contribution of these types of users and their interaction benefit Wikidata item quality. Furthermore, it examined the effects of tenure and interest diversity across registered human users on outcome quality. Ordinal logistic regression analysis revealed that the interaction between human and algorithmic users is necessary to create high quality items. Contributions from anonymous users are instead detrimental for quality. Concerning tenure and interest diversity, both these features have a positive influence on quality. More heterogeneous groups seem likely to benefit from the different experiences and skills of their members. One of the goals of the current study was to identify what are the characteristics of successful groups working on Wikidata items. These groups are slightly larger than average. Their members are both human and bots and contribute in a balanced proportion. Human editors in these groups are likely to have diverse levels of experience and interests in Wikidata.

Regarding the limitations of this work, cross-sectional approaches such as the one employed in the current paper may suffer from reverse causation and uncontrolled confounding factors [15]. Longitudinal analyses are effective for addressing these issues. Nevertheless, no measures of quality over time are currently available for Wikidata, to the best of our knowledge. This is a relevant research topic for the future of Wikidata and should be addressed by further studies. Several variables are at play in group work, such as the coordination among their members. Future research should explore how group diversity interact with other variables.

Acknowledgements. This project is supported by funding received from the European Union's Horizon 2020 research and innovation programme under the Marie Skłodowska-Curie grant agreement No. 642795 (WDAqua ITN).

References

1. Adler, B.T., de Alfaro, L.: A content-driven reputation system for the Wikipedia. In: Williamson, C.L., Zurko, M.E., Patel-Schneider, P.F., Shenoy, P.J. (eds.) Proceedings of the 16th International Conference on World Wide Web, WWW 2007, Banff, Alberta, Canada, 8–12 May 2007, pp. 261–270. ACM (2007). http://doi.acm.org/10.1145/1242572.1242608
2. Ancona, D.G., Caldwell, D.F.: Demography and design: predictors of new product team performance. Organ. Sci. **3**(3), 321–341 (1992)
3. Arazy, O., Nov, O., Patterson, R., Yeo, L.: Information quality in Wikipedia: the effects of group composition and task conflict. J. Manag. Inf. Syst. **27**(4), 71–98 (2011)
4. Bedeian, A.G., Mossholder, K.W.: On the use of the coefficient of variation as a measure of diversity. Organ. Res. Methods **3**(3), 285–297 (2000)
5. Bender, R., Grouven, U.: Ordinal logistic regression in medical research. J. Roy. Coll. Phys. Lond. **31**(5), 546–551 (1997)
6. Brant, R.: Assessing proportionality in the proportional odds model for ordinal logistic regression. Biometrics 1171–1178 (1990)
7. Brasileiro, F., Almeida, J.P.A., Carvalho, V.A., Guizzardi, G.: Applying a multilevel modeling theory to assess taxonomic hierarchies in Wikidata. In: Proceedings of the 25th International Conference Companion on World Wide Web, pp. 975–980. International World Wide Web Conferences Steering Committee (2016)
8. Chen, J., Ren, Y., Riedl, J.: The effects of diversity on group productivity and member withdrawal in online volunteer groups. In: Proceedings of the 28th International Conference on Human Factors in Computing Systems - CHI 2010, p. 821. ACM, New York, April 2010

9. Erxleben, F., Günther, M., Krötzsch, M., Mendez, J., Vrandečić, D.: Introducing Wikidata to the linked data web. In: Mika, P., et al. (eds.) ISWC 2014. LNCS, vol. 8796, pp. 50–65. Springer, Cham (2014). doi:10.1007/978-3-319-11964-9_4

10. Färber, M., Bartscherer, F., Menne, C., Rettinger, A.: Linked data quality of DBpedia, Freebase, OpenCyc, Wikidata, and YAGO. Semantic Web (Preprint), pp. 1–53 (2016)

11. Färber, M., Ell, B., Menne, C., Rettinger, A.: A comparative survey of DBpedia, freebase, OpenCyc Wikidata and YAGO. Seman. Web 1, 1–5 (2015)

12. Harrison, D.A., Klein, K.J.: What's the difference? Diversity constructs as separation, variety, or disparity in organizations. Acad. Manag. Rev. 32(4), 1199–1228 (2007)

13. Haythornthwaite, C.: Crowds and communities: light and heavyweight models of peer production. In: Proceedings of the 42nd Annual Hawaii International Conference on System Sciences, HICSS (2009)

14. Jehn, K.A., Northcraft, G.B., Neale, M.A.: Why differences make a difference: a field study of diversity, conflict, and performance in workgroups. Adm. Sci. Q. 44(4), 741–763 (1999)

15. Kittur, A., Kraut, R.E.: Harnessing the wisdom of crowds in Wikipedia: quality through coordination. In: Proceedings of the ACM 2008 Conference on Computer Supported Cooperative Work - CSCW 2008, p. 37 (2008)

16. Lam, S.K., Karim, J., Riedl, J.: The effects of group composition on decision quality in a social production community. In: Proceedings of the 16th ACM International Conference on Supporting Group Work - GROUP 2010, p. 55 (2010)

17. Levine, J.M., Moreland, R.L.: Progress in small group research. Ann. Rev. Psychol. 41(1), 585–634 (1990)

18. Lukyanenko, R., Parsons, J., Wiersma, Y.F.: The IQ of the crowd: understanding and improving information quality in structured user-generated content. Inf. Syst. Res. 25(4), 669–689 (2014). https://doi.org/10.1287/isre.2014.0537

19. Milliken, F.J., Martins, L.L.: Searching for common threads: understanding the multiple effects of diversity in organizational groups. Acad. Manag. Rev. 21(2), 402–433 (1996)

20. Moreland, R.L., Levine, J.M.: Socialization in organizations and work groups. In: Groups at Work: Theory and Research, p. 69 (2014)

21. Müller-Birn, C., Karran, B., Lehmann, J., Luczak-Roesch, M.: Peer-production system or collaborative ontology development effort: what is Wikidata? In: OpenSym 2015 - Conference on Open Collaboration, San Francisco, US, 19–21 August 2015 (2015)

22. Niederer, S., van Dijck, J.: Wisdom of the crowd or technicity of content? Wikipedia as a sociotechnical system. New Media Soc. 12(8), 1368–1387 (2010). https://doi.org/10.1177/1461444810365297

23. Pelled, L.H., Eisenhardt, K.M., Xin, K.R.: Exploring the black box: an analysis of work group diversity, conflict, and performance. Adm. Sci. Q. 44(1), 1–28 (1999)

24. Piscopo, A., Phethean, C., Simperl, E.: Wikidatians are born: paths to full participation in a collaborative structured knowledge base. In: 50th Hawaii International Conference on System Sciences, HICSS 2017, Hilton Waikoloa Village, Hawaii, USA, 4–7 January 2017. AIS Electronic Library (AISeL) (2017)

25. Ribón, I.T., Vidal, M., Kämpgen, B., Sure-Vetter, Y.: GADES: a graph-based semantic similarity measure. In: SEMANTICS, pp. 101–104. ACM (2016)

26. Staab, S., Studer, R.: Handbook on Ontologies. Springer Science & Business Media, Heidelberg (2013)

27. Steiner, T.: Bots vs. wikipedians, anons vs. logged-ins. In: Proceedings of the Companion Publication of the 23rd International Conference on World Wide Web Companion, pp. 547–548. International World Wide Web Conferences Steering Committee (2014)

28. Surowiecki, J.: The Wisdom of Crowds. Anchor, Daman (2005)

29. Thakkar, H., Endris, K.M., Garica, J.M., Debattista, J., Lange, C., Auer, S.: Are linked datasets fit for open-domain question answering? A quality assessment. In: Proceedings of the 6th International Conference on Web Intelligence, Mining and Semantics (WIMS16). ACM (2016)

30. Van Knippenberg, D., De Dreu, C.K., Homan, A.C.: Work group diversity and group performance: an integrative model and research agenda. J. Appl. Psychol. **89**(6), 1008 (2004)

31. Vrandečić, D., Krötzsch, M.: Wikidata: a free collaborative knowledgebase. Commun. ACM **57**(10), 78–85 (2014)

32. Wagner, C.: Wiki: a technology for conversational knowledge management and group collaboration. Commun. Assoc. Inf. Syst. **13**(1), 58 (2004)

33. Yapinus, G., Sarabadani, A., Halfaker, A.: Wikidata item quality labels (2017). https://figshare.com/articles/Wikidata_item_quality_labels/5035796

Multimodal Analysis and Prediction of Latent User Dimensions

Laura Wendlandt[1]([⊠]), Rada Mihalcea[1], Ryan L. Boyd[2],
and James W. Pennebaker[2]

[1] University of Michigan, Ann Arbor, MI, USA
{wenlaura,mihalcea}@umich.edu
[2] University of Texas at Austin, Austin, TX, USA
{ryanboyd,pennebaker}@utexas.edu

Abstract. Humans upload over 1.8 billion digital images to the internet each day, yet the relationship between the images that a person shares with others and his/her psychological characteristics remains poorly understood. In the current research, we analyze the relationship between images, captions, and the latent demographic/psychological dimensions of personality and gender. We consider a wide range of automatically extracted visual and textual features of images/captions that are shared by a large sample of individuals ($N \approx 1,350$). Using correlational methods, we identify several visual and textual properties that show strong relationships with individual differences between participants. Additionally, we explore the task of predicting user attributes using a multimodal approach that simultaneously leverages images and their captions. Results from these experiments suggest that images alone have significant predictive power and, additionally, multimodal methods outperform both visual features and textual features in isolation when attempting to predict individual differences.

Keywords: Analysis of latent user dimensions · Multimodal prediction · Joint language/vision models

1 Introduction

Personalized image data has become widespread: over 1.8 billion digital images are added to the internet each day [29]. Despite this tremendous quantity of visual data, the relationship between the images that a person shares online and his/her demographic and psychological characteristics remains poorly understood. One of the most appealing promises of this data is that it can be used to gain a deeper understanding into the thoughts and behaviors of people.

Specifically, in this work, we examine the relationship between images, their captions, and the latent user dimensions of personality and gender to address several basic questions. First, from a correlational perspective, how do image and caption attributes relate to the individual traits of personality and gender? We extract an extensive set of visual and textual features and use correlational

© Springer International Publishing AG 2017
G.L. Ciampaglia et al. (Eds.): SocInfo 2017, Part I, LNCS 10539, pp. 323–340, 2017.
DOI: 10.1007/978-3-319-67217-5_20

techniques to uncover new, interpretable psychological insight into the ways that image attributes (such as objects, scenes, and faces) as well as language features (such as words and semantic categories) relate to personality and gender. Second, do image attributes have predictive power for these traits? We demonstrate that visual features alone have significant predictive power for latent user dimensions. While previous work has extensively explored the connection between textual features and user traits, we are among the first to show that images can also be used to predict these traits. Finally, how can we combine visual and textual features in a multimodal approach to achieve better predictive results? We develop multimodal models that outperform both visual features and textual features in isolation when attempting to predict individual differences. We also show that these models are effective on a relatively small corpus of images and text, in contrast to other published multimodal approaches for tasks such as captioning, which rely on very large visual and textual corpora.

2 Related Work

When studying individuals, we are often trying to get a general sense of who they are as a person. These types of evaluations fall under the broader umbrella of *individual differences*, a large area of research that tries to understand the various ways in which people are psychologically different from one another, yet relatively consistent over time [2]. A large amount of research in the past decade has been dedicated to the assessment and estimation of individual characteristics as a function of various behavioral traces. In our case, these traces are images and captions collected from undergraduate students.

Personality Prediction. Much of the work in individual differences research focuses on the topic of *personality*. Generally speaking, "personality" is a term used in psychology to refer to constellations of feelings, behaviors, and cognitions that co-occur within an individual and are relatively stable across time and contexts. Personality is most often conceived within the Big 5 personality framework, and these five dimensions of personality are predictive of important behavioral outcomes such as marital satisfaction [16] and even health [36].

From a computational perspective, the problem of predicting personality has primarily been approached using Natural Language Processing (NLP) methods. While the textual component of our work focuses on short image captions, most previous research used longer bodies of text such as essays or social media updates [33]. N-grams, as well as psychologically-derived linguistic features such as those provided by LIWC, have been shown to have significant predictive power for personality [25,34].

In addition to textual inference, there has been a recent movement towards incorporating images into the study of individual differences. Similar to our work, Segalin et al. have found that both traditional computer vision attributes and convolutional neural networks can be used to infer personality [38,39]. Liu et al. have also discussed the possibility of inferring personality from social media profile pictures [22]. However, unlike our work, these studies do not make use of higher-level image features (e.g. scenes, objects), and they do not consider any image captions or any interaction between visual and textual modalities.

Gender Prediction. Contemporary research on individual differences extends well beyond personality evaluations to include variables such as gender, age, life experiences, and so on – facets that differ between individuals but are not necessarily caused by internal psychological processes. In addition to personality, we also consider gender in this work.

As with personality, predicting gender has primarily been approached using NLP techniques [18,21,31]. Relevant to the current work, however, is recent work by You et al. [43], who have explored the task of predicting gender given a user's selected images on Pinterest, an online social networking site.

Inference from Multiple Modalities. Our work also relates to the recent body of research on the joint use of language and vision. Our multimodal approach is particularly related to automatic image annotation, the task of extracting semantically meaningful keywords from images [44]. Other related multimodal approaches can be found in the fields of image captioning [15] and joint text-image embeddings [3]. Some of these approaches rely on very large corpora. For example, Johnson et al. train an image captioning algorithm using Visual Genome, a dataset with greater than 94,000 images [14].

3   Dataset

We use a dataset collected at the University of Texas at Austin in the context of a Fall 2015 online undergraduate introductory psychology class.[1] The dataset includes free response data and responses to standard surveys collected from 1,353 students ages 16 to 46 (average 18.8 ± 2.10). The ethnicity distribution is 40.3% Anglo-Saxon/White, 27.1% Hispanic/Latino, 22.3% Asian/Asian American, 5.5% African American/Black, and 4.8% Other/Undefined.

Three elements of this dataset are of particular interest to our research:

Free Response Image Data. Each student was asked to submit and caption five images that expressed who he/she is as a person. As Fig. 1 illustrates, students submitted a wide range of images, from memes to family photos to landscapes. Some students chose to submit fewer than five images.

Big 5 Personality Ratings. Each student completed the BFI-44 personality inventory, which is used to score individuals along each of the Big 5 personality dimensions using a 1-to-5 scale [13]. The Big 5 personality dimensions include [28]: *Openness* (example adjectives: artistic, curious, imaginative, insightful, original, wide interests); *Conscientiousness* (efficient, organized, planful, reliable, responsible, thorough); *Extraversion* (active, assertive, energetic, enthusiastic, outgoing, talkative); *Agreeableness* (appreciative, forgiving, generous, kind, sympathetic, trusting); and *Neuroticism* (anxious, self-pitying, tense, touchy, unstable, worrying).

---

[1] This data was collected under IRB approval at UT Austin.

(a)   (b)   (c)   (d)   (e)

Fig. 1. Five images from the dataset submitted by a single student (with student faces blurred out for privacy). The accompanying captions are: (a) I'd rather be on the water. (b) The littlest things are always so pretty (and harder to capture). (c) I crossed this bridge almost every day for 18 years and never got tired of it. (d) The real me is right behind you. (e) Gotta find something to do when I have nothing to say.

Gender. Finally, demographic data is also associated with each student, including gender, which we use in our work. The gender distribution is 61.6% female, 37.8% male, and 0.5% undefined. Gender-unspecified students are omitted from our analyses.

Computing Correlations. An important contribution of our work is gathering new insights into textual and image attributes that correlate with personality and gender. Each of the personality dimensions is continuous, therefore, a version of the Pearson correlation coefficient is used to calculate correlations between personality and visual and textual features. Because there are, in some cases, thousands of image or text features, we must account for inferential issues associated with multiple testing (e.g., inflated error rates); we address such issues using a multivariate permutation test [42].

This approach is done by first calculating the Pearson product-moment correlation coefficient r for two variables. Then, for a high number of iterations (in our case, 10,000), the two variables are randomly shuffled and the Pearson coefficient is re-calculated each time. At the end of the shuffling, a two-tailed p-test is conducted, comparing the true correlation r with the values of r attained from randomly shuffling the data. The original result is considered to be legitimate only when the original Pearson's r is found to be statistically significant in comparison to all of the random coefficients. As discussed in [42], for small sample sizes, this multivariate permutation test has more statistical power than the common Bonferroni correction.

Unlike personality, gender is a categorical variable. Thus, Welch's t-tests are used to look for significant relationships between gender and image and text features. These relationships are measured using effect size (Cohen's d), which measures how many standard deviations the two groups differ by, and is calculated by dividing the mean difference by the pooled standard deviation. In using Welch's t-tests, we make the assumption that within each gender, image and text features follow a normal distribution.

4   Analysing Images

In order to explore the relationship between images and psychological attributes, we want to extract meaningful and interpretable image features that have some connection to the user.

4.1   Raw Visual Features

We begin by describing low-level raw visual features of an image.

Colors. Past research has shown that colors are associated with abstract concepts [35]. For instance, red is associated with excitement, yellow with cheerfulness, and blue with comfort, wealth, and trust. Furthermore, research has shown that men and women respond to color differently. In particular, one study found that men are more tolerant of gray, white, and black than are women [17].

To characterize the distribution of colors in an image, we classify each pixel as one of eleven named colors using the method presented by Van De Weijer et al. [41]. This method trains a Probabilistic Latent Semantic Analysis model over retrieved Google images, using the model to assign color names to individual pixels. For our experiments, we use Van De Weijer et al.'s pre-trained model. The percentage of each color across an image is used as a feature.

Brightness and Saturation. Images are often characterized in terms of their brightness and saturation. Here, we use the HSV color space, where brightness is defined as the relative lightness or darkness of a particular color, from black (no brightness) to light, vivid color (full brightness). Saturation captures the relationship between the hue of a color and its brightness and ranges from white (no saturation) to pure color (full saturation). We calculate the mean and the standard deviation for both the brightness and the saturation.

Previous work has also used brightness and saturation to calculate metrics measuring pleasure, arousal, and dominance, as expressed in the following formulas: $Pleasure = 0.69y + 0.22s$; $Arousal = -0.31y + 0.60s$; $Dominance = -0.76y + 0.32s$, where y is the average brightness of an image and s is its average saturation [40].[2]

Texture. The texture of an image provides information about the patterns of colors or intensities in the image. Following [23], we use Grey Level Co-occurrence Matrices (GLCMs) to calculate four texture metrics: contrast, correlation, energy, and homogeneity.

Static and Dynamic Lines. Previous work has shown that the orientation of a line can have various emotional effects on the viewer [24]. For example, diagonal lines are associated with movement and a lack of equilibrium. To capture some of these effects, we measure the percentage of static lines with respect to all of

---

[2] For prediction experiments, we use a slightly different version of dominance ($Dominance = 0.76y + 0.32s$), as formulated in [24].

the lines in the image.[3] Static lines are defined as lines that are within $\pi/12$ radians of being vertical or horizontal.

Circles. The presence of circles and other curves in images has been found to be associated with emotions such as anger and sadness [35]. Following the example of [35], we calculate the number of circles in an image.[4]

Correlations. Once the entire set of raw features is extracted from the images, correlations between raw features and personality/demographic features are calculated. Table 1 presents significant correlations between visual features and personality traits. One correlation to note is a positive relationship between the number of circles in an image and extraversion. This is likely because the circle detection algorithm often counts faces as circles, and faces have a natural connection with the social facets of extraversion. Our results also validate the findings of Valdez and Mehrabian, who suggest that pleasure, arousal, and dominance have emotional connections [40]. Here we show that these metrics also have connections to personality. While these correlations are weak, they are statistically significant.

Table 2 shows effect sizes for features significantly different between men and women. As suggested by previous research, men are more likely to use the color black [17]; other correlations appear to confirm stereotypes, e.g., a stronger preference by women for pink and purple.

4.2   Scenes

Previous research has linked personal spaces (such as bedrooms and offices) with various personality attributes, indicating that how a person composes his/her space provides clues about his/her psychology, particularly through self-presentation and related social processes [11].

In order to identify the scene of an image, we use Places-CNN [45], a convolutional neural network (CNN) trained on approximately 2.5 million images and able to classify an image into 205 scene categories. To illustrate, Fig. 2 shows sample images. For each image, we use the softmax probability distribution over all scenes as features.

Correlations. Scenes strongly correlated with personality traits are shown in Table 1. The strongest positive correlation is between extraversion and ballrooms, and the strongest negative correlation is between extraversion and home offices. Findings such as these are conceptually sound, as individuals tend to engage in personality-congruent behaviors. In other words, individuals scoring high on extraversion are expected to feel that inherently social locations, such as ballrooms, are more relevant to the self than locations indicative of social isolation, such as home offices.

---

[3] We use the OpenCV probabilistic Hough transform function with an accumulator threshold of 50, a minimum line length of 50, and a maximum line gap of 10.

[4] We use the OpenCV Hough circles function, with a minimum distance of 8 and method-specific parameters set to 170 and 45.

Table 1. Significant correlations between image attributes and Big 5 personality traits. These correlations are corrected using a multivariate permutation test, as described in Sect. 3. Only scenes and basic WordNet domains that have one of the top five highest correlations or one of the top five lowest correlations are shown.

Image Attributes	Big 5 Personality Dimensions				
	Openness	Conscientiousness	Extraversion	Agreeableness	Neuroticism
Raw Visual Features					
Black	-	-	-	−0.06	-
Blue	-	-	0.06	-	−0.07
Grey	0.06	-	−0.11	-	-
Orange	-	-	0.07	-	-
Purple	-	-	0.06	-	-
Red	−0.06	-	-	-	-
Brightness Std. Dev	-	-	0.07	-	-
Saturation Mean	-	-	0.07	-	−0.06
Saturation Std. Dev	−0.06	-	0.06	-	−0.06
Pleasure	-	-	0.07	-	−0.05
Arousal	-	-	-	-	0.06
Dominance	-	-	0.08	-	−0.05
Homogeneity	-	0.05	-	-	-
Static Lines %	-	-	−0.07	-	-
Num. of Circles	-	-	0.10	-	−0.06
Scenes					
Ballroom	-	-	0.12	0.06	−0.06
Bookstore	-	-0.06	−0.11	-	0.08
Canyon	0.11	-	-	-	-
Home Office	-	-	−0.12	-	-
Mansion	-	-	-	0.10	-
Martial Arts Gym	-0.09	-	0.06	-	-
Pantry	-	-	-0.11	-0.10	-
Playground	-	-	0.07	0.09	−0.06
River	-	0.09	0.07	0.07	-
Shower	-	-	−0.09	-	-
Faces	−0.07	0.08	0.17	0.11	-
WordNet Supersenses					
Animal	-	-	0.06	-	-
Person	-	-	-	-	−0.06
Basic WordNet Domains					
History	-	-	0.06	-	-
Play	−0.10	-	-	-	-
Sport	−0.10	-	-	-	-
Home	-	−0.06	−0.09	-	-
Biology	-	-	0.07	-	-
Physics	-	−0.08	-	−0.09	-
Anthropology	-	0.06	-	-	-
Industry	-	-	−0.08	-	-
Fashion	−0.07	0.06	0.11	0.05	-

Table 2. Image and text features where there is a significant difference ($p < 0.05$) between male and female images. Only scenes, basic WordNet domains, and unigrams with the highest ten effect sizes (by magnitude) are shown. All text features except for the word count itself are normalized by the word count. Positive effect sizes indicate that women prefer the feature, while negative effect sizes indicate that men prefer the feature.

Image Attributes	Effect Size	Text Attributes	Effect Size
Raw Visual Features		**Stylistic Features**	
Pink	0.455	Num. of Words	0.174
Static Lines %	-0.360	Readability - GFI	-0.161
Black	-0.325	Readability - SMOG	-0.146
Brightness Mean	0.266	Readability - FRE	-0.136
Saturation Std. Dev.	-0.176	**Unigrams**	
Purple	0.167	Boyfriend	0.361
Brown	0.166	Girlfriend	-0.360
Homogeneity	0.118	Was	0.287
Red	0.111	Play	-0.285
Faces	0.160	She	0.264
Scenes		Them	0.262
Beauty Salon	0.347	Sport	-0.254
Ice Cream Parlor	0.340	Sister	0.244
Office	-0.290	Game	-0.242
Slum	0.286	Enjoy	-0.236
Football Stadium	-0.267	**LIWC Categories**	
Basement	-0.235	Prepositions	-0.198
Herb Garden	0.224	Past Focus	0.176
Gas Station	-0.222	Sports	-0.173
Music Studio	-0.222	Work	-0.167
Baseball Stadium	-0.222	Period	-0.157
WordNet Supersenses		Other References	0.145
Artifact	-0.213	Quote	-0.133
Person	-0.173	Other	0.123
Food	0.107	1st Person Plural Personal Pronouns	0.123
Basic WordNet Domains		**MRC Categories**	
Play	-0.236	Kucera-Francis Written Freq.	-0.139
Sport	-0.235	Kucera-Francis Num. of Samples	-0.134
Transport	-0.186		
Military	-0.182		
Animals	-0.155		
History	-0.153		
Art	-0.142		
Food	0.136		
Plants	0.120		
Tourism	-0.118		

We also measure the relationship between scenes and gender. Table 2 shows scenes that are associated with either males or females. Men are more commonly characterized by sports-related scenes, such as football and baseball stadiums, whereas women are more likely to have photos from ice cream and beauty parlors. As illustrated in Fig. 2, the scene detection algorithm tends to conflate coffee shops and ice cream parlors, so this observed preference for ice cream parlors could be partially attributed to a preference for coffee shops.

(a) Coffee Shop (0.53), Ice Cream Parlor (0.24)   (b) Parking Lot (0.57), Sky (0.26)

Fig. 2. Top scene classifications for two images, along with their probabilities.

4.3 Faces

Most aspects of a person's personality are expressed through social behaviors, and the number of faces in an image can capture some of this behavior. We use the work by Mathias et al. to detect faces [27]. Specifically, we use their pre-trained *HeadHunter* model, an advanced evolution of the Viola-Jones detector.

Correlations. Significant correlations between faces and personality traits are shown in Table 1. Of particular note is the strong positive correlation between the number of faces and extraversion, which is intuitive because extraverts are often thought of as enjoying social activities. With respect to gender, Table 2 shows that women tend to have more faces in their images than men.

4.4 Objects

Previous research has indicated that people can successfully predict other's personality traits by observing their possessions [10]. This indicates that object detection has the ability to capture certain psychological insight.

To detect multiple objects per image, we break each image into multiple regions, apply object detection to each region, and post-process each detection to create interpretable features. To identify image regions, we use *Edge Boxes* [46] to detect a maximum of 2,000 regions;[5] to avoid falsely detecting objects, regions that are less than 3% of the total image area are discarded.

Objects are detected by sending each region through CaffeNet, a version of AlexNet [12,19]. CaffeNet assumes that each region contains one object and outputs a softmax probability over 1,000 ImageNet objects [37]. The final score for an object in a region is the *Edge Boxes* score for the region multiplied by CaffeNet's softmax probability. We remove any objects with a score below a certain threshold, where the threshold is optimized on the PASCAL VOC image set [7]. For each object type, the scores of all of the detected objects in a particular image are added up, creating a 1,000-dimensional feature vector.

---

[5] We use the *Edge Boxes* parameters $\alpha = 0.65$ and $\beta = 0.55$.

Because of the small size of our dataset and the large number of ImageNet objects, this feature vector is somewhat sparse and hard to interpret. To increase interpretability for correlational analysis, we consider two coarser-grained systems of classification: WordNet supersenses and WordNet domains. WordNet [8] is a large hierarchical database of English concepts (or synsets), and each ImageNet object is directly associated with a WordNet concept. Supersenses are broad semantic classes labeled by lexicographers (e.g., communication, object, animal) [5]. WordNet domains [1] is a complementary synset labeling. It groups WordNet synsets into various domains, such as medicine, astronomy, and history. The domain structure is hierarchical, but here we consider only basic WordNet domains, which are domains that are broad enough to be easily interpretable (e.g., history, chemistry, fashion). An object is allowed to fall into more than one domain.

Correlations. WordNet supersenses and domains correlate significantly with multiple personality traits, as shown in Table 1. Table 2 shows object classes that are different for males and females. These object classes connect back to scenes associated with men and women. For example, men are more likely to have sports objects in their images, reflected in the fact that men are more likely to include scenes of sports stadiums.

4.5 Captions

When available, captions can be considered another way of representing image content via a textual description of the salient objects, people, or scenes in the image. Importantly, the captions have been contributed by the same people who contributed the images, and they represent the views that the image "owners" have about their content.

Stylistic Features. To capture writing style, we consider surface-level stylistic features, such as the number of words and the number of words longer than six characters. We also use the Stanford Named Entity Recognition system to extract the number of references to people, locations, and organizations [9]. Finally, we look at readability and specificity metrics. For readability, we consider a variety of metrics: Flesch Reading Ease (FRE), Automated Readability Index (ARI), Flesch-Kincaid Grade Level (FK), Coleman-Liau Index (CLI), Gunning Fog Index (GFI), and SMOG score (SMOG). For specificity, we use Speciteller [20].

N-grams. In addition to style, we want to capture the content of each caption. We do this by considering unigrams, bigrams, and trigrams. Each caption is tokenized (split into tokens on punctuation other than periods) and stemmed using the Lancaster Stemmer [4]. Only n-grams that occur more than five times are considered. N-grams that occur less than this are replaced by an out-of-vocabulary (OOV) symbol. We also consider part-of-speech (POS) unigrams, bigrams, and trigrams, tokenized using the Penn Treebank tagset [26].

Table 3. Significant correlations between language attributes and Big 5 personality traits. All features except for the word count itself are normalized by the word count. Only unigrams, LIWC categories, and MRC categories that have one of the top five highest correlations or one of the top five lowest correlations are shown.

Language Attributes	Big 5 Personality Dimensions				
	Openness	Conscientiousness	Extraversion	Agreeableness	Neuroticism
Stylistic Features					
Num. of Words	0.14	-	-	-	0.07
Words Longer than Six Characters	-	0.09	0.06	-	-
Num. of Locations	-	0.07	-	-	−0.07
Readability - FRE	−0.13	-	-	-	-
Readability - ARI	-	0.06	-	-	-
Readability - GFI	−0.14	-	-	-	-
Readability - SMOG	−0.13	-	-	-	−0.06
Specificity	-	0.08	-	-	−0.06
Unigrams					
Decide	-	−0.12	-	-	-
Different	0.11	-	-	-	-
In	0.11	-	-	-	-
It	0.11	-	-	-	-
King	-	0.06	-	−0.15	-
Level	-	-	−0.12	-	-
My	−0.14	0.07	-	-	-
Photoshop	0.10	-	-	-	-
Sport	−0.14	-	-	-	-
Write	0.10	-	-	-	-
LIWC Categories					
Achievement	-	0.08	-	-	-
All Punctuation	-	0.08	-	-	−0.07
Discrepancies	-	-	0.10	-	−0.07
1st Person Singular Personal Pronouns	−0.10	-	-	-	-
Inclusive	-	-	-	0.08	-
Occupation	-	0.08	0.06	-	-
Other References	−0.10	-	-	-	−0.06
1st Person Personal Pronouns	−0.10	-	-	-	-
Sports	−0.11	0.07	-	-	-
Unique	-	0.07	-	0.08	−0.09
MRC Categories					
Imagery	−0.07	0.06	-	0.06	−0.07
Kucera-Francis Num. of Categories	−0.07	0.06	-	0.07	−0.09
Kucera-Francis Num. of Samples	−0.08	-	-	-	−0.07
Mean Pavio Meaningfulness	−0.08	-	-	-	−0.07
Num. of Letters in Word	-	0.08	-	0.07	−0.08
Num. of Phonemes in Word	-	0.08	-	0.07	−0.08
Num. of Syllables in Word	-	0.08	-	0.08	−0.08

LIWC Features. Linguistic Inquiry and Word Count (LIWC) is a word-based text analysis program [34]. It focuses on broad categories such as language composition, as well as emotional, cognitive, and social processes. We analyze each piece of text using LIWC in order to capture psychological dimensions of writing. For each of the 86 LIWC categories, we calculate a feature that reflects the percentage of caption words belonging to that category.

MRC Features. The MRC Psycholinguistic Database contains statistics about word use [6]. MRC features are calculated by averaging the values of all of the words in the caption. In our correlational analysis, certain MRC features emerge as particularly relevant. These include word frequency counts, which capture how common a word is in standard English usage, as well as measures for meaningfulness, imagery, and length (e.g., number of letters, phenomes, and syllables). These features provide a complementary perspective to the LIWC features.

Word Embeddings. For our prediction tasks, we also consider each word's embedding. *Word2vec (w2v)* is a method for creating a multidimensional embedding for a particular word [30]. Google provides pre-trained word embeddings on approximately 100 billion words of the Google News dataset.[6] For each caption in our dataset, we average together all of the word embeddings to produce a single feature vector of length 300. We use the Google embeddings for this, discarding words that are not present in the pre-trained embeddings.

Correlations. For correlational analysis, we normalize all text features by word count. Table 3 shows correlations between language features and personality. Interestingly, there are very few strong correlations for extraversion. This is complementary to what we see with images, where there are many strong correlations for extraversion, suggesting that we are gleaning different aspects of personality from both images and text. Many of these textual correlations have been discussed in previous literature (e.g. [25,34]), and our work confirms previous results.

Table 2 shows language features that are different between men and women. Things to note here are that women tend to write longer captions and men again exhibit a preference for talking about sports.

5   Multimodal Prediction

The task of prediction can provide valuable insights into the relationship between images, captions, and user dimensions. Here, we consider six coarse-grained classification tasks, one for each personality trait and one for gender. For each prediction, we divide the data into high and low segments. The high segment includes any person who has a score greater than half a standard deviation above the mean, while the low segment includes any person who has a score lower than half a standard deviation below the mean. All other data points are discarded.

---

[6] Available at https://code.google.com/archive/p/word2vec/.

This binary division of personality traits results in mostly balanced data, with the high segment for each trait containing 47.7–51.8% of the data points. For gender, 61.6% of the data is female. In doing these coarse-grained classification tasks, we follow previous work [25,32], which suggested that classification serves as a useful approximation to continuous rating.

We use a random forest with 500 trees and 10-fold cross validation across individuals in the dataset. Table 4 shows the classification results. As a baseline, we include a model that always predicts the most common training class. In addition to the random forest model, we also considered other approaches to this problem, primarily neural network-based. These approaches were not successful, partially because of the small size of our dataset, though they suggest some interesting future avenues to explore.

To enable direct comparison to previously published results, we use our data to re-train the personality prediction models from Mairesse et al. [25]; the re-trained classifier with the highest accuracies on our data, SMO, is shown in Table 5. We also include the relative error rate reduction between this model and our best multimodal model.

Single Modality Methods. To understand the predictive power of images and captions individually, we consider a series of predictions using feature sets derived from either only visual data or only textual data. These feature sets are the same features that we described in Sect. 4.

As shown in Table 4, image features in isolation are able to significantly classify both extraversion and gender. Text features are also able to significantly classify these traits, with slightly less accuracy than image features. Text features have additional predictive power for openness.

Multimodal Methods. We experiment with several methods of combining visual and textual data. First, we concatenate both the image and text feature vectors (excluding *w2v* embeddings). These results are shown in Table 4 under the *All* row in the *Image and Caption Attributes* section.

To provide a more nuanced combination of features, we introduce the idea of image-enhanced unigrams (IEUs). This is a bag-of-words representation of both an image and its corresponding caption. It includes all of the caption unigrams, as well as unigrams derived from the image. We consider two methods, macro and micro, for generating image unigrams. For the macro method, we examine each individual image. If a color covers more than one-third of the image, the name of the color is added to the bag-of-words. The scene with the highest probability and any objects detected in the image are also added. The unigrams from each individual image are then combined with the caption unigrams to form the set of macro IEUs. To generate micro IEUs, instead of considering individual images, we consider aggregated image characteristics. First, for each student, we average his/her image feature vectors into a single vector, and then we extract image unigrams from this combined vector. For example, if the average percentage of a particular color across all images is greater than 33%, the name of that color is added to the bag-of-words. These unigrams are mixed with the caption unigrams to form the set of micro IEUs.

Table 4. Classification accuracy percentages. O, C, E, A, and N stand for openness, conscientiousness, extraversion, agreeableness, and neuroticism, respectively. * indicates significance with respect to the baseline ($p < 0.05$). Only image features that produce significant results and text features that score highest in one of the categories are shown.

Feature Set Used	Predicted Attributes					
	O	C	E	A	N	Gender
Baseline: Most Common Class	51.4	52.0	49.2	51.8	52.3	59.8
Image Attributes Only						
Object	**55.6**	51.7	57.2*	51.3	51.7	64.7*
Scene	55.5	53.8	59.8*	55.0	55.2	66.8*
Face	50.7	51.2	58.5*	54.1	51.1	59.7
All	54.8	**54.3**	**59.9***	**55.3**	55.3	**68.6***
Caption Attributes Only						
Unigrams	60.2*	53.1	54.3	54.2	53.4	**67.6***
Bigrams	58.0*	**53.2**	**57.6***	53.4	**57.3**	65.1*
LIWC	59.6*	**53.2**	54.1	53.4	54.2	64.9*
All (except pre-trained *w2v*)	61.2*	52.2	53.3	54.6	55.2	65.1*
Pre-trained *w2v* (caption only)	**61.8***	51.4	55.4	**55.4**	56.5	67.1*
All + Pre-trained *w2v* (caption only)	61.2*	52.3	55.5	53.0	56.1	65.6*
Image and Caption Attributes						
All	60.5*	55.1	57.9*	55.3	56.8	67.1*
Macro IEU	58.5*	56.6	58.5*	54.2	54.7	**71.0***
Micro IEU	58.7*	54.4	58.9*	54.0	52.7	**71.0***
All + Macro IEU	60.0*	**57.1**	58.3*	54.2	56.9	68.1*
All + Micro IEU	59.1*	55.6	60.3*	54.8	**58.3***	69.1*
Pre-trained *w2v* (w/Micro IEU)	**61.4***	54.8	59.6*	56.4*	56.5	68.6*
Pre-trained *w2v* (w/Macro IEU)	61.0*	55.6	**60.5***	**57.0***	56.6	69.0*
All + Pre-trained *w2v* (w/Micro IEU)	59.5*	54.8	59.1*	55.3	55.3	70.1*
All + Pre-trained *w2v* (w/Macro IEU)	**61.4***	54.7	59.4*	55.2	56.5	70.8*

We use IEUs in several different ways for prediction. First, we consider them both in isolation and concatenated with all of the previous visual and textual features (excluding *w2v*). We also explore using the pre-trained *w2v* model to represent the IEUs and produce richer embeddings. Instead of only averaging together the embeddings of each caption unigram, we average together the embeddings of each IEU. Finally, we consider these enriched embeddings concatenated with all of the previous features.

A significant advantage of these multimodal approaches is that they can be used with relatively small corpora of images and text. Large background corpora

Table 5. Comparison between our best classification model and the best model (SMO) from Mairesse et al. * indicates significance with respect to the baseline ($p < 0.05$).

Feature Set Used	Predicted Attributes					
	O	C	E	A	N	Gender
Baseline: Most Common Class	51.4	52.0	49.2	51.8	52.3	59.8
Mairesse et al.: SMO	59.1*	51.3	53.3	54.4	54.7	63.0
Our model: Pre-trained *w2v* (w/Macro IEU)	61.0*	55.6	60.5*	57.0*	56.6	69.0*
Relative error rate reduction (our model vs. Mairesse et al.)	4.6%	8.8%	15.4%	5.7%	4.2%	16.2%

are used for training (e.g., for training the scene CNN), but these models have already been trained and released. Our approaches work when there is only a small amount of training data, as is often the case when ground truth labels are expensive to obtain. This is demonstrated on our dataset, which consists of short captions and a relatively limited set of images.

The results obtained with the multimodal methods are shown in the bottom part of Table 4. As seen in the table, when compared to the methods that rely on individual modalities, these multimodal models outperform image features in all six categories and text features in all but one category. The methods using IEUs achieve the best results and are able to significantly classify both neuroticism and agreeableness, something that neither visual features nor textual features are able to do in isolation.

As shown in Table 5, our multimodal approaches also outperform the method from Mairesse et al., achieving relative error rate reductions between 4% and 16%.

6   Conclusion

This paper explores the connection between images, captions, and the latent user dimensions of personality and gender. While there is a large body of previous work that has considered the use of text as a way to analyse and predict user traits, there is very little work on the use of images for this task. The paper makes several contributions. First, using a new dataset of captioned images associated with user attributes, we extract a large set of visual and textual features and identify significant correlations between these features and the user traits of personality and gender. Second, we demonstrate the effectiveness of image features in predicting user attributes; we believe this result can have applications in many areas of the web where textual data is limited. Finally, we show that a multimodal predictive approach outperforms purely visual and textual methods. Our multimodal methods are also effective on relatively small corpora.

Acknowledgments. This material is based in part upon work supported by the National Science Foundation (NSF #1344257), the John Templeton Foundation (#48503), and the Michigan Institute for Data Science (MIDAS). Any opinions, findings, and conclusions or recommendations expressed in this material are those of the authors and do not necessarily reflect the views of the NSF, the John Templeton Foundation, or MIDAS. We would like to thank Chris Pittman for his aid with the data collection, Shibamouli Lahiri for the readability code, and Steven R. Wilson for the implementation of Mairesse et al.

References

1. Bentivogli, L., Forner, P., Magnini, B., Pianta, E.: Revising the WordNet domains hierarchy: semantics, coverage and balancing. In: Proceedings of the Workshop on Multilingual Linguistic Resources, pp. 101–108. Association for Computational Linguistics (2004)
2. Boyd, R.L.: Psychological text analysis in the digital humanities. In: Hai-Jew, S. (ed.) Data Analytics in the Digital Humanities. MMSA, pp. 161–189. Springer Science, New York City (2017). doi:10.1007/978-3-319-54499-1_7. In Press
3. Bruni, E., Tran, N.K., Baroni, M.: Multimodal distributional semantics. J. Artif. Intell. Res. **49**, 1–47 (2014)
4. Chris, D.P.: Another stemmer. In: ACM SIGIR Forum, vol. 24, pp. 56–61 (1990)
5. Ciaramita, M., Johnson, M.: Supersense tagging of unknown nouns in WordNet. In: Proceedings of the 2003 Conference on Empirical Methods in Natural Language Processing, pp. 168–175. Association for Computational Linguistics (2003)
6. Coltheart, M.: The MRC psycholinguistic database. Q. J. Exp. Psychol. **33**(4), 497–505 (1981)
7. Everingham, M., Van Gool, L., Williams, C.K., Winn, J., Zisserman, A.: The PASCAL visual object classes (VOC) challenge. Int. J. Comput. Vis. **88**(2), 303–338 (2010)
8. Fellbaum, C.: WordNet. Wiley Online Library, Hoboken (1998)
9. Finkel, J.R., Grenager, T., Manning, C.: Incorporating non-local information into information extraction systems by Gibbs sampling. In: Proceedings of the 43rd Annual Meeting on Association for Computational Linguistics, pp. 363–370 (2005)
10. Gosling, S.D., Craik, K.H., Martin, N.R., Pryor, M.R.: Material attributes of personal living spaces. Home Cultures **2**(1), 51–87 (2005)
11. Gosling, S.D., Ko, S.J., Mannarelli, T., Morris, M.E.: A room with a cue: personality judgments based on offices and bedrooms. J. Personal. Soc. Psychol. **82**(3), 379 (2002)
12. Jia, Y., Shelhamer, E., Donahue, J., Karayev, S., Long, J., Girshick, R., Guadarrama, S., Darrell, T.: Caffe: convolutional architecture for fast feature embedding. In: Proceedings of the 22nd ACM International Conference on Multimedia, pp. 675–678 (2014)
13. John, O.P., Srivastava, S.: The big five trait taxonomy: history, measurement, and theoretical perspectives. Handb. Personal.: Theory Res. **2**(1999), 102–138 (1999)
14. Johnson, J., Karpathy, A., Fei-Fei, L.: DenseCap: Fully convolutional localization networks for dense captioning. arXiv preprint arXiv:1511.07571 (2015)
15. Karpathy, A., Fei-Fei, L.: Deep visual-semantic alignments for generating image descriptions. In: Proceedings of the IEEE Conference on Computer Vision and Pattern Recognition, pp. 3128–3137 (2015)

16. Kelly, E.L., Conley, J.J.: Personality and compatibility: a prospective analysis of marital stability and marital satisfaction. J. Personal. Soc. Psychol. **52**(1), 27 (1987)
17. Khouw, N.: The meaning of color for gender. In: Colors Matters-Research (2002)
18. Koppel, M., Argamon, S., Shimoni, A.R.: Automatically categorizing written texts by author gender. Literary Linguist. Comput. **17**(4), 401–412 (2002)
19. Krizhevsky, A., Sutskever, I., Hinton, G.E.: ImageNet classification with deep convolutional neural networks. In: Advances in Neural Information Processing Systems, pp. 1097–1105 (2012)
20. Li, J.J., Nenkova, A.: Fast and accurate prediction of sentence specificity. In: AAAI, pp. 2281–2287 (2015)
21. Liu, H., Mihalcea, R.: Of men, women, and computers: data-driven gender modeling for improved user interfaces. In: International Conference on Weblogs and Social Media (2007)
22. Liu, L., Preotiuc-Pietro, D., Samani, Z.R., Moghaddam, M.E., Ungar, L.: Analyzing personality through social media profile picture choice. In: Tenth International AAAI Conference on Web and Social Media (2016)
23. Lovato, P., Bicego, M., Segalin, C., Perina, A., Sebe, N., Cristani, M.: Faved! biometrics: tell me which image you like and I'll tell you who you are. IEEE Trans. Inf. Forensics Secur. **9**(3), 364–374 (2014)
24. Machajdik, J., Hanbury, A.: Affective image classification using features inspired by psychology and art theory. In: Proceedings of the 18th ACM International Conference on Multimedia, pp. 83–92. ACM (2010)
25. Mairesse, F., Walker, M.A., Mehl, M.R., Moore, R.K.: Using linguistic cues for the automatic recognition of personality in conversation and text. J. Artif. Intell. Res. **30**, 457–500 (2007)
26. Marcus, M.P., Marcinkiewicz, M.A., Santorini, B.: Building a large annotated corpus of English: the Penn treebank. Comput. Linguist. **19**(2), 313–330 (1993)
27. Mathias, M., Benenson, R., Pedersoli, M., van Gool, L.: Face detection without bells and whistles. In: Fleet, D., Pajdla, T., Schiele, B., Tuytelaars, T. (eds.) ECCV 2014. LNCS, vol. 8692, pp. 720–735. Springer, Cham (2014). doi:10.1007/978-3-319-10593-2_47
28. McCrae, R.R., John, O.P.: An introduction to the five-factor model and its applications. J. Personal. **60**(2), 175–215 (1992)
29. Meeker, M.: Internet trends 2014-Code conference (2014). Accessed 28 May 2014
30. Mikolov, T., Sutskever, I., Chen, K., Corrado, G.S., Dean, J.: Distributed representations of words and phrases and their compositionality. In: Advances in Neural Information Processing Systems, pp. 3111–3119 (2013)
31. Newman, M.L., Groom, C.J., Handelman, L.D., Pennebaker, J.W.: Gender differences in language use: an analysis of 14,000 text samples. Discourse Process. **45**(3), 211–236 (2008)
32. Oberlander, J., Nowson, S.: Whose thumb is it anyway? Classifying author personality from weblog text. In: COLING/ACL, pp. 627–634 (2006)
33. Park, G., Schwartz, H.A., Eichstaedt, J.C., Kern, M.L., Kosinski, M., Stillwell, D.J., Ungar, L.H., Seligman, M.E.P.: Automatic personality assessment through social media language. J. Personal. Soc. Psychol. **108**(6), 934–952 (2014)
34. Pennebaker, J.W., King, L.A.: Linguistic styles: language use as an individual difference. J. Personal. Soc. Psychol. **77**(6), 1296 (1999)
35. Redi, M., Quercia, D., Graham, L., Gosling, S.: Like partying? Your face says it all. Predicting the ambiance of places with profile pictures. In: Ninth International AAAI Conference on Web and Social Media (2015)

36. Roberts, B., Kuncel, N., Shiner, R., Caspi, A., Goldberg, L.: The power of personality: the comparative validity of personality traits, socioeconomic status, and cognitive ability for predicting important life outcomes. Perspect. Psychol. Sci. 4(2), 313–345 (2007)
37. Russakovsky, O., Deng, J., Su, H., Krause, J., Satheesh, S., Ma, S., Huang, Z., Karpathy, A., Khosla, A., Bernstein, M., et al.: ImageNet large scale visual recognition challenge. Int. J. Comput. Vis. 115(3), 211–252 (2015)
38. Segalin, C., Cheng, D.S., Cristani, M.: Social profiling through image understanding: personality inference using convolutional neural networks. Comput. Vis. Image Understanding 156, 34–50 (2016)
39. Segalin, C., Perina, A., Cristani, M., Vinciarelli, A.: The pictures we like are our image: continuous mapping of favorite pictures into self-assessed and attributed personality traits. IEEE Trans. Affect. Comput. 8(2), 268–285 (2016)
40. Valdez, P., Mehrabian, A.: Effects of color on emotions. J. Exp. Psychol.: Gen. 123(4), 394 (1994)
41. Van De Weijer, J., Schmid, C., Verbeek, J., Larlus, D.: Learning color names for real-world applications. IEEE Trans. Image Process. 18(7), 1512–1523 (2009)
42. Yoder, P.J., Blackford, J.U., Waller, N.G., Kim, G.: Enhancing power while controlling family-wise error: an illustration of the issues using electrocortical studies. J. Clin. Exp. Neuropsychol. 26(3), 320–331 (2004)
43. You, Q., Bhatia, S., Sun, T., Luo, J.: The eyes of the beholder: gender prediction using images posted in online social networks. In: 2014 IEEE International Conference on Data Mining Workshop, pp. 1026–1030. IEEE (2014)
44. Zhang, D., Islam, M.M., Lu, G.: A review on automatic image annotation techniques. Pattern Recogn. 45(1), 346–362 (2012)
45. Zhou, B., Lapedriza, A., Xiao, J., Torralba, A., Oliva, A.: Learning deep features for scene recognition using places database. In: Advances in Neural Information Processing Systems, pp. 487–495 (2014)
46. Zitnick, C.L., Dollár, P.: Edge boxes: locating object proposals from edges. In: Fleet, D., Pajdla, T., Schiele, B., Tuytelaars, T. (eds.) ECCV 2014. LNCS, vol. 8693, pp. 391–405. Springer, Cham (2014). doi:10.1007/978-3-319-10602-1_26

Characterizing Videos, Audience and Advertising in Youtube Channels for Kids

Camila Souza Araújo[1(✉)], Gabriel Magno[1], Wagner Meira Jr.[1],
Virgilio Almeida[1,2], Pedro Hartung[3], and Danilo Doneda[4]

[1] Universidade Federal de Minas Gerais, Belo Horizonte, Brazil
{camilaaraujo,magno,meira,virgilio}@dcc.ufmg.br
[2] Berkman Klein Center, Harvard University, Cambridge, USA
[3] Harvard Law School, Cambridge, USA
[4] Universidade do Estado do Rio de Janeiro, Rio de Janeiro, Brazil
danilo@doneda.net

Abstract. Online video services, messaging systems, games and social media services are tremendously popular among young people and children in many countries. Most of the digital services offered on the internet are advertising funded, which makes advertising ubiquitous in children's everyday life. To understand the impact of advertising-based digital services on children, we study the collective behavior of users of YouTube for kids channels and present the demographics of a large number of users. We collected data from 12,848 videos from 17 channels in US and UK and 24 channels in Brazil. The channels in English have been viewed more than 37 billion times. We also collected more than 14 million comments made by users. Based on a combination of text-analysis and face recognition tools, we show the presence of racial and gender biases in our large sample of users. We also identify children actively using YouTube, although the minimum age for using the service is 13 years in most countries. We provide comparisons of user behavior among the three countries, which represent large user populations in the global North and the global South.

1 Introduction

All over the world, digital technologies are shaping children's lives for better or for worse. Policy makers, researchers and educators who work with children's rights agenda recognize the social impact of digitization for young people's lives [4,5,8,9,13]. Online video services (e.g., YouTube, Netflix, BBC, etc.), messaging systems (e.g., Whatsapp, Messenger, etc.), games (e.g., Apple, Google Play, IGN, Gamespot, etc.) and social media services (e.g., Snapchat, Facebook, etc.) are tremendously popular among young people in many countries [11]. YouTube in particular has been viewed as an alternative to traditional children's TV [6]. Millions of children are already watching videos on YouTube, most of them logged in from their parents' accounts. For example, the channel of a popular

---

C.S. Araújo and G. Magno—These authors contributed equally to this work.

© Springer International Publishing AG 2017
G.L. Ciampaglia et al. (Eds.): SocInfo 2017, Part I, LNCS 10539, pp. 341–359, 2017.
DOI: 10.1007/978-3-319-67217-5_21

youtuber, Joseph Garrett, has 7.8 million subscribers and its videos have been viewed 5.3 billion times, making it one of the most popular British YouTube channels for children [7]. Most of the digital services offered in the Web are funded by advertising, which makes advertising ubiquitous in children's everyday life. YouTube offers ad-funded video channels. As a consequence, several questions about the role of advertising in children's life arise. What forms of advertising do children face on the internet? How do children react to online advertising? The goal of this paper is to provide a detailed quantitative characterization of users, videos and advertising in a sample based on several popular YouTube channels for kids in US, UK and Brazil.

There are several types of ads. For example, advergames are video games created by a company with the intention of promoting the company itself or its products. Usually these games are distributed freely as a marketing tool. There are cases of food and drink companies that target children with advertising unhealthy products on various internet platforms. An European Commission study [11] reports that online marketing to children and young people is widespread, and in some cases various marketing techniques used are not always transparent to the child consumer. There are marketing strategies that target children on YouTube with advertising disguised as other content. They use popular youtubers to pitch products and brands as non-commercial content in videos that are viewed worldwide. Characterizing and understanding these strategies and their effectiveness is a key task for making the internet and the web a better place for children.

Recent figures published by ITU (International Telecommunication Union) in 2016 show that developing countries now account for the vast majority of internet users, with 2.5 billion users compared to one billion in developed countries. According to [14], one of every three internet users in the world is a child. internet is becoming the main medium through which children collaborate, share, learn and play. In order to understand rights, risks and opportunities for children on the internet, it is important to look at countries from both the global North and the global South [9]. Because of its worldwide penetration, YouTube channels for kids is a good scenario to understand advertising campaigns that target children. The paper provides a study of interaction of online advertising and Youtube for Kids audience in US, UK and Brazil. The survey on digital marketing by the company GroupM[1] in April 2017, estimates 44 million YouTube users in UK and 72 million in Brazil. The Statistics Portal[2] estimates 180 million YouTube users in US.

In order to collect and analyze YouTube usage data, we developed an experimental methodology based on the combination of free APIs and open source tools available on the internet. The results of the characterization presented in this paper can be useful for policy makers in different countries to assess the need of public policies to protect children online. To the best of our knowledge, this

---

[1] www.groupm.com.

[2] www.statista.com.

paper is the first one to study and characterize videos, audience and advertising in internet channels for children.

Overall, we make the following contributions:

1. We develop a simple experimental methodology to collect and analyze large amounts of YouTube usage data based on APIs and open source tools available on the internet.
2. We integrate free text-analysis and face recognition tools to identify age, race and gender of YouTube channel users as well as to characterize the behavior of those users.
3. We identify children actively using YouTube, although the minimum age for using the platform is 13 years, according to their Terms of Service. Even if some usage of under 13 is generally considered as fair due to parents' or legal responsible consent and supervision, the fact is that if children are actually using the platform they can be exposed to advertising, what raise concerns about compliance with publicity regulation in several countries.
4. We show the presence of racial and gender bias in the large sample of YouTube users in our data sets. The percentage of black users is very small when compared to white and Asian users.
5. We analyze the behavior of YouTube users in three countries, US and UK in the global North and Brazil in the global South. We show differences and similarities in the demographics of YouTube channel audience as well as in the categories of products and brands associated with the videos of the channels.

The rest of the paper is organized as follows. We begin with a description of research questions associated with online advertising for children in Sect. 2. In Sect. 4, we discuss the computational approach used to gather and analyze data from different internet channels for kids. A detailed description of the datasets collected from YouTube channels is given in Sect. 5.1. Next, in Sects. 5.2 and 5.3, we characterize videos and advertising of popular YouTube channels. Finally we describe and characterize the behaviors of users of YouTube channels in Sect. 5.4. Section 6 summarizes our findings and discusses future work.

2   Research Questions

In this section we discuss the research questions that we address in our work. The expansion of the use of social and digital media led to the expansion of the presence of marketing to children through digital platforms. As mentioned, advergames, product placement in YouTube videos and online games, marketing in social networks and other strategies are commonly used by companies to attract the attention of children and persuade them to consume certain products or services. However, unlike traditional media, marketing in the digital environment takes new forms and many of them are more difficult to be clearly identified.

By providing a detailed characterization of YouTube channels for kids, this paper aims at shedding some light on streaming video-on-demand programming that target children all over the world. It also seeks to understand how the children's audience interacts with channels and videos through the children's engagement in the conversations in the video comments in YouTube [4]. As a consequence of our research goal, we ask the following questions:

- What are the characteristics of the content of the most recurrent videos on children's channels?
- What does characterize the audience to the videos for children (e.g., is there a predominance of gender in the audience and also in the young youtubers)?
- Which classes of products are marketed to a specific target (i.e., gender, age, ethnicity)?
- Is it possible to measure the percentage of children's audience in the YouTube channels examined?
- What are the gender, specific age and ethnicity among the children identified?
- What is the content of the most recurrent videos on children's channels?
- Is it possible to identify publicity directly aimed at children on the channels?

In order to investigate the stated research questions, this study relies on data collected from popular YouTube channels in US, UK and Brazil. We developed a computational methodology based on open source code to analyze the data.

3   Related Work

We now briefly summarize existing studies related to YouTube analysis, as well as studies of user behavior in Social Media.

Online social networks are popular platforms for people to connect and interact with each other [15]. According to Benevenuto et al. [3], understanding users behavior on social networking sites creates several opportunities. For example, accurate models of user behavior are important in social studies and viral marketing, since viral marketers may exploit models of user interaction to spread their content quickly and widely. Nowadays, many children use the Internet and mobile technologies as part of their everyday lives. The overlap of the online and offline world comes with a range of digitally-mediated opportunities and risks. Reference [13] provides a qualitative analysis of different social media sites to assess if they provide healthy environments for children and teenagers. In [17], the authors investigate the effectiveness of Internet filtering tools designed to shield teenagers from aversive online experiences. Based on 1,030 in-home interviews conducted with early teenagers aged from 12 to 15 years, the paper shows that Internet filters were not effective at shielding early teenagers from aversive online experiences, that include scary online videos. Magno et al. [12] studied the Google+ environment and compared its network structure with Facebook and Twitter, and noticed that it has a higher average path length and higher reciprocity. They also compare the user profile characteristics between different countries, and found that some countries are more private than others.

As pointed out by Benevenuto et al. [2], online video sharing systems have been increasing and gaining popularity. These environments allow several kinds of interactions between users and videos, such as publication of comments. This is the most related work to ours in terms of characterization methodologies, however the authors presented an in-depth workload characterization of sessions and requests on an video server different than YouTube. In terms of sociological studies of the impact of YouTube on kids, according to the authors of [18], the evidence on how use of the Internet impacts on child rights and well-being is still scattered and patchy in most countries. Livingstone and Local [10] discussed the problem of audience measurement techniques regarding children's television viewing, because of the diversification in devices on which television content can be viewed. It is already well known that television content can be viewed on Internet-enabled devices and Internet content can be accessed via Internet-enabled television sets, but such viewing cannot be measured satisfactorily at present.

There are few articles in the literature that address quantitative analysis of online advertising for children in Internet video channels. For example, Dehghani et al. [5] uses data collected from Italian students to analyze the perception of YouTube by young people. Data were obtained from 315 questionnaires. The results show positive aspects of YouTube in terms of entertainment, informativeness and customization. The negative aspect is related to YouTube advertising. Unlike this reference, our paper relies on a large scale datasets collected from YouTube channels.

4 Experimental Methodology

In this section we describe the computational approach adopted to answer the aforementioned research questions.

4.1 Rationale

The research questions outlined in Sect. 2 are hard to verify and quantify, mainly considering that most of our input data that are publicly available and are composed of free text and images. One immediate consequence is that it is unfeasible, in practice, to get fully accurate and complete datasets about the video body we want to analyze. Then, we adopt an approach based on identifying evidences. Each evidence makes explicit a piece of information about the entity being analyzed. Considering YouTube users, examples of evidences are his or her gender, age and race, as extracted from a profile picture. In this work, we chose a set of evidences that demonstrate the occurrence of advertising in child-oriented videos, as described in Sect. 4.2.

These evidences should be conservative, although it is possible to improve the gathering techniques and be able to identify evidences. For instance, when we label a video as an advertising piece, we should be as sure as possible that it really is. The immediate impact of our approach is that all our figures are lower bounds of the actual evidence counts. Although we are usually not able to perform analyses that demand accurate counts, they demonstrate clearly the occurrence of targeted phenomenon or behavior. It is important to emphasize that our strategy also leverages on the fact that there are already a huge number of techniques and tools that may be promptly used for identifying evidence, as we discuss next.

4.2   Methodology

In this section we present our methodology for assessing the occurrence of not only advertising in YouTube videos, but may also serve to analyze the occurrence of various phenomena associated with Internet applications. As we discussed in Sect. 2, we look for identifying and modeling three groups of evidences: (i) content characterization; (ii) audience profiles; and (iii) detection of products and their publicity in videos.

The starting point of our methodology is the set of research questions we want to answer. We then select the data sources from which we will gather data for each question. We also map the questions into evidences to be identified, which demand the application of one or more techniques to the data, usually enhancing them. Examples of evidence employed in this paper are the positivity of video meta-data and user profile inferred based on face snapshots, which add attributes to both video and users, respectively. The evidences may be characterization findings, descriptive models or predictive models. Characterization may use summary statistics, among other techniques, to detect invariants, trends and other properties. Descriptive models comprise patterns and models inherent to the data, such as clusters and correlations. Predictive models estimate samples' class or numerical dependent variables. It is worth mentioning that there is a large spectrum of techniques for identifying and modeling evidences, most of them freely available in the Internet. The enriched data, characterization findings and derived models are then used for analysis and answering of the original research questions. The last step is to, considering the correctness and completeness of the answers, improve the whole process towards increasing its quality. Figure 1 depicts the methodology proposed.

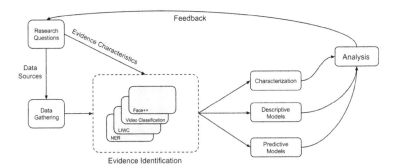

Fig. 1. Methodology

In the next sections we discuss the techniques used for evidence identification and modeling in more detail, as well as how they help our analysis.

4.3   Data Gathering

YouTube is a large-scale video sharing online platform where users can produce and/or consume content. On YouTube users need first to create a channel to upload videos. Users do not need to be logged in to watch videos, but they need to be logged in to comment and 'like' videos. We collect information of YouTube videos and comments using Google's YouTube Data API[3], accessing it directly with Python 3 scripts. The data collection process was performed in 5 phases:

1. **Select list of channels:** we manually select a list of 41 popular YouTube channels targeted to children. This selection was performed by children's rights experts and based on their popularity and also empirical evidence they may employ advertising strategies.
2. **Retrieve list of videos:** for each channel, we collect its list of videos. Due to API limits, we only get the last 500 videos published in the channel.
3. **Retrieve video statistics:** for each video, we collect its information and statistics.
4. **Retrieve comments:** for each video, we gather the comments published by users about it.
5. **Retrieve replies:** YouTube users may reply to a video comment, thus for each comment we collect its list of replies as well. In our analysis we handle replies as normal comments.

As we discuss later, the collected information allows extensive analysis about the video characteristics, the marketing strategies it may employ, and the observed impact of such strategies.

4.4   Evidence Identification and Modeling

In this section we present the various strategies and techniques used in this study for sake of evidence identification and modeling.

Entity Recognition. In order to characterize the videos we need to extract entities (names, brands, products etc.) that are mentioned in it. We use a technique called Named Entity Recognition (NER), a method that labels sequences of words into categories of things, such as company names, person and cities. We use the Stanford NER[4] tool with the English pre-trained model. Unfortunately, it does not have a pre-trained model for Portuguese, so we use this technique only for the videos of U.S channels. For both Portuguese and English, we also detected entities, in particular products and brands, by assessing the video meta-data, as discussed in Sect. 4.4.

---

[3] http://developers.google.com/youtube/v3/.
[4] http://nlp.stanford.edu/software/CRF-NER.shtml.

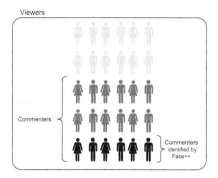

Fig. 2. 'Viewers' are all users who watched the video and 'commenters' are users who left comments. We still have a subset of commenters for whom Face++ has identified a face.

Table 1. Categories of products used to classify videos

Product categories		
Footwear	Water	School Suplies
Clothes	Snacks	Electronics
Fast Food	Fresh Food	Pet Products
Chocolate	Food (other)	Books
Candies	Cosmetics	Travel and Recreation
Sodas	Make Up	Services
Juices	Toys	Movies and Shows
Yogurts	Games	

Sentiment Analysis. We assess the public perception on the videos published by analyzing the content of the comments written about them. To attain this task, we use the Language Inquiry and Word Count (LIWC) [16], a lexicon used to verify the occurrence of words from several grammatical (e.g., pronouns, verbs, and articles, among others) and semantic (e.g., positive emotion, social, motion) categories. We use the LIWC 2007 dictionary, whose complete list of categories and word examples is available at LIWC's website[5]. For sake of our analysis in this work, we calculate the proportion of comments that contained at least one word of a particular category and label the comment to all categories that match.

Product Category Identification. A key component for our analysis is the identification of products and respective products categories that may be marketed and advertised in the videos being analyzed. However, watching and labeling thousands or millions of videos is unfeasible. We adopt the strategy described next for identifying product categories present in each video. We start by extracting the tags of the "video tags" field for each video, which is a list of labels manually inserted by the owner of the channel. For the videos of U.S channels, we also consider the entities mentioned in the "description" field, which are extracted using the NER tool (as described in Sect. 4.4).

The next step is, given the list of tags (manual tags and NER tags) for each video, we calculate the frequency of the tags among all videos, and compile a sorted list of the most popular tags for each country. Then, we retrieve the top 1,000 tags in each list and manually check the assignment of each tag to one of the 23 categories of products presented in Table 1. If the tag does not match any of the categories, we ignore it.

Video Classification. Once we assigned tags to product categories, we may classify the videos by simply verifying whether it contains one of the tags of a particular category. It is important to notice that a tag might have been classified into more than one category (e.g. "Disney toys" is both from "Toys" and "Movies and Shows" category). In the same sense, a video might be assigned to two or more categories. Notice that the process we employed provides good precision, but not necessarily a good recall, since it relies on the channel owner, who provides the tag definition and description information. It is beyond the scope of this work to assess how complete, accurate, and consistent across videos and channels these data are.

User Visual Profiling. The user visual profiling aims to determine user information such as gender, age and race of the users who comment the videos. As previously stated, after selecting a channel list, we collect information from the last 500 videos of each channel, which includes the URL of the YouTube profile image of all users who left comments. We then download the profile pictures associated with all users and use Face++[6] to extract information such as age, race and gender about each face in the photo. Face++ is an online API for facial recognition and its accuracy is known to be over 90% for face detection [1]. It is important to note that not all users use real photos as a profile image, so Face++ is not always able to identify a face. In the next section, we will present the number of identified faces that composes our dataset. It is important to mention that, although we employed just visual profiling, any technique that provides such information may be used. The key issue here is the coverage of the profiling information acquired considering the user population and their accuracy.

5   Data Analysis and Results

5.1   Datasets

Now we present a brief characterization of the datasets collected for this work. We chose to collect data from 24 Brazilian YouTube channels, and 17 YouTube channels for kids produced in English from United States and United Kingdom. The rationale for selecting US, UK and Brazil is the following. Most of the YouTube content is produced in English[7]. However, Brazil is the second largest market considering time spent on YouTube[8]. The three countries represent a large number of YouTube users in the global North and global South. Our Brazilian dataset comprises data about 7,664 videos and 10,940,565 comments associated with them, issued by 2,982,595 distinct users. That is, the same user

---

[6] www.faceplusplus.com/.

[7] http://medium.com/@synopsi/what-youtube-looks-like-in-a-day-infographic-d23f8 156e599.

[8] http://googlediscovery.com/2017/03/23/google-brasil-dados-importantes-sobre-o- google-no-brasil/.

may leave more than one comment. It is important to emphasize that throughout the work when we refer to 'users' we do not refer to all users who watched
the video, we refer to the subset of users who made comments, as shown in
the Fig. 2. From now on, we will call those users - users who left comments -
of 'commenters', in this way we avoid confusing them with the users who only
watch the videos. Of this total of commenters we were able to extract information of 129,286 faces. Table 2 summarizes the size of the dataset collected from
the channels of both countries. In Table 3 (Appendix) we summarize the dataset
composition.

Table 2. Dataset summary

	#channels	#videos	#views	#comments	#commenters	#faces
Brazil	24	7,664	4,614,161,928	10,940,565	2,982,595	129,286
US+UK	17	5,184	37,401,690,211	3,569,553	2,013,419	9,248

5.2   Analysis I: Videos and Channels

In this section we will present a characterization of the videos present in our
dataset. Figure 3 shows the number of comments and commenters - users who
have left comments - per channel. In general, Brazilian videos have more commenters and comments, but this may only be a consequence of the selected
channels and not a result of the behavior of the audience from the two countries.

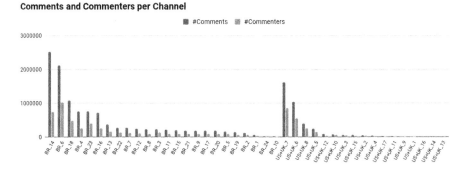

Fig. 3. Number of commenters and comments per channel.

Interestingly, the ranking of channels regarding the number of comments
and the number of commenters is different. For instance, the channel with more
comments in Brazil is BR_14, while the one with more commenters is BR_6. This

result comes from the fact that the consumers of some channels are more active than others with respect to interacting (i.e., commenting) with the video.

In Fig. 9 (Appendix) we present the number of comments and likes by video duration in seconds. From the chart we observe that the number of comments and likes does not correlate to the duration of the video, the most popular videos (i.e., videos that receive more likes and comments) are the shortest videos.

Figure 4 presents the cumulative distributions of four video metrics (number of visualizations, number of comments, duration in seconds and proportion of likes), comparing between the countries. We fitted the metrics to a Lognormal distribution and we estimate the parameters μ (mean) and σ (sd) using the maximum likelihood estimation technique. We present the corresponding function of distribution and the estimated parameters in the plots.

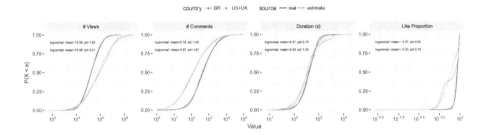

Fig. 4. Distribution of video statistics

As we observe, the shape of the curves are similar between both datasets, although presenting different values. For instance, US and UK videos have more visualizations, while Brazil videos have more comments and a higher proportion of likes.

5.3   Analysis II: Advertising

According to Westenberg [19], YouTubers are viewed as authentic by their audience, when reviewing a product or brand. Followers believe that Youtubers' recommendations are honest. In order to look more honest and transparent to their followers, Youtubers label their promoted videos with special hashtags, meaning the content, product or brand is sponsored. Thus, we take advantage of the presence of hastags to identify the commercial nature of a video. Videos may contain explicit or implicit advertising. The former involves direct sales messages to a target audience. Implicit advertising, on the other hand, works best when businesses want to associate their brand or products with a psychological or symbolic element. We argue that if a video mentions products or brands, it potentially has advertising messages. To verify whether a video has advertisement, we employ the methodology of video classification explained in Sect. 4.4.

We were able to classify 219 out of 1,055 tags for Brazil, and 249 out of 1,010 tags for channels in English. In total, 6,017 videos in Brazil were classified, and 4,109 videos in English.

Figure 5 shows the distribution of the video categories for both Brazil and English channels. The categories "Toys", "Movies and Shows" and "Games" are very popular in both countries, while "Services" is popular only in Brazil.

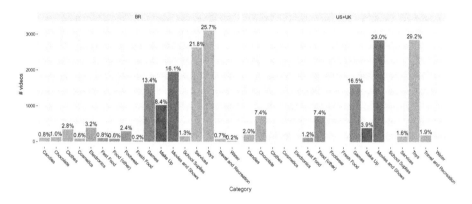

Fig. 5. Frequency of video categories by country

Figure 6 presents the distribution of categories among all the 41 channels. We observe that there are some channels specialized in a certain kind of content. For instance, channels BR_15 and US+UK_11 have a high proportion of videos about Toys. Channels BR_6 and US+UK_7 are mostly about Games.

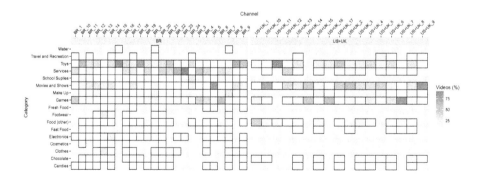

Fig. 6. Frequency of video categories by channel

5.4   Analysis III: Audience

In this section our analysis focuses on YouTube audience. Considering only videos that have some kind of advertisement (i.e. those we were able to classify into one of the categories). The average number of comments per user is 3.19, for Brazilian videos, and 1.74, for English channels.

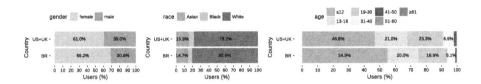

Fig. 7. Demographics of audience by country

First, we show gender, race and age distributions of commenters in Fig. 7 - considering only videos with advertisement. The difference between men and women is smaller for users in English channels, but the proportion of women is higher in both countries. In the race distribution (middle) we observe a similar distribution for both countries showing that the proportion of white people commenting on videos is higher than the proportion of Asian and black people. On the bottom chart we observe that the user age distribution for both countries present similar behavior, the only difference is that in Brazilian videos the second age group who most commented on youtuber are children and teenagers between 13 and 18 years and, for the English channels, they are young people from 19 to 30 years. We choose these age intervals to distinguish from children under 12 years old, who should not have a YouTube account, and children and teenager audience between the ages of 13 and 18 who may have an account under parental supervision.

Figure 10 (Appendix) shows the demographics with respect to gender, race and age groups for each channel. We observe that the profile of the audience might be very different. For instance, 90% of channel US+UK_1's audience is female, while this is only 52% for channel BR_3. Regarding age, some channels have a child audience of nearly 70%, such as channels US+UK_15 and BR_10.

Figure 8 shows the demographics for each category, for both countries. We observe that the Games category is the one with higher proportion of male audience, although still having more women comparatively. Also, the audience for Games is older, presenting lower frequencies of children.

Brazilian legal framework considers publicity aimed at children as abusive and, therefore, illegal. The legal definition of children includes any person under 12 years, and the Consumer Code, which specifies a set of abusive conducts, lists as one of them the act of directly approach children with publicity of products or services, considering they haven't reached a certain degree of bio-physical development which is necessary to identify and understand the marketing discourse

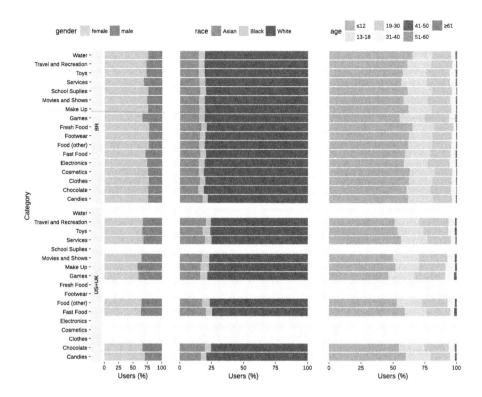

Fig. 8. Demographics of audience by category

and, therefore, is legally regarded as vulnerable. Brazilian law regarding Internet - basically the Internet Civil Rights Framework, or Marco Civil da Internet - basically follows this same rationale and recognizes the need for special information and education about children's access to Internet. There is no general data protection framework enacted in Brazil which could impact children's privacy.

The collection and use of Children's personal data is subject to the standards of COPPA (Children's Online Privacy Protection Act of 1998), which dictates that no data regarding persons under 13 years can be collected without their parents or caregivers explicit consent. COPPA also includes a series of obligations for site owners, makes it mandatory for a website to include in its privacy policy a set of rules and warranties for the its usage by children, and also clarifies how the consent from the parent or responsible has to be collected.

6   Conclusions

Google has some clear age policies for its products[9]. The minimum age requirements to own a Google account in the United States is 13 or older (i.e., except

---

[9] http://support.google.com/accounts/answer/1350409?hl=en.

for Google Accounts created in Family Link for kids under 13), 14 or older in Spain and South Korea, 16 or older in Netherlands and 13 or older in all other countries. Some services have specific rules, such as YouTube that specifies that age-restricted video should be watched only by users who are 18 or older. In Brazil, however, the use of YouTube itself is restricted to those over 18, according to the terms of service of the platform that is clear in stating that the YouTube website is not designed for young people under 18 years[10].

Among outcomes of this paper we could also mention that it can lead to a discussion about Google's politics on the age limit if it is confirmed the active presence of under 13 on YouTube. Also, data gathered and analyzed about the profile of users under 13 may be used in future research about (i) the presence of racial and gender bias, (ii) the means publicity approaches children on YouTube and (iii) the way private data from children is collected and commercialized in digital media.

Out of the data analyzed, we believe the major impact may result from the identification and characterization of children actively using YouTube. Even if some usage of under-18 is generally considered as fair due to parents' or legal responsible consent and supervision, the fact is that if children are actually using the platform they can be exposed to different challenges, as advertising, inappropriate content, privacy issues and crimes in the digital world, which raise concerns about compliance with regulations in several countries.

Other questions addressed by this work could be investigated in greater detail to highlight possible nuances not captured by the experiments done. For example, an evaluation of how exactly Face++ accuracy is impacted by the particularities of the pictures in the user profile could help to know whether there are adjustments to be made in this respect. A detailed analysis of usage patterns and spread of YouTube channels across countries may reveal how local differences affect the overall temporal dynamics found. Analysis of the influence of geographic and cultural location on the user behavior would be interesting for promoting educational and healthy food videos among children. Considering that many videos blur the boundaries between entertainment and advertising [6], another possible direction would be to dig further into the transcripts of the videos to analyze the texts and characterize the different types of advertising that are exhibited to children.

Acknowledgements. This work was partially supported by CNPq, CAPES, FAPE-MIG, and the projects InWeb, MASWEB, and INCT-Cyber.

---

[10] www.youtube.com/static?gl=BR\&template=terms\&hl=pt.

A   Appendix 1

Table 3. Dataset fields

Dataset Fields		
Video	channel id	Video id
	channel name	Id of channel where video was posted
	video id	Video channel name
	video title	Title of the video
	video description	Video description (made manually by youtuber)
	transcript	Automatic textual transcription from the audio
	subtitle	Manual subtitle (made by youtuber or by third parties)
	video tags	List of tags (made manually by youtuber)
	video date	Video posting date and time
	video duration	Video duration in seconds
	view count	Number of views
	comment count	Number of comments
	like count	Number of likes
Comment	comment id	Comment id
	author name	Name of the commenter
	author id	Id of the commenter
	author image	YouTube profile picture of the commenter
	comment date	Date and time the comment was posted
	comment text	Content of the comment
	video id	Id of the video (in which the comment was posted)
	parent id	Id of the original comment (if it is a comment reply)
User	gender, age and race	Features extracted by Face++

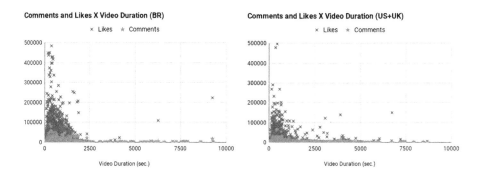

Fig. 9. Comments and Likes X Video Duration.

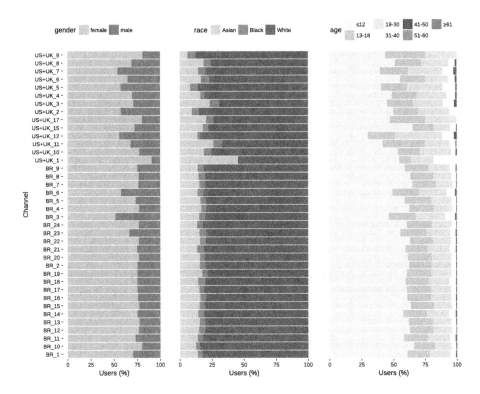

Fig. 10. Demographics of audience by channel

B   Appendix 2 - Semantics

In this analysis we want to measure how the video was evaluated by the viewers. We use the text of the comments as a proxy for the perception of the audience, looking into the semantics it contains. We focus on only two categories of LIWC: Positive Emotions and Negative Emotions. Since the LIWC is available only for the English language, we inspect only comments from the U.S. channels.

Figure 11 (Appendix) presents the percentage of the comments that contain words related to positive emotions or negative emotions, according to LIWC. We aggregate the comments by channel, video category, gender and age group. The predominance of positive emotions is notorious, indicating that the videos are, in general, well evaluated by the public. Interestingly, some channels have a higher proportion of positive words than others, such as US+UK_11 and US+UK_9. Regarding the video categories, we observe that videos with make up are more positive than the others. Looking into the social groups, there are no huge differences, although we observe an indication that the use of positive words seems to decrease as the audience get older.

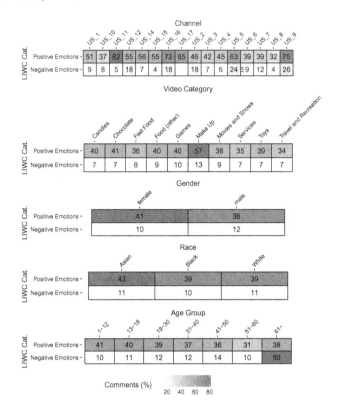

Fig. 11. Percentage of comments containing words of positive and negative emotion

References

1. Bakhshi, S., Shamma, D.A., Gilbert, E.: Faces engage us: photos with faces attract more likes and comments on instagram. In: Proceedings of the 32nd Annual ACM Conference on Human Factors in Computing Systems, pp. 965–974. ACM (2014)
2. Benevenuto, F., Pereira, A.C.M., Rodrigues, T., Almeida, V.A.F., Almeida, J.M., Gonçalves, M.A.: Characterization and analysis of user profiles in online video sharing systems. JIDM **1**(2), 261–276 (2010)
3. Benevenuto, F., Rodrigues, T., Cha, M., Almeida, V.: Characterizing user behavior in online social networks. In: Proceedings of the 9th ACM SIGCOMM Conference on Internet Measurement, IMC 2009, pp. 49–62. ACM, New York (2009)
4. Chester, J.: How Youtube, big data and big brands mean trouble for kids and parents (2015). http://www.alternet.org/media/how-youtube-big-data-and-big-brands-mean-trouble-kids-and-parents. Accessed 13 June 2017
5. Dehghani, M., Niaki, M.K., Ramezani, I., Sali, R.: Evaluating the influence of Youtube advertising for attraction of young customers. Comput. Hum. Behav. **59**, 165–172 (2016)

6. Dredge, S.: Why Youtube is the new children's tv... and why it matters (2015). https://www.theguardian.com/technology/2015/nov/19/youtube-is-the-new-childrens-tv-heres-why-that-matters. Accessed 15 Mar 2017

7. Dredge, S.: Joseph garrett, the children's presenter with 7.8 million subscribers (2016). https://www.theguardian.com/technology/2016/aug/28/stampy-joseph-garrett-youtube-childrens-presenter-millions-of-viewers. Accessed 13 June 2017

8. Livingstone, S.: Children's digital rights: a priority. Intermedia **42**(4/5), 20–24 (2014)

9. Livingstone, S.: Digital media and children's rights (2014). http://blogs.lse.ac.uk/mediapolicyproject/2014/09/12/sonia-livingstone-digital-media-and-childrens-rights/. Accessed 15 Mar 2017

10. Livingstone, S., Local, C.: Measurement matters: difficulties in defining and measuring children's television viewing in a changing media landscape. Media Int. Aust. **163**(1), 67–76 (2017)

11. Lupianez-Villanueva, F., Gaskell, G., Veltri, G., Theben, A., Folkford, F., Bonatti, L., Bogliacino, F., Fernandez, L., Marek, E., Codagnone, C.: Study on the impact of marketing through social media, online games and mobile applications on children's behaviour (2016). http://ec.europa.eu/consumers/consumer_evidence/behavioural_research/impact_media_marketing_study/index_en.htm. Accessed 15 Mar 2017

12. Magno, G., Comarela, G., Saez-Trumper, D., Cha, M., Almeida, V.: New kid on the block: exploring the Google+ social graph. In: Proceedings of the 2012 Internet Measurement Conference, IMC 2012, pp. 159–170. ACM, New York (2012)

13. O'Keeffe, G.S., Clarke-Pearson, K.: The impact of social media on children, adolescents, and families. Pediatrics **127**(4), 800–804 (2011)

14. Global Commission on Internet Governance. One internet (2016). https://www.ourinternet.org/sites/default/files/inline-files/GCIG_Final%20Report%20-%20USB.pdf. Accessed 15 Mar 2017

15. Ottoni, R., Pesce, J.P., Las Casas, D.B., Franciscani Jr., G., Meira Jr., W., Kumaraguru, P., Almeida, V.A.: Ladies first: analyzing gender roles and behaviors in Pinterest. In: ICWSM. The AAAI Press (2013)

16. Pennebaker, J.W., Chung, C.K., Ireland, M., Gonzales, A., Booth, R.J.: The Development and Psychometric Properties of LIWC2007. This article is published by LIWC Inc, Austin, Texas 78703 USA in conjunction with the LIWC2007 software program

17. Przybylski, A.K., Nash, V.: Internet filtering technology and aversive online experiences in adolescents. J. Pediatrics (2017)

18. Stoilova, M., Livingstone, S., Kardefelt-Winther, D.: Global kids online: researching children's rights globally in the digital age. Global Stud. Childhood **6**(4), 455–466 (2016)

19. Westenberg, W.: The influence of Youtubers on teenagers: a descriptive research about the role Youtubers play in the life of their teenage viewers. M.Sc dissertation, University of Twente, September 2016

Comparing Influencers: Activity vs. Connectivity Measures in Defining Key Actors in Twitter *Ad Hoc* Discussions on Migrants in Germany and Russia

Svetlana S. Bodrunova[1(✉)] ⓘ, Anna A. Litvinenko[1,2] ⓘ,
and Ivan S. Blekanov[1] ⓘ

[1] St. Petersburg State University, 7-9, Universitetskaya nab.,
St. Petersburg 199004, Russia
s.bodrunova@spbu.ru
[2] Freie Universitaet Berlin, 55 Garystr., 14195 Berlin, Germany

Abstract. Today, a range of research approaches is used to define the so-called influencers in discussions in social media, and one can trace both conceptual and methodological differences in how influencers are defined and tracked. We distinguish between 'marketing' and 'deliberative' conceptualization of influencers and between metrics based on absolute figures and those from social network analytics; combining them leads to better understanding of user activity and connectivity measures in defining influential users. We add to the existing research by asking whether user activity necessarily leads to better connectivity and by what metrics in online *ad hoc* discussions, and try to compare the structure of influencers. To do this, we use comparable outbursts of discussions on inter-ethnic conflicts related to immigration. We collect Twitter data on violent conflicts between host and re-settled groups in Russia and Germany and look at top20 user lists by eight parameters of activity and connectivity to assess the structure of influencers in terms of pro/contra-migrant cleavages and institutional belonging. Our results show that, in both discussions, the number of users involved matters most for becoming an influencer by betweenness and pagerank centralities. Also, contrary to expectations, Russian top users all in all are, in general, more neutral, while Germans are more divided, but in both countries pro-migrant media oppose anti-migrant informal leaders.

Keywords: Twitter · Influencers · Inter-ethnic conflict · Germany · Russia · Web crawling

1 Introduction

Uneven representation of group interest in mediatized public discussions has been established in the research literature [1] as one of the fundamental problems of public communication and public decision-making. Among the reasons for that, there is representation of newsmakers privileging institutional actors vs. ordinary citizens as *vox populi* [2]. Since Internet had emerged as a public communicative space less

© Springer International Publishing AG 2017
G.L. Ciampaglia et al. (Eds.): SocInfo 2017, Part I, LNCS 10539, pp. 360–376, 2017.
DOI: 10.1007/978-3-319-67217-5_22

dependent on media, scholars expressed hopes that networked communication would provide for equalizing citizens with institutional actors within public discussions [3] bypassing media who used to serve as gatekeepers of public agendas [4]. But, till today, horizontalization of discursive relations online remains highly disputable [5]; moreover, new societal cleavages emerge in hybrid media systems [6] due to digital divide, interest- and value-based variance in media diets, and growing platform-oriented fragmentation of public arenas.

In online communicative milieus, the figures of *newsmaker, informer,* and *opinion leader* are re-conceptualized as that of *influencer* [7], partly based on an older idea of 'influential' [8]. Influencers combine beyond-the-average capacities of information dissemination with those of casting impact upon users' opinions and formation of discussion circles often described as echo chambers [9], and thus are key structural elements of networked discussions [10, 11].

Despite influencers' expected crucial role in reshaping power relations between institutional and non-institutional participants of online discussions, they are, till today, under-studied in such aspects as dependence of influencer position upon user activity, institutional status, or taking sides in conflict. Social network analysis (SNA) tries to predict influencers technically, based on their activity and metadata, as well as on the discussion graph structure; other important works explore the interplay between the nature of the publics and constellations of influencers [12–16]. Within this research cluster, Twitter as a microblogging platform has gained particular attention, but it is yet unclear whether this platform tends to democratize influencers in the so-called *ad hoc* public discussions that rapidly rise and disseminate on events of high social relevance or on issues with high potential of social polarization.

To a large extent, this is due to the fact that very different approaches to defining and detecting influencers co-exist in computer science and communication disciplines. Earlier, we traced at least two concepts of influencer (based on user activity and user connectivity, respectively), as well as a methodological divide in detecting influencers via absolute-figure metrics and SNA metrics [17]; we also stated that few attempts had been made to juxtapose these ways of detecting influencers. Also, comparative studies beyond the Western and Arab Spring countries remain rare [18].

Thus, the aim of this paper is twofold. First, we assess whether user activity necessarily leads to better connectivity, and by what metrics. Then, we try to compare the structure of influencers across countries in terms of their institutional belonging and pro-/anti-migrant stance. We do this by collecting and analyzing data on the Twitter discussion around anti-migrant bashings in Biryuliovo (Moscow) in 2013 and the one around the mass harassment in Cologne in 2016. To accomplish this, we have collected the discussion content, selected the metrics, applied them and formed user lists by activity and connectivity metrics (betweenness and pagerank centralities). We manually assessed the listed accounts to position them institutionally and politically.

Section 2 presents our conceptualization of 'marketing' vs. 'deliberative' influencers, while Sect. 3 reviews today's approaches to defining influencers, including those based on user activity and connectivity metrics. Section 4 describes the cases, research hypotheses, and our methodology. Section 5 discusses our results.

2 Actor Disparities in *Ad Hoc* Twitter Discussions

By 1990s, the public sphere theory had already stated that public discussions were arenas of high disparities in terms of who formed the opinions and influenced the discussion agendas. As mentioned above, institutional and elite representatives were naturally preferred by media; moreover, media themselves became the key nodes in information networks and performed agenda setting [19, 20]. Another reason for criticism of media-based public spheres was their oppressive majority-oriented discourse [21–24]; a lot of efforts have been put by countries in Europe and beyond to establish public media that would encompass at least some minority views.

With the rise of online platforms, hopes for better access of citizens to public discussion first rose [5] and then faded, as both social [25] and communicative [26] offline divides were accompanied by new disparities emerging due to divergent media consumption [27, 28] and digital divide [29, 30], among other reasons. Not even asking whether Twitter discussions have any impact upon real-world policymaking, scholars doubt even whether 'Habermas is on Twitter' [16] [31: 31]. Out of this, a range of research agendas have emerged on who become discussion leaders (influencers) and whether the disparities in influence persist. Also, we need to know how we define and detect the influencers, as their detection appears to be measure-dependent.

Defining an Influencer. SNA is widely used to show deviant users in Twitter discussions. As we stated before [17], there are at least three major divisions in SNA-based influencer studies that define influencers in differing ways.

Here, we will only shortly reconstruct our logic and show applicability of this logic to comparative studies. Thus, the three divisions may be conceptualized as follows. The first one is between 'marketing' and 'deliberative' influencers. The former generates a self-oriented 'long tail' of attention and support [32: 1261] [33]; here, key characteristics of an influencer are $N_{followers}$, the quantity and regularity of posting, and the vastness of 'support waves' of liking and retweeting. The latter, 'deliberative' influencer, helps in formation of a politically relevant and effective discussion by linking user groups with varying or even opposing views, as well as of intertwining topic-based echo chambers; also, such a user is linked to the maximum number of other users within the discussion by interacting with them. As inclusiveness and horizontality [34], along with rationality and orientation to consensus, are key features of an effective 'field of discursive connections' [35: 37], deliberative influencers are key for formation of 'opinion crossroads' [28, 30] as a metaphor of an all-involving public discussion. Structurally, inter-linkage between clusters in a discussion and N_{users} involved in commenting and retweeting becomes the feature that defines an influencer. We consider these approaches mutually amplifying, as they both, in a way, are extensions of theory of two-step communication flow via opinion leaders [36].

To add, two more divisions may be traced: first, the one between user activity metrics (N_{posts}, N_{likes}, $N_{retweets}$, $N_{comments}$ left, N_{users} followed, N_{users} involved by a given user into any type of interaction) and user connectivity metrics (N_{likes}, $N_{retweets}$, $N_{comments}$ received, $N_{followers}$, N_{users} interacting with a given user, and centrality metrics that describe a user's position in the web graph). And second, the same metrics are divided into absolute-figure ones measured for every user independently and graph-based metrics that, for every user, depend on the overall graph configuration [17].

Conceptual Limitations in Twitter Studies of Influencers. But before discussing particular ways of detecting influencers on Twitter, we need to mention that there are limitations for that; they are linked to the nature of the discussion, its level of rationality, and inherent Twitter mechanisms that technically privilege certain actors [17].

In short, the first limitation is linked to the fact that 'issue publics' [12: 422] [30: 108], or *ad hoc* publics [14], become affective [15] and quickly rise and dissolve [13: 74]. This, in its turn, raises two issues: (1) that of representability of *ad hoc* discussion for stable discursive patterns outside the time of the event; (2) comparability of ad hoc discussions in terms of their structure and the conclusions they allow for. In response to this, we may state that our experiments (work in progress) show that the structure of *ad hoc* discussions changes the same way in six different discussions if isolated users are eliminated; that is, the patterns of *ad hoc* discussions are, at least partly, comparable. In future, we will also test their comparability with stable discussions.

The issue of rationality has been debated among scholars since the appearance of Twitter itself. Twitter pessimists claim that the platform is home for depoliticized trivial content full of 'white noise' [37] and subjected to slacktivist practices [38]. Other studies, though, show that migroblogging changes news agendas [39], generates 'sub-political' discussion topics [40], and may result into 'self-generated public opinion', as in long-text blogs [41]; we share the latter opinion. Also, scholars have called Twitter the quickest platform for expression of public sentiment [42]; this is why we cannot dismiss the Twitter influencers' potential of shaping the discussions.

The third limitation poses the question of structural limitations for all-involving discussion. Twitter networks resemble information-sharing ones and not offline social networks [43: 264] and, thus, privilege 'gatewatchers' [44] or 'gateways' [43] who multiply and disseminate information from both outside the network and from influencers, as Twitter networks demonstrate 'highly skewed distribution of followers and a low rate of reciprocated ties' [43: 263]. But in our paper we try to see whether active users with a particular position towards migrants get to the influencer lists; later, we may check whether the structure of the network played a role in their promotion.

3   Absolute Figures vs. Centrality Metrics in Detecting Influencers

In our earlier case study, we have showed that existing research actually rarely links absolute-figure metrics to SNA-based graph-dependent metrics (centralities) [45]. Extremely wide SNA literature is dedicated to predicting the key nodes in discussion networks; a smaller bunch of works applies the network-based metrics to Twitter discussions (as examples, see [32, 46]), using not only single metrics but also their combinations [47, 48] and case-specific derivatives [49].

Several of these works have focused on the institutional nature of the key network nodes; mainly, researchers are looking at whether media continue to be information flow hubs – and express significant doubts. Thus, authors [43] have shown that it was content that mattered for generating 'highly replicated messages… without relying on the activity of user hubs' [43: 260], and that the role of media outlets in forming retweet waves was much exaggerated [46: 269]. Other authors [32] have shown that media remained influencers only by indegree and eigenvalue metrics; another research group [50] has demonstrated that new groups of influential users join experts and media. Thus, we expect that media would still be among network-detected influencers but they will not be the leading ones.

But at the same time, research that uses absolute-figure metrics provides a more nuanced picture on who is labeled as influencer, which metrics to use for detecting them, and whether institutional (political, media, economic etc.) users remain among them. Earlier, we have shown that the majority of researchers have named $N_{retweets}$ the most efficient metric to detect an influencer [17]. But other authors warn that $N_{retweets}$ cannot actually help differentiate between 'having a following' due, e.g., a big number of tweets by a given user or a celebrity – and 'being seen as an expert' whose tweets are genuinely shared more than those of other users [32: 1263]; N_{tweets} has been shown to be a mediating factor for other metrics [51]. This understanding corresponds to our 'marketing' vs. 'deliberative influencers' division.

Also, most of these works insist that institutionalized users remain highly influential in how discussions develop. Of course this partly due to another view on influencer as on 'prestigious actor whose position is approved by the audience and who initiates more support than criticism' [52], which does not take into account the user's position in the network. In this line of research, several case studies have proved that Twitter strengthens the pre-existing hierarchies with media and political leaders [53–55], as well as experts and long-established institutions [56, 57], still playing the key role in information dissemination. Using a composite measure named 'mentions' (that comprises several absolute-figure metrics), author [58] shows that journalists and mainstream media were dominating the top100 accounts in the Twitter coverage of the UK 2011 riots. Similar results were received for New Zealand [59] where, of top16 Twitter accounts by retweet & comment, 11 were institutional and included media. This may happen because journalists often retweet other journalists [60], but this can hardly influence the top lists selected out of several hundred thousand user.

So far, only rare works tried to combine or juxtapose the absolute and network-based metrics [17, 52, 61, 62]. To see the correlations between the two types of metrics, we will use the scheme we had elaborated earlier [17]. We will use both activity/connectivity and absolute/network-based divisions to describe the metrics we will juxtapose. Thus, the metrics we will use for top list formation are the following:

- activity, absolute: N_{tweets};
- activity, network-based: outdegree centrality;
- connectivity, absolute: $N_{retweets}$, $N_{comments}$, N_{recom} – retweets and comments combined (as it was conceptualized in [59]);
- connectivity, network-based: indegree, betweenness, and pagerank centralities.

4 The Cases, Research Hypotheses, and Methodology of the Study

To formulate our research questions more precisely, we also need to take into consideration the context of the cases under scrutiny. The relevant aspects include the expectations from the Russian and German Twittersphere formulated in the existing research; the description of the cases; the societal cleavages inside it. This is done to help form our expectations of who would be the influencers within the discussions.

4.1 The Inter-ethnic Conflicts in Germany and Russia and Their Social and Communicative Context

To explore the issues described above, we have focused on comparable conflictual *ad hoc* discussions. The topic of migrant crime and the following anti-migrant uprising provides cases that possess the following features: they have a rapid violent trigger, cause social polarization and street action, involve authorities, and get to national Twitter trending topics.

The German case. According to statista.com, the number of regular Twitter users in Germany in 2015 was only 1.73 million (2% of the population), with about twice that number using it occasionally [63], and it seems not to grow since 2010 [64].

The German media system belongs to the democratic corporatist model [65] with a strong tradition of freedom of expression combined with the tradition of corporatism, including the leading role of public TV. Also, the press market, despite the adherence to the notion of objectivity, is characterized by a degree of political polarization and media-political parallelism, as well as by powerful tabloids. The German Twitter, though being an undeniable news alert arena and one of the political facilitation tools in mass actions, has generated virtually no research on its structure and discussion features. Thus, our expectations are based on the overall structure of the media market, traditions of balanced reporting and public deliberation, and specific features of the German media market and civil society stated above. Thus, we expect German state actors and NGOs to be present in the discussion and perhaps even to become the discussion centers; supra-national mainstream media (like foreign newspapers or Euronews TV channel) will also be present.

The event under our scrutiny is the Köln mass harassment. During the New Year's Eve 2015/2016 in Köln (Cologne), numerous sexual assaults were committed on women by groups of young men, allegedly mainly from the North African and Arab countries. The attacks triggered a new wave of far-right protests of the ultraconservative party 'Alternative für Deutschland' (AfD) and anti-migrants movement 'Pegida'. Public support for refugee-welcoming politics of Angela Merkel has significantly dropped within several weeks [66]. The national media reported about the attacks with delay of several days, which led to new accusations of the mainstream media in pro-migrant bias and to escalation of the debate about the 'lying press ('Lügenpresse') by AfD and Pegida. The Parliamentary Assembly of the Council of Europe reacted with a debate under urgent procedure on January 25, 2016, stating in Resolution 13961 that 'media hold an important responsibility to report on objective facts without stigmatization. Partial, late or dishonest media reporting on crimes can feed in conspiracy theories and fuel hatred against a part of the population. It can also contribute to mistrust in the authorities and the media'.

The Russian Case. After 1991, the Russian media system has seen fundamental transformation but, in political respect, it remained mostly post-Soviet [67]. Today, the country's media sphere is highly fractured along the lines of value-based cleavages between small cosmopolitan hyper-urban and huge mid-urban post-Soviet population clusters [68, 69]. Online, this division shows up in formation of platform-wide political echo chambers [69], with the Russian Facebook serving as the best example.

Research on Russian Twitter is as well extremely scarce; it is hard even to estimate the overall use of Twitter in Russia. As for August 2015, figures varied from 8 to 11 mln subscribers, of which around 50% seemed to be active users (used Twitter once a month or more, as estimated by TASS). The existing research on Russian Twitter provides mixed evidence on whether Twitter in Russia can play a role of an 'opinion crossroads'. Several works have proved that political representation of pro- and anti-'systemic' actors on the Russian Twitter is virtually equal [70, 71], but at the same time others stated that topic-based clusters with clear political bias were evident in earlier years [72]. Importantly, the latter work also stated the absence of any distinct nationalist clusters in the Russian blogs and on Twitter in particular. Except for our earlier works [17, 45], there was no substantial attempt to study the nature and structural roles of influencers on the Russian Twitter. The newest work [73] also proved extremely high 'botization' of political topics on the Russian Twitter; this is why we take as case the discussion of almost 4 years ago when it was not yet the case.

The events we analyze – anti-migrant bashings in Biryuliovo district of Moscow – happened in October 2013 and were in Twitter Trending Topics for over two days. The timeline included akilling of a Muscovite Egor Scherbakov by an Uzbek named Orkhan Zeinalov, the bashings at Biryuza trade center, its warehouse and the surroundings in Biryuliovo where the alleged killer should have resided along with many of his fellows, and the subsequent police street actions, several 'gatherings' of the locals, and arrest and trial of the suspect; the events were also accompanied by statements of federal and Moscow authorities. Thus, the actors that we may trace were: authorities (federal, Moscow, local); police; eyewitnesses; migrants. As the case was reported in federal and local media, we also expect high level of media involvement.

Expectations in Terms of Influencer Structure and Positioning. In both countries, we expect institutional actors to dominate top user lists, despite high levels of eyewitness posting. We expect national and local authorities, media, and police to be the main influencers; to a smaller extent, we expect NGOs and other pro-migrant speakers to form the lists. According to earlier research, we expect neither nationalists nor migrants to be highly influential in the Russian case, while we may expect anti-migrant citizens to show up in both cases; but taking into consideration the traditions of public discussion in Germany, we expect users and media to be mostly neutral.

4.2   Research Questions

Based on everything aforementioned, we have formulated four research questions.

RQ1. Do the users that post most become discussion centers in both absolute and network-based metrics? That is, does N_{tweets} significantly correlates to $N_{retweets}$, $N_{comments}$, N_{recom}, outdegree, betweenness, and pagerank centralities in both cases?

RQ2. Do institutionalized users dominate over ordinary users by both activity and connectivity metrics? Do the patterns of institutionalization differ a lot? We expect that, for Russia, pro- and anti-migrant users (like NGOs and nationalists) will be absent from both the lists of active (N_{tweets}, indegree) and 'central' (betweenness and pagerank) top user lists; but in Germany we expect more political actors, social organizations, and NGOs to form the lists.

RQ3. Do media occupy significant place in top user lists? Within the lists, are media of all views are represented?

RQ4. Are institutional and most non-institutional top users neutral in terms of taking sides in the conflict?

4.3   Methodology and Research Process

To collect the discussion bulk, we conducted vocabulary-based web crawling; then, we reconstructed the discussion web graphs. For this, we developed a specialized web crawler [74]. We used our own software to overcome limitations common for openly available API-based analogs; our algorithm is human-like, which allowed for unfolding of the discussion in the past and trespassing the time and quantity upload limits. To form the vocabularies, we first collected relevant keywords and hashtags at trendinalia.com and double-checked the lists on two other Twitter trending topics trackers.

Then, we added more hashtags based on manual snowballing of tweets in over 1,000 tweets for both cases. The vocabularies for Russia included 6 main hashtags/keywords, and for Germany – 15 hashtags/keywords.

For Russia, the research period chosen was October 1 to 31, 2013, to capture the outburst of the discussion and its long tail. 3,574 users with 10,715 posts were identified as a result of crawling and formed the core dataset. One step further in crawling was made to identify those who commented or retweeted the collected tweets, to calculate properly the number of comments and retweets; this returned 12,040 users. For Germany, a similar strategy of uploading (January 1 to 31, 2016) discovered a significantly bigger discussion of 12,382 users involved with 64,874 posts posted; one step further returned 40,117 users.

For comparison, we used the user lists from the core datasets, but the data on commenting and retweeting for individual users are taken from the bigger datasets.

Then, we have conducted the following procedures:

1. To calculate the SNA metrics, we reconstructed the discussion graphs. The graphs themselves were non-directed (as we were not interested in directions of interactions, only in numbers), but our data allowed for calculating in-/outdegrees independently.

2. From the graphs, we received the values for the chosen variables: N_{tweets}, $N_{retweets}$, $N_{comments}$, N_{recom}, indegree, outdegree, betweenness, and pagerank for the core datasets.
3. After that, we formed additional dataset of users with $N_{tweets} \geq 10$ to include only those who actively participated in the discussion. This was done in order to exclude the discussion 'long tails' with large number of users who, though, posted only a few tweets each and, thus, would distort the results true for active users. For Germany, the list included 1,211 users; for Russia, only 178 users.
4. Then, we conducted descriptive statistics (Spearman rho) to see to what extent the chosen metrics correlate in the core datasets and the datasets with $N_{tweets} \geq 10$ (see Tables 1 and 2 for Russia and Tables 3 and 4 for Germany). We considered the use of Spearman's rho appropriate despite we realized that absolute figures, including N_{tweets}, and in-/outdegree values may play a role in formation of other centrality metrics, and we expect them to correlate, but it is the strength of correlation that we will be looking at. Also, as stated above, betweenness and pagerank are network-dependent, while in-/outdegree are calculated as absolute numbers of user interactions.
5. We manually checked the user top lists, to assess the patterns user transposition from the lists by activity metrics to the lists by connectivity metrics, and those by absolute figures – to those by network metrics; we also marked their institutional belonging and pro-/anti-migrant position (see Figs. 1 and 2). To do so, we checked a user's self-description, the collected tweets, and the user's tweets closer to nowadays.

The results assessed in comparative perspective are presented below.

Table 1. Spearman's correlation between activity and connectivity measures in Russia for the core dataset ($N_{users} = 3,574$)

	Tweets	Retweets	Comments	Recom	Indegree	Outdegree	BC	PRC
Tweets	1,000							
Retweets	,472**	1,000						
Comments	,408**	,482**	1,000					
Recom	,489**	,893**	,753**	1,000				
Indegree	,486**	,226**	,219**	,238**	1,000			
Outdegree	,345**	,168**	,154**	,179**	,430**	1,000		
Betweenness	,410**	,215**	,200**	,227**	,493**	,532**	1,000	
Pagerank	,403**	,186**	,185**	,194**	,808**	,453**	,513**	1,000

Note for Figs. 1 and 2.

Regular – 'ordinary user'
Bold – institutional user/representative
Bold italic – media account/journalist
Italic – 'Twitter media'
Green – strong/institutional support of migrants (absent from picture)

Table 2. Spearman's correlation between activity and connectivity measures in Russia for the dataset of active users, $N_{tweets} \geq 10$ ($N_{users} = 178$)

	Tweets	Retweets	Comments	Recom	Indegree	Outdegree	BC	PRC
Tweets	1,000							
Retweets	,461**	1,000						
Comments	,417**	,753**	1,000					
Recom	,453**	,954**	,893**	1,000				
Indegree	,443**	,444**	,354**	,429**	1,000			
Outdegree	,182*	,190*	,233**	,208**	,505**	1,000		
Betweenness	,335**	,320**	,344**	,340**	,646**	,754**	1,000	
Pagerank	,414**	,437**	,357**	,420**	,873**	,850**	,644**	1,000

Table 3. Spearman's correlation between activity and connectivity measures in Germany for the core dataset ($N_{users} = 12{,}382$)

	Tweets	Retweets	Comments	Recom	Indegree	Outdegree	BC	PRC
Tweets	1,000							
Retweets	,502**	1,000						
Comments	,799**	,683**	1,000					
Recom	,644**	,968**	,845**	1,000				
Indegree	,519**	,905**	,668**	,893**	1,000			
Outdegree	,418**	,260**	,330**	,304**	,298**	1,000		
Betweenness	,791**	,558**	,780**	,678**	,555**	,676**	1,000	
Pagerank	,529**	,721**	,648**	,571**	,804**	,267**	,557**	1,000

Table 4. Spearman's correlation between activity and connectivity measures in Germany for the dataset of active users, $N_{tweets} \geq 10$ ($N_{users} = 1{,}211$)

	Tweets	Retweets	Comments	Recom	Indegree	Outdegree	BC	PRC
Tweets	1,000							
Retweets	,470**	1,000						
Comments	,481**	,681**	1,000					
Recom	,503**	,941**	,864**	1,000				
Indegree	,485**	,960**	,777**	,958**	1,000			
Outdegree	,368**	,309**	,431**	,369**	,378**	1,000		
Betweenness	,446**	,608**	,654**	,662**	,687**	,748**	1,000	
Pagerank	,395**	,786**	,767**	,843**	,861**	,285**	,629**	1,000

Light green – weak support of migrants

White – neutral user

Light orange – weak anti-migrant attitude

Orange – strong anti-migrant attitude/nationalist account.

Ntweets	Nretweets	Ncomments	Nrecom	In-Degree	Out-Degree	BC	PR
mvnameisphilipp	vitbullet	lifenews_ru	vitbullet	lifenews_ru	BorisALV	lifenews_ru	lifenews_ru
lifenews_ru	lifenews_ru	sgromov	lifenews_ru	IlyaYashin	Antiputja	MedvedRu	SultanHamzaev
BorisALV	sgromov	polozovs	sgromov	mvnameisphilipp	MedvedRu	BorisALV	Izvestia_ru
White76chkniblog	mvnameisphilipp	mastka	mvnameisphilipp	RT_russian	mishailv	ivanmazurin	MaximParshin
topoprf	Evgenyi_K	belogolovcev	Evgenyi_K	polozovs	Sergey Sergey G	mishailv	mvnameisphilipp
ruspoker	dlogattai	RT_russian	polozovs	belogolovcev	irynka_korf	dternovskiy	IlyaYashin
mastka	topoprf	mvnameisphilipp	topoprf	izvestia_ru	Iarto	IlyaYashin	RT_russian
volya_naroda	polozovs	MaxPupkin	dlogattai	SvobodaRadio	Filosof	Elena Baturyna	VasilyKonov
MetroRussia	RT_russian	MedvedRu	RT_russian	MaloverjanBBC	RTVRU	polozovs	Medvedru
ruvr_ru	vb05091979	CallmJoker	belogolovcev	ru_rbc	Elena Baturyna	the outreach	belogolovcev
ipotechniy	roman_primorye	topoprf	roman_primorye	RomanPomych	ivanmazurin	izvestia_ru	rodnyansky
Mir24TV	KarpovVitaly	jack_crust	CallmJoker	BorisALV	helenascorpion	mvnameisphilipp	White_technolog
MedvedRu	ZakharovaOksana	ruvr_ru	vb05091979	GrantTweet	lifenews_ru	vvehunanov	ruspoker
NoviniRosii	CallmJoker	vsemail1975	ruvr_ru	ruvr_ru	pell3132	pell3132	polozovs
krgzr	filelo	ruspoker	filelo	ARTEM KLYUSHIN	AlexSavinovv	Antiputja	rentvchannel
Estraniero	izvestia_ru	INadtochey	ZakharovaOksana	rodnyansky	DerUnabomber	RTVRU	Ericamarat
ciperovich	ruvr_ru	BorisALV	KarpovVitaly	MetroRussia	VladMatveev	DerUnabomber	mitya_kalinkin
urannews	ElenaZev	JohnsonRussiaLi	izvestia_ru	onlinekpru	conspirologorg	dasorel	ruredaktor
istina	MetroRussia	Evgenyi_K	jack_crust	dternovskiy	arl_spb	pilodship	ELukyanov
RomanPomych	ru_rbc	DerUnabomber	ru_rbc	Pavel XII	roman_primorye	BlossomGeorge	sashakots

Fig. 1. Institutional belonging and pro/contra-migrant positioning of top users in Russia

Ntweets	Nretweets	Ncomments	Nrecom	Indegree	Outdegree	Betweenness	Pagerank
gamergateblogde	zeltonline	ThomasMichael71	ThomasMichael71	tagesschau	chris65110	gamergateblogde	tagesschau
ThomasMichael71	tagesschau	gamergateblogde	gamergateblogde	LarsWinter	gamergateblogde	chris65110	gamergateblogde
BukowskisNephew	ThomasMichael71	tagesschau	tagesschau	dwnews	ColdSweetness	ThomasMichael71	ThomasMichael71
TarekFatta	LarsWinter	BukowskisNephew	zeltonline	BukowskisNephew	Lucifer6	tagesschau	PaulWilko057
Chester_LTP	LadyAodh	LarsWinter	LarsWinter	aktuelle_stunde	kwisatz_h	balleryna	dwnews
chris65110	balleryna	faznet	BukowskisNephew	ThomasMichael71	IllyrioM	dwnews	PatrickOensing
abdejan	BukowskisNephew	SPIEGELONLINE	balleryna	SPIEGELONLINE	ThomasMichael71	Welt_im_Chaos	MickyBeisenherz
zoolbase	gamergateblogde	zeltonline	LadyAodh	faznet	Welt_im_Chaos	TarekFatta	aktuelle_stunde
weidenkatzl	dwnews	TarekFatta	dwnews	zeltonline	EthicalFuture	LarsWinter	LarsWinter
vonRomberg	heuteshow	aktuelle_stunde	aktuelle_stunde	gamergateblogde	Deutschland77	mundaufmachen	M000X
krixx5	aktuelle_stunde	vonRomberg	heuteshow	balleryna	CH2CH2CH2CH2CH2	zoolbase	TarekFatta
CitizenCane	BlondJedi	ZDFheute	SPIEGELONLINE	BlondJedi	Artrad	marthsdear	ThomasWalde
DEmergencyBrake	SPIEGELONLINE	tagesspiegel	BlondJedi	tagesspiegel	MrBadGuy5270	SPIEGELONLINE	Vildkvittran
LarsWinter	Bedburg_Puetz	Nikil100001	faznet	Bedburg_Puetz	FrankiLilli	vonRomberg	LadyAodh
Tschonka	faznet	BinBerlinerIn	Bedburg_Puetz	AltRight	mundaufmachen	Chester_LTP	faznet
EthicalFuture	AltRight	POTTROIT	MatthiasMeisner	MatthiasMeisner	von_Steiner	FrankiLilli	MatthiasMeisner
visstgoerdetcost	MatthiasMeisner	aotto1968_2	aotto1968_2	aotto1968_2	zoolbase	EthicalFuture	BukowskisNephew
dl2dby	AnjaReuchkel	OppressedFart	AltRight	AlexiaStellar	LWaff	BukowskisNephew	balleryna
CHerwartz	aotto1968_2	Bedburg_Puetz	ZDFheute	OnlineMagazin	balleryna	inka3396815	DocTinaK
brigitte_cv	AlexiaStellar	Chester_LTP	AlexiaStellar	LadyAodh	haut_drauf	zeltonline	SPIEGELONLINE

Fig. 2. Institutional belonging and pro/contra-migrant positioning of top users in Germany

5   Results

RQ1. Number of Tweets and Discussion Centers. For both countries, the more users post, the more likely they become both 'marketing' (by $N_{retweets}$ and $N_{comments}$) and 'deliberative' (by betweenness and pagerank) influencers, despite the difference in the size of datasets. The correlations remain in place for all the metrics for full and active-user datasets, despite the fact that elimination of 'the crowd' significantly drops outdegree for the Russian discussion and high values for $N_{comments}$ and betweenness centrality for Germany. All in all, strength of the correlations remains comparable for all four of our datasets (though higher for Germany for the two aforementioned metrics), which might be telling of the nature of *ad hoc* discussions on Twitter, but can also support the idea of the mediating role of N_{tweets}; this needs further exploration.

But if we look closer at correlation values, we will see that outdegree correlates more weakly with N_{tweets} than other metrics throughout our data; this might mean that tweeting a lot does not provide for necessarily becoming commented or retweeted; the value is never higher than 0,418, and thus, the correlation is weak enough. Also, only in the German case, $N_{retweets}$ matters for getting higher betweenness and pagerank, while in Russia their correlation is much weaker. But what, instead, seems to be important for becoming an influencer is a user's indegree, that is – how many users have interacted with you. This parameter becomes more important for becoming an authoritative node than the number of tweets, retweets, or comments – the metrics that many works stated as markers of influencers. For all four of our datasets, the strength of ties between indegree and pagerank is 0,804 or higher. That is, a successful strategy within an *ad hoc* discussion might be not to comment many times or get into a long meaningful discussion but to make a bigger number of users comment on you, perhaps by commenting them as well. On the other hand, outdegree does not seem to matter much for both betweenness and pagerank; this brings us to the conclusion that attractive content (which makes users interact with it) may be more important within such discussions than user activity.

RQ2. Institutionalization of the Discussion. In Figs. 1 and 2, we have marked institutional users, including media, bold (media – bold italic). In general, the picture is similar in both countries and may be described as 'liberal media against individual nationalists'. What is similar (and striking) in both countries is the absence of the much-awaited national/regional authorities, as well as NGOs and human rights watchers. We cannot prove dominance of institutional accounts over 'ordinary users', unlike in previous research [62], as we find only two politicians and one account of Public Advisory Chamber among the Russian top users, and two NGO-like organizations in the German top user lists.

Also, we cannot prove absence of nationalists as top users: in both countries, they are not only present but demonstrate blooming activity, and if in Russia they are most active in commenting, in Germany they lead both tweeting and commenting activities, all of them being non-institutionalized.

We call the picture similar, despite that, from Figs. 1 and 2, the German discussion seems highly radicalized and the Russian one shows a lot of neutral users. But this may be explained by two factors. First, Biryuliovo happened over three years ago, and assessment of the accounts of top users does not bring over a lot of anti-migrant posts; this has cast its impact upon our allocation of users as neutral or biased. But we need to state that we have discovered a dominant mood among Russian 'ordinary people' which may be described as 'angry patriotism': today, such users (over a dozen in the Russian top lists) express 'patriotic' views like supporting Donbass population or tweeting on national pride (e.g. on leading industries like aviation, military equipment etc.) but at the same demonize the current country's leaders as corrupt and ineffective. Thus, these users are highly politicized, no less than the German users; it is just not always possible to deduce their attitude from the tweets of the discussion (especially if they retweeted other accounts) and today's tweets. Second, some media accounts in the Russian list (like lifenews_ru, izvestia_ru, or RT_russian) were marked neutral, as we could not find direct proof of their anti-migrant bias, but their overall tone is pro-establishment, and thus their position fluctuates from supporting the state views on open visa regime for Central Asian post-Soviet ethnicities to populism of attaching social and cultural threats to their communities. Having said this, we can consider the situation similar indeed in both cases, as it is highly polarized, full of political criticism, and intolerant.

RQ3. The Place of Media in the Discussions. Media, indeed, occupy a significant place in the discussion and represent a variety of political views and positions. Unlike on Russian Facebook, in this discussion both pro-establishment and highly oppositional media (ru_rbc, GraniTweet), as well as foreign liberal media and journalists (MaloverjanBBC, fulelo, SvobodaRadio) are present, and the liberal-oppositional media show their efficacy, as they become retweeted and commented by many people without tweeting a lot. In Germany, it is mainstream media, and mostly newspapers, that also become influencers without posting a lot; they get retweeted and commented in general and by a lot of users in particular, and gain high pageranks. But even if so, media do not outperform nationalist users, and they do not get high betweenness centrality, which means that they do not play the role of 'information mini-hubs' as the basic nodes of the online public sphere. They remain authoritative (especially in Germany), but the niche of 'deliberative connectors' remains free and is occupied by the most polarized users. Thus, the 'opinion crossroads' may be there in terms of representation of views within the whole discussion but it is still a question whether the opposing views actually have a chance to meet.

RQ4. Neutrality of Top Users. As already stated above, neutrality of users cannot be proven, especially in case of Germany. In Russia, general negative politicization of the audience goes along with nationalist and pro-nationalist views, and in Germany the discussion after a major public harassment is shaped not by the forces countering intolerance but by openly anti-migrant discussants; in both cases, it is individuals that polarize the discourse against re-settlers and media that counter this – even if due to different reasons. Thus, for most of the German media, supporting immigrants is a non-valent issue, and expressing an alternative position would amount to a scandal. In Russia, the division between pro-establishment and oppositional media is also true for the migration issues, and thus liberal-oppositional media support their political standing by expressing pro-migrant views.

6   Conclusion

We have looked at two *ad hoc* discussions on violent inter-ethnic conflicts, namely the Biryuliovo bashings in 2013 and mass harassment in Cologne in 2016, to see whether in such discussions user activity leads to higher positions within the discussion network and higher connectivity. Along with this, we assessed the substantial features of top users, such as their institutional status and opinion positioning.

Despite the differences in samples, we have managed to show that comparing influencers is possible, and there are patterns in the structure of influencing that are similar. The main methodological finding is that, in both discussions, the number of users involved mattered more for becoming an influencer (by BC and PRC) than the number of actual tweets, retweets, or comments received by a user.

Though direct comparisons were not always possible by our methodology, we have found more similarities in the two cases than we had expected. Thus, in both countries, the situation may be described as opposition 'liberal media vs. nationalist users', and the absence of both authorities and NGOs is striking. Media do become influencers, but in terms of authority (or 'marketing' approach) rather than in deliberative terms, as they do not get high betweenness centrality and thus may have difficulties in performing the roles of shapers of information flows. In both countries, the discussion was highly opinionated and emotionally heated even within several weeks after the events, and seemingly higher neutrality of the Russian users was compensated by their overall politicization and rebuttal modus.

Thus, as to the question of whether and how 'opinion crossroads' are forming, there is evidence that, in general, left-right or in-system/oppositional views are well represented by media within the discussions. But virtual absence of pro-migrant institutions and opposition of liberal media to pro-nationalist 'ordinary users' shows that, in both countries, the discussion is far from being balanced, rational, and inclusive.

Acknowledgements. This research has been supported in full by Russian Science Foundation (research grant 16-18-10125).

References

1. Nieminen, H.: Hegemony and the public sphere: essays on the democratisation of Communication. Department of Media Studies, School of Art, Literature and Music, University of Turku (2000)
2. Scheufele, D.A., Tewksbury, D.: Framing, agenda setting, and priming: the evolution of three media effects models. J. Commun. **57**(1), 9–20 (2007)
3. White, C.S.: Citizen participation and the internet: prospects for civic deliberation in the information age. Soc. Stud. **88**(1), 23–28 (1997)
4. White, D.M.: The gate keeper: a case study in the selection of news. Journal. Mass Commun. Q. **27**(4), 383 (1950)
5. Fuchs, C.: Social Media: A Critical Introduction. Sage, London (2013)
6. Chadwick, A.: The Hybrid Media System: Politics and Power. Oxford University Press, Oxford (2013)
7. Patterson, K., Grenny, J., et al.: Influencer: The Power to Change Anything. Tata McGraw-Hill Education, London (2007)
8. Rogers, E.M.: Diffusion of Innovations, 4th edn. Free Press, New York (2010)
9. Wallsten, K.: Political blogs and the bloggers who blog them: is the political blogosphere and echo chamber. In: American Political Science Association's Annual Meeting, Washington, DC, pp. 1–4 (2005)
10. Castells, M.: Communication, power and counter-power in the network society. Int. J. Commun. **1**(1), 238–266 (2007)
11. Bakshy, E., Rosenn, I., Marlow, C., Adamic, L.: The role of social networks in information diffusion. In: Proceedings of the 21st International Conference on World Wide Web, pp. 519–528. ACM (2012)
12. Habermas, J.: Political communication in media society: does democracy still enjoy an epistemic dimension? The impact of normative theory on empirical research. Commun. Theory **16**(4), 411–426 (2006)

13. Dahlgren, P.: Media and Political Engagement: Citizens, Communication, and Democracy. Cambridge University Press, Cambridge (2009)
14. Bruns, A., Burgess, J.E.: The use of Twitter hashtags in the formation of ad hoc publics. In: Proceedings of the 6th European Consortium for Political Research (ECPR) General Conference 2011 (2011)
15. Papacharissi, Z.A.: Affective Publics. Oxford University Press, Oxford (2015)
16. Bruns, A., Highfield, T.: Is Habermas on Twitter? Social media and the public sphere. In: Christensen, C., Bruns, A., Enli, G., Skogerbo, E., Larsson, A. (eds.) The Routledge Companion to Social Media and Politics, pp. 56–73. Routledge, London (2016)
17. Bodrunova, S.S., Litvinenko, A.A., Blekanov, I.S.: Influencers on the Russian Twitter: institutions vs. people in the discussion on migrants. In: ACM International Conference Proceeding Series, 22–23 November 2016, pp. 212–222 (2016)
18. Hladík, R., Štětka, V.: The powers that tweet: social media as news sources in the Czech Republic. Journal. Stud. **1**, 1–21 (2015)
19. McCombs, M.E., Shaw, D.L.: The agenda-setting function of mass media. Public Opin. Q. **36**(2), 176–187 (1972)
20. McCombs, M.: A look at agenda-setting: past, present and future. Journal. Stud. **6**(4), 543–557 (2005)
21. Fraser, N.: Rethinking the public sphere: a contribution to the critique of actually existing democracy. Soc. Text **25/26**, 56–80 (1990)
22. Laclau, E., Mouffe, C.: Hegemony and Socialist Strategy: Towards a Radical Democratic Politics. Verso, London (2001)
23. Fenton, N., Downey, J.: Counter public spheres and global modernity. Javnost - Public **10**(1), 15–32 (2003)
24. Dahlberg, L.: The internet, deliberative democracy, and power: radicalizing the public sphere. Int. J. Media Cult. Politics **3**(1), 47–64 (2007)
25. Nakamura, L.: Cybertypes: Race, Ethnicity, and Identity on the Internet. Routledge, London (2013)
26. Daniels, J.: Race and racism in internet studies: a review and critique. New Media Soc. **15**(5), 695–719 (2013)
27. Pfetsch, B., Adam, S.: Media agenda building in online and offline media–comparing issues and countries. In: Proceedings of the 6th ECPR General Conference, Reykjavik, Iceland, pp. 25–27 (2011)
28. Bodrunova, S., Litvinenko, A.: Fragmentation of society and media hybridisation in today? Russia: how Facebook voices collective demands. Zhurnal Issledovanii Sotsial'noi Politiki **14**(1), 113–124 (2016)
29. Norris, P.: Digital Divide: Civic Engagement, Information Poverty, and the Internet Worldwide. Cambridge University Press, Cambridge (2001)
30. Van Deursen, A.J., Van Dijk, J.A.: The digital divide shifts to differences in usage. New Media Soc. **16**(3), 507–526 (2014)
31. Murthy, D.: Twitter: Social communication in the Twitter age. Wiley, London (2013)
32. Dubois, E., Gaffney, D.: The multiple facets of influence identifying political influentials and opinion leaders on Twitter. Am. Behav. Sci. **58**(10), 1260–1277 (2014)
33. Aquino, J.: Boost brand advocates and social media influencers. CRM Mag. **17**(1), 30–34 (2013)
34. Papacharissi, Z.A.: A Private Sphere: Democracy in a Digital Age. Polity, London (2010)
35. Calhoun, C.: Introduction: Habermas and the public sphere. In: Calhoun, C. (ed.) Habermas and the public sphere, pp. 1–50. MIT Press, Cambridge (1992)
36. Katz, E.: The two-step flow of communication: an up-to-date report on an hypothesis. Public Opin. Q. **21**(1), 61–78 (1957)

37. Hartley, J., Green, J.: The public sphere on the beach. Eur. J. Cult. Stud. **9**(3), 341–362 (2006)
38. Morozov, E.: The brave new world of slacktivism. Foreign Policy **19**(05) (2009). http://foreignpolicy.com/2009/05/19/the-brave-new-world-of-slacktivism/
39. Broersma, M., Graham, T.: Social media as beat: tweets as a news source during the 2010 British and Dutch elections. Journal. Pract. **6**(3), 403–419 (2012)
40. Lindgren, S., Lundström, R.: Pirate culture and hacktivist mobilization: the cultural and social protocols of# WikiLeaks on Twitter. New Media Soc. **13**(6), 999–1018 (2011)
41. Koltsova, O., Koltcov, S.: Mapping the public agenda with topic modeling: the case of the Russian Livejournal. Policy Internet **5**(2), 207–227 (2013)
42. Bruns, A., Burgess, J.E., Crawford, K., Shaw, F.: #qldfloods and @QPSMedia: Crisis Communication on Twitter in the 2011 South East Queensland Floods. Centre of Excellence for Creative Industries and Innovation. ARC, Brisbane (2012)
43. Bastos, M.T., Raimundo, R.L.G., Travitzki, R.: Gatekeeping Twitter: message diffusion in political hashtags. Media Cult. Soc. **35**(2), 260–270 (2013)
44. Bruns, A.: Gatewatching: Collaborative Online News Production. Peter Lang, London (2005)
45. Bodrunova, S.S., Blekanov, I.S., Maksimov, A.: Measuring influencers in Twitter ad-hoc discussions: active users vs. internal networks in the discourse on Biryuliovo bashings in 2013. In: Proceedings of the AINL FRUCT 2016 Conference, item #7891853 (2017). Authors (2016-2)
46. Almind, T.C., Ingwersen, P.: Informetric analyses on the World Wide Web: methodological approaches to 'webometrics'. J. Doc. **53**(4), 404–426 (1997)
47. Kwak, H., Lee, C., Park, H., Moon, S.: What is Twitter, a social network or a news media? In: Proceedings of the 19th International Conference on World Wide Web, pp. 591–600. ACM (2010)
48. González-Bailón, S., Borge-Holthoefer, J., Moreno, Y.: Broadcasters and hidden influentials in online protest diffusion. Am. Behav. Sci. **57**(7), 943–965 (2013). doi:10.1177/0002764213479371
49. Maireder, A., Weeks, B.E., de Zúñiga, H.G., Schlögl, S.: Big data and political social networks introducing audience diversity and communication connector bridging measures in social network theory. Soc. Sci. Comput. Rev. (2015). doi:10.1177/0894439315617262
50. Hilbert, M., Vásquez, J., Halpern, D., Valenzuela, S., Arriagada, E.: One step, two step, network step? Complementary perspectives on communication flows in Twittered citizen protests. Soc. Sci. Comput. Rev. (2016). doi:10.1177/0894439316639561
51. Jungherr, A.: Twitter as political communication space: publics, prominent users, and politicians. In: Jungherr, A. (ed.) Analyzing Political Communication with Digital Trace Data. CPS, pp. 69–106. Springer, Cham (2015). doi:10.1007/978-3-319-20319-5_4
52. Adam, S.: Medieninhalte aus der Netzwerkperspektive. Publizistik **53**(2), 180–199 (2008)
53. Wu, S., Hofman, J.M., Mason, W.A., Watts, D.J.: Who says what to whom on Twitter. In: Proceedings of the 20th International Conference on World Wide Web, pp. 705–714. ACM (2011)
54. Vaccari, C., Valeriani, A., Barberá, P., Bonneau, R., Jost, J.T., Nagler, J., Tucker, J.: Social media and political communication: a survey of Twitter users during the 2013 Italian general election. Rivista italiana di scienza politica **43**(3), 381–410 (2013)
55. Jungherr, A., Juergens, P.: Through a glass, darkly tactical support and symbolic association in Twitter messages commenting on stuttgart 21. Soc. Sci. Comput. Rev. **32**(1), 74–89 (2014)
56. Fox, S., Zickuhr, K., Smith, A.: Twitter and status updating, fall 2009. Pew Internet Am. Life Proj. **21** (2009)

57. Page, R.: The linguistics of self-branding and micro-celebrity in Twitter: the role of hashtags Discourse. Communication **6**(2), 181–201 (2012)
58. Vis, F.: Twitter as a reporting tool for breaking news: journalists tweeting the 2011 UK riots. Digit. Journal. **1**(1), 27–47 (2013)
59. Bruns, A.: Social media and journalism during times of crisis. In: Hunsinger, J., Senft, T. (eds.) The Social Media Handbook, pp. 159–175. Routledge, London (2014)
60. Lotan, G., Graeff, E., Ananny, M., Gaffney, D., Pearce, I.: The arab spring: the revolutions were tweeted: information flows during the 2011 Tunisian and Egyptian revolutions. Int. J. Commun. **5**, 31 (2011)
61. Gruzd, A., Roy, J.: Investigating political polarization on Twitter: a Canadian perspective. Policy Internet **6**(1), 28–45 (2014)
62. Xu, W.W., Sang, Y., Blasiola, S., Park, H.W.: Predicting opinion leaders in twitter activism networks the case of the Wisconsin recall election. Am. Behav. Sci. (2014). doi:10.1177/0002764214527091
63. Kissane, D.: How many Twitter users are there in Germany? Quoracom, 27 January 2016. https://www.quora.com/How-many-Twitter-users-are-in-Germany. Accessed 01 Feb 2017
64. Tumasjan, A., Sprenger, T.O., Sandner, P.G., Welpe, I.M.: Election forecasts with Twitter: how 140 characters reflect the political landscape. Soc. Sci. Comput. Rev. (2010). doi:10.1177/0894439310386557
65. Hallin, D.C., Mancini, P.: Comparing Media Systems: Three Models of Media and Politics. Cambridge University Press, Cambridge (2004)
66. Dearden, L.: Cologne attacks: support for refugees in Germany falling amid far-right protests and vigilante attacks. The Independent, 13 January 2016. http://www.independentcouk/news/world/europe/cologne-attacks-support-for-refugees-in-germany-plummeting-amid-far-right-protests-and-vigilante-a6808616html. Accessed 01 Feb 2017
67. Vartanova, E.L.: Post-Soviet Transformations of Media and Journalism. MediaMir, Moscow (2013)
68. Bodrunova, S.S., Litvinenko, A.A.: New media and political protest: the formation of a public counter-sphere in Russia, 2008–12. In: Russia's Changing Economic and Political Regimes: The Putin Years and Afterwards, pp. 29–65 (2013)
69. Bodrunova, S.S., Litvinenko, A.A., Gavra, D.P., Yakunin, A.V.: Twitter-based discourse on migrants in Russia: the case of 2013 bashings in Biryulyovo. Int. Rev. Manag. Mark. **5**, 97–104 (2015)
70. Greene, S.A.: Twitter and the Russian street: memes, networks and mobilization. Working Materials of Center for the Study of New Media Society, Moscow New Economic School (2012). https://ru.scribd.com/document/94393092/Twitter-and-the-Russian-Street-CNMS-WP-2012-1. Accessed 01 Feb 2017
71. Nikiporets-Takigawa, G.: Tweeting the Russian protests. Digit. Icons: Stud. Russ. Eurasian Central Eur. New Media **9**, 1–25 (2013)
72. Barash, V., Kelly, J.: Salience vs commitment: dynamics of political hashtags in Russian Twitter. Berkman Center Research Publication, no. 2012-9 (2012)
73. Sanovich, S., Stukal, D., Penfold-Brown, D., Tucker, J.: Turning the virtual tables: government strategies for addressing online opposition with an application to Russia. Proceedings of the Paper Presented at the 2015 Annual Conference of the International Society of New Institutional Economics, June 2015
74. Blekanov, I.S., Sergeev, S.L., Martynenko, I.A.: Constructing topic-oriented web crawlers with generalized core. Sci. Res. Bull. St. Petersburg State Polytech. Univ. **5**(157), 9–15 (2012)

The President on Twitter: A Characterization Study of @realDonaldTrump

Brooke Auxier[(⊠)] and Jennifer Golbeck

University of Maryland, College Park, MD 20742, USA
{bauxier, jgolbeck}@umd.edu

Abstract. US President Donald Trump is perhaps the most powerful man on Twitter in terms of both his office and his ability to impact world events through his tweets. The way he uses the platform is unusual for someone in his position and is divisive among US citizens. Some tweets are posted by staff while others are posted by Trump himself, and in the time period of our dataset, the platform used to post distinguishes the author. We use this data to study the behavioral characteristics of the tweet sources and the public reaction to this content. Trump tweets tended to be more focused on himself or and other people, rather than the audience, and are more negative, angry, and anxious than staffers' tweets. Liberals and conservatives alike found some of the tweets inappropriate for someone in Trump's position to be posting, and the majority of inappropriate tweets came from Trump himself. The language characteristics are so distinctive that they may be used in a predictive model to correctly classify a tweet's author with 87% accuracy. Our predictive model will low for authorship determination, even when platform information is not informative, and our analysis suggests directions for future research on the rise of populist candidates and how they communicate on social media.

Keywords: Twitter · Trump

1 Introduction

Donald Trump was a prolific Twitter user at @realDonaldTrump before he became a candidate with a serious chance at the US Presidency. Throughout the 2016 Presidential primaries, his formal candidacy, his transition, and his early presidency, people questioned whether he would change his brusk style to better fit with what might be expected of someone in his position. He has continued to use the platform in a way that certainly breaks from how high-ranking officials typically conduct themselves online, and while some appreciate his style as "refreshing", others find it improper and disrespectful to the institution of the Presidency.

The Trump tweets that garner the most media attention tend to be the more blustery or controversial ones, but there is a lot of nuance to be found in the Trump Twitter stream. As has been widely reported and analyzed, Trump tweets are authored by multiple people. Having staff-authored tweets is a common practice, but in this case, the author of the tweet appears to be identifiable based on the platform. Trump posted (at least in the time we were collecting our data) from an Android and his staff posted from

© Springer International Publishing AG 2017
G.L. Ciampaglia et al. (Eds.): SocInfo 2017, Part I, LNCS 10539, pp. 377–390, 2017.
DOI: 10.1007/978-3-319-67217-5_23

iPhone. This original analysis was posted online in non-peer reviewed analysis[1], but the text and social media analysis community online has supplied a lot of supportive evidence for this theory. Comments from staff also suggest it is true and scholarly literature has begun accepted this insight (e.g. Ott 2017). While we recognize platform may not be a perfect proxy for authorship, it appears to be a solid theory and we rely on it in this paper. Our prediction results discussed later add strength to the theory as well.

Knowing with high probability who is authoring any given tweet at @realDonaldTrump supports a content-based analysis of the tweets. As one of the most successful candidates among the populist movements that have arisen since 2016, Trump's communications in general are important. And since Twitter is Trump's main communication platform, understanding the nuances between Trump's own tweets and those of his staff can provide insight into their different types of language and interaction patterns and how those are perceived by the public. Thus, we undertake this characterization study with two major research questions:

1. RQ 1: What are the characteristics of iPhone (Staff) vs. Android (Trump) tweets, in terms of their social connections, timing, perceived appropriateness, and linguistic style attributes?
2. RQ 2: Are the social media characteristics of these tweets predictive of the source of the tweet? Can the text of a tweet identify its author?

Our findings suggest that Trump's tweets are more focused on the media, are more negative, and are perceived by citizens as less appropriate than those posted by his staff. The linguistic differences are so stark that a word vector approach can be used to classify a tweet as Trump-authored or staff-authored with $\sim 87\%$ accuracy. We discuss the implications of this work for more deeply analyzing the Trump Twitter phenomenon and for understanding communication of populist figures like Trump.

2   Related Work

Though Trump's official political career and presidency have just begun, there is much research about how politicians – both from the U.S. and other countries – use Twitter as a platform for communication. The literature related to our case study and analysis looks at the interactivity of politicians on Twitter and the social networks of politicians on Twitter. Perhaps more relevant, however, are a few more recent pieces of scholarship that examine Donald Trump's use of the platform. This is a small but growing body of scholarship, which our research aims to contribute to.

2.1   Politicians on Twitter: Promotional Platform or Interactive Communication Tool?

Though social media is lauded as a democratizing, interactive, accessible communication tool, some scholars suggest that politicians on Twitter are not communicating

---

[1] http://varianceexplained.org/r/trump-tweets/.

often, or well, with their audiences and constituents. On one side of the argument is Gunn Enli and her article on how Donald Trump and Hillary Clinton used social media throughout their presidential bids. Enli states that political campaigns fail to use social media as a way to interact with voters or encourage dialogue, rather they use the platforms as channels for political marketing (Enli, p. 53). The 2016 campaigns were no different and Enli notes that campaign websites in 2016 lacked comments sections altogether, which meant the campaigns were clearly using social media platforms as "channels to promote candidates and mobilise voters, not to engage with the public" (Enli citing Pew Research 2016, p. 54).

The findings from more research, from Golbeck, et al., from 2009, found a similar trend: politicians, particularly Congresspeople in the United States, are using Twitter for information-sharing purposes rather than as a direct communication tool. All of this analysis suggests that politicians may not be using the platform to directly communicate with other users, but rather they see it as a one-way communication tool to share information and details about their event attendance.

Standing on the other side of the argument are scholars Graham et al. who examine the use of Twitter by British and Dutch politicians in general election campaigns. The authors suggest that social media (Twitter, in particular) allows for connections between ordinary people and the "popular, powerful and influential" (Graham et al. 2016, p. 766). They also call it an "interesting tool to reach out to voters" (Graham et al. 2016, p. 767). As of December 2012, 87% of democratic countries had a leader using Twitter (Graham et al. 2016, citing Digital Daya, 2012, p. 767).

Several studies have found that microblogging by politicians is used as a one-way broadcasting tool and for self-promotion, information dissemination, negative campaigning, party mobilization and impression management, rather than used for conversation and collaboration (Graham et al. 2016, p. 768). They also cite studies (Bruns and Highfield 2013; Burgess and Bruns 2012; Grant et al. 2010; Larsson and Moe 2011, 2013; Verweij 2012) that suggest politicians mainly interact with politicians, journalists and activists (p. 768). Other research (Ausserhofer and Maireder 2013) suggests that Twitter is in fact a place that can be joined by outsiders (p. 768). This is a lively debate, and is one that our case study and analysis of Trump's Twitter use hopes to contribute to.

The analysis done by Graham, Jackson and Broersma examines Twitter use by politicians (members of Parliament) in the United Kingdom and the Netherlands in 2010. Their research examined, among other things, the most common type of tweet and with whom candidates were interacting. They found that both British and Dutch politicians used @-replies frequently, 31.8% and 47.4% of tweets respectively. They also found that the politicians interacted most frequently with members of the public, 59.1% and 61.8% of tweets, respectively (Graham et al. 2016, pp. 774–775). Though this research is not based on US politicians, it lays important groundwork for further examining how politicians use of Twitter, especially when considering who their tweets are directed towards.

Other authors agree that conversations trump politics on Twitter. In 2012, Hemphill, Shapiro and Otterbacher examined how politicians in Chicago, Illinois use Twitter as a communication tool. The authors found that "politicians in Chicago are using Twitter (and potentially other social media) to engage in social conversations rather than formal politicking," (Hemphill et al. 2012, p. 3). The authors, did not look into who the politicians were communicating with and they did not analyze the communities and connections in their network analysis, but their findings related to politicians using the platform for conversations is relevant to our work.

2.2   @realDonaldTrump on Twitter

While it is important to examine how politicians use Twitter more broadly, in the United States and abroad, it is also critical to explore how other scholars have approached Donald Trump's use of Twitter – especially in his new role as politician and now, President of the United States – directly. Because Donald Trump is relatively new to the political sphere and has only been in office as president for a short time, the scholarship is limited, though this is an area ripe for research.

Enli's research, which focused on the 2016 presidential campaign cycle, looked closely at the interactions of the two candidates on Twitter. Through her analysis, she found that Donald Trump retweeted more frequently than Hillary Clinton (Enli 2017, p. 54). Approximately 25% of his tweets were retweets. He also engaged more with "ordinary users," as 78% of his retweets were from the general public (Enli 2017, p. 54). This suggests, according to Enli, that the Trump camp was more willing to engage with the general public and willing to "take the risk of retweeting content it did not control" (Enli 2017, p. 54). Enli also discusses the issue of authorship of tweets. She states that Donald Trump was more involved in social media strategy, tweeting from his @realDonaldTrump account, as though to "underline that the tweets came directly from Trump himself and were not managed and crafted solely by his campaign" (Enli 2017, p. 57).

Authors Lee and Lim examined the use of Twitter by both Donald Trump and Hillary Clinton during the campaign season in their own 2016 article. They examined 295 tweets from President Trump and 228 tweets from Clinton from two time frames in 2015 (based around dates of primary debates). They analyzed the tweets for the following traits: feminine traits, masculine traits, tweet type, tweet content, use of multimedia and civility (Lee and Lim 2016, p. 851). In examining the use of masculine and feminine language, they found that among 91 gendered trait words, Donald Trump used 38: 23 masculine (60.5%) and 15 feminine (39.5%) (Lee and Lim 2016, p. 852). As for tweet type, their analysis found that only 42.4% of Trump's tweets were original (i.e. not retweets). They also found that Trump is keen to retweet citizens. They found that almost half of Trump's tweets were retweets of constituents' accounts and over 80% of his total retweets were from citizen accounts (Lee and Lim 2016, p. 852). Eleven percent of his retweets were media organizations, almost 3% were his campaign staff and 2.5% of retweets were other public figures (Lee and Lim 2016, p. 852). As for the content of his tweets, 25% of his tweets were supportive comments and endorsements from others and another 25% of his tweets were found to be criticisms or attacks of others (Lee and Lim 2016, p. 852). The researchers also evaluated the civility of Trump's tweets and found that 10% of Trump's tweets included uncivil wording or attacks on other candidates (Lee and Lim 2016, p. 852).

Another recent article by Ahmadian et al. looked at the communication styles of Republican candidates in the U.S. presidential election, with an emphasis on Donald Trump's communication style. In order to conduct their research, they combined data from candidates' campaign speeches and their Twitter accounts (Ahmadian et al. 2017, p. 51). Though this study is not entirely focused on his use of Twitter, it gives insights into his conversation style, both on- and off-line. Most relevant to this research, the authors found that Trump's conversation style was rated highest in grandiosity—identified by the use of first person pronouns, or I-talk—when compared to other Republican candidates (Ahmadian et al. 2017, p. 51). Trump's was also rated highly informal—categorized by four variables: analytical thinking, formality, words per sentence and words with less than letters—when compared to other Republican candidates (Ahmadian et al. 2017, p. 51).

3   Data Collection

3.1   Tweet Collection and Platform Identification

Using the Twitter API, we collected all the tweets from the @realDonaldTrump Twitter account that were posted between January 1, 2016 and February 5, 2017. This time period covered his candidacy, transition, and the first few weeks of his Presidency. There were 4,590 total tweets.

Embedded in the tweet is the platform from which it was posted. Of the over 4,500 tweets, the Android and iPhone platforms were by far the most common sources. There were 291 tweets from the web client, especially leading up to the election, and 88 tweets from other platforms (ads, Instagram, etc.). However, 4,287 were from one of the two main mobile platforms.

Conventional wisdom, media reports, and comments from Trump's social media director all suggest that, during the period we are addressing, Trump was tweeting from the Android and the staff was tweeting from the iPhone. This appears to have changed – Trump may now be tweeting from an iPhone[2]. However, as we will discuss later on, classification algorithms can easily distinguish a Trump tweet from a staff tweet, so this platform distinction is not critical in research going forward.

3.2   Appropriateness Ratings

Trump's use of Twitter is unusual for someone in his position. They are often personal in nature, including personal attacks, they stray into topics not typically addressed by a candidate for President, and may appear unfiltered. The strongly partisan political environment in the US ensures that many people will have strong feelings about the politics reflected in the tweets. However, there is a different question that we found especially interesting in his case: which tweets are *appropriate*.

---

[2] https://twitter.com/DanScavino/status/846918912793083904.

By appropriateness, we consider whether the content is something that a citizen believes befits the role of Presidential candidate or the President of the United States, regardless of whether they agree with it politically. To determine appropriateness, we polled American workers on Mechanical Turk.

For this part of our analysis, we eliminated retweets and quoted tweets so we only considered posts written by someone using the account. This gave us 3,666 total tweets.

Next, we asked Americans to rate the tweets. We created a pool of about 175 people on Mechanical Turk. We restricted the HIT to workers based in the US, listed a requirement that workers be American citizens, and everyone in our pool passed a qualification test that posed several American cultural questions. We also had workers describe their political beliefs on a liberal-conservative scale. Each of the 3,666 tweets was rated by 10 self-described liberals and 10 self-described conservatives, randomly selected from the pool. Raters were asked if the tweet was "Appropriate", "Neutral", or "Inappropriate".

Instructions made it explicit that workers should not to rate a tweet based on whether they agreed *politically* with the statement but rather to rate if it was an appropriate statement that a Presidential candidate or the President should be making. We also included an attention check in the instructions:

> Please rate whether you personally believe these are appropriate tweets for the President of the United States or a candidate for President to be posting.
> This does not necessarily mean you agree with the politics of the tweet. For example, a tweet that says "Today I signed a bill that cuts taxes by 1% in all income brackets." may not reflect what you personally believe is good policy, but it is an appropriate tweet for the President to make. You would mark a tweet like that as Appropriate. To make sure you read instructions, always mark tweet 3 as neutral. However, a tweet that said "My hands are HUGE and anyone who says otherwise is spreading FAKE NEWS!" may be marked either way depending on whether you think this is something the President should be saying on Twitter.

We assigned perceived "appropriate" tweets a score of 1, "inappropriate" a score of -1, and "neutral" a score of 0. We averaged the rating of all 20 raters to get a score for each tweet. An average of 0.9 would mean 19 people labeled the tweet "appropriate" (1) and 1 person labeled it "inappropriate" (-1). An average score of -1 would mean all 20 people labeled the tweet "inappropriate".

3.3   Mention and Retweet Coding

President Trump reaches a wide audience with his 140-characters, with over 32.1M followers on the platform. And although he keeps his following list tight-knit (following just 45 accounts) he interacts quite frequently on the platform with other users. And rather than looking at the language used in the interactions, we can look at the type of accounts the tweets mention to understand behavioral differences between the platforms (Table 1).

From our original dataset, we extracted 550 retweets and 774 tweets that contained one or more account mentions. Some tweets mentioned multiple accounts, yielding 874 mentioned accounts in total. Using an open coding approach, we established a set of

Table 1. Codes for account types in Trump mentions

Category	Code	Details
Family	fam	Twitter handles of people related to Trump (including children and wife)
Media	med	Twitter handles of news media organizations and journalists
Politicians	pol	Twitter handles of politicians, including VP, Senators, House Reps and local politicians (governors, mayors, etc.)
Constituents/citizens	cit	Twitter handles of average Twitter users, including constituents
Official businesses	bus	Twitter handles of non-government businesses and companies
Government entities	gov	Twitter handles of government organizations, departments, branches
Celebrity	cel	Twitter handles of celebrities, well-known individuals
Trump admin	adm	Trump administration/campaign handles
Union	uni	Twitter handles for local unions

categories in order to better understand the populations within Trump's retweet and mentions network. The categories included: family, media, politicians, citizens, businesses, government entities, celebrities and members of the Trump administration.

4   RQ1: Content Characterization

4.1   Mentions and Retweets

Nearly all of the retweets on the @realDonaldTrump account came from the Android device. Of the 550 retweets, only 11 were from iPhone, including 3 administration members, 3 media retweets, and 2 citizens.

The Android retweets were dominated by retweets of citizens: 429 of the 536 (81.2%). Another 10% were retweets of media. Some of the retweeted accounts were no longer accessible: 13 were suspended and 19 were completely deleted.

Mentions follow a much different pattern. From Android, the vast majority of Trump's mentions are of media (81%) with another 10% addressing politicians. iPhone-based tweets have a more diverse set of mentioned account types, as shown in Fig. 1.

4.2   Appropriateness

Using the ratings from our Mechanical Turk workers, we can analyze the appropriateness of the @realDonaldTrump tweets. Recall 0 is neutral, 1 is appropriate, and −1 is inappropriate. The average tweet scored a 0.51, halfway between neutral and appropriate. 780 (23%) of tweets had an average negative score, putting them on the inappropriate end of the scale.

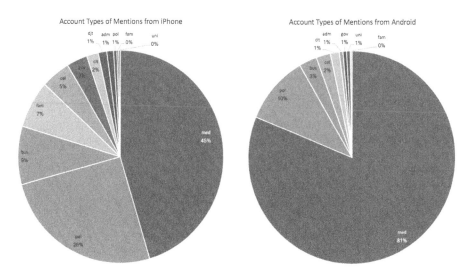

Fig. 1. Distribution of mention types from iPhone (left) and Android (right)

Not surprisingly, liberals and conservatives differ in what they find appropriate. The average rating from liberals is 0.38 while conservatives gave an average of 0.64. Liberals gave 1,064 (29%) tweets an average negative score, indicating they felt a sizable minority of the tweets were not befitting someone in Trump's position.

Breaking down the tweets by device also shows large differences in appropriateness ratings. Android-originating tweets were rated significantly lower than iPhone tweets. Among the 780 "inappropriate" tweets with average scores less than 0, 482 (61.9%) were posted from Android. Further dividing the ratings according to the rater's political leanings, we find dramatic results. Liberals give Trump's Android tweets an average score of only 0.1. Nearly half (49%) of Trump's tweets averaged neutral to inappropriate scores when rated by liberals. On the other hand, conservatives give Trump much higher marks and the staff tweets have quite a high rating. These results are shown in Fig. 2.

There are many tweets (1,297) that all of our raters agreed were neutral to appropriate (i.e. no one said they were "inappropriate"); 647 tweets were ranked totally appropriate by all 20 raters. Most of these came from iPhones, but some (118 of the 647, or 18%) came from Trump's Android device. These were typical campaign tweets for the most part, e.g. "It was so great being in Nebraska last week Today is the big day —get out and vote!" (Fig. 3).

However, there were some tweets that were considered inappropriate by liberals and conservatives alike. Trump's tweet threatening to "spill the beans" on Ted Cruz's wife received the lowest score; it was ranked inappropriate by everyone except one conservative (an average score of −0.9).

Some additional tweets received very low average ratings from all sides. The following tweets were the lowest rated, with overall average scores of −0.75 or lower:

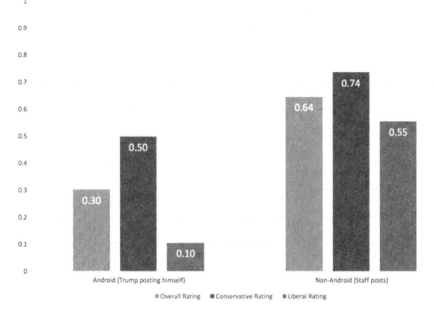

Fig. 2. Appropriateness ratings by platform and rater's political leanings

Fig. 3. Trump's most inappropriate tweet according to our raters with an average score of −0.9. The tweet originates from the Android platform, indicating Trump himself authored it.

Wall Street paid for ad is a fraud, just like Crooked Hillary! Their main line had nothing to do with women, and they knew it. Apologize? (−0.85)

Explain how the women on The View, which is a total disaster since the great Barbara Walters left, ever got their jobs. @abc is wasting time (−0.85)

HILLARY FAILED ALL OVER THE WORLD. #BigLeagueTruth ✗LIBYA ✗SYRIA ✗IRAN ✗IRAQ ✗ASIA PIVOT ✗RUSSIAN RESET ✗BENGHAZI... https://t.co/H1UH0svtt2 (-0.75)

.@FoxNews is so biased it is disgusting. They do not want Trump to win. All negative! (−0.75)

There are 53 tweets that liberals unanimously deemed inappropriate. These include the tweets mentioned below, criticisms of Megyn Kelly, John McCain, Elizabeth Warren, and Mitt Romney, and comments on pop culture. Below are four representative tweets from this pool:

Pocahontas is at it again! Goofy Elizabeth Warren, one of the least productive U.S. Senators, has a nasty mouth. Hope she is V.P. choice.

Really dumb @CheriJacobus. Begged my people for a job. Turned her down twice and she went hostile. Major loser, zero credibility!

.@NBCNews is bad but Saturday Night Live is the worst of NBC. Not funny, cast is terrible, always a complete hit job. Really bad television!

Mitt Romney, who was one of the dumbest and worst candidates in the history of Republican politics, is now pushing me on tax returns. Dope!

There were also some tweets where liberals and conservatives had major disagreements, where the majority of liberals said they were inappropriate and the majority of conservatives said they were appropriate. The tweets below all had a difference of 1.5 between the average liberal rating and average conservative rating, except for the first which had a difference of 1.6.

Taxpayers are paying a fortune for the use of Air Force One on the campaign trail by President Obama and Crooked Hillary. A total disgrace!

Goofy Senator Elizabeth Warren @elizabethforma has done less in the U.S. Senate than practically any other senator. All talk, no action!

Watching John Kasich being interviewed - acting so innocent and like such a nice guy. Remember him in second debate, until I put him down.

What Barbara Res does not say is that she would call my company endlessly, and for years, trying to come back. I said no.

People forget, it was Club for Growth that asked me for $1 million. I said no & they went negative. Extortion! https://t.co/oq8jmoep7i

Hillary Clinton has been involved in corruption for most of her professional life!

#CrookedHillary is outspending me by a combined 31 to 1 in Florida, Ohio, & Pennsylvania. I haven't started yet! https://t.co/BcoPrwqFMe

These tweets are particularly notable for those interested in the political divisions in the United States, as they reflect not just a difference in politics but a stark difference in how people believe political discourse should take place.

4.3   Linguistic Style

As part of RQ1, we hope to characterize linguistic differences between the Staff and Trump tweets as well as differences in the appropriate and inappropriate tweets. We are focused on two categories of linguistic differences: pronoun usage and affective words. Pronouns are likely to capture differences in who the tweets are talking about. With a focus on affective processes, we anticipate differences in positive vs. negative emotional words and language relating to anger and anxiety.

We removed mentions and retweets from this analysis, using 3,287 total tweets: 1,842 iPhone tweets and 1,445 Android tweets. We used LIWC2007 (Pennebaker et al. 2001) to analyze the text.

When comparing between the devices, we found significant differences in all the hypothesized areas. Statistics are calculated with Student's t-tests with a Bonferroni correction and are significant for $p < 0.01$.

Android (i.e. Trump) tweets used "I", "he/she", and "they" significantly more often than iPhone (i.e. Staff) tweets. iPhone tweets, on the other hand, used "you" significantly more than Android tweets, at 5.98 times the rate. These indicate that Trump uses his tweets to talk about himself and other people while the staffers address the audience.

There was no significant difference in the overall number of affective words used based on device, but there were large differences in the types of affective words. iPhone tweets used significantly more positive emotion words and Android tweets used significantly more negative emotion words, anxiety words, and anger words.

These differences were mimicked in the analysis of appropriate vs. inappropriate tweets. We separated tweets into Fully Appropriate (received scores of appropriate from all raters—647 tweets, 82% of which were non-Android) and Inappropriate (had an average negative score—780 tweets, 62% of which were Android posts). Since the prevalence of Android vs. iPhone tweets is related to the appropriateness ratings, we expect some overlap in findings. That did occur, but some results were more extreme than what we found in the platform analysis. All results reported are significant for $p < 0.01$ with the same tests and corrections as described above.

Inappropriate tweets use "he/she" over 16 times more often than appropriate tweets. Appropriate tweets use "we" 3.3 times as often than inappropriate tweets; there was no significant difference in the use of "we" based on platform. Appropriate tweets also used "you" more than 17 times as often as inappropriate tweets.

Emotional content also differs in that inappropriate tweets are more negative. The inappropriate tweets used words related to negative emotions more than 8 times as often as the appropriate tweets; words associated with anger 6.6 times as frequently; and words associated with anxiety 7.4 times as frequently. Appropriate tweets use words related to positive emotions at 3.3 times the rate of the inappropriate tweets.

5   RQ2: Prediction

Our content analysis echoes discussions in the media about who is authoring tweets on the @realDonaldTrump account. Trump representatives appear to have confirmed that, until recently, the platform was a fairly accurate distinguishing source but this appears to no longer be the case with all recent tweets to the account coming from an iPhone. Thus, being able to automatically connect a tweet to its author becomes more important as a tool for Trump Twitter Analysts.

We use the words of the tweets themselves as features to predict authorship. Each tweet is represented as a word vector and it is labeled with its source (Android or iPhone) as a class. We used standard 10-fold cross validation for evaluation. We trained the Weka SimpleLogistic classifier, the best performing of five different types of classifiers we tested. We report precision, recall, F-measures, ROC AUC, and accuracy.

Results are shown in Table 2. We are able to predict the source, and thus the authorship, of tweets in our dataset with 86.7% accuracy and a ROC AUC of 0.924.

Table 2. Results for classification with SimpleLogistic algorithm for classifying tweets

TP Rate	FP Rate	Prec.	Recall	F-Meas	MCC	ROC area	PRC	Class
0.927	0.193	0.827	0.927	0.874	0.74	0.924	0.911	Android
0.807	0.073	0.918	0.807	0.859	0.74	0.924	0.935	iPhone
0.867	0.133	0.872	0.867	0.867	0.74	0.924	0.923	Weighted average

Given that device is connected to authorship for the tweets in our dataset, this classifier will allow prediction of authorship on new tweets just with the language of the tweet, regardless of what device is used.

We achieve similar results using the Word Vector approach with the SimpleLogistic algorithm to classify tweets as "Appropriate" or "Inappropriate". Tweets were classified as Inappropriate if their average was < 0 and "Appropriate" otherwise. The classifier achieved and 87.3% accuracy rate with ROC AUC of 0.917.

6   Discussion

6.1   Identifying Tweet Authorship and Impact

Our predictive model shows that tweet authorship can be accurately predicted with a word vector. This means that even as indicators like platform change, the language of the tweet itself can identify the author. Thus, going forward, such models will allow differentiation of content for analysis.

We were also able to classify perceived appropriateness with high accuracy. While there is some overlap in authorship and appropriateness, it is only partial. Being able to predict bi-partisan disapproval of tweet content ahead of time can be especially useful for communications professionals. It is possible that Trump and even members of his team are unconcerned with citizens' perception of what is appropriate. However, there are certainly candidates and legislators who are concerned with this, and the success of the classifier suggests promise in future work that can provide algorithmic feedback about social media posts before they are made public.

6.2   The Language of Populism

This characterization study was not designed to describe the entire populist movement. However, as an outspoken and successful populist, Trump serves as an interesting case study. His staff's tweets from the period we studied are often more traditional in their online communication approach when compared with Trump's own comments. Our results that show a focus on himself and others – both through his linguistic patterns and heavy use of media mentions – as well as tweets rooted in negative emotions, anger, and anxiety.

These results suggest an approach to analyzing the language of populists on Twitter may yield interesting linguistic insights about the movement itself and how it differentiates itself from mainstream political communication online.

7   Conclusions

Trump is changing what we expect in public statements from our leaders. In this paper, we leveraged the observation that the platform from which a tweet was posted to @realDonaldTrump can identify its author as Trump or Staff. Our results show that Trump himself tends to more actively tweet about the media, speak about himself or others (rather than the audience), and to communicate about anger, anxiety, and negative emotions when compared with staff tweets. We also found that citizens' perceive Trump's tweets as less appropriate for someone in his position to be posting. Using language features, we were able to develop predictive models for tweet authorship and for tweet appropriateness that perform with high accuracy. Our findings have implications for the study of Trump specifically and for understanding the online language and behaviors of the populist movement.

References

Ahmadian, S., Azarshahi, S., Paulhus, D.L.: Explaining Donald Trump via communication style: grandiosity, informality, and dynamism. Pers. Individ. Differ. **107**, 49–53 (2017). doi:10.1016/j.paid.2016.11.018

Enli, G.: Twitter as arena for the authentic outsider: exploring the social media campaigns of Trump and Clinton in the 2016 US presidential election. Eur. J. Commun. **32**(1), 50–61 (2017). doi:10.1177/0267323116682802

Golbeck, J., et al.: Twitter use by the U.S. congress. J. Am. Soc. Inf. Sci. Technol. **61**(8), 1612–1621 (2010). doi:10.1002/asi.21344

Graham, T., Jackson, D., Broersma, M.: New platform, old habits? Candidates' use of Twitter during the 2010 British and Dutch general election campaigns. N. Media Soc. **18**(5), 765–783 (2016)

Hemphill, L., Shapiro, M.A., Otterbacher, J.: Chicago Politicians on Twitter (2012)

Hsu, C.L., Park, H.W.: Mapping online social networks of Korean politicians. Gov. Inf. Q. **29**(2), 169–181 (2012)

Lee, J., Lim, Y.: Gendered campaign tweets: the cases of Hillary Clinton and Donald Trump. Publ. Relat. Rev. **42**(5), 849–855 (2016). doi:10.1016/j.pubrev.2016.07.004

Ott, B.L.: The age of Twitter: Donald J. Trump and the politics of debasement. Crit. Stud. Media Commun. **34**(1), 59–68 (2017)

Pennebaker, J.W., Francis, M.E., Booth, R.J.: Linguistic Inquiry and Word Count (LIWC): A Computerized Text Analysis Program, vol. 7. Lawrence Erlbaum, Mahwah (2001)

Social Networking Sites Withdrawal

Carlos Osorio[1](✉) ⓘ, Rob Wilson[2], and Savvas Papagiannidis[3]

[1] University of Manizales, Manizales, Colombia
cosoriot@umanizales.edu.co
[2] Centre for Knowledge, Innovation, Technology and Enterprise,
Newcastle University Business School, 5 Barrack Road,
Newcastle upon Tyne NE1 4SE, UK
Rob.Wilson@newcastle.ac.uk
[3] Goldman Chair of Innovation, Newcastle University Business School,
5 Barrack Road, Newcastle upon Tyne NE1 4SE, UK
savvas.papagiannidis@ncl.ac.uk

Abstract. The importance of the users for the survival of a social networking site is vital. For this reason, most of the research about this topic is focused about how to make the user to participate on the network. However, little has been researched about the reasons why a user would decide to close its account and leave the network for good. This research is aimed to study this phenomenon based on the Social Identity Theory, specifically the disidentification concept. The research implemented the means-end chain methodology using the data collected from in-depth interviews to 26 adults who have closed an SNS account. This data was analyzed through content analysis and using Social Network Analysis as an alternative to map the chains suggested by the means end chain methodology, as well as providing more information based on the centrality measures. The findings suggest that impression management, friendship, time management and emotional stability play a central role to take the withdrawal decision.

Keywords: Social networking sites · Withdrawal · Identity · Disidentification · Means-end chain · Social Network Analysis · Social Identity Theory

1 Introduction

Researchers and practitioners in Social Networking Services are in a constant search of the next big thing. This search has witnessed rise and falls of many social networks. Cases like Friendster and Myspace, show how a Social Networking Service, also known as Social Networking Site (SNS), that were on top of its popularity are now relegated with a fraction of the users they had in the past. Another example is country based SNSs, which were popular a couple of years ago being now replaced by Facebook as the top network on the market.

An SNS without users is doomed to disappear. For this reason, researchers and practitioners in SNSs have focused on SNSs' growth and searched for new ways to encourage users to join and participate in the network [1, 2]. However, a very limited

© Springer International Publishing AG 2017
G.L. Ciampaglia et al. (Eds.): SocInfo 2017, Part I, LNCS 10539, pp. 391–408, 2017.
DOI: 10.1007/978-3-319-67217-5_24

body of research has addressed the reasons why a user decides to cease using a SNS in which he/she has been active member [3]. Research regarding SNS shows how researchers have focused their efforts on network usage and user retention [2, 4–10], leaving SNS withdrawal as the complementary outcome when the usage is not continued. Some authors have adopted a mathematical modelling approach using techniques such as epidemiologic models and Social Network Analysis-SNA (static and dynamic) to study SNS decline as an approximation to SNS withdrawal. However, the understanding of the reasons for closing the account still needs further research, reflecting Vandenberghe [11] criticism about the simplification of the SNA, transforming the person into a node with certain attributes, but still missing the human condition.

2   Literature Review

Reviewing the literature available about SNS withdrawal, Sillaber et al. [12] identified different types of status on SNS (Others or non-members, Guests, Passive Members, Active Members and Developers, as shown in Fig. 1) based on previous research about SNS usage. The transition between statuses, denoted by '~Ca,b,c', includes three processes: the first one is the temporary inactivity, defined as user inactivity for an unspecified period of time, but still reachable through the SNS platform. The second state is permanent inactivity, consisting on when a user stops using the SNS for good but without deleting the profile and leaving the information that the user posted in the profile available. The third stage is the purge, defined as closing the SNS profile, deleting the content and cutting all the ties created in the network.

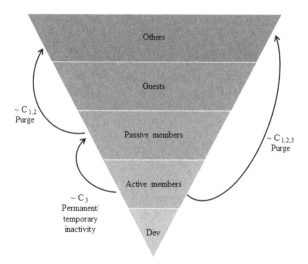

Fig. 1. User withdrawals from social network services [12]

Sillaber's contribution is based on the different statuses that a user can have in an SNS and how the transition from one status to another represents usage decline. However, his work does not explain the reasons for changing the status nor proposes a clear distinction between temporary and permanent inactivity definitions, there is a lack of clarity concerning cases like users with a long inactivity time, e.g. people who visit their profile yearly or people who visit their profile after receiving a reminder to visit the network. These long periods of inactivity generate confusion whether to assign users into a certain category or not. For the sake of clarity, the definition coined in this research for SNS withdrawal adopts the purge transition definition proposed by Sillaber et al. [12]. This definition is selected because it makes it possible to identify who is a user and who is not in a clearer way. In addition, the fact that a person took the time and effort to close its account implies a stronger conviction about this decision, hence stronger reasons to do it. This strong conviction makes it possible to assume that salient characteristics and motivations to take this decision are easier to identify. It is worth clarifying as well that SNS withdrawal is understood as closing the profile in a specific SNS, not closing all the profiles and discontinuing the use of SNS altogether. The following section will show the main elements of the Social Identity Theory that will help understand SNS user withdrawal.

2.1 Social Identity Theory (SIT)

An SNS gives the user the chance to create, one or more identities on an SNS and become a member of several groups based on the user interests. The link attaching self-concept given by the identity and membership of a group is known as social identification [13–15]. The definition of social identification adopted for this paper comes from the seminal paper by Kreiner and Ashforth, who defined it as "self-descriptions based on a perceived overlap of individual and group identities" [14, p. 1] having elements in common with the definition by Sluss and Ashfort proposed as "the extent to which one defines oneself in terms of a given role-relationship" [16, p. 11]. This dynamic process of identification between the self and the group is the central idea of Social Identity Theory [17], which is presented next.

Baker and White introduce Social Identity Theory (SIT)'s main idea by identifying the importance of memberships of social groups in the definition of the self- concept [18], which is based on the work of Tajfel and Turner [17], Hogg and Abrams [19].

SIT considers three possible cognitive states: identification, disidentification and ambivalent identification [13, 15, 20], which are defined by Kreiner et al. as follows:

"Identification refers to the definition of self-vis-à-vis some group, such as an occupation or organisation (citing Ashforth and Mael, 1989), whereas disidentification involves defining oneself as being not the same as the group (citing Elsbach and Bhattacharya, 2001). Ambivalent identification (also called schizo-identification) is said to occur when one simultaneously identifies and disidentifies with the group or various facets of the group (citing Pratt, 2000)" [20, p. 620].

These cognitive states proposed by Kreiner show how (dis)identification is based on the overlap between the identity of the individual and the identity of the group which is a central element for SNS users' withdrawal. This overlap suggests the identification as a process with different stages going from a full overlap (identification) passing by a partial overlap (ambivalent identification) and ending with no overlap (disidentification). The stages of this identification process are similar to SNS usage decline model proposed by Sillaber et al. [12], in which SNS users may feel completely identified with the SNS, identified with some aspects of the network and disentified with others at the same time (e.g. identified with the people in their network, but not with some practices such as sponsored posts), or completely disidentified with the SNS. The case of disidentification is similar to the purge in Sillaber's model, wherein if there is nothing in common or is not satisfying of any need, the user feels disidentified with the network. These three states are illustrated in Fig. 2, showing how identification/disidentification processes help to understand SNS permanence and withdrawal.

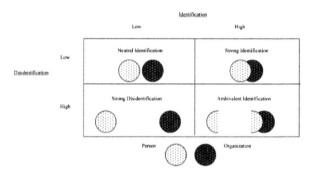

Fig. 2. Expanded model of identification [14]

Disidentification as Foundation of SNS Withdrawal

Given the similarities between disidentification and SNS withdrawal, the definitions and explanations for disidentification can be applied to SNS withdrawal as well. Steele defines disidentification as "a re-conceptualisation of the self and of one's values so as to remove the domain as a self-identity, as a basis of self-evaluation. Disidentification offers the retreat of not caring about the domain in relation to the self" [21, p. 614]. This definition highlights a continuous self-evaluation process regarding the overlap between self-identity and social or group identity, which is used by Woodcock et al. [22] on their research about stereotypes. This continuous self-assessment makes it possible to understand that, as people grow and change interests, groups can have changes as well as part of their evolution. As a consequence, disidentification may happen, causing the person to stop caring about the group, which is labelled as domain disidentification by Woodcock et al. [22]. These authors define domain disidentification as "when a formerly valued social identity is significantly reduced or abandoned" [22, p. 3], which is in alignment with Sillaber's definition about withdrawal.

Disidentification has been studied from diverse fields, such as ethnic identification for first and second generations [21, 23–27], ethnocentrism [23, 28] and gender and sexuality [29]. Literature regarding disidentification in SNS, produced few results which was a motivation for this article to contribute to the theory by extending the application of the disidentification process to the SNS context.

3 Methodology

Research on SNS is a growing body of knowledge, but as stated before, little attention has been paid to SNS withdrawal. The lack of information about this phenomenon leads to the adoption of an exploratory approach, in order to gain an initial understanding of this phenomenon.

The definitions reviewed about disidentification present this process as a cognitive state in which the self-identity is found to be different from the identity of the group [13, 15, 20, 30]. In addition to the definitions aforementioned, Bhattacharya and Elsbach define disidentification as "schemes that help define a person's self-concept" [31, p. 28]. Thus, taking disidentification as a part of a cognitive scheme makes it possible considering the application of a methodology that helps identify the elements involved in the disidentification decision and how they are related in a structured way. Taking into account these requirements, the Means-End Chain (MEC) approach appears as a valid alternative to understand the cognitive decision-making process by identifying the attributes, consequences and values of the subject of study [32–35].

3.1 The Means-End Chain Approach

Means-End Chain (MEC) is an approach used for understanding decision making processes based on a model of consumers' cognitive structures, making it possible to identify how product or service characteristics are associated to a value (or end) de-sired by the consumer [32, 34]. MEC is based on the linkage of three cognitive levels: the attributes (or means) of the product/service; the consequences for the consumer, which are a result of the attributes; and the personal values (or ends), related to the satisfaction of consequences and values which are relevant to the person [36]. As a result, a hierarchical chain connecting concepts, going from the more concrete (the attributes) to more abstract (the values), illustrates the elements and their relationships to explain the subject of study [37]. MEC argues that attributes of the product per-se are not very relevant for the consumer, as their relevance come from the consequences that the attributes are expected to bring. In turn, the ends of the chain are often a desired personal goal or life values [37]. In other words, the decision maker bases his/her choices not on the product or service itself, but on the extent to which the product/service may contribute to achieving his/her goals.

Comparing the characteristics of MEC with SIT, both study cognitive processes (decision making and identification processes) that are ultimately concerned with the creation/reaffirmation of the self-concept. Thus, the use of MEC as the main method makes sense as it will help to understand the SNS withdrawal/disidentification process as it can help identify the elements involved in the decision, as well as relations be-tween these elements using the techniques proposed for this method.

Definitions about these elements are similar across researchers using this model, originally proposed by [38]. One of the clearest definitions is provided by Reynolds and Gutman as follows:

> "Attributes are features or aspects of products or services. Consequences accrue to people from consuming products or services. They may be desirable (benefits) or undesirable. Values, or end states, are important beliefs people hold about themselves and about their feelings concerning others' beliefs about them." [39 p. 31]

Latter models established different categories for each element. For example, the model proposed by Olson and Reynolds [40] offers a higher level of detail about the attributes, consequences and values. However, Olson and Reynolds [37] argue that six levels tend to overcomplicate the data analysis, thus proposing the standard three elements model.

In the IS – online context, MEC has gained popularity due to its usefulness for uncovering users' motivation in the decision-making process [41–44]. Abeele and Zaman [45] did a review about how MEC has been applied to Human-Computer Interaction (HCI) allowing them to understand user's choices. Likewise, [42] applied the MEC theory to SNS, combining this theory with Uses and Gratification in order to elicit the reasons for SNS adoption. MEC theory proposes a mixed methodology combining qualitative techniques for data collection using laddered interviews which are codified using content analysis, with quantitative analysis by quantifying the relationships between the codes. The nodes and relationships obtained are presented graphically using a Hierarchical Value Map (HVM). For a detailed explanation of each technique see the work of Reynolds and Gutman [36], Bech-Larsen and Nielsen [46] and Reynolds et al. [47].

Applying Social Network Analysis

A number of MEC researchers have questioned the application of a Hierarchical Value Map (HVM) as an accurate way of representing relationships among the elements identified [33, 34, 48–50]. The main argument against the HVM is related to the rigid structure of the map, which does not allow recursive relationships (loops) as well as the assumption that the asymmetry of the relationships cannot be taken for granted, as explained by [34]. Implementing Social Network Analysis (SNA) techniques is an alternative growing in popularity, due to the flexibility in analysing laddering data graphically and quantitatively.

The analysis is based on centrality, as the main concept for the analysis, having a similarity between the in-degree and out-degree summary to the From–To table proposed by Gutman [38] in the original MEC method. Both of them aim to find the most influential elements on the ladders. One of the earliest publications using SNA in MEC was by Pieters et al. [51], who used abstractedness, centrality and prestige as measures to analyse consumer goal structures. According to Pieters, the higher the abstractedness, the more connections are established with elements in a higher level. Applying this definition to the MEC, nodes with a high abstractness index are associated to high level elements in the chain. (i.e. the Values) Conversely, low values of abstractedness are associated with low levels in the chain (i.e. attributes). An element with high centrality has a large proportion of connections passing through it. Finally, high prestige suggests that the element is the destination of other elements.

On the practical side, each chain created for the MEC analysis has to be translated into the SNA format, in which the chains have to be decomposed in dyads. The literature suggests using direct relationships to create the implication matrix for the net-work. Consequently, the chain (a) SNS dependency (c) addiction (v) keep regain control (codes: 32 – 38- 87- 80) is decomposed by 32 -38, 38-87 and 87-80 dyads.

Due to the numbers of elements (or nodes in the SNA jargon), the network became quite large, making it necessary to introduce an extra step before creating the map [52]. Hansen et al. [52] recommend merging duplicated dyads, due to the inflating effect that this can have for some measures such as the centrality degree. Following this rec-ommendation, duplicated dyads were merged, producing a new column called edge weight which was created to keep the information about the repetition of the dyads. The importance of this step is that the edge weight is what MEC researchers use as the cut-off level [48, 49].

Sample

The participants were sought based on two conditions: The first is that the person must have had a closed SNS account at the time of the interview to be considered for the sample and the second is being resident in the UK, preferably in Newcastle upon Tyne, the city where the researcher was based at the time of the study. The first condition was required in order to follow the definition adopted for SNS withdrawal. In addition, closing an SNS account requires going through a process that is not always easy, as users who have closed their profile may have stronger reasons than those who just stop using the SNS.

This research aims to understand withdrawal based on the detail of the information that the interviewees provide to find the similarities as well as the differences between different networks and individuals. Once the data collection was started, it was found that there was a scarcity of people satisfying the condition of having an account closed which enforced the decision of keeping the sample open to different networks rather than focusing on a specific SNS. Due to the characteristics of the profile, participants were recruited through a snowball sampling which is a common method among SNS researchers [42, 53–56] as well as SIT [57–59]. Participation was completely voluntary and before starting each interview, every person was informed about the purpose of the research, followed by signing a consent form.

A total of 26 face to face interviews were held, exceeding the accepted rule of thumb of at least 20 respondents for laddered interviews (Reynolds et al. [47]). About the sample, 61.54% were women (with an age average age of 31.18 years old) and 38.46% men (average age 27.8 years old). Regarding the occupation, the main groups were people working and postgraduate students with 42.31% each. From the first group, 38.46% are full-time employees and 3.85% part-time; of the students, 34.62% were doing their PhD 7.69% and a Master. The SNS they were part of were Facebook (50%), Twitter (19.23%), MySpace (15.38%), Bebo (11.54) (there were two cases who had closed their profiles in both Networks) and other SNS represented 11.54% of the sample.

4   Data Analysis

All the interviews were transcribed verbatim using NVIVO 10 for the codification phase. As a result, 37 Attributes, 39 Consequences and 18 Values were identified and a total of 401 chains were identified in total. Each chain was loaded into Microsoft Excel to create the implication matrix and undertake further analysis related to the MEC and SNA indices.

For creating the map of the chains using SNA, the first decision for the analysis was the selection of the cut-off level. The traditional MEC method recommends a level between 3 and 5, whereas a level around 6 is recommended for network analysis [33, 50]. To find the most appropriated cut-off level, a top-down ranking strategy was implemented [60] using the software NodeXL [52, 61] to compare the different outputs.

In Fig. 3, attributes are represented by circles, consequences by squares and values by triangles. The size of the figures represents the degree centrality, in which the bigger the size of the figure (circles for attributes, squares for consequences and triangles for values) the more important is its role in the network. The layout selected for the network was the Harel-Koren Fast Multi-scaling as this method places adjacent nodes close to each other [52], making the analysis more straightforward. A cut-off level of four offers enough level of detail with a moderate level of complexity.

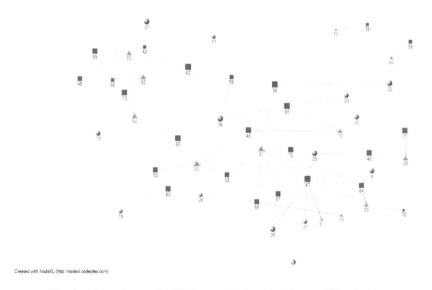

Fig. 3. Network map for SNS user withdrawal with cut-off level = 4

An additional criterion for defining the cut-off level in MEC is the proportion of active links in relation to the number of active cells [42, 49, 51]. This proportion is calculated based on the whole universe of elements (cells and links) to evaluate the loss of information out of the total data set. In this case, levels three and four offered the best balance between data reduction and retention [42]. Based on the graphics and the cells/links criteria, a cut-off level of four was selected as this provides 36% of information using 7% of the elements present in the implication matrix.

4.1 Social Network Analysis

An initial analysis of the SNA indices shows how abstractedness and prestige values follow previous research patterns, in which lower scores are related to low levels of abstraction (attributes), whereas the higher scores of abstractedness and prestige are for values. The advantage of prestige is that it is calculated over the total of the connections, giving a better measure of the importance of this reason for the whole network. Table 1 presents the top reasons by prestige wherein the highest score is to keep – regain control, making this the most prominent reason to leave the network. This means that the former SNS users felt that they were not in control of SNS, and therefore withdrawing from the networks could help them regain control. This finding contrast with the findings of Buffardi and Campbell [62] and Papacharissi [63] about the control of the image that people want to portray in SNS. The second value is the emotional stability, meaning that the SNS they were using was causing trouble, affecting their emotional wellbeing or their mental stability. This varied from relation-ship break-ups to negative or offensive content on the network. The third item is exposure of self which represents the issues related with the exposure of personal information or exposure of the user in general terms to others, for example, being tagged in photos by other people.

Table 1. Abstractedness and prestige

ID	Reason	Abstractedness	Prestige
87	Keep - regain control	89%	7.3%
80	Emotional stability	100%	5.5%
47	Exposure of self	49%	4.5%
85	Image - impression management	98%	4%
94	Time management	95%	3.8%
92	Productivity – work	100%	3.4%
93	Simplify life	91.9%	3.4%

Analysing centrality in Table 2, it shows how the consequence Exposure of self plays an important role as connector between attributes and values, meaning that many of the reasons given by the interviewees involved the exposure of self as part of the problem. It is interesting to find evidence suggesting that to keep – regain control and emotional stability play a role not only as a receiver of consequences, illustrated in its prestige score, but also in terms of connecting with other less frequent values. Likewise, personal information out there plays a similar role within the attributes. Based on the centrality personal information out there (26) -> exposure of self (47) -> keep - regain control (87) and the fact that they are connected, it can be said that this is the most frequent path within the network or, in MEC terms, the strongest ladder.

Table 2. Centrality

ID	Reason	Centrality
47	Exposure of self	9.1%
87	Keep - regain control	8.2%
80	Emotional - mental stability	5.5%
64	Others' perception	5.5%
62	Not useful anymore	5.5%
26	Personal information out there	5.3

5 Discussion

The combination of Social Network Analysis and Means-End Chain make it possible to establish the main reasons that move a user to close the profile in an SNS and, furthermore, to conceptualise the relationships between these reasons. From the analysis, the elements with high out-degree levels make it possible to identify the main triggers to close the SNS, which are usually related to the MEC attributes. Similarly, the elements with a high in-degree level make it possible to identify the ultimate reasons that motivated the SNS withdrawal which are related to the values in the ACV chain.

First Group: Impression Management
Considering the elements present on the ladders identified, it was found that the main reason is related with the control that former users wanted to have over their profile, including who can access their information, as well as privacy issues. The attributes presented in the ladders show how most of the interviewees were concerned about the personal information being available in the network and the people looking at their profile. Both attributes were connected to the values through the consequence "exposure of self". Consequently, the exposure of the online persona and the information attached to it were identified as the main concerns for the former SNS users. These elements show that users have the need to feel in control of their online persona, on the one hand, controlling the information available about them, and on the other hand, the people that are looking at their information. This last point reveals an interesting situation in which the privacy becomes a blurry line related with who can see the user's information and the awareness that people have about the things they post on the SNS.

The control of the perceptions that other people create about the individual has been acknowledged through the research, namely, Impression Management Theory [25], and more recently in SNS environments by Krasnova et al. [1], Ellison et al. [64], Ellison et al. [65], Nadkarni and Hofmann [66]. These aforesaid authors have highlighted the opportunity that these networks provide for having a better control of the self-presentation process. [1, 62, 64, 67, 68].

Second Group: Friendship
A second group of ladders is related with friendship and how users are related to others. The values included in this group are related with the importance of the people in the network and the quality of relationships. These ladders give an insight into the changes

that relationships have had since the SNS became popular. Now the word 'friend' has different implications and being in a relationship is official when it is public on Facebook. In the words of Interviewee 13, "I think it's a distorted idea of a friends list I think". But curiously, despite the virtual component of the SNS interactions, there are still some manners inherited from the offline world that are applied here, making the SNS relations something more complex. For example, Interviewee 13 will not deny any friend request out of politeness and would rather ignore or unfriend afterwards.

Talking about the amount and relevance of the information posted by the members of the personal network, the growing number of posts in the timeline generates an overwhelming feeling in the users. Interviewee 8 commented: "Posting too much, yes that's one that would get on my wick..., I don't want to see pictures of their kids, pictures of their dogs, I don't care, I don't want to know if they're lying in bed eating nachos or something like that". The annoyance with the overload of information is mainly due to the perception of it being unnecessary which is based not only on the content of the post, but also the frequency of posting and the opinion that the person has about the author of the post. Interviewee 8 commented in this regard that the continuous post of a close friend on his vacations is not the same as the continuous post of an acquaintance talking about everyday activities. This point is evidence of the level of subjectivity of the information on the SNS, and how information gains or loss relevance is consequently based on who is posting. This situation contrasts with the networking gratifications which have been identified as an important factor for participating in an SNS [69–78]. The problem of an overflow of information has been identified by different SNSs who have different alternatives to manage this issue. Facebook developed an algorithm to select the posts that will be displayed on the wall; Twitter proposed the lists to group the contacts they are following and Google + created circles.

Third Group: Time Management

The third group includes values related with the users' concern about the time spent on the network and the impact on their productivity. The interviewees agreed on how once the hype of the SNS is gone, they started to be more conscious about their time management or started spending the SNS time on other types of activity. The values in this group find their origins in the unnecessary information posted on the timeline, generating the perception that the SNS is not as useful as before, hence the time spent on it is taken as a waste of time. Likewise, former users found themselves spending too much time looking at other people's profiles, reducing the time for the other tasks they were supposed to do during the day (Interviewees 1, 5, 14, 23 and 24). In fact, once people stop using the SNS they realise how much time they have on their hands, as in the case of Interviewee 20, who felt she had recovered four hours per day of her time. In addition to the time spent reading content on the network, some people found themselves spending a fair amount of time planning what they were going to post on their profiles. Interviewee 24 said in this regard "I would spend 10 min to get a good sentence. I will get the wording right, the syntax right, etc." This example shows how the efforts to project a certain image to others results in the time spent planning their post, including the decision whether to publish the post, and if the post is not published the time lost is even worse. One factor that has an influence on the impact of time management and productivity is the age group of the sample, as adult people have more responsibilities that require their time and attention, and if they spend the time on the SNS these responsibilities will be affected.

Fourth Group: Emotional Stability

In the fourth group, the ladders are related with making life simpler and emotional stability. The interviews revealed how SNS are becoming an extra source of situations that can complicate users' lives. The first ladder is identified by usability issues, showing how when the user finds difficulties at the time of using the network, it leads to a decrease in the frequency of use to the point of closing the account. Ease of use has been studied by models like Theory of Planned Behaviour [1, 76] and Technology Adoption Model [79, 80] among others, showing its relevance for SNS adoption and participation. The perception of the difficulties of use comes from two sources mainly. The first one is related with the fact that users could not figure out the way the SNS works, not only from the technical aspect, but the purpose of the network. This difficulty was frequently found on Twitter users, as people were used to Facebook and the change ended in a bad experience, as in the case of Interviewee 17. The second case comes from SNS updating the layout, tools and policies. These changes discourage the use and produce frustration for the users (Interviewees 5, 6, 14 and 17) as they feel that they cannot cope with the pace of the updates and they are used to finding the buttons and menus at specific places. So, whenever there is any change they feel annoyed, especially when the changes are frequent, as Interviewee 14 who said "they keep changing the damn thing as well! And as soon as you get used to one, well sort of, used to the buttons that I know how to use, they damn well move them!" showing how changes affect the intention of use.

The ladders related with emotional stability show how people can be affected by the content of the post they find in their timelines (Offensive negative comments- 19). But it is not only the presence of explicit negative comments, as happened to Interviewee 19, who was bullied through the SNS, but also the positive posts of other people that produce negative reactions in the readers (i.e. jealousy or envy, as happened to Interviewee 13, 15 and 20). The feeling of other people achieving things that you as the reader have not, makes the reader feel bad or inferior. This happened to Interviewee 5 with some friends and their photos of engagement, kids or the happy life they portrayed which made her feel uncomfortable. Interviewee 13 pointed out how people can still feel bad even when they know that what others have posted is not true (or partially true), showing the impact of others' publications on the self-esteem of the people. People's fake posts are explained by narcissistic behaviour on the SNS [67], but the impact of these posts on others' self-esteem needs further re-search, as well as how and why people think that posts are not true. Some researchers have studied the opposite case of people feeling happy with the bad news of others which is known as "schadenfreude" [58], which is an open field for further research.

5.1   The SIT Perspective

From the SIT perspective, the ladders related with the loss of control follow the uncertainty reduction process as the users' effort at projecting an identity (real or desired) is challenged by the control that other users and the network itself are taking by being able to post/filter information about them. As a consequence, users prefer to close the profile in order to take back the control of the image they want to portray. This is exemplified by Interviewee 1 saying "if somebody wants to meet me, he can call", showing how being away from the network allows him to control the image and the information he wants to share with other people who are interested in that. In contrast, the ladders related with impression management and employability follow the self-enhancement process as they are trying to create and maintain an image of professionalism that otherwise could affect their future career as well as personal projects. Thus, the distinctiveness from previous stages in their lives or from groups that may impact on the image they want to portray now allows them to reinforce the belief that their identity does not fit the identity of the group they belong to on the SNS, generating the disidentification process explained by [30]. Disidentification can be due to differences with the organisation or with the members. In this case, the organisation is the platform, and users are the members. To some extent, former users now consider their previous SNS a necessary evil, like Interviewee 1, showing characteristics of the negative relational categorisation proposed by Elsbach and Bhattacharya.

The need to improve the quality of the relationships can be explained by the need for belongingness [66, 81], as users need meaningful interactions that provide part of feeling part of the group. In addition, belongingness can be analysed from the self-enhancement process from the SIT via the distinctiveness that the users are trying to create which is related to the difference of the group that the user belongs to. This in turn reinforces his/her identity [13] maintaining and enhancing the identity of the group [82]. Additionally, the distinctiveness is reinforced in the fact that the user is the one who is withdrawing from the group rather than being excluded or isolated, showing that the decision to retire from the group was their choice which implies a rational process of assessing whether they belong to the group they were in on the SNS. The ladders related with time management and productivity follow the uncertainty reduction process. Former users were trying to block an undesired behaviour that was generating a problem to keep their identity aligned to the groups and activities they are interested in participating in, e.g. keeping their jobs or keeping their place in the university and progress in their degree.

The noxious information present in the SNS impacts on the emotional stability of the user, especially their self-esteem which is one of the pillars of the identification process, making the user avoid people who are a source of negative information. This is a distinctiveness strategy, as they do not want to be in the same group, and in some cases, do not want to be associated with the authors of noxious information. Thus, the self-enhancement process from the SIT makes it possible to understand SNS disidentification, as this process is based on the differences with the people posting the unwanted information. On the other hand, the difficulties with the SNS usage follow the uncertainty reduction process as the interviewees showed a preference for platforms that are more stable. The reason for this preference is that they are used to the layout, so they know where to find the tools and services they use regularly and changes in the SNS make them feel they need to learn how to use it again. Accordingly, the disidentification process occurs from the users to the platform as they do not feel comfortable/confident using the SNS.

6   Conclusions

The research was aimed to identify the main reasons for SNS withdrawal which were grouped in four major categories. For the first category, former users felt that they were not in control of their information any more, as other users had the chance to read and post information related to them. For the second category, former SNS users were in the pursuit of more meaningful relationships with the members of their network. This group suggested that when talking about friendship online quantity does not mean quality. Closing the SNS profile helped them to concentrate on fewer contacts that are closer to the person, making the friendship relation more meaningful.

Regarding the third category, time management and productivity, the interviewees agreed when it came to the impact that the SNS was having on their available time and time management and how they found themselves spending several hours just looking around others' profiles or editing the information on their profiles. The age of the sample allowed inferring how the everyday responsibilities made former users more critical about the time spent on the SNS and how they felt guilty after spending time on the network. For the fourth category, emotional stability and how SNS had complicated modern life instead of making it easier, the emotional stability was affected by negative information appearing on the SNS affecting users' self-concept and self-esteem. Negative information includes even positive information that had a negative effect on the user. The part related with making life easier is related with the complications that SNS users have when they work with a new network or when the SNS updated its features. It is very common to read of Facebook users complaining every time there is a change to the Network.

As part of the contributions, it was found that people continuously assess their identification with the people there (peer identification), but also their identification with the platform. SNS is a trendy world, so people want to be associated with the trendy ones and non-related with the outdated ones. For example, adults have a bad perception of their peers still using Myspace, as this SNS is associated with teenagers. Given the exploratory nature of this research, further investigation is required to expand the findings obtained in this research and to what extend each of the four groups identified influence the SNS withdrawal decision.

References

1. Krasnova, H., et al.: Why participate in an online social network: an empirical analysis. In: 16th European Conference on Information Systems ECIS 2008, National, Galway, Ireland (2008)

2. Al-Debei, M.M., Al-Lozi, E., Papazafeiropoulou, A.: Why people keep coming back to Facebook: explaining and predicting continuance participation from an extended theory of planned behaviour perspective. Decis. Support Syst. **55**(1), 43–54 (2013)
3. Garcia, D., Mavrodiev, P., Schweitzer, F.: Social resilience in online communities: the autopsy of friendster. In: Proceedings of the First ACM Conference on Online Social Networks. ACM (2013)
4. Hargittai, E.: Whose space? Differences among users and non-users of social network sites. J. Comput.-Mediat. Commun. **13**(1), 276–297 (2007)
5. Joinson, A.N.: 'Looking at', 'looking up' or 'keeping up with' people? Motives and uses of Facebook, Florence (2008)
6. Shi, N., et al.: The continuance of online social networks: how to keep people using Facebook? Koloa, Kauai, HI (2010)
7. Ellison, N.B., Steinfield, C., Lampe, C.: The benefits of facebook "friends:" social capital and college students' use of online social network sites. J. Comput.-Mediat. Commun. **12**(4), 1143–1168 (2007)
8. Nadkarni, A., Hofmann, S.G.: Why do people use Facebook? Pers. Individ. Differ. (2011)
9. Robards, B.: Leaving MySpace, joining Facebook: 'growing up' on social network sites. Continuum **26**(3), 385–398 (2012)
10. Valenzuela, S., Park, N., Kee, K.F.: Is there social capital in a social network site?: Facebook use and college student's life satisfaction, trust, and participation. J. Comput.-Mediat. Commun. **14**(4), 875–901 (2009)
11. Vandenberghe, F.: Reconstructing humants: a humanist critique of actant-network theory. Theor. Cult. Soc. **19**(5–6), 51–67 (2002)
12. Sillaber, C., Chimiak-Opoka, J., Breu, R.: Understanding and modeling usage decline in social networking services. In: Uden, L., Herrera, F., Bajo Pérez, J., Corchado Rodríguez, J. (eds.) 7th International Conference on Knowledge Management in Organizations: Service and Cloud Computing. Advances in Intelligent Systems and Computing, vol. 172. Springer, Heidelberg (2013). doi:10.1007/978-3-642-30867-3_34
13. Ashforth, B.E., Mael, F.: Social identity theory and the organization. Acad. Manag. Rev. **14**(1), 20–39 (1989)
14. Kreiner, G.E., Ashforth, B.E.: Evidence toward an expanded model of organizational identification. J. Organ. Behav. **25**(1), 1–27 (2004)
15. Anand, V., Joshi, M., O'Leary-Kelly, A.M.: An organizational identity approach to strategic groups. Organ. Sci. **24**(2), 571–590 (2013)
16. Sluss, D.M., Ashforth, B.E.: Relational identity and identification: defining ourselves through work relationships. Acad. Manag. Rev. **32**(1), 9–32 (2007)
17. Tajfel, H., Turner, J.C.: The social identity theory of intergroup behavior. In: Austin, W.G., Worchel, S. (eds.) Psychology of Intergroup Relations. Nelson-Hall Publishers, Chicago (1986)
18. Baker, R.K., White, K.M.: Predicting adolescents' use of social networking sites from an extended theory of planned behaviour perspective. Comput. Hum. Behav. **26**(6), 1591–1597 (2010)
19. Hogg, M.A., Abrams, D.: Social Identifications: A Social Psychology of Intergroup Relations and Group Processes. Routledge, London (1988)
20. Kreiner, G.E., Ashforth, B.E., Sluss, D.M.: Identity dynamics in occupational dirty work: integrating social identity and system justification perspectives. Organ. Sci. **17**(5), 619–636 (2006)
21. Steele, C.M.: A threat in the air: how stereotypes shape intellectual identity and performance. Am. Psychol. **52**(6), 613 (1997)

22. Woodcock, A., et al.: The consequences of chronic stereotype threat: domain disidentification and abandonment. J. Pers. Soc. Psychol. **103**(4), 635 (2012)

23. Chen, F.F., Kenrick, D.T.: Repulsion or attraction? Group membership and assumed attitude similarity. J. Pers. Soc. Psychol. **83**(1), 111 (2002)

24. Eidelman, S., Biernat, M.: Derogating black sheep: individual or group protection? J. Exp. Soc. Psychol. **39**(6), 602–609 (2003)

25. Leary, M.R., Kowalski, R.M.: Impression management: a literature review and two-component model. Psychol. Bull. **107**(1), 34 (1990)

26. Zou, X., Morris, M.W., Benet-Martínez, V.: Identity motives and cultural priming: cultural (dis) identification in assimilative and contrastive responses. J. Exp. Soc. Psychol. **44**(4), 1151–1159 (2008)

27. Verkuyten, M., Yildiz, A.A.: National (dis) identification and ethnic and religious identity: a study among Turkish-Dutch Muslims. Pers. Soc. Psychol. Bull. **33**(10), 1448–1462 (2007)

28. Josiassen, A.: Consumer disidentification and its effects on domestic product purchases: an empirical investigation in the Netherlands. J. Mark. **75**(2), 124–140 (2011)

29. Scharff, C.: Young women's negotiations of heterosexual conventions: theorizing sexuality in constructions of 'the feminist'. Sociology **44**(5), 827–842 (2010)

30. Elsbach, K.D., Bhattacharya, C.B.: Defining who you are by what you're not: organizational disidentification and the national rifle association. Organ. Sci. **12**(4), 393–413 (2001)

31. Bhattacharya, C., Elsbach, K.D.: Us versus them: the roles of organizational identification and disidentification in social marketing initiatives. J. Publ. Policy Mark. **21**(1), 26–36 (2002)

32. McIntosh, A.J., Thyne, M.A.: Understanding tourist behavior using means–end chain theory. Ann. Tour. Res. **32**(1), 259–262 (2005)

33. Morandin, G., Bagozzi, R.P., Bergami, M.: Brand community membership and the construction of meaning. Scand. J. Manag. (2013)

34. van Rekom, J., Wierenga, B.: On the hierarchical nature of means-end relationships in laddering data. J. Bus. Res. **60**(4), 401–410 (2007)

35. Botschen, G., Thelen, E.M., Pieters, R.: Using means-end structures for benefit segmentation: an application to services. Eur. J. Mark. **33**(1/2), 38–58 (1999)

36. Reynolds, T.J., Gutman, J.: Laddering theory, method, analysis, and interpretation. J. Advert. Res. **28**(1), 11–31 (1988)

37. Olson, J.C., Reynolds, T.J.: The means-end approach to understanding consumer decision making. In: Reynolds, T.J., Olson, J.C. (eds.) Understanding Consumer Decision Making: The Means-end Approach to Marketing and Advertising Strategy. L. Erlbaum, New Jersey (2001)

38. Gutman, J.: A means-end chain model based on consumer categorization processes. J. Mark. **46**(2), 60–72 (1982)

39. Reynolds, T.J., Gutman, J.: Advertising is image management. J. Advert. Res. 27–37 (1984)

40. Olson, J.C., Reynolds, T.J.: Understanding consumers' cognitive structures: implications for advertising strategy. Advert. Consum. Psychol. **1**, 77–90 (1983)

41. Subramony, D.P.: Why users choose particular web sites over others: introducing a "means-end" approach to human-computer interaction. J. Electron. Commer. Res. **3**(3), 144–161 (2002)

42. Pai, P., Arnott, D.C.: User adoption of social networking sites: eliciting uses and gratifications through a means–end approach. Comput. Hum. Behav. (2012)

43. Xiao, L.: Consumer motivations in online group buying: a means-end chain approach. In: PACIS 2013 Proceedings (2013)

44. Leão, A.L.M., Mello, S.C.: The means-end approach to understanding customer values of a on-line newspaper. BAR-Braz. Adm. Rev. **4**(1), 1–20 (2007)

45. Abeele, V.V., Zaman, B.: Laddering the User Experience! (2009)
46. Bech-Larsen, T., Nielsen, N.A.: A comparison of five elicitation techniques for elicitation of attributes of low involvement products. J. Econ. Psychol. **20**(3), 315–341 (1999)
47. Reynolds, T.J., Dethloff, C., Westberg, S.J.: Advancements in Laddering. Understanding Consumer Decision Making: The Means-End Approach to Marketing and Advertising Strategy, pp. 91–118 (2001)
48. Matook, S.: Conceptualizing means-end chains of user goals as networks. Inf. Manag. **50**(1), 24–32 (2013)
49. Bagozzi, R.P., Sekerka, L.E., Hill, V.: Hierarchical motive structures and their role in moral choices. J. Bus. Ethics **90**(4), 461–486 (2009)
50. Gengler, C.E., Klenosky, D.B., Mulvey, M.S.: Improving the graphic representation of means-end results. Int. J. Res. Mark. **12**(3), 245–256 (1995)
51. Pieters, R., Baumgartner, H., Allen, D.: A means-end chain approach to consumer goal structures. Int. J. Res. Mark. **12**(3), 227–244 (1995)
52. Hansen, D.L., Shneiderman, B., Smith, M.A.: Analysing social media networks with NODEXL. In: Insights from a Connected World 2010. Elsevier Inc., Burlington (2010)
53. Bagozzi, R.P., Dholakia, U.M.: Intentional social action in virtual communities. J. Interact. Mark. **16**(2), 2–21 (2002)
54. Vasalou, A., Joinson, A.N., Courvoisier, D.: Cultural differences, experience with social networks and the nature of "true commitment" in Facebook. Int. J. Hum. Comput. Stud. **68** (10), 719–728 (2010)
55. Ren, Y., Kraut, R., Kiesler, S.: Applying common identity and bond theory to design of online communities. Organ. Stud. **28**(3), 377–408 (2007)
56. Hou, J.: Uses and gratifications of social games: blending social networking and game play. First Monday **16**(7) (2011)
57. Terry, D.J., Hogg, M.A., White, K.M.: The theory of planned behaviour: self-identity, social identity and group norms. Br. J. Soc. Psychol. **38**(3), 225–244 (1999)
58. Havard, C.T.: Glory out of reflected failure: the examination of how rivalry affects sport fans. Sport Manag. Rev. **17**, 243–253 (2013)
59. Valentine, G., Sporton, D.: How other people see you, it's like nothing that's inside': the impact of processes of disidentification and disavowal on young people's subjectivities. Sociology **43**(4), 735–751 (2009)
60. Leppard, P., Russell, C., Cox, D.N.: Improving means-end-chain studies by using a ranking method to construct hierarchical value maps. Food Qual. Prefer. **15**(5), 489–497 (2004)
61. Smith, M., et al.: NodeXL: a free and open network overview, discovery and exploration add-in for Excel 2007/2010 (2010)
62. Buffardi, L.E., Campbell, W.K.: Narcissism and social networking web sites. Pers. Soc. Psychol. Bull. **34**(10), 1303–1314 (2008)
63. Papacharissi, Z.: The presentation of self in virtual life: characteristics of personal home pages. Journal. Mass Commun. Q. **79**(3), 643–660 (2002)
64. Ellison, N., Heino, R., Gibbs, J.: Managing impressions online: self-presentation processes in the online dating environment. J. Comput.-Mediat. Commun. **11**(2), 415–441 (2006)
65. Ellison, N., Steinfield, C., Lampe, C.: Spatially bounded online social networks and social capital. Int. Commun. Assoc. **36**(1–37) (2006)
66. Nadkarni, A., Hofmann, S.G.: Why do people use Facebook? Pers. Individ. Differ. **52**(3), 243–249 (2012)
67. Mehdizadeh, S.: Self-presentation 2.0: narcissism and self-esteem on Facebook. Cyberpsychol. Behav. Soc. Netw. **13**(4), 357–364 (2010)
68. Zhao, S., Grasmuck, S., Martin, J.: Identity construction on Facebook: digital empowerment in anchored relationships. Comput. Hum. Behav. **24**(5), 1816–1836 (2008)

69. Cha, J.: Factors affecting the frequency and amount of social networking site use: motivations, perceptions, and privacy concerns. First Monday **15**(12) (2010)

70. Dimmick, J., Kline, S., Stafford, L.: The gratification niches of personal e-mail and the telephone competition, displacement, and complementarity. Commun. Res. **27**(2), 227–248 (2000)

71. Dimmick, J., et al.: Extending society': the role of personal networks and gratification-utilities in the use of interactive communication media. New Media Soc. **9**(5), 795 (2007)

72. Foregger, S.K.: Uses and gratifications of Facebook.com. Michigan State University (2008)

73. Kim, Y., Sohn, D., Choi, S.M.: Cultural difference in motivations for using social network sites: a comparative study of American and Korean college students. Comput. Hum. Behav. **27**(1), 365–372 (2011)

74. Nyland, R.: The gratification niches of online social networking, e-mail and face-to-face communication. Brigham Young University (2007)

75. Papacharissi, Z., Rubin, A.M.: Predictors of internet use. J. Broadcast. Electron. Media **44**(2), 175–196 (2000)

76. Park, N., Kee, K.F., Valenzuela, S.: Being immersed in social networking environment: Facebook groups, uses and gratifications, and social outcomes. CyberPsychol. Behav. **12**(6), 729–733 (2009)

77. Ramirez Jr., A., et al.: Revisiting interpersonal media competition the gratification niches of instant messaging, e-mail, and the telephone. Commun. Res. **35**(4), 529–547 (2008)

78. Sangwan, S.: Virtual community success: a uses and gratifications perspective. In: HICSS 2005, Proceedings of the 38th Annual Hawaii International Conference on System Sciences 2005 (2005)

79. Kwon, O., Wen, Y.: An empirical study of the factors affecting social network service use. Comput. Hum. Behav. **26**(2), 254–263 (2010)

80. Lorenzo-Romero, C., Del Chiappa, G.: Adoption of social networking sites by Italian. Inf. Syst. e-Bus. Manag. 1–23 (2013)

81. Baumeister, R.F., Leary, M.R.: The need to belong: desire for interpersonal attachments as a fundamental human motivation. Psychol. Bull. **117**(3), 497 (1995)

82. Griepentrog, B.K., et al.: Integrating social identity and the theory of planned behavior: predicting withdrawal from an organizational recruitment process. Pers. Psychol. **65**(4), 723–753 (2012)

When *Follow* is Just One Click Away: Understanding Twitter *Follow* Behavior in the 2016 U.S. Presidential Election

Yu Wang[1]([⊠]), Jiebo Luo[2], and Xiyang Zhang[3]

[1] Laserlike Inc., Mountain View, USA
yu.wang@laserlike.com
[2] Department of Computer Science, University of Rochester, Rochester, USA
jluo@cs.rochester.edu
[3] School of Psychology, Beijing Normal University, Beijing, China
zxy2013@mail.bnu.edu.cn

Abstract. Motivated by the two paradoxical facts that the marginal cost of following one extra candidate is close to zero and that the majority of Twitter users choose to follow only one or two candidates, we study the Twitter *follow* behaviors observed in the 2016 U.S. presidential election. Specifically, we complete the following tasks: (1) analyze Twitter *follow* patterns of the presidential election on Twitter, (2) use negative binomial regression to study the effects of gender and occupation on the number of candidates that one follows, and (3) use multinomial logistic regression to investigate the effects of gender, occupation and celebrities on the choice of candidates to follow.

1 Introduction

President Obama is often credited as the first to extend his political campaign onto social media during his first presidential run in 2008 [36]. Eight years later in the 2016 presidential election, social media was considered to be Donald Trump's most powerful weapon [1,23]. After winning the election, Donald Trump himself commented that tweeting "is a great way of communication" [35]. In his book *Our Revolution*, which reflects on the 2016 presidential campaign, Bernie Sanders suggests that one of the reasons why his campaign did well is the campaign team's success with social media [32]. One opinion shared by both Trump and Sanders is that having a large number of followers on Twitter is an invaluable campaign asset [32,35].

Given the prominent role that Twitter played in the presidential election, a systematic study of how individuals behave on Twitter and the informing factors underlying the observed behavior is warranted. Our work is motivated (1) by the paradoxical observation that most individuals choose to follow only one or two presidential candidates, when the marginal cost of following the fifteen others is just one click away and therefore technically close to zero, and (2) by the common criticism that Twitter *follow* is not a strong signal of support. We started by compiling the entire universe of the 2016 U.S. presidential election on Twitter.

© Springer International Publishing AG 2017
G.L. Ciampaglia et al. (Eds.): SocInfo 2017, Part I, LNCS 10539, pp. 409–425, 2017.
DOI: 10.1007/978-3-319-67217-5_25

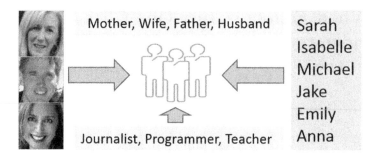

Fig. 1. We use first names, profile images and family roles to identify gender, and we extract from self-descriptions individuals' occupations.

We recorded all the 15.5 million individuals who were following one or more of the 16 candidates in early April, 2016. With such a rich dataset, we are able to (1) explore the most frequent *follow* patterns among these 15.5 million individuals, (2) explore the correlation between following two different candidates and examine the question of electorate polarity, (3) study the effects of gender and occupation on the number of candidates that one chooses to follow with negative binomial regression, and (4) study the effects of gender, occupation and the endorsement of celebrities on the choice of candidates. When coding the variable *gender*, we integrate information from first names, profile images and self descriptions (Fig. 1) and we show in the paper that the effect of gender is consistent across all the three channels.

The contributions of our paper are as follows: (1) we demonstrate to what extent the leading presidential candidates have dominated the Twitter sphere using a weighted follower metric, (2) we quantitatively measure how polarized Twitter followers are when it comes to choosing presidential candidates across party lines, (3) we show that women tend to follow fewer candidates than men and that journalists are more likely to follow a large number of candidates, (4) we find that women tend to follow Democratic candidates, which supports the idea that women vote following party lines [27], and (5) we find that people who follow celebrities such Beyoncé, Lebron James and Lady Gaga are more likely to be following candidates of both parties.

2   Related Literature

Our paper builds on previous literature on electoral studies, data mining and computer vision.

Previous work has studied the increasing polarization of American politics at both the elite level [14,25] and the mass level [6,7]. Druckman *et al.*, in particular, study how elite partisan polarization affects public opinion formation and find that party polarization decreases the impact of substantive information [9]. Social clustering, on the other hand, is analyzed in [2,26]. In our work, we contribute to analyzing political polarization at the public level on Twitter.

Gender plays an important role in the forming and dissolving of relationships [5], in online behavior [30] and in political voting [3,8,19,38]. One common observation is that women tend to vote for women, which is usually referred to as gender affinity effect. In this paper we will analyze specifically the effects of gender on the number of presidential candidates that an individual chooses to follow and on which party that one chooses to follow.

Given the importance of gender in real applications, a large number of studies have attempted to classify gender based on user names [28,29], tweets, screen name and description [4] and friends [40]. Following this line of research, our study will take advantage of information from both user names and user-provided descriptions.

Recent advances in computer vision [15,20,33,34], on the other hand, have made object detection and classification increasingly accurate. In particular, face detection and gender classification [10,17,22] have both achieved very high accuracy, largely thanks to the adoption of deep learning [21] and the availability of large datasets [16,18,31] and more recently [12]. Our paper extracts gender-related information based on Twitter profile images and is related to gender classification using facial features [22,29,37–39].

3   Data

Our dataset includes two components, both of which come from Twitter. The first component consists of the followers' Twitter ID information for all the presidential candidates in April, 2016. This component is exhaustive in the sense that we have recorded all the followers' IDs. In total, there are 15,455,122 individuals following the 16 presidential candidates and some of them are following more than 1 candidate. We transform this component into a 15.5 million by 16 matrix of 1's and 0's, with each row representing an individual and each column a presidential candidate. We report the summary statistics in Table 1[1]. It can be easily observed that Donald Trump and Marco Rubio have the largest numbers of followers among the Republican candidates and that Hillary Clinton and Bernie Sanders have the largest numbers of followers among the Democratic candidates.

The second component of our dataset has 1 million individuals, randomly sampled from the first component.[2] Based on these individuals, we extract user name, user-provided description, the starting year of using Twitter, social capital [38], and the profile image [39].

The third component comprises follower information of Beyoncé, Lady Gaga, Lebron James, three media celebrities all of whom have explicitly endorsed Hillary Clinton. These three celebrities constitute a significant presence among individuals who follow the presidentail candidates: 5.65% of the individuals in the dataset follow Beyoncé, 15.9% follow Lebron James and 19.58% follow Lady

---

[1] The data sets and codes used in our paper are available for download at https://sites.google.com/site/wangyurochester/papers.

[2] To facilitate replication of our results, we have set the random seed (Python) to 11.

Table 1. The number of followers (April, 2016)

Candidate	# Followers	Candidate	# Followers
Chafee (D)	23,282	Clinton (D)	5,855,286
O'Malley (D)	130,119	Sanders (D)	1,859,856
Webb (D)	25,731	Bush	529,820
Carson (R)	1,248,240	Christie (R)	120,934
Cruz (R)	1,012,955	Fiorina (R)	672,863
Kasich (R)	266,534	Huckabee (R)	460,693
Paul (R)	841,663	Rubio (R)	1,329,098
Trump (R)	7,386,778	Walker (R)	226,282

Note: Sorted by party affiliation and alphabetically.

Table 2. Variable definitions

Name	Definition
Independent variables:	
Tweets	Count, number of tweets posted
Social capital	Count, number of followers
Journalist	Binary, a journalist
Name	Binary, female based on first names
Image	Binary, female based on profile images
Description	Binary, female based on self-provided descriptions
Female	Binary, female by first name or image or description
Beyoncé	Binary, follow Beyoncé
Lady Gaga	Binary, follow Lady Gaga
Lebron James	Binary, follow Lebron James
Celebrity	Binary, follow Beyoncé or Lady Gaga or Lebron James
Dependent variables:	
# candidates	Count, number of candidates that one follows
Democrat follower	Binary, follow Democrats only
Republican follower	Binary, follow Republicans only
Independent follower	Binary, follow both Democrats and Republicans
Bernie Sanders	Binary, follow Bernie Sanders
Hillary Clinton	Binary, follow Hillary Clinton

Note: Following [38], we define social capital on Twitter as the raw number of followers.

Gaga. In the book *Our Revolution*, Bernie Sanders also emphasizes the importance of celebrity support [32]. Donald Trump, by contrast, contended that he does not need celebrities to fill up rallies, when Jay Z and Beyoncé held public events to rally votes for Clinton.[3] This data component then enables us to analyze the celebrity effect in a quantitative manner: whether individuals who follow these celebrities are also more likely to follow the candidates who have won the celebrities' endorsement.

We summarize the variables used in this work and their definitions in Table 2.

4   Methodology

4.1   Gender Classification

We employ three methods to extract information on gender. As in several prior studies [28,29], we first compile a list of 800 names, based on appearance frequency on Twitter, that are gender-revealing, such as Mike, Jake, Emily, Isabella and Sarah.[4] This constitutes our first channel. We then use this list to classify individuals whose names are contained in this list. As one would expect, a large number of individuals can not be classified with this list.

Our second channel is the profile image. We train a convolutional neural network using 42,554 weakly labeled images, with a gender ratio of 1:1. These images come from Trump's and Clinton's followers. We infer their labels using the followers' names (channel 1). For validation, we use a manually labeled data set of 1,965 profile images for gender classification. The validation images come from Twitter as well so we can avoid the cross-domain problem. Moreover, they do not intersect with the training samples as they come exclusively from individuals who unfollowed Hillary Clinton before March 2016.

The architecture of our convolutional neural network is reported below in Fig. 2, and we are able to achieve an accuracy of 90.18%, which is adequate for our task.[5]

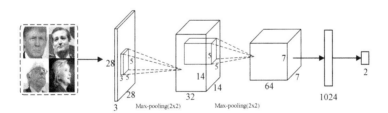

Fig. 2. The CNN model consists of 2 convolutional layers, 2 max-pool layers, and a fully connected layer.

Third, we extract gender-revealing keywords from user-provided descriptions. These keywords are *papa, mama, mom, father, mother, wife* and *husband.*

---

[3] https://www.washingtonpost.com/video/politics/trump-we-dont-need-jay-z-to-fill-up-arenas/2016/11/05/25d536e2-a365-11e6-8864-6f892cad0865_video.html.

[4] The complete name list is available for download on the first author's website.

[5] The trained model has been deployed at our demo website: www.ifacetoday.com/iface.

We prioritize the first channel (first names) most and the third channel (self description) the least. Only when the more prioritized channels are missing do we use the less prioritized channels. Based on this ranking, we are able to label 38.7% of the observations from first names, another 17.2% with profile images and 0.7% with self descriptions. In total, we are able to classify 56.6% of the 1 million individuals. We summarize the number of labeled individuals and the net contribution of each channel in Table 3.

Table 3. 3-channel classification of gender

Channel	First name	Profile image	Self description
Priority	1	2	3
Identification	387,148	304,278	30,786
Contribution	38.7%	17.2%	0.7%

4.2 Negative Binomial Regression

Our work is motivated by the observation that the majority of individuals choose to follow only one or two candidates when the marginal cost of "following" other candidates is just one click away. In order to understand this phenomenon, especially the role that gender plays, we apply the negative binomial regression [11] and link the number of candidates that one follows, which is count data, to the explanatory gender variable. In this regression, the conditional likelihood of the number of candidates that individual j follows, y_j, is formulated as

$$f(y_j|v_j) = \frac{(v_j\mu_j)^{y_j}e^{-v_j\mu_j}}{\Gamma(y_j+1)}$$

where $\mu_j = exp(\mathbf{x_j}\boldsymbol{\beta})$ is the link function that connects our explanatory variables to the number of candidates that one chooses to follow and v_i is a hidden variable with a Gamma($\frac{1}{\alpha}$, α) distribution. After plugging in the explanatory variables, the unconditional log-likelihood function takes the form:

$$\begin{aligned}
\ln L &= \sum_{j=1}^{N}[ln(\Gamma(m+y_j)) - ln(\Gamma(y_j+1)) - ln(\Gamma(m)) \\
&\quad + mln(p_j) + y_jln(1-p_j)] \\
p &= 1/(1+\alpha\mu) \\
m &= 1/\alpha \\
\mu &= exp(\beta_0 + \beta_1\text{Tweets Posted} + \beta_2\text{Follower Count} \\
&\quad + \beta_3\text{Journalist} + \beta_4\text{Year Fixed Effects} \\
&\quad + \boldsymbol{\beta_5} \cdot \textbf{Name} + \boldsymbol{\beta_6} \cdot \textbf{Image} \\
&\quad + \boldsymbol{\beta_7} \cdot \textbf{Description} + \boldsymbol{\beta_8} \cdot \textbf{Female})
\end{aligned}$$

where α is the over-dispersion parameter and will be estimated as well.

4.3   Multinomial Logistic Regression

Besides the number of candidates, another question we try to answer is which candidates one chooses to follow. For this purpose, we identify three classes: (1) follow Democratic candidates only, (2) follow candidates from both parties, and (3) follow Republican candidates only. We use the class c as the dependent variable and formulate the probability of each observation in a multinomial logistic setting [24]:

$$P1 = Pr(c = 1) = \frac{e^{\mathbf{x}\beta_1}}{e^{\mathbf{x}\beta_1} + 1 + e^{\mathbf{x}\beta_3}}$$

$$P2 = Pr(c = 2) = \frac{1}{e^{\mathbf{x}\beta_1} + 1 + e^{\mathbf{x}\beta_3}}$$

$$P3 = Pr(c = 3) = \frac{e^{\mathbf{x}\beta_3}}{e^{\mathbf{x}\beta_1} + 1 + e^{\mathbf{x}\beta_3}}$$

where $\mathbf{x}$ is the vector of explanatory variables: number of posted tweets, number of followers, being a journalist (binary), gender, following a celebrity and year controls. Notice that the coefficients for the second class (following candidates from both parties) have been normalized to 0 to solve the identification problem.

The log-likelihood function then takes the form:

$$\ln L = \sum_{i=1}^{n} [\delta_{1i}\ln(P1) + \delta_{2i}\ln(P2) + \delta_{3i}\ln(P3)]$$

where $\delta_{ij} = 1$ if $i = j$ and 0 otherwise. Note that logistic regression, which we will use to differentiate the celebrity effects on Hillary Clinton and Bernie Sanders, is a special case of the multinomial logistic regression with β_3 set to zero.

5   Results

In this section, we report on (1) election *follow* patterns observed on Twitter (2) negative binomial regression analysis of the number of candidates that one follows (3) multinomial logistic regression analysis of gender affinity effects on the choice of candidates and (4) logistic regression analysis of celebrity effects.

5.1   Election *Follow* Patterns on Twitter

In Table 4, we report on how "committed" each candidate's followers are. By commitment, we mean how many of the followers follow only that one specific candidate. It can be seen that Clinton, Trump and Sanders have highest percentages of 'committed' followers in the Twitter sphere, whereas only 9% of Bush's 529,820 followers follow him alone and 89% of Cruz's 1,012,955 followers follow other candidates besides Cruz. This suggests that while having a large number of followers is always beneficial, not all followers are equally committed.

Table 4. Follower engagement for each candidate (in decimals)

Candidate	# 1	# 2	# 3	# 4	# 5+
Chafee	0.39	0.13	0.08	0.06	0.34
Clinton	0.75	0.16	0.04	0.02	0.04
O'Malley	0.29	0.23	0.17	0.07	0.24
Sanders	0.6	0.23	0.07	0.03	0.07
Webb	0.15	0.13	0.1	0.09	0.52
Bush	0.09	0.16	0.14	0.11	0.51
Carson	0.24	0.19	0.14	0.12	0.3
Christie	0.11	0.13	0.12	0.09	0.56
Cruz	0.11	0.17	0.18	0.15	0.39
Fiorina	0.41	0.15	0.08	0.07	0.29
Kasich	0.25	0.13	0.1	0.08	0.44
Huckabee	0.28	0.15	0.11	0.09	0.37
Paul	0.2	0.16	0.14	0.12	0.38
Rubio	0.25	0.16	0.15	0.13	0.32
Trump	0.72	0.14	0.05	0.03	0.06
Walker	0.14	0.08	0.08	0.08	0.62

Note: '#5+' stands for following five or more presidential candidates. For example, six percent of Trump followers follow five or more candidates.

To overcome this problem, we propose a simple and intuitive method to weight each follower by the reciprocal of the total number of candidates that he or she is following. For example, an individual who follows Bernie Sanders, Donald Trump and Ted Cruz will receive a weight of $\frac{1}{3}$, and an individual who follows Hillary Clinton only will receive a weight of 1. Mathematically, the Twitter share of candidate j is then calculated as:

$$\text{share}_j = \frac{\sum_{i=1}^{n} \delta_{ij} \text{weight}_i}{\sum_{k=1}^{m} \sum_{i=1}^{n} \delta_{ik} \text{weight}_i}$$

$$\text{weight}_i = \frac{1}{\sum_{k=1}^{m} \delta_{ik}}$$

where n is the total number of followers $(15,455,122)$, m is the total number of candidates (16), δ_{ik} is 1 if individual i follows candidate k and 0 otherwise.

After applying this weighting mechanism, we find the Twitter share of the leading candidates, such as Donald Trump, Hillary Clinton and Bernie Sanders, further increases. Their aggregated share of Twitter followers rises from 68.7% to 80.1% (Fig. 3).

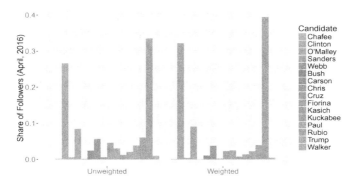

Fig. 3. Share of the three leading candidates further increases after weighting the followers.

We further analyze the top 15 most frequent patterns present in the Twitter sphere (Table 5). One immediate observation is that Trump, Clinton and Sanders are the three dominant forces in the Twitter sphere. 34.5% of the individuals recorded in our exhaustive dataset are following Donald Trump alone. 28.4% are following Hillary Clinton alone. 7.2% are following Sanders alone. These three groups account for 69.9% of the entire recorded population in our dataset. Individuals who follow only Marco Rubio or Carson or Fiorina make up no more than 2% of the population. Individuals who follow both Clinton and Trump constitute 3% of the entire recorded population.[6] Other frequent 2-itemsets [13] include Carson and Trump (1%), Sanders and Trump 0.6/% and Rubio and Trump (1%). The only 3-itemset among the top 15 frequent pattern is Clinton, Sanders and Trump (0.5%).

Table 5. Top 15 most frequent items in the election's Twitter sphere

1	0.345	Trump	9	0.011	Paul
2	0.284	Clinton	10	0.010	Carson Trump [2-itemset]
3	0.072	Sanders	11	0.008	Kuckabee
4	0.030	Clinton Trump [2-itemset]	12	0.007	Cruz
5	0.021	Rubio	13	0.006	Sanders Trump [2-itemset]
6	0.021	Clinton Sanders [2-itemset]	14	0.006	Rubio Trump [2-itemset]
7	0.020	Carson	15	0.005	Clinton Sanders Trump [3-itemset]
8	0.018	Fiorina			

---

[6] This number is surprisingly low and suggests that Twitter 'follow' behavior is more of a signal of support/interest than communication as far as the presidential campaign is concerned.

We further examine how the decision of following one candidate correlates with that of following another candidate using the Pearson correlation coefficient. One immediate observation is that correlation between following candidates from the same party tends to be positive and correlation between following candidates from different parties tends to be negative (Fig. 4). In particular, the correlation is -0.51 between Clinton and Trump and -0.22 between Sanders and Trump. By contrast, Marco Rubio and Ted Cruz have a strong and positive correlation coefficient of 0.43. This constitutes our first piece of evidence that individuals on Twitter are also polarized [6].

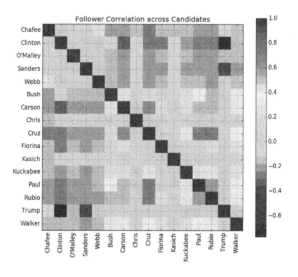

Fig. 4. Party clustering observed in Twitter following behavior. Individuals who follow Trump are more likely to follow Ted Cruz and Marco Rubio and less likely to follow Hillary Clinton or Bernie Sanders.

Motivated by the fact that Twitter *follow* behavior appears to cluster around the two parties, we refer to individuals who follow Democratic candidates exclusively as *Democrat followers* and refer to individuals who follow Republican candidates exclusively as *Republican followers* and lastly we refer to those who follow candidates from both parties as *Independent followers*.[7] It turns out that 92% of the 15.5 million followers are either Democrat followers or Republican followers, i.e., they are following candidates from only one party not both parties, which lends further support to the idea that the public are polarized on Twitter [6].

---

[7] Note that this definition is based on Twitter *follow* behavior not on real party affiliation.

5.2   Negative Binomial: Follow the Candidates

Having summarized the election *follow* patterns as a whole, we are now ready to analyze the factors behind an individual's decision to follow a certain number of candidates. In particular, while the marginal cost of following an extra candidate is close to zero, most individuals choose to follow only 1 or 2 candidates (Fig. 5).

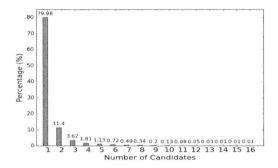

Fig. 5. This figure is generated using all 15.5 million observations. In spite of the low marginal cost of following extra people on Twitter, most individuals chose to follow no more than 2 candidates during the 2016 U.S. presidential election.

In the regression, we use the number of candidates that one follows (# candidates) as the dependent variable. *social capital, journalist* and gender are the three variables that we are particularly interested in. The coefficient on *social capital* would enable us to learn whether more prominent individuals tend to follow more candidates or not. The coefficient on *journalist* measures whether journalists tend to follow a larger number of the presidential candidates (and we expect the answer to be yes). *gender* measures the effects of being female. Following [5,38], we expect the coefficient on *gender* to be negative, i.e., women tend to follow fewer candidates.

We report our regression results in Table 6. Across all the four specifications, we find that *tweets, social capital* and *journalist* are all positively correlated with the number of candidates that one chooses to follow. With respect to gender, we find that regardless of the channel that we use (name in Column 1, image in Column 2, description in Column 3, all the three in Column 4), the coefficient on *female* is consistently negative, suggesting that women are more likely to follow fewer candidates.[8]

5.3   Multinomial Logistic Regression: Gender Affinity Effect

Having demonstrated that women behave differently from men in the number of candidates that they choose to follow, in this subsection we analyze whether

---

[8] In all the specifications, we have controlled for the year fixed effects.

Table 6. Negative binomial: the number of candidates one follows

	Name	Image	Descr.	All
# candidates				
Tweets	2.906***	2.180***	3.543***	2.427***
	(0.146)	(0.134)	(0.418)	(0.105)
Social capital	2.168***	1.153***	0.753	1.282***
	(0.482)	(0.329)	(0.920)	(0.298)
Journalist	0.249***	0.223***	0.0444	0.201***
	(0.0234)	(0.0208)	(0.0646)	(0.0181)
Name	−0.0817***			
	(0.00270)			
Image		−0.0286***		
		(0.00340)		
Description			−0.150***	
			(0.00936)	
Female				−0.0536***
				(0.00230)
Year F.E	Yes	Yes	Yes	Yes
Constant	0.257*	0.268*	0.546	0.299**
	(0.129)	(0.134)	(0.319)	(0.108)
$\ln(\alpha)$				
Constant	−3.804***	−4.327***	−2.046***	−4.320***
	(0.0441)	(0.0826)	(0.0330)	(0.0600)
Observations	387148	294987	30786	557777

Standard errors in parentheses
$^*p < 0.05$, $^{**}p < 0.01$, $^{***}p < 0.001$.

women also differ from men in choosing *which* candidates to follow. We summarize the gender ratio of each candidates' followers in Fig. 6.[9] It can be seen that Clinton has the highest female to male ratio, followed closely by Bernie Sanders. Rand Paul (R) and Jim Webb (D) on the other hand have the lowest female to male ratio. In general, the Democratic candidates mostly have a gender ratio close to or over 40%, while the Republican candidates tend to have a gender ratio well below 40%. Carly Fiorina, the only female candidate in the Republican party, is the only Republican to reach 40%.

Building from previous studies [3, 8, 19, 38], we construct a multinomial logistic regression model to test whether women are more likely to follow Democratic candidates. In addition, we examine whether followers of Beyoncé, Lady Gaga and Lebron James, all of whom have explicitly endorsed Hillary Clinton, thus

---

[9] We used all the three channels to extract gender-related information.

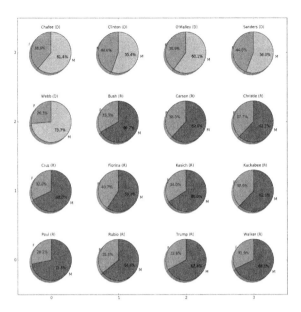

Fig. 6. In percentage, the leading Democratic candidates have more female followers than the leading Republican candidates.

revealing support for Democratic causes, are more likely to follow Democratic candidates exclusively.

We report our results in Table 7. Using *Independent* as the baseline for comparison, we examine the role of social capital, occupation, gender and celebrities. Across all specifications, we find that people with higher social capital and people working as a journalist are more likely to be *Independent* followers, i.e., following candidates from both parties.

From Columns 1 to 4, we examine the role of gender in determining whom to follow. The coefficient on gender is negative for Republican, positive for Democrat and 0 for Independent, suggesting that women are more likely to follow Democrats and less likely to follow Republicans (Fig. 7). This result is consistent across all the four specifications.

From Columns 5 to 8, we examine the role of celebrities in determining whom to follow. The coefficient on celebrity (Beyoncé, Lebron James and Lady Gaga) is negative for both *Democratic follower* and *Republican follower* and 0 for *Independent follower*, suggesting that individuals who are following these celebrities are more likely to follow candidates from both parties. This result is also consistent across all the four specifications (5–8).

Table 7. Multinomial logistic analysis of the choice of candidates to follow

	Name	Image	Descr.	All	Beyoncé	James	Gaga	Celebrity
Democratic follower								
Tweets	−0.909	−0.856	1.561	−0.384	−0.149	−0.296	−0.333	−0.180
	(0.605)	(0.543)	(1.707)	(0.446)	(0.452)	(0.450)	(0.447)	(0.451)
S. Capital	−5.104*	−6.716*	−1.351	−7.334**	−6.521**	−7.145**	−6.831**	−6.757**
	(2.568)	(3.038)	(2.537)	(2.579)	(2.515)	(2.593)	(2.543)	(2.525)
Journalist	−0.749***	−0.677***	−0.536**	−0.640***	−0.646***	−0.668***	−0.651***	−0.664***
	(0.0801)	(0.0686)	(0.206)	(0.0608)	(0.0609)	(0.0610)	(0.0609)	(0.0610)
Name	0.644***							
	(0.0128)							
Image		0.316***						
		(0.0149)						
Description			0.732***					
			(0.0426)					
Female				0.490***	0.516***	0.438***	0.506***	0.490***
				(0.0106)	(0.0107)	(0.0107)	(0.0106)	(0.0106)
Beyoncé					−0.424***			
					(0.0179)			
James						−0.594***		
						(0.0131)		
Lady Gaga							−0.302***	
							(0.0121)	
Celebrity								−0.391***
								(0.0107)
Year F.E	Yes	Yes	Yes	Yes	Yes	Yes	Yes	Yes
Constant	1.924***	1.767**	1.172	1.588***	1.595***	1.619***	1.627***	1.654***
	(0.534)	(0.540)	(1.125)	(0.413)	(0.413)	(0.413)	(0.413)	(0.414)
Independent follower (baseline)								
Republican follower								
Tweets	−25.61***	−18.03***	−14.99***	−22.70***	−21.87***	−22.62***	−22.66***	−22.22***
	(0.842)	(0.741)	(2.059)	(0.618)	(0.619)	(0.619)	(0.619)	(0.619)
S. Capital	−38.05***	−22.61***	−59.30**	−29.51***	−27.58***	−29.51***	−27.82***	−28.07***
	(7.154)	(5.235)	(18.91)	(4.992)	(4.937)	(5.000)	(4.918)	(4.924)
Journalist	−1.838***	−1.804***	−1.506***	−1.838***	−1.851***	−1.859***	−1.858***	−1.871***
	(0.0911)	(0.0834)	(0.222)	(0.0716)	(0.0718)	(0.0717)	(0.0717)	(0.0718)
Name	−0.130***							
	(0.0123)							
Image		−0.0207						
		(0.0148)						
Description			−0.0888*					
			(0.0393)					
Female				−0.0518***	−0.00658	−0.0895***	−0.0237*	−0.0525***
				(0.0104)	(0.0104)	(0.0104)	(0.0104)	(0.0104)
Beyoncé					−0.895***			
					(0.0180)			
James						−0.406***		
						(0.0123)		
Lady Gaga							−0.577***	
							(0.0118)	
Celebrity								−0.545***
								(0.0103)
Year F.E	Yes	Yes	Yes	Yes	Yes	Yes	Yes	Yes
Constant	1.393*	1.422*	0.859	1.203**	1.215**	1.226**	1.265**	1.286**
	(0.582)	(0.575)	(1.226)	(0.449)	(0.449)	(0.449)	(0.450)	(0.450)
Observations	387148	294987	30786	557777	557777	557777	557777	557777

Standard errors in parentheses

$^*p < 0.05$, $^{**}p < 0.01$, $^{***}p < 0.001$.

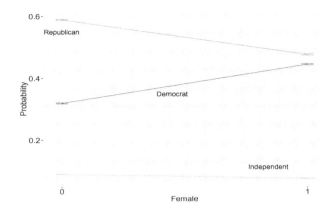

Fig. 7. As indicated by the slope, the effects of being female are positive on Democrat, negative on Republican and slightly negative on Independent.

6   Conclusion

This paper studies the paradoxical observation that while technically the marginal cost of following one extra presidential candidate is just a click a way, most individuals choose to follow only 1 or 2 candidates. Building from an exhaustive dataset that includes 15.5 million records, taking advantage of three information channels (name, image, description), and applying various regression models, we (1) explored the frequent patterns of the 2016 U.S. presidential campaign on Twitter, calculated the weighted presence for each candidate, and measured the extent to which individuals on Twitter are polarized, (2) studied how gender has had an effect on the number of candidates that one chooses to follow, (3) found that females are more likely to be following Democratic candidates exclusively and (4) demonstrated that instead of choosing to follow candidates from the party that has won the celebrities' endorsement, followers of celebrities tend to be more open and more likely to be following candidates from both parties.

Acknowledgments. We acknowledge support from the Department of Political Science at the University of Rochester, from the New York State through the Goergen Institute for Data Science, and from our corporate sponsors. We also thank the three anonymous reviewers for their insightful comments and suggestions.

References

1. Alaimo, K.: Where Donald Trump got his real power. CNN (2016)
2. Barberá, P.: Birds of the same feather tweet together. Bayesian ideal point estimation using Twitter data. Polit. Anal. **23**(1), 76–91 (2015)
3. Brians, C.L.: Women for women? Gender and party bias in voting for female candidates. Am. Polit. Res. (2005)

4. Burger, J.D., Henderson, J., Kim, G., Zarrella, G.: Discriminating gender on Twitter. In: Proceedings of the 2011 Conference on Empirical Methods in Natural Language Processing (2011)
5. Burt, R.S.: Decay functions. Soc. Netw. **22**, 1–28 (2000)
6. Campbell, J.E.: Polarized: Making Sense of a Divided America. Princeton University Press, Princeton (2016)
7. Doherty, C.: 7 things to know about polarization in America. Pew Research Center (2014)
8. Dolan, K.: Is there a "gender affinity effect" in American politics? Information affect, and candidate sex in U.S. House elections. Polit. Res. Q. (2008)
9. Druckman, J.N., Peterson, E., Slothuus, R.: How elite partisan polarization affects public opinion formation. Am. Polit. Sci. Rev. **107**(1), 57–79 (2013)
10. Farfade, S.S., Saberian, M., Li, L.-J.: Multi-view face detection using deep convolutional neural networks. In: ICMR (2015)
11. Greene, W.: Functional forms for the negative binomial model for count data. Econ. Lett. **99**, 585–590 (2008)
12. Guo, Y., Zhang, L., Hu, Y., He, X., Gao, J.: MS-Celeb-1M: a dataset and benchmark for large-scale face recognition. In: Leibe, B., Matas, J., Sebe, N., Welling, M. (eds.) ECCV 2016. LNCS, vol. 9907, pp. 87–102. Springer, Cham (2016). doi:10.1007/978-3-319-46487-9_6
13. Han, J., Kamber, M., Pei, J.: Data Mining: Concepts and Techniques. Morgan Kaufmann, Burlington (2011)
14. Hare, C., Poole, K.T.: The polarization of contemporary american politics. Polity **46**(3), 411–429 (2014)
15. He, K., Zhang, X., Ren, S., Sun, J.: Deep residual learning for image recognition. In: CVPR (2016)
16. Huang, G.B., Ramesh, M., Berg, T., Learned-Miller, E.: Labeled faces in the wild: a database for studying face recognition in unconstrained environments. Technical report, University of Massachusetts (2007)
17. Jia, S., Cristianini, N.: Learning to classify gender from four million images. Pattern Recogn. Lett. (2015)
18. Ricanek Jr., K., Tesafaye, T.: Morph: a longitudinal image database of normal adult age-progression. In: 7th International Conference on Automatic Face and Gesture Recognition (FGR06) (2006)
19. King, D.C., Matland, R.E.: Sex and the grand old party: an experimental investigation of the effect of candidate sex on support for a republican candidate. Am. Polit. Res. (2003)
20. Krizhevsky, A., Sutskever, I., Hinton, G.E.: Imagenet classification with deep convolutional neural networks. In: NIPS (2012)
21. LeCun, Y., Bengio, Y., Hinton, G.: Deep learning. Nature (2015)
22. Levi, G., Hassner, T.: Age and gender classification using deep convolutional neural networks. In: Proceedings of the IEEE Conference on Computer Vision and Pattern Recognition, pp. 34–42 (2015)
23. Lockhart, K.: Watch: why social media is Donald Trump's most powerful weapon. The Telegraph, September 2016
24. Maddala, G.S.: Limited-Dependent and Qualitative Variables in Econometrics. Cambridge University Press, Cambridge (1983)
25. McCarty, N., Poole, K.T., Rosenthal, H.: Does gerrymandering cause polarization? Am. J. Polit. Sci. **53**(3), 666–680 (2009)
26. McPherson, M., Smith-Lovin, L., Cook, J.M.: Birds of a feather: homophily in social networks. Ann. Rev. Sociol. (2001)

27. Miller, C.C.: Why women did not unite to vote against Donald Trump. The New York Times, November 2016

28. Mislove, A., Lehmann, S., Ahn, Y.-Y., Onnela, J.-P., Rosenquist, J.N.: Understanding the demographics of Twitter users. In: Proceedings of the Fifth International AAAI Conference on Weblogs and Social Media (2011)

29. Nilizadeh, S., Groggel, A., Lista, P., Das, S., Ahn, Y.-Y., Kapadia, A., Rojas, F.: Twitter's glass ceiling: the effect of perceived gender on online visibility. In: Proceedings of the Tenth International AAAI Conference on Web and Social Media (2016)

30. Ottoni, R., Pesce, J.P., Casas, D.L., Franciscani Jr., G., Meira Jr., W., Kumaraguru, P., Almeida, V.: Ladies first: analyzing gender roles and behaviors in Pinterest. In: Proceedings of the Seventh International AAAI Conference on Weblogs and Social Media (2013)

31. Phillips, P.J., Wechslerb, H., Huangb, J., Raussa, P.J.: The feret database and evaluation procedure for face-recognition algorithms. Image Vis. Comput. 295–306 (1998)

32. Sanders, B.: Our Revolution: A Future to Believe In. Thomas Dunne Books, New York City (2016)

33. Simonyan, K., Zisserman, A.: Very deep convolutional networks for large-scale image recognition. In: International Conference on Learning Representations 2015 (2015)

34. Srivastava, R.K., Greff, K., Schmidhuber, J.: Highway network. arXiv:1505.00387v2 (2015)

35. Stahl, L.: President-elect trump speaks to a divided country on 60 minutes. CBS (2016)

36. Tumasjan, A., Sprenger, T.O., Sandner, P.G., Welpe, I.M.: Predicting elections with Twitter: what 140 characters reveal about political sentiment. In: Proceedings of the Fourth International AAAI Conference on Weblogs and Social Media (2010)

37. Wang, Y., Feng, Y., Luo, J.: Gender politics in the 2016 U.S. Presidential election: a computer vision approach. In: International Conference on Social Computing, Behavioral-Cultural Modeling and Prediction and Behavior Representation in Modeling and Simulation, pp. 35–45 (2017)

38. Wang, Y., Feng, Y., Zhang, X., Luo, J.: Voting with feet: who are leaving Hillary Clinton and Donald Trump? In: Proceedings of the IEEE Symposium on Multimedia (2016)

39. Wang, Y., Li, Y., Luo, J.: Deciphering the 2016 U.S. Presidential campaign in the Twitter sphere: a comparison of the Trumpists and Clintonists. In: Tenth International AAAI Conference on Web and Social Media (2016)

40. Zamal, F.A., Liu, W., Ruths, D.: Homophily and latent attribute inference: inferring latent attributes of Twitter users from neighbors. In: Proceedings of the Sixth International AAAI Conference on Weblogs and Social Media (2012)

Inferring Spread of Readers' Emotion Affected by Online News

Agus Sulistya[1,2(✉)], Ferdian Thung[1], and David Lo[1]

[1] School of Information Systems, Singapore Management University,
Singapore, Singapore
{aguss.2014,ferdiant.2013,davidlo}@smu.edu.sg
[2] Human Capital Center, PT Telekomunikasi Indonesia, Bandung, Indonesia

Abstract. Depending on the reader, A news article may be viewed from many different perspectives, thus triggering different (and possibly contradicting) emotions. In this paper, we formulate a problem of predicting readers' emotion distribution affected by a news article. Our approach analyzes affective annotations provided by readers of news articles taken from a non-English online news site. We create a new corpus from the annotated articles, and build a domain-specific emotion lexicon and word embedding features. We finally construct a multi-target regression model from a set of features extracted from online news articles. Our experiments show that by combining lexicon and word embedding features, our regression model is able to predict the emotion distribution with RMSE scores between 0.067 to 0.232 for each emotion category.

Keywords: Social emotion · Multi target regression · Machine learning

1 Introduction

Nowadays, online news platforms are popular due to their up-to-date contents, and have become important sources of information. The platforms provide a convenient way for publishers to share latest news that can quickly reach online readers. The platforms also allow readers to interact by providing comments and votes, and by sharing news articles on social media.

Publishers, writers, and many others can potentially benefit from news readers' responses. The responses can be used to measure degree of user engagement. More comments or feedbacks given by readers indicate higher popularity of a news article. The responses can also be used as a clue for placing advertisement. Moreover, readers' responses can help publishers, writers, individuals, and organizations to learn how a certain issue is viewed by the public in general. Such insight can potentially be used by decision makers to make more informed decisions (e.g., on policy and business strategy). Given the value of readers' responses, it would be beneficial to be able to predict *early* how public are likely to respond to a particular issue described in a news article.

A news article should be objective as it is intended only to report facts. This means that readers' opinions to a news article is not contained in the article itself.

© Springer International Publishing AG 2017
G.L. Ciampaglia et al. (Eds.): SocInfo 2017, Part I, LNCS 10539, pp. 426–439, 2017.
DOI: 10.1007/978-3-319-67217-5_26

To give an impression of objectivity, the writers often avoid using overly positive or negative vocabulary, or resort to other means to express their opinion, such as embedding statements in a more complex discourse or argument structure, and quoting other persons who said what they feel [2]. Separate responses to the news, when available, contain readers' opinions and emotions toward the content of the news.

Predicting readers' emotion for a particular article is an emerging research area. Most studies on predicting readers' emotion translate the task into a classification problem, either by considering it as a multi-class classification (assign an article into one of the emotion categories) [7,9,11,19] or a multi-label classification (assign to each articles a set of emotion categories) [21] problem. In this paper, we formulate the problem as a multi-target regression with the goal of predicting readers' *emotion distribution*. By knowing the predicted emotion distribution, we can get a deeper insight on likely readers' responses, e.g., estimated proportion of readers who are happy with a piece of news.

We explore lexicon-based and word-vector-based features, and input them to a regression model to predict emotion distribution. As a case study, we use a popular Indonesian online news, namely detik.com. Our work complements existing works on readers' emotion analysis and prediction. Specifically, our contributions are as follows:

1. We create a new corpus consisting of Indonesian news articles for predicting readers' emotion distribution affected by news articles.
2. We compare the effectiveness of using different parts of news articles (headlines only, contents only, and both headlines and contents) to predict the spread of readers' emotion.
3. We compare the effectiveness of *domain-specific* emotion lexicon and word embeddings with *general purpose* lexicon and word embeddings for the problem of predicting emotion distribution of a news article readers.

The structure of the remainder of this paper is as follows. Related work is presented in Sect. 2. In Sect. 3, we describe the methodology of our proposed approach which consists of 5 main steps: corpus creation, word vector construction, emotion lexicon formation, feature extraction, and regression model learning. We describe our experiments and evaluate the effectiveness of our proposed approach in Sect. 4. Threats to validity is discussed in Sect. 5. We finally conclude and mention future work in Sect. 6.

2   Related Work

Predicting social emotions has been studied in past few years. Most existing works focus on building emotion lexicons or devising prediction algorithm. In this section, we briefly summarize research efforts conducted on these two focuses.

Building Emotion Lexicon. A popular resource for emotion lexicon is WordNetAffect [20], which contains manually assigned affective labels (anger, joy, etc.) to WordNet synsets (i.e., set of synonyms). AffectNet, which is a part of SenticNet project [5], contains around 10,000 words taken from ConceptNet and aligned with WordNetAffect. AffectNet maps common sense knowledge to affective knowledge (i.e., WordNetAffect affective labels). Another popular resource is NRC-EmoLex [13], which consists of 10,000 lemmas (i.e., a base word form that is indexed in the lexicon) annotated with an intensity label for each emotion. These data are manually labeled by multiple annotators. Another approach for building lexicons is through automated means. Staiano and Guerini presented DepecheMood [18], an emotion lexicon that is built by harvesting crowd-sourced affective annotation from a social news network. In the domain of non-English lexicon, Abdaoui et al. [1] built a French lexicon by performing semi-automatic translation and synonym expansion for words in NRC-EmoLex. Nguyen et al. [14] proposed an approach to mine public opinions from Vietnamese text using a domain-specific sentiment dictionary that was built incrementally. In this paper, we extend Staiano and Guerini work [18]. Specifically, we automatically build emotion lexicon using affective-annotated news articles in an under-resource language (Indonesian) from a popular online news platform.

Predicting Social Emotion. SemEval-2007 [19] is considered the first research effort in predicting readers' emotions by analyzing news article headlines. It used news headlines as its data source. Rao et al. [15] proposed an algorithm and pruning strategies to automatically build a word-level emotion dictionary, in which each word is associated with a distribution of social emotions. They also proposed to use topic modeling for constructing a topic-level emotion dictionary, in which each topic is associated with a distribution of social emotions. Lei et al. [9] proposed an approach that performs document selection, Part-Of-Speech (POS) tagging, and social emotion lexicon generation system to detect social emotion. Hsieh et al. [7] proposed a document modeling method that utilizes embeddings of emotion keywords to perform readers' emotion classification. Recent work by Bandhakavi et al. [3] compared General Purpose Emotion Lexicons (GPELs) and Domain-Specific Emotion Lexicons (DSELs) for emotion detection from text. They confirmed the superiority of DSELs for emotion detection. Lin and Chen [10] proposed the use of a regression model to estimate readers' emotion towards news article. They use Chinese character bi-gram, Chinese words, and news metadata as features, and use Support Vector Regression (SVR) as the regression model. Our work complements these research efforts by exploring different sets of features by combining word vectors and emotion lexicon generated from different parts of news articles (headlines, contents and both).

3   Methodology

Overall framework of our approach is depicted in Fig. 1. In *Construct Corpus* step, we collect a set of online news' links that are mentioned in Twitter, and crawl the corresponding news headlines and contents to build our news article corpus. By analyzing the corpus, we build emotion lexicon and train word vectors in *Build Emotion Lexicon* and *Build Word Vector* step, respectively. We

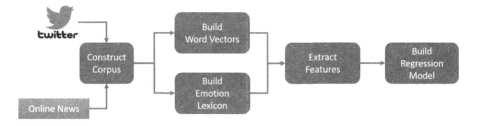

Fig. 1. Our approach's overall framework to predict readers' emotion distribution

extract features based on emotion lexicon and word vectors in *Extract Features* step. In *Build Regression Model* step, we use different combinations of extracted features to build regression models that predict reader's emotion distribution. We elaborate the above-mentioned steps in the following subsections.

3.1 Problem Definition

In this paper, we aim to predict readers' emotion distribution affected by reading a news article. Given a corpus of documents D, with their emotion scores E, where E_i is the emotion score vector for a news article D_i, we want to predict emotion scores E' for a set of new articles D'. An example of a document-emotion score vector of a particular article is: $\langle$ happy:0.4; amused:0.0; inspired:0.0; dont_care:0.6; sad:0.0; afraid:0.0; angry:0.0 $\rangle$.

3.2 Step 1: Construct Corpus

Many news organizations have recognized the potential of social media and have used social media marketing to attract online audiences; for example, by using Twitter to promote certain articles that might interest their readers. Therefore, we are interested in an online news platform that actively tweets news article headlines, and also provide emotion scoring and commenting features for the readers.

We identify an online news platform in Indonesia, namely detik.com. According to Alexa web ranking[1], it is ranked as the most popular online news and the fourth most popular website in Indonesia. The news platform provides features that allow users to give emotion score to a particular article, as shown in Fig. 2. There are eight different emotion categories, which can be translated in English as: *Happy, Amused, Inspired, Don't Care, Annoyed, Sad, Afraid* and *Angry*. The emotion score for each category will be shown in the same page as the article that the scores correspond to.

The online news platform (detik.com) also has a Twitter account: *detikcom*. It has a huge number of followers (13.7 millions as of April 2017) and ranked

---

[1] http://www.alexa.com/topsites/countries/ID.

Fig. 2. A sample of emotion scores of an article published in online news

number 3 in Indonesia in terms of number of followers[2]. This makes detik.com a good source of data for analyzing the sentiment distribution of news articles' readers.

We initially collect news articles that were mentioned in detik.com's Twitter account from November 2016–February 2017. We use Python Tweepy[3] module to get its Twitter timeline. We find that there are many duplicate tweets that refer to the same news article. Online media tend to repost the same content in order to get more traffic, hit multiple time zones, and reach new followers. We remove duplicate tweets by keeping the earliest tweet and removing newer ones. After removing duplicate tweets, we have 36,587 distinct tweets.

We then process the tweets, get their contents, numbers of retweets, and favorite counts. To get the corresponding articles from the online news platform, we extract URLs from the tweets. We build a custom webpage scraper and download the articles pointed to by the URLs. For each article, we get its headline, content and emotion scores.

We remove news articles that have no emotion scores; after this step, we have 11,704 news articles. However, some of these articles may only receive very few emotion votes. We further remove articles that are likely to receive few emotion votes. We use number of comments as a proxy to number of votes[4]. We believe that the number of comments should be less than the number of votes, since it is more difficult and time consuming to write a comment, as compared to providing a vote. Therefore, we further filter our dataset to exclude articles that have less than 10 comments. At the end of this step, we have 1,575 articles remaining as our final dataset. Since we want to predict emotion distribution of unseen documents, we order the dataset based on the article's date, and use 80% from the ordered data as our training corpus. This corpus is used for building emotion lexicon and word vector features. The remaining 20% of the ordered set is used as our testing corpus. This corpus is used to evaluate the performance of emotion distribution prediction approaches.

Table 1 reports the average proportion of votes for each emotion for articles in our detik.com dataset. Note that "happy" emotion has a higher score (i.e., most articles receive higher proportion of "happy" votes than other votes) than other

---

[2] https://www.socialbakers.com/statistics/twitter/profiles/indonesia/.

[3] http://www.tweepy.org/.

[4] The website does not provide the number of votes but only the proportion of votes for the various emotions.

Table 1. Average emotion scores from our detik.com dataset

Sentiment	Mean score
Happy	0.41
Amused	0.05
Inspired	0.05
Don't Care	0.18
Annoyed	0.04
Sad	0.09
Afraid	0.02
Angry	0.18

emotions. Possible explanations for this observation is due to characteristics of commenters, or our dataset selection process. The predominance of "happy" emotion has also been found in other datasets used in a related work by Staiano and Guerini [18].

3.3   Step 2: Build Word Vector

Word embedding is a technique to represent words in a form of continuous value vectors. These vectors encode meanings of words. One of the most popular word embedding technique is *word2vec*. *word2vec* uses a shallow neural network to reconstruct contexts of words. Two architectures can be used to generate the vectors: continuous bag-of-words (CBOW) or continuous skip-gram (SG) [12]. For CBOW, a neural network is trained to predict a word based on its surrounding words. In this architecture, the continuous value vector for a word is the vector that is input to the last layer in the network after we input its surrounding words to the network. For SG, a neural network is trained to predict surrounding words based on the current word. In this architecture, the continuous value vector for a word is the vector that is output by the first layer in the network.

Continuous value vectors that are generated by *word2vec* contain semantic meanings of words. Words that appear in similar contexts tend to have similar vector representations. The vectors also have an interesting arithmetic feature. For example, the resultant vector of the following arithmetic operation (vector of brother − vector of man + vector of woman) is pretty similar to the vector of sister. This is related to analogical reasoning where brother is to sister as man is to woman, which is encoded in the vector representation learned by *word2vec*.

Building on top of the success of word embeddings, we learn a custom word embedding from our training corpus. In practice, SG tends to be more effective than CBOW when larger datasets are available [8]. However, due to relatively small size of our training corpus, we use CBOW model to build word vectors. To create word vectors, we first split news articles in the corpus into sentences.

Indonesian texts use the same sentence end symbols as those used in English texts (sentences can end with "?", "!", or "."). We use NLTK's punkt tokenizer[5] for sentence splitting. Given the generated sentences, we train *word2vec* model using Python's gensim module [16]. We compute 300-dimensional word embeddings with CBOW model on our training corpus, without removing stop words. We have 76,752 word vectors generated from our training set.

3.4 Step 3: Build Emotion Lexicon

Emotion lexicon is a dictionary that associates words with emotion categories, such as anger, fear, surprise, sadness, etc. It is typically constructed via crowd-sourcing. In the crowdsourcing process, a group of people is asked to label a set of words by associating each word with one or more basic emotions. Labels from the group of people are then aggregated for each word by summing up vote for each basic emotion. The resultant sums are then normalized across basic emotions, which represent emotion distribution for the corresponding word. The resultant collection of words along with their corresponding emotion distribution is the constructed emotion lexicon.

Another approach to create emotion lexicon is to use a crowd-sourced affective annotation from a social news network, such as the one used in Staiano and Guerini work [18]. Typically, an automated tools such as web crawler is used to get news articles and related emotion scores tagged by readers. By splitting a news article into words, emotion scores for each word in the article are calculated.

To create an emotion lexicon, we first construct a document-by-emotion matrix containing the eight emotion scores for each document. We follow a previous work to create a word-by-emotion matrix [18]. We also create a word-by-document matrix containing normalized word frequency across documents. We multiply the document-by-emotion matrix and the word-by-document matrix to produce a word-by-emotion matrix. In the end, we have 22,346 words and their corresponding eight emotion scores that we refer to as our generated Emolex (Emotion Lexicon). An excerpt of the matrix is shown in Table 2.

Table 2. Sample taken from *word-by-emotion* matrix generated by analyzing our detik.com training corpus

Word	Happy	Amused	Inspired	Don't Care	Annoyed	Sad	Afraid	Angry
Walikota (Mayor)	0.488	0.032	0.087	0.209	0.010	0.028	0.006	0.142
Membunuh (Kill)	0.246	0.038	0.091	0.055	0.017	0.152	0.047	0.354
Pahlawan (Hero)	0.442	0.050	0.051	0.058	0.040	0.080	0.016	0.264

---

[5] http://www.nltk.org/.

3.5   Step 4: Extract Features

A news article contains headline and content. We explore different combinations of news article parts to extract features from, i.e., use only headlines, contents or both. We follow emotion lexicon construction process (described in Sect. 3.4) and word vectors training process (described in Sect. 3.3).

Lexicon Features. We build around 22,000 lexicons tagged with emotion scores as described in Sect. 3.4. We transform each news article in our corpus into a document-by-emotion feature vector by following these steps:

1. We split the considered portion of a news article into words, and then remove the stop words.
2. For each word, we retrieve its emotion score vector from our word-by-emotion matrix.
3. We calculate the emotion vector for the news article by averaging emotion vectors of the words in the news article.

In the end, we have a document-by-emotion matrix of the following dimension: total number of articles in the corpus (1,575) × emotion scores (8). Each document-emotion vector in the matrix represents emotion lexicon features for the corresponding news article.

Word Vector Features. Our set of trained word vectors model include around 76,000 vectors of 300 dimensions. We generate a vector for each news article. To do this, we use a vector-averaging approach, which consists of the following steps:

1. We split the considered portion of a news article into words, and then remove the stop words.
2. For each word, we retrieve its word vector from our trained *word2vec* model.
3. We generate a vector for the news article by averaging word vectors that corresponds to the words in the news article.

As a result, we have a vector for each news article in the corpus. Since we have 1,575 news articles, we get 1,575 × 300 matrix.

3.6   Step 5: Build Regression Model

We formulate our problem as a multi-target regression task. Multi-target regression is a family of regression techniques where there are multiple output variables. In multi-target regression task, a set of training example E is given, where each example is in the form of $(\mathbf{x}, \mathbf{y})$. $\mathbf{x} = \{x_1, x_2, x_3, ..., x_A\}$ is a vector of A attributes and $\mathbf{y} = \{y_1, y_2, y_3, ..., y_T\}$ is a vector of T target values. Multi-target regression learns a model that, given $\mathbf{x}$, predicts all T target values in $\mathbf{y}$ simultaneously. Multi target regression is generally solved by transforming it to multiple single-target regression or adapting the regression algorithm to directly deal with multiple outputs.

Given features extracted from our training corpus, we build a multi-target regression model to predict spread of readers' emotions. We explore different sets of features, i.e. emotion lexicon features (with 8 independent variables), word vector features (with 300 variables), and combination of both.

4   Experiments and Results

In this section, we first describe our experiment setting, baselines used and evaluation metrics. Then, we present our research questions and results of our experiments which answer the questions.

4.1   Experiment Setting and Evaluation

Experiment Setting. Our dataset consists of 1,575 articles. We use 80% of this data as training corpus, and the remaining as testing corpus. Before we build word vector model as described in Sect. 3.3, we preprocess the corpus using Python NLTK and Scikit module. We remove punctuations and non-word characters, and convert the remaining characters into lowercase.

We use Scikit-Learn[6] module to build a multi-target regression model. The module supports multi-target regression by transforming it into multiple single-target regression tasks. The single-target regression algorithm is determined by choosing a base regressor. For choosing a good base regressor, we experimented with different regressors such as Linear Model, Random Forest Regressor, Support Vector Regressor, and Gradient Boosted Regressor. We found that Gradient Boosted regressor achieves the best overall performance compared to other regressors. Therefore, we use this regressor in our experiments.

All experiments were done on an Intel Core i7 CPU, 8 GB RAM notebook running Windows 10 64 bit.

Baseline. We compare our model with two general purpose models that can be used for emotion prediction:

1. We use Sentic-API [6] as a general purpose emotion lexicon. Sentic-API supports Indonesian language. It contains denotative (i.e., semantics) and connotative information (sentics) associated with 50,000 common sense concepts. A word-emotion lexicon that associates words with four dimensions of sentics (pleasantness, attention, sensitivity, and aptitude) is also provided. For each news article, we take the sentics values for each word and compute the average value for each sentics dimension. The generated four average values (i.e., each corresponding to a particular sentics dimension) is the news sentics. These average values are converted to a feature vector that is input to a multi-target regression model. An excerpt of the word-sentics matrix is shown in Table 3.

---

[6] http://scikit-learn.org.

Table 3. An excerpt of Sentic-API's word-sentics matrix

Word	Aptitude	Attention	Pleasantness	Sensitivity
Gembira (Happy)	0.193	0.156	0.504	−0.176
Sedih (Sad)	−0.051	0.266	−0.826	−0.461
Walikota (Mayor)	0.000	0.152	0.079	−0.061

2. We use a freely available word vector model trained using FastText [4] as the general purpose word vector. This model is trained on Wikipedia dataset, and it is available for 294 languages including Indonesian. The pre-trained model has word vectors with dimension of 300, and were obtained using the skip-gram model described in Bojanowski et al.'s paper [4]. For each news article, the word vector associated with each word is collected and averaged. The averaged word vector is considered as the news representation and input to a multi-target regression model.

Evaluation. To measure the effectiveness of our approach and the baselines, we use RMSE (Root Mean Squared Error). RMSE is a widely used evaluation metric when estimating continuous values. It is the square root of the average of squared differences between prediction and actual observation. The metric is defined below:

$$RMSE = \sqrt{\frac{1}{N}\sum_{i=1}^{N}(y_i - \hat{y}_i)^2}$$

where N is the number of documents, y_i is the ground truth of emotion score, and $\hat{y}_i$ is the predicted emotion score.

4.2 Research Questions and Results

RQ1: How effective is the use of different portions of news article (headlines only, contents only, headlines+contents) in predicting emotion scores?

Approach: In this research question, we investigate the effectiveness of using three different portions of news articles: news headlines only, news contents only and combination of news headlines and contents. For each of them, we trained separate *word2vec* models using gensim. We also create different word-by-emotion matrix. Based on the extracted features, we build regression models and calculate RMSE for each emotion category.

Results: Table 4 shows the results of our experiments. We can see that generally, using headline combined with contents performs at least as good as using headline

Table 4. RMSE scores of the emotion lexicon (EM) and word vectors (WV) when considering different portions of news articles: Headlines (H), Contents (C), and Headlines+Contents (H+C)

	Features	Happy	Amused	Inspired	Don't Care	Annoyed	Sad	Afraid	Angry	Average
H	WV	0.299	0.105	0.105	0.230	0.068	0.149	0.039	0.259	0.157
C	WV	0.284	0.107	0.113	0.235	0.063	0.148	0.058	0.243	0.156
H+C	WV	0.278	0.098	0.120	0.213	0.060	0.145	0.077	0.252	0.155
H	EM	0.308	0.071	0.118	0.242	0.071	0.143	0.051	0.239	0.155
C	EM	0.299	0.079	0.111	0.257	0.046	0.142	0.056	0.252	0.155
H+C	EM	0.277	0.103	0.095	0.203	0.056	0.131	0.034	0.216	0.151

or content only. This finding suggests that both headlines and contents contain useful information that can be combined together to create a better model.

RQ2: How effective are the generated emotion lexicon (EM) and word vectors (WV) as compared to the general purpose baselines?

Approach: In this research question, we compare the effectiveness of using emotion lexicon and word vector generated by our approach against the general purpose baselines (see Sect. 4.1) to predict emotion scores distribution. Our previous experiment shows that using news headline combined with news content generally produces better result. Therefore, we use this combination for this experiment.

Results: Table 5 shows the results of our experiments. Our generated emotion lexicon features achieve better performance for predicting scores in all emotion categories, when compared to using Sentics. Similarly, our generated word vectors achieves a better performance, as compared to using a general pre-trained word vector from Wikipedia using FastText. Comparing average RMSE over all emotions, EM outperforms Sentics by 14.7%, while WV outperforms FastText by 84.9%. These results show the usefulness of building domain specific emotion lexicon and training domain specific word vectors.

Table 5. RMSE scores of our generated emotion lexicon (EM) and word vectors (WV) as compared to a general purpose lexicon (Sentics) and word vectors trained on Wikipedia (FastText) on predicting emotion distribution scores

Features	Happy	Amused	Inspired	Don't Care	Annoyed	Sad	Afraid	Angry	Average
EM	0.277	0.103	0.095	0.203	0.056	0.131	0.034	0.216	0.151
Sentics	0.328	0.105	0.114	0.297	0.059	0.154	0.083	0.272	0.177
WV	0.278	0.098	0.120	0.213	0.060	0.145	0.077	0.252	0.155
FastText	0.373	1.695	1.314	0.494	1.385	1.127	1.293	0.54	1.028

RQ3: Can combining emotion lexicon and word embedding vectors improve the performance of the prediction model?

Approach: To answer this question, we combine emotion lexicon and word vector features (EM+WV), and compare it with using emotion lexicon features alone (EM) and word vector features alone (WV). Similar like RQ2, we extract features from both headlines and contents of news articles.

Results: Table 6 shows the results of our experiments. By combining emotion lexicon features and word embedding vector features (EM+WV), the average RMSE score is reduced from 0.151 to 0.130 (13.91%) as compared to EM, and from 0.155 to 0.130 (16.13%) as compared to WV. Therefore, by combining emotion lexicon and word vector features, we can improve performance of the regression model.

Table 6. RMSE scores of the combination of emotion lexicon and word vector features (EM+WV) compared to when each set of features is used alone (EM or WV)

Features	Happy	Amused	Inspired	Don't Care	Annoyed	Sad	Afraid	Angry	Average
EM	0.277	0.103	0.095	0.203	0.056	0.131	0.034	0.216	0.151
WV	0.278	0.098	0.120	0.213	0.060	0.145	0.077	0.252	0.155
EM+WV	0.232	0.090	0.102	0.158	0.067	0.129	0.067	0.193	0.130
Sentics+WV	0.304	0.132	0.133	0.207	0.090	0.166	0.083	0.256	0.171

5   Threats to Validity

There are a number of threats that may affect the validity of our findings. In this section, we discuss threats to internal validity, external validity, and construct validity.

Internal Validity. Threats to internal validity relates to experimenter bias and errors in our implementation. We have checked our implementation, but there could still be errors that we do not notice.

External Validity. Threats to external validity relate to the generalizability of our findings. We have evaluated the effectiveness of our approach to infer readers' emotion scores in a corpus of 1,575 online news articles. In the future, we plan to reduce this threat further by considering a larger set of articles from various online news platforms.

Construct Validity. Threats to construct validity relate to the suitability of our evaluation metric. In this work, we use RMSE as the evaluation metric. RMSE is a standard metric and it has been used as evaluation metrics in past studies such as in [10]. Thus, we believe that threats to construct validity are minimal.

6 Conclusion and Future Work

In this paper, we have presented an approach that use emotion lexicon and word embedding in order to predict readers' emotion scores distribution towards an online news article. We build a new corpus containing around 1,5k Indonesian news articles taken from detik.com along with affective annotations provided by readers of those articles. Our experiments show that, by using combined features of domain-specific emotion lexicon together with word embeddings vectors, we are able to predict the distribution of readers' emotion scores with a Root Mean Squared Error (RMSE) score ranging from 0.067 to 0.232. Our approach is generic and can be easily replicated to other online news platforms that allow readers to provide affective annotations. Our approach can benefit publishers by giving them early insight on expected public response to a particular article, before they actually publish it.

In the future, we plan to evaluate our proposed approach on another corpus. To improve the accuracy of our approach further, we plan to experiment with more features to better characterize different reader emotions. One possibility is by improving accuracy of the emotion lexicon using bag-of-concepts [17] instead of bag-of-words.

Acknowledgments. This research is supported by the National Research Foundation, Prime Minister's Office, Singapore under its International Research Centres in Singapore Funding Initiative, and PT Telekomunikasi Indonesia (Telkom).

References

1. Abdaoui, A., Azé, J., Bringay, S., Grabar, N., Poncelet, P.: Expertise in French health forums. Health Inf. J. 1460458216682356 (2016)
2. Balahur, A., Steinberger, R., Kabadjov, M., Zavarella, V., Van Der Goot, E., Halkia, M., Pouliquen, B., Belyaeva, J.: Sentiment analysis in the news. arXiv preprint (2013). arXiv:1309.6202
3. Bandhakavi, A., Wiratunga, N., Massie, S., Padmanabhan, D.: Lexicon generation for emotion detection from text. IEEE Intell. Syst. **32**(1), 102–108 (2017)
4. Bojanowski, P., Grave, E., Joulin, A., Mikolov, T.: Enriching word vectors with subword information. arXiv preprint (2016). arXiv:1607.04606
5. Cambria, E., Hussain, A.: Sentic Computing: Techniques, Tools, and Applications, vol. 2. Springer Science & Business Media, Netherlands (2012)
6. Cambria, E., Poria, S., Bajpai, R., Schuller, B.W.: Senticnet 4: a semantic resource for sentiment analysis based on conceptual primitives. In: COLING, pp. 2666–2677 (2016)
7. Hsieh, Y.L., Chang, Y.C., Chu, C.H., Hsu, W.L.: How do i look? Publicity mining from distributed keyword representation of socially infused news articles. In: Conference on Empirical Methods in Natural Language Processing, p. 74 (2016)
8. Lai, S., Liu, K., He, S., Zhao, J.: How to generate a good word embedding. IEEE Intell. Syst. **31**(6), 5–14 (2016)
9. Lei, J., Rao, Y., Li, Q., Quan, X., Wenyin, L.: Towards building a social emotion detection system for online news. Future Gener. Comput. Syst. **37**, 438–448 (2014)

10. Lin, K.H.Y., Chen, H.H.: Ranking reader emotions using pairwise loss minimization and emotional distribution regression. In: Proceedings of the Conference on Empirical Methods in Natural Language Processing, pp. 136–144. Association for Computational Linguistics (2008)
11. Lin, K.H.Y., Yang, C., Chen, H.H.: Emotion classification of online news articles from the reader's perspective. In: 2008 IEEE/WIC/ACM International Conference on Web Intelligence and Intelligent Agent Technology, WI-IAT 2008, vol. 1, pp. 220–226. IEEE (2008)
12. Mikolov, T., Chen, K., Corrado, G., Dean, J.: Efficient estimation of word representations in vector space. arXiv preprint (2013). arXiv:1301.3781
13. Mohammad, S.M., Turney, P.D.: Crowdsourcing a word-emotion association lexicon. Comput. Intell. **29**(3), 436–465 (2013)
14. Nam Nguyen, H., Van Le, T., Son Le, H., Vu Pham, T.: Domain specific sentiment dictionary for opinion mining of vietnamese text. In: Murty, M.N., He, X., Chillarige, R.R., Weng, P. (eds.) MIWAI 2014. LNCS, vol. 8875, pp. 136–148. Springer, Cham (2014). doi:10.1007/978-3-319-13365-2_13
15. Rao, Y., Lei, J., Wenyin, L., Li, Q., Chen, M.: Building emotional dictionary for sentiment analysis of online news. World Wide Web **17**(4), 723–742 (2014)
16. Rehurek, R., Sojka, P.: Software framework for topic modelling with large corpora. In: Proceedings of the LREC 2010 Workshop on New Challenges for NLP Frameworks. Citeseer (2010)
17. Sahlgren, M., Cöster, R.: Using bag-of-concepts to improve the performance of support vector machines in text categorization. In: Proceedings of the 20th International Conference on Computational Linguistics, p. 487. Association for Computational Linguistics (2004)
18. Staiano, J., Guerini, M.: Depechemood: a lexicon for emotion analysis from crowd-annotated news. arXiv preprint (2014). arXiv:1405.1605
19. Strapparava, C., Mihalcea, R.: Semeval-2007 task 14: affective text. In: Proceedings of the 4th International Workshop on Semantic Evaluations, pp. 70–74. Association for Computational Linguistics (2007)
20. Strapparava, C., Valitutti, A., et al.: Wordnet affect: an affective extension of wordnet. In: LREC, vol. 4, pp. 1083–1086 (2004)
21. Zhang, Y., Su, L., Yang, Z., Zhao, X., Yuan, X.: Multi-label emotion tagging for online news by supervised topic model. In: Cheng, R., Cui, B., Zhang, Z., Cai, R., Xu, J. (eds.) APWeb 2015. LNCS, vol. 9313, pp. 67–79. Springer, Cham (2015). doi:10.1007/978-3-319-25255-1_6

How Polarized Have We Become? A Multimodal Classification of Trump Followers and Clinton Followers

Yu Wang[(⊠)], Yang Feng, Zhe Hong, Ryan Berger, and Jiebo Luo

University of Rochester, Rochester, NY 14627, USA
yu.wang@laserlike.com

Abstract. Polarization in American politics has been extensively documented and analyzed for decades, and the phenomenon became all the more apparent during the 2016 presidential election, where Trump and Clinton depicted two radically different pictures of America. Inspired by this gaping polarization and the extensive utilization of Twitter during the 2016 presidential campaign, in this paper we take the first step in measuring polarization in social media and we attempt to predict individuals' Twitter following behavior through analyzing ones' everyday tweets, profile images and posted pictures. As such, we treat polarization as a classification problem and study to what extent Trump followers and Clinton followers on Twitter can be distinguished, which in turn serves as a metric of polarization in general. We apply LSTM to processing tweet features and we extract visual features using the VGG neural network. Integrating these two sets of features boosts the overall performance. We are able to achieve an accuracy of 69%, suggesting that the high degree of polarization recorded in the literature has started to manifest itself in social media as well.

Keywords: Polarization · American politics · Donald Trump · Hillary Clinton · LSTM · VGG · Multimedia

1 Introduction

> To see a World in a Grain of Sand
> And a Heaven in a Wild Flower,
> Hold Infinity in the palm of your hand.
> And Eternity in an hour.
> —William Blake

Polarization in American politics has been extensively documented and analyzed for decades, and it became all the more apparent in the 2016 presidential election, with Trump and Clinton depicting two radically different pictures of America and targeting "two different Americas".[1] According to a survey by the Pew

---

[1] http://www.denverpost.com/2016/11/04/clinton-derides-trumps-fitness-he-disparages-her-honesty.

© Springer International Publishing AG 2017
G.L. Ciampaglia et al. (Eds.): SocInfo 2017, Part I, LNCS 10539, pp. 440–456, 2017.
DOI: 10.1007/978-3-319-67217-5_27

Research Center, only 8% of Democrats and Democratic-leaning independents approve of Trump's job performance during the first month of his presidency, as compared to 84% approval rate by Republicans and Republican leaners.[2] A better understanding of the polarization phenomenon is urgently called for (Fig. 1).

Fig. 1. Top left: profile images and tweets from Clinton followers. Bottom right: profile images and tweets from Trump followers. These everyday details constitute the source from which we detect polarization.

Twitter played an important role in the 2016 U.S. presidential election. All the major candidates including Donald Trump, Hillary Clinton, Bernie Sanders and Ted Cruz, have millions of Twitter followers, to whom they can easily reach out to. Candidates formulate issue policies, attack rival candidates and gauge the public opinions via 'likes' [34] over Twitter. Some of the candidates' tweets have even entered into the Democratic and the Republican debates. After winning the election, Donald Trump himself commented that tweeting "is a great way

---

[2] http://www.people-press.org/2017/02/16/in-first-month-views-of-trump-are-already-strongly-felt-deeply-polarized.

of communication" [30]. In his book *Our Revolution*, which reflects on the 2016 presidential campaign, Bernie Sanders suggests that one of the reasons why his campaign did well is the campaign team's success with social media [28]. One opinion shared by both Trump and Sanders is that having a large number of followers on Twitter is an invaluable campaign asset [28,30]. Naturally, being able to distinguish between Trump followers and Clinton followers and understand why individuals choose to follow one candidate but not the other becomes important.

In this paper, we take a first step in analyzing polarization of the public on social media. We treat polarization as a classification problem and study to what extent Trump followers and Clinton followers on Twitter can be distinguished. Our work differs from previous research in two different ways. First, previous work relies on expert-designed questions that have explicit political intonation. Our work, by contrast, tries to gauge one's Twitter following inclination by sifting through their daily tweets, profile images and posted pictures. Second, previous studies focus exclusively on American citizens and rely on small-sized surveys. Our work, boosted by the international reach of social media, includes individuals from all around the world and is several magnitudes larger than any survey-based studies.

We apply LSTM to processing tweet features and we extract visual features using the VGG network. Combining two sets of features, our model attains an accuracy of 69%, indicating that the high degree of polarization recorded in surveys has already manifested itself in social media.

Our contributions can be summarized as follows:

- We analyze the everyday language and pictures of Trump followers and Clinton followers and examine their high-level differences.
- We study political polarization from a completely new, non-invasive and more challenging angle that at the same time covers a larger portion of the population.
- We have made our data publicly available to facilitate replication and stimulate further analysis.

2   Literature Review

Earlier works have studied the increasing polarization of American politics at both the elite level [10,21] and the mass level [3,5,7]. Druckman *et al.*, in particular, study how elite partisan polarization affects public opinion formation and find that party polarization decreases the impact of substantive information [6]. Social clustering, the opposite side of polarization, is analyzed in [1,22]. We contribute to this literature by analyzing polarization at the public level on the social media site Twitter.

There also exist a series of social media studies on the 2016 U.S. presidential election that are the inspiration of ours. The social demographics of Trump followers and Hillary followers are analyzed in [35] using exclusively profile images. Again using profile images, [31,33] further tracked and compared the 'unfollow' behavior of Trump followers and Hillary followers. [34,37], on the other hand, analyze the tweets posted the presidential candidates and draw inference about the followers' preferences based on the observed number of 'likes.' Our work follows this line of research. Compared with previous studies, we utilize both text information and images.

Recursive neural networks (RNN), in particular its variant Long Short Memory Networks (LSTM) [12], have been very successful in modeling sequential data [23,42], with wide applications in text classification [16], especially in sentiment analysis [14,19]. A recent study [27] that is most related to ours uses word embeddings and LSTM to classify as either Democratic or Republican the social media messages posted by people who are known to be either Democrats or Republicans. Our study, by comparison, is more challenging as we attempt to capture political leaning among ordinary Trump/Clinton followers, who may not be Democrats or Republicans and may not even be American voters.

Deep convolutional neural networks (CNN), on the other hand, have proven extremely powerful in image classification, usually reaching or surpassing human performance [11,29,36]. There exist quite a few studies that analyze selfies and other images posted on the social network [4,41]. In particular, researchers have attempted to capture demographic differences (e.g. gender and race) between Trump followers and Clinton followers by examining exclusively the profile images [33,35]. Our work analyzes the same profile images to detect Twitter following inclinations from these images.

3   Problem Definition

We define the problem of measuring polarization on social media as a classification problem: whether the individual under study is following Trump or Clinton. The high-level formulation is

$$\Pr(\text{Predicted Class} = \text{Trump} \mid \text{Tweet, Picture, Trump follower})$$

$$\Pr(\text{Predicted Class} = \text{Clinton} \mid \text{Tweet, Picture, Clinton follower})$$

where **Tweet** and **Picture** are two sets of features and the classes of Trump and Clinton followers are balanced. Tweets and pictures that exhibit a low level of polarization will bring accuracy close to 0.5, whereas a high level of polarization on social media could push accuracy substantially over 0.5.

Note that *follower* is a rather weak concept: it implies neither support nor opposition. At a minimum, it suggests interest. We are acutely aware that polarization might be too strong a word to be associated with Twitter following which is technically just "one click away" [38]. Referring back to William Blake, "to see a world in a grain of sand," we strive to detect traces of polarization as millions of individuals cluster around two most polarized candidates.

4   Data and Preprocessing

On May 8th 2016, Donald Trump had 8.02 million followers and Hillary Clinton had 6.18 million followers. To collect ground-truth data, we first use binary search to identify and remove individuals who were following both candidates and second we randomly select 3905 individuals who are following Donald Trump but not following Hillary Clinton and 3668 individuals who are following Hillary Clinton but not Donald Trump. In order to make our classification task easier, we do not select individuals that were following both candidates[3]. We choose to collect data from a pre-election date because this will partially insulate our study from the effect of Trump winning the election and subsequently becoming the President. The data collection period is reported in Fig. 2.

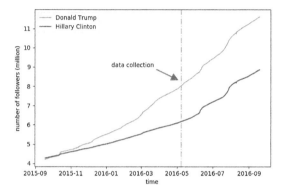

Fig. 2. We collected the IDs of the original seed individuals on May 8th, six months before the election day.

The selected individuals in turn serve as seed users, and we collect their profile images, tweets and posted pictures. While each individual could only have one profile image, the number of tweets and posted pictures is virtually limited. In Table 1, we present the summary statistics of the data used in this paper. Compared with questionnaire-based studies, which have been the norm, our approach is substantially more subtle and voluminous.

4.1   Tweets

Tweets constitute an integral part of our data source. From these tweets we attempt to detect signs of Twitter following inclination. Compared with questionnaires where the surveyed subject takes a passive role and answers a limited

---

[3] Individuals who follow both candidates constitute a surprisingly small portion of the entire follower population. For a more detailed analysis that includes also Bernie Sanders, please see [38].

Table 1. Summary statistics

	Trump followers	Clinton followers
Individuals	3,905	3,668
Tweets	2, 214, 898	2, 172, 591
Profile images	3,096	2,956
Posted pictures	110,000	110,000

number of carefully crafted questions, tweets represent the spontaneous flow of emotions, ideas, thoughts and events.

For example, in what follows we show two questions that are typically used for the study of political polarization [13].

Question 1:
A. Government is almost always wasteful and inefficient.
B. Government often does a better job than people give it credit for.
Question 2:
A. Poor people today have it easy because they can get government benefits without doing anything in return.
B. Poor people have hard lives because government benefits don't go far enough to help them live decently.

Answers to these questions are then transformed into binary values and their mean value is then used to represent an individual's political leaning between left and right.

By comparison, our text data are substantially subtler. Below are four tweets posted by followers of Donald Trump and Hillary Clinton:

@markhoppus how much you gettin an hour out there?
@wizkhalifa like when you finally release your load into the sock
RT @somizi: Topic at church: WISDOM. With it u will be able to survive anything anywhere
@allinwithchris My mom actually went to high school with Dick Cheney in Wyoming. So he is "from there" - just not Lynn. :-) (Weird)
@afc33125: OK ALREADY It's time to CUT OFF #Christie's FREE AIR TIME!!!!!!

To process these tweets, we first tokenize the text using Python's *nltk.tokenize* library which is able to preserve punctuations. An illustrative example is reported below:

Original tweet:
Today is the anniversary of Congress' most deplorable act, an apt day ponder what a petty, partisan, tribal, prick @morning_joe is.
After tokenization:
Today is the anniversary of Congress' most deplorable act, an apt day ponder what a petty, partisan, tribal, prick @morning_joe is.

The summary statistics of the tweets after tokenization is reported in Table 2 and the Fig. 3 shows the distribution of these tweets for each group. It can be observed that while Donald Trump is usually thought of using short and easy-to-understand language, his tweets are statistically longer than Clinton's. Interestingly, the tweets posted by Clinton's followers tend to be longer than those of Trump's followers.

Second, we use a pre-trained word embedding [15,25] to translate each token into an array of dimension 25 and 50 respectively. Word embeddings map words into a higher dimensional vectors that can capture syntactic and semantic patterns and have been widely used in text classification tasks [18,27]. To overcome the limited length of a tweet, we concatenate every 20 tweets from the same individual into a super-tweet and in our final processing super-tweets that are shorter than 100 tokens are discarded. Eventually, we obtain 197,440 training

Table 2. Distribution of tweet lengths

	Mean	Variance	# observations
Clinton	20.4	40.8	3234
Clinton followers	16.2	80.4	2, 172, 591
Trump	21.4	50.2	3602
Trump followers	14.7	69.6	2, 214, 898

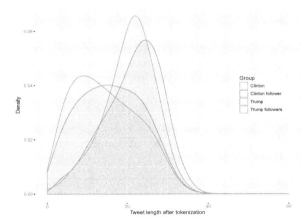

Fig. 3. The length distribution of tweets posted by Clinton, Clinton followers, Trump and Trump followers respectively.

examples (the ratio is balanced with 97,528 for Clinton followers and 99,912 for Trump followers), and 10,000 examples for validation and 10,000 for testing.

4.2 Profile Pictures

With the recent success of deep convolutional neural networks (CNN), profile pictures and selfies have emerged as an integral data source for understanding individuals' demographics, sentiments and habits [4,36,41]. In particular, several studies of the 2016 presidential election have demonstrated the efficacy of using images for modeling political events. [33] studies the unfollowing behavior of men and women, and it relies on a neural network to infer individuals' gender. So does [32], which studies the effects of the 'woman card' controversy.

As each one is confined to having only one profile image, we are able to collect 6,052 profile images. We will attempt to make predictions of one's Twitter following behavior based on the deep features in the these profile images.

4.3 Posted Pictures

Besides profile images, we also collect pictures posted by the seed individuals to train our integrated LSTM-CNN model. In total we have 220,000 posted pictures.

In order to have a better understanding of these images, we first use the VGG neural network to extract deep features. Then we use k-means to cluster these images and use the silhouette coefficient to set the proper number of clusters (i.e., k) to 27. We subsequently merge the clusters that we judge to be of the same category and eventually we get 24 clusters. For each cluster, we are able to label it according to the images therein. The names of these 24 clusters and the associated numbers of images are reported in Table 3.

We notice that the two dominant clusters are text and people indoor respectively and that they are several times larger than the smaller clusters such as food and animal. This indicates that Trump followers and Clinton followers are most likely to post pictures that fall into these two categories. Figure 4 shows that top clusters from our clustering result.

Besides the large variation in cluster sizes, we further explore with-in cluster differences between Trump followers and Clinton followers. In Fig. 5, we show the distribution of images for Trump followers and Clinton followers separately. We observe, for example, more images fall into the sports cluster and the car cluster for Trump clusters. At the same time, more *crowd* and *cartoon* images are posted by Clinton followers than by Trump followers in relative terms.

To test for the statistical significance of these differences, we use score test [33] to each cluster. The test results suggest that Clinton followers have a statistically higher representation in *leader & speaker, table, crowd, catoon, suit & tie, and female*. Trump followers have a statistically higher representation in *sports, vehicle, screenshot, round object, food, and scenery*. Differences in the other clusters, including the top two clusters, *text* and *people indoor*, are not statistically significant. Figure 6 at the end of our paper summarizes our test results.

Table 3. Cluster labeling and sizes

ID	Cluster	# images	ID	Cluster	# images
1	People indoor	3820	13	Screenshot	1542
2	Text	5462	14	Building	1323
3	Leader & speaker	1793	15	Dog & cat	916
4	Sports	1649	16	Round object	1070
5	Soldier	1604	17	Cartoon	1820
6	Car & bus	1086	18	Food	699
7	Table	1381	19	Scenery	1233
8	Animal	676	20	Poster	1604
9	Selfie	1475	21	Square object	1473
10	People outdoor	1715	22	Suit & tie	1463
11	Nature	949	23	Other	1738
12	Crowd	1795	24	Female	1714

Fig. 4. Top left: text; top right: people indoor; bottom left: crowd; bottom right: cartoon.

These variations in distribution among clusters offer us some first evidence that posted pictures can be useful for detecting Twitter following inclination.

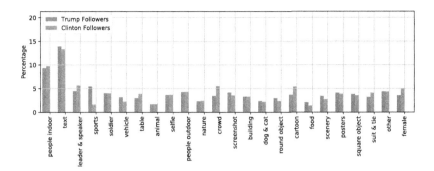

Fig. 5. The distribution of the 24 clusters for Trump followers and Clinton followers. Notice that the weight on the sports cluster is much higher for Trump followers than that for Clinton followers. The opposite holds for the crowd cluster, the cartoon cluster and the female cluster.

5 Experimental Setup

Our experimental design consists of four steps. First we classify tweets only, second we classify posted pictures, third we classify profile images, and fourth we integrate the two using a fusion model.

5.1 Tweet-Based Classification

We first use a pre-trained word embedding (with dimension $D = 25, 50$) [25] to transform the tokens into word vectors. We then set the number of timesteps to 150. Super-tweets that were shorter than 150 are padded with vectors generated from a normal distribution with mean 0 and variance 0.1. For super-tweets longer than 150, we only take the first 150 word vectors. In this way we transform each super-tweet into a matrix of dimension D × 150.

These matrices in turn serve as the input of our LSTM network. To identify the best performing model, we set the dimension of the hidden state to 100 and 200 alternatively. To link the outputs of the LSTM cells to the class label, we experiment with (1) using the output of the last timestep, which has the same dimension as the hidden state, and (2) using the mean output of all the timesteps [9]. The highest accuracy achieved by this model is 67.9%.

Next we compare the performance of SVM with LSTM. Following [18,40], we compute the vector representation of a super-tweet by averaging all the word vectors contained in the super-tweet. Given the padding and truncation operations discussed above, in effect, super-tweet (i) is represented as follows:

$$C_i = (\sum_{j=1}^{150} w_{i,j})/150$$

where $w_{i,j}$ is the word vector for the jth word in super-tweet i and 150 is the number of timesteps that we have previously chosen.

As with LSTM, we experiment with two different dimensions of the input: 25 and 50, both using the RBF kernel. For SVM we find that word representations of dimension 50 yield better performance. Nonetheless, LSTM outperforms SVM in all specifications. We report the details in Table 4.

5.2   Picture-Based Classification

Given the large number of posted pictures in our dataset, we are able to finetune the entire VGG network rather than only the last few fully connected layers. We use 200,000 examples for training (class ratio 1:1), 10,000 samples for validation and another 10,000 samples for testing. The highest accuracy that we obtain is 59.4%.

In absolute terms, this accuracy is low and it reminds of the findings in picture clusters: there are a few clusters where Trump followers and Clinton followers weigh differently, but these are only minor clusters. For the dominant two clusters, *text* and *people indoor*, there is not statistical difference. In relative terms, however, this result is surprisingly high, as it confirms that it is feasible to predict individuals' Twitter following behavior by directly looking at their posted pictures.

Besides finetuning the entire architecture, we also experiment with extracting deep features using the VGG network and then feed these features into an RBF kernel SVM, reminiscent of the classical R-CNN architecture [8,20]. This approach is particularly helpful when the number of training samples is small [24]. With this approach, we are able to achieve an accuracy of 57.0%, which is slightly lower than finetuning the whole architecture.

5.3   Profile Image-Based Classification

Next, we examine the feasibility of predicting Twitter following inclinations using profile images. We have 3,096 profile images from Trump followers and 2,956 profile images of Clinton followers. For each class, we take 500 samples out for validation and another 500 samples for testing.

As explained in the last subsection, we use the VGG network to extract deep features instead of finetuning it. Considering that the deep feature is of dimension 1,000, we further apply a maxpool operation of dimension 10 with stride 10 to the deep feature to obtain a final feature of length 100. We train an SVM using these features and the accuracy is 55.8% (Table 4).

5.4   Tweet and Picture-Based Classification

Lastly, we develop an integrated approach that leverages both tweets and posted pictures. The model is illustrated in Fig. 7. On the left is the LSTM model that processes the super-tweets, and on the right is the VGG model that processes pictures and generates deep features. At the bottom lies the softmax function that incorporates both text features and visual features:

Fig. 6. Clusters within red bounding boxes have a higher representation among Trump followers. Clusters within blue bounding boxes are better represented among Clinton followers. (Color figure online)

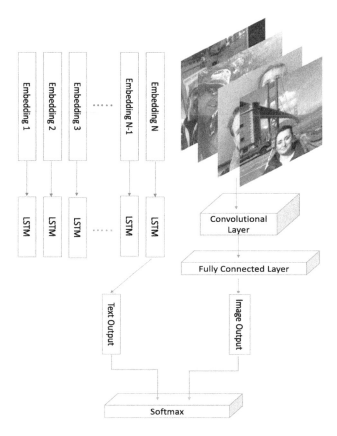

Fig. 7. The left part represents the LSTM component, which generates the text feature. The right part represents the CNN component, which generates the visual feature. The softmax function takes both features as input and generates the prediction.

$$\text{softmax}(W_{text}X_{text} + W_{visual}X_{visual} + Bias)$$

where W_{text} and W_{visual} represent two weight matrices that are to be learned from the data.

As with LSTM, we experiment with different configurations on the dimension of the word embedding, the dimension of the hidden state and the final output feature vector. The highest accuracy achieved by this fusion model is 68.9%, when the word vectors are of length 25, the hidden state is of dimension 100, and the mean output is used as the final output feature (Table 4). It should also be noted that across all specifications, the fusion model uniformly yields the best result.

Table 4. Experiment results

Experiment setup	Tweet		Profile image	Posted picture		Tweet and picture
	SVM*	LSTM	SVM**	SVM**	VGG**	LSTM + VGG
Hidden 100, Embedding 25, Last	61.1	67.8	55.8	57.0	59.4	**68.5**
Hidden 100, Embedding 50, Last	62.1	67.0	55.8	57.0	59.4	**67.6**
Hidden 200, Embedding 25, Last	61.1	67.5	55.8	57.0	59.4	**68.6**
Hidden 200, Embedding 50, Last	62.1	66.8	55.8	57.0	59.4	**67.2**
Hidden 100, Embedding 25, Mean	61.1	67.1	55.8	57.0	59.4	**68.6**
Hidden 100, Embedding 50, Mean	62.1	67.8	55.8	57.0	59.4	**68.9**
Hidden 200, Embedding 25, Mean	61.1	67.2	55.8	56.7	59.4	**68.1**
Hidden 200, Embedding 50, Mean	62.1	67.9	55.8	57.0	59.4	**68.1**

*For the SVM on tweets, we experiment with dimension of 25 and of 50. **These models are not changed as we experiment with different LSTM specifications.

6   Discussion and Future Research

Individual attributes such as age, gender, sentiment and even income, can be estimated using either texts [2,26,39] or images [17,41]. Both data sources certainly contain informative cues about these attributes. Our study suggests that these two approaches are at least capturing some shared hidden information, as the net gain of fusion model is less than than sum of the LSTM model and the VGG model.

Whiles texts and pictures both contribute to a better understanding of an individual's following inclinations, our experiments suggest that 4.4 million tweets contain more information than 220,000 pictures with regard to understanding Twitter following inclinations. Moreover, the best model is the one that uses both texts and pictures.

In terms of time complexity, the fusion model (LSTM + VGG) also outperforms finetuning VGG. For the fusion model, where deep visual features are extracted only once, training 20,000 samples for one epoch takes only about 9.3 min, compared with 2.8 hours for fine-tuning the VGG network for one epoch.

Polarization has been developing for decades, and now we have shown that the phenomenon has started to manifest itself in social media as well. A natural next step is measure and track the evolution of polarization in social media each year parallel with survey-based research. To facilitate this initiative, we have made our data and code available[4].

7   Conclusion

Inspired by the gaping polarization in our society and the increasing popularity of social media, we took a first step in measuring political polarization on Twitter. By assembling a large dataset and applying state-of-the-art algorithms, we achieved a high accuracy of 69% in predicting candidate followers. Methodologically, we demonstrated incorporating both text features and visual features

---

[4] The datasets and codes are available at https://sites.google.com/site/wangyuro chester/papers.

could improve the model performance. Substantively, we provided first evidence that the gaping polarization observed in our society has crept into social media as well.

Acknowledgement. We acknowledge support from the Department of Political Science at the University of Rochester, from the New York State through the Goergen Institute for Data Science, and from our corporate sponsors. We also thank the four anonymous reviewers for their insightful comments and suggestions.

References

1. Barberá, P.: Birds of the same feather tweet together: Bayesian ideal point estimation using twitter data. Polit. Anal. **23**(1), 76–91 (2015)
2. Burger, J.D., Henderson, J., Kim, G., Zarrella, G.: Discriminating gender on twitter. In: Proceedings of the 2011 Conference on Empirical Methods in Natural Language Processing (2011)
3. Campbell, J.E.: Polarized: Making Sense of a Divided America. Princeton University Press, Princeton (2016)
4. Chen, T., Chen, Y., Luo, J.: A selfie is worth a thousand words: mining personal patterns behind user selfie-posting behaviours. In: Proceedings of the 26th International World Wide Web Conference (2017)
5. Doherty, C.: 7 things to know about polarization in America. Pew Research Center, Washington, D.C. (2014)
6. Druckman, J.N., Peterson, E., Slothuus, R.: How elite partisan polarization affects public opinion formation. Am. Polit. Sci. Rev. **107**(1), 57–79 (2013)
7. Fiorina, M.P., Abrams, S.J.: Political polarization in the American public. Annu. Rev. Polit. Sci. **11**, 563–588 (2008)
8. Girshick, R., Donahue, J., Darrell, T., Malik, J.: Rich feature hierarchies for accurate object detection and semantic segmentation. In: Proceedings of the 2014 IEEE Conference on Computer Vision and Pattern Recognition, pp. 580–587 (2014)
9. Goodfellow, I., Bengio, Y., Courville, A.: Deep Learning. The MIT Press, Cambridge (2016)
10. Hare, C., Poole, K.T.: The polarization of contemporary American politics. Polity **46**(3), 411–429 (2014)
11. He, K., Zhang, X., Ren, S., Sun, J.: Deep residual learning for image recognition. In: CVPR (2016)
12. Hochreiter, S., Schmidhuber, J.: Long short-term memory. Neural Comput. **9**(8), 1735–1780 (1997)
13. Political Polarization in the American Public
14. Irsoy, O., Cardie, C.: Opinion mining with deep recurrent neural networks. In: Proceedings of the 2014 Conference on Empirical Methods in Natural Language Processing (EMNLP), pp. 720–728 (2014)
15. Kim, Y.: Convolutional neural networks for sentence classification. In: Proceedings of the 2014 Conference on Empirical Methods in Natural Language Processing (EMNLP), pp. 1746–1751 (2014)
16. Lai, S., Xu, L., Liu, K., Zhao, J.: Recurrent convolutional neural networks for text classification. In: Proceedings of the Twenty-Ninth AAAI Conference on Artificial Intelligence (2015)

17. Levi, G., Hassner, T.: Age and gender classification using deep convolutional neural networks. In: Proceedings of the IEEE Conference on Computer Vision and Pattern Recognition, pp. 34–42 (2015)
18. Lin, Y., Lei, H., Wu, J., Li, X.: An empirical study on sentiment classification of Chinese review using word embedding. In: Proceedings of the 29th Pacific Asia Conference on Language, Information and Computation (2015)
19. Liu, P., Joty, S., Meng, H.: Fine-grained opinion mining with recurrent neural networks and word embeddings. In: Proceedings of the 2015 Conference on Empirical Methods in Natural Language Processing, pp. 1433–1443 (2015)
20. Liu, Z., Luo, P., Wang, X., Tang, X.: Deep learning face attributes in the wild. In: 2015 IEEE International Conference on Computer Vision, pp. 3730–3738 (2015)
21. McCarty, N., Poole, K.T., Rosenthal, H.: Does gerrymandering cause polarization? Am. J. Polit. Sci. **53**(3), 666–680 (2009)
22. McPherson, M., Smith-Lovin, L., Cook, J.M.: Birds of a feather: homophily in social networks. Ann. Rev. Sociol. **27**, 415–444 (2001)
23. Pascanu, R., Gulcehre, C., Cho, K., Bengio, Y.: How to construct deep recurrent neural networks. In: Proceedings of the Second International Conference on Learning Representations (ICLR 2014) (2014)
24. Paul, R., Hawkins, S.H., Hall, L.O., Goldgof, D.B., Gillies, R.J.: Combining deep neural network and traditional image features to improve survival prediction accuracy for lung cancer patients from diagnostic CT. In: 2016 IEEE International Conference on Systems, Man, and Cybernetics (2016)
25. Pennington, J., Socher, R., Manning, C.D.: Glove: global vectors for word representation. In: Empirical Methods in Natural Language Processing (EMNLP), pp. 1532–1543 (2014)
26. Preotiuc-Pietro, D., Volkova, S., Lampos, V., Bachrach, Y., Aletras, N.: Studying user income through language, behaviour and affect in social media. PLoS One **10**(9), e0138717 (2015)
27. Rao, A., Spasojevic, N.: Actionable and political text classification using word embeddings and LSTM. arXiv:1607.02501 (2016)
28. Sanders, B.: Our Revolution: A Future to Believe. Thomas Dunne Books, New York (2016)
29. Simonyan, K., Zisserman, A.: Very deep convolutional networks for large-scale image recognition. In: International Conference on Learning Representations 2015 (2015)
30. Stahl, L.: President-elect trump speaks to a divided country on 60 minutes. CBS (2016)
31. Wang, Y., Feng, Y., Luo, J.: Gender politics in the 2016 U.S. presidential election: a computer vision approach. In: International Conference on Social Computing, Behavioral-Cultural Modeling and Prediction and Behavior Representation in Modeling and Simulation, pp. 35–45 (2017)
32. Wang, Y., Feng, Y., Luo, J., Zhang, X.: Pricing the woman card: gender politics between Hillary Clinton and Donald Trump. In: IEEE International Conference on Big Data (2016)
33. Wang, Y., Feng, Y., Zhang, X., Luo, J.: Voting with feet: who are leaving Hillary Clinton and Donald Trump? In: Proceedings of the IEEE Symposium on Multimedia (2016)
34. Wang, Y., Feng, Y., Zhang, X., Luo, J.: Inferring follower preferences in the 2016 US presidential primaries with sparse learning. In: Lee, D., Lin, Y.R., Osgood, N., Thomson, R. (eds.) SBP-BRiMS 2017. LNCS, vol. 10354, pp. 3–13. Springer, Cham (2017). doi:10.1007/978-3-319-60240-0_1

35. Wang, Y., Li, Y., Luo, J.: Deciphering the 2016 U.S. presidential campaign in the twitter sphere: a comparison of the Trumpists and Clintonists. In: Tenth International AAAI Conference on Web and Social Media (2016)
36. Wang, Y., Liao, H., Feng, Y., Xue, X., Luo, J.: Do they all look the same? Deciphering Chinese, Japanese and Koreans by fine-grained deep learning. arXiv:1610.01854v2 (2016)
37. Wang, Y., Luo, J., Niemi, R., Li, Y., Hu, T.: Catching fire via 'likes': inferring topic preferences of Trump followers on twitter. In: Tenth International AAAI Conference on Web and Social Media (2016)
38. Wang, Y., Luo, J., Zhang, X.: When follow is just one click away: understanding twitter follow behavior in the 2016 U.S. presidential election. In: International Conference on Social Informatics (2017)
39. Wang, Y., Yuan, J., Luo, J.: To love or to loathe: how is the world reacting to China's rise? In: Workshop Proceedings International Conference on Data Mining 2015 (2015)
40. Ounis, I., Yang, X., Macdonald, C.: Using word embeddings in twitter election classification. arXiv:1606.07006 (2016)
41. You, Q., Luo, J., Jin, H., Yang, J.: Robust image sentiment analysis using progressively trained and domain transferred deep networks. In: Proceedings of the 29th AAAI Conference on Artificial Intelligence (2015)
42. Zaremba, W., Sutskever, I., Vinyals, O.: Recurrent neural network regularization (2015). https://arxiv.org/pdf/1409.2329v5.pdf

Can Cross-Lingual Information Cascades Be Predicted on Twitter?

Hongshan Jin[1(✉)], Masashi Toyoda[2], and Naoki Yoshinaga[2]

[1] The University of Tokyo, Tokyo, Japan
jhs@tkl.iis.u-tokyo.ac.jp
[2] Institute of Industrial Science, The University of Tokyo, Tokyo, Japan
{toyoda,ynaga}@tkl.iis.u-tokyo.ac.jp

Abstract. Social network services (SNSs) have provided many opportunities for sharing information and knowledge in various languages due to their international popularity. Understanding the information flow between different countries and languages on SNSs can not only provide better insights into global connectivity and sociolinguistics, but is also beneficial for practical applications such as globally-influential event detection and global marketing. In this study, we characterized and attempted to detect influential cross-lingual information cascades on Twitter. With a large-scale Twitter dataset, we conducted statistical analysis of the growth and language distribution of information cascades. Based on this analysis, we propose a feature-based model to detect influential cross-lingual information cascades and show its effectiveness in predicting the growth and language distribution of cascades in the early stage.

1 Introduction

Online social network services (SNSs) have become more global and multilingual due to their widespread adoption. Let us take Twitter as an example. As of June 2016, there were 313 million monthly active users, 79% of accounts were outsides the United States, and more than 40 languages are supported. Other popular SNSs, such as Facebook and Google+, have millions of monthly active users worldwide and support many languages as well.

With easy access and less limitation, SNSs have become a new type of information platform. Posts are easily and quickly shared among users, with convenient functions, such as "retweet" and "mention" in Twitter and "share" in Facebook (hereafter, referred to as *reshare*). A set of all subsequent reshares starting from the root post that originally created the content is considered an information cascade (or cascade) [4].

Along with cascade growth, some cascades can spread over different regions and languages. We could find several internationally influential cascades. One example is the "ALS Ice Bucket Challenge," which went viral on social media in 2014. The hashtag of the Ice Bucket Challenge was used worldwide and translated into other languages. As a result, this campaign attracted many participants and

© Springer International Publishing AG 2017
G.L. Ciampaglia et al. (Eds.): SocInfo 2017, Part I, LNCS 10539, pp. 457–472, 2017.
DOI: 10.1007/978-3-319-67217-5_28

successfully increased donations for ALS patients worldwide [16]. Another example, the "Oscars selfie," became the most retweeted post in 2014 [15], which was posted by talk show host Ellen DeGeneres on her Twitter account. People reposted and imitated this photo, diffusing them across regions and languages at amazing speed. At the same time, DeGeneres's selfie, taken during the broadcast on a Samsung smart phone affected Samsung's global marketing.

Goal. In this paper, we focus on characterizing and detecting influential cross-lingual information cascades that are widely spread and internationally reshared. Though there has been a large amount of research on information cascades, much of the focus has been on just predicting the cascade size and structure [3,4,6,11–13]. Language is an interesting and significant, but understudied research topic on information cascades. In this work, we define, analyze and predict growing large cross-lingual information cascades on Twitter. We address the following new problems: what is the linguistic properties of cascades; why and how can information diffuse cross-linguistically and can these information cascades be predicted in an early stage?

Motivation. Understanding the cross-lingual characteristics and factors of why information can diffuse beyond language barriers is valuable for sociological research. It can help uncover the global connectivity of social networks and determine relationships among different languages and regions. In addition, accurate prediction of influential cross-lingual information cascades in the early stage is an important enabler of several possible applications. First, knowing the probabilities of information being propagated into difference languages can be used to generate a ranked list of issues for users providing early detection of international breaking news and recommendation of globally-influential events. Second, knowing possible reaction of the multilingual users for a post that advertises a new product, we can quickly evolve (elaborate) the marketing strategy of globally-influential products in the global viral marketing.

Outline of Results. In this paper, we analyzed the information cascades from 74 million root posts among 1.5 million users based on a six-week data set aggregated from Twitter. We first defined the notion of cross-lingual information cascade on the basis of the main language of root users and resharers, and measured several statistical properties such as cross-lingual ratio (formally defined in Sect. 4.1) of the actual information cascades on Twitter. First, large cascades are rare and 98% of the reshares appear within one week. Accordingly, we focused on the cascades having size larger than ten which grew within one week. After having observed several reshares of cascades, half of them grew 1.6 times irrespective of the observed number of reshares. Second, most of the information reshares and cascades were monolingual. The mean value of the cross-lingual ratio of the cascades was only about 11%. We also found that only a small fraction of cross-lingual information cascades keeps their cross-lingual ratio over time.

Based on the above empirical observations, we define the cascade prediction problem. By analyzing six types of features including content features and language features of the root node and several observed nodes, we propose a feature-based model to predict the size and language distribution of cascades.

Our model detected influential cross-lingual information cascades with better performance than a baseline which uses features for predicting cascade size [4]. The evaluation revealed that language features contributed to the improvement for prediction accuracy both for size and cross-lingual ratio. Specially, multilingual users and users having international followers are likely to produce cross-lingual cascades.

2   Related Work

2.1   Information Cascade

The popularity of online SNSs has resulted in many new research topics of information cascades or diffusion [12]. Some researchers analyzed and cataloged the properties of information cascades [3,6,12,13], while others considered predicting the speed, final size, and structure of cascade growth [1,4].

Existing empirical analysis of information cascades on SNSs [3,6,12,13], revealed common properties of the cascades. Most cascades are small [6,13] and usually grow in a short time [3,12]. Based on these properties, researchers have attempted to predict the final size of cascades. They considered the cascade prediction task as a regression problem [1,11] or binary classification problem [4,11]. One widely used approach to predicting cascade size is the feature-based method [4]. These studies extracted an exhaustive list of potentially relevant features, mainly including content, root user, and network-structural and temporal features. They then applied various learning algorithms to predict cascade size.

Although the increasing multilingual Web indicates the increasing importance of multilingual/cross-lingual studies on information cascades, little work has been done on their cross-lingual behaviors. In this work, we studied cross-lingual characteristics of information cascades.

2.2   Language Community

Several recent studies have examined language distribution and multilingualism in global SNSs [5,8]. Multiple languages are used in global SNSs, and Hale [8] found that 11% of users are multilingual and use more than two languages in Twitter. Social network services are international in scope, but not as multilingual as they should be [7]. Distance and language serve as barriers in social communication [7,9]. They lead to networks having many isolated clusters or groups of individuals with the same language called language communities [9]. Most content is only shared within communities.

Some researchers analyzed the role of multilingual users [5,8] and languages [8,9] in language communities. Social network analysis of multilingual users indicates that multilingual individuals can help diminish the barriers among different language communities [5]. When users form cross-language communities, these users are likely to engage in larger languages, particularly, English [8]. These studies did not analyze in detail the linguistic influence on information cascades, but have inspired us to argue that large languages and multilingual users may contribute to cross-lingual information cascades.

3   Twitter Datasets

3.1   Data Collection

Twitter is one of the most global and multilingual SNSs and its data is publicly available through Twitter API.[1] We have crawled for more than six years worth of Twitter data using Twitter API from 2011. Our crawling started from 26 famous Japanese users by obtaining their past timelines. We then repeatedly expanded the set of users by following retweets and mentions appearing in their timelines. We continuously expanded users and tracked their timelines. Since we did not limit the language and country of users during expansion, most languages on Twitter were included in the dataset.

Our archive included more than 2 billion tweets and 1.5 million users from March 1 to July 5, 2014. We used tweets from March 1 to May 31 to analyze users and their friendship properties. Based on the user network, we observed the information cascades in tweets from June 1 to July 5.

3.2   Language Detection

Most research on social network analysis has been focused on a single language, regardless of its multilingual characteristic. As a multilingual platform, Twitter has supported more than 40 languages. We identified the language of each tweet using the Language Detection API[2] developed by Nakatani, the precision of which reaches 99% for 53 types of languages on long, clean text such as news articles. Because language identification is difficult in noisy, short text like tweets [14], we temporally removed less language-dependent strings such as URLs, hashtags, and mentions from the text of tweets and detected the languages of tweets containing more than 20 characters. This pre-processing cut only 0.8% of tweets.

After detecting the languages of the tweets, we built a language profile for each user. For each user u_i, we counted the frequency of each language in their tweets and built a language distribution vector, $L_i = (f(l_1), f(l_2), \cdots, f(l_{53}))$. Then we defined the *main language of user* and determined whether a user is multilingual. The main language of a user is defined as the language that is most frequently used in user's tweets. Table 1 shows the language distribution of tweets and languages from March 1 to May 31. The first two columns show the frequency and proportion of the top-10 languages of tweets, ordered by decreasing number, and the distribution of users' main language is shown in the last two columns.

---

[1] https://dev.twitter.com/overview/api.
[2] https://github.com/shuyo/language-detection.

Table 1. Top-10 languages used in tweets and as main languages by users.

Language	# of tweets (K)	%	# of users (K)	%
English	534,683	38.8	583	39.2
Japanese	316,902	23.0	433	29.2
Arabic	138,139	10.0	157	10.6
Spanish	81,103	5.89	73	4.92
French	60,263	4.37	67	4.55
Thai	59,101	4.29	32	2.14
Indonesian	41,062	2.98	53	3.55
Portuguese	23,157	1.68	15	0.99
Korean	15,235	1.11	18	1.20
Dutch	15,125	1.10	8	0.56

A *monolingual user* is he/she who uses only one language and a *multilingual user* is he/she who uses two or more languages. Due to the difficulties in language detection for short text Twitter, it is useful to set a threshold to determine whether a user uses a certain language. For each user, the *usage rate* of each language is defined as the percentage of that language in the user's tweets. In this study, one user is considered to use a certain language when the usage rate and number of tweets is more than 20% and 4. The usage rate of languages other than the main language is defined as the *multilingual ratio* of the user. Among all users in our dataset, 8% met our requirement for multilingual users.

Because we initially expand users from 26 Japanese users, the percentage of Japanese tweets was a little higher than that in related studies. However, the top-10 languages were in line with those studies [5,8,10], which shows our dataset is a reasonable subset of Twitter for studying of cross-lingual cascades.

4   Information Cascades

4.1   Definitions

Twitter allows convenient conventions, such as "retweet" and "mention." If user u_j retweeted or mentioned a tweet of user u_i, user u_i is called the *root user* and user u_j is called a *resharer*. Accordingly, the retweet or mention is called the *information reshare* (or *reshare*) and the tweet of the root user is called the *root tweet*. A set of all subsequent reshares starting from the root tweet that originally created the content is considered as an *information cascade* (or *cascade*) and the number of reshares in one information cascade is defined as *cascade size k*.

A majority of reshares are done by retweets that just copy the content of the root tweet. Therefore we cannot observe changes in language by retweets even when they are done by foreign users. Instead of observing changes in language, we define the monolingual/cross-lingual information cascades based on the main language of users.

Definition 1 *Monolingual information cascade. If the main languages of all resharers in a cascade is the same as that of the root user, the cascade is called a monolingual information cascade.*

Definition 2 *Cross-lingual information cascade. If a cascade contains a resharer whose main language differs from that of the root user, the cascade is considered a cross-lingual information cascade.*

Accordingly, the language distribution of each cascade refers to the fraction of resharers grouped by their main languages in one cascade. The proportion of cross-lingual resharers in a cascade is defined as the *cross-lingual ratio* $r_k(>0)$. For a monolingual cascade, r_k is 0.

4.2   Cascade Properties

We extracted 74 million information cascades from June 1 to July 5, 2014 and investigated the distribution of their cascade size. Information cascades follow a heavy-tailed distribution and large information cascades are quite rare, as has been confirmed in the literature [4,12]. 96% of cascades had less than five reshares and only 2% of cascades consisted of more than ten reshares. We investigated how soon information reshares appears and an information cascade grows. By observing the time intervals between each reshare and root tweet in June, we found that only less than 2% of the reshares occurred after one month. For the cascades which root tweets appeared during June 1 to 7, we observed the cascade size during one month and investigated the speed of cascade growth and found that 98% of the cascades grew within one week and tended to stabilize after one week.

Distribution of Cascades. According to the above size and speed analysis of cascades, we define one week as the duration of cascade growth and define the *final cascade size* $g(k)$ as the size of reshares in a cascade after one week has passed since the root tweet is posted. Similarly, the *final cross-lingual ratio* $f(r_k)$ is ratio of cross-lingual reshares after one week. For the following analysis, we selected about 1.4 million cascades with the final cascade size $g(k)$ larger than ten and the root tweets of which appeared during June 1 to 28 for. The distribution of the $g(k)$ and $f(r_k)$ is shown in Fig. 1.

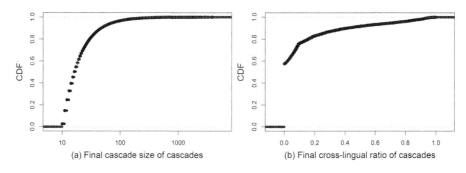

Fig. 1. Cumulative distribution function (CDF) of final cascade size (left) and final cross-lingual ratio of information cascades (right).

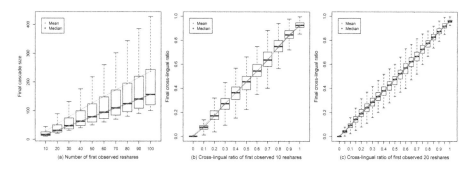

Fig. 2. Box-plot of $g(k)$ and $f(r_k)$ after observing k reshares.

Figure 1(a) shows the cumulative distribution function of cascade size. Less than 10% of cascades will exceed 100 and large cascades are really rare. From Fig. 1(b), we can observe that more than half of the cascades were monolingual. The median value of the cross-lingual ratio was 0 and the mean value of $f(r_k)$ was just 11%. This means that predicting cascades with high $f(r_k)$ is quite difficult.

Final Size of Cascades. In order to detect influential cross-lingual cascades in the early stage, we observed the first k reshares of a cascade and the final cascade size $g(k)$ [4]. This allowed us to study how cascade growth varies with k. From a box-plot of $g(k)$ after observing the first k reshares (Fig. 2(a)), we found that the median value of $g(k)$ is about 1.6 times that of k and the mean value of $g(k)$ is 2.5 times that of k. This indicates that there is a linear relation between the final cascade size and firstly-observed reshares.

Final Cross-Lingual Ratio of Cascades. Similarly to the analysis of cascade growth, we observed the correlation between the cross-lingual ratio r_k of the firstly-observed k resharers and the final cross-lingual ratio $f(r_k)$. Figure 2(b) shows a box-plot of $f(r_k)$ after observing the r_k of the firstly-observed ten/twenty resharers. We found that the median value of $f(r_k)$ had a linear relationship (0.9 times) with the r_k of the firstly-observed resharers. Even if we observe more k, the median value of $f(r_k)$ would show a linear relationship with the r_k of the observed k resharers. Only about 20% of cascades will exceed the value of r_k after observing k resharers. It means that maintaining cross-lingual ratio over time is quite difficult. We therefore focus on predicting whether $f(r_k)$ exceeds the cross-lingual ratio r_k based on firstly-observed k reshares.

4.3   Factors Behind Cross-Lingual Cascades

Section 4.2 revealed that cross-lingual cascades are rare and predicting large cross-lingual cascades is challenging. In this section, we discuss several factors of root users and tweets that may influence cross-linguality of information cascades.

Influence of Root Users' Main Language. Commonly used languages such as English can serve as bridges between language communities [8]. By connecting language communities, information can spread across language barriers [5].

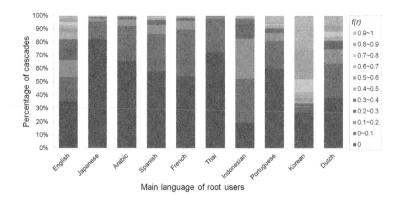

Fig. 3. Main language of root users vs. cross-lingual ratio of cascades.

We assume root users using different main languages have different potential to produce cross-lingual cascades. For each main language of root users, we investigated the frequency of cascades with a varied range of $f(r_k)$ (Fig. 3).

The main language of root users affects the cross-lingual ratio of their cascades. As we had expected, root users whose main language is English produce more cross-lingual cascades than monolingual cascades and cascades with higher $f(r_k)$ are less. Most cascades starting from root users whose main languages are Japanese, Arabic or Thai are monolingual. The cascades of root users whose main language is European languages and Indonesian tend to be more cross-lingual.

Influence of Multilingual Root Users. Since multilingual users may belong to several language communities, they have the potential to propagate information across languages. We grouped the cascades by the root users' multilingual ratio and calculated the average $f(r_k)$ of their cascades. The multilingual ratio of root users has a positive correlation to the $f(r_k)$ of their cascades, as shown in Fig. 4. The cascades from multilingual root users tend to be cross-lingual.

Influence of Internationally Popular Root Users. In some cases, root users are not multilingual, but are internationally famous and have followers worldwide; thus, their tweets can also be cross-lingual and influential. To define the international popularity of users, we analyzed the directed *reshare graph* and defined their *monolingual* and *multilingual neighbors*.

Reshare graph is extracted from users' previous reshares. Nodes represents the root user and resharers. A directed edge e_{ij} represents a user u_j is the resharer of user u_i and u_j is a follower of u_i. We call users connected with each user in the reshare graph as neighbors of the users. Monolingual neighbors refer to neighbors who share one dominant main language and multilingual neighbors refer to neighbors who share more than one language and the proportion of the second language is larger than 0.2. The multilingual ratio of neighbors is defined as the proportion of languages other than the dominant main language, which reflects the internationality of the user.

We investigated the average $f(r_k)$ of cascades whose root users' neighbors were monolingual and multilingual (Fig. 5). Cascades from root users with a

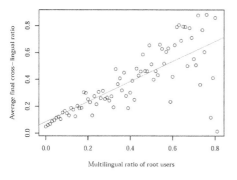
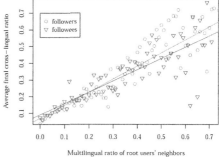

Fig. 4. Multilingual ratio of root users vs. average of $f(r_k)$.

Fig. 5. Multilingual ratio of root users' neighbors vs. average of $f(r_k)$.

higher multilingual ratio of neighbors had higher $f(r_k)$. In particular, multilingual followers, which represent the international popularity of root users, had higher $f(r_k)$. By analyzing the effect of the main language of root users and multilingualism of root users and their neighbors, we found that these language factors are important for predicting cross-lingual cascades.

Influence of Content of Root Tweets. The content or topics of tweets can be an important factor affecting cross-lingual cascades. We extracted frequently used words of cascades with different $f(r_k)$ and in different languages. For instance, for cascades with $f(r_k)$ larger than 0.8, the main languages were Korean and Thai containing keywords related to famous Korean singers and stars. Cascades with $f(r_k)$ from 0.2 to 0.7, contained topics related to World Cup 2014 in English and European languages. The top languages used in monolingual cascades were English, Japanese and Arabic. The analysis of root tweets indicates that the languages and topics of root tweets are also important for cross-lingual cascade prediction.

Influence of Network Structures of Root Users. We investigated the correlation between network structure and cross-lingual ratio of cascades. We extracted an ego network of each root user. Each node in the ego network represents a Twitter user connected to the root user and each weighted, directed edge e_{ij} represents the number of tweets that are authored by user i and mentions and retweets to user j.

We extracted main features including number of nodes/edges, degree assortativity, and density or clusters of the networks, and then calculated the coefficient correlation between these features and $f(r_k)$. As a result, root users who had more denser networks tended to produce cross-lingual cascades.

5   Cascade Prediction

5.1   Problem Definition

Previous studies considered the cascade size prediction task as a binary classification problem [1,11] or regression problem [4,11]. To predict both of the cascade growth and cross-lingual ratio, we define our task as a classification problem and regression problem.

Classification Task. For the influential cross-lingual cascade prediction task, we define a binary classification problem based on whether $g(k)$ and $f(r_k)$ will reach threshold values after one week. Following the observations in Sect. 4.2, this classification problem is divided into two parts: cascade size prediction and cross-linguality prediction.

Following previous research [4], we define the cascade size prediction task as a binary classification problem to predict whether the $g(k)$ of a cascade reaches the median size (1.6 times of k) after observing the first k reshares of that cascade.

For predicting cross-lingual cascades, we predicted the $f(r_k)$ of cascades. We define the cross-lingual ratio prediction task as a binary classification problem to predict whether $f(r_k)$ exceeds the r_k of the firstly-observed k reshares after one week. As shown in Sect. 4.2, the percentage of such cascades is only 20%. We evaluated the performance of our prediction model by adjusting the task to predict higher $f(r_k)$ from lower r_k.

Regression Task. Besides predicting $f(r_k)$, we are also interested in predicting the final distribution of languages in cascades. This problem can be solved by a multi-output regression task. The model predicts the final distribution of the resharers' main languages.

5.2   Approach

Our approach to the cascade prediction problem is to represent a cascade by a set of features and then use machine learning methods to predict its future size, cross-lingual ratio and language distribution. For the classification task, we used a linear support vector machine[3] to train the classifier and performed 10-fold cross validation to tune the parameters. In the regression task, we used multi-output regression with random forest and the multi-output meta-estimator.[4] Multi-output meta-estimator performed slightly better than random forest.

We now describe the features for prediction. The cascade size prediction problem is not a new topic, and a previous study [4] showed the importance of structural and temporal features of the root and first k reshares in a cascade to predict growth. When predicting $f(r_k)$, language and content features are important as stated in Sect. 4.3. We grouped the features of the root post and firstly-observed k reshares into six types: root-user, resharer, content, structural, temporal, and language (refer to Appendix). We focus on introducing novel language and content features in this section.

Language Features. From the previous section, we found that the language features of root users are important for cross-lingual cascades. Accordingly, those features of k resharers may also be important. Therefore, we calculated the language features containing the main language, multilingualism, multilingual

---

[3] Liblinear: https://www.csie.ntu.edu.tw/~cjlin/liblinear/.

[4] Multi-output regression: http://scikit-learn.org/stable/modules/multiclass.html.

ratio of the main language, and language distribution vector of the root user and k resharers.

For the root users, we extracted their main language, multilingual ratio and multilingualism of the users and their neighbors. For a more detailed language profile, we include the language distribution vector of tweets and main language distribution vector of their neighbors. For the resharers, we calculated the ratio of multilingual resharers and multilingual neighbors. We also computed the average language distribution vector of their tweets and that of their neighbors.

Content Features. Content is an important feature for cross-lingual cascades, but is less relevant than user features in the cascade size prediction task [1]. We extracted preliminary content features, *e.g.*, the language of the root tweet and whether it contained a hashtag, mention, and URL.

To deal with multilingual content data, we trained a topic model based on Wikipedia articles written in the top-10 languages used in our Twitter datasets. We grouped the multilingual articles into one document by using the inter-language link[5] of articles and modeled using Latent Dirichlet Allocation (LDA) [2]. By testing the perplexity of several specified topic numbers, we finally chose 200 as the number of topics and inferred the probabilities of topics for each tweet by using this multilingual LDA model.

5.3   Experiments

We extracted 1.4 million cascades larger than ten from June 1 to July 5, 2014. As a training set, we sampled more than 300,000 cascades, the root tweets of which appeared during June 1 to 21. As a test set, we sampled 100,000 cascades, the root tweets of which appeared from June 22 to 28. User and structural features were extracted from March 1 to May 31.

Predicting Influential Cross-Lingual Cascades. To illustrate the general performance of the features described in the previous section, we observed the root post and first ten reshares of the cascades and predicted whether the final size $g(k)$/final cross-lingual ratio $f(r_k)$ would reach the median $(1.6 * 10)$/cross-lingual ratio r_10 of the firstly-observed ten reshares. We trained classifiers on the training set using 10-fold cross validation and evaluated the performance of our model from the precision, recall, and F_1-score on the test set. The *baseline1* (all positive) classifies all cascades to reach the threshold. The *baseline2* uses features for growth prediction and the r_k of the firstly-observed k reshares. The overall performance of our feature-based prediction model for the final cascade size $g(k)$ and the final cross-lingual ratio $f(r_k)$ prediction tasks after observing ten resharers is shown in Table 2. The proposed method performed better than the baselines on all the tasks.

In what follows, we (1) evaluated the importance of each feature, (2) examined the predictability of cross-lingual cascades by changing the threshold of

---

[5] https://en.wikipedia.org/wiki/Help:Interlanguage_links.

Table 2. Results of influential cross-lingual prediction task after observing 10 resharers.

$g(k)$	$f(r_k)$	Model	Precision	Recall	F_1-score
>median	-	Baseline1	0.42	1	0.60
		Baseline2	0.56	0.78	0.65
		Our model	0.54	0.86	**0.66**
-	$>r_k$	Baseline1	0.17	1	0.29
		Baseline2	0.24	0.63	0.35
		Our model	0.42	0.70	**0.41**
>median	$>r_k$	Baseline1	0.12	1	0.22
		Baseline2	0.27	0.37	0.31
		Our model	0.26	0.59	**0.36**

cross-lingual ratio, and (3) examined how the prediction performance of our model changed as more resharers were observed.

Feature Importance. To evaluate the importance of each feature type, we measured the performance when using each feature type separately. As shown in [4], temporal features most significantly affected the performance of $g(k)$ prediction, followed by structural features. When predicting the $f(r_k)$ of cascades, we found that language features were more effective than other features (Fig. 6). The temporal and structural features were not useful for cross-lingual ratio prediction.

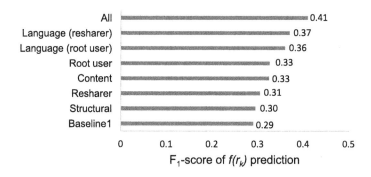

Fig. 6. F_1-score of $f(r_k)$ prediction when using each feature type separately.

In addition, we measured correlation coefficient between each feature and $g(k)$ or $f(r_k)$. The average time interval between the first half of reshares and average time interval beetween the rest reshares proved to be the most correlated with $g(k)$. Among structural features, the total number of unique followers of the root user and first k resharers showed higher relevance than the others. For the $f(r_k)$ of cascades, we found that the multilingual ratio of users' neighbors was the most significant. This was followed by the multilingual ratio of the root user and k resharers. Among content features, we found that some of the topics, such as music and movies, resulted in cross-lingual information cascades.

Sensitivity to Threshold Values. We examined the sensitivity of prediction performance to the thresholds of cross-lingual ratio. In the first experiment, we predicted whether $f(r_k)$ would exceed the observed r_k. In more realistic applications, we would like to know whether $f(r_k)$ would exceed a constant threshold. Since r_k and $f(r_k)$ have a linear relationship, cascades having large r_k values would exceed the threshold with high probability. We thus chose cascades with r_k less than or equal to 0.1, and predicted the performance of our model when changing the threshold value (0.1 and 0.3). As shown in Table 3, our model performed far better than the baseline, even when the threshold was 0.3.

Table 3. Results of $f(r_k)$ prediction with different threshold.

$f(r_k)$	Model	Precision	Recall	F_1-score
>0.1	Baseline1	0.04	1	0.08
	Baseline2	0.23	0.06	0.09
	Our model	0.29	0.45	**0.35**
>0.3	Baseline1	0.002	1	0.004
	Baseline2	0.22	0.07	0.014
	Our model	0.25	0.21	**0.23**

Sensitivity to Prediction Timing. We examined how the prediction performance of our model changed as more resharers were observed. Table 4 lists the F_1-scores when we changed the number of the firstly-observed resharers (k) from 10 to 80. Our model showed better prediction performance regardless of k. The performance of the cascade size prediction slightly improved as k increased, while that of the cross-lingual ratio prediction also improved as k increased, but the improvement from the baselines became smaller. This is because the percentage of cross-lingual cascades tended to increase after observing more resharers, which made prediction easier and decreased the effectiveness of our model.

Predicting Language Distribution of Cascades. In this experiment, a baseline used only the main language distribution of the first ten resharers as features for regression, whereas our model used all the features discussed in Sect. 5.2. We evaluated the performance in terms of the mean absolute error of regression loss for each language. Table 5 shows the language-wise errors of the most frequent languages. Among those top languages, the error of English was the highest, since the most cross-lingual cascades tended to flow into English. Thai showed relatively high error, since most of the cross-lingual cascades that started from Korean tended to flow into Thai. As shown in Table 5, our model could consistently decrease the regression loss of most top languages, and showed the effectiveness of the proposed features.

Table 4. F_1-score of $g(k)$ and $f(r_k)$ prediction with different k.

k	Task	Baseline1	Baseline2	Our model
10	$g(k) >$ median	0.60	0.65	0.66
	$f(r_k) > r_k$	0.29	0.35	0.42
20	$g(k) >$ median	0.62	0.68	0.70
	$f(r_k) > r_k$	0.37	0.42	0.48
40	$g(k) >$ median	0.61	0.70	0.72
	$f(r_k) > r_k$	0.45	0.48	0.52

Table 5. Mean absolute error of estimated language distribution on top-10 languages.

Language	Baseline	Our model
English	0.072	0.065
Japanese	0.022	0.020
Arabic	0.023	0.019
Spanish	0.019	0.018
French	0.027	0.025
Thai	0.038	0.032
Indonesian	0.014	0.012
Portuguese	0.015	0.013
Korean	0.013	0.012
Dutch	0.006	0.006

6   Conclusions

We analyzed and detected influential cross-lingual information cascades using a large dataset on Twitter. We studied the language usage on Twitter and observed the growth and cross-lingual properties of information cascades. We analyzed the factors behind cross-lingual cascades and proposed a feature-based model, which enables the accurate prediction of size and language distribution of information cascades that performed better than the baseline.

This study is just the preliminary stage in detecting influential cross-lingual information diffusion. The prediction performance is still low, which means more error analysis and more detailed observation related to cultural, content, and structural factors is necessary. For future work, we will consider the translated version of content and cluster the cascades written in different languages to paint a more holistic picture of cross-lingual information diffusion.

Acknowledgments. This work was supported by the Research and Development on Real World Big Data Integration and Analysis program of RIKEN, and the Ministry of Education, Culture, Sports, Science, and Technology, JAPAN.

A   List of Features Used for Learning

Root user features
Whether a user is verified number of friends/followers/followees
Number of listed/statues/favorites
Number of original/total tweets
Number of reshares
Number of reshared tweets
Resharer features
Ratio of k resharers who are verified
Average/max number of friends of k resharers
Average/max number of followers of k resharers
Average/max number of listed of k resharers
Average/max number of statues of k resharers
Average/max number of favorites of k resharers
Average/max number of original tweets of k resharers
Average/max number of total tweets of k resharers
Average/max number of reshares of k resharers
Average/max number of reshared tweets of k resharers
Content features
Language of root tweet
Whether a hashtag/mention/url is contained
Topic distribution of the root tweet
Structural features
Out-degree of root user and kth resharers
In-degree of root user and kth reshares
Number of common followers between the root user and kth resharers
Total number of unique followers of the root user and k resharers
Ratio of k resharers who are not first-degree connections of the root user
Temporal features
Time interval between the root user and kth resharers
Time interval between $k - 1th$ resharers and kth resharers
Average time interval between first half of reshares
Average time interval between second half of reshares
Language features
Main language of root user
Whether a root user is a multilingual user
Usage rate of main language of the root user
Whether the follower community of the root user is multilingual
Whether the followee community of the root user is multilingual
Language distribution of tweets of the root user
Main language distribution of followers of the root user
Main language distribution of followees of the root user
Cross-lingual ratio of k resharers
Ratio of k resharers who are multilingual users
Ratio of k resharers whose follower community are multilingual users
Ratio of k resharers whose followee community are multilingual users
Average main language distribution of k resharers' tweets
Average main language distribution of k resharers' followers
Average main language distribution of k resharers' followees

References

1. Bakshy, E., Karrer, B., Adamic, L.A.: Social influence and the diffusion of user-created content. In: Proceedings of the 10th ACM conference on Electronic commerce, pp. 325–334. ACM (2009)
2. Blei, D.M., Ng, A.Y., Jordan, M.I.: Latent Dirichlet allocation. J. Mach. Learn. Res. **3**(Jan), 993–1022 (2003)
3. Borge-Holthoefer, J., Baños, R.A., González-Bailón, S., Moreno, Y.: Cascading behaviour in complex socio-technical networks. J. Complex Netw. **1**(1), 3–24 (2013)
4. Cheng, J., Adamic, L., Dow, P.A., Kleinberg, J.M., Leskovec, J.: Can cascades be predicted? In: Proceedings of the 23rd International Conference on World Wide Web, pp. 925–936. ACM (2014)
5. Eleta, I., Golbeck, J.: Bridging languages in social networks: how multilingual users of twitter connect language communities? Proc. Am. Soc. Inf. Sci. Technol. **49**(1), 1–4 (2012)
6. Goel, S., Watts, D.J., Goldstein, D.G.: The structure of online diffusion networks. In: Proceedings of the 13th ACM Conference on Electronic Commerce, pp. 623–638. ACM (2012)
7. Halavais, A.: National borders on the world wide web. New Media Soc. **2**(1), 7–28 (2000)
8. Hale, S.A.: Global connectivity and multilinguals in the twitter network. In: Proceedings of the SIGCHI Conference on Human Factors in Computing Systems, pp. 833–842. ACM (2014)
9. Herring, S.C., Paolillo, J.C., Ramos-Vielba, I., Kouper, I., Wright, E., Stoerger, S., Scheidt, L.A., Clark, B.: Language networks on livejournal. In: 40th Annual Hawaii International Conference on System Sciences, 2007, HICSS 2007, p. 79. IEEE (2007)
10. Hong, L., Convertino, G., Chi, E.H.: Language matters in twitter: a large scale study. In: Proceedings of the 5th International AAAI Conference on Weblogs and Social Media (ICWSM 2011) (2011)
11. Kupavskii, A., Umnov, A., Gusev, G., Serdyukov, P.: Predicting the audience size of a tweet. In: Proceedings of the 7th International AAAI Conference on Weblogs and Social Media (2013)
12. Kwak, H., Lee, C., Park, H., Moon, S.: What is twitter, a social network or a news media? In: Proceedings of the 19th International Conference on World Wide Web, pp. 591–600. ACM (2010)
13. Leskovec, J., McGlohon, M., Faloutsos, C., Glance, N.S., Hurst, M.: Patterns of cascading behavior in large blog graphs. In: Proceedings of the 2007 SIAM International Conference on Data Mining, vol. 7, pp. 551–556. SIAM (2007)
14. Papalexakis, E., Doğruöz, A.S.: Understanding multilingual social networks in online immigrant communities. In: Proceedings of the 24th International Conference on World Wide Web, pp. 865–870. ACM (2015)
15. Reed, M.: Who owns ellen's oscar selfie: deciphering rights of attribution concerning user generated content on social media. J. Marshall Rev. Intell. Prop. L. **14**, 564 (2014)
16. Townsend, L.: How much has the ice bucket challenge achieved? BBC News Mag. (2014)

An Analysis of Individuals' Behavior Change in Online Groups

David Jurgens[1]([⊠]), James McCorriston[2], and Derek Ruths[2]

[1] Stanford University, Stanford, CA 94095, USA
jurgens@stanford.edu
[2] McGill University, Montreal, QC H3A 2A7, Canada
mccorriston@mail.mcgill.ca, druths@networkdynamics.org

Abstract. Many online platforms support social functions that enable their members to communicate, befriend, and join groups with one another. These social engagements are known to shape individuals' future behavior. However, most work has focused solely on how peers influence behavior and little is known what additional role online groups play in changing behavior. We investigate the capacity for group membership to lead users to change their behavior in three settings: (1) selecting physical activities, (2) responding to help requests, and (3) remaining active on the platform. To do this, we analyze nearly half a million users over five years from a popular fitness-focused social media platform whose unique affordances allow us to precisely control for the effects of social ties, user demographics, and communication. We find that after joining a group, users readily adopt the exercising behavior seen in the group, regardless of whether the group was exercise and non-exercise themed, and this change is not explained by the influence of pre-existing social ties. Further, we find that the group setting equalizes the social status of individuals such that lower status users still receive responses to requests. Finally, we find, surprisingly, that the number of groups one joins is negatively associated with user retention, when controlling for other behavioral and social factors.

1 Introduction

In both online and offline settings, groups and communities provide individuals with opportunities for tie formation and social learning [12] and also expose individuals to new information and peer influence [17]. However, individuals also change their behavior on the basis of their explicit social ties [3,6], raising the question of what impact group membership specifically has on individuals. Here, we examine how users change their behavior as members of a group in three different settings when controlling for the effects of social ties.

Significant work has shown that individuals change their behavior through explicit peer influence and implicitly observing their peers' actions. For example, the effects of explicit ties within a social network have been shown to manifest in a number of social phenomena such as information diffusion [9,16], peer influence

© Springer International Publishing AG 2017
G.L. Ciampaglia et al. (Eds.): SocInfo 2017, Part I, LNCS 10539, pp. 473–498, 2017.
DOI: 10.1007/978-3-319-67217-5_29

[74], and exercise frequency [3,6]. Similarly, other work has examined communities as a whole, showing their potential influence on behavioral aspects such as linguistic norms [24], visual presentation [84], and content moderation [51]. However, little is known about how online groups affect behavior independent of effects from the social network and the whole community, with only a few studies examining their lifecycle [44,85], their effect on social network formation [8,54], and how they facilitate political engagement [21,83] and dietary choice [56].

In this this study, we examine how individuals change their behavior on the basis of group membership, employing a longitudinal dataset from Fitocracy over five years with 477 K users and 12 K groups. We measure individuals' exercise and communication activities to test for the behavioral effects of group memberships in three contexts: (1) **Physical Activity**: When joining a group, do users change their behavior by becoming more similar to the behaviors seen in the group? (2) **Communication**: How do groups impact a user's requests for help and do they tend to respond to such requests? (3) **User Retention**: Does joining a group make it more likely for a user to stay on the site? Due to the presence of both groups and a social network on Fitocracy, we can disentangle the interaction of these two sources of behavior influence.

Our work offers three main insights into groups' effects on behavior. First, we demonstrate that joining a group correlates strongly with changes in individuals' behavior, with individuals adopting the exercise behaviors they observe, regardless of whether the group was focused on exercise. Second, individuals modulate their communication strategy for which audience they direct questions to, using groups to answer subjective advice-seeking questions, while asking fact-seeking questions to friends. Further, we find that the penalty for low social status is negated in groups, with individuals of all statuses being equally likely to have their questions answered—unlike when users ask either their social network or others directly in which case high status is critical for a response. Third, surprisingly, increased social and group engagements are not positively associated with new user retention; instead new users are more likely to stay if they engage in the core fitness-related functionality of Fitocracy.

2   Fitocracy Groups

Platform. Fitocracy is a social networking platform designed for individuals interested in fitness. Users track activities on a daily basis by selecting from a predefined list of 1,090 exercises, which enables the ability to precisely measure any changes in the activities that were performed. Users, all of whose profiles are public, may optionally self-report their age, gender, and height, with 91% reporting at least two attributes.

Beyond recording workouts, Fitocracy includes common social functionalities. Users may post status updates and comment on others' workouts and statuses. Notably, Fitocracy supports directed communication by enabling users to post comments to another user's wall. All posts are public and may be replied to by any users. No private communication exists on Fitocracy which allows full observability of communication.

Fitocracy includes gamification elements where users receive points for recording workouts. Points determine a user's *level*, which serves as a indicator of their degree of fitness and intensity. Notably, the platform highlights the highest-leveled users and those scoring the most points over different durations. Thus, because of its visibility on the platform, ties to physical prowess, and generalizability across different exercising disciplines, level is a reasonable proxy for *social status*.

During the lifetime of the platform, Fitocracy added the ability for individuals to find paid coaching and added a knowledge base section with information on diet and exercise. These elements, combined with gamification, can potentially drive an individual to change their behavior beyond what they would do independently.

Dataset. User activities, profile, social data, and group memberships were crawled using a web scraper to collect the complete profiles and workout histories of 476,716 users who recorded at least one workout. The total dataset contains 12,522,959 workouts (55.1M activities) over nearly a five year span from February 2011 to December 2015. Users were roughly balanced between genders (48.7% female) and, while skewed slightly younger, contain a sizable older population with a mean age of 29.2 and standard deviation of 19.5 years.

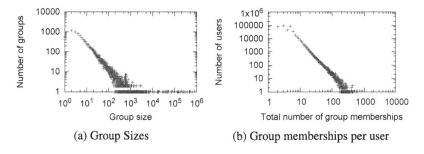

(a) Group Sizes   (b) Group memberships per user

Fig. 1. Group membership and size rates.

Group Statistics. Groups are a widely-used social feature on the platform and are commonly based on sports, diet, lifestyle, or location. Once a user joins a group, the activities recorded by that group's members appear in a separate feed on the user's home page, exposing them to how people in the group exercise. Furthermore, group members may make posts to the group's feed, such as to ask a question.

The membership lists were gathered for 12,669 groups. Group sizes follow a power law curve with $\alpha = 1.96$ (Fig. 1a), which was determined to be a better fit than a log-normal distribution at $p < 0.01$ [1,20]; the largest groups have hundreds of thousands of members. Individuals typically join a handful of groups, with 94% of users belonging to ten or fewer groups (Fig. 1b). Groups had low social connectivity with an average clustering coefficient of 0.152, indicating that most people in a group do not follow each other. Further, a group's size and clustering coefficient were not correlated (Pearson's $r = -0.01$; $p = 0.22$), indicating that smaller groups are not necessarily more connected.

3   Exercise Behavior Change

Individuals exercise for a variety of fitness goals. On Fitocracy, groups can provide social and informational support to individuals for attaining their fitness goals, e.g., observing what types of exercises are done by successful runners and motivation for continued exercise. Here, we ask to what degree do users change their behavior after joining a group? Our study is motivated by recent work [3,6] showing that the formation of new friendships in a user's social network increases their exercise frequency as measured by daily step count. We examine an analogous condition, asking to what degree do individuals change their exercising behavior when joining a new group and observing the exercises performed by its members.

Experimental Setup

Cohorts. Our analysis focuses on individuals who regularly exercise with a minimum level of activity, defined as recording at least one activity twice per week. This selection process controls for the possible effects of changes in exercise frequency (e.g., stopping exercise for several weeks) and ensures accurate estimates of individuals' behavior at any point. To estimate their average behavior, groups are only included if they have at least 100 active members who in total record at least ten workouts a week. Ultimately before-and-after-joining workout histories were gathered for 109,772 individuals across 996 groups. To contrast with the change seen by the study cohort, a *control cohort* was constructed of all users with the same exercise frequency but whom did not join a group during the study period; it consists of 29,520 users.

Groups. Groups may form for different purposes so all groups in this study were categorized as either exercise-focused (27.7%), such as Running or Powerlifting, or those focused on a non-exercise theme (72.3%) such as Vegans or Video Games. This distinction allows comparing groups where the expected impact of the group's knowledge and conversation is on an individual's exercising behavior versus another aspect of their life. We further divide these groups into one of eight themes: social (40.8%), shared interests (18.3%), general fitness (10.6%), challenge (8.8%), sport-specific (6.3%), city or regional affiliation (6.3%), dietary (4.6%), and weight-loss (2.3%). A small number of groups (1.2%) were unable to be categorized due to no clear description or title and are excluded from this study. Challenge groups ask members to perform specific exercises and show members' rankings according to the challenge goal.

Exercise Measurement. A natural method of comparing individuals' exercising behavior is to simply compare the frequencies with which they perform each exercise. However, directly comparing exercises can fail to recognize thematic similarities in behavior, e.g., that "trail running" and "jogging" are highly related, and that individuals performing such exercises have the same behavior in practice. Therefore, we adopt the approach of Jurgens *et al.* [43] for capturing high-level fitness behaviors. Here, behaviors are probability distributions over exercises and are learned by training a Latent Dirichlet Allocation (LDA) model [13] on individuals' workout histories. Much like how an LDA model identifies topics of related words in text documents, our model identifies behaviors of thematically-related exercises. The authors show that the LDA model is robust to number of topics and captures salient behaviors for a wide-range of choices. Here, we opt for 100 behaviors to capture fine-grained changes.

The LDA model is trained from documents where each represents all the exercises performed by a user; to provide more behavioral consistency when learning the model, we construct the training data from documents consisting of the exercises recorded by a user within a single month, where that user has recorded at least two workouts a week. The final training contains a total of 656,802 documents.

Measuring Behavioral Similarity. The LDA model infers a probability distribution over exercise-based behaviors (topics) from a user's activities. To compare behaviors, we calculate the distance between two distributions by computing Jensen-Shannon Divergence (JSD). Behavior similarity is then measured as $1 - JSD$, where 1 indicates maximal similarity. We note that when comparing the behaviors of a group and one of its members, the distribution of the group is inferred from the activities of all other members, *excluding* those of the individual under analysis.

Did Users Change Behavior After Joining a Group?

To assess whether joining a group was associated with behavior change, we compared the behaviors for individuals in the study cohort for their activities in the month prior to joining and the month after. By contrasting these differences with the changes seen in an analogous period for the control cohort, shown in Fig. 2, we observe that users who join a group change their behavior significantly more than those in the control cohort. This initial result should not be directly interpreted as the group causing the change itself. An alternative interpretation is that joining a group signals an intent to change behavior; therefore any observed difference in the groups could be due to selection bias, rather than the effects of group memberships. Nonetheless, there is a clear signal that when a user does join a group, their behavior is likely to change more.

Do Users Adopt the Group's Behavior?

When an individual joins the group, do they change by adopting the behaviors of the group? We test for group-specific change by measuring behavioral similarity

Fig. 2. The cohort of users who joined a group (shown left in green) had a statistically significant increase in the amount of change in the following month, compared with the control cohort of users who did not join a group but had equivalent levels of activity (shown right in blue). Bars show 95% confidence intervals computed through bootstrap resampling and points denote the mean change. (Color figure online)

before and after joining with respect to the group's behavior during the relevant time periods. Here, we consider two cohorts: (1) users who join an *Exercise-focused group*, e.g., Running, (2) users who join a *Non-exercise focused group*, e.g., Vegetarians. Behavior change is compared against a *Null model* of the same individuals but where change is measured as if they had joined a *random group* at that same point in time. This null model captures the scenario where the user has the same motivation for change (as signaled by joining a group) but is not exposed to the exercises of that group. For the null model, we sample 30 random groups per user and require that a random group have the same activity level.

The exercise, non-exercise, and null conditions allow testing for different hypotheses of exercise behavior change:

H1: The platform as a whole is converging towards a common behavior so all users become more similar to each other every month. If true, we should expect an increase in user similarity with the random group's behavior in the null model.

H2: An individual joins a group due to interest in the group's theme and therefore are likely to adopt behaviors with respect to that theme. If true, we should expect only users who joined exercise-related groups to become more similar to the group's exercise behavior.

H3: Individuals adopt the behavior they are exposed to within a group. If true, we should expect to see increased similarity for both exercise and non-exercise groups.

Results. At the outset, it is important to note that most studies on community-driven behavior change (including the present study) are observational, which limits the extent to which causality can be inferred unless experimental conditions allow for a natural experiment. That said, the findings of prior work and the findings here are strongly suggestive of some kind of causal mechanism. Establishing such causality is an important direction for future work. Here, we consider the alternative ways in which our findings could inform such investigations.

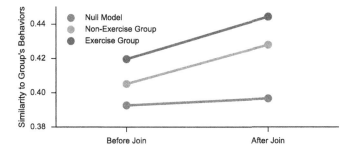

Fig. 3. Users had a substantially larger change towards the behavior of the group they joined than would be expected than by chance, as shown with the null model. Bars show bootstrapped 95% confidence intervals but are too small to be seen and points denote mean similarity.

Individuals adopted the exercise behavior they observed in groups, *independent of the exercise-focus of the group*, as seen in Fig. 3. Individuals in both exercise-related and non-exercise groups became substantially more similar to the group's behavior, far beyond what is expected by chance, as reflected in the null model. The increase in behavioral similarity was consistent across group types, shown Fig. 4 in Appendix A, However, the degree of adoption varied by type of group, with users joining Challenge groups changing the most and those joining location, sports, or shared-interests groups changing the least. Individuals are known to adopt the norms and behaviors of communities upon joining [47] and this tendency has been seen in topical online communities with changes to linguistic behaviors [14,24,55,59,76]. Hence, we interpret the consistent shift in user exercise behavior towards the group's behavior as evidence that individuals adopt the offline norms of online groups. Our result also concurs with the observations of prior work's surveys of Fitocracy that showed perceived social norms and feedback from "likes" provided strong incentives for sustained behavior [35]. Examining the null model, we found weak support for H1, where there was a tiny but statistically-significant increase in user similarity month-over-month for the platform as a whole ($p < 0.01$ using the two-sample Kolmogorov-Smirnov test); given the exercise focus the platform, we speculate that this effect is due individuals' continued lifestyle improvements. The consistent trend of users in all group types to adopt their group's exercises supports H3, with a substantially larger effect size than H1 ($p < 0.01$ using the two-sample Kolmogorov-Smirnov test), and did not support evidence of change only for exercise-focused groups only (H2). Thus, our results suggest that an individual observing a group could drive behavior change, though our experimental conditions cannot fully establish causality.

Is Change Driven by Explicit Social Ties?

Given that prior studies have shown that an individual's behavior is influenced by their friends [5,82], one possible explanation for the behavior change is the presence of friends within the group. That is, when a user joins a group that contains their friends, they change to match the behavior of their friends within the group, rather than being influenced by the group itself. However, an individual's demographics and prior behavior are also known to affect the degree to which they change their exercising behavior [22,58,69,77,78]. Thus, we test two hypotheses for what factors explain the degree of change seen by an individual: (1) **H4**: behavior change is driven by the influence of existing relationships in the group and thus the percentage of the group that is the user's friends predicts the magnitude of the behavior change and (2) **H5**: behavior change is driven by demographic factors of the individual.

To test the impact of friendship, we construct a mixed-effect linear regression model to predict the degree of change towards the group's mean behavior. We include random effects for both the individual and group to control for within-subject and within-group variation. As fixed effects, we include an individual's demographic features, their frequency of posting to the group, group size, and group type. Following common practice when regressing on variables from different scales, all numeric variables are centered and standardized to enable comparison in effect sizes per standard deviation of change.

Results. The regression results in Table 1 show that an individual's demographics and prior behavior have a much larger impact on the degree of their change than prior social ties. An individual's prior similarity to the group's behavior is the largest predictor of increased conformity, indicating that people change the most when joining groups whose activities are more familiar. Further, users who have exercised more frequently or more intensely (i.e., have a high level) change more. The coefficients for age and gender concur with prior work that had shown that (1) older individuals perceive more limitations in their exercise abilities [22,78] and thus, may be less likely to attempt new behaviors and (2) inconclusive results of gender on exercising behavior when controlling for age [10,68], suggesting its effect should not be significant. These results confirm H5 that demographics are in part responsible for the degree of change.

Examining group variables, the percentage of friends in the group has a statistically-significant positive association with behavior change towards the groups, which confirms H6. However, its effect size is the second smallest of all significant variables; i.e., having a standard deviation more friends in a group will have a smaller behavior change than having a similar magnitude of change in another variable. As such, *we do not interpret the change seen when joining a group to be primarily explained by explicit friendships within the group.*

More generally, our findings offer potential insight for how to introduce behavioral interventions where individuals are placed into online groups to support behavior change [11,57,66], e.g., dietary or exercise. Given the choice between placing the individual in a group with more friends versus a group with a more familiar behavior, our results suggest that the individual would change more if placed in the latter group.

Table 1. Regression coefficients for predicting the degree of behavior change towards the group's behavior show demographic and behavior factors were stronger predictors of change than the percentage of friends in the group. This suggests that peer influence from friends is not the driving force behind behavior change seen when a user joins a group. *** denotes $p < 0.01$. Due to normalization, coefficients should be interpreted as change per standard deviation of difference in the variable. For categorical coding, the reference gender is female and group type is challenge.

Variable	Coefficient	Variable	Coefficient
User's initial similarity to the group	0.062***	Type: dietary	−0.012***
User's level	0.015***	Type: fitness	0.003
User's age	−0.007***	Type: interests	−0.016***
Gender: male	−0.002	Type: location	−0.027***
Gender: unspecified	0.065***	Type: social	−0.010***
% of group friended	0.002***	Type: sport	−0.001
# of posts to group wall	0.001***	Type: weight-loss	−0.003
Group's mean level	0.004***	Group size	−0.002***
Intercept	0.029***		
N 109,772	Marginal R^2 0.404	Conditional R^2 0.676	

4   Requesting Help from Peers

Individuals frequently ask questions to their peers in online platforms [52,73]. This behavior, known as social search, leverages the social capital of an individual for mobilizing their peers to respond [62,67,80]. On Fitocracy, individuals have the three communication forms (posting to your own wall, another's wall, or to a group), with each reaching distinct audiences and incurring different social capital costs. We examine how individuals modulate their communication behavior on the basis of being members of groups in two settings: (1) how audience affects the types of questions asked, (2) what social factors predict whether a question will be answered.

Who is Asked What?

Groups provide an avenue for individuals to pose questions to a large audience and, due to their membership, potentially increase the diversity in response beyond that available through existing ties. We hypothesize that the low social capital cost associated with asking the social ties implicit in a group should cause users to modulate their behavior in terms of which questions are asked to groups versus friends (directly). To underscore, our question here is not about the *topic* a user might ask about. Rather, the hypothesis concerns what kind of questions a user might pose on a given topic and how those questions would be posed: the null hypothesis being that the user does not differentiate between the user-to-user and group contexts.

Methodology. A question-response dataset was created by automatically extracting posts with at least one sentence ending with a '?' and then using a series of heuristics to remove noise from platform-generated messages and messages not expressing a question, e.g., "huh?" In total, users posted 44,543 questions on their own wall, 87,205 questions to the wall of another users, and 61,969 questions to groups.

Questions were classified using a scheme adapted from Ellison *et al.* [27] and Morris *et al.* [62] to match the question types seen in Fitocracy (described in full in Appendix B, Table 5). Question types capture the broad intentions of users during social search, e.g., asking for advice. Two hundred questions from each setting were then randomly sampled and annotated by two annotators, who had an agreement of 0.657, measured using Krippendorff's α, which indicates substantial agreement [7]. After annotation was complete, both annotators adjudicated all items for the final labels.

Table 2. Individuals modulate the questions they ask by audience as seen in the stark differences in question distributions. No offer type questions were seen.

Type	Own wall		Other's wall		Group	
	Asked	w. reply	Asked	w. reply	Asked	w. reply
Advice	35.0	25.7	6.5	76.9	51.5	90.2
Fact seeking	29.5	35.6	7.0	71.4	20.5	92.6
Invitation	1.5	33.3	2.5	100.0	3.5	57.1
Participation	1.5	33.3	0.0	-	6.0	75.0
Favor	2.5	20.0	0.0	-	0.0	-
Rhetorical	18.5	37.8	5.5	63.6	4.5	88.8
Personal	5.5	36.3	53.5	76.6	11.0	95.4
Social	6.0	25.0	25.0	70.0	3.0	66.7

Results. Given the three potential audiences to which a question could be posed, individuals displayed clear preferences for the types of questions asked to each. Table 2 displays the breakdown of question types seen for each audience and the percentage of the questions that received a response. Two main trends are seen in these results.

First, individuals used groups and their social network primarily for seeking information rather than for social purposes. However, the type of information asked for differed: subjective questions for advice were posed more to groups, while factual questions were asked more frequently to followers; both differences are significant at $p < 0.01$. This result contrasts with the analysis of Morris *et al.* [62], who found no statistically-significant difference between factual and advice question frequencies on Facebook and Twitter, which are analogous to own-wall and group posting conditions, respectively. We interpret this difference as suggesting that, given equal opportunity between asking a peer or group audience, individuals may choose not to mobilize their social capital when asking a question without an objective answer—thereby incurring the social costs associated with asking peers [62]—and instead seek out answers to subjective questions from individuals with whom they have no social relationship.

Despite the features on the Fitocracy site designed to highlight and promote highly proficient individuals, the questions directly posed to other individuals on their wall were primarily social and personal in nature, rather than requests for advice from experts. This result is made more striking in comparison to the clear information gathering behavior seen for questions posted to a user's wall and groups. Surprisingly, despite the social nature of the questions, the majority of questions were asked to those without social relationships. Indeed, 85.7% questions were replied to by strangers while only 14.3% were replied to by friends, suggesting a general openness beyond that predicted by social ties.

Second, groups provide a significantly higher response rate for questions that a user posted to their own wall and are in line with those seen for community question-answering sites [36,38]. In contrast, the response rate when an individual asks their social network via a wall post is similar to that seen on Twitter when using general-purpose hashtags [40] rather than those when asking on social networking sites [61]. One explanation could be that friends tend to answer questions posted in groups, which was seen for Twitter Q&A hashtags [73], where most responses were from individuals with established social connections. However, we find that few questions posted to groups had responses by friends (13.9%). We examine the social factors in these responses next.

Who Receives a Response?

As potential members of each audience, individuals have the option of responding to questions. Social theory suggests that individuals with high social status are more likely to have their questions answered, as lower-status individual aim to acquire social capital through fulfilling these requests [33,42,70]. Alternatively, group membership may elicit altruistic behavior due to the perception of a shared social affiliation [12,30]. As a result, group members may respond without incentivization regardless of an individual's status. Finally, linguistic signals of politeness convey deference and respect and can incentivize individuals to respond [4,18,37,72,75]. These behavioral theories can be operationalized as three hypotheses for whether a question receives a response.

H6: High social status individuals are more likely to receive a response.
H7: Group members are more likely to receive a response due to affiliation benefits.
H8: Asking politely increases the likelihood of a response.

These hypotheses offer alternate explanations of how individuals behave when choosing to answer questions, raising the question of which hypotheses are valid for each Fitocracy audience, e.g., do group members still require high social status to receive response or is the group affiliation alone sufficient? Following, we test each hypothesis for the three audiences to understand the impact of group membership.

Methodology. We construct separate mixed-effect logistic regression models for each audience on the binary variable of whether a question receives a response. The models use fixed effects for sociological and textual variables to predict whether the question has a response, described in full in Appendix C. We use random effects for the location where the question is asked and the individual asking the question. As in previous models, all numeric variables are normalized such that coefficients reflect impact per standard deviation of change. To control for collinearity between variables, models were constructed using step-wise variable deletion, also described in Appendix C. We fit the model to using 116,607 questions for which we have users' demographic information.

Table 3. Regressions on whether a question will receive an answer. Results for additional question content variables are reported in Appendix D in Tables 6, 7, and 8. All numeric variables are z-scored. For categorical coding, the reference gender is female.

	Own wall	Other's wall	Group
Gender: male	-0.510^{***}	-0.110^{***}	-0.196^{***}
Age	0.045^{*}	-0.124^{***}	-0.129^{***}
Level	0.256^{***}	0.261^{***}	-0.003
# of Followers	0.647^{***}	-0.008	-0.020
# of Friends	0.027	0.005	-0.026
# of Previously asked questions to this audience	0.020	-0.100^{***}	-0.022
Message length	0.099^{***}	0.204^{***}	0.106^{***}
Message politeness	0.013	0.046^{***}	0.060^{***}
Intercept	-1.656^{***}	-1.049^{***}	-0.508^{***}
N	28,712	55,987	31,908
Marginal R^2	0.120	0.077	0.078
Conditional R^2	0.263	0.252	0.280

Note: *p < 0.1; **p < 0.05; ***p < 0.01.

Results. Audiences differed widely according to which social factors were predictive of them replying to a question (Table 3), with our three hypotheses varying by audience. Individuals posting to groups did not require high social status (i.e., level) to receive a response, confirming H7 that group membership affords social benefits and provides no evidence for the role of status (H6); in contrast, high status plays a substantial role when a user asks on their own wall or the wall of another, suggesting H6 holds in these settings. Surprisingly, politeness (H8) was only significantly associated with increased response rates for questions posted to groups or to other's walls, though its effect size was relatively small. Demographic factors played a substantial role in response rates, with men and older users being much less likely to receive a response. However, social connectedness did not play a significant role except for the number of followers when an individual posts to their own wall, which is expected since it reflects how may people might see the question. More broadly, these findings suggest that groups can a play critical role for new users. Because a new user is unlikely to have high social status or a large number of followers, they are much less likely to have their questions answered *unless* they ask in a group setting where these factors do not matter.

5   User Retention

Online communities often change over time, with new users joining a site and older users departing at certain intervals. The departure of users can come from a variety of reasons, such as a lack of active connections to other users [26,29] or changes in culture [24]. While relationships may fill the social needs of individuals, groups can potentially provide another form of social support, creating a sense of virtual community that keeps users engaged on the platform [65].

In examining group's impact on user retention, prior work has largely examined groups on social platforms where social engagement and communication are the primary uses of the platform [45,46,50,81]. In contrast, as an exercise-oriented platform, Fitocracy provides workout tracking functionality as its core service, with social and group functionalities as additions. This distinction enables us to study the impact of groups on retention independent of the purpose of the platform. Therefore, we test how the likelihood of retention of new users is affected by (a) joining a group and communicating within it and (b) engaging in social networking and directed communication.

Methodology. The Fitocracy platform publicly displays the dates when users record each workout and when users join groups. However, no information is provided about when users begin following another user. Therefore, to precisely track the impact of social network, we created a complete longitudinal dataset for 10,000 new users, by crawling these users profiles every day over a four month period to capture how their social network evolved, in addition to their workout and group activities. We construct our set of users from the "WTF – Welcome to Fitocracy" group, which all new users automatically join upon signing up for the site. Once crawled, we restrict our analyses to those that report their age, leaving a total of 7,781 users.

To analyze user retention, we construct logistic regression models with the dependent variable of whether a user will record any kind of activity (post, comment, or workout) in the following month. Two models were designed with different blocks of variables to highlight the separate contributions of (a) user demographics and (b) social and group interactions. Due to access limitations, we were unable to continuously track changes to who follows each user. As in previous models, all numeric variables were standardized so that the variable coefficients can be compared. To reduce collinearity, we used step-wise variable deletion on the fixed effects to remove the variable with the largest variance inflation factor (VIF) until all variables had VIF ≤ 5; ultimately eight variables were removed. Each model is provided with the first month of the user's activity on the site.

Table 4. Regression coefficients for user retention show that workout-associated variables were positive predictive of user retention, rather and social variables. *, **, and *** denote p<, 0.10, 0.05 and 0.01, respectively. All numeric variables are z-scored. For categorical coding, the reference gender is female.

	Null model	Social model
Intercept	−4.02***	−3.93***
# of workouts	0.39***	0.33***
Age	−0.33***	−0.23**
Gender: male	0.28*	0.11
Gender: unstated	1.99***	1.31***
Level	1.45***	1.55***
# of friends		−0.02
# of groups joined		−0.30***
# of posts received		−0.44
# of group comments		0.26
# of posts to others		0.65*
# of wall posts		0.16**
# of questions replied to		−0.12
Pseudo R^2	0.47	0.48
N	7773	7773

Results. Most of the variance in user retention is explained by individuals' demographic information and whether they actively engage in the site's core functionality of recording activities. Table 4 shows the results of the two regression models, with only small improvements to the model when adding social and group variables. The positive relations from the combination of the level and number of recorded workouts variables suggests that fitness enthusiasts are more likely to stay on the site, as these are the cohort of users who workout frequently or who record intensive exercises.

Surprisingly, for the most part, increases in social connectivity, interactions, and group memberships were not associated with increased retention. Indeed, of the social variables, only users posting to their own wall was positively associated and significant at $p < 0.05$; however, these posts often describe fitness-related content, rather than being social. The number of group memberships was strongly negatively associated with user retention. We speculate that this behavior is analogous to that seen in social platforms such as Facebook when individuals are overexposed to other individuals and become dissatisfied [19,28,32,63]. Here, when new users rapidly join a large number of groups immediately upon joining, they increase their exposure to individuals with much higher fitness status; this exposure in turn leads to lower satisfaction with their own activities and eventual dropout. Further, we can hardly expect community membership and user retention to be a simple function. For these reasons, future work is needed to test this hypothesis.

We interpret the negative association of social and group variables with increased user retention as reflecting the purpose of the Fitocracy website itself. While the site provides many social features, its core functionality is for tracking workouts. Users who actively seek such functionality are more likely to stay, whereas making friends and joining groups are not central to the focus of the platform and therefore do not keep them active. More broadly, this insight suggests that the success of an online platform with social features is dependent on the site's ability to engage users with its core functionality and is less dependent on the social networking functionality available.

Our finding that social and group features do not strongly predict user retention stands in contrast to the Fitocracy user surveys [34,35] that found social factors were strongly associated with the user's perceived enjoyment of the platform and planned continued use. However, they surveyed individuals who had been actively using the site, rather than new users, which we examine. This difference suggests that social connections enrich the experience of established users, keeping them engaged longer, but that when initially joining, in the absence of social capital and strong ties, the core functionality drives longevity rather than the formation of social ties.

More broadly, our finding also relates to studies showing that social connections lead to increased user engagement [8,15,53] and retention [25,41,71]. While our results initially seem conflicting, these studies were done on social platforms where interpersonal communication is central to the platform's service, in contrast to the functionality of Fitocracy. Thus, our findings actually confirm those of earlier studies: because the sites are designed for social engagement, increased use of its core functionality should be strongly associated with user retention.

Furthermore, we observed Simpson's paradox in our regression: when using only the number of groups joined as the predictive variable, its coefficient was positive (0.151) and significant at $p < 0.01$; however, when the full list of variables are included, its coefficient flips its sign, indicating a confounder variable was missing from the simplified regression and the overall impact of group joins is detrimental to retention.

In light of other work, our results point to a deeper mechanism behind retention: the ability of a site to attract and engage individuals in its core functionality predicts the size of its user base. More broadly, our results suggest that for online platforms, the addition of social and group functionality is not immediately necessary nor beneficial; such features only benefit the retention of established users, rather than new users.

6   Conclusion

Groups in online social networks can have a profound impact on the behaviors of individuals. Through a large-scale analysis of hundreds of thousands of users on Fitocracy, a social media platform dedicated to fitness and workout tracking, we demonstrate the impact of groups in three core contributions. First, the act of joining a group is strongly associated with an individual changing their behavior to be more similar to the group's; further, this behavior change is not explained through social influence and is substantially larger than expected by chance. Second, we demonstrate that individuals modulate their communication strategy by preferring to seek subjective answers and advice from group members, while asking factual questions more to friends. This difference suggests a strategic choice in the willingness to mobilize social capital when a objective answer may not be available. Additionally, we find that when individuals had the option of answering a question, they are more likely to respond to those asked in a group, independent of the relative social status of the asker, which suggests online groups promote in-group altruistic behavior. Third, we find that neither group nor social activities strongly contribute to the retention of new users on the platform, but rather retention is explained most by the individual's engagement with the platform's core functionality, i.e., workout tracking. Viewed with prior studies on user churn in social networking sites which found retention was increased by social relationships, our work points to the more fundamental mechanism being user engagement in the platform itself (e.g., tracking for Fitocracy, being social for social platform) rather than participation in social functionalities. Beyond Fitocracy, our results demonstrate that social groups can serve as a primary form of information for individuals aiming to change their behavior, which has broader implications when designing policies and campaigns to raise awareness about health topics [64], which to-date have seen only modest benefits from incorporating social media [49,57].

Acknowledgments. We thank the reviewers for their insightful and detailed comments, with special thanks to Reviewer 3 for their nuanced analysis. The first author would also like to thank Tim Althoff, Will Hamilton, and Jure Leskovec for their helpful discussion and feedback. Finally, we thank the Fitocracy developers for creating their platform and making it accessible to all.

A   Appendix: Additional Behavior Change Results

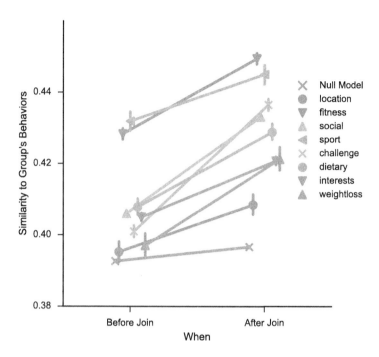

Fig. 4. Users change their behavior to be more similar to the group's behavior in the month after joining, regardless of group type. Symbols have added x-axis jitter for improved visual clarity. Bars show bootstrapped 95% confidence intervals. The large effect seen in the challenge groups suggests that public competition in online groups can facilitate individuals changing their behavior to meet their goals. Indeed, surveys, Fitocracy users rated the gamification aspects of the site highly for their enjoyment and motivation [31,34].

B   Appendix: Question Classification

Table 5. The classification of user question on social search and applied in Sect. 4, adapted from Ellison et al. [27] and Morris et al. [62]

Class	Description
Advice	Asking for a recommendation or opinion ("What is the best leg exercise?")
Fact seeking	Asking a concrete question ("What's the world record marathon time?")
Invitation	Inviting others to a social event ("Anyone want to train together in Boston?")
Participation	Asking about attending or participating in an event or social activity ("Is anyone doing this road race this weekend?")
Offer	Offering services or help ("Does anyone want a used treadmill?")
Favor	Requesting a favor from another user ("Mind checking my form in this video?")
Rhetorical	Asking with no intention for a response ("am I right or what?")
Personal	A factual question posed to a user or group about their habits, lifestyle, or some other aspect of their person ("what's your diet like?").
Social	An open-ended, generic question to group or person, often with a subjective nature ("hows everyone doing today?")

C   Appendix: Details on Question Response Regression

Social variables include the user's gender, age, level, number of followers, number of friends, and the number of times the user has asked this audience a question previously. Text features are partially drawn from the setup for Althoff *et al.* [2], which examined requests for favors on Reddit. We measure the overall politeness of a request with the model of Danescu-Niculescu-Mizil *et al.* [23]. To capture broad content variations, we (1) train a 20-topic LDA model [13] to generate a distribution of topics for each question, described in Appendix B, Table 9 and (2) count the relative frequency of word categories from the Linguistic Inquiry and Word Count (LIWC) [79] lexicon. Question sentiment is measured using word frequencies from the NRC sentiment and emotion lexicons [48,60]. Finally, we include the relative frequency of hedges and modals in the question [39].

The mixed-effect logistic regression was constructed using step-wise variable deletion, which removed the variable with the highest variance inflation factor (VIF) until all variables had a VIF < 5. This process removed 9 variables all of which were LIWC lexical categories. The final model had 94 variables.

D   Appendix: Additional Question Response Regression Results

Table 6. Additional regression coefficients for textual features in the mixed-effect logistic regression model predicting whether a question will receive a response, shown in Table 3. All numeric variables are z-scored.

	Own wall	Other's wall	Group
hedges	0.001	−0.028**	0.016
modals	−0.019	−0.078***	−0.103***
NRC_trust	−0.007	0.013	0.086***
NRC_fear	0.008	0.037**	−0.060**
NRC_negative	0.020	−0.020	0.039
NRC_sadness	−0.024	−0.032*	0.045*
NRC_anger	0.034	0.022	−0.020
NRC_surprise	−0.004	−0.043***	−0.060**
NRC_positive	0.053*	−0.019	0.036
NRC_disgust	−0.029	−0.021	−0.006
NRC_joy	−0.025	0.008	−0.088***
NRC_anticipation	−0.019	0.012	0.019
LIWC_Inhib	0.024	−0.004	0.018
LIWC_Space	0.008	−0.042***	−0.048**
LIWC_Filler	0.040*	0.009	0.003
LIWC_Ipron	0.041	0.031***	0.073***
LIWC_Time	−0.051**	−0.007	0.001
LIWC_Quant	0.071***	−0.001	0.094***
LIWC_Discrep	−0.004	−0.018	−0.013
LIWC_You	0.081	−0.023	0.029
LIWC_Cause	−0.035	0.056***	0.026
LIWC_Prep	0.109***	0.044***	0.132***
LIWC_Relig	−0.039	−0.002	−0.001
LIWC_Body	0.001	−0.002	−0.001
LIWC_We	−0.061*	−0.019*	−0.040**
LIWC_Assent	0.019	−0.026**	−0.057**
LIWC_Incl	0.017	−0.025**	0.026
LIWC_Leisure	−0.039	−0.026**	0.055***
LIWC_AuxVb	0.102***	0.030**	0.158***
LIWC_Hear	0.048**	−0.006	0.013
LIWC_They	0.011	0.006	0.015
LIWC_Posemo	−0.029	−0.049***	0.002
LIWC_Article	0.045**	0.018	0.062***
LIWC_Excl	0.074***	0.002	0.099***
LIWC_Home	−0.018	−0.006	−0.021
LIWC_Friends	0.012	0.017*	−0.007
LIWC_Present	−0.014	−0.021	0.035
LIWC_Numbers	0.028	0.001	−0.011

Note: $^*p < 0.1$; $^{**}p < 0.05$; $^{***}p < 0.01$.

Table 7. Additional regression coefficients for textual features in the mixed-effect logistic regression model predicting whether a question will receive a response, shown in Table 3. All numeric variables are z-scored.

	Own wall	Other's wall	Group
LIWC_I	0.160***	0.022	0.113***
LIWC_Work	−0.034	0.007	−0.066***
LIWC_Tentat	0.023	0.037**	0.044**
LIWC_Ingest	0.045**	0.017	0.046***
LIWC_Motion	−0.001	−0.033***	−0.006
LIWC_Anger	−0.021	0.004	−0.038
LIWC_Achiev	0.005	−0.011	0.050**
LIWC_Swear	−0.004	0.00002	−0.028
LIWC_Death	−0.019	−0.0004	0.005
LIWC_Social	0.036	0.051***	0.125***
LIWC_Nonflu	0.020	0.016*	−0.023
LIWC_Family	0.022	−0.023**	0.005
LIWC_Feel	−0.0004	0.008	0.030*
LIWC_Certain	0.024	−0.004	0.022
LIWC_Insight	0.069***	0.052***	0.027*
LIWC_Humans	0.099***	−0.005	0.037**
LIWC_Sad	0.013	0.032**	−0.005
LIWC_Past	−0.054*	−0.045***	−0.094***
LIWC_See	−0.011	−0.0002	−0.008
LIWC_Future	−0.008	−0.028**	−0.009
LIWC_Adverbs	−0.031	−0.035***	0.039*
LIWC_SheHe	0.006	0.001	−0.009
LIWC_Money	−0.004	−0.014	0.011
LIWC_Negate	−0.002	−0.065***	0.006
LIWC_Health	0.020	−0.006	0.027
LIWC_Conj	0.026	0.037***	0.057**
LIWC_Anx	0.009	0.003	0.022
LIWC_Negemo	0.054*	−0.012	0.102***
LIWC_Sexual	0.025	−0.015	0.028

Note: *p < 0.1; **p < 0.05; ***p < 0.01.

Table 8. Additional regression coefficients for textual features in the mixed-effect logistic regression model predicting whether a question will receive a response, shown in Table 3. All numeric variables are z-scored.

	Own wall	Other's wall	Group
topic_1	0.066	-0.139^{***}	-0.129^{***}
topic_2	0.034	-0.053^{***}	-0.008
topic_3	0.076^{**}	-0.048^{**}	0.046^{**}
topic_4	0.073^{**}	-0.021	0.057^{***}
topic_5	0.110^{*}	-0.095^{***}	-0.044
topic_6	0.034	-0.144^{***}	-0.090^{***}
topic_7	0.099	-0.305^{***}	-0.106^{*}
topic_8	0.023	-0.001	-0.115^{***}
topic_9	0.083^{**}	-0.039^{**}	0.060^{***}
topic_10	0.057^{*}	-0.024^{*}	-0.051^{**}
topic_11	0.069^{**}	-0.087^{***}	0.011
topic_12	0.056^{*}	-0.063^{***}	-0.006
topic_13	0.034	-0.119^{***}	-0.053^{**}
topic_14	0.022	-0.128^{***}	-0.076^{***}
topic_15	-0.008	-0.148^{***}	-0.141^{***}
topic_16	-0.005	-0.087^{***}	-0.045^{**}
topic_17	0.059^{**}	-0.051^{***}	0.027^{*}
topic_18	0.028	-0.072^{***}	-0.113^{***}
topic_19	0.068^{*}	-0.095^{***}	-0.021

Note: $^{*}p < 0.1$; $^{**}p < 0.05$; $^{***}p < 0.01$.

Table 9. The most probable words for the topics used in predicting whether a question receives a response using the mixed-effect regression analysis in Table 2. Topics regression coefficients are reported in Table 8.

Topic #	Most probable 20 words
0	follow play i'm back game hey playing love games read martial favorite kind practice good you're arts book i've video
1	hey how's hope haven't workouts what's you're man back props things time prop good long bro miss dude coming workout
2	run running i'm week time training miles marathon half mile i've minutes today distance runs day long ran start tips
3	protein eat i'm good eating food healthy day diet drink water don't meal make breakfast i've ideas suggestions sugar it's
4	weight i'm fat i've lbs lose body calories day muscle week loss eating diet days eat lost pounds gain good
5	follow back goals hey you're fitness fito how's good awesome great luck happy fitocracy nice workouts what's training i'm coming
6	app fitocracy i'm group post workouts people find can't runkeeper don't it's site workout track iphone friends fito hey feed
7	starting check strength log running routine don't workouts forget show started amazing wanted bodyweight exercise view case guide guides trainers
8	i'm run hey area race year weekend tough running mudder live good marathon training group meet gym half follow spartan
9	i'm gym good weight strength lifting training i've program week start weights starting workout work don't routine exercises body workouts
10	people don't gym i'm it's guy you're make friends feel love didn't today that's girl time awesome told friend life
11	i'm i've time back it's feel work working week don't months weeks gym year tips started hard good ago exercise
12	back pain i'm i've knee it's left hurt good squats running sore shoulder lower today advice suggestions leg don't exercises
13	day today workout i'm work gym week days time morning tomorrow feel back rest good night it's feeling working run
14	workout log points workouts track fitocracy exercises i'm add exercise can't quests don't find time logging quest today day class
15	challenge level points group i'm join start challenges fitocracy day today hey duel time you're gonna month make i'll quests
16	bike points log count walking work hours today ride stairs exercise track walk workout miles day time cycling i'm running
17	shoes running i'm good wear pair suggestions i've buy music don't recommendations it's run fit wearing thinking love size nike
18	follow pic profile back props thx picture love prop nice based workout hey awesome you're fast what's lol where's great
19	weight press squats bar bench ups squat i'm exercises pull log barbell reps exercise leg set sets dumbbell machine back

References

1. Alstott, J., Bullmore, E., Plenz, D.: Powerlaw: a python package for analysis of heavy-tailed distributions. PLoS ONE **9**(1), e85777 (2014)
2. Althoff, T., Danescu-Niculescu-Mizil, C., Jurafsky, D.: How to ask for a favor: a case study on the success of altruistic requests. In: ICWSM (2014)
3. Althoff, T., Jindal, P., Leskovec, J.: Online actions with offline impact: how online social networks influence online and offline user behavior. In: WSDM (2017)
4. Andersson, L.M., Pearson, C.M.: Tit for tat? the spiraling effect of incivility in the workplace. Acad. Manag. Rev. **24**(3), 452–471 (1999)
5. Aral, S., Muchnik, L., Sundararajan, A.: Distinguishing influence-based contagion from homophily-driven diffusion in dynamic networks. Proc. Nat. Acad. Sci. **106**(51), 21544–21549 (2009)
6. Aral, S., Nicolaides, C.: Exercise contagion in a global social network. Nat. Commun. 8 (2017). https://www.nature.com/articles/ncomms14753
7. Artstein, R., Poesio, M.: Inter-coder agreement for computational linguistics. Comput. Linguist. **34**(4), 555–596 (2008)
8. Backstrom, L., Huttenlocher, D., Kleinberg, J., Lan, X.: Group formation in large social networks: membership, growth, and evolution. In: KDD (2006)
9. Bakshy, E., Rosenn, I., Marlow, C., Adamic, L.: The role of social networks in information diffusion. In: WWW (2012)
10. Bauman, A.E., Sallis, J.F., Dzewaltowski, D.A., Owen, N.: Toward a better understanding of the influences on physical activity: the role of determinants, correlates, causal variables, mediators, moderators, and confounders. Am. J. Prev. Med. **23**(2), 5–14 (2002)
11. Van den Berg, M.H., Schoones, J.W., Vlieland, T.P.V.: Internet-based physical activity interventions: a systematic review of the literature. J. Med. Int. Res. **9**(3), e26 (2007)
12. Billig, M., Tajfel, H.: Social categorization and similarity in intergroup behaviour. Eur. J. Soc. Psychol. **3**(1), 27–52 (1973)
13. Blei, D.M., Ng, A.Y., Jordan, M.I.: Latent dirichlet allocation. J. Mach. Lear. Res. **3**, 993–1022 (2003)
14. Budak, C., Agrawal, R.: On participation in group chats on twitter. In: WWW (2013)
15. Burke, M., Marlow, C., Lento, T.: Feed Me: motivating newcomer contribution in social network sites. In: CHI (2009)
16. Cheng, J., Adamic, L., Dow, P.A., Kleinberg, J.M., Leskovec, J.: Can cascades be predicted? In: WWW, pp. 925–936. ACM (2014)
17. Cheung, C.M., Chiu, P.Y., Lee, M.K.: Online social networks: why do students use facebook? Comput. Hum. Behav. **27**(4), 1337–1343 (2011)
18. Chilton, P.: Politeness, politics and diplomacy. Discourse Soc. **1**(2), 201–224 (1990)
19. Chou, H.T.G., Edge, N.: They are happier and having better lives than i am: the impact of using facebook on perceptions of others' lives. Cyberpsychology Behav. Soc. Netw. **15**(2), 117–121 (2012)
20. Clauset, A., Shalizi, C.R., Newman, M.E.: Power-law distributions in empirical data. SIAM Rev. **51**(4), 661–703 (2009)
21. Conroy, M., Feezell, J.T., Guerrero, M.: Facebook and political engagement: a study of online political group membership and offline political engagement. Comput. Hum. Behav. **28**(5), 1535–1546 (2012)

22. Cross, S., Markus, H.: Possible selves across the life span. Hum. Dev. **34**(4), 230–255 (1991)
23. Danescu-Niculescu-Mizil, C., Sudhof, M., Jurafsky, D., Leskovec, J., Potts, C.: A computational approach to politeness with application to social factors. In: ACL (2013)
24. Danescu-Niculescu-Mizil, C., West, R., Jurafsky, D., Leskovec, J., Potts, C.: No country for old members: user lifecycle and linguistic change in online communities. In: WWW (2013)
25. Dror, G., Pelleg, D., Rokhlenko, O., Szpektor, I.: Churn prediction in new users of yahoo! answers. In: WWW, pp. 829–834. ACM (2012)
26. Ducheneaut, N., Yee, N., Nickell, E., Moore, R.J.: Alone together?: exploring the social dynamics of massively multiplayer online games. In: CHI, pp. 407–416. ACM (2006)
27. Ellison, N.B., Gray, R., Vitak, J., Lampe, C., Fiore, A.T.: Calling all facebook friends: exploring requests for help on facebook. In: ICWSM (2013)
28. Garcia, D., Mavrodiev, P., Casati, D., Schweitzer, F.: Understanding popularity, reputation, and social influence in the twitter society. Policy Int. (2017). http://onlinelibrary.wiley.com/doi/10.1002/poi3.151/full
29. Garcia, D., Mavrodiev, P., Schweitzer, F.: Social resilience in online communities: the autopsy of friendster. In: COSN (2013)
30. Goette, L., Huffman, D., Meier, S.: The impact of group membership on cooperation and norm enforcement: evidence using random assignment to real social groups. Am. Econ. Rev. **96**(2), 212–216 (2006)
31. Goh, D.H.-L., Razikin, K.: Is gamification effective in motivating exercise? In: Kurosu, M. (ed.) HCI 2015. LNCS, vol. 9170, pp. 608–617. Springer, Cham (2015). doi:10.1007/978-3-319-20916-6_56
32. Gonzales, A.L., Hancock, J.T.: Mirror, mirror on my facebook wall: effects of exposure to facebook on self-esteem. Cyberpsychology Behav. Soc. Net. **14**(1–2), 79–83 (2011)
33. Gray, R., Ellison, N.B., Vitak, J., Lampe, C.: Who wants to know?: question-asking and answering practices among facebook users. In: CSCW (2013)
34. Hamari, J., Koivisto, J.: Social motivations to use gamification: an empirical study of gamifying exercise. In: ECIS, p. 105 (2013)
35. Hamari, J., Koivisto, J.: "Working out for likes": an empirical study on social influence in exercise gamification. Comput. Hum. Behav. **50**, 333–347 (2015)
36. Harper, F.M., Raban, D., Rafaeli, S., Konstan, J.A.: Predictors of answer quality in online Q&A sites. In: CHI (2008)
37. Holmes, J., Stubbe, M., et al.: Power and Politeness in the Workplace: A Sociolinguistic Analysis of Talk at Work. Routledge, Abingdon (2015)
38. Horowitz, D., Kamvar, S.D.: The anatomy of a large-scale social search engine. In: WWW (2010)
39. Hyland, K.: Metadiscourse: Exploring Interaction in Writing. Continuum, London (2005)
40. Jeong, J.W., Morris, M.R., Teevan, J., Liebling, D.J.: A crowd-powered socially embedded search engine. In: ICWSM (2013)
41. Joyce, E., Kraut, R.E.: Predicting continued participation in newsgroups. J. Comput.-Mediat. Commun. **11**(3), 723–747 (2006)
42. Jung, Y., Gray, R., Lampe, C., Ellison, N.: Favors from facebook friends: unpacking dimensions of social capital. In: CHI, pp. 11–20. ACM (2013)
43. Jurgens, D., McCorriston, J., Ruths, D.: An analysis of exercising behavior in online populations. In: ICWSM (2015)

44. Kairam, S.R., Wang, D.J., Leskovec, J.: The life and death of online groups: predicting group growth and longevity. In: WSDM (2012)
45. Karnstedt, M., Rowe, M., Chan, J., Alani, H., Hayes, C.: The effect of user features on churn in social networks. In: WebScience (2011)
46. Kayes, I., Chakareski, J.: Retention in online blogging: a case study of the blogster community. IEEE Trans. Comput. Soc. Syst. **2**(1), 1–14 (2015)
47. Kelman, H.: Social influence and linkages between the individual and the social system: further thoughts on the processes of compliance, identification, and internalization. In: Tedeschi, J. (ed.) Perspectives on Social Power (1974)
48. Kiritchenko, S., Zhu, X., Mohammad, S.M.: Sentiment analysis of short informal texts. J. Artif. Intell. Res. (JAIR) **50**, 723–762 (2014)
49. Korda, H., Itani, Z.: Harnessing social media for health promotion and behavior change. Health Promot. Pract. **14**(1), 15–23 (2013)
50. Kumar, S., Zafarani, R., Liu, H.: Understanding user migration patterns in social media. In: AAAI (2011)
51. Lampe, C., Resnick, P.: Slash (dot) and burn: distributed moderation in a large online conversation space. In: CHI, pp. 543–550. ACM (2004)
52. Lampe, C., Vitak, J., Gray, R., Ellison, N.: Perceptions of facebook's value as an information source. In: CHI (2012)
53. Lento, T., Welser, H.T., Gu, L., Smith, M.: The ties that blog: examining the relationship between social ties and continued participation in the wallop weblogging system. In: WWW (2006)
54. Li, H., Bhowmick, S.S., Sun, A.: CASINO: towards conformity-aware social influence analysis in online social networks. In: CIKM (2011)
55. Luczak-Roesch, M., Tinati, R., Simperl, E., Van Kleek, M., Shadbolt, N., Simpson, R.J.: Why won't aliens talk to us? content and community dynamics in online citizen science. In: ICWSM (2014)
56. Ma, X., Chen, G., Xiao, J.: Analysis of an online health social network. In: Proceedings of the 1st ACM International Health Informatics Symposium, pp. 297–306. ACM (2010)
57. Maher, C.A., Lewis, L.K., Ferrar, K., Marshall, S., De Bourdeaudhuij, I., Vandelanotte, C.: Are health behavior change interventions that use online social networks effective? a systematic review. J. Med. Int. Res. **16**(2), e40 (2014)
58. Marcus, B.H., Selby, V.C., Niaura, R.S., Rossi, J.S.: Self-efficacy and the stages of exercise behavior change. Res. Q. Exerc. Sport **63**(1), 60–66 (1992)
59. Michael, L., Otterbacher, J.: Write like i write: herding in the language of online reviews. In: ICWSM (2014)
60. Mohammad, S.M., Kiritchenko, S.: Using hashtags to capture fine emotion categories from tweets. Comput. Intell. **31**(2), 301–326 (2015)
61. Morris, M.R., Teevan, J., Panovich, K.: A comparison of information seeking using search engines and social networks. In: ICWSM (2010)
62. Morris, M.R., Teevan, J., Panovich, K.: What do people ask their social networks, and why?: a survey study of status message q&a behavior. In: CHI (2010)
63. Muise, A., Christofides, E., Desmarais, S.: More information than you ever wanted: does facebook bring out the green-eyed monster of jealousy? CyberPsychology behav. **12**(4), 441–444 (2009)
64. Nakhasi, A., Shen, A.X., Passarella, R.J., Appel, L.J., Anderson, C.A.: Online social networks that connect users to physical activity partners: a review and descriptive analysis. J. Med. Int. Res. **16**(6), e153 (2014)

65. Newell, E., Jurgens, D., Saleem, H.M., Vala, H., Sassine, J., Armstrong, C., Ruths, D.: User migration in online social networks: a case study on reddit during a period of community unrest. In: ICWSM (2016)
66. Norman, G.J., Zabinski, M.F., Adams, M.A., Rosenberg, D.E., Yaroch, A.L., Atienza, A.A.: A review of ehealth interventions for physical activity and dietary behavior change. Am. J. Prev. Med. **33**(4), 336–345 (2007)
67. Paul, S.A., Hong, L., Chi, E.H.: Is twitter a good place for asking questions? a characterization study. In: ICWSM (2011)
68. Plotnikoff, R.C., Mayhew, A., Birkett, N., Loucaides, C.A., Fodor, G.: Age, gender, and urban-rural differences in the correlates of physical activity. Prev. Med. **39**(6), 1115–1125 (2004)
69. Prochaska, J.O., Velicer, W.F.: The transtheoretical model of health behavior change. Am. J. Health Promot. **12**(1), 38–48 (1997)
70. Raban, D., Harper, F.: Motivations for answering questions online. New Media Innov. Technol. **73** (2008)
71. Ren, Y., Harper, F.M., Drenner, S., Terveen, L.G., Kiesler, S.B., Riedl, J., Kraut, R.E.: Building member attachment in online communities: applying theories of group identity and interpersonal bonds. MIS Q. **36**(3), 841–864 (2012)
72. Rogers, P.S., Lee-Wong, S.M.: Reconceptualizing politeness to accommodate dynamic tensions in subordinate-to-superior reporting. J. Bus. Tech. Commun. **17**(4), 379–412 (2003)
73. Rzeszotarski, J.M., Spiro, E.S., Matias, J.N., Monroy-Hernández, A., Morris, M.R.: Is anyone out there?: unpacking Q&A hashtags on Twitter. In: CHI (2014)
74. Salganik, M.J., Dodds, P.S., Watts, D.J.: Experimental study of inequality and unpredictability in an artificial cultural market. Science **311**(5762), 854–856 (2006)
75. Samuel, G.O.: Language and politics: indirectness in political discourse. Discourse Soc. **8**(1), 49–83 (1997)
76. Schoenebeck, S.Y.: The secret life of online moms: anonymity and disinhibition on YouBeMom.com. In: ICWSM (2013)
77. Sherwood, N.E., Jeffery, R.W.: The behavioral determinants of exercise: implications for physical activity interventions. Annu. Rev. Nutr. **20**(1), 21–44 (2000)
78. Stults-Kolehmainen, M.A., Ciccolo, J.T., Bartholomew, J.B., Seifert, J., Portman, R.S.: Age and gender-related changes in exercise motivation among highly active individuals. Athl. Insight **5**(1), 45 (2013)
79. Tausczik, Y.R., Pennebaker, J.W.: The psychological meaning of words: LIWC and computerized text analysis methods. J. Lang. Soc. Psychol. **29**(1), 24–54 (2010)
80. Teevan, J., Morris, M.R., Panovich, K.: Factors affecting response quantity, quality, and speed for questions asked via social network status messages. In: ICWSM (2011)
81. Teng, C.Y., Adamic, L.A.: Longevity in second life. In: ICWSM (2010)
82. Umberson, D., Crosnoe, R., Reczek, C.: Social relationships and health behavior across life course. Ann. Rev. Sociol. **36**, 139 (2010)
83. Vissers, S., Stolle, D.: Spill-over effects between facebook and on/offline political participation? evidence from a two-wave panel study. J. Inf. Technol. Politics **11**(3), 259–275 (2014)
84. Yee, N., Bailenson, J.N., Urbanek, M., Chang, F., Merget, D.: The unbearable likeness of being digital: the persistence of nonverbal social norms in online virtual environments. CyberPsychology Behav. **10**(1), 115–121 (2007)
85. Zhu, H., Kraut, R.E., Kittur, A.: The impact of membership overlap on the survival of online communities. In: CHI (2014)

The Message or the Messenger?
Inferring Virality and Diffusion Structure from Online Petition Signature Data

Chi Ling Chan[1], Justin Lai[1], Bryan Hooi[2], and Todd Davies[1(✉)]

[1] Stanford University, Stanford, CA, USA
callmechiling@gmail.com, {jzlai,davies}@stanford.edu
[2] Carnegie Mellon University, Pittsburgh, PA, USA
bhooi@andrew.cmu.edu

Abstract. Goel et al. [14] examined diffusion data from Twitter to conclude that online petitions are shared more virally than other types of content. Their definition of structural virality, which measures the extent to which diffusion follows a broadcast model or is spread person to person (virally), depends on knowing the topology of the diffusion cascade. But often the diffusion structure cannot be observed directly. We examined time-stamped signature data from the Obama White House's We the People petition platform. We developed measures based on temporal dynamics that, we argue, can be used to infer diffusion structure as well as the more intrinsic notion of virality sometimes known as infectiousness. These measures indicate that successful petitions are likely to be higher in both intrinsic and structural virality than unsuccessful petitions are. We also investigate threshold effects on petition signing that challenge simple contagion models, and report simulations for a theoretical model that are consistent with our data.

Keywords: Petitions · Virality · Broadcast · Diffusion

1 Introduction

This study infers the "virality" and diffusion structure of petitions by examining the temporal dynamics of petition signatures. Viral characteristics can be understood as the opposite of broadcast characteristics. Whereas a *broadcast* structure refers to large diffusion events in which a single source spreads content to a large number of people, *viral* diffusion refers to a cascade of sharing events each between a sender and their associates. Intuitively, a petition that exhibits virality is more likely to attract signatures, in part, through the intrinsic appeal of its *message*, whereas a petition that exhibits more broadcast characteristics is dependent on mass distribution by one or more well-connected senders (the *messenger(s)*) in order to gain signatures.

ⓒ Springer International Publishing AG 2017
G.L. Ciampaglia et al. (Eds.): SocInfo 2017, Part I, LNCS 10539, pp. 499–517, 2017.
DOI: 10.1007/978-3-319-67217-5_30

We used time- and location-coded signature data from the Obama White House's We The People (WTP) petition site.[1] Whereas MoveOn.org and Change.org provide "continuous user engagement" through social media and email, WTP simply provides a static page for each petition, with standard sharing buttons. Since petitions on WTP are less likely to be broadcast, at least directly, than on other petition sites, we reasoned that they would be more likely to depend on person-to-person sharing, and hence viral characteristics, to reach the signature threshold for success [26]. We wished to infer how petitions were shared without direct access to diffusion data. The data we did have – about signatures and the success or failure of each petition, constitute the variables of greatest interest for petitions, and, as is usually the case, the true diffusion data were not observable because they involve an unknown amount of private communication (including emails, phone calls, and face to face dialogue). We therefore sought indirect ways to measure viral and broadcast components of diffusion.

2   Related Work

Virality. Recent literature has examined the virality of online petitions and their differences from other social media. Compared to other online activities, petition-signing typically requires personal endorsement/commitment before sharing. As such, researchers have noted that Twitter cascades about petitions exhibit more *structural virality* than those for news, pictures, and videos [14,15]. Structural virality (SV) is a continuous measure that distinguishes between a single, large broadcast (high SV) and viral spread over multiple generations (low SV).

Structural virality is defined as the average distance between all pairs of nodes in a diffusion tree, a quantity that, for a given cascade size (number of Tweets and Re-Tweets) is minimized when all Re-Tweets are direct offspring of a single source Tweet (pure broadcast diffusion). It is maximized when each Re-Tweet is itself directly Re-Tweeted just once, indicating a string of successors influenced by each predecessor, rather than one predecessor with a great deal of influence. Goel et. al found little to no correlation between structural virality and popularity (cascade size) within any given type of shared content, including petitions (for which they found $r = .04$) [14].

Temporal Adoption Patterns. In the literature on diffusion and contagion, the dominant model posits an S-shaped cumulative adoption curve [5,9,23,37, 42,49], which exhibits an initial period of exponential growth that levels off when the population runs out of potential adopters (see Fig. 1).

Whether this diffusion pattern applies in the online setting has been a question of interest, given the increasing prominence of online mobilization. Investigations of online network mobilizations have identified an S-shaped curve, with

---

[1] We the people petitions from the Obama years are archived at https://petitions.obamawhitehouse.archives.gov.

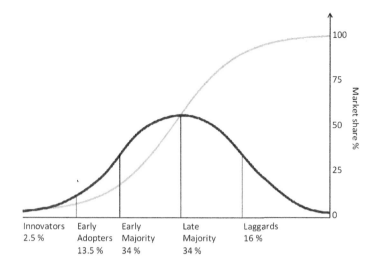

Fig. 1. The classical adoption pattern, showing different phases of adoption for a cumulative S-shaped curve. (Graph from Wikimedia Commons, https://commons. wikimedia.org/wiki/File:Diffusionofideas.PNG, Public Domain.)

critical mass reached only after participants have responded to evidence from early participants [17]. However, evidence remains mixed. In a study that tracks the growth curves of 20,000 petitions on the government petitioning site in the United Kingdom, Yasseri et al. [48] noted that a petition's fate is virtually set after the first 24 h of its introduction, a finding echoed in a study [20] which tracked 8000 petitions on the UK petitioning site No. 10 Downing Street. The S-shaped period of stasis before reaching a critical point appears largely absent, consistent with most studies of online petitioning. These findings call into question the explanatory power of the S-curve model for online petitions. Given that research on online petitions is a relatively new area of study [46], however, there remains a lack of empirical calibration and external validity - a point acknowledged by authors of most of these studies [17,20].

A second question has to do with the diffusion mechanism behind observed patterns. Empirical studies have largely interpreted the S-curve as evidence of social contagion [5,37], but others suggest that the same curve could arise from broadcast distribution mechanisms such as mass media sharing [43]. It remains ambiguous whether viral diffusion is in fact the diffusion mechanism driving growth momentum, as is typically assumed in classical diffusion studies. Related research has shown that information cascades in online networks occur rarely, and studies of online petitions have found that the vast majority of signatures are dominated by a tiny fraction of massively successful petitions [19,25,48]. Events that 'go viral' are an exception rather than the rule [14]. Untangling broadcast from viral diffusion mechanisms, however, has been difficult largely because these studies have based themselves on aggregate diffusion data.

Recent studies have been able to overcome this limitation by analyzing cascade structures directly. Goel et al. analyzed cascades from a billion diffusion events on Twitter and offered a fine-grained analysis of how viral and broadcast diffusion interact [14]. They found that large diffusion events exhibit extreme diversity of structural forms, and demonstrate various mixes of viral and broadcast diffusion, such that the S-curve is but one of many combinations. Extending Goel's analysis of viral and broadcast diffusion, we might ask related questions about how patterns develop over time: When do viral and/or broadcast diffusion set in, and how do they combine to generate the adoption patterns observed? Hale et al. observed that signatures are typically gathered via "punctuated equilibria," specific points that trigger large cascades within a short time, resulting in leptokurtic distributions (characterized by sharp peaks in signature counts) [20], which suggest broadcast events.

Goal Thresholds. A related but less well-studied aspect of online petitioning and diffusion has to do with the effects of threshold requirements that define petition success. Signature thresholds are a typical feature in most online petitions and are crucial for goal-setting by campaigners. Social psychology studies demonstrate that people invest greater effort as they approach a goal [8,29,30], a phenomenon known as the goal-gradient hypothesis, first described by behaviorist Hull (1934) observing rats running faster as they approach a food reward in a maze [22]. For online petitions, there is suggestive evidence in Hale (2013) for threshold effects at the 500-signature mark (the minimum required for an official response on No. 10 Downing Street) [19], but it remains unclear if this can be extrapolated across other petition platforms such as WTP.

3   Data and Methods

3.1   WTP Petitions Data

In this observational study, we relied on an aggregated adoption dataset of 3682 publicly searchable petitions using the public API of WTP.gov, the official online petitioning platform of the White House. These petitions were created within a time period that began from the inception of the platform on September 20, 2011 and ended on March 30, 2015, as our study commenced.

Two critical thresholds for We the People should be noted. First, to be publicly listed and searchable within the site, a petition had to reach 150 signatures within 30 days. Second, to cross the second threshold for review by the White House and be distributed to policy officials for an official response, a petition had to obtain 100,000 signatures (25,000 until January 2013) within 30 days. Responses were posted and linked to the petition on WhiteHouse.gov, and emailed to all petition signers. All petitions in our dataset crossed the 150 signatures threshold, and were publicly listed (the API allowed the retrieval of only petitions that were publicly searchable).

3.2 Variables in Signatures and Petitions Dataset

The WTP API provided data on both petitions and their individual signatures submitted via the petition site. Data on petitions included timestamp of creation, the body of text that campaigners submitted, status at the time of the API query (open/pending response/responded/closed), and the signature count. The data included the time a signature was submitted, as well as geographical details (state, Zipcode if the signature was from the U.S., country, city) of the signatory.

From the API, we assembled a dataset comprising all signatures and petitions and organized them into the following variables: (1) petition ID; (2) signature ID; (3) Unix timestamp of signature; and (4) Zipcode of signatory. This was then merged with a dataset of petitions containing the following data: (1) petition ID; (2) petition title; (3) petition description; (4) signature count; (5) signature status; and (6) Unix timestamp of creation (Unix timestamps were recoded to reflect number of days since a petition's creation).[2]

For this study, a petition was considered successful if it reached the 100,000 (or 25,000) signature threshold necessary for White House review.[3] Using this criterion, a large majority (98.4%) of petitions failed. Of all visible petitions, 1.6% reached the 100,000 threshold. This success rate is consistent with the predicted pattern that only a small fraction of campaigns eventually succeed [48].

3.3 Some Measures of Virality

Because we could not observe the diffusion network of a petition on WTP, we could not use the same measure of structural virality (SV) used by Goel et al. [14]. Furthermore, as they note, their concept of SV may have no relationship to the concept of "infectiousness," or the probability that, in this case, a recipient of a petition announcement will sign the petition.[4] Therefore, we propose indirect measures of SV, which we also distinguish from infectiousness which we call *intrinsic virality* (IV). An indirect measure of SV is the *exceed ratio*, while IV may be assessed through the *first-day, second-day signature comparison*.

Exceed Ratios. The *exceed ratio* is a measure indicating the contribution of temporal peaks to a petition's total signature count. A temporal peak is a period (e.g. day or hour) when the signature count exceeds those within both of its adjacent time periods of the same duration. For every temporal peak, we calculate the signatures received on that peak day minus the number received on either the day before or the day after, whichever is larger. The total exceed ratio E_{Tot} is the sum of these differences across all temporal peaks, divided by the total signature count. Notationally, E_{Tot}, for a given petition over T time periods, in which $S[i]$ signatures are obtained in period i, and L refers to the set of all peak periods within T, is thus defined as:

---

[2] Our data are available at https://github.com/justinlai/petitiondata.

[3] For an alternative perspective on e-petition "success," see Wright [47].

[4] Indeed, for some other types of content such as the spread of memes, initial infectiousness appears not to be a good predictor of later success [39,45].

$$E_{Tot} = \frac{\Sigma_{i \in L}(S(i) - \max[S(i-1), S(i+1)])}{\Sigma_{i=1}^{T} S(i)}$$

The total exceed ratio is a measure of broadcast-ness, and therefore are inverse measure of structural virality. Broadcast content is more likely to rely on large diffusion events in which a period's signature count is larger than those in its adjacent periods, whereas viral content would likely have fewer such events.

We can also calculate a global-peak-only exceed ratio E_{GPO} by dividing the adjacent-periods signature difference for just the global peak period by total signatures, as an indication of the effect of the largest broadcast event.

First-Day, Second-Day Signature Comparison. The *first-day, second-day signature comparison* (FDSD) for a given petition asks whether the number of signatures received on the first day is exceeded by those on the second day. We posit this as a simple measure of intrinsic virality (IV, or infectiousness, viz, intrinsic message appeal for signing and sharing), on the assumption that a petition with high IV will be more likely both to be passed on and to be signed by recipients than will one with lower IV. The first day is the best day to make this follow-on comparison if we assume petitions are most likely to be announced in broadcast events on their first day. If this is the case, then FDSD provides the best standard comparison across petitions, which on other days are likely to vary in whether or not they are broadcast. Since many petitions gain no traction after the first day, the FDSD also allows us to capture that lack of enthusiasm for the largest number of petitions under study.

4   Results

4.1   Overall Adoption Patterns

Overall, a total of 24.5 million signatures were collected by 3682 petitions in our dataset, of which 59 (1.6%) reached the 100,000 signature threshold required for a response from the White House. Successful petitions garnered 31.8% of total signatures.

Each petition's signature data can be plotted as an adoption curve, showing the number of signatures reached day by day. Figures 3 and 4 in Appendix A show temporal signature histograms for randomly chosen successful and unsuccessful petitions, to give a sense of how these look. Figures 5 and 6 of Appendix B show aggregated cumulative adoption patterns and the 30 day temporal thresholds for all the petitions (successful and unsuccessful).

4.2   Structural Virality vs. Broadcast Events

We found that unsuccessful petitions have a **47.4%** higher average total exceed ratio E_{Tot} than successful petitions in the daily distribution of signatures. For the hourly distribution of signatures, this rises to **55.4%** ($p < .0001$ for both

Table 1. Average total exceed ratio E_{Tot} for all petitions: successful versus unsuccessful.

	Successful (N = 59)	Unsuccessful (N = 3623)
Daily	0.152 (sd = .13)	0.224 (sd = .04)
Hourly	0.148 (sd = .09)	0.230 (sd = .03)

comparisons by a two-tailed t-test). This suggests that successful petitions are less dependent on broadcast events (peaks) for growth, and therefore higher in structural virality (Table 1).

The daily global-peak-only exceed ratio E_{GPO} for successful petitions was 0.105 (sd = .11), and for unsuccessful ones was 0.155 (sd = .19). This appears to conflict with the statement by Goel et al. that "if popularity is consistently related to any one feature, it is the size of the largest broadcast," since in our data the indicator of a larger single broadcast is higher for unsuccessful (therefore less popular) petitions ($p = .042$ by a two-tailed t-test).[5]

4.3   Intrinsic Virality (Infectiousness)

Among the 59 successful petitions, 68% had more signatures in their second day than their first day, but among the 3623 unsuccessful petitions, this percentage was only 38%. Thus, there is a clear relationship between a petition's success and having more signatures in its second than its first day (χ^2 test p-value $< 10^{-5}$).

This finding agrees with our earlier intuition that poorly performing petitions tend to receive an initial burst of signatures but then decay quickly. Moreover, this measure is particularly interesting as it only relies on the first two days, and thus can be used as an early indicator of whether a petition is likely to succeed. By the reasoning in Subsect. 3.3, we infer that successful petitions are higher in intrinsic virality than are unsuccessful ones. This may seem like an obvious truth, but it contradicts influential models of diffusion which imply that "the largest and most viral cascades are not inherently better than those that fail to gain traction, but are simply more fortunate" [14] (citing [44]).

4.4   Additional Measures: Viral and Broadcast Diffusion Across All Petitions

We can also analyze our dataset as a whole, without distinguishing between petitions that do and do not pass the success threshold. Additional measures of interest for looking at virality across all petitions are described in Table 2. A petition's 'global peak' is the day during which it received the most signatures (where day 1 is the day the petition was introduced). This is another indirect way to measure intrinsic virality, on the assumption that a petition with more appeal

---

[5] In footnote 10 on p. 187, Goel et al. clarify that this statement applies to normalized and not just to absolute size [14].

will be more likely to grow in its signature count rather than die out, and hence would be expected to have a later global peak. The dependent variable, *total*, is the total number of signatures a petition acquires over the 60 day period. Here we will refer to more and less popular petitions to indicate numerical differences rather than the binary, successful and unsuccessful categories.

Table 2. Measures of shape examined in this section (with the type of virality measured noted in brackets)

Measure of Shape	Interpretation
Skewness	Whether distribution has larger 'tails' extending to right (positive) [IV]
Kurtosis	How peaked a distribution is [SV]
Location of global peak	The day on which the petition received the most signatures [IV]
Number of local peaks	Number of days on which the petition received more signatures than on adjacent days [SV]

Regression Results. We perform linear regressions of the number of signatures over our measures in Table 2. The results are shown in Table 3.

As shown in Columns 1, 3 and 4 of Table 3, we find that skewness and kurtosis are also significantly correlated with signature count. Under all three model specifications, petitions with right skewed distributions (i.e. larger right tails) tend to end up with more signatures (which indicates intrinsic virality, i.e. more signatures late in the process due to more people signing and passing on the petition), as do petitions with lower kurtosis (i.e. having less sharp peaks). This latter finding would be predicated by higher structural virality, since kurtosis is related to our exceed ratio as an indicator of events (the inverse of virality).

As shown in column 2 of Table 3, linear regression suggests that on average, a petition that peaks 1 day later ends up with 262.89 more signatures ($p \approx 1.3 \times 10^{-9}$). The relationship remains about as strong, and still highly significant, when we control for the number of local peaks, and the skewness and kurtosis of the petition's temporal distribution (column 3) as well as when we replace the dependent variable by its logarithm (to ensure that petitions with large signature counts do not excessively influence the fitted coefficients).

Hence, we find that petitions with later global peak days tend to end up with more signatures than petitions with earlier peaks, which we take to be an indication of intrinsic virality. This finding is also illustrated in Fig. 2, in which petitions are separated into those with global peaks on day 1, 2, and so on; and we observe, the mean numbers of signatures seems to broadly increase as the peak gets later, which agrees with the regression findings.

As noted above, more popular petitions have more local peaks. However, further analysis reveals that this phenomenon occurs mainly because less popular

Table 3. Linear regression shows a highly significant positive relationship between peak_day and total signatures (total). Model 3 shows that this relationship remains significant when controlling for the number of peaks, variance, skewness, and kurtosis. Model 4 shows that this remains significant when log transforming the dependent variable (number of signatures).

	Dependent variable:			
	total signatures			log(total)
	(Model 1)	(Model 2)	(Model 3)	(Model 4)
skewness	5,009.992***		5,875.782***	0.558***
	p = 0.00003		p = 0.00000	p = 0.000
kurtosis	−585.658***		−532.246***	−0.062***
	p = 0.00001		p = 0.00003	p = 0.000
global_peak.day		262.890***	227.812***	0.008**
		p = 0.000	p = 0.00000	p = 0.013
num_local_peaks			2,103.878***	0.150***
			p = 0.000	p = 0.000
Constant	−342.411	4,985.854***	−22,660.150***	5.455***
	p = 0.860	p = 0.000	p = 0.000	p = 0.000
Observations	3,682	3,682	3,682	3,682
R^2	0.006	0.010	0.087	0.089
Adjusted R^2	0.005	0.010	0.086	0.088
Residual Std. Error	19,316.340 (df = 3679)	19,271.360 (df = 3680)	18,518.850 (df = 3677)	1.364 (df = 3677)
F Statistic	10.355*** (df = 2; 3679)	36.997*** (df = 1; 3680)	87.054*** (df = 4; 3677)	90.216*** (df = 4; 3677)

Note: *p<0.1; **p<0.05; ***p<0.01

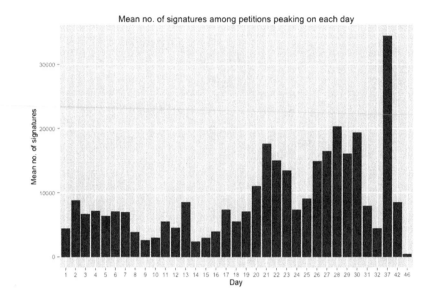

Fig. 2. The chart indicates the mean number of signatures of petitions with a global peak on a given day (with missing days after day 32 to a lack of instances). Petitions which peak on later days tend to end up with a higher total number of signatures than those which peak on earlier days.

petitions receive very few signatures after day 30 (as discussed in our threshold section) particularly when they do not reach the 100, 000 mark, and hence have fewer local peaks. Indeed, when we consider only days 1 to 30 and perform another regression of $\log(total)$ against num_local_peaks, the regression coefficient becomes much smaller and no longer statistically significant (coefficient of $-0.009, p = 0.437$).

4.5   Threshold Effects

Our analysis of petition adoption curves reveals: (a) a goal-gradient threshold effect, i.e. petitions start to receive fewer signatures after reaching the 100, 000 signatures mark; and (b) a temporal threshold effect, i.e. if a petition becomes 30 days old without receiving 100, 000 signatures, it suddenly starts to receive fewer signatures. (See Figs. 5 and 6 in Appendix B) We take this as evidence that WTP site users are paying attention to the social context when they decide to sign, which is at odds with a "simple contagion" model in which the probability of signing as a result of each new communication remains the same (see, e.g. [6, 14, 18]).

5   A Theoretical Model

In this section we describe a model that explains the observed signatures as a mixture of broadcasts (which induce a group of users to sign the petition, e.g. a news broadcast) and viral spreading of the petition from people who have just signed it to new users. Under this model, at each time step, a petition has a small probability of a broadcast occurring. Each broadcast brings in a number of users, where the number is drawn from a log-normal distribution, which allows for large variance in broadcast sizes similar to what we observe in actual data. Naturally, this distribution can be replaced by any appropriate distribution in other applications depending on the researcher's prior beliefs.

At the same time, viral spread is happening constantly - each user who has just signed the petition has a small probability of spreading the petition to each other user who has not signed it yet. The strength of the viral spread can be parametrized by the basic reproduction number R_0, the average number of people that each signer spreads the petition to in a completely susceptible population. In addition, since we observe in the real data a fairly constant and low 'background' level at which users sign the petition, we also add a similar low background probability for each user in the population to sign the petition at each time step, independent of the existing broadcast and viral mechanism.

For our simulations, the probability of broadcasts was chosen to give an average of 3 broadcasts per petition, with broadcast size following a log-normal distribution: if X is a broadcast size, then $\log X \sim \mathcal{N}(\mu, \sigma^2)$, where we use $\mu = 5, \sigma = 1.5$. There is always at least one broadcast, and the first broadcast occurs on day 1. For viral spread, the initial susceptible population is set at 10000, and R_0 is chosen from a uniform distribution between 0.7 and 1.9. The background level is set such that each user who has not signed the petition has a 0.002 chance of signing it at each time step.

In this model, R_0 could be thought of as what we have called "instrinsic virality" (IV) of the *message*, in that it varies across petitions and measures the likelihood of signing and passing along that petition across all recipients in the population. The average broadcast size, by contrast, is assumed to be the same for each petition, since we assume that to be a feature of the population (the *messengers*) rather than of the petition itself.

Replicating Empirical Findings on Shape and Success. Are the empirical findings from Subsect. 4.4 relating the shape of a petition's adoption curve and its popularity also present in the simulations? If they are, this provides a possible explanation for the empirical findings; if not, they suggest a way of improving the model. To answer this question, we simulate 5000 petitions using the broadcast and viral model, and do a linear regression of the logarithm of the total number of signatures received by a petition against measures of shape as we did earlier (in Table 3). As before, we use the logarithm of the number of signatures as the response variable to prevent outliers from excessively influencing the fit. Table 4 shows the regression coefficients when using these simulations (col. 1) compared

Table 4. Comparison between regression coefficients using simulated data (left col.) vs. actual data (right col.). Regression coefficients are all significant and match by sign; however, there is a stronger effect of num_local_peaks for the actual data. Variables: global_peak_day: which day the most signatures were received. num_local_peaks: number of days at which more signatures were received than the previous and next day.

	Dependent variable:	
	log(total)	
	Simulated	Actual Data
	(1)	(2)
global_peak_day	0.007***	0.008**
	p = 0.000	p = 0.013
num_local_peaks	0.024***	0.150***
	p = 0.000	p = 0.000
skewness	0.453***	0.558***
	p = 0.000	p = 0.000
kurtosis	−0.028***	−0.062***
	p = 0.000	p = 0.000
Constant	5.991***	5.455***
	p = 0.000	p = 0.000
Observations	5,000	3,682
R^2	0.298	0.089
Adjusted R^2	0.298	0.088
Residual Std. Error	0.403 (df = 4995)	1.364 (df = 3677)
F Statistic	530.431*** (df = 4; 4995)	90.216*** (df = 4; 3677)
Note:		*p<0.1; **p<0.05; ***p<0.01

to the original regression coefficients for the actual data (col. 2). Table 4 shows that all the coefficients for the regression on simulated data are significant with the same sign as in the original petition data. Most are of fairly similar magnitudes, with the exception of num_local_peaks, which has a stronger effect in the actual data. However, we observed earlier that this variable is significant in the actual data largely as an artifact of the long runs of zeros for less successful petitions.

Since the simulations are based on a simple model, we can explain these regression findings. Petitions with low R_0 peak early when they receive an initial broadcast but then lose momentum extremely quickly due to the lack of strong viral spread; hence, they have earlier global peaks, short right tails, and a highly peaked distribution. Petitions with high R_0 accumulate signatures more gradually due to having stronger viral spread, then lose momentum gradually as the population runs out of users who have not signed the petition, thus having later global peaks, larger right tails, and a less peaked distribution. Since petitions with high R_0 end up with more total signatures, these account for the regression coefficients.

This does not necessarily imply that the same effects are present in the actual data. But these simulations provide a plausible explanation for the empirical findings that more successful petitions have later global peaks, more skewed and less peaked distributions. The simulation results suggest that under a simple model of viral spread, as long as different petitions have varying values of R_0 (i.e. rate of viral spread), we should expect correlations between total number of signatures and these measures of petition shape. As we have observed in our simulations, this is because higher R_0 petitions have different characteristic shapes than low R_0 petitions, and also end up with more signatures.

6   Discussion and Future Work

We have studied the temporal dynamics of adoption and diffusion patterns in online petition-signing, in order to understand what makes petitions gain traction and growth momentum. In this final section, we return to the questions that motivated this study and discuss theoretical and practical implications of our observations and modeling.

While Goel et al. noted that there is a very weak correlation for popularity and structural virality (the average distance between nodes) for petition sharing on Twitter [14], our research finds that our measures of intrinsic virality (first-day second-day comparison, skewness, and global peak day) are highly predictive of petition popularity/success. Our measures of exceed ratio and kurtosis indicate further that threshold-successful and/or more popular petitions are higher in structural virality. Intrinsic virality we take to be a property of a petition's message, whereas structural virality is the inverse of broadcast-ness, which we take to be a feature of its messengers.

The fact that intrinsic virality, which is based on the appeal of the message rather than how it is spread, appears to predict success for petitions on We the People, is a partial answer to a question posed by Goel et al. about the relationship between structural virality and what they call "infectiousness" (intrinsic virality). They look at different models in which infectiousness is assumed to be either fixed or varying between different messages (petitions, in our case), and remain uncommitted about which one better describes real data. Our results for the first-day, second-day comparison and other intrinsic virality measures argue that not all messages are created equal, and that early indications of a message's intrinsic appeal, before the diffusion structure has had a chance to be determined, are correlated with eventual success for petitions. Two other findings challenging whether the assumptions of Goel et al. apply to WTP are that (a) the global-peak-only exceed ratio for daily signature totals was lower for successful than for failed petitions on We the People, which indicates that the largest (relative) broadcast event may not be the best predictor of petition popularity/success; and (b) signatures on WTP exhibit a strong threshold effect (consistent with the goal gradient hypothesis), which is at odds with a simple contagion model, of which theirs is a special case ([14], p. 189, footnote 14).

Regression analysis over all the petitions, in Subsect. 4.4, indicated that more successful petitions exhibit: (1) a later global peak; (2) a larger right tail (positive skewness); (3) a less peaked distribution (lower kurtosis). Features 1 and 2 are indicative of intrinsic virality (IV), while feature 3 is indicative of structural virality (SV). Petitions that under-perform often experience early bursts of momentum at the outset, but the decay of such spikes is usually rapid. Based on our simulations, we find that a simple model combining broadcasts and viral diffusion, in which different petitions have different strength of viral diffusion (or R_0) (analogous to IV) can account for these three findings, primarily due to the different characteristic shapes between high and low R_0 petitions.

Our FDSD variable finding revealed that a petition is likely to fail if the number of signatures gathered on its second day is lower than its first day, indicating it has low intrinsic virality. But previous research has shown the first day alone to be a very important predictor of petition success [20,48]. This could be taken as evidence for the importance of the initial broadcast event, in addition to structural and intrinsic virality, for petition popularity. Absent an effective broadcast, it is highly unlikely that a viral effect will set in and bring about the necessary momentum for growth in support.

The WTP data contain location- as well as timestamped signatures. This opens the possibility of further testing for geographical diffusion effects. An initial attempt to predict petition success from average land distance between Zipcodes in adjacent signature pairs did not uncover a difference between successful and unsuccessful petitions. However, this may be due to the fact that the overall average distance confounds both diffusion distance between signers (which might be lower for viral transmission) and the fact that more popular petitions are likely eventually to find an audience across larger distances than are less popular ones that fizzle early. This question awaits a good measure that can disentangle these potentially opposing effects.

Acknowledgements. We wish to thank Marek Hlavac for technical assistance, and Lee Ross and Howard Rheingold for timely and valuable feedback on an earlier version of this work (which was submitted by the first author as her masters thesis [7]), as well as three anonymous reviewers for their helpful comments.

Appendix A: Signature Graphs for Individual Petitions

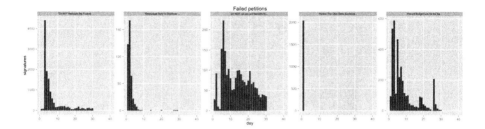

Fig. 3. Temporal distribution of 5 randomly chosen petitions which did not reach the 100,000 signature mark.

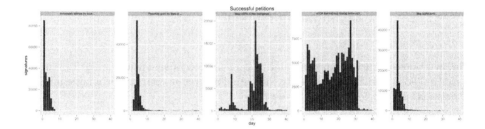

Fig. 4. Temporal distribution of 5 randomly chosen petitions which succeeded in reaching the 100,000 signature mark

Appendix B: Aggregated Temporal Signature Graphs

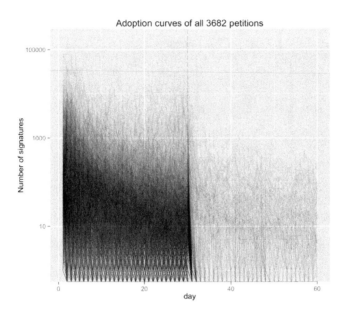

Fig. 5. Adoption curves capturing daily accumulation of signatures in 3682 petitions across a 60-day period. A clear spike indicating a surge in support for a large number of petitions right before the 30-day deadline.

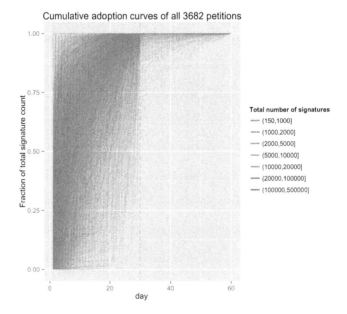

Fig. 6. Adoption curves capturing daily accumulation of signatures in 3682 petitions across a 60-day period. A clear spike indicating a surge in support for a large number of petitions right before the 30-day deadline.

References

1. Adar, E., Adamic, L.: Tracking information epidemics in blogspace. In: IEEE/WIC/ACM International Conference on Web Intelligence. IEEE Computer Society, Compiegne University of Technology, France (2005)
2. Bandura, A., Cervone, D.: Differential engagement of self-reactive influences in cognitive motivation. Organ. Behav. Hum. Decis. Process. **38**(1), 92–113 (1986)
3. Bakshy, E., Hofman, J.M., Mason, W.A., Watts, D.J.: Everyone's an influencer: quantifying influence on twitter. In: Proceedings of the Fourth ACM International Conference on Web Search and Data Mining, pp. 65–74. ACM (2011)
4. Bakshy, E., Karrer, B., Adamic, L.: Social influence and the diffusion of user-created content. In: Proceedings of the Tenth ACM Conference on Electronic Commerce, pp. 325–334. Association of Computing Machinery (2009)
5. Bass, F.M.: A new product growth for model consumer durables. Manag. Sci. **15**(5), 215–227 (1969)
6. Centola, D., Macy, M.: Complex contagions and the weakness of long ties. Am. J. Sociol. **113**(3), 702–734 (2007)
7. Chan, C.L.: Temporal dynamics of adoption and diffusion patterns in online petitioning. M.S. thesis, Stanford University (2015)
8. Cheema, A., Bagchi, R.: The effect of goal visualization on goal pursuit: implications for consumers and managers. J. Mark. **75**(2), 109–123 (2011)
9. Coleman, J., Katz, E., Menzel, H.: The diffusion of an innovation among physicians. Sociometry **20**, 253–270 (1957)
10. Cryder, C.E., Loewenstein, G., Seltman, H.: Goal gradient in helping behavior. J. Exp. Soc. Psychol. **49**(6), 1078–1083 (2013)
11. Dodds, P.S., Watts, D.J.: A generalized model of social and biological contagion. J. Theor. Biol. **232**(4), 587–604 (2005)
12. Gladwell, M.: The Tipping Point: How Little Things can Make a Big Difference. Little, Brown and Company, Boston (2002)
13. Gleeson, J.P., Cellai, D., Onnela, J.-P., Porter, M.A., Reed-Tsochas, F.: A simple generative model of collective online behaviour (2013). arXiv preprint arXiv:1305.7440
14. Goel, S., Anderson, A., Hofman, J., Watts, D.: The structural virality of online diffusion. Manag. Sci. **62**(1), 180–196 (2016)
15. Goel, S., Watts, D.J., Goldstein, D.G.: The structure of online diffusion networks. In: Proceedings of the 13th ACM Conference on Electronic Commerce, pp. 623–638. ACM (2012)
16. Goldenberg, J., Libai, B., Muller, E.: Talk of the network: a complex systems look at the underlying process of word-of-mouth. Mark. Lett. **12**(3), 211–223 (2001)
17. Gonzalez-Bailon, S., Borge-Holthoefer, J., Rivero, A., Moreno, Y.: The dynamics of protest recruitment through an online network. Sci. Rep. **1**, 197 (2011)
18. Granovetter, M.: Threshold models of collective behavior. Am. J. Sociol. **83**(6), 1420–1443 (1978)
19. Hale, S.A., John, P., Margetts, H.Z., Yasseri, T.: Investigating political participation and social information using big data and a natural experiment. In: APSA 2014 Annual Meeting Paper (2014)
20. Hale, S.A., Margetts, H., Yasseri, T.: Petition growth and success rates on the UK no. 10 downing street website. In: Proceedings of the 5th Annual ACM Web Science Conference, pp. 132–138. ACM (2013)

21. Heath, C., Larrick, R.P., Wu, G.: Goals as reference points. Cogn. Psychol. **38**(1), 79–109 (1999)
22. Hull, C.L.: The rat's speed-of-locomotion gradient in the approach to food. J. Comp. Psychol. **17**(3), 393 (1934)
23. Iyengar, R., Van Den Bulte, C., Valente, T.W.: Opinion leadership and social contagion in new product diffusion. Mark. Sci. **30**, 195–212 (2011)
24. Jones, B.D., Baumgartner, F.R.: The Politics of Attention: How Government Prioritizes Problems. University of Chicago Press, Chicago (2005)
25. Jungherr, A., Jrgens, P.: The political click: political participation through E? Petitions in Germany. Policy Internet **2**(4), 131–165 (2010)
26. Karpf, D.: Analytic Activism: Digital Listening and the New Political Strategy. Oxford University Press, Corby (2017)
27. Kempe, D., Kleinberg, J., Tardos, E.: Maximizing the spread of influence through a social network. In: 9th ACM SIGKDD International Conference on Knowledge Discovery and Data Mining. Association of Computing Machinery (2003)
28. Kitsak, M., Gallos, L.K., Havlin, S., Liljeros, F., Muchnik, L., Stanley, H.E., Makse, H.A.: Identification of influential spreaders in complex networks. Nat. Phys. **6**(11), 888–893 (2010)
29. Kivetz, R., Urminsky, O., Zheng, Y.: The goal-gradient hypothesis resurrected: purchase acceleration, illusionary goal progress, and customer retention. J. Mark. Res. **43**(1), 39–58 (2006)
30. Koo, M., Fishbach, A.: The small-area hypothesis: effects of progress monitoring on goal adherence. J. Consum. Res. **39**(3), 493–509 (2012)
31. Leskovec, J., Singh, A., Kleinberg, J.: Patterns of influence in a recommendation network. In: Ng, W.-K., Kitsuregawa, M., Li, J., Chang, K. (eds.) PAKDD 2006. LNCS, vol. 3918, pp. 380–389. Springer, Heidelberg (2006). doi:10.1007/11731139_44
32. Lin, Y.-R., Margolin, D., Keegan, B., Baronchelli, A., Lazer, D.: #bigbirds never die: understanding social dynamics of emergent hashtags (2013)
33. Locke, E.A.: Toward a theory of task motivation and incentives. Organ. Behav. Hum. Perform. **3**(2), 157–189 (1968)
34. Lopez-Pintado, D., Watts, D.: Social influence, binary decisions and collective dynamics. Ration. Soc. **20**(4), 399–443 (2008)
35. Margetts, H.Z., John, P., Escher, T., Reissfelder, S.: Social information and political participation on the Internet: an experiment. Eur. Polit. Sci. Rev. **3**(3), 321–344 (2011)
36. Margetts, H.Z., John, P., Hale, S.A., Reissfelder, S.: Leadership without leaders? Starters and followers in online collective action. Polit. Stud. **63**, 278–299 (2013)
37. Rogers, E.: Diffusion of Innovations. Free Press, New York (1962)
38. Rothkopf, E.Z., Billington, M.J.: Goal-guided learning from text: inferring a descriptive processing model from inspection times and eye movements. J. Educ. Psychol. **71**(3), 310 (1979)
39. Salganik, M.J., Dodds, P.S., Watts, D.J.: Experimental study of inequality and unpredictability in an artificial cultural market. Science **311**(5762), 854–856 (2006)
40. Staab, S., Domingos, P., Golbeck, J., Ding, L., Finin, T., Joshi, A., Nowak, A.: Social networks applied. IEEE Intell. Syst. **20**(1), 80–93 (2005)
41. Sun, E., Rosenn, I., Marlow, C., Lento, T.: Gesundheit! modeling contagion through facebook news feed. In: Proceedings of International AAAI Conference on Weblogs and Social Media (2009)
42. Valente, T.W.: Network Models of the Diffusion of Innovations, vol. 2. Hampton Press, Cresskill (1995)

43. Van den Bulte, C., Lilien, G.L.: Medical innovation revisited: social contagion versus marketing effort. Am. J. Sociol. **106**(5), 1409–1435 (2001)
44. Watts, D.J.: A simple model of global cascades on random networks. Proc. Nat. Acad. Sci. **99**(9), 5766–5771 (2002)
45. Weng, L., Menczer, F., Ahn, Y.Y.: Predicting successful memes using network and community structure. In: ICWSM, March 2014
46. Wright, S.: E-petitions. In: Handbook of Digital Politics, p. 136 (2015). Chapter 9
47. Wright, S.: Success and online political participation: the case of Downing Street E-petitions. Inf. Commun. Soc. **19**(6), 843–857 (2016)
48. Yasseri, T., Hale, S.A., Margetts, H.: Modeling the rise in internet-based petitions (2013). arXiv preprint arXiv:1308.0239
49. Young, H.P.: Innovation diffusion in heterogeneous populations: contagion, social influence, and social learning. Am. Econ. Rev. **99**(5), 1899–1924 (2009)

Proximity, Location, Mobility, and Urban Analytics

Measuring Ambient Population from Location-Based Social Networks to Describe Urban Crime

Cristina Kadar$^{(\boxtimes)}$, Raquel Rosés Brüngger, and Irena Pletikosa

Information Management Chair, D-MTEC, ETH Zurich, Zürich, Switzerland
{ckadar,rroses,ipletikosa}@ethz.ch

Abstract. Recently, a lot of attention has been given to crime prediction, both by the general public and by the research community. Most of the latest work has concentrated on showing the potential of novel data sources like social media, mobile phone data, points of interest, or transportation data for the crime prediction task and researchers have focused mostly on techniques from supervised machine learning to show their predictive potential. Yet, the question remains if indeed this data can be used to better describe urban crime. In this paper, we investigate the potential of data harvested from location-based social networks (specifically Foursquare) to describe urban crime. Towards this end, we apply techniques from spatial econometrics. We show that this data, seen as a measurement for the ambient population of a neighborhood, is able to further describe crime levels in comparison to models built solely on census data, seen as measurement for the resident population of a neighborhood. In an analysis of crime on census tract level in New York City, the total number of incidents can be described by our models with up to $R^2 = 56\%$, while the best model for the different crime subtypes is achieved for larcenies with roughly 67% of the variance explained.

Keywords: Urban computing · Social computing · Computational social science · Crime analysis · Spatial econometrics · Location-based social networks

1 Introduction and Related Work

Many past criminological studies have already highlighted the relationship between urban crime and various characteristics of the *resident population* in the area, like e.g. ethnicity [12], income level [12], and residential stability [26]. The theoretical underpinning of these studies lies in the *social disorganization theory* [24] which links the ecological attributes of a neighborhood to its crime levels. In these empirical studies, scholars have exploited traditional census data to measure the population at risk.

Yet, with the advent of internet-enabled mobile devices, citizens have become sensors [16] that produce rich data revealing the intensity and nature of

© Springer International Publishing AG 2017
G.L. Ciampaglia et al. (Eds.): SocInfo 2017, Part I, LNCS 10539, pp. 521–535, 2017.
DOI: 10.1007/978-3-319-67217-5_31

human activity in cities. Specifically, location-based social networks (LBSNs) like Foursquare bridge the physical and digital worlds by allowing their users to share their location when visiting different spots in a city. Such services expose information on the location, time, and nature of the activities their users engage in (like shopping, eating out, commuting, being at home, etc.). Moreover, the users can be seen as exponents of the *ambient population* in an area, a more loyal measure of the population at risk expected in that area at any given time. We argue that characteristics of such data can be integrated in models of urban crime.

The relationship between human dynamics and crime in urban environments has been loosely captured by criminologists under the umbrella of the *routine activity theory* [11] or hypothesized by urban planners in quantitative studies (e.g. *eyes on the street* in [18]). Under the routine activity theory paradigm, crime is seen as occurring when a motivated offender meets an unguarded target at a suitable point in time and space [11]. Even further, Brantingham and Brantingham [7] argue that one common way offenders encounter their targets is through overlapping or shared activity spaces, like the offenders home, work, school, and places of recreation as nodes. Furthermore, the same authors go on in [8] and classify some urban hot spots as *crime attractors* (particular places where strongly motivated offenders are attracted due to the known criminal opportunities, like bar and prostitution areas), and others as *crime generators* (particular areas to which large numbers of people are attracted for reasons unrelated to any particular level of criminal motivation, like shopping and entertainments areas). On the other hand, the visionary author and activist Jane Jacobs postulated in her 1961 book *The Death and Life of Great American Cities*, that higher densities and diversities of people and human activities would act as crime deterrents [18].

Very recently, computational social scientists have started to test such theories at scale in descriptive studies by leveraging human dynamics data such as mobile phone data [30]. The authors find significant negative correlations between crime and the diversity of age and ratio of visitors and positive correlations between crime and the ration of residents in an area, as computed using footfall counts extracted from telecommunication data. Finally, latest literature from the data mining community has concentrated on showing the potential of novel data sources of human dynamics like social media [15], mobile phone data [6], or transportation data [31] in a *crime prediction setup*. They prove that machine learning techniques can achieve competitive predictive scores on features mined from such alternative data sources.

In this work, we focus on showing the novelty of the LBSN data in a *crime description setup*. Shmueli outlays in [29] the three different scenarios in which statistical modeling can be used to develop and test theories: causal explanation, prediction, and description. In a descriptive setup, a model is used for capturing the association between the dependent and the independent variables, rather than for causal inference or for predictive modeling [29]. In this work, we are applying linear models from spatial econometrics that are able to produce an interpretable model. The contribution of the new factors to the dependent variable is precisely quantified in a multivariate setup (as compared to the correlation analyses in [30]) and tested for statistical significance (as compared to the non-parametric machine learning models in [6], e.g.).

In the remainder of the paper we: present the leveraged datasets and derived factors in Sect. 2, elaborate on the methods and results of the analysis in Sect. 3, and summarize the conclusions, implications and limitations in Sect. 4.

2   Datasets and Factors

In our empirical study, we use data from New York City (NYC), a city that is sufficiently large, diverse, and high-tech savvy to assure a high degree of penetration for location-sharing services.

The dependent variable are incident counts from years 2011 through 2015 at census tract level: $N = 2{,}167$ census tracts. A census tract is a stable geographical unit for the presentation of statistical data with a population size between 1,200 and 8,000 people, with an optimum size of 4,000[1]. To account for the heterogeneity of the unit of analysis, we include the census tract's **area** as a control variable. In terms of independent variables, we will be crafting two sets of variables: one set describing the resident population and one set describing the ambient population. In trying to keep the variables count low, we will be relying heavily on aggregate metrics like fractions and diversity indexes. Even more, we will attempt to craft suitable counterparts of the established resident population metrics when using proxy data of the ambient population.

2.1   Crime

The full crime dataset was downloaded from the NYC Open Data platform[2] and all incidents from 2011–2015 were mapped to the census tracts of the city. Each incident belongs to one of the following sub-types: grand larceny, robbery, burglary, felony assault, and grand larceny of motor vehicle, rape, or murder. In the following, we will be analyzing the total number of incidents, as well as the specific sub-types of crimes that can be described by population characteristics: grand larcenies, robberies, burglaries and assaults. First, to address the skewed distribution of the count data – see Fig. 1 (upper left) for the raw counts –, we apply a log-transformation. This operation will yield the dependent variable in the models.

2.2   Residential Population

The census data for NYC have been derived from the 2010 Decennial Census and the 2010–2014 American Community Survey[3] and it has been employed to derive the crime correlates as per the *social disorganization theory*.

---

[1] https://www.census.gov/geo/reference/gtc/gtc_ct.html.
[2] https://nycopendata.socrata.com/.
[3] http://www.census.gov/.

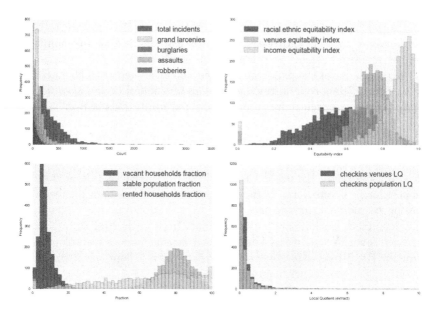

Fig. 1. Histograms of raw variables: crime counts (upper left), equitability indexes (upper right), fractions (lower left), and local quotients (lower right).

The first variable is the **total population** and it is a measure of the resident population at risk. The population diversity has been shown to play a role in the crime phenomenon [17] so we compute two diversity indexes based on the socio-demographic and economical information: a **racial-ethnic equitability index** and an **income equitability index**. The racial-ethnic index measures the presence of multiple ethnic and racial groups within a certain area and is computed based on five exhaustive and mutually exclusive aggregates (non-Hispanic whites, non-Hispanic blacks, Hispanics of any race, Asians, and others – Native Americans, members of other races, and multi-racial persons), and the income index measures the variance in household income across three main income levels (low, medium, and high-income households). To compute these indexes, we utilize the Shannon diversity index [27], initially developed in information theory, and later used in ecology to summarize the diversity of species [23]. Finally, the Shannon equitability index [28] is simply the Shannon diversity index divided by the maximum diversity, yielding a normalized value within [0, 1]:

$$-\sum_{i=1}^{k} p_i \ln p_i / \ln k$$

where p_i is denoting the proportion of the population in group i and k is the total number of groups. Note that lower values indicate the relative abundance of a given group, while higher values indicate equiprobability of all groups. We plot the histograms of all equitability indexes in Fig. 1 (upper right). Finally, we calculate the **fraction of vacant households**, the **fraction of rented households** from the occupied ones, and the **fraction of stable population** (individuals who moved in prior to 2010) as measures for the neighborhood instability which has been shown to be associated with violence [26] – see Fig. 1 (lower left).

2.3   Ambient Population

The factors describing the ambient population were derived based on a dataset collected over the Foursquare API[4] in May–June 2016, consisting of 250,926 venues covering the whole area of NYC, and spanning following 10 broad categories: Arts and Entertainment (11,794 venues), College and University (7,082), Event (84), Food (47,590), Nightlife Spot (11,140), Outdoors and Recreation (18,011), Professional and Other Places (64,055), Residence (14,632), Shop and Service (62,627), Travel and Transport (13,911). These venues have experienced in total almost 122 million checkins since their creation in the app.

The **number of total venues**, **number of total checkins** and in typical **week and weekend afternoons** within a census tract reflect the popularity of that area [5] are all potential metrics of the ambient population at risk, similarly to how the census's total population is a measure of the resident population at risk.

The **venues equitability index**, computed by an analog equitability formula to the one introduced for the residential population, is then a metric capturing the functional decomposition of a neighborhood. Previous work in urban computing has used similar metrics of neighborhood diversity based on LBSN data [19] or on mobile phone data [13,22], as pioneered in [14]. The higher the equitability index, the more heterogeneous the area is in terms of types of places, and following that, in terms of functions and activities of the neighborhood. On the other hand, a least entropic area would indicate an area with a dominant function. For example, an area dominated by College and University venues would indicate an area where people primarily study, like an university campus.

Finally, inspired by recent work on digital neighborhoods [4], we compute **local quotients** of (digital) social activity within an area as concentrations of checkins relative to the number of businesses and to the reference census population:

$$\frac{1 + C(t_i)}{total\_checkins} \times \frac{total\_venues}{1 + V(t_i)}$$

$$\frac{1 + C(t_i)}{total\_checkins} \times \frac{total\_population}{1 + P(t_i)}$$

where $P(t_i)$ is the total population count within a census tract, $C(t_i)$ is the total number of checkins, and $V(t_i)$ is the total number of venues. Neighborhoods with

---

[4] https://developer.foursquare.com/.

local quotients $>>1$ can be considered (digital) hot spots, while neighborhoods with local quotients $<<1$ can be considered (digital) deserts. A zoom-in on the $[0, 10]$ interval of the local quotients distributions is plotted in Fig. 1 (lower right).

3   Analysis

3.1   Transformations

As seen in Sect. 2, many of the raw explanatory variables exhibit skewed distributions. Therefore we first transform them towards a normal distribution by using the *Box-Cox method* [9], making them more suitable for linear regression and correlation analysis. As in this work we aim at interpreting and comparing the different regression coefficients, the values of the explanatory variables need to be on the same numerical scale. Towards this end, we apply a second transformation by computing their *z-values* (subtracting the mean μ and normalizing by standard deviation σ).

3.2   Correlation Analysis

Before we delve into building the explanatory models, we run a series of tests first. First, Table 1 shows the Pearson correlation coefficients between the different factors and the log-transformed number of total crime incidents within a census

Table 1. Pearson correlation between all considered factors and the dependent variable: total number of incidents in a census tract (significance levels: $^{***}p \leq 0.001$, $^{**}p \leq 0.01$, $^{*}p \leq 0.05$).

ID	Factor	Pearson Corr.
0	area	-0.1184^{***}
1	population	$+0.5046^{***}$
2	racial_ethnic_div_index	$+0.1410^{***}$
3	income_div_index	-0.1024^{***}
4	vacant_fraction	$+0.1256^{***}$
5	rented_fraction	$+0.5516^{***}$
6	stable_fraction	-0.1217^{***}
7	venues	$+0.5875^{***}$
8	checkins	$+0.4679^{***}$
9	ven_pop_we_afternoon	$+0.4012^{***}$
10	ven_pop_week_afternoon	$+0.4406^{***}$
11	venues_div_index	$+0.2516^{***}$
12	checkins_venues_lq	$+0.2162^{***}$
13	checkins_population_lq	$+0.1764^{***}$

tract. We observe that all correlations are significant at 0.1%. Furthermore, most of the factors are positively correlated with the crime levels, with the exception of the census tract's area, income diversity index, and fraction of stable population.

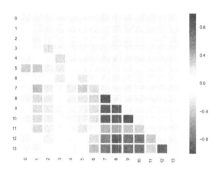

Fig. 2. Correlation matrix of all factors.

We proceed by looking at the correlation matrix of variables defined above to identify potentially correlated factors – depicted in Fig. 2. While multicollinearity does not reduce the reliability of the whole model within the sample set, it is a problem if we are interested in the effects of individual factors on the outcome, since we cannot separate out their individual contributions. As expected from the way they were constructed, the number of venues, checkins, and popular venues are correlated between each other. Also, the two local quotients values are highly correlated. Furthermore, we compute the variance inflation factor (VIF) which quantifies the severity of multicollinearity in an ordinary least squares regression analysis. The lower the VIF value, the better, while an upper limit value of 10 is accepted in the literature [20]. The first column in Table 2 lists the VIF scores considering a specification with all factors. Based on the results from the correlation matrix and the VIF analysis, we keep one variable per group of correlated variables: the number of venues, and the local quotient relative to the population, respectively. We recompute the VIF values in a specification with the remaining 9 factors – see second column in Table 2 –, and conclude that all kept factors have VIF values smaller than 5, which is well below the accepted threshold.

Finally, Fig. 3 presents the linear relations between the crime counts and the the remaining variables. These initial results support our assumption that specific old and novel attributes of the resident and ambient population of a neighborhood are related to the crime levels. We keep all 9 factors for further analysis.

In addition, we perform a Moran's test [10] to test wether spatial dependencies are present in the crime data. As we obtain a significant global Moran's Index of 0.5552 (***$p \leq 0.001$), we conclude that the spatial distribution of high values and/or low values in the dataset is more spatially clustered than would be expected if underlying spatial processes were random. This result confirms

Table 2. Variance Inflation Factor for all factors and for the remaining factors (*marks an accepted value under 10).

ID	Factor	VIF (all factors)	VIF (remaining factors)
0	area	1.4248*	1.3987*
1	population	3.4659*	2.4226*
2	racial_ethnic_div_index	1.1999*	1.1599*
3	income_div_index	1.4420*	1.3985*
4	vacant_fraction	1.2127*	1.1986*
5	rented_fraction	2.0193*	1.9871*
6	stable_fraction	1.4591*	1.4241*
7	venues	40.0859	4.5949*
8	checkins	64.3999	-
9	ven_pop_we_afternoon	9.1538*	-
10	ven_pop_week_afternoon	8.3502*	-
11	venues_div_index	1.3938*	1.3065*
12	checkins_venues_lq	30.0767	-
13	checkins_population_lq	12.8960	4.0846*

the choice of the spatial lag model. Even more, in addition to the global auto-correlation statistics, we calculate a local indicator of spatial association (LISA) [2], which can help identify and visualize local hot-spots and cold-spots of crime – see Fig. 4.

3.3   Multivariate Explanatory Models

To explain the relationship between the descriptors of the resident and ambient populations and crime levels, we opt for regression models. In a first attempt, which serves as a benchmark, we build a **linear model**:

$$C = \alpha + \beta_0 A + \beta_1 RP + \beta_2 AP + \epsilon$$

where C is the level of crime in a neighborhood, α is the intercept term, A is the area of the neighborhood, RP is the set of variables relating to the resident population in a neighborhood, AP is a set of variables describing the different characteristics of the ambient population, and ϵ is the error term. The parameters β_0, β_1, and β_2 are capturing the effect of these metrics on the crime levels at an intra-urban level.

This technique requires the independence of the observations, yet the distribution of crime across NYC is likely to have a marked spatial dimension. If so, failing to account for the spatial correlation of the dependent variable in an econometric model leads to a biased model [1]. For this reason, we expand the baseline linear model by including the so-called *spatial lag* – an explanatory

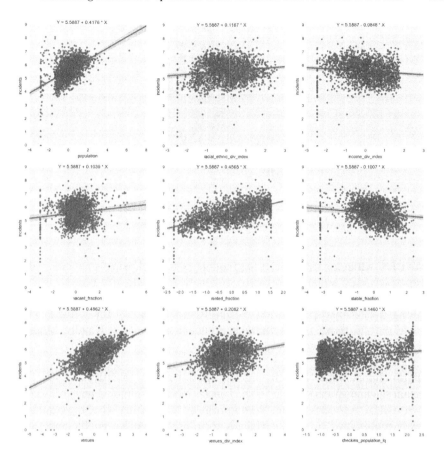

Fig. 3. Total incident counts regressed on the final resident and ambient population metrics. The dependent variable is log-transformed. All independent variables are Box-Cox-transformed and normalized.

variable that captures the values of the dependent variable in the surrounding neighborhood and obtain following **spatial lag model** [1]:

$$C = \alpha + \rho W \times C + \beta_0 A + \beta_1 RP + \beta_2 AP + \epsilon$$

where the new term W is a spatial weights matrix encoding the spatial relationships between the census tracts in the dataset (we use a queens contiguity matrix which considers as neighbors any pair of cells that share a vertex) and ρ is the spatial autoregressive parameter.

Total Incidents. Table 3 presents the regression results, reporting the R^2 measure for model fit, as well as the value and sign of the coefficients and whether they are significant or not. Specifically, we use the PySAL library in Python [25] and for the linear models estimated using ordinary least squares we report the

Fig. 4. Crime hot-spots and cold-spots.

adjusted R^2, while for the spatial lag models estimated using a generalized spatial two-stage least squares we report the spatial pseudo R^2. Firstly, in Model *(1)* the regression was run with only the area and the independent variables describing the resident population. Secondly, in Model *(2)*, the crime levels are described only in terms of the ambient population variables. Finally, Model *(3)* makes use of the whole set of descriptors.

Although results are comparable across the standard and spatial models some details do change when introducing the spatial effects. Firstly, the size of the significant coefficients is smaller in the spatial model – a known effect of ignoring positive spatial autocorrelation. When properly accounting for the spatial effect, variation is absorbed by the spatial lag term and the other coefficients display more conservative values. The presence of relevant spatial auto-correlation is further confirmed by the significance and large size of the spatial parameter w_incidents (ρ) in all three models.

We now turn at comparing the three model specifications. Overall, in terms of significance, we observe that the racial-ethnic index and the census tract area lose significance when moving from the resident population only model to the full model, while the stable fraction gains significance. The ambient population factors remain significant throughout the models, with the exception of the local quotient of digital activity, which loses significance in some of the specifications. The sign of the significant variables remain stable for the control variable, resident and ambient population variables.

Most importantly, overall, the two models in *(3)* achieve best explanatory performance, with roughly 56% explained variance! This confirms the hypothesis that, the novel factors contribute towards more performant descriptive models of crime. By looking at the spatial-lag formulation of the full model, we interpret that, in the multivariate setup defined previously:

– the population of an area, the fraction of vacant and rented households, the fraction of stable population, the number of venues in the area, and the crime

Table 3. Results of the three regression models. Dependent variable: total number of incidents in a census tract. (significance levels: $^{***}p \leq 0.001$, $^{**}p \leq 0.01$, $^{*}p \leq 0.05$).

	(1)		(2)		(3)	
	Linear	Spatial lag	Linear	Spatial lag	Linear	Spatial lag
Adj./spatial pseudo R^2	43.90%	43.93%	46.88%	46.91%	56.15%	56.33%
constant	+5.5887***	+2.5020***	+5.5887***	+3.7853***	+5.5887***	+3.8228***
area	+0.0336*	+0.1005***	−0.1236***	−0.0454**	−0.0271	+0.0249
population	+0.3109***	+0.2359***			+0.1152***	+0.0919***
racial_ethnic_div_index	+0.0404**	+0.0321**			+0.0062	+0.0082
income_div_index	−0.0813***	−0.0240			−0.1084***	−0.0704***
vacant_fraction	+0.1240***	+0.0944***			+0.0447***	+0.0384***
rented_fraction	+0.3245***	+0.2036***			+0.2355***	+0.1809***
stable_fraction	−0.0269	−0.0205			+0.0462***	+0.0545***
venues			+0.7296***	+0.6342***	+0.5104***	+0.4602***
venues_div_index			+0.0284*	+0.0007	−0.0174	−0.0355**
checkins_population_lq			−0.3498***	−0.3294***	−0.1832***	−0.1864***
w_incidents		+0.5478***		+0.3201***		+0.3134***

in the surrounding areas are positively and significantly related to the area's crime levels.
- the income diversity of the population in an area, as well as the venues diversity and the level of (digital) social activity in that area are negatively and significantly related to the area's crime levels;
- the racial-ethnic diversity of a neighborhood, as well as the neighborhood area are not significantly related to the overall crime levels in that neighborhood.

In terms of implications, the resident population factors derived from the *social disorganization theory* have therefore found strong support in our empirical results. The one exception is the racial-ethnic diversity of a neighborhood, which is actually a pleasant finding: the expectation is that the model will perform similarly well when leaving out this race-based factor. Most importantly, the activity of the ambient population in terms of its diversity and intensity have been found to be statistically significant and negatively related to the crime counts of a neighborhood – result which is in line with Jacob's *Eyes on the Street* theory. Finally, the other factor derived from LBSN data, the number of venues in a neighborhood is found to be statistically significant and positively related to crime – result which supports the *criminogenic places* theory of Brantingham and Brantingham.

Finally, comparing the actual number of incidents versus the estimated number of incidents we obtain a Pearson's $r = 0.6779$ ($^{***}p \leq 0.001$) and $MSE = 0.2434$ on the whole dataset.

Crime Types. So far, the analysis investigated the total number of incidents. Yet, some types of crime can be better described by the attributes of the resident and ambient population than others. We proceed by employing model *(3)* for all crime sub-types. Larcenies, as they include all types of thefts, including e.g. pick-pocketing, seem to be best described by the complete set of population factors with a spatial pseudo R^2 of 66.98%. The models for burglaries and assaults are also competitive with metrics of 45.09% and 45.29%, respectively. Finally, the model for robberies managed to explain 34.56% of the variance, while the remaining types of incidents could not be well described by the population factors.

Table 4. Contribution of the different explanatory variables across different crime types (red – positive coefficient, blue – negative coefficient).

	total incidents	grand larcenies	robberies	burglaries	assaults
Adj./ spatial pseudo R^2	56.33%	66.98%	34.56%	45.09%	45.29%
area	0.0249	0.0178	0.0604	0.0265	0.1168
population	0.0919	0.1150	0.0165	0.1054	0.0722
racial_ethnic_div_index	0.0082	0.0210	0.0312	0.0028	0.0205
income_div_index	0.0704	0.0649	0.0202	0.0113	0.0578
vacant_fraction	0.0384	0.0496	0.0375	0.0796	0.0266
rented_fraction	0.1809	0.1123	0.1553	0.1519	0.2774
stable_fraction	0.0545	0.0620	0.0413	0.0007	0.0414
venues	0.4602	0.5656	0.3876	0.3804	0.3520
venues_div_index	0.0355	0.0328	0.0706	0.0406	0.0703
checkins_venues_lq	0.1864	0.0331	0.2264	0.2468	0.2654
w_incidents	0.3134	0.1994	0.7580	0.0966	0.6020

Table 4 visualizes the contribution of each factor in the explanatory models of the different crime types. We can observe that, in general, the sign and relative size of the coefficients stays similar across the models, with some notable exceptions. The geographical influence of crime in the neighboring areas plays a much greater role in the case of robberies and assaults. On the other hand, for grand larcenies and burglaries the influence of the surrounding areas is smaller in comparison to the general model of total incidents. For the category of grand larcenies, which include cases of street thefts, the number of venues in the areas has a higher contribution in comparison to the general model, while the other two ambient population factors have lower negative coefficients. For the category of assaults, which include more violent types of crimes, the neighborhood's fraction of rented house units and the neighborhood's area have higher positive coefficients in comparison to the general model.

4   Conclusions and Discussion

In this paper, inspired by literature in criminology and urban computing, we have leveraged a location-based online service to craft a series of factors describing the ambient population and used these as describing factors for urban crime.

First, we proved that these novel factors are significantly related to the crime levels in an area. We then built linear and spatial econometric models of crime and concluded that these factors and the geographical influence improve the explanation models based only on factors describing the resident population. Specifically, we found support for both Jacobs *Eyes on the Street* and Brantingham and Brantinghams *criminogenic places* theories, as the diversity and intensity of the ambient population's activities was found to be negatively related to the crime counts, while the number of venues within the neighborhood was positively related to the crime counts. We have repeated the analysis and built models for the various criminal incident types and found that the results hold across the specific models. In the case of street thefts, the positive influence of the number of venues was more substantial, while in the case of more violent types of incidents like assaults and robberies, the geographical influence was found more pronounced.

Limitations of this work reside in the geographical and demographic biases of the users active in such services, as well as in limiting the analysis to one city. Future work will address these points, by including further ubiquitous data sources in the models and by analyzing other urban areas. We ought also to stress the fact, that this is an observational study and not a controlled experiment, therefore the results should be seen as correlation and not causality between the observed variables and the target variable.

Note: We have tested alternative specifications that included further explanatory variables mentioned in the literature, like household diversity index, age diversity index, and venues offering advantages. We do not include these because of space limitations and also because they do not contribute fundamentally new insights or improve R^2 significantly anymore. Furthermore, we believe the true interesting result of this work is the systematic comparison of the two sets of resident and ambient population variables. Details are, however, available from the authors.

Data accessibility: All raw data used in this study is available from the public sources listed in the text (NYC OpenData platform for the crime data, FTP pages of the US Census Bureau for the census data, and Foursquare API for the LBSN data). In case of interest, readers are welcome to contact the authors for the processed data and used source code.

References

1. Anselin, L.: Spatial Econometrics Methods and Models. Studies in Operational Regional Science, vol. 4. Springer, Dordrecht (1988)
2. Anselin, L.: Local indicators of spatial association LISA. Geograph. Anal. **27**(2), 93–115 (1995)
3. Anselin, L., Cohen, J., Cook, D., Gorr, W., Tita, G.: Spatial analyses of crime. Crim. Justice **4**(2), 213–262 (2000)
4. Anselin, L., Williams, S.: Digital neighborhoods. J. Urban.: Int. Res. Placemaking Urban Sustain. **9175**, 24 (2015)

5. Arribas-Bel, D., Kourtit, K., Nijkamp, P.: The sociocultural sources of urban buzz. Environ. Plan. C: Gov. Policy **34**(1), 188–204 (2016)
6. Bogomolov, A., Lepri, B., Staiano, J., Oliver, N., Pianesi, F., Pentland, A. Once upon a crime: towards crime prediction from demographics and mobile data. In: ICMI 2014 (2014)
7. Brantingham, P.J., Brantingham, P.L.: Nodes, paths, and edges: consideration on the complexity of crime and the physical environment. J. Environ. Psychol. **13**, 328 (1993)
8. Brantingham, P.L., Brantingham, P.J.: Criminality of place: crime generators and crime attractors. Eur. J. Crim. Policy Res. **3**, 526 (1995)
9. Box, G.E.P., Cox, D.R.: An analysis of transformations. J. R. Stat. Soc. Ser. B (Methodol.) **26**(2), 211–252 (1964)
10. Cliff, A.D., Ord, J.K.: Spatial Processes: Models & Applications. Taylor & Francis (1981)
11. Cohen, L.E., Felson, M.: Social change and crime rate trends: a routine activity approach. Am. Sociol. Rev. **44**(4), 588 (1979)
12. Cohen, L.E., Kluegel, J.R., Land, K.C.: Social inequality and predatory criminal victimization: an exposition and test of a formal social inequality and predatory criminal victimization: an exposition and test of a formal theory. Am. Sociol. Rev. **5**, 505–524 (1981)
13. De Nadai, M., Staiano, J., Larcher, R., Sebe, N., Quercia, D., Lepri, B.: The death and life of great Italian Cities. In: WWW 2016 (2016)
14. Eagle, N., Macy, M., Claxton, R.: Network diversity and economic development. Science **328**(5981), 1029–1031 (2010)
15. Gerber, M.S.: Predicting crime using Twitter and kernel density estimation. Decis. Support Syst. **61**(1), 115–125 (2014)
16. Goodchild, M.F.: Citizens as sensors: the world of volunteered geography. Geo-Journal **69**, 211–211 (2007)
17. Graif, C., Sampson, R.J.: Spatial heterogeneity in the effects of immigration and diversity on neighborhood homicide rates. Homicide Stud. **13**(3), 242–260 (2009)
18. Jacobs, J.: The Death and Life of Great American Cities. Vintage Books, New York City (1961)
19. Karamshuk, D., Noulas, A., Scellato, S., Nicosia, V., Mascolo, C.: Geo-spotting: mining online location-based services for optimal retail store placement. In: KDD 2013 (2013)
20. Kutner, M.H., Nachtsheim, C.J., Neter, J.: Applied Linear Regression Models, 4th edn. McGraw-Hill Irwin, New York (2004)
21. Lee, B.A., Iceland, J., Sharp, G.: Charting Change in American Communities Over Three Decades Key Findings, Gregory Racial and Ethnic Diversity Goes Local (2012)
22. Pappalardo, L., Vanhoof, M., Gabrielli, L., Smoreda, Z., Pedreschi, D., Giannotti, F.: An analytical framework to nowcast well-being using mobile phone data. Int. J. Data Sci. Anal. **2**(12), 75–92 (2016)
23. Peet, R.K.: The measurement of species diversity. Ann. Rev. Ecol. Syst. **5**(1), 285–307 (1974)
24. Pratt, T.C., Cullen, F.T.: Assessing macro-level predictors and theories of crime: a meta-analysis. Crime Justice **32**, 373–450 (2005)
25. Rey, S., Anselin, L.: PySAL: a Python library of spatial analytical methods. In: Fischer, M., Getis, A. (eds.) Handbook of Applied Spatial Analysis, vol. 37, pp. 175–193. Springer, Heidelberg (2009)

26. Sampson, R., Rauenbush, S., Earls, F.: Neighborhoods and violent crime: a multi-level study of collective efficacy. Science **277**, 918–924 (1997)
27. Shannon, C.E.: A mathematical theory of communication. Bell Syst. Tech. J. **27**, 379–423 (1948)
28. Sheldon, A.L.: Equitability indices: dependence on the species count. Ecology **50**(3), 466–467 (1969)
29. Shmueli, G.: To explain or to predict? Stat. Sci. **25**(3), 289–310 (2010)
30. Traunmueller, M., Quattrone, G., Capra, L.: Mining mobile phone data to investigate urban crime theories at scale. In: Aiello, L.M., McFarland, D. (eds.) SocInfo 2014. LNCS, vol. 8851, pp. 396–411. Springer, Cham (2014). doi:10.1007/978-3-319-13734-6_29
31. Wang, H., Kifer, D., Graif, C., Li, Z.: Crime rate inference with big data. In: KDD 2016 (2016)

Robust Modeling of Human Contact Networks Across Different Scales and Proximity-Sensing Techniques

Michele Starnini[1,2]([⊠]), Bruno Lepri[3], Andrea Baronchelli[4], Alain Barrat[5,6],
Ciro Cattuto[5], and Romualdo Pastor-Satorras[7]

[1] Departament de Física Fonamental, Universitat de Barcelona,
Martí i Franquès 1, 08028 Barcelona, Spain
michele.starnini@gmail.com
[2] Universitat de Barcelona Institute of Complex Systems (UBICS),
Universitat de Barcelona, Barcelona, Spain
[3] Fondazione Bruno Kessler, via Sommarive 18, 38123 Trento, Italy
lepri@fbk.eu
[4] Department of Mathematics, City, University of London, Northampton Square,
London EC1V 0HB, UK
Andrea.Baronchelli.1@city.ac.uk
[5] ISI Foundation, Torino, Italy
alain.barrat@cpt.univ-mrs.fr, ciro.cattuto@isi.it
[6] Aix Marseille Univ, Université de Toulon, CNRS, CPT, Marseille, France
[7] Departament de Física, Universitat Politàcnica de Catalunya,
Campus Nord B4, 08034 Barcelona, Spain
romualdo.pastor@upc.edu

Abstract. The problem of mapping human close-range proximity networks has been tackled using a variety of technical approaches. Wearable electronic devices, in particular, have proven to be particularly successful in a variety of settings relevant for research in social science, complex networks and infectious diseases dynamics. Each device and technology used for proximity sensing (e.g., RFIDs, Bluetooth, low-power radio or infrared communication, etc.) comes with specific biases on the close-range relations it records. Hence it is important to assess which statistical features of the empirical proximity networks are robust across different measurement techniques, and which modeling frameworks generalize well across empirical data. Here we compare time-resolved proximity networks recorded in different experimental settings and show that some important statistical features are robust across all settings considered. The observed universality calls for a simplified modeling approach. We show that one such simple model is indeed able to reproduce the main statistical distributions characterizing the empirical temporal networks.

Keywords: Social computing · Computational social science · Social network analysis · Mobile sensing · Mathematical modeling · Wearable sensors

© Springer International Publishing AG 2017
G.L. Ciampaglia et al. (Eds.): SocInfo 2017, Part I, LNCS 10539, pp. 536–551, 2017.
DOI: 10.1007/978-3-319-67217-5_32

1   Introduction

Being social animals by nature, most of our daily activities involve face-to-face and proximity interactions with others. Although technological advances have enabled remote forms of communication such as calls, video-conferences, e-mails, etc., several studies [34,50] and the constant increase in business traveling, provide evidence that co-presence and face-to-face interactions still represent the richest communication channel for informal coordination [29], socialization and creation of social bonds [28,48], and the exchange of ideas and information [14,35,51]. At the same time, close-range physical proximity and face-to-face interactions are known determinants for the transmission of some pathogens such as airborne ones [31,39]. A quantitative understanding of human dynamics in social gatherings is therefore important not only to understand human behavior, creation of social bonds and flow of ideas, but also to design effective containment strategies and contrast epidemic spreading [21,40,44].

Hence, face-to-face and proximity interactions have long been the focus of major attention in social sciences and epidemiology [4,5,7,18] and recently various research groups have developed sensing devices and approaches to automatically measure these interaction networks [1,10,16,30,32,39,47,49]. Reality Mining (RM) [16], a study conducted in 2004 by the MIT Media Lab, was the first one to collect data from mobile phones to track the dynamics of a community of 100 business school students over a nine-month period. Following this seminal project, the Social Evolution study [32,33] tracked the everyday life of a whole undergraduate dormitory for almost 8 months using mobile phones (i.e. call logs, location data, and proximity interactions). This study was specifically designed to model the adoption of political opinions, the spreading of epidemics, the effect of social interactions on depression and stress, and the eating and physical exercise habits. More recently, in the Friends and Family study 130 graduate students and their partners, sharing the same dormitory, carried smartphones running a mobile sensing platform for 15 months [1]. Additional data were also collected from Facebook, credit card statements, surveys including questions about personality traits, group affiliations, daily mood states and sleep quality, etc.

Along similar lines, the SocioPatterns (SP) initiative [10,26] and the Sociometric Badges projects [30,36,37] have been studying since several years the proximity patterns of human gatherings, in different social contexts, such as scientific conferences [45], museums [9], schools [20,46], hospitals [26] and research institutions [30] by endowing participants with active RFID badges (SocioPatterns initiative) or with devices equipped with accelerometers, microphones, Bluetooth and Infrared sensors (Sociometric Badges projects) which capture body movements, prosodic speech features, proximity, and face-to-face interactions respectively.

However, the different technologies (e.g., RFID, Bluetooth, Infrared sensors) employed in these studies might imply potentially relevant differences in measuring contact networks. Interaction range and the angular width for detecting contacts, for instance, vary in a significant way, from less than 1 m using Infrared sensors to more than 10 m using Bluetooth sensors, and from 15° using Infrared sensors to 360° using Bluetooth sensors. In many cases, data cleaning and post-processing is based on calibrated power thresholds, temporal smoothing, and other assumptions that introduce their own biases. Finally, experiments themselves are diverse in terms of venue (from conferences to offices), size (from $N \simeq 50$ to $N \simeq 500$ individuals), duration (from a single day to several months) and temporal resolution. The full extent to which the measured proximity networks depends on experimental and data-processing techniques is challenging to assess, as no studies, to the best of our knowledge, have tackled a systematic comparison of different proximity-sensing techniques based on wearable devices.

Here we tackle this task, showing that empirical proximity networks measured in a variety of social gatherings by means of different measurement systems yield consistent statistical patterns of human dynamics, so we can assume that such regularities capture intrinsic properties of human contact networks. The presence of such apparently universal behavior, independent of the measurement framework and details, calls, within a statistical physics perspective, for an explanatory model, based on simple assumptions on human behavior. Indeed, we show that a simple multi-agent model [41,43] accurately reproduces the statistical regularities observed across different social contexts.

2   Related Work

The present study takes inspiration from the emerging body of work investigating the possibilities of analyzing proximity and face-to-face interactions using different kinds of wearable sensors. At present, mobile phones allow the collection of data on specific structural and temporal aspects of social interactions, offering ways to approximate social interactions as spatial proximity or as the co-location of mobile devices, e.g., by means of Bluetooth hits [1,15,32,33,47]. For example, Do and Gatica Perez have proposed several topic models for capturing group interaction patterns from Bluetooth proximity networks [12,13]. However, this approach does not always yield good proxies to the social interactions occurring between the individuals carrying the devices.

Mobile phone traces suffer a similar problem: They can be used to model human mobility [8,22] with the great advantage of easily scaling up to millions of individuals; they too, however, offer only coarse localization and therefore provide only rough co-location information, yielding thus only very limited insights into the social interactions of individuals.

An alternative strategy for collecting data on social interactions is to resort to image and video processing based on cameras placed in the environment [2,11]. This approach provides very rich data sets that are, in turn, computationally very complex: They require line-of-sight access to the monitored spaces and people, specific effort for equipping the relevant physical spaces, and can hardly cope with large scale data.

Since 2010, Cattuto *et al.* [10] have used a technique for monitoring social interactions that reconciles scalability and resolution by means of proximity-sensing systems based on active RFID devices. These devices are capable of sensing spatial proximity over different length scales and even close face-to-face interactions of individuals (1 to 2 m), with tunable temporal resolution. The SocioPatterns initiative has collected and analyzed face-to-face interaction data in many different contexts. These analyses have shown strong heterogeneities in the contact duration of individuals, the robustness of these statistics across contexts, and have revealed highly non-trivial mixing patterns of individuals in schools, hospitals or offices as well as their robustness across various timescales [20,23,26,27,46]. These data have been used in data-driven simulations of epidemic spreading phenomena, including the design and validation of containment measures [21].

Along a similar line, Olguín *et al.* [36] have designed and employed Sociometric Badges, platforms equipped with accelerometers, microphones, Bluetooth and Infrared sensors which capture body movements, prosodic speech features, proximity and face-to-face interactions respectively. Some previous studies based on Sociometric Badges revealed important insights into human dynamics and organizational processes, such as the impact of electronic communications on the business performance of teams [36], the relationship between several behavioral features captured by Sociometric Badges, employee' self-perceptions (from surveys) and productivity [36], the spreading of personality and emotional states [3].

3   Empirical Data

In this section, we describe datasets gathered by five different studies: The "Lyon hospital" and "SFHH" conference datasets from the SocioPatterns (SP) initiative [10], the Trento Sociometric Badges (SB) dataset [30], the Social Evolution (SE) dataset [32,33], the Friends and Family (FF) [1] dataset, and two datasets (Elem and Mid) collected using wireless ranging enabled nodes (WRENs) [49]. The main statistical properties of datasets under consideration are summarized in Table 1, while the settings of the studies are described in detail in the following subsections.

3.1   SocioPatterns (SP)

The measurement infrastructure set up by the SP initiative is based on wireless devices embedded in badges, worn by the participants on their chests. Devices exchange radio packets and use them to monitor for proximity of individuals (RFID). Information is sent to receivers installed in the environment, logging contact data. They are tuned so that the face-to-face proximity of two individuals wearing the badges are sensed only when they are facing each other at close range (about 1 to 1.5 m). The time resolution is set to 20 s, meaning that a contact between two individuals is considered established if their badges exchange at least one packet during such interval, and lasts as long as there is at least one packet exchanged over subsequent 20-s time windows. More details on the experimental setup can be found in Ref. [10]

Here we consider the dataset "Hospital", gathered by the SP initiative at a Lyon Hospital, during 4 workdays, and the dataset "SFHH", gathered by the SP initiative at the congress of the Société Francaise d'Hygiène Hospitaliére, where the experiment was conducted during the first day of a two-days conference. See Ref. [45] for a detailed description.

3.2 Sociometric Badges (SB)

The Sociometric Badges data [30] has been collected in a research institute for over a six week consecutive period, involving a population of 54 subjects, during their working hours. The Sociometric Badges, employed for this study, are equipped with accelerometers, microphones, Bluetooth and Infrared sensors which capture body movements, prosodic speech features, co-location and face-to-face interactions respectively [36]. For the purposes of our study we have exploited the data provided from the Bluetooth and Infrared sensors.

Infrared Data. Infrared (IR) transmissions are used to detect face-to-face interactions between people. In order for a badge to be detected by an IR sensor, two individuals must have a direct line of sight and the receiving badge's sensor must be within the transmitting badge's IR signal cone of height $h \leq 1$ m and a radius of $r \leq h \tan \theta$, where $\theta = \pm\, 15°$. The infrared transmission rate (TR_{ir}) was set to 1 Hz.

Bluetooth Data. Bluetooth (BT) detections can be used as a coarse indicator of proximity between devices. Radio signal strength indicator (RSSI) is a measure of the signal strength between transmitting and receiving devices. The range of RSSI values for the radio transceiver in the badge is $(-128\,\text{dBm}, 127\,\text{dBm})$. The Sociometric Badges broadcast their ID every five seconds using a 2.4 GHz transceiver $(TR_{radio} = 12$ transmissions per minute).

3.3 Social Evolution (SE)

The Social Evolution dataset was collected as part of a longitudinal study with 74 undergraduate students uniformly distributed among all four academic years (freshmen, sophomores, juniors, seniors). Participants in the study represents 80% of the residents of a dormitory at the campus of a major university in North America. The study participants were equipped with a smartphone (i.e. a Windows Mobile device) incorporating a sensing platform designed for collecting call logs, location and proximity data. Specifically, the software scanned for Bluetooth wireless devices in proximity every six minutes, a compromise between short-term social interactions and battery life [17]. With this approach, the BT log of a given smartphone would contain the list of devices in its proximity, sampled every six minutes.

Participants used the Windows Mobile smartphones as their primary phones, with their existing voice plans. Students had also online data access with these phones due to pervasive Wi-Fi on the university campus and in the metropolitan area. As compensation for their participation, students were allowed to keep the smartphones at the end of the experiment. Although relevant academic and extra-curricular activities might have not been covered either because the mobile phones may not be permanently on (e.g., during classes), or because of contacts with people not taking part to the study, the dormitory may still represent the preferential place where students live, cook, and sleep. Additional information on the SE study is available in Madan *et al.* [32,33].

3.4 Friends and Family (FF)

The Friends and Family dataset was collected during a longitudinal study capturing the lives of 117 subjects living in a married graduate student residency of a major US university [1]. The sample of subjects has a large variety in terms of provenance and cultural background. During the study period, each participant was equipped with an Android-based mobile phone incorporating a sensing software explicitly designed for collecting mobile data. Such software runs in a passive manner and does not interfere with the every day usage of the phone.

Proximity interactions were derived from Bluetooth data in a manner similar to previous studies such as [16,32]. Specifically, the Funf phone sensing platform was used to detect Bluetooth devices in the participant's proximity. The Bluetooth scan was performed periodically, every five minutes in order to keep from draining the battery while achieving a high enough resolution for social interactions. With this approach, the BT log of a given smartphone would contain the list of devices in its proximity, sampled every 5 min. See Ref. [1] for a detailed description of the study.

3.5 Toth et al. Datasets (Toth et al.)

The datasets, publicly available, were collected by Toth *et al.* [49] deploying wireless ranging enabled nodes (WRENs) [19] to students in Utah schools. Each WREN was worn by a student and collected time-stamped data from other WRENs in proximity at intervals of approximately 20 s. Each recording included a measure of signal strength, which depends on the distance between and relative orientation of the pair of individuals wearing each WREN. More specifically, Toth *et al.* [49] have applied signal strength criteria such that each retained data point was most likely to represent a pair of students, with face-to-face orientation, located 1 m from each other.

In the current paper, we resort to the data collected from two schools in Utah: One middle school (Mid), an urban public school with 679 students (age range 12–14); and one elementary school (Elem), a suburban public school with 476 students, (age range 5–12). The contact data were captured during school hours of two consecutive school days in autumn 2012 from 591 students (87% coverage) at Mid and in winter 2013 from 339 students (71% coverage) at Elem.

4 Temporal Network Formalism

Proximity patterns can be naturally analyzed in terms of temporally evolving graphs [24,25], whose nodes are defined by the individuals, and whose links represent interactions between pairs of individuals. Interactions need to be aggregated over an elementary time interval Δt_0 in order to build a temporal network [38]. This elementary time step represents the temporal resolution of data, and all the interactions established within this time interval are considered as simultaneous. Taken together, these interactions constitute an "instantaneous" network, formed by isolated nodes and small groups of interacting individuals (not necessarily forming cliques). The sequence of such instantaneous networks forms a temporal, or time-varying, network. The elementary time step Δt_0 is set to $\Delta t_0 = 20\,$s in the case of SP data, $\Delta t_0 = 60\,$s for SMBC data, $\Delta t_0 = 300\,$s for SE and FF data, and $\Delta t_0 = 20\,$s for Toth $et\ al.$ datasets. Note that temporal networks are built by including only non-empty instantaneous graphs, i.e. graphs in which at least a pair of nodes are connected.

Table 1. Some average properties of the datasets under consideration. SP-hosp = "SocioPatterns Lyon hospital", SP-sfhh = "SocioPatterns SFHH conference", SB = "Sociometric Badges", SE = "Social Evolution", FF = "Friends and Family", Elem = "Toth's Elementary school", Mid = "Toth's Middle school"

Experiment	Dataset	dev	Δt_0	N	T	$\overline{p}$	$\langle k \rangle$	$\langle s \rangle$
SP	hosp	RFID	20 s	84	20338	0.049	30.4	1146
SP	sfhh	RFID	20 s	416	3834	0.075	53.9	502
SB	SB	IR	60 s	56	10238	0.064	14.2	734
SB	SB	BT	60 s	53	28604	0.029	44.1	20481
SE	SE	BT	300 s	70	64068	0.29	66.2	48265
FF	FF	BT	300 s	82	48839	0.33	56.1	26418
Toth et al.	Elem	WREN	20 s	339	2242	0.20	46.2	634
Toth et al.	Mid	WREN	20 s	590	2488	0.21	82.8	605

Each data set is thus represented by a temporal network with a number N of different interacting individuals, and a total duration of T elementary time steps. Temporal networks can be described in terms of a characteristic function $\chi(i,j,t)$ taking the value 1 when individuals i and j are connected at time t, and zero otherwise [42]. Integrating the information of the time-varying network over a given time window T produces an aggregated weighted network, where the weight w_{ij} between nodes i and j represents the total temporal duration of the contacts between agents i and j, $w_{ij} = \sum_t \chi(i,j,t)$, and the strength s_i of a node i, $s_i = \sum_j w_{ij}$, represents the cumulated time spent in interactions by individual i.

In Table 1 we summarize a number of significant statistical properties, such as the size N, the total duration T in units of elementary time steps Δt_0, and the average fraction of individuals interacting at each time step, $\overline{p}$. We also report the average degree, $\langle k \rangle$, defined as the average number of interactions per individual, and average strength, $\langle s \rangle = N^{-1} \sum_i s_i$, of the aggregated networks, integrated over the whole sequence. One can note that the data sets under consideration are highly heterogeneous in terms of the reported statistical properties. Aggregated network representations preserve such heteogeneity, even though it is important to remark that aggregated properties are sensitive to the time-aggreagating interval [38] and therefore to the specificity of data collection and preprocessing.

5   Comparison Among the Different Datasets

In this section we perform a comparison of several statistical properties of the temporal networks, as defined above, representing the different datasets under consideration.

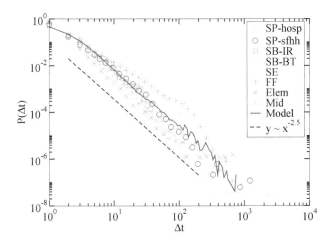

Fig. 1. Probability distribution of the duration Δt of the contacts between pairs of agents, $P(\Delta t)$, for the different datasets under consideration, compared with numerical simulations of the attractiveness model. A power law form, $P(\Delta t) \sim \Delta t^{-\gamma_{\Delta t}}$, with $\gamma_{\Delta t} = 2.5$, is plotted as a reference in dashed line. (Color figure online)

The temporal pattern of the agents' contacts is probably the most distinctive feature of proximity interaction networks. We therefore start by considering the distribution of the durations Δt of the contacts between pairs of agents, $P(\Delta t)$, and the distribution of gap times τ between two consecutive proximity events involving a given individual, $P(\tau)$. The bursty dynamics of human interactions [6] is revealed by the long-tailed form of these two distributions, which can be described in terms of a power-law function. Figures 1 and 2 show the distribution of the contacts duration $P(\Delta t)$ and gap times $P(\tau)$ for the various sets of empirical data. In both cases, all dataset shows a broad-tailed behavior,

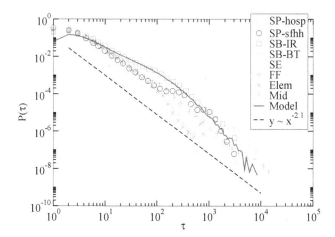

Fig. 2. Probability distribution of the gap times τ between consecutive contacts of pairs of agents, $P(\tau)$, for the different datasets under consideration, compared with numerical simulations of the attractiveness model. A power law form, $P(\tau) \sim \tau^{-\gamma_\tau}$, with $\gamma_\tau = 2.1$, is plotted as a reference in dashed line. (Color figure online)

that can be loosely described by a power law distribution. In Figs. 1 and 2 we plot, as a guide for the eye, power-law forms $P(\Delta t) \sim \Delta t^{-\gamma_{\Delta t}}$, with exponent $\gamma_{\Delta t} \sim 2.5$, and $P(\tau) \sim \tau^{-\gamma_\tau}$, with exponent $\gamma_\tau \sim 2.1$, respectively.

The probability distributions of strength, $P(s)$, and weight, $P(w)$, are a signature of the topological structure of the corresponding aggregated, weighted networks. Since the duration T of the datasets under consideration is quite heterogeneous, see Table 1, we do not reconstruct the aggregated networks by integrating over the whole duration T, but we integrate each temporal network over a time window of fixed length, $\Delta T = 1000$ elementary time steps. That is, we consider a random starting time T_0 (provided that $T_0 < T - \Delta T$), and reconstruct an aggregated network by integrating the temporal network from T_0 to $T_0 + \Delta T$. We average our results by sampling 100 different starting times. Note that, since the elementary time step Δt_0 is different across different experiments, the real duration of the time window considered is different across different datasets.

Figures 3 and 4 show the weight and strength distributions, $P(w)$ and $P(s)$, of the aggregated networks over ΔT, for the considered datasets. Again, all datasets display a similar heavy tailed weight distribution, roughly compatible with a power-law form, meaning that the heterogeneity shown in the broad-tailed form of the contact duration distribution, $P(\Delta t)$, persists also over longer time scales. Data sets SB-BT, SE and FF present deviations with respect to the other data sets. The strength distribution $P(s)$ is also broad tailed and quite similar for all data sets considered, but in this case it is not compatible with a power law.

Finally, Fig. 5 shows the average strength as a function of the degree, $s(k)$, in the aggregated networks integrated over an interval ΔT. One can see that if the

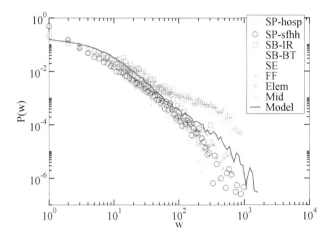

Fig. 3. Weight distribution $P(w)$, for the different datasets under consideration, compared with numerical simulations of the attractiveness model. (Color figure online)

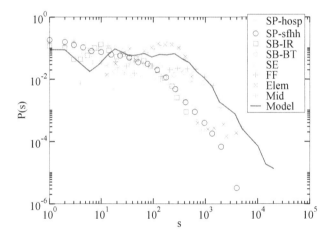

Fig. 4. Strength distribution $P(s)$, for the different datasets under consideration, compared with numerical simulations of the attractiveness model. (Color figure online)

strength is rescaled by the total strength of the network in the considered time window, $\langle s \rangle = N^{-1} \sum_{t=T_0}^{T_0+\Delta T} \sum_{ij} \chi(i,j,t)$, the different data sets show a similar correlation between strength and degree. In particular, Fig. 5 shows that all data sets considered present a slightly superlinear correlation between strength and degree, $s(k) \sim k^\gamma$ with $\gamma > 1$, as highlighted by the linear correlation plotted as a dashed line.

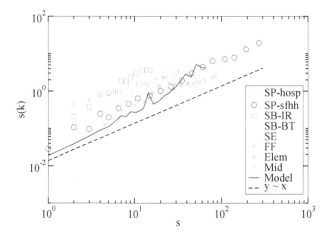

Fig. 5. Strength as a function of the degree, $s(k)$, for the different datasets under consideration, compared with numerical simulations of the attractiveness model. A linear correlation $s(k) \sim k$ is plotted in dashed line, to highlight the superlinear correlation observed in data and model. (Color figure online)

6   Modeling Human Contact Networks

In the previous Section, we have shown that the temporal networks representing different datasets, highly heterogeneous in terms of size, duration, proximity-sensing techniques, and social contexts, are characterized by very similar statistical properties. Here we show that a simple model, in which individuals are endowed with different social attractiveness, is able to reproduce the empirical distributions.

6.1   Model Definition

The social contexts in which the data were collected can be modeled by a set of N mobile agents free to move in a closed environment, who interact when they are close enough (within the exchange range of the devices) [41]. The simplifying assumption of the model proposed in [41] is that the agents perform a random walk in a box of linear size L with periodic boundary conditions (the average density is $\rho = N/L^2$). Whenever two agents are within distance d (with $d \ll L$), they start to interact. The key ingredient of the model is that each agent is characterized by an "attractiveness", a_i, a quenched random number, extracted from a distribution $\eta(a)$, representing her power to raise interest in the others, which can be thought of as a proxy for social status or the role played in the considered social gathering. Attractiveness rules the interactions between agents in a natural way: Whenever an individual is involved in an interaction with other peers, she will continue to interact with them with a probability proportional to the attractiveness of her most interesting neighbor, or move away otherwise.

Finally, the model incorporates the empirical evidence that not all agents are simultaneously present in system: Individuals can be either in an active state, where they can move and establish interactions, or in an inactive one representing absence from the premises. Thus, at each time step, every active individual becomes inactive with a constant probability r, while inactive individuals can go back to the active state with the complementary probabillty $1 - r$. See Refs. [41, 43] for a detailed description of the model.

6.2   Model Validation

Here we contrast the results obtained by the numerical simulation of the model against empirical data sets. We average our results over 100 runs with parameters $N = 100$, $L = 50$, $T = 5000$. The results of numerical experiments are reported in Figs. 1, 2, 3, 4 and 5, for the corresponding quantities considered, represented by a continuous, blue line.

In the case of the contact duration distribution, $P(\Delta t)$, Fig. 1, numerical and experimental data show a remarkable match, with some deviations for the SB-BT and FF datasets. Numerical data also show a close behavior to the mentioned power-law distribution with exponent $\gamma_{\Delta t} = 2.5$. Also in the case of the gap times distribution, $P(\tau)$, Fig. 2, the distribution obtained by numerical simulations of the model is very close to the experimental ones, spanning the same orders of magnitude. The weight distribution $P(w)$ of the model presents a very good fit to the empirical data, see Fig. 3, with the exception of data sets SB-BT, SE and FF, as mentioned above. The strength distribution $P(s)$, Fig. 4, is, as we have commented above, quite noisy, especially for the datasets of smallest size. It follows however a similar trend across the different datasets that is well matched by numerical simulations of the model. Finally, in the case of the average strength of individuals of degree k, $s(k)$, Fig. 5, the most striking feature, namely the superlinear behavior as a function of k, is correctly captured by the numerical simulations of the model.

7   Discussion

All datasets under consideration show similar statistical properties of the individuals' contacts. The distribution of the contact durations, $P(\Delta t)$, and the inter-event time distribution, $P(\tau)$, are heavy tailed and compatible with power law forms, and the attractiveness model is able to quantitavely reproduce such behavior. The weight distribution of the aggregated networks, $P(w)$, is also heavy tailed for all datasets and for the attractiveness model, even though some datasets show deviations. The strength distribution $P(s)$ and the correlation between strength and degree, $s(k)$, present a quite noisy behavior, especially for smaller datasets. However, all datasets show a long tailed form of $P(s)$ and a superlinear correlation of the $s(k)$, correctly reproduced by the attractiveness model.

Previous work [10, 20, 27] have shown that the functional shapes of contact and inter-contact durations' distributions were very robust across contexts, for data collected by the SocioPatterns infrastructure as well as by similar RFID sensors. Our results show that this robustness extends in fact to proximity data collected through different types of sensors (e.g., Bluetooth, Infrared, WREN, RFID).

This is of particular relevance in the context of modeling human behavior and building data-driven models depending on human interaction data, such as models for the spread of infectious diseases, from two points of view. On the one hand, the robust broadness of these distributions implies that different contacts might play very different roles in a transmission process: Under the common assumption that the transmission probability between two individuals depends on their time in contact, the longer contacts, which are orders of magnitude longer than average, could play a crucial role in disease dynamics. The heterogeneity of contact patterns is also relevant at the individual level, as revealed by broad distributions of strengths and the superlinear behavior of $s(k)$, and is known to have a strong impact on spreading dynamics. In particular, it highlights the existence of "super-contactors", i.e. individuals who account for an important proportion of the overall contact durations and may therefore become super-spreaders in the case of an outbreak.

On the other hand, the robustness of the distributions found in different contexts represents an important information and asset for modelers: It means that these distributions can be assumed to depend negligibly on the specifics of the situation being modeled and thus directly plugged into the models to create for instance synthetic populations of interacting agents. From another modeling point of view, they also represent a validation benchmark for microscopic models of interactions, which should correctly reproduce such robust features. In fact, as we have shown, a simple model based on mobile agents, and on the concept of social appealing or attractiveness, is able to reproduce most of the main statistical properties of human contact temporal networks. The good fit of this model hints towards the fact that the temporal patterns of human contacts at different time scales can be explained in terms of simple physical processes, without assuming any cognitive processes at work.

It would be of interest to measure and compare several other properties of the contact networks, such as the evolution of the integrated degree distribution $P_T(k)$ and of the aggregated average degree in $k(T)$, or the rate at which the contact neighborhoods of individuals change. Unfortunately, these quantities are difficult to measure in some cases due to the small sizes of the datasets.

Acknowledgments. M.S. acknowledges financial support from the James S. McDonnell Foundation. R.P.-S. acknowledges financial support from the Spanish MINECO, under projects FIS2013-47282-C2- 2 and FIS2016-76830-C2-1-P, and additional financial support from ICREA Academia, funded by the Generalitat de Catalunya. C.C. acknowledges support from the Lagrange Laboratory of the ISI Foundation funded by the CRT Foundation.

References

1. Aharony, N., Pan, W., Ip, C., Khayal, I., Pentland, A.: Social fMRI: investigating and shaping social mechanisms in the real world. Pervasive Mobile Comput. **7**(6), 643–659 (2011)
2. Alameda-Pineda, X., Staiano, J., Subramanian, R., Batrinca, L., Ricci, E., Lepri, B., Lanz, O., Sebe, N.: SALSA: a novel dataset for multimodal group behavior analysis. IEEE Trans. Pattern Anal. Mach. Intell. **38**(8), 1707–1720 (2016)
3. Alshamsi, A., Pianesi, F., Lepri, B., Pentland, A., Rahwan, I.: Beyond contagion: reality mining reveals complex patterns of social influence. Plos One **10**(8), e0135740 (2015)
4. Arrow, H., McGrath, J., Berdahl, J.: Small Groups as Complex Systems: Formation, Coordination, Development, and Adaptation. Sage-Publications, Thousand Oaks (2000)
5. Bales, R.: Interaction Process Analysis: A Method for the Study of Small Groups. Addison-Wesley, Boston (1950)
6. Barabasi, A.L.: The origin of bursts and heavy tails in human dynamics. Nature **435**, 207 (2005)
7. Bion, W.: Experiences in Groups and Other Papers. Routledge, Abingdon (2013)
8. Blondel, V., Decuyper, A., Krings, G.: A survey of results on mobile phone datasets analysis. EPJ Data Sci. **4**, 10 (2015)
9. Van den Broeck, W., Quaggiotto, M., Isella, L., Barrat, A., Cattuto, C.: The making of sixty-nine days of close encounters at the science gallery. Leonardo **45**(3), 285 (2012)
10. Cattuto, C., Van den Broeck, W., Barrat, A., Colizza, V., Pinton, J.F., Vespignani, A.: Dynamics of person-to-person interactions from distributed RFID sensor networks. Plos One **5**(7), e11596 (2010)
11. Cristani, M., Bazzani, L., Paggetti, G., Fossati, A., Tosato, D., Del Bue, A., Menegaz, G., Murino, V.: Social interaction discovery by statistical analysis of F-formations. In: Proceedings of the British Machine Vision Conference (2011)
12. Do, T., Gatica-Perez, D.: Human interaction discovery in smartphone proximity networks. Pers. Ubiquit. Comput. **3**, 413–431 (2013)
13. Do, T., Kalimeri, K., Lepri, B., Pianesi, F., Gatica-Perez, D.: Inferring social activities with mobile sensor networks. In: Proceedings of the International Conference on Multimodal Interaction, pp. 405–3412 (2013)
14. Doherty-Sneddon, G., Anderson, A., O'Malley, C., Langton, S., Garrod, S., Bruce, V.: Face-to-face and video-mediated communication: a comparison of dialogue structure and task performance. J. Exp. Psychol.: Appl. **3**(2), 105–125 (1997)
15. Dong, W., Lepri, B., Pentland, A.: Modeling the co-evolution of behaviors and social relationships using mobile phone data. In: Proceedings of the Mobile and Ubiquitous Multimedia, pp. 134–143 (2011)
16. Eagle, N., Pentland, A.: Reality mining: sensing complex social systems. Pers. Ubiquit. Comput. **10**(4), 255–268 (2006)
17. Eagle, N., Pentland, A.S., Lazer, D.: Inferring friendship network structure by using mobile phone data. Proc. Natl. Acad. Sci. **106**(36), 15274–15278 (2009)
18. Eames, K., Bansal, S., Frost, S., Riley, S.: Six challenges in measuring contact networks for use in modelling. Epidemics **10**, 72–77 (2015)
19. Forys, A., Min, K., Schmid, T., Pettey, W., Toth, D., Leecaster, M.: WRENMining: large-scale data collection for human contact network research. In: Proceedings of the 1st International Workshop on Sensing and Big Data Mining, pp. 1–6 (2013)

20. Fournet, J., Barrat, A.: Contact patterns among high school students. Plos One **9**(9), e107878 (2014)
21. Gemmetto, V., Barrat, A., Cattuto, C.: Mitigation of infectious disease at school: targeted class closure vs school closure. BMC Infect. Dis. **14**, 695 (2014)
22. Gonzaléz, M., Hidalgo, C., Barabasi, A.L.: Understanding individual human mobility patterns. Nature **7196**(453), 779–782 (2010)
23. Gnois, M., Vestergaard, C.L., Fournet, J., Panisson, A., Bonmarin, I., Barrat, A.: Data on face-to-face contacts in an office building suggest a low-cost vaccination strategy based on community linkers. Netw. Sci. **3**(03), 326–347 (2015)
24. Holme, P., Saramäki, J.: Temporal networks. Phys. Rep. **519**, 97–125 (2012)
25. Holme, P.: Modern temporal network theory: a colloquium. Eur. Phys. J. B **88**(9), 234 (2015)
26. Isella, L., Romano, M., Barrat, A., Cattuto, C., Colizza, V., Van den Broeck, W., Gesualdo, F., Pandolfi, E., Ravá, L., Rizzo, C., Tozzi, A.: Close encounters in a pediatric ward: measuring face-to-face proximity and mixing patterns with wearable sensors. Plos One **6**(2), e17144 (2011)
27. Isella, L., Stehlé, J., Barrat, A., Cattuto, C., Pinton, J.F., Van den Broeck, W.: What's in a crowd? Analysis of face-to-face behavioral networks. J. Theor. Biol. **271**(1), 166–180 (2011)
28. Kendon, A., Harris, R., Key, R.: In: Hinds, P., Kiesler, S. (eds.) Organization of Behavior in Face-to-Face Interaction. De Gruyter Mouton, Berlin (1975)
29. Kraut, R., Fish, R., Root, R., Chalfonte, B.: Informal communication in organizations: form, function, and technology. In: Groupware and Computer-Supported Cooperative Work, pp. 287–314 (1993)
30. Lepri, B., Staiano, J., Rigato, G., Kalimeri, K., Finnerty, A., Pianesi, F., Sebe, N., Pentland, A.: The SocioMetric badges corpus: a multilevel behavioral dataset for social behavior in complex organizations. In: IEEE Proceedings of Social-Com/PASSAT, pp. 623–628. IEEE (2012)
31. Liljeros, F., Edling, C., Amaral, L., Stanley, H., Aberg, Y.: The web of human sexual contacts. Nature **6840**, 907–908 (2001)
32. Madan, A., Cebrian, M., Lazer, D., Pentland, A.: Social sensing for epidemiological behavior change. In: Proceedings of the ACM International Conference on Ubiquitous Computing, pp. 291–300 (2010)
33. Madan, A., Cebrian, M., Moturu, S., Farrahi, K., Pentland, A.: Sensing the "health state" of a community. IEEE Pervasive Comput. **11**(4), 36–45 (2012)
34. Nardi, B., Whittaker, S.: The place of face to face communication in distributed work. In: Hinds, P., Kiesler, S. (eds.) Distributed Work, pp. 351–360. MIT Press, Cambridge (2002)
35. Nohria, N., Eccles, R.: Face-to-face: making network organizations work. In: Technology, Organizations and Innovation: Critical Perspectives on Business and Management, pp. 1659–1681 (2000)
36. Olguín, O.D., Waber, B., Kim, T., Mohan, A., Ara, K., Pentland, A.: Sensible organizations technology and methodology for automatically measuring organizational behavior. IEEE Trans. Syst. Man Cybern. Part B (Cybern.) **39**, 43–55 (2009)
37. Onnela, J.P., Waber, B.N., Pentland, A., Schnorf, S., Lazer, D.: Using sociometers to quantify social interaction patterns. Sci. Rep. **4** (2014). Article no. 5604
38. Ribeiro, B., Perra, N., Baronchelli, A.: Quantifying the effect of temporal resolution on time-varying networks. Sci. Rep. **3** (2013). Article no. 3006
39. Salathé, M., Kazandjieva, M., Lee, J.W., Levis, P., Feldman, M.W., Jones, J.H.: A high-resolution human contact network for infectious disease transmission. Proc. Natl. Acad. Sci. **107**(51), 22020–22025 (2010)

40. Smieszek, T., Salathé, M.: A low-cost method to assess the epidemiological importance of individuals in controlling infectious disease outbreaks. BMC Med. **11**(1), 35 (2013). http://www.biomedcentral.com/1741-7015/11/36
41. Starnini, M., Baronchelli, A., Pastor-Satorras, R.: Modeling human dynamics of face-to-face interaction networks. Phys. Rev. Lett. **110**, 168701–168706 (2013)
42. Starnini, M., Baronchelli, A., Barrat, A., Pastor-Satorras, R.: Random walks on temporal networks. Phys. Rev. E **85**, 056115 (2012)
43. Starnini, M., Baronchelli, A., Pastor-Satorras, R.: Model reproduces individual, group and collective dynamics of human contact networks. Soc. Netw. **47**, 130–137 (2016)
44. Starnini, M., Machens, A., Cattuto, C., Barrat, A., Pastor-Satorras, R.: Immunization strategies for epidemic processes in time-varying contact networks. J. Theor. Biol. **337**, 89–100 (2013)
45. Stehlé, J., Voirin, N., Barrat, A., Cattuto, C., Colizza, V., Isella, L., Régis, C., Pinton, J.F., Khanafer, N., Van den Broeck, W., Vanhems, P.: Simulation of an SEIR infectious disease model on the dynamic contact network of conference attendees. BMC Med. **9**, 87 (2011)
46. Stehlé, J., Voirin, N., Barrat, A., Cattuto, C., Isella, L., Pinton, J.F., Quaggiotto, M., Van den Broeck, W., Régis, C., Lina, B., Vanhems, P.: High-resolution measurements of face-to-face contact patterns in a primary school. Plos One **6**(8), e23176 (2011)
47. Stopczynski, A., Sekara, V., Sapiezynski, P., Cuttone, A., Larsen, J.E., Lehmann, S.: Measuring large-scale social networks with high resolution. PLOS One **9**(4), e95978 (2014)
48. Storper, M., Venables, A., Pastor-Satorras, R.: Buzz: face-to-face contact and the urban economy. J. Econ. Geogr. **4**, 351–360 (2004)
49. Toth, D.J.A., Leecaster, M., Pettey, W.B.P., Gundlapalli, A.V., Gao, H., Rainey, J.J., Uzicanin, A., Samore, M.H.: The role of heterogeneity in contact timing and duration in network models of influenza spread in schools. J. R. Soc. Interface **12**(108), 20150279 (2015)
50. Whittaker, S., Frohlich, D., Daly-Jones, O.: Informal workplace communication: what is it like and how might we support it? In: Proceedings of the ACM Conference on Human Factors in Computing Systems CHI 1994, pp. 131–137. ACM Press, New York (1994)
51. Wright, M., Li, Y.: The associations between young adults' face-to-face prosocial behaviorsand their online prosocial behaviors. Comput. Hum. Behav. **27**, 1959–1961 (2011)

Personalized Recommendation
of Points-of-Interest Based on Multilayer
Local Community Detection

Roberto Interdonato and Andrea Tagarelli[✉]

DIMES, University of Calabria, Rende, Italy
rinterdonato@dimes.unical.it, andrea.tagarelli@unical.it

Abstract. When visiting a touristic venue, building personalized itineraries is often non-trivial, mainly because of the variety of types of points-of-interest (PoIs) that might be considered by an individual. Several online platforms exist to support the tourists by providing them with detailed PoI-related information in a certain area, such as routes, distances, reviews, and ratings. However, integrating all these aspects can be tricky, and finding a reasonable trade-off between spatial/temporal proximity, amount and serendipity of the PoIs to visit can be challenging even for expert tourists. In this work, we propose a novel approach to the recommendation of a set of PoIs for a geographic area set around a given seed PoI, by leveraging a multilayer local community detection framework. The seed-centric communities are discovered in a complex network system, whose nodes correspond to PoIs and relations in the different layers correspond to services provided by different online platforms, i.e., *Google Maps*, *Foursquare* and *Wikipedia*. Experimental evaluation on renowned Italian touristic venues unveiled interesting findings on the significance of the proposed approach.

1 Introduction

Touristic planning has experienced increasing benefits since the early days of the Web. Until a decade ago a major advantage was the possibility of booking a flight or hotel electronically, also upon comparing prices and getting the best offer; nowadays, online social networks and geo-tagged crowd-sourced data have introduced new scenarios, so that massively using Web sources has become extremely popular for planning a travel and booking related choices. In the attempt of maximizing the benefits from using Web sources for personal purposes, a user might in principle access several online services, including route planning (e.g., Google Maps, Bing Maps), user-provided reviews and ratings (e.g., Foursquare, Tripadvisor, Yelp), comparing and booking accommodations (e.g., Booking, AirBnb, Trivago), and looking for encyclopedic descriptions about venues (e.g., Wikipedia). Even though the availability of all these services is certainly precious, at the same time it often implies information overload for the user. Therefore, combining data from heterogeneous sources, and eventually filtering the information that mostly suits the user's specific needs, is not trivial at all.

© Springer International Publishing AG 2017
G.L. Ciampaglia et al. (Eds.): SocInfo 2017, Part I, LNCS 10539, pp. 552–571, 2017.
DOI: 10.1007/978-3-319-67217-5_33

In this context, large amounts of data relevant to the travel domain have been produced and made publicly available, such as geo-referenced data and mobile-based geo-tagged data. Such data are recognized as highly attractive for various research tasks, and in fact they have been extensively used in order to ease travel planning experiences. Examples of approaches that widely use data coming from platforms like TripAdvisor, Foursquare and Google Maps include new generation recommender systems, e.g., package-based recommenders [7], smart serendipity-oriented route recommenders [15,17], retrieval systems of walkability information [18]; also, travel-oriented online sources have been exploited to support several analysis tasks, such as describing the distinctive features of a neighborhood [20] or its well being [13].

Nevertheless, there is a lack of computational approaches that are capable of exploiting data coming from multiple Web sources, to provide effective support in the personalization of a user's traveling experience. In particular, we are not aware of studies that are designed to discover knowledge about a user's preferred location venue and its *points-of-interest* (PoIs), from heterogeneous online data, in an automatic and integrated way. In this work, we make a first step towards filling this gap in the literature, by pursuing a twofold research goal:

1. Integrate online networked data coming from different travel-oriented platforms, in order to support advanced analysis tasks in the travel domain, and
2. Define a novel PoI recommendation approach that employs personalized (i.e., query-dependent) community detection techniques designed to effectively work on such integrated data.

We accomplish the first goal by developing a methodology to build cross-platform PoI databases and networks. We make use of publicly available geo-referenced, social geo-tagged, lexical and semantic information about PoIs and their relations, gathered from three popular online platforms: *Google Maps*, *Foursquare* and *Wikipedia*. We exploit our cross-platform PoI databases and networks to accomplish the second research goal, by leveraging a *local community detection* framework, named ML-LCD, recently developed for *multilayer networks* [8–10]. The ML-LCD framework allows us to provide personalized recommendations in terms of PoIs, for any given user-specified query PoI, by discovering local (i.e., centered on the query PoI) communities in a complex network model representing the previously integrated cross-platform data. In this scenario, the discovery of a densely connected portion of the graph around a query node will represent a structured set of geographically, conceptually, and socially related PoIs. Unlike classic community detection methods, local approaches have small memory-footprint requirements, and are beneficial for any scenario, like the one treated in this work, in which computing a global community structure is not feasible (e.g., big network data, streaming and dynamic networks), or it is not required (e.g., only community memberships of a subset of nodes are needed).

In the remainder of the paper, Sect. 2 discusses related work, Sect. 3 introduces the ML-LCD framework, Sect. 4 describes the proposed PoI recommendation framework, Sect. 5 contains our experimental evaluation, finally Sect. 6 concludes the paper.

2   Related Work

Local Community Detection. One of the earliest works on local community detection is the Clauset's framework [4], which is designed to explore a graph through local expansion starting from a seed node. More recent studies have investigated and evaluated different strategies that account for the internal and external connectivity of the community being formed [1,2,5,21]. The Lemon algorithm proposed in [16] exploits truncated random walks and approximate invariant subspace to discover a local community for any given seed set.

Only few works in literature deal with local communities in multilayer networks. In [11], the solution of a personalized PageRank is approximated for a local partition of the multilayer network in order to find communities. However, the approach assumes complete knowledge about the network structure, and the local perspective is intended as the way the random walk is personalized, which differs from identifying local communities using multilayer features. The ML-LCD framework [8–10] is the first to address the problem of local community detection in multilayer networks, which will be discussed in detail in Sect. 3. In this work, we will resort to ML-LCD in order to discover recommendations for a given PoI in the form of a local community of PoIs built upon information coming from different social media services.

Clustering of Geo-Referenced and Geo-Tagged Data. Skovsgaard et al. [19] define a clustering technique based on nearest neighbor chains, which exploits spatial and textual data from microblog posts in order to discover PoIs. Han and Lee [6] use geo-tagged photos extracted from Flickr in order to extract landmarks and obtain adaptively personalized recommendations for individual travelers and their trips. León et al. [14] design a learning and clustering approach based on the analysis of Fuzzy Cognitive Maps in order to describe users' preferences and behaviors in terms of modes of transport given specific circumstances.

We are not aware of studies addressing PoI exploration or prediction analysis tasks as a community detection problem. One exception is given by [3], which aims to discover an organization of communities in a spatial network that are characterized both by high topological density and geographical closeness. However, the above approach refers to a classic global community detection task (i.e., it is not query-dependent), nor it deals with PoI recommendation. To the best of our knowledge, in this work we first address a personalized PoI recommendation problem under a framework of local community detection. Moreover, we are also the first to integrate geo-referenced, geo-tagged, and descriptive semantic data, from different social media sources, into a multilayer network model.

3   Multilayer Local Community Detection

Multilayer Network Model. A multilayer network [12] models a set $\mathcal{V}$ of *entities* (e.g., users) and their relations over a set of *layers* $\mathcal{L} = \{L_1, \ldots, L_\ell\}$. Each layer hence corresponds to a given type of entity relation, or edge-label.

If we denote with $V_{\mathcal{L}} \subseteq \mathcal{V} \times \mathcal{L}$ the set containing the occurrences of each entity on each layer, and with $E_{\mathcal{L}} \subseteq V_{\mathcal{L}} \times V_{\mathcal{L}}$ the set of undirected links between such entity-layer pairs, the graph defined as $G_{\mathcal{L}} = (V_{\mathcal{L}}, E_{\mathcal{L}}, \mathcal{V}, \mathcal{L})$ is a *multilayer network* for $\mathcal{V}$ on $\mathcal{L}$. Entities (i.e., elements of $\mathcal{V}$) are not required to participate to all layers, however each entity has to appear in at least one layer. Moreover, in this work the only inter-layer edges are regarded as "couplings" of nodes representing the same entity between different layers, according to a *multiplex* network representation.

General Scheme of Local Community Detection. Local community detection methods generally implement some strategy that iteratively considers a node from one of three sets, namely: the community under construction (initialized with the seed node), the "shell" of nodes that are neighbors of nodes in the community but do not belong to the community, and the unexplored portion of the network. A key aspect is hence how to select, at each step, the *best* node in the shell to add to the community to be identified. Most algorithms, which are designed to deal with monoplex (i.e., simple) graphs, try to maximize a function in terms of the *internal* edges, i.e., edges that involve nodes in the community, and to minimize a function in terms of the *external* edges, i.e., edges to nodes outside the community. By accounting for both kinds of edges, nodes are evaluated as candidates to be added to a community in proportion to their contribution to the internal-to-external *connection density* ratio of the local community being discovered.

The ML-LCD Method. The M*ulti*L*ayer* L*ocal* C*ommunity* D*etection* (ML-LCD) method proposed in [8–10] follows the above general scheme and extends it to identify local communities over a multilayer network. Essentially, ML-LCD takes as input a multilayer graph $G_{\mathcal{L}}$ and a seed node v_0, and computes the local community C associated to v_0 by performing an iterative search that seeks to maximize the value of *similarity-based local community function* for C ($LC(C)$), which is defined as the ratio of an *internal community relation* $LC^{int}(C)$ to an *external community relation* $LC^{ext}(C)$.

Both internal and external community relations are based on a notion of similarity that expresses the topological affinity of any two nodes in a multilayer graph, e.g., Jaccard coefficient of the two nodes' sets of neighbors. In this paper, we revisit the definitions provided for the *within-layer similarity-based local community functions* in [8–10] by introducing two new elements: (i) layer-specific edge weighting functions, and (ii) a layer relevance weighting scheme. The former, by quantifying the strength of connection between any two nodes in the network, will be coupled with a neighborhood-based similarity function, properly adapted to account for weighted edges in the network. The latter is useful to reflect any a-priori knowledge or user-predetermined relevance scheme to assign with the layers in the network.

Given a community C, the shell set of C is defined as $S = \{v \in \mathcal{V} \setminus C \mid \exists((u, L_i), (v, L_j)) \in E_{\mathcal{L}} \wedge u \in C\}$ and the boundary set of C as $B = \{u \in$

$C \mid \exists((u, L_i), (v, L_j)) \in E_{\mathcal{L}} \wedge v \in S\}$. Moreover, we will use symbol E_h^C to denote the set of edges in layer L_h between nodes that belong to C, and symbol E_h^B to denote the set of edges in layer L_h between nodes in B and nodes in S. Also, $N_h(i)$ will denote the set of nodes that are neighbors to node v_i in the graph of L_h.

Given $G_{\mathcal{L}} = (V_{\mathcal{L}}, E_{\mathcal{L}}, \mathcal{V}, \mathcal{L})$ and a local community C, we define the *weighted similarity-based community internal relation* as:

$$LC^{int}(C) = \frac{1}{|C|} \sum_{j \in C} \sum_{L_h \in \mathcal{L}} \alpha_h \left[\sum_{(i,j) \in E_h^C \ i \in C} w_h(i,j) \cdot sim_h(i,j) \right] \quad (1)$$

and the *weighted similarity-based community external relation* as:

$$LC^{ext}(C) = \frac{1}{|B|} \sum_{j \in B} \sum_{L_h \in \mathcal{L}} \alpha_h \left[\sum_{(i,j) \in E_h^B, \ i \in S} w_h(i,j) \cdot sim_h(i,j) \right] \quad (2)$$

where, for each layer L_h $(h = 1..\ell)$, α_h are positive, real-valued coefficients, by default set to one, $w_h(i,j)$ denotes the weight of edge (i,j) in the graph of L_h, and

$$sim_h(i,j) = \frac{\displaystyle\sum_{p \in N_h(i) \cap N_h(j)} \frac{w_h(i,p) + w_h(j,p)}{2}}{\left(\displaystyle\sum_{p \in N_h(i) \cup N_h(j)} w_h(i,p) + w_h(j,p) \right) - \left(\displaystyle\sum_{p \in N_h(i) \cap N_h(j)} \frac{w_h(i,p) + w_h(j,p)}{2} \right)} \quad (3)$$

4 Proposed PoI Recommendation Framework

In this section we describe the methodology adopted to build our cross-platform PoI databases and networks. The backbone of our framework corresponds to publicly available information gathered from three popular online platforms: *Google Maps*, *Foursquare* and *Wikipedia*. We identified these platforms as a particularly suited ensemble for integrating geographical, social tagging, lexical and semantic information about PoIs and their relations. Figure 1 shows the main data modules and flows of the crawling process we performed to build the cross-platform PoI databases and, upon it, a PoI multilayer network system. In the following, we first describe our crawling strategy, then we define the PoI multilayer network.

4.1 Crawling Methodology

Our defined crawling strategy is comprised of 5 main steps, which are easily recognized in Fig. 1. We elaborate on each of them next.

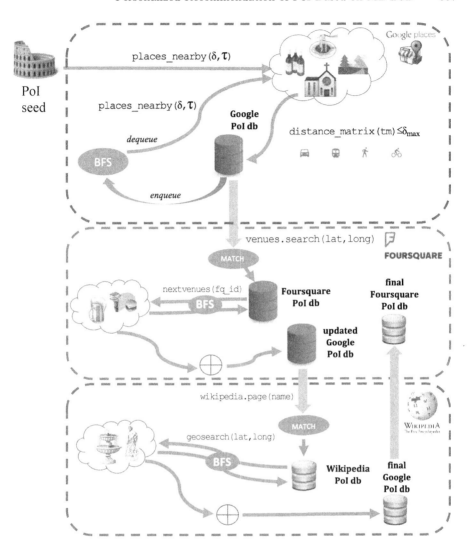

Fig. 1. Workflow of the crawling process from *Google Maps*, *Foursquare* and *Wikipedia*, for the construction of our cross-platform PoI databases and networks.

Step 1: Seed PoI Selection. The first step is the selection of a venue (geographical area) and an initial (*seed*) PoI from which a crawling process started. An intuitive choice for the seed PoI corresponds to a popular place, centrally located in the selected venue (e.g., the city park, the cathedral square, etc.).

Step 2: Google Maps Database. We started by gathering geolocation information about the area surrounding the seed PoI, using public Google Maps APIs, namely Google Places[1] and Google Distance Matrix.[2] Google Places offers a service to get information about a geographic location given its coordinates. In particular, by means of the `places_nearby` method, all PoIs can be retrieved within an area of a given radius, centered on specific coordinates. A set of categories, $\mathcal{T}$, valid for the PoIs[3] can also be selected, in order to retrieve neighboring PoIs in a focused way. Given two locations, the `distance_matrix` method available in Google Distance Matrix returns distance information, both in time and space.

We retrieved, and stored in our first database, PoIs in the area surrounding the seed, in a Breadth-First-Search (BFS) fashion. At each iteration of the BFS process, we searched for neighboring PoIs within a distance δ from the PoIs found at the previous iteration, by iteratively invoking the `places_nearby` method. The exploration process was terminated when we reached a PoI far away a certain δ_{max} from the seed—note that `places_nearby` evaluates distances δ and δ_{max} as airline distances. For each pair of retrieved PoIs, we extracted information about the minimum spatial distance and time between them, for different modes of transport: pedestrian paths, public transport and private transport.

Step 3: Foursquare Database. To benefit from social media contents concerning PoIs, in the form of user-generated feedbacks (e.g., reviews and ratings), we resorted to Foursquare public APIs.[4] The objective of the third step was to retrieve new PoIs and also to enrich the information about the PoIs of a certain area previously gathered through Google Maps tools. To this purpose, we used the `venues.search` method to match PoIs discovered at the previous step with Foursquare PoIs, based on their coordinates. For any given PoI, the `nextvenues` method was invoked to obtain the most frequently visited PoIs, which are neighbors up to a certain distance—this is set fixed to 800 m in the current version of Foursquare APIs. We explored the Foursquare knowledge base by iteratively invoking the `nextvenues` method in a BFS fashion, up to a certain maximum distance from the seed. The new PoIs extracted from Foursquare were added into the Google database (in Fig. 1, this merging operation is indicated by graphical symbol $\oplus$).

Step 4: Wikipedia Database. The last crawling step consisted in extracting descriptive information about PoIs from Wikipedia. The reason for retrieving this kind of information is twofold. First, through the data obtained from Wikipedia we were able to represent conceptual relations between PoIs, i.e., by exploiting hyperlinks between the corresponding Wiki-pages. Second, we observed that the two previous crawling steps, due to limitations of the Google and Foursquare APIs, were not able to retrieve many potentially attractive PoIs, especially monuments and other historical areas. Therefore, we tried to match

---

[1] https://developers.google.com/places/.
[2] https://developers.google.com/maps/documentation/distance-matrix/.
[3] https://developers.google.com/places/supported_types/.
[4] https://developer.foursquare.com/.

wiki-concepts with each of the PoIs gathered at the previous steps, according to their names and using the `wikipedia.page` method available from the Wikipedia APIs.[5] We then looked for neighboring PoIs using the `geosearch` method, which returns PoIs valid in Wikipedia (i.e., with an associated wiki-page), in a geographic area around specific coordinates. We again used a BFS approach, iteratively calling the `geosearch` method within range δ, until a maximum distance from the seed was reached. We retrieved and stored information about description, backlinks and coordinates of each discovered PoI/Wiki-concept.

Step 5: Refinement. All new PoIs discovered via Foursquare and Wikipedia APIs (*Step 3* and *Step 4*) were used to update the Google database. In this regard, we completed missing information about distance between PoIs, referring again to the Google Distance Matrix APIs. Note that, since coordinates were also available for PoIs discovered in Wikipedia, it was possible to compute corresponding distances in Google Maps. Similarly, PoIs discovered at Step 4 in Wikipedia were matched with corresponding PoIs in Foursquare, using the `venues.search` function of the Foursquare APIs, and used to update the Foursquare database.

4.2   Multilayer Network System

Our integrated cross-platform PoI databases store relational information that we used to generate a multilayer network system. Even though relations in these platforms were retrieved as directed, we treated them as undirected edges in our multilayer network, in order not to bias the PoI recommendation procedure with a specific visiting order.

According to the model introduced in Sect. 3, we define our PoI multilayer network $G_\mathcal{L} = \langle V_\mathcal{L}, E_\mathcal{L}, \mathcal{V}, \mathcal{L} \rangle$ such that $\mathcal{V}$ is the set of PoI-entities in the three platforms, $V_\mathcal{L}$ and $E_\mathcal{L}$ denote the set of PoI-nodes and edges, respectively, and

$$\mathcal{L} = \mathcal{L}^{(gm)} \cup \mathcal{L}^{(fs)} \cup \mathcal{L}^{(wiki)}$$

is the set of layers comprised of three layer subsets, each corresponding to one of the platforms, i.e., $\mathcal{L}^{(gm)}$ for Google Maps, $\mathcal{L}^{(fs)}$ for Foursquare, and $\mathcal{L}^{(wiki)}$ for Wikipedia. We next provide details on each of these platform-specific layer subsets.

Google Maps Layer-Graphs. The Google Maps layer subset $\mathcal{L}^{(gm)}$ identifies a 6-layer network $G_{\mathcal{L}^{(gm)}} = \langle V^{(gm)}, E^{(gm)}, \mathcal{V}, \mathcal{L}^{(gm)} \rangle$, with

$$\mathcal{L}^{(gm)} = \mathcal{L}_d^{(gm)} \cup \mathcal{L}_t^{(gm)} = \{L_{1,d}^{(gm)}, L_{2,d}^{(gm)}, L_{3,d}^{(gm)}\} \cup \{L_{1,t}^{(gm)}, L_{2,t}^{(gm)}, L_{3,t}^{(gm)}\},$$

where subscripts d and t refers to measures of *spatial distance* and *duration*, respectively. Using $h = 1..3$ as layer index, we define the graphs in $G_{\mathcal{L}^{(gm)}}$

---

[5] https://www.mediawiki.org/wiki/API:Main_page.

corresponding to the layers $L_{h,d}^{(gm)}$ as $G_{h,d}^{(gm)} = \langle V_h^{(gm)}, E_h^{(gm)}, w_{h,d}^{(gm)} \rangle$, where $w_{h,d}^{(gm)} : E_h^{(gm)} \mapsto \mathbb{R}$ are edge weighting functions. For any two PoI nodes $p_i, p_j \in V_h^{(gm)}$, we define the edge $(p_i, p_j) \in E_h^{(gm)}$ if p_j and p_j are connected via a *pedestrian walk* ($h = 1$), a *public transport* ($h = 2$), or a *private transport* ($h = 3$). Edge weights are defined as $w_{h,d}^{(gm)}(i,j) = dist_h(p_i, p_j)$, where $dist_h(\cdot, \cdot)$ is a distance function that measures the length of the walk between two PoIs via pedestrian walk, public or private transport, respectively. Analogous definitions hold for the graphs in $G_{\mathcal{L}^{(gm)}}$ corresponding to the layers $L_{h,t}^{(gm)}$, with the exception of the edge weights $w_{h,t}^{(gm)}(i,j)$ that measure the time needed to reach PoI p_j from PoI p_i via pedestrian walk, public or private transport, respectively. Please note that, even though in Google Maps distance and time between two PoIs may vary depending on the starting and arrival point, we always followed the PoI visiting order to set weights.

Foursquare Layer-Graphs. The Foursquare layer subset $\mathcal{L}^{(fs)}$ identifies a 3-layer network $G_{\mathcal{L}^{(fs)}} = \langle V^{(fs)}, E^{(fs)}, \mathcal{V}, \mathcal{L}^{(fs)} \rangle$, with $\mathcal{L}^{(fs)} = \{L_1^{(fs)}, L_2^{(fs)}, L_3^{(fs)}\}$. For $h = 1..3$, we define the layer graphs in $G_{\mathcal{L}^{(fs)}}$ as $G_h^{(fs)} = \langle V_h^{(fs)}, E_h^{(fs)}, w_h^{(fs)} \rangle$, with edge weighting functions $w_h^{(fs)} : E_h^{(fs)} \mapsto \mathbb{R}$. To define the edges, we exploited the Foursquare functionality (provided by the `nextvenues` API method) of recommending a set of PoIs to visit from an input one; formally for any two PoI nodes p_i, p_j $V_h^{(fs)}$, there exists an edge in $E_h^{(fs)}$ if p_j is contained in the set of *recommended* PoIs from p_i. To define the edge weights, we benefited from social media contents available for Foursquare PoIs; specifically, edge weights are defined as $w_h^{(fs)}(i,j) = 1 + \sqrt{\frac{\widehat{n_{i_h}} \times \widehat{n_{j_h}}}{\widehat{n_{i_h}} + \widehat{n_{j_h}}}}$, where $\widehat{n_{i_h}} = \log_2(2 + n_{i_h})$, and n_{i_h} measures the number of *ratings* ($h = 1$), *likes* ($h = 2$), or *comments* ($h = 3$) received by PoI p_i. The ratio behind using these weighting schemes is to have a joint popularity of the path connecting two PoIs.

Wikipedia Layer-Graph. Finally, the Wikipedia layer subset $\mathcal{L}^{(wiki)}$ identifies a single network $G_{\mathcal{L}^{(wiki)}} = \langle V^{(wiki)}, E^{(wiki)}, \mathcal{V}, \{L^{(wiki)}\} \rangle$, equipped with edge weighting function $w^{(wiki)} : E^{(wiki)} \mapsto \mathbb{R}$, and such that $V^{(wiki)}$ is the set of nodes corresponding to wikipages describing PoIs in $\mathcal{V}$. An edge $(p_i, p_j) \in E^{(wiki)}$ exists if the wikipage of PoI p_i contains hyperlinks to the wikipage of PoI p_j, and the weight $w^{(wiki)}(i,j)$ expresses the content affinity between the wikipages p_i, p_j based on the number of wikipages jointly pointed to by p_i, p_j (denoted as $nlinks_{i,j}$), i.e., $w^{(wiki)}(i,j) = \log_2(2 + nlinks_{i,j})$.

5 Experimental Evaluation

5.1 Framework Settings

We used our defined PoI recommendation framework to build four cross-platform databases and multilayer networks corresponding to major Italian touristic venues: *Florence, Milan, Rome,* and *Venice.* For each of these venues, we selected a popular, central square as seed PoI, namely: "Piazza del Duomo" (Cathedral Square) in *Florence* and in *Milan,* "Piazza del Popolo" (People's Square) in *Rome,* "Piazza San Marco" (San Marco Square) in *Venice.* Our reason for the above choices is that all of the four cities are rich of PoIs of different types (historical, gastronomical, etc.). For each seed PoI, we carried out an independent instance of our PoI recommendation framework, and finally obtained four distinct multilayer networks.

To drive the crawling process, the radius δ at each step of exploration in Google Maps was set to 4 km. For each of the platforms, the BFS expansion process was iterated until a PoI distant more than $\delta_{max} = 20$ km from the seed PoI was reached. We initially selected the following PoI types ($\mathcal{T}$) supported by Google Places: *restaurant, cafe, bar, store, museum, movie theater, park, casino, art gallery, stadium, zoo, library, church, mosque, amusement_park, shopping mall.* Moreover, since the PoIs identified in Foursquare and Wikipedia induced new types of PoIs not necessarily covered by the Google ones, we organized the PoIs in the cross-platform databases into 13 macro-types, namely: CULTURE, ENTREPRENEURSHIP, FOOD & DRINK, HEALTH, LODGING, MONUMENT, NATURE, RELAX, SPORT, STORE, TRANSPORT, WORSHIP, Miscellanea. Details can be found in Appendix 1 of this paper.

5.2 Evaluation Goals

For each of the evaluation venues, besides analyzing the associated multilayer network in its entirety, we were also interested in assessing the performance of our ML-LCD method over different subsets of multilayer network corresponding to different combinations of the layers provided by the Google Maps, Foursquare and Wikipedia platforms. Specifically, we devised the following seven combinations of the layer graphs: full multilayer network (*All layers*), only Google Maps layers, either with distance or temporal weights ($\mathcal{L}_d^{(gm)}$ and $\mathcal{L}_t^{(gm)}$), only Foursquare layers ($\mathcal{L}^{(fs)}$), all layers with the exclusion of Wikipedia (*All but* $\mathcal{L}^{(wiki)}$), Foursquare (*All but* $\mathcal{L}^{(fs)}$), or Google Maps (*All but* $\mathcal{L}^{(gm)}$). Table 1 summarizes main characteristics of our evaluation network datasets and their configurations. Node relations in all datasets are treated as symmetric. We denote with A_{deg} the average degree of a node considering multiple edges, and with A_{layer} the average number of layers in which a node is present.

Moreover, we examined three selections of local communities produced by ML-LCD for each of the layer configurations and venue dataset. The first scenario, hereinafter referred to as *seed*, corresponds to the single local community centered on the seed PoI of the dataset; the second selection corresponds to the *top-k popular* PoIs in the dataset, where popularity was estimated according to the ratings provided in Foursquare; the third selection corresponds to the *top-k central* PoIs in the dataset, where centrality referred to the total (i.e., multilayer) degree of a PoI node. We will show results corresponding to $k = 10$.

Table 1. Main characteristics of the multilayer networks, and their configurations, obtained for the four evaluation venues (i.e., seed PoIs)

Configuration	# Nodes	# Edges	# Layers	Density	A_{deg}	A_{layer}	# Nodes	# Edges	# Layers	Density	A_{deg}	A_{layer}
Florence							*Milan*					
All layers	1359	48803	10	0.007	71.822	8.072	1918	81006	10	0.006	84.469	8.176
$\mathcal{L}_d^{(gm)}$ *only*	1359	20099	3	0.007	29.579	3.000	1918	32213	3	0.006	33.590	2.998
$\mathcal{L}_t^{(gm)}$ *only*	1359	20099	3	0.007	29.579	3.000	1918	32213	3	0.006	33.590	2.998
$\mathcal{L}^{(fs)}$ *only*	751	7385	3	0.011	19.667	2.710	1355	16341	3	0.006	24.120	2.885
All but $\mathcal{L}^{(wiki)}$	1359	47583	9	0.008	70.026	7.497	1918	80767	9	0.006	84.220	8.035
All but $\mathcal{L}^{(fs)}$	1359	41418	7	0.007	60.954	6.575	1918	64665	7	0.006	67.430	6.138
All but $\mathcal{L}^{(gm)}$	1123	8605	4	0.009	15.325	2.508	1462	16580	4	0.006	22.681	2.858
Rome							*Venice*					
All layers	2181	89908	10	0.005	82.447	8.007	728	23234	10	0.012	63.830	8.427
$\mathcal{L}_d^{(gm)}$ *only*	2181	37049	3	0.005	33.974	2.994	728	8738	3	0.011	24.005	2.990
$\mathcal{L}_t^{(gm)}$ *only*	2181	37049	3	0.005	33.974	2.994	728	8738	3	0.011	24.005	2.990
$\mathcal{L}^{(fs)}$ *only*	1341	15239	3	0.006	22.728	2.834	545	5489	3	0.014	20.143	2.837
All but $\mathcal{L}^{(wiki)}$	2181	89337	v9	0.005	81.923	7.732	728	22965	9	0.012	63.091	8.104
All but $\mathcal{L}^{(fs)}$	2181	74669	7	0.005	68.472	6.265	728	17745	7	0.011	48.750	6.304
All but $\mathcal{L}^{(gm)}$	1593	15810	4	0.006	19.849	2.763	635	5758	4	0.013	18.135	2.805

5.3   Results

We discuss here our main results, which include evaluation of the benefits from integrating the three online platforms, and analysis of the size, similarity and PoI-type coverage of the local communities (i.e., recommendations) provided by ML-LCD.

Impacts of Using Google Maps, Foursquare and Wikipedia Sources. For each of the evaluation datasets, we investigated how much the set of PoIs initially extracted via Google Maps API (Step 2 in our framework) was expanded thanks to the exploitation of Foursquare and Wikipedia sources (Steps 3–5). We found the following percentage increases in the Google PoIs due to Foursquare (resp. in the Google *plus* Foursquare PoIs due to Wikipedia): 51.62% (resp. 249.26%) in *Florence*, 105.64% (resp. 86.74%) in *Milan*, 68.51% (resp. 132.73%) in *Rome*, and 196% (resp. 286.4%) in *Venice*. This confirmed the beneficial effect of integrating Google Maps with PoI information available from Foursquare and Wikipedia.

We then specialized this analysis according to the categorization of PoIs into macro-types previously introduced in Sect. 5.1. Figure 2 shows the percentage of PoIs newly contributed by Foursquare and from Wikipedia, in *Florence* (results on the other evaluation venues are also shown in Fig. 4 in Appendix 2). In general, Foursquare and Wikipedia jointly led to a substantial enrichment of PoIs of types *Culture* (from 8% in Rome to 20% in Venice), *Food & Drink* (from 19% in Venice to 30% in Milan), and *Monument* (from 23% in Milan to 33% in Florence). Information extracted from Foursquare was particularly useful to expand the set of PoIs of types falling into the *Food & Drink* macro-type, whereas *Monument* PoIs benefited from the support provided by Wikipedia pages.

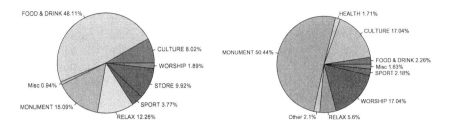

Fig. 2. Percentage contributions, for different PoI macro-types, from Foursquare to the Google Maps PoIs (left side), and from Wikipedia to the Google Maps plus Foursquare PoIs (right side), in *Florence*.

Table 2. Size of the local communities extracted by ML-LCD for different venues and configurations. Punctual values are reported for *seed* PoI, whereas mean ± standard deviation values over 10 PoIs are reported for *top*-10_*popular* and *top*-10_*central* evaluation cases.

Configuration	seed	top-10_central	top-10_popular	seed	top-10_central	top-10_popular
	Florence			Milan		
All layers	15	12.7 ± 5.478	9.5 ± 6.83	10	17.5 ± 16.317	6.0 ± 2.966
$\mathcal{L}_d^{(gm)}$ *only*	11	14.6 ± 6.406	10.5 ± 8.755	10	14.7 ± 12.634	6.2 ± 3.4
$\mathcal{L}_t^{(gm)}$ *only*	11	13.8 ± 6.177	10.8 ± 9.432	10	14.4 ± 12.729	6.2 ± 3.4
$\mathcal{L}^{(fs)}$ *only*	9	13.9 ± 8.938	5.6 ± 3.981	10	13.9 ± 11.777	6.1 ± 3.477
All but $\mathcal{L}^{(wiki)}$	10	12.3 ± 5.46	9.4 ± 6.406	10	17.5 ± 16.317	5.7 ± 3.002
All but $\mathcal{L}^{(fs)}$	11	14.6 ± 6.515	10.2 ± 8.829	10	14.7 ± 12.634	6.2 ± 3.4
All but $\mathcal{L}^{(gm)}$	11	11.7 ± 6.885	6.3 ± 3.848	10	13.9 ± 11.777	6.0 ± 3.521
	Rome			Venice		
All layers	11	11.0 ± 6.648	6.2 ± 1.833	13	7.7 ± 2.571	6.9 ± 3.081
$\mathcal{L}_d^{(gm)}$ *only*	11	11.0 ± 6.588	6.2 ± 1.661	13	8.1 ± 2.486	6.9 ± 3.081
$\mathcal{L}_t^{(gm)}$ *only*	11	11.0 ± 6.588	6.2 ± 1.661	14	8.2 ± 2.676	7.0 ± 3.286
$\mathcal{L}^{(fs)}$ *only*	10	13.5 ± 7.446	5.6 ± 2.691	12	8.2 ± 2.441	6.7 ± 2.865
All but $\mathcal{L}^{(wiki)}$	11	11.0 ± 6.648	6.2 ± 1.833	13	7.7 ± 2.571	6.9 ± 3.081
All but $\mathcal{L}^{(fs)}$	9	11.0 ± 6.588	6.2 ± 1.661	14	8.1 ± 2.7	6.9 ± 3.27
All but $\mathcal{L}^{(gm)}$	10	13.4 ± 6.1	5.5 ± 1.2	12	8.2 ± 2.441	6.7 ± 2.865

Size of the Local Communities. Table 2 reports on the size of the local communities identified by ML-LCD for the different venues and layer configurations. Focusing on the local communities obtained for the *seed* PoI, we observed that the different layer configurations have a low impact on the community size, with variations in terms of few units of PoIs. One exception corresponds to the community obtained for *seed* in *Florence* using configuration *All layers*, which is larger than the other ones. Few variations also are observed in the average size of local communities obtained for the *top*-10_*central* and *top*-10_*popular* PoIs. Conversely, variations in size can be evident when comparing local communities obtained for different PoIs of the same venue, i.e., standard deviation is relatively high in the majority of cases (with the exception of *top*-10_*popular* PoIs in *Rome*). More interestingly, the average size of local communities centered on each of the *top*-10_*popular* PoIs is always lower than the one observed for the *top*-10_*central* PoIs and the seed PoI, while local communities obtained for *top*-10_*central* PoIs are generally larger than seed-centric local communities, with the exception of *Venice*.

Similarity of Local Communities. We evaluated the similarity between the sets of PoIs belonging to the local communities respectively extracted for the seed PoI, the *top*-10_*popular* PoIs and the *top*-10_*central* PoIs. Table 3 summarizes mean and standard deviation of Jaccard similarity values aggregated over different sets of local communities. As a general remark, mean Jaccard similarities are relatively low in all cases, even if there can be significant variations in similarity when comparing different communities (i.e., standard deviations are always relatively high, and generally higher than mean values). The lowest mean value

Table 3. Pairwise comparison of communities produced by ML-LCD for *seed*, *top*-10_*popular* and *top*-10_*central* PoIs, for different layer configurations. Mean and standard deviation of Jaccard similarity values are computed over: (X_1) *seed* community vs. *top*-10_*central* communities, (X_2) *seed* community vs. *top*-10_*popular* communities, (X_3) *top*-10_*central* communities vs. each other, (X_4) *top*-10_*popular* communities vs. each other, (X_5) *top*-10_*popular* communities vs. *top*-10_*central* communities. Number of comparisons was 10 for X_4 and X_5 and 45 for X_1, X_2 and X_3.

	All layers	$\mathcal{L}_d^{(gm)}$ only	$\mathcal{L}_t^{(gm)}$ only	$\mathcal{L}^{(fs)}$ only	All but $\mathcal{L}^{(wiki)}$	All but $\mathcal{L}^{(fs)}$	All but $\mathcal{L}^{(gm)}$
Florence							
X_1	0.243 ± 0.323	0.109 ± 0.298	0.109 ± 0.298	0.308 ± 0.417	0.331 ± 0.417	0.1 ± 0.3	0.196 ± 0.315
X_2	0.193 ± 0.303	0.16 ± 0.306	0.191 ± 0.362	0.306 ± 0.455	0.312 ± 0.451	0.142 ± 0.312	0.169 ± 0.307
X_3	0.121 ± 0.258	0.067 ± 0.214	0.072 ± 0.232	0.183 ± 0.315	0.142 ± 0.295	0.064 ± 0.233	0.109 ± 0.236
X_4	0.042 ± 0.151	0.04 ± 0.158	0.031 ± 0.132	0.071 ± 0.249	0.075 ± 0.248	0.028 ± 0.134	0.026 ± 0.085
X_5	0.109 ± 0.266	0.078 ± 0.234	0.063 ± 0.218	0.118 ± 0.296	0.134 ± 0.31	0.059 ± 0.219	0.073 ± 0.208
Milan							
X_1	0.17 ± 0.341	0.175 ± 0.339	0.175 ± 0.339	0.17 ± 0.341	0.17 ± 0.341	0.175 ± 0.339	0.17 ± 0.341
X_2	0.18 ± 0.363	0.18 ± 0.363	0.18 ± 0.363	0.19 ± 0.381	0.18 ± 0.363	0.18 ± 0.363	0.19 ± 0.381
X_3	0.025 ± 0.132	0.027 ± 0.133	0.028 ± 0.134	0.026 ± 0.133	0.025 ± 0.132	0.028 ± 0.134	0.026 ± 0.133
X_4	0.04 ± 0.187	0.04 ± 0.187	0.04 ± 0.187	0.042 ± 0.196	0.04 ± 0.187	0.04 ± 0.187	0.042 ± 0.196
X_5	0.046 ± 0.201	0.052 ± 0.203	0.057 ± 0.207	0.046 ± 0.201	0.046 ± 0.201	0.057 ± 0.207	0.046 ± 0.201
Rome							
X_1	0.275 ± 0.341	0.267 ± 0.33	0.267 ± 0.33	0.284 ± 0.361	0.275 ± 0.341	0.324 ± 0.402	0.291 ± 0.37
X_2	0.157 ± 0.262	0.148 ± 0.244	0.148 ± 0.244	0.139 ± 0.247	0.157 ± 0.262	0.18 ± 0.295	0.145 ± 0.264
X_3	0.153 ± 0.314	0.159 ± 0.324	0.159 ± 0.324	0.163 ± 0.32	0.153 ± 0.314	0.159 ± 0.324	0.157 ± 0.309
X_4	0.073 ± 0.222	0.075 ± 0.227	0.075 ± 0.227	0.074 ± 0.23	0.073 ± 0.222	0.075 ± 0.227	0.07 ± 0.225
X_5	0.12 ± 0.272	0.124 ± 0.279	0.124 ± 0.279	0.113 ± 0.265	0.12 ± 0.272	0.124 ± 0.279	0.108 ± 0.257
Venice							
X_1	0.229 ± 0.325	0.233 ± 0.335	0.231 ± 0.329	0.254 ± 0.341	0.229 ± 0.325	0.233 ± 0.335	0.254 ± 0.341
X_2	0.136 ± 0.307	0.133 ± 0.306	0.136 ± 0.307	0.146 ± 0.316	0.136 ± 0.307	0.133 ± 0.306	0.146 ± 0.316
X_3	0.085 ± 0.244	0.09 ± 0.234	0.09 ± 0.231	0.105 ± 0.259	0.095 ± 0.244	0.09 ± 0.234	0.105 ± 0.259
X_4	0.023 ± 0.115	0.025 ± 0.124	0.025 ± 0.125	0.024 ± 0.11	0.023 ± 0.115	0.025 ± 0.124	0.024 ± 0.11
X_5	0.092 ± 0.267	0.088 ± 0.257	0.088 ± 0.57	0.109 ± 0.285	0.092 ± 0.267	0.088 ± 0.257	0.109 ± 0.285

(0.023 ± 0.115) is obtained for *Venice*, when comparing *top-10_popular* PoIs' communities, for configurations *All Layers* and *All but* $\mathcal{L}^{(wiki)}$, while the highest mean value (0.331 ± 0.417) is observed for *Florence* when comparing *seed* PoI's community with *top-10_popular* PoIs' communities, for configuration *All but* $\mathcal{L}^{(wiki)}$. Higher similarity values correspond to the comparison of seed-centric communities with those obtained for *top-10_popular* and *top-10_central* PoIs, for all venues and configurations. Conversely, lower similarity values correspond to the pairwise comparison of communities obtained for *top-10_popular* PoIs (followed by the values obtained when comparing *top-10_central* PoIs' communities). These results would indicate that the *seed* PoI, due to its geographical centrality (i.e., strategic location), is likely to have a certain number of PoIs belonging to its local community that are shared by *top-10_central* and *top-10_popular* PoIs' communities; conversely, both *top-10_central* and *top-10_popular* PoIs' communities are likely to be found in different geographical locations, and thus tend to belong to disjoint local communities.

Coverage of Types in the PoI Distributions of the Local Communities. In this evaluation stage, we analyzed the composition of the obtained local communities in terms of PoIs of different macro-types. We first focused on the local communities centered on the *seed* of each venue, using the whole multilayer network for that venue (*All Layers* configuration). Results are shown in Fig. 3. As a general remark, the majority of PoIs for all venues were selected among the *Monument* and *Food & Drink* macro-types, with a predominance of the former for *Florence* and *Rome*, and of the latter for *Milan* and *Venice*. This is actually not surprising, since monuments and restaurants are likely the most attractive and popular PoIs to consider during a trip. The most heterogeneous local communities were obtained for *Florence* and *Venice*, where six different PoI macro-types are covered. By contrast, the *seed* local community obtained

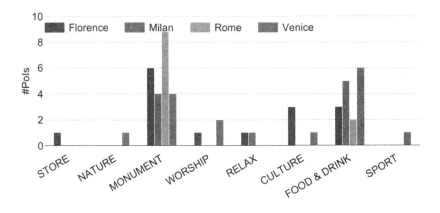

Fig. 3. PoI distribution over different macro-types for the *seed*-centric local communities, with *All Layers* configuration, for the various venues. *(Best viewed in color)* (Color figure online)

for *Rome* was much less heterogeneous, where most PoIs belong to the *Monument* and *Food & Drink* macro-types, which can be explained due to the larger extension of the popular historical site in *Rome* w.r.t. the other venues. It should be emphasized that ML-LCD, being multilayer and query-dependent, is able to extract (i.e., recommend) both communities focused on a small set of PoI types, as well as communities distributed on several PoI types, depending on the seed PoI. As regards the *seed* local communities obtained for different configurations (results not shown), we observed that the impact on the PoI type distribution was relatively low, similarly to what we found for the community sizes in Table 2. In fact, for all venues, the *seed* local community is always characterized mostly by *Monument* and *Food & Drink* PoIs, regardless of the specific combinations of layers.

We also analyzed the PoI distribution over different macro-types for the local communities discovered around the *top*-10_*popular* PoIs, on the various venues (results are shown in Fig. 5 in Appendix 3). We observed that substantial differences emerge in the type distribution trends for different PoIs. Depending on the peculiar characteristics of each venue, some local communities were found to be strongly unbalanced towards a single type; for instance, in *Florence* and *Milan*, several communities are characterized by a strong presence of *Store* PoIs (a macro-type scarcely represented in *seed* communities), which is sometimes the unique macro-type in the local community (e.g., for PoIs located in large shopping areas, such as "Gucci Store" and "Louis Vuitton Store" in *Milan*). Concerning the communities extracted for the *top*-10_*popular* PoIs in *Rome*, a few of them are mainly characterized by *Monument* PoIs, consistently with what we found in the *seed* community analysis. As a final remark, also in this case the impact of different layer configurations was relatively low. The only significant (and expected) outcome is that local communities obtained for the $\mathcal{L}^{(fs)}$ *only* configuration were generally characterized by a massive presence of *Food & Drink* PoIs, due to the popularity of this type in Foursquare data. Analogous observations were drawn for the local communities extracted for the *top*-10_*central* PoIs for the different venues (results not shown).

6   Conclusions

We presented a novel approach to the recommendation of Points-of-Interest, which employs a multilayer local community detection method on cross-platform networked data. We defined an integrated crawling methodology for travel-oriented social media networks, which allowed us to extract information about PoIs of a given geographical area from different sources, i.e., geo-referenced information from Google Maps, geo-tagged social information from Foursquare, lexical and semantic information from Wikipedia. Upon the consolidated databases, we defined a cross-platform PoI multilayer network, and used it to input our PoI recommender system based on multilayer local community detection. Empirical evidence unveiled interesting outcomes of our approach.

As a future work, it would be useful to further enrich our PoI integrated databases with online social data about user profiles, in order to improve the expressiveness of our model in terms of a user's budget constraints and preferences. Our cross-platform PoI networks are made available at http://people.dimes.unical.it/andreatagarelli/poi-rec/.

Appendix 1. PoI Macro-types

See Table 4.

Table 4. Macro-types of PoIs and their descriptions

Macro-type	List of PoI types
STORE	shopping malls, department stores, hardware, food, super-dealers, dealers, local stores, markets, outlets, mini markets, groceries, florists, storages
WORSHIP	churches, basilicas, abbeys, monasteries, churches, chapels, cloisters, synagogues, cathedrals, tabernacles
RELAX	villas, gardens, parks, cinemas, camps, beaches, harbors, discos, panoramas, music, spas, casinos, aquariums, racecourses, locales, salons, night clubs, circles, venues, gyms, Zoo
MONUMENT	squares, bridges, municiparks, buildings, archaeological sites, towers, bell towers, clocks, walls, doors, temples, tombs, arenas, sculptures, obelisks, castles, streets, fountains, lungars, catacombs, amphitheater palaces, crypts, historic centers, Domes, baptistery, residences, columns, lamps, skyscrapers, fortifications, farmhouses
CULTURE	theaters, museums, art galleries, libraries, schools, universities, academies, cemeteries, fairs, institutions, barracks, offices, archives, planetaries, art formations, embassies, observers, institutes
TRANSPORT	stations, airports, vehicle repair, transportation, rentals
NATURE	canals, lagoons, rivers, tributaries, lakes, hills, mountains, bays, forests, dams
HEALTH	hospitals, pharmacies, health care centers
Misc	area, location, fractions, islands, neighborhoods, streets, places, cities
ACCOMMODATION	accommodation, hotels, hotels, hostels
FOOD & DRINK	restaurants, pubs, bars, taverns, taverns, bars, wineries, cocktail bars, ice-cream parlors, pizzerias, bakeries, lounges, steakhouses, banquets, bistros, pastry shops
SPORT	stadiums, soccer fields, tennis courts, basketball courts, swimming pools
ENTREPRENEURSHIP	companies, companies, agencies, offices, post offices, central factories, associations

Appendix 2. Impacts of Using Google Maps, Foursquare and Wikipedia Sources: *Other Venues*

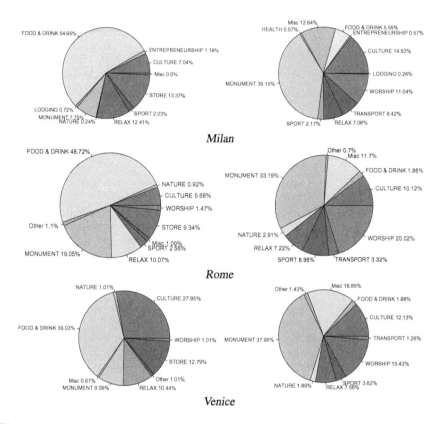

Fig. 4. Percentage contributions, for different PoI macro-types, from Foursquare to the Google Maps PoIs (left side), and from Wikipedia to the Google Maps plus Foursquare PoIs (right side).

Appendix 3. Coverage of Types in the PoI Distributions of the Local Communities Centered on Most Popular PoIs

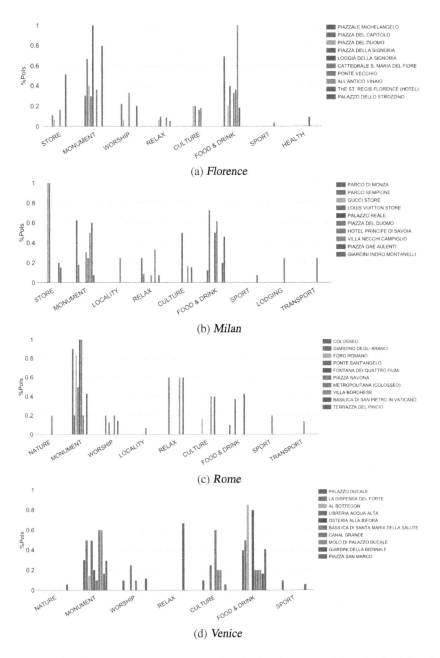

Fig. 5. PoI distribution over macro-types for the local communities obtained for the *top-10_popular* PoIs, with *All Layers* configuration, for the various venues.

References

1. Branting, K.: Context-sensitive detection of local community structure. Soc. Netw. Anal. Min. **2**(3), 279–289 (2012)
2. Chen, J., Zaïane, O.R., Goebel, R.: Local community identification in social networks. In: Proceedings of IEEE/ACM International Conference on Advances in Social Networks Analysis and Mining (ASONAM), pp. 237–242 (2009)
3. Chen, Y., Xu, J., Xu, M.: Finding community structure in spatially constrained complex networks. Int. J. Geogr. Inf. Sci. **29**(6), 889–911 (2015)
4. Clauset, A.: Finding local community structure in networks. Phys. Rev. E **72**(2), 026132 (2005)
5. Fagnan, J., Zaïane, O.R., Barbosa, D.: Using triads to identify local community structure in social networks. In: Proceedings of IEEE/ACM International Conference on Advances in Social Networks Analysis and Mining (ASONAM), pp. 108–112 (2014)
6. Han, J., Lee, H.: Adaptive landmark recommendations for travel planning: personalizing and clustering landmarks using geo-tagged social media. Pervasive Mob. Comput. **18**, 4–17 (2015)
7. Interdonato, R., Romeo, S., Tagarelli, A., Karypis, G.: A versatile graph-based approach to package recommendation. In: Proceedings of International Conference on Tools with Artificial Intelligence (ICTAI), pp. 857–864 (2013)
8. Interdonato, R., Tagarelli, A., Ienco, D., Sallaberry, A., Poncelet, P.: Local community detection in multilayer networks. In: Proceedings of IEEE/ACM International Conference on Advances in Social Networks Analysis and Mining (ASONAM), pp. 1382–1383 (2016)
9. Interdonato, R., Tagarelli, A., Ienco, D., Sallaberry, A., Poncelet, P.: Local community detection in multilayer networks. Data Min. Knowl. Disc. 1–36 (2017). doi:10.1007/s10618-017-0525-y
10. Interdonato, R., Tagarelli, A., Ienco, D., Sallaberry, A., Poncelet, P.: Node-centric community detection in multilayer networks with layer-coverage diversification bias. In: Gonçalves, B., Menezes, R., Sinatra, R., Zlatic, V. (eds.) CompleNet 2017. SPC, pp. 57–66. Springer, Cham (2017). doi:10.1007/978-3-319-54241-6_5
11. Jeub, L.G.S., Mahoney, M.W., Mucha, P.J., Porter, M.A.: A local perspective on community structure in multilayer networks. Netw. Sci. **5**(2), 144–163 (2017)
12. Kivela, M., Arenas, A., Barthelemy, M., Gleeson, J.P., Moreno, Y., Porter, M.A.: Mutilayer networks. J. Complex Netw. **2**(3), 203–271 (2014)
13. Lathia, N., Quercia, D., Crowcroft, J.: The hidden image of the city: sensing community well-being from urban mobility. In: Kay, J., Lukowicz, P., Tokuda, H., Olivier, P., Krüger, A. (eds.) Pervasive 2012. LNCS, vol. 7319, pp. 91–98. Springer, Heidelberg (2012). doi:10.1007/978-3-642-31205-2_6
14. León, M., Mkrtchyan, L., Depaire, B., Ruan, D., Vanhoof, K.: Learning and clustering of fuzzy cognitive maps for travel behaviour analysis. Knowl. Inf. Syst. **39**(2), 435–462 (2014)
15. Li, Y., Barbieri, N., Quercia, D.: Applying space syntax to online mapping tools. In: Proceedings of ACM Conference on Web Search and Data Mining (WSDM), pp. 273–282 (2017)
16. Li, Y., He, K., Bindel, D., Hopcroft, J.E.: Uncovering the small community structure in large networks: a local spectral approach. In: Proceedings of ACM Conference on World Wide Web (WWW), pp. 658–668 (2015)

17. Quercia, D., Schifanella, R., Aiello, L.M.: The shortest path to happiness: recommending beautiful, quiet, and happy routes in the city. In: Proceedings of ACM Conference on Hypertext and Social Media (HT), New York, USA, pp. 116–125 (2014)
18. Rijurekha, S., Quercia, D., Ruiz, C.V., Gummadi, K.P.: Scalable urban data collection from the web. In: Proceedings of AAAI Conference on Web and Social Media (ICWSM) (2016)
19. Skovsgaard, A., Idlauskas, D., Jensen, C.S.: A clustering approach to the discovery of points of interest from geo-tagged microblog posts. In: Proceedings of IEEE International Conference on Mobile Data Management, pp. 178–188. IEEE (2014)
20. Venerandi, A., Quattrone, G., Capra, L., Quercia, D., Saez-Trumper, D.: Measuring urban deprivation from user generated content. In: Proceedings of ACM Conference on Computer Supported Cooperative Work and Social Computing (CSCW), pp. 254–264 (2015)
21. Zakrzewska, A., Bader, D.A.: A dynamic algorithm for local community detection in graphs. In: Proceedings of IEEE/ACM International Conference on Advances in Social Networks Analysis and Mining (ASONAM), pp. 559–564 (2015)

Designing for Digital Inclusion: A Post-Hoc Evaluation of a Civic Technology

Claudia López[1(✉)] and Rosta Farzan[2]

[1] Universidad Técnica Federico Santa María, Av. Espana 1680, Valparaíso, Chile
claudia@inf.utfsm.cl
[2] University of Pittsburgh, 135 North Bellefield, Pittsburgh, PA 15213, USA
rfarzan@pitt.edu

Abstract. Digital inequalities are a major obstacle in diversifying the public discourse on the Internet. To explore the potential of a system design to help bridging digital inequalities across gender and race, we conducted a post-hoc evaluation of design decisions within a civic technology that were particularly dedicated to increase participation of women and people of color. While many aspects of digital inequality stay unresolved, our results provide evidence in support of such dedicated design decisions. Our work also makes a methodological contribution by providing an approach to use external public data sets to supplement user demographic data, without which studies of digital inclusion could only rely on self-reported, potentially biased data. We discuss the empirical and ethical implications of our research approach and results.

Keywords: Digital inclusion · Gender · Race · Civic technology

1 Introduction

With the strong perception of prevalence of social technologies in people's lives comes an intense discussion of to what extent various groups of the population are involved in these new social media. Presumably, social technologies are designed to empower the general public to exchange information and interact with each other; everyone is encouraged to voice out their point of views, their opinions, and their knowledge; e.g. everyone can contribute to a Wikipedia article, anyone can post on Twitter, and individuals can participate on various online discussion forums.

However, there is a rich body of research highlighting the phenomena of digital gaps that denote systematic inequalities of access and use of digital and Internet technologies [7,27,34]. Early research on digital inequalities often reported lower rates of Internet use among females and people of color as a result of their lower level of access to digital technologies [17,25]. More recent research reports that the access gap is diminishing [7] and the differences on uses of the Internet are more nuanced [17,31]. The differences might be linked to other variables such as social class [31], the development of Internet skills [13], and a sense of self-efficacy [15]. These variables are often significantly lower among women and

© Springer International Publishing AG 2017
G.L. Ciampaglia et al. (Eds.): SocInfo 2017, Part I, LNCS 10539, pp. 572–588, 2017.
DOI: 10.1007/978-3-319-67217-5_34

people of color compared to white men. This explains why there is still evidence of gender and racial digital gaps in online participation even in developed countries where the access inequalities have been disappearing.

While designing technology for underrepresented or under-served populations has drawn sizable attention from researchers, these efforts have seldom addressed under-representation of females and people of color. The concept of *universal design* has been adapted to highlight the importance of engaging in a conscious effort to design computer-mediated interactions that can be "experienced and effectively used by the broadest possible end user communities" [2]. Part of these efforts aim to address regional digital divides by investigating technology-mediated interactions among people living in developing countries [30] or rural communities [26]. Another stream of research has advanced the guidelines, methods and tools to design for populations with, so called, "special needs" within regions where the Internet access is similar for all potential users. Examples of these populations are older adults [20], children [8], people with disabilities [22,32], persons who are illiterate [21], and economically distressed individuals [16].

The challenge of addressing racial and gender digital under-representation from a designer perspective has remained understudied. Significant attention has being drawn to gender imbalances among Wikipedia editors [4,18], the gaming and open source communities. While some design lessons have been proposed to address these inequalities [5,28] and a few existing studies have acknowledged the importance of design decisions on individuals' participation patterns [11], there are still few attempts to assess how the design of technologies can help to narrow the gender and racial inequalities in online participation, especially in developed countries.

Our research goal is to assess whether a civic technology can be designed (or redesigned) to increase gender and racial diversity among its members and active participants. In this work, we have studied participation of women and people of color in E-Democracy.org, a pioneer example of a civic technology, that had similarly been facing unenthusiastic participation of these two populations. To address such inequalities, E-Democracy.org enacted specific design decisions aiming to foster digital inclusion and diversify the online public discourse. This paper reports on our post-hoc investigation of these design decisions and whether they were related to a more diverse participation.

We examined participation of women and people of color as represented in the archival data of 37 E-Democracy forums with respect to their specific design decisions in engaging these populations. As the platform does not collect information about the gender and race of their users but strongly encourage them to use their real names as usernames, we employed an alternative approach to estimate these user demographics. Following the approaches proposed in [9,24], we used external data sets (from the US Social Security Administration and Census) to estimate the probability of gender and race associated with the first and last name provided by the platform's users. Using these probabilities, we computed the proportions of women and people of color who joined and contributed to the forums. Our analyses indicate mixed results in terms of the relationship between the design decisions enacted by E-Democracy and digital inclusion; thus revealing opportunities and challenges of effectively designing for fostering gender and racial inclusion in a civic technology.

Our work contributes to research and practice on computer-mediated interaction by: (1) Bringing attention to a less regarded area within universal design to study whether and how the design of computer-mediated interactions can help bridging digital inequalities related to gender and race in a developed country; (2) Presenting an approach in connecting research and practice by studying association of design decisions made by technology practitioners with research outcomes; (3) Providing methodological insight on how to estimate missing demographic data such as the gender and race using external data sources while discussing the implications of such approaches to supplement missing data.

The rest of this paper is structured as follows. First, we review the literature on the intersection between digital inclusion and computer-mediated interaction. We define our research questions and, then, we describe E-Democracy, our research platform. We detail our research method and the results of our analyses. Finally, we provide a discussion of our contributions and the practical and ethical implications of our methods and results.

2   Related Work and Research Question

A recent research report from civic technology practitioners has found that women and racial minorities are systematically under-represented among civic technology users in both developed and developing countries [29].

These findings are aligned with other evidence of gender and racial digital inequalities. While recent US surveys conclude that women are as likely as men to participate in social media in general, there are significant differences among specific social media platforms [3]. Women are more likely than men to engage in Pinterest, Facebook, and Instagram; however, they are significantly less likely to participate in online production communities such as Wikipedia [4,18] and online discussion forums [3].

In terms of race inequalities and in the context of civic participation, there is significant inequality of participation across races, after controlling for the effect of social class. White people are more likely than African-Americans and Hispanics to engage in civic communications, including political communications, both offline and online [33].

There has been various studies on investigating the factors influencing race and gender digital inequalities [3,13,15,17,18,25]. These factors span across various dimensions such as socio-demographics, nature of contribution, self-efficacy, privacy concerns, and technical skills. For example, through a survey of Wikipedia contributors and non-contributors, Hargittai and Shaw identify Internet skills as an important factor influencing gender gap in Wikipedia [13]. In addition to individual characteristics contributing to online participation inequality, there are features of the online platforms that can influence the participation of women and people of color. For example, individual biases and antagonistic environment of online platforms have been shown to discourage active participation of women and ethnic minorities in online discussion forums, online games, or open source software communities [19,28,35].

As highlighted here, abundance of studies have drawn attention to gender gap and racial gap. They acknowledge the importance of bridging the gap to achieve more effective online platforms and serve a more diverse population. The designs themselves can be influenced by the various factors identified in these studies to be contributing to participation inequalities. Practitioners and researchers have been investigating ways to design for a more diverse population. While such practices have been motivated by existing research, there has been less research on evaluating whether technology designs can help narrowing such gaps. There have been few studies in the context of Wikipedia and games that have started the conversation on lessons for addressing gender imbalance [5,10,28] and designing for racial minorities [12,36]. However, it is still unknown whether enacting a design decision can be related to more online participation of women or people of color. In this work we aim to extend the scope of existing work on gender and racial inequality in online communities by focusing on the assessment of design decisions. Therefore, we have framed our research around the following question:

What is the relationship between design decisions and participation of women and people of color in a civic technology?

3   Research Platform: E-Democracy

Founded in 1994, E-Democracy is a non-profit organization with the mission "to harness the power of online tools to support participation in public life, strengthen communities, and build democracy."[1] Originally, E-Democracy was designed as a virtual space (implemented through an email listserv) to obtain and disseminate information about political candidates in the state of Minnesota.[2,3] E-Democracy also hosted pioneer e-debates in which candidates got involved in week-long online conversations (including answers and rebuttals) around topics that residents had raised through the platform.[4] Over time, especially during election times, E-Democracy became stable discussion forums that had attracted more than 1,300 residents of Minnesota. With this user base, E-Democracy later decided to launch their web-based platform version and modified their email listserv to an announcement-only email list to allow residents to promote their civic events without the need to follow political discussions.[5]

Around 2000, E-Democracy launched online discussion forums for few cities in the state of Minnesota and adopted a metaphor of an online town hall to

---

[1] http://forums.e-democracy.org/about/.

[2] http://www.e-democracy.org/1994/Project_description.html.

[3] http://blog.e-democracy.org/archives.

[4] http://www.e-democracy.org/1994/E-Debates/.

[5] http://www.e-democracy.org/mn-politics/explain.html.

describe the dynamics and goals of these forums.[6] These city-wide forums have a strong focus on political discussion and deliberation about local issues. For example, the description of the Minneapolis' forum invites users "to discuss local-level Minneapolis civic issues. With over 1,600 registered participants, this is a vibrant online space where citizens, elected officials, and community leaders - with diverse ideas and backgrounds - can discuss the important local issues facing our city in a civil and respectful manner."[7] With those forums, E-Democracy had attracted enough users to keep the online public debate going. However, the online debates were also dominated by the typical, non-diverse participants of face-to-face town hall meetings; i.e. white, highly educated, well-off males. As a result, diversifying participation and digital inclusion became an important goal of E-Democracy.[8] To identify the main design decisions that E-Democracy enacted to achieve this goal, we interviewed the founder and a senior staff member of E-Democracy and conducted a content analysis of the organization's blog,[9] which describes important events in the platform's development. We concluded that E-Democracy undertook three major design decisions as explicit attempts to bridge the digital divide in participation in their platform:

City vs. Neighborhood Forums: As the first attempt to reach a more diverse audience, E-Democracy created neighborhood forums that aim to increase community involvement as opposed to encourage political discussion. As highlighted by the founder of E-Democracy, providing a platform for residents to discuss community life is essential to encourage participation from diverse members of the community [1]. By capitalizing on residents' interest and connection to local issues, they aimed to create a less polarized virtual space that might be more welcoming for newcomers, especially those who might be less accustomed to participating in political discussions.

Offline Outreach: To encourage participation of under-represented populations, E-Democracy implemented a user engagement strategy in neighborhoods with high racial diversity, focusing on reaching out to the neighborhoods' residents through offline channels in order to increase awareness about the forums and to sign up new users. This strategy was implemented through several mechanisms, including hosting workshops about how to use the forums, attending neighborhoods' festivals to publicize the forums, and conducting door-to-door advertisement. Due to budgetary issues, the offline outreach was only conducted in some neighborhoods with high racial diversity, but not all them.

Maximum Daily Number of Posts: All E-Democracy forums constrain the number of daily posts that a user can add, in order to diversify voices and to avoid domination in the forum by a few members [6]. Majority of forums restrict number of posts to two per user per day, with a considerable number of them using three as the threshold and a few other ones allowing between four to six posts per user per day.

---

[6] http://blog.e-democracy.org/posts/624.

[7] http://forums.e-democracy.org/groups/mpls/charter.

[8] http://forums.e-democracy.org/projects/engage/inclusive-social-media/.

[9] http://blog.e-democracy.org/.

These design decisions were implemented from the start of the neighborhood forums, except the max number of daily posts which was updated after the creation time. Unfortunately, we were unable to trace back the exact timing of that decision in each forum. Therefore, our analysis could not account for it.

4 Methods

4.1 Determining Gender and Race of Users

To be able to assess the impact of design decisions on participation of female and people of color, first we needed to determine the gender and race of the E-Democracy users as the platform does not collect that information. Given that the users are strongly encouraged to provide their real names to register in the system, we attempted to estimate users' gender and race by matching their first and last names against aggregated names data from The United States Social Security Administration (SSA) and the US Census. The estimation provide us with a probability of a name belonging to a specific gender and race. We adopted these approaches from prior research [9,24].

We used an iterative process to retrieve the probability of each user's first name belonging to a male or female person. In this process, we employed data of the most frequent baby names by gender in the US,[10] according to the SSA. The data includes the frequency of all first names that have more than five occurrences for the same gender in the period of one year. We used the list of names corresponding to the beginning of each decade from 1920 until 2010. For all E-Democracy users' first names, we initially examined the 1960's Census data that corresponds to the average birth year of E-Democracy users.[11] If the name was found, the corresponding frequencies were assigned to the user's first name in order to compute the probability of each gender. Otherwise, we followed the same procedure of looking for the name in other Censuses from 1920 to 2010 in chronological order. Once the process was over, all found names had been associated with a probability of belonging to a male or female person.

To compute the users' probability of belonging to a racial group, we used two kinds of data: the list of most-frequently occurring surnames from the 2000 US Census,[12] and the racial distribution of the neighborhoods in the cities of Minneapolis and St. Paul according to the 2010 US Census, as compiled by Minnesota Compass.[13] The first dataset includes all last names with more than 100 occurrences in the 2000 Census and their distribution across people of different races. For each user's last name, we retrieved its probability of belonging to a person of each of the races and ethnicities coded in the US Census: White, Black, Asian and Pacific Islander (API), American Indian and Alaska Native (AIAN), Two or More Races, and Hispanic. As the E-Democracy users are affiliated with

---

[10] http://www.ssa.gov/oact/babynames/limits.html.
[11] According to the 2014 E-Democracy's user survey.
[12] http://www.census.gov/topics/population/genealogy/data/.
[13] http://www.mncompass.org/profiles/neighborhoods/minneapolis-saint-paul.

either a neighborhood or a city forum, we also gathered the racial distribution of these geographical areas from our second source of data. Finally, we computed the joint probability of each race considering both the probability of such race given the user's last name and the user's geographical area. To determine gender and race, we employed a pseudo-random sampling according to the probability distributions of each user's name.

4.2   Longitudinal Analysis of Digital Inclusion

We integrated the gender and race data to the archival data of 35 neighborhood forums and two city forums in Minnesota. These forums varied in tenure from 4 to 39 quarters with an average of 16 quarters. For each forum and for each quarter, we calculated the proportion of females and people of color who joined each forum and contributed to the forum as well as proportion of content contributed by women and people of color. These variables were used as dependent variables to measure the effect of the E-Democracy design decisions on digital inclusion. We modeled the relationship between the design decisions and the participation factors, using a series of longitudinal linear regressions[14] for nested data to control for repeated measures of the forums over time. The independent variables in the regression models were the design decisions in each forum. Moreover, in the analyses, we controlled for the year that the forum was created, and the forum's tenure at each observation period.

4.3   Additional Analysis Consideration

As described earlier, three design decisions were the focus of the study: the kind of forums (city vs. neighborhoods), if the forums have had offline outreach, and the daily maximum number of posts. Offline outreach and the variation of maximum number of posts was only enacted for the neighborhood forums; therefore, we limited our analysis of these two design decisions to the 35 neighborhood forums. The assignment of forums to these decisions was neither balanced nor random. Therefore, our analyses had to deal with unbalanced samples and potential co-linearity among the variables that denote the design decisions and other neighborhood demographics. To reduce the imbalance and sparsity of forums within different categories of maximum daily posts, we created a binary variable to indicate if the maximum number of daily posts was above three. The correlation between this variable and the offline outreach variable was not significant (Spearman's $\rho = 0.22$, p $= 0.18$). Therefore, we included both of them in the same regression analyses. Table 1 presents the number of forums that enacted each of these design decisions.

The neighborhood forums were also aggregated regarding their year of creation in order to avoid very unbalanced samples. This variable had two levels: if the forum was created before 2011 or later.

---

[14] To ensure normal distribution of dependent variables, we used log transformation in any case that the variable was not normally distributed.

Table 1. Neighborhood forums by design decisions

Daily max. # of posts	Without outreach	With outreach	Total
Two or three	20	6	26
Four or five or six	6	5	11

5 Results

Overall, the data included 13,705 E-Democracy users. We were able to estimate the gender for 10,105 users (74.39%) and race for 11,120 users (81%). Our analysis focuses on the users who were matched to gender and/or race probabilities.

Although these results will not describe the whole user base of the system, we believe that they are a good representative of the trends of participation of women and people of color on E-Democracy because the datasets that we used to determine these variables are not likely to over-represent these populations. First, the SSA data is unlikely to be biased towards any gender as it record all American babies' gender and given names, regardless of how frequent each combination is. Second, the US census data includes information about surnames with more than 100 occurrences. This dataset might be less likely to have information about people of color given that they are minorities in the US. This bias might result in an underestimation of participation of people of color on E-Democracy. Hence, we believe that the results we obtain about participation of people of color in the forums will represent a conservative estimate that could only be higher if this bias indeed exists.

5.1 Descriptive Statistics About Gender and Race

The results indicate that there are more female than male users who have contributed posts to the E-Democracy forums (see Table 2). There is 7% higher percentage of female contributors on E-Democracy. However, women provide a significantly smaller share of the posts. On average, men post about twice more messages than women.

Our results reveal a great deal of inequality of participation between white people and people of color in the E-Democracy forums. Table 3 presents the descriptive statistics of user contribution across different races. Most contributors are white and they account for a majority of posts. 68% of the users who added content to the forums are white and only 13% of the users belong to any other race or ethnicity. Among the minorities, people whose race is Black and Asian Pacific Islander comprise larger shares of the contributor base than Hispanics or other races. The white majority among contributors is further extended by an even larger proportion of posts provided by it. White people contributed 83% of the content in the forums. Members belonging to other races added only 7% of the posts. On average, white members contribute more posts (14.68) than users from any other race (at most 8.51).

Table 2. Contributors and posts by gender

	Women	Men
Contributors	5,445 (53%)	4,750 (46%)
Posts	53,267 (38%)	88,220 (62%)
Posts/contributors	9.78	18.57

Table 3. Contributors and posts by race

	Contributors	Posts	Posts/contributors
White	9,316 (68%)	136,748 (83%)	14.68
Black	698 (5%)	5,938 (4%)	8.51
API	675 (5%)	1,208 (1%)	1.79
AIAN	8 (<1%)	14 (<1%)	1.75
2 + races	37 (<1%)	83 (<1%)	2.24
Hispanics	386 (3%)	2,529 (2%)	6.55

Overall, these results signify indication of strong racial inequality in active participation in the forums. The E-Democracy platform still attracts majority of its users from white population who are also more prone to express their voices on the platform than users from other races. The rest of our analyses aims to delve deeper to assess whether any of the design decisions enacted in E-Democracy have helped to re-shape the contribution patterns of women and people of color at the forum level.

5.2   Neighborhood vs City Forums

Our first set of regression analyses consider longitudinal data (in quarters) of all forums to estimate whether city and neighborhood forums vary significantly in terms of participation of women and people of color while controlling for the forum tenure. Tables 4 show the results of the population-averaged GEE (Generalized Estimating Equation) model. GEE models are appropriate for estimating the coefficients of a generalized linear model with possible correlation between outcomes that allows us to account for repeated measures of forums.

The results provide strong support in favor of neighborhood forums attracting more participation from women and people of color both in terms of new membership and active contribution. Compared to city forums, neighborhood forums attract a 10 units larger proportion of women in each quarter. The proportion of female contributors in neighborhood forums is predicted to be 27 units higher. Women also contribute significantly larger shares of content in neighborhood forums than in city-wide forums. Compared to a city forum, the content on a neighborhood forum which is provided by women is predicted to be 12.6 units larger.

Table 4. Participation of women and people of color in city vs neighborhood forums

IVs	Women	People of color
	% new members	log % new members
Neighborhood	10.38***	9.28***
Tenure	0.20*	0.26*
	% contributors	log % contributors
Neighborhood	27.03***	7.52***
Tenure	0.37***	0.07***
	% posts	log % posts
Neighborhood	12.60***	5.75*
Tenure	0.04	0.06

* $p < 0.05$, ** $p < 0.01$, *** $p < 0.001$; Light gray
denotes a non-significant regression.

Regarding race, the analyses show that, as opposed to city-wide forums, neighborhood forums have larger proportions of new members and contributors who are people of color. Given that we used a log transformation of these dependent variables, the interpretation of the results considers changes in percent (instead of units) of user proportion. In particular, compared to city forums, neighborhood forums are expected to have a 9.28% increase in proportion of new members who are people of color. They are also predicted to have a 7.52% increase in proportion of contributors who race is not white. A positive relationship between neighborhood forums and production of content can not be confirmed as the regression model was not significant.

Beyond the forum type, time turned out to be a significant factor on the representation of women and people of color. Over time (i.e. longer tenure), the proportion of female new members and contributors grows by 0.20 and 0.37 units by every quarter of tenure, respectively. This result can be related to a recent general trend of wider female participation in social media [3]. Similarly, the proportions of people of color who joins the forums and contributes grow by 0.28 and 0.07% by every quarter of tenure, respectively. Nevertheless, tenure is not significantly associated with growth in the proportion of content created by these groups of users.

Together, these findings provide evidence that the decision to create neighborhood based forums is associated with attracting larger proportions of women and people of color as new members and contributors to the E-Democracy platform. Furthermore, neighborhood forums also gather larger proportions of content provided by people in these populations. Therefore, in the case of E-Democracy, we found that limiting the geographical scope from cities to neighborhoods and shifting the focus from political discussion to community engagement is indeed related to attracting populations that had been elusive in the platform's early days. These results are encouraging with regard to the impact of particular design decisions on fostering digital inclusion in the context of civic technologies.

Table 5. Participation of women and people of color by conditions

IVs	Women	People of color
	% new members	log % new members
Created 2010-	0.81	-0.13*
Tenure	0.11	0.01**
Outreach	1.09	0.27***
4+ max posts	-0.24	0.02
R-square	**0.01**	**0.21**
	% contributors	log % contributors
Created 2010-	-7.48**	-0.15
Tenure	.43***	0.00
Outreach	2.98	0.39***
4+ max posts	2.58	0.17
R-square	**0.16**	**0.42**
	% posts	log % posts
Created 2010-	5.57	-0.19
Tenure	-0.04	0.01
Outreach	3.68	0.31*
4+ max # of posts	-0.77	0.29
R-square	**0.03**	**0.22**

* $p < 0.05$, ** $p < 0.01$, *** $p < 0.001$, Light gray denotes a non-significant regression.

5.3 Impact of Offline Outreach and Daily Post Restriction

The next set of regression analyses aimed to model the effect of the other two design decisions, *offline outreach* and *daily maximum number of posts*, on digital inclusion. These analyses were conducted using data only from the neighborhood forums because city-wide forums never enacted offline outreach strategies and they allow the same maximum number of posts daily. We also controlled for the year of creation of each forum and their tenure at the observation period. Table 5 shows the results.

On the one hand, our results do not provide any support for the an association between offline outreach activities and more participation from women. On the other hand, the results suggest that outreach activities are associated with a small increases in the proportions of new members and contributors who are people of color (0.3% and 0.4%, respectively). There is also support for a positive relationship between this design decision and the proportion of content provided by people of color. Compared to forums with no offline outreach, neighborhood forums that were subject to offline outreach are expected to have a 0.39% increase in proportion of content shared by people of color.

In terms of the daily maximum number of posts, our results show no support for its association with attracting users from neither of the populations under study. The year of creation of a forum is significantly related to digital inclusion in the E-Democracy neighborhood forums. Compared to newer forums, older forums (those created in 2010 or earlier) had smaller proportions of female contributors and smaller proportions of new members who are people of color. In the older forums, proportion of women contributors expected to decrease by 7.48 units and proportion of people of color is expected to decrease by 0.13%. Over time, some measures of inclusion change significantly. The proportion of female contributors increased along with the forum tenure by a factor of 0.43 units and proportion of people of color members increases by 0.01%.

In general, the models of female participation achieve lower explanatory power than the models of participation of people of color as demonstrated by R-squared values in Table 5; this suggests that these two design decisions and time variables better explain the variability of the data about racial digital inequality than gender digital inequality.

6 Alternative Approach to Estimate Race and Gender

As described earlier, in face of lack of true race and gender data, we utilized external data sources to estimate race and gender. This means that our results can be highly sensitive to the precision of the approximation method. At the same time, there is neither a ground truth nor a non-intrusive way to systematically assess the precision of our method. Therefore, to assess the reliability of our study, we employed an alternative mechanism to our pseudo-random sampling approach. Using the same external data sources, our alternative mechanism estimated race and gender using a threshold-based approach. A threshold had to be met to assign the top category as the user's gender and race. We used two different thresholds, a conservative (high) threshold of 90% for both race and gender, and a more relaxed (lower) threshold of 2/3 (66%) for gender and 50% for race. The relaxed threshold is higher for gender as 50% for gender can be the same as a random selection of any class given the only two possible values.

Table 6 shows the contrast between the number of users classified as female or male by each method. The relaxed threshold-based approach is quite close to the pseudo-random approach but the most conservative threshold classifies lower number of users into each of the gender classes. However, the direction of the results stays the same with either of the approaches; i.e. there is a larger number of female contributors on the site but smaller number of posts are contributed by women. Overall, female contributors add significantly fewer posts.

Table 7 shows the classification of users regarding race by each method. While the absolute numbers of users who are classified into each race by threshold-based approaches are considerably different from each other and from the pseudo-random approach, the patterns repeat across different approaches. All three approximations suggest that a significant majority of users are white and they account for a larger majority of posts. Compared to the pseudo-random approach, the relaxed threshold mechanism generates a larger proportion of white people and the conservative threshold mechanism generates a smaller proportion. On the other hand, with regards to black races, both threshold mechanisms generate smaller proportion. This is due to the large amount of last names that have comparable probabilities of belonging to either of these two races.

Table 6. Contributors and posts by gender

		Pseudo-random	t = 0.66	t = 0.90
Contributors	Women	5,445	5,406	4,948
	Men	4,750	4,771	4,170
Posts	Women	53,267	52,378	49,013
	Men	88,220	89,077	83,368
Posts/contributors	Women	9.78	9.68	9.90
	Men	18.57	18.67	19.99

Table 7. Contributors and posts by race

		Pseudo-random	t = 0.50	t = 0.90
Contributors	White	9,316 (68%)	9,715 (71%)	7,613 (56%)
	People of color	1767 (15%)	1276 (11%)	647 (6%)
Posts	White	136,748 (83%)	144,003 (87%)	121,022 (73%)
	People of color	9,689 (8%)	3181 (3%)	1003 (2%)
Posts/contr.	White	14.68	14.82	15.90
	People of color	18.6	14.75	7.75

We further explored differences in the results across these alternative approaches of gender and race approximation. Results vary depending on what method has been used to identify gender. In case of neighborhood vs. city forums, while the direction of the results stays the same along the three different approaches, the effect size drops significantly from pseudo-random based approach to the threshold approaches. Similarly, there is a smaller drop from the relaxed to the conservative threshold.

In turn, the effect size of the neighborhood variable on the proportion of people of color joining a forum also drops from the pseudo-random approach to the threshold-based approaches. Nevertheless, the effect remains significant. For other dependent variables, the differences across our estimation approaches were milder. Nevertheless, the results highlight the importance of methodological considerations with regards to automatic estimation of gender and race.

7 Discussion

In this work, we conducted a post-hoc evaluation of digital inclusion in E-Democracy, as an example of a civic technology. As acknowledge by prior research as well, platforms decision decisions are not always visible to researchers studying those platforms. Researchers have been employing various approaches in bridging this gap, such as utilizing users' behavior discontinuity in data dumps from systems such as Netflix or Facebook [23]. In this work, we demonstrated yet another approach in studying the impact of design decisions as a post-hoc evaluation using various sources of archival data available. We studied how design decisions enacted by designers of such platform relate to the dynamics of the user population and their active participation. In particular, we studied the relationship of three design decisions with gender and racial digital inclusion. In order to determine members' race and gender, we adopted an approach to automatically estimate them using members' first and last names.

We believe our study contributes significantly as a distinct longitudinal study of design decisions across a number of discussion forums sharing the same platform while serving neighborhoods with different demographics. Our results show that E-Democracy attracts more women than men as contributors but women add significantly smaller proportions of content on the platform. We also observed that the broad majority of the E-Democracy contributors are white people who, on average, generate more content than people of color.

While many aspects of the challenge of digital inequality cannot be solved by technology design as they result from larger social inequalities, our results provide evidence in support of dedicated attention to fostering a diverse online participation in civic technologies. Design decisions employed by E-Democracy have been successful in achieving the goal of digital inclusion. We found strong evidence that creating neighborhood forums to encourage community involvement, as an alternative to city-wide forums focusing on political deliberation, had a significant positive impact on digital inclusion in E-Democracy. We also found partial support for a positive relationship between offline outreach strategies and broader participation of people of color in the online forums.

At the same time, our evaluation provide insights for designers on decisions that might not be achieving the desired goal. E-Democracy has always enacted rules to constrain the maximum number of posts a user can provide in a single day as an attempt to avoid monopolization of the online discussion and one-to-one seemingly endless arguments that could discourage newcomers to join in the online conversation. This constraint would in turn encourage more people to contribute their opinions to the online conversation. Overall, we found no evidence that this policy significantly influence the participation of women and people of color. Although this result does not support or challenge the overall goal of diversifying public discourse, it provides evidence that it does not contribute to gender or racial diversity.

Our work also makes a methodological contribution by providing an approach to use external datasets to supplement limited self-reported demographic information. This approach offers an alternative to self-reported demographic data that can be difficult to obtain and might also be significantly biased, as discussed on research studying gender imbalance in Wikipedia [14]. While this approach is useful for research purposes, it has ethical and practical implications that should be taken into consideration. To protect users' privacy, we made a decision to analyze the data at aggregate levels (not individual level) to avoid singling out users and their behavior based on features that were based on external data. Besides, the use of last names to determine race may be a simplistic approach that fails to acknowledge multi-racial families. For this reason, our work also provides a sensitivity analysis of the results. The impact of design decisions on digital inclusion on some cases was sensitive to the approach in estimating gender and race. It is important to highlight this aspect to draw attention to the potential pitfalls of algorithmic approximations of missing data.

As the future direction of our research, we aim to explore design decisions in relation to digital inclusion experimentally to be able to draw stronger conclusions about the impact of such decisions and to be able to understand the mechanism by which the decision increase or decrease inclusive participation.

Acknowledgements. The authors would like to thank E-Democracy.org for providing its data and domain knowledge. The work of the first author was supported by CONICYT Chile, under grant Conicyt-Fondecyt Iniciación #11161026.

References

1. Abdullah, C., Karpowitz, C.F., Raphael, C.: Equity and inclusion in online community forums: an interview with Steven Clift. J. Public Delib. **12**(2), 3 (2016)
2. Akoumianakis, D., Stephanidis, C.: Universal design in HCI: a critical review of current research and practice. In: Adjunct Proceedings of the ACM Conference on Human Factors in Computing Systems, pp. 499–500 (2001)
3. Anderson, M.: Americans Internet Access: 2000–2015. Technical report, Pew Research Center (2015)
4. Antin, J., Yee, R., Cheshire, C., Nov, O.: Gender differences in Wikipedia editing. In: Proceedings of the 7th International Symposium on Wikis and Open Collaboration, WikiSym 2011, pp. 11–14. ACM, New York (2011). http://doi.acm.org/10.1145/2038558.2038561
5. Collier, B., Bear, J.: Conflict, confidence, or criticism: an empirical examination of the gender gap in Wikipedia. In: Proceedings of the ACM 2012 Conference on Computer Supported Cooperative Work, CSCW 2012, pp. 383–392 (2012)
6. Dahlberg, L.: Extending the public sphere through cyberspace: the case of Minnesota e-democracy. First Monday **6**(3) (2001)
7. Dijk, J.A.V.: Digital divide research, achievements and shortcomings. Poetics **34**(4), 221–235 (2006)
8. Druin, A.: Cooperative inquiry: developing new technologies for children with children. In: Proceedings of the SIGCHI Conference on Human Factors in Computing Systems, CHI 1999, pp. 592–599. ACM, New York (1999). http://doi.acm.org/10.1145/302979.303166
9. Elliott, M.N., Morrison, P.A., Fremont, A., McCaffrey, D.F., Pantoja, P., Lurie, N.: Using the census bureaus surname list to improve estimates of race/ethnicity and associated disparities. Health Serv. Outcomes Res. Method. **9**(2), 69–83 (2009)
10. Farzan, R., Savage, S., Saviaga, G.: Bring on board new enthusiasts! A case study of impact of Wikipedia art + feminism edit-a-thon events on newcomers. In: Proceedings of the International Conference on Social Informatics, SocInfo 2016 (2016, to appear)
11. Hale, S.A., John, P., Margetts, H.Z., Yasseri, T.: Investigating political participation and social information using big data and a natural experiment. In: APSA 2014 Annual Meeting (2014)

12. Hankerson, D., Marshall, A.R., Booker, J., El Mimouni, H., Walker, I., Rode, J.A.: Does technology have race? In: Proceedings of the 2016 CHI Conference Extended Abstracts on Human Factors in Computing Systems, pp. 473–486. ACM (2016)
13. Hargittai, E., Shaw, A.: Mind the skills gap: the role of internet know-how and gender in differentiated contributions to Wikipedia. Inf. Commun. Soc. **18**(4), 424–442 (2015)
14. Hill, B.M., Shaw, A.: The Wikipedia gender gap revisited: characterizing survey response bias with propensity score estimation. PloS ONE **8**(6), e65782 (2013)
15. Hoffmann, C.P., Lutz, C., Meckel, M.: Content creation on the Internet: a social cognitive perspective on the participation divide. Inf. Commun. Soc. **18**(6), 696–716 (2015)
16. Jen, B., Kaur, J., De Heus, J., Dillahunt, T.R.: Analyzing employment technologies for economically distressed individuals. In: Extended Abstracts on Human Factors in Computing Systems, CHI 2014, pp. 1945–1950. ACM, New York (2014). http://doi.acm.org/10.1145/2559206.2581290
17. Joiner, R., Stewart, C., Beaney, C.: Gender Digital Divide. The Wiley Blackwell Handbook of Psychology, Technology and Society, p. 74. Wiley, Chichester (2015)
18. Lam, S.K., Uduwage, A., Dong, Z., Sen, S., Musicant, D., Terveen, L., Riedl, J.: WP:Clubhouse? An exploration of Wikipedia's gender imbalance. In: WikiSym 2011. ACM (2011)
19. Kofink, A.: Contributions of the under-appreciated: gender bias in an open-source ecology. In: Companion Proceedings of the 2015 ACM SIGPLAN International Conference on Systems, Programming, Languages and Applications: Software for Humanity, pp. 83–84. ACM (2015)
20. Kurniawan, S., Mahmud, M., Nugroho, Y.: A study of the use of mobile phones by older persons. In: CHI 2006 Extended Abstracts on Human Factors in Computing Systems, pp. 989–994. ACM (2006)
21. Lalji, Z., Good, J.: Designing new technologies for illiterate populations: a study in mobile phone interface design. Interact. Comput. **20**(6), 574–586 (2008)
22. Lazar, J., Dudley-Sponaugle, A., Greenidge, K.D.: Improving web accessibility: a study of webmaster perceptions. Comput. Hum. Behav. **20**(2), 269–288 (2004)
23. Malik, M.M., Pfeffer, J.: Identifying platform effects in social media data. In: ICWSM, pp. 241–249 (2016)
24. Mislove, A., Lehmann, S., Ahn, Y.Y., Onnela, J.P., Rosenquist, J.N.: Understanding the demographics of Twitter users. In: ICWSM, vol. 11, p. 5 (2011)
25. Novak, T.P.: Bridging the racial divide on the Internet. Sci. (AAAS-Wkly. Pap. Ed.) **280**(5362), 390–391 (1998)
26. Oreglia, E., Liu, Y., Zhao, W.: Designing for emerging rural users: experiences from China. In: Proceedings of the SIGCHI Conference on Human Factors in Computing Systems, CHI 2011, pp. 1433–1436. ACM, New York (2011). http://doi.acm.org/10.1145/1978942.1979152
27. Radovanović, D., Hogan, B., Lalić, D.: Overcoming digital divides in higher education: digital literacy beyond facebook. New Media Soc. **17**(10), 1733–1749 (2015)
28. Richard, G.T.: Designing games that foster equity and inclusion: encouraging equitable social experiences across gender and ethnicity in online games. In: Proceedings of the CHI 2013 Workshop: Designing and Evaluating Sociability in Online Video Games, Paris, France, pp. 83–88 (2013)
29. Rumbul, R.: Who benefits from civic technology? Demographic and public attitudes research into the users of civic technologies. Technical report, mySociety (2015)

30. Sambasivan, N., Cutrell, E., Toyama, K., Nardi, B.: Intermediated technology use in developing communities. In: Proceedings of the SIGCHI Conference on Human Factors in Computing Systems, pp. 2583–2592. ACM (2010)
31. Schradie, J.: The trend of class, race, and ethnicity in social media inequality: who still cannot afford to blog? Inf. Commun. Soc. **15**(4), 555–571 (2012)
32. Small, J., Schallau, P., Brown, K., Appleyard, R.: Web accessibility for people with cognitive disabilities. In: CHI 2005 Extended Abstracts on Human Factors in Computing Systems, pp. 1793–1796. ACM (2005)
33. Smith, A.: Civic engagement in the digital age. Technical report, Pew Research Center (2013)
34. Van Dijk, J.A.: Digital divide research, achievements and shortcomings. Poetics **34**(4–5), 221–235 (2006)
35. Vasilescu, B., Capiluppi, A., Serebrenik, A.: Gender, representation and online participation: a quantitative study of StackOverflow. In: 2012 International Conference on Social Informatics (SocialInformatics), pp. 332–338. IEEE (2012)
36. Yardi, S., Bruckman, A.: Income, race, and class: exploring socioeconomic differences in family technology use. In: Proceedings of the SIGCHI Conference on Human Factors in Computing Systems, pp. 3041–3050. ACM (2012)

Security, Privacy, and Trust

The Cognitive Heuristics Behind Disclosure Decisions

Vincent Marmion$^{(\boxtimes)}$, Felicity Bishop, David E. Millard,
and Sarah V. Stevenage

University of Southampton, Highcliff Campus, Southampton SO17 1BJ, UK
v.marmion@soton.ac.uk

Abstract. Despite regulatory efforts to protect personal data online, users knowingly consent to disclose more personal data than they intend, and they are also prone to disclose more than they know. We consider that a reliance on cognitive heuristics is key to explaining these aspects of users' disclosure decisions. Also, that the cues underpinning these heuristics can be exploited by organisations seeking to extract more data than is required. Through the lens of an existing credibility heuristic framework, we qualitatively analyse 23, one-to-one, semi-structured interviews. We identify six super-ordinate classes of heuristics that users rely upon during disclosures: PROMINENCE, NETWORK, RELIABILITY, ACCORDANCE, NARRATIVE, MODALITY, and a seventh non-heuristics TRADE class. Our results suggest that regulatory efforts seeking to increase the autonomy of the informed user are inapt. Instead the key to supporting users during disclosure decisions could be to positively nudge users through the cues underpinning these simple heuristics.

Keywords: Cognitive heuristics · Privacy paradox · Informed consent

1   Introduction

Disclosing personal data is self-managed. It is users that decide whether to consent to disclosure requests or whether to withhold their data. This consent-based model aligns appealingly with the ideals of information self-determinism [48]. However, in practice these ideals are not being met. Although regulations such as the UK Data Protection Act (1998) stipulate that organisations inform users of the operation of data processing, the explanation of risk is left to organisational discretion, making it incumbent on users to make the necessary risk calculation [40]. If we adopt the long-standing definition regarding consent in a medical context [49], the reality of consent in disclosure is akin to simple rather than informed consent. Simple consent involves a brief explanation of operations, followed by a trust-based agreement or refusal; to elevate this to informed consent, a detailed discussion of risks is also required. Regardless of likelihood, high risk necessitates informed consent. Because the consequences of data misuse are increasingly high and decreasingly rare [18], simple consent is unsatisfactory.

© Springer International Publishing AG 2017
G.L. Ciampaglia et al. (Eds.): SocInfo 2017, Part I, LNCS 10539, pp. 591–607, 2017.
DOI: 10.1007/978-3-319-67217-5_35

Unfortunately, increasing the autonomy of informed users may not be sufficient. This is because disclosure decisions are inherently uncertain, and when data is stored indefinitely there is no means of accounting for future uses or future capabilities, so the 'data controller' may also be ignorant of the risk [47]. Even if organisations were able to explain the risk, users rarely read privacy policies [45], and when there is an attempt, they lack the time and/or the capacity for the required uncertainty calculus ('privacy calculus') to comprehend them [13,27]. Users are essentially left to trust that the data controller will behave in an expected and innocuous manner [33,38], and to make heuristic judgements (i.e. using 'rules of thumb') about whether to disclose [44].

We share the view of [14,41] in considering cognitive heuristics as key to understanding these decisions, and illuminating the problem of the privacy paradox - the tendency of user's to disclose more in their actual behaviour than in their previously stated intention [37].

In this paper we present a qualitative study to understand the heuristics that people use when making disclosure decisions. Using established credibility heuristics as a starting point we present an analysis of 23 semi-structured interviews, with the aim of exploring whether the heuristics related to credibility judgements are a general enough framework to also apply to disclosure decisions. We also seek to identify superordinate classes of similarly themed heuristics, and to explore the importance and limitations of heuristics within those classes, and therefore within the disclosure decision process as whole.

2   Background

When faced with difficult, uncertain, or intractable problems, using heuristics can be rational [17] as they fit with observations of decision-making *in the wild*. Nonetheless, they are prone to misjudgement and bias [44] and with that are prone to manipulation, or 'nudges'. While these nudges might be used to limit over-disclosure, they can also be used to encourage users to disclose more than they might otherwise be comfortable with [2,19]. In this section we will look at exactly what is meant by heuristics, how they have been linked to credibility, and used when exploring disclosure decisions.

2.1   Heuristics and Credibility

Heuristics are used to reduce difficult decisions to solvable simple decisions [15]. For example, whether to invest in company A or B is a difficult decision, which depends on many complex factors. Whereas, an associated heuristic may be that size is related to success. Then the heuristic's decision variable, i.e., the cue, could be the number of service users or stock price. So, whether $A(cue) > B(cue)$ substitutes for whether A is a better investment than B.

Early research around activities such as *phishing* and *fake news* showed the impact that online cues have on users' trust of web sites, and their judgements of the credibility and legitimacy of those sites [12,42]. Fogg [12] finds that rather

Table 1. Heuristic approaches to credibility evaluation online

Heuristic	Description
Authority	An official or primary authority
Recognition	Familiarity, even in name only
Reputation*	A prestigious service would not knowingly be wrong
Endorsement*	Recommendation from known others
Bandwagon	Recommendations or perceived actions of unknown others
Consistency*	Agreement with another source or procedure
Consensus	Agreement between many sources or procedures
Self-Confirmation*	Alignment with a pre-existing belief
Coolness	New modalities of the technology
Novelty	New encounters with the technology
Expectancy Violation*	Inferior site design, errors, poor visual appearance
Persuasive Intent*	A feeling of bias or being pushed

Note: Twelve (* six prominent) credibility heuristics collated from [34].

than users seeking a particular cue, prominent cues affect users, and that with new digital interfaces comes changes in the prominent cues (e.g., the padlock shown on a search bar). Understanding how to manipulate these effects is an active research agenda for behavioural economists [2,6,8].

The MAIN model [42] structures ten years of psychological research into the cues that have been empirically shown to affect users. This model assembles the cues in terms of four technological affordances of digital media: Modality, Agency, Interactivity, and Navigability. The result is an extensive array of cues and associated heuristics, providing a framework for more applied research. Drawing from this model, Metzger et al. [35] conducted 11 focus groups, and found five prominent credibility heuristics: *Reputation, Endorsement, Consistency, Expectancy Violation and Persuasive Intent*; later adding *Self-confirmation* as a sixth [34]. For instance, determining the credibility of a website is a difficult decision. An associated heuristic may be the Expectancy Violation heuristic that illegitimate websites appear unprofessional. So, whether the website has spelling mistakes can substitute for whether the website is credible.

The value of [34,35] is in representing an expansive array of cues and decision variables, as in the MAIN model, into something simple and coherent (as summarised in Table 1). In addition, this table contains the six additional heuristics that [34] discussed as relevant, yet omitted for their purposes[1]. A concern is that the original six may be overly fitted to credibility judgements.

2.2   The Role of Heuristics in Disclosure

Credibility and disclosure decisions are both trust-based decisions [33,41], and heuristics are somewhat abstracted from the *weeds* of a problem [26]. In fact, is it

---

[1] Metzger et al., found six heuristics through a process of reduction, i.e., Recognition is subsumed under Reputation, as to perceive reputation involves a prior recognition.

predicted that in some circumstances one simple heuristic can take an individual through a cycle of disclosure through related yet independent decisions, flowing from a credibility judgement regarding the legitimacy of a service, through a judgement to determine a service's trustworthiness as a data controller, and finally to whether the individual is willing to disclose a particular item of data.

In similar work, [14] used grounded theory, on data from eight focus groups, to reveal eight heuristics that underpin disclosure; four of which promote disclosure (Gatekeeping, Safety-net, Bubble and Ephemerality), and four that inhibit it (Fuzzy-boundary, Intrusiveness, Uncertainty, Mobility). Where the work of Metzger et al. provided the motivation for this work, the findings here have been refactored in light of these eight newly revealed heuristics.

There is a question however, as to the value of producing an ever-expansive set of heuristics separated only by subtleties. For instance the Intrusiveness heuristic, i.e. unsolicited communications inhibiting disclosure willingness from [14], shares similarities with the Persuasive Intent heuristic i.e. a feeling of bias or being pushed that inhibits the willingness to disclose [34]. A balance is required to avoid returning to the extensive set of decision cues such as in the MAIN model, and remaining in the scope of the simple findings bespoke to credibility. Hence our focus on developing superordinate classes of similarly themed heuristics that might accommodate emerging work.

3   Method

A series of semi-structured, one-to-one, face-to-face interviews were conducted. This approach was consistent with the qualitative nature of the focus groups in [14,35], but had an advantage of providing for a deeper focus on individual experience. The interview structure followed that of a cognitive walk-through, this was chosen as it is productively used for heuristic evaluations within human computer interaction (HCI) studies [22,36]. However, instead of a specific target system as in HCI studies, the interviewee were asked to recall an interaction with an online service. This meant that no one system had to be contrived, and also the focus on what had already occurred avoided talk of ideals that misalign with actual behaviour (i.e., the privacy paradox) [37].

Furthermore, focusing on interviewee interpretation (the heuristic) means that the actual system, and the content of the cues was of less importance than the type of cues. For instance, one person may look for a NUS seal of approval, whereas another looks for a Royal Warrant mark, either way they can both be using the Endorsement heuristic. This meant that the required sample were those who regularly engaged with online actives and services, and who could also reason and articulate about these engagements. With this in mind we recruited from the Psychology department's participant pool, resulting in 23 Interviewees, all of whom were 18 to 25 years old.

The interviews were all under an hour (43 to 57 min), and were conducted on campus. Interviewees were briefed, and given the opportunity for questions before signing a consent form, the audio recording then commenced for the duration of the interview, and at the end they were debriefed. Participants were paid a small amount of compensation for their time. Finally, the audio files were transcribed verbatim by the interviewer, and imported into NVivo for analysis.

The interviews comprised three stages. Stage one (approx. 5 min), involved simple questions that established the interviewee's general digital engagement, whilst also easing them into the interview process.

In stage two (approx. 40 min), each interviewee was asked to recall a recent instance whereby they registered with an online service. Then, interviewees were primed to think within one of two possible self-regulatory mindsets [21]; twelve were *promotion primed* to recall a system relating to social activities, entertainment or freebies (in the analysis these are denoted with S, for social, i.e., S1, S2,...S12), and eleven were *prevention primed* to recall a system relating to responsibilities or financial and commercial transactions (denoted with T, for transaction, i.e., T1, T2,...T11).

Once a relevant situation had been recalled they were asked to discuss the process from first considering the service, through to completing the registration or transaction. They were allowed to speak freely around the task, however, when recall became disjointed a prompt sheet of short questions that moved chronologically through the process was referred to. While the interviewer steered the conversation around the contexts of the original primer, some contextual cross-over was unavoidable, and in many cases these instances were insightful.

Finally, stage three (approx. 5 min), included questions regarding the general concept of identity and privacy in the media. As well as a winding down exercise, this section allowed the interviewees to express any related thoughts or concerns that may have occurred during the interview.

3.1 Analysis

The analysis was undertaken in three parts.

The first part was ensuring familiarity with the data. The first author conducted the interviews, and transcribed the audio recordings, which ensured a base level of familiarity with the data. The data was then divided into; (A) the data relating to disclosure decisions, and (B) the data not relating to disclosure decisions. Before being set aside, data set B was examined to provide context and validity as to the interviewees' suitability for, and engagement with the process.

The second part involved coding the interview data into distinct categories. To do this, the transcripts were examined using an interpretivist approach [10, 23], wherein the interviewee constructs the theoretical connection between cue and decision, the analyst is then left to categorise the self-reported 'rules of thumb' [42]. An analysis challenge stems from people combining heuristics or interweaving heuristic and non-heuristic interpretations to inform decisions [16].

To help address this data set A was first categorised into; (A1) heuristic-based, and (A2) non-heuristic decisions. Then by matching the language used and the cues mentioned with those outlined in the literature, data set A1 were deductively categorised to align with the heuristics in Table 1 as described in [34]. Data not aligned with Table 1 were then inductively coded, as described in

[39], to reveal additional heuristics. Data set A2 provided a set of non-heuristic decisions, that coded inductively acted as deviant cases to counterbalance any confirmatory-bias residing in the efforts to explore heuristics.

While part two teased the results apart, part three of the analysis serves to recombine them by identifying super-ordinate classes that encapsulate the results from part two. For example, while the Reputation and Recognition heuristics involve different interpretations and reasoning, they seem to be based upon similar underlying cues (for instance the size of the organisation) therefore, they are discussed within a parent *prominence* class. This allows the extension of the original credibility framework whilst maintaining its richness, and also helps to keep the overall results concise and pragmatic.

4   Interviewee Context and Validity

Interviewees reported habitual engagement with digital living, with typical comments such as; "Oh, literally, all the time", and "when I wake in the morning, I just look in bed on Facebook." However, we remain mindful of the temporal nature of the responses [28], as summed up by interviewee T6 when they said "I was 15, now I'm 19, so I have different interests."

The Interviewees were open and candid within the interviews, this was exemplified by a common revelation about having only two or three passwords across all online systems, a finding that mirrors those of [29]. For example, one participant admitted "when I am creating a password they say you need a capital or a punctuation so it might vary, but generally I use one of three." In some cases the participants even admitted to writing them down for ease, "I just created a word document to remember all of my passwords."

While the similar age and educational status of the participants naturally scopes our findings to a particular demographic, it is a key demographic for the problem of disclosure. Our analysis of the first stage of the interview shows that our participants were engaged with the problem of disclosure in their everyday lives, and prepared to give rich answers to the interview questions.

5   Findings

Table 2 summarises the results of the second and third parts of our analysis (coding, and identifying super-ordinate classes), and contains sample dialogue to illustrate the coding process. Six super-ordinate classes are discussed; PROMINENCE, NETWORK, RELIABILITY, ACCORDANCE, NARRATIVE, and MODALITY. A seventh non-heuristics TRADE class was also identified. Within the following sections, the interview extracts address the flow of decisions through the cycle of disclosure, leading an interviewee from an initial assessment of service legitimacy, through the assessment of the service as a trustworthy data controller, and finally to the assessment as to whether the interviewee actually disclosed an item of PII.

Table 2. Superordinate classes and heuristic coding reference

CLASS	Heuristic: Description	Example Extract -*Interviewee*
PROMINENCE	**Reputation:** Prestigious services would not knowingly do wrong	"FIFA is well-known and probably not evil." $_{S3}$
	Recognition: A familiarity with a service, even in name only	"it is just a very small app that I have not heard much about, I think I wouldn't put my information on it." $_{S4}$
NETWORK	**Endorsement:** A recommendation from known others	"My brother has been telling me it is more secure, it is easier, better and safer." $_{S1}$
	Authority: A recommendation from official or primary authority	"He was a journalist, so he knows a lot of those sort of things." $_{T7}$
	Bandwagon: Perceiving the actions of unknown peers or general population	"I was quite influenced by what everyone was doing." $_{T7}$
RELIABILITY	**Consistency:** Interacting with a familiar process	"I tried another website, and also they ask for the same thing. The same questions. You have to sign up first, and it was the same thing. So I signed up." $_{S1}$
	Consensus: A normative or standardised process	"Just the normal, name, date of birth and the important one is the mobile number to create an account." $_{S10}$
	Expectancy:[a] Inferior site design, errors, poor visual appearance	"this looked fashionable and genuine." $_{S6}$
ACCORDANCE	**Intent:**[b] A feeling of bias or being pushed	"they wanted all my details to tell me how much it would cost. So I provided false details." $_{T3}$
	Self-confirmation: Feeling a consistency with pre-existing beliefs	"Why do you need ID? I'm only buying make-up." $_{T11}$
MODALITY	**Coolness:** Gratifying features of a technology	"I like the effect on the photos, I only did it for that, I don't like the privacy really, but I don't really use it very often, it is just on there in case." $_{S6}$
	Novelty: An new encounter with a technology	"When I actually started, I was so happy about it, that I completed absolutely everything." $_{S3}$
NARRATIVE[c]	**Availability:** The ability to recall similar instances	"there has never been a dodgy situation when I don't want to give [my location data] because it is harmless games like Flappy Bird" $_{S3}$
	Coherence: The ability to envisage the result of an action	"if someone hacked my Twitter account I honestly wouldn't care because it is utter rubbish, nothing important, it is only entertainment" $_{S2}$

a: Violation aspect removed from the Expectancy heuristic to provide neutral label, [See Sect. 5.3]
b: Persuasive aspect removed from the Intent heuristic to provide neutral label. The Intent heuristic also incorporate the Intrusiveness heuristic from [14] [See Sect. 5.4]
c: Not part of the original Credibility heuristics framework as described in Table 1

5.1   PROMINENCE: Recognition and Reputation

Many of the participants expressed terms aligning with the **Reputation** heuristic, by implying that a prestigious service would not knowingly do wrong, as described in [34]. When asked for location data, Interviewee S3 says; "I mean FIFA is well-known and probably not evil." This is the first example of a simple heuristic, reputation, being sufficient to complete the cycle of disclosure. We know that reputation relates to credibility judgements regarding an organisation's legitimacy, also, within this exchange with S3 it also provided an implicit trustworthiness of FIFA as a data controller, and then specifically in regards to their willingness to disclose their location data.

Interpreting cues related to size, being low-key, or being a known brand were typical. Such as when Interviewee S5 suggests that "Twitter is such a big company you assume they would not [...] pass your information on." In a related tone, Interviewee T11 associates size and risk "because smaller companies don't have as many resources for security." Meaning that an organisation would want to protect their reputation, and thus protect the user, and the bigger the organisation the better the protection. There was an overall sense that if something has gained prominence then it must be doing something right, whereas lacking prominence suggests otherwise.

This sentiment is also reflected in the **Recognition** heuristic; trust occurring due to a basic familiarity with an entity [17,35]. T6 makes the connection from the prominence of a high-street presence, and thus being "well-known", and them "not trying to scam me". This may seem similar to reputation, but there is value in the distinction. Reputation seems to involve other people, as in "well-known" compared to an inwards reflection, as in "I have not heard".

Perhaps the most notable difference between recognition and reputation, is that reputation extends beyond the original entity towards subsidiaries. Gambino et al. [14] refer to this as a safety-net heuristic, exemplified by Interviewee T10 when they state "with independent people, you need a barrier". This is a repeated factor in disclosure decisions, yet it is still a factor of reputation because reputation is acting as a form of collateral for the data exchange, as something "to live up to", T1. For instance, online organisations acting as a trust intermediary for other associated organisations, because the parent "company image is that valuable", S11. This protection is also inherited by other service users, as S4 finds it "really dodgy" being young and female on "a site that isn't well-known", yet on Twittter they "wouldn't worry too much".

Seemingly, being of prominence provides organisations with many cues interpreted towards trust and willingness to disclose. We have a scenario where credible organisations are "not trying to scam", which attracts users, which in turn adds to them being "so well-known and so big you can trust it", and this trustworthiness is reinforced by having the "resources for security" against outside threats, and being "probably not evil" to cause inside threats. This cocktail of credibility and trustworthiness leading to willing to disclosure is a prime example of the simplicity in the cycle of disclosure. However, from Interviewee T2's perspective, "it is not really about the reputation it is about the price", reminding us that although these are simple heuristics, the decision cues remain diverse, and moreover, that when finance is involved it changes the decision further.

5.2   NETWORK: Endorsement, Authority and Bandwagon

Evident from the interviews was that an individual's interpersonal network has a considerable influence on disclosure decisions. This was also reflected in [34] through the Endorsement and Bandwagon heuristics. These heuristics are similar to the heuristics in the Prominence class, the difference being that the Prominence class regàrds a service's place in the world, i.e., a high-street presence, whereas the network class has a personal characteristic, i.e., my friends were doing it.

Focusing first on the **Endorsement** heuristic; testimonial by known others, Interviewee S2 found "that two of my housemates were already there made it seem more comfortable". These findings mirror that of [35], suggesting that in some cases individuals prefer recommendations to their own decision. Interviewee S1 reflects delegation to others to make decision for them, when admitting; "I am more affected by what people tell me as I am not really an IT person". This type of sentiment, by an educated individual with habitual use of technology, runs counter to the notion that disclosure is to be self-managed.

The **Authority** heuristic is when trust stems from expert or official authority endorsements [42]. When Interviewee T7's father convinced T7 to allow electoral roll information to be traded, he was the authority but not as a parent, "he was a journalist, so he knows a lot of those sort of things". In effect it is an endorsement from an individual with reputation, but is not passive like the reputation heuristic. This feature was seldom present in the interviews.

Similarly, the **Bandwagon** heuristic involves recommendations and often shares decision cues with the Endorsement heuristic [35]. However, the findings here agree with [42], that the two are meaningfully different. Instead of a personal endorsement from friends and family, in the Bandwagon heuristic the recommendations can be from unknown others via less personal factors such as aggregated testimonials or star ratings embedded within the interface. This places the Bandwagon heuristic conceptually close to the Prominence class, illustrated by "many thousands of people have downloaded them they can't be that bad", S4. Yet, it is also has a socially compelling aspect to it, as T7 explains, "I wasn't 100% satisfied with the [privacy policy]" but, "everyone is doing it" or as T10 reflects "I thought everyone else was. I assumed you had to fill it in".

Throughout this Network class of heuristics, there is a degree of delegating the decisions within the cycle of disclosure, through direct council and endorsement or indirectly through the assumed behaviours of peers. There is a free-riding aspect, whereby there is an expectation of others doing the risk discovery [45]. But this is a self-fulfilling 'social proof' [9], whereby a herd mentality can follow without due consideration of the circumstances [5].

5.3   RELIABILITY: Expectancy, Consistency and Consensus

The **Expectancy Violation** heuristic has negative connotations surrounding poor design, central to which is an expectation of professionalism [34]. In this regard, on numerous occasions interviewees were cued by presentation details, with features such as poor layout, inferior design or errors impacting on perceptions of service trustworthiness. To this end T6 trusted their judgement "by looking at their website or social networking site, whether it looks professional or not", or for T7 it was that, "something in my mind saying it is not right". We have chosen to remove the 'violation' label and simply use Expectancy, because the cues can work both ways, in that "you sort of get the feeling that it is not right, but this looked fashionable and genuine" (S6), this relabelling reflects that writing inconsistency, non-consensus, or disreputable would be unproductive.

This Reliability class also contains the **Consistency** heuristic; trust based on the agreement between two independent sources [35]. When S1 says "I didn't want to sign up, so I tried another website, and also they ask for the same thing. The same questions. You have to sign up first, and it was the same thing. So I signed up.", we say they are using the Consistency heuristic. In this case, S1 expected to engage without registering, however, when it became apparent that the seemingly non-standard requirement for registration was a consistent requirement across similar TV services, the user became willing to disclose.

Similarly, the Reliability class includes the **Consensus** heuristic; a normalised and general agreement [42]. Consensus has a broader application than the Consistency heuristic. These situations are exemplified by the use of normative terms, such as Interviewee S4 noting that "obviously name, email address" and "obviously it wanted a photo" to describe an interaction with a social networking site. Likewise, Interview S10 with "Just the normal, name, date of birth", and T6 with "obviously name and email", however, the data within these normal and obvious requests did tend to differ. The result is that "it almost bypasses you because you have done it so many times, but if something unexpected came up like a page you have not seen before that would make you doubt it. [...]. If it is the same process as usual I would assume it was fine".

The three heuristics are linked by the idea that if something is broken, has mistakes, or if something changes, it can cue users against disclosure, whereas a professional and as-expected interaction goes unnoticed. Problematically, this manner of thinking could incentivise service providers to request more information than is currently required, because in waiting to do so at a later occasion, the service risks disturbing the user's sense of routine and invoke questions such as S6's when a TV service started asking for information; "why are you doing that? It used to be different. They didn't use to ask for details".

5.4   ACCORDANCE: Self-confirmation and Persuasion

When Interviewee S6 expressed that a TV service "didn't use to ask for details" they were disrupted as a factor of the consistency heuristic, however, when they then reflected on "why are you doing that" this is closer to the **Self-Confirmation** heuristic; when something aligns with one's prior belief [35]. S6 later went on to reflect on why the BBC iPlayer "need[s] to check up on me, and my full name? To see what I'm watching?". Then as a result, "I just put my initials in, because I'm just watching TV".

The Accordance class differs from the Reliability class, in that it refers to beliefs and understanding rather than process or interface. Also, the Self-confirmation heuristics does not require a norm to the request, as long as there is an understanding that the request "comes up for good reasons" such as a store requesting a delivery address from S3. Whereas, when asked for ID for a birthday promotion, T11 refrains because "that is not a good reason to give my ID, especially when I just want to buy make-up. I wasn't happy, so I didn't sign up". They could not justify the disclosure when told the reason, although in contrast T11 did give their ID to a storage company when told it was in case "something happened" despite being vague and not particularly compelling.

Also in the Accordance class is the **Persuasive Intent** heuristic, the underlying principle of which is that perceived manipulation leads to negative judgements [35]. For instance, pop-up messages have been shown to produce a negative psychological effect [11,46]. Throughout the interviews, such instances related to unsettling aspects of an interaction being "too violent, in your face" or annoying features that "as you try and get a page and they are flashing up at you". Gambino et al. [14] recognise such aspects as being an *intrusiveness* heuristics, leading users to "question the integrity" of the service. Removing the 'persuasion' part of the name of this heuristic to leave it labelled simply as 'intent' serves the purpose of being close to the 'integrity' element in Gambino et al., whilst maintaining a neutral description. Intent better describes the grey area between it being "quite helpful if they have picked up on what you are trying to find" and "it seems to be everywhere, [...]. It is annoying and unnecessary. I suppose there is two sides to it".

We learn more about this class when Interviewee T7 implies that paying for prominence on a search result was something to be "wary about", as if it was not in the spirit of things, compared to those who achieve prominence through merit of popularity. Or when Interviewee T2 was deterred by an insurance company because "they wanted all my details to tell me how much it would cost". In this instance, T2 realised it was a 'consistent' process for insurance companies to request this, yet the feeling of being pushed meant they "provided false details".

5.5   MODALITY: Coolness and Novelty

Sundar [42] associates the **Coolness** heuristic with new technological features, or the bells and whistles of existing technologies, with positive credibility evaluations. For instance, Interviewee S6 consents [Instagram] access to all their photos, despite that they "don't particularly like to, but you can't download it without giving that permission", and they "like the effect on the photos".

The **Novelty** heuristic is subtly distinct from the Coolness heuristic as it is invoked by a user's initial experience with a technology [42]. S3 describes two instances of "when I first started Facebook I think I got a bit carried away", and "when I actually started [Deviant Art] I was so happy about it, that I completed absolutely everything". However, that early exuberance waned and "looking back on my profile I used to disclose more information than I do now".

In Sundar's MAIN model [42], these heuristics are seen as a factor of modality. Instances of these heuristics were sparse, and limited to social and entertainment situations, perhaps aligned with the explanation that in these instances individuals are mostly concerned with gains and immediate gratification [1,21].

5.6 NARRATIVE: Availability and Coherence

The framework in Table 1 was insufficient to explain all of what the interviewees described. This is mainly because the credibility framework referred to individuals establishing trust, it does not account for individuals considering risk. Instead of "why are you doing that" type questions, interviewees would engage with past examples, and/or hypothetical situations, asking themselves "why would they be interested in me", or more pertinent, "if I had been affected" type reflections.

To frame these instances of introspection, we refer to the description by [43, p. 15] of the **Availability** heuristic; a judgement of the likelihood of an event based on the 'ease with which relevant instances come to mind'. A example is S4's work insight meaning they "would not sign up for anything like [comparison websites], because I worked in insurance and basically if anyone put information on GoCompare it would come straight to us".

Interviewee S4's experience was not typical in relation to those less aware, such as Interviewee S3's lack of risk availability in that "there has never been a dodgy situation when I don't want to give [my location data] because it is harmless in games like Flappy Bird". There were many similarities between the perspectives of the interviewees here and [7] as when the extent of data leakages were revealed to their participants they were 'very surprised' by the frequency and the destination of data leakage from mobile games.

The overriding difference is that in [7] the full extent of data disclosures as a result of playing a game was demonstrated, which in turn, allowed their participants to envisage a list of possible negative outcome, thus completing a disclosure narrative. In the end, these participants stated a desire to change future behaviours, and one participant even changed from perceiving disclosure as useful for customisation, to later referring to the game as being 'slime'.

It is unsatisfactory to wait for users' negative experiences to instil a more cautious, considered approach to disclosure. Instead, it may be possible to inform users of disclosure risk through a relatable narrative. In this regard we refer to a **Coherence** heuristic; being able to envisage the result of a decision as a plausible outcome. For example, S11 does not profess to having been mugged, yet they can reason that "when you post a picture you can add your location then people in the area can look at the picture and they can find you and they could mug you or something like that". For S2, they can envisage that it is possible to hack a Twitter account, yet "honestly wouldn't care because it is utter rubbish, nothing important, it is only entertainment". Seemingly, the interviewee does not have the available recall or imagination to see the potential negative results, such as those increasingly experienced by victims of facility takeovers [24,25].

Norberg et al. [37] finds that people abstractly perceive risks in over-disclosure, yet when faced with a specific disclosure decision they most likely disclose. The evidence in this study contributes to that observation, and further suggests that the often missing narrative could play a significant role. In practice however, due to the consent model being 'simple', such narrative is rarely available to the user, and therefore, the resulting behaviour is similar to that observed in Norberg et al. Furthermore, there is an expectation of sorts that this narrative will be brought to them as noted by T1 who "assume[s] that if I had been affected [...] I would be contacted by eBay. [...]. Only at that point if that happened would I care about it a bit more". Or T3 suggesting that "[i]f there was a serious problem I'm sure it would be in the news".

5.7   TRADE: Gains and Worth

Despite the primary focus on heuristics, we examined the data for deviant cases to counter some confirmation bias. From this, it was evident that along with heuristics, interviewees were also weighing up their disclosures in terms of trading utility gains versus losses [3,4]. In many ways the Modality class (coolness and novelty) reflects the notion of a trade. Interviewee S3 considering that "it doesn't seem like a good investment" to disclose location data to a poorly designed game, seemingly interpreted in a manner associated with the Effort Heuristic [32] in that lack of effort reduces utility. Likewise, S6 explains that it was "quite a lot of details, but I felt like I was getting something back with the [rail] voucher".

Trade-type behaviours were often imbalanced in favour of disclosure. For instance, S9 perceived a lack of real option "[w]hen Google linked Gmail and YouTube [...] I didn't have much of a choice, I would have had to close my YouTube account, and I didn't want to do that", because "I didn't want to lose" my "personal videos" and "amateur stuff". Likewise, S11 described how "they force you to have it on your phone", with the sentiment that "I sort of need it. I have 100–200 friends on there that I need to contact". S11 also reflected on "why would they be interested in me?" Conveying a common sentiment of insignificance around personal data [20], hence apportioning a low overall value to the data disclosed, compared to a clear understanding of Facebook's utility.

Within efforts to disclose in a more calculative manner, the variables under-pinning the decision often remain heuristics based. When S2 explains a differences when disclosing "name, phone number, that I need to give, that is fine. But I wouldn't tell them where I'm working or what I study", they rely on the Coherence heuristic when envisaging someone turning up at their work. Equally, S1 can envisage the risk and therefore caution "in terms of card and bank details. That will put me off subscribing or buying online", but this is only a relative value as "mobile, or equally email, is the least worrying compared to card".

Whilst in some instances there was a relative value to single identifiers, i.e., name vs. place of work, in other instances, disclosing a combination of identifiers impacted the valuation. Interviewee S4 talked of less willingness to disclose their age once gender had already been disclosed. Seemingly, being a female was a satisfactory disclosure, but not in conjunction with being young. Not evident is whether age in isolation holds the same value as when in combination with gender, or how this value may change over time. In contrast, from S9's perspective there is a threshold effect; "I consider my phone number a pretty private thing to begin with it, so if someone has it, they already probably know my name."

6   Conclusion

The interviews that we have conducted have provided a rich qualitative account of users interaction with the disclosure decision points of online systems. Looking at the simplicity of such decisions through the lens of credibility heuristics, we find that our prediction that the heuristics are also being used for disclosure decisions to be valid. Also, we find disclosure heuristics outside of the credibility framework, mainly the importance of narrative in how users make disclosure decisions. These results were then encapsulated within superordinate groups (Table 2), revealing PROMINENCE, NETWORK, RELIABILITY, ACCORDANCE, NARRATIVE, MODALITY and a seventh non-heuristics TRADE class.

The main implication of this paper is that the self-managed model whereby self-informed individuals are responsible for consenting or withholding personal data, is idealistic. The evidence here is that users tend to make impoverished decisions. They evaluate trustworthiness from heuristics formed of prominence and social networks, using decision cues such as popularity, brand exposure or word of mouth, resulting in somewhat of a herd mentality. Alternatively, users evaluate trustworthiness from heuristics formed of accordance with beliefs and a sense of reliability, using cues such as familiarity and regularity. However, this reasoning has inductive pitfalls based on the idea that if nothing negative occurred before as a result of a disclosure, then future like-for-like instances are deemed safe. Our results agree with [14,41] that a reliance on such cognitive heuristics is key to understanding users knowingly consenting to give more than intended (i.e., privacy paradox). But also, we find this key to understanding users consenting to give more than they know (i.e., simple consent).

Norberg [37] calls it a privacy paradox when describing how users base their disclosure intentions on risk, yet base their disclosure behaviours on trust. The result is behaviour that favours disclosure because in disclosure environments there are many trust based cues yet scarce information about the risks. Therefore, on occasions when users attempt a considered approach to disclosure, qualitative accounts of what may happen are not adequately portrayed, and users find it difficult to complete a coherent narrative which diminishes their ability to adequately conduct the 'privacy calculus' [31] required for informed consent.

Our new super-ordinate set of heuristics for disclosure is envisaged to allow future research into the heuristics, and also to provide a place for emerging heuristics. Our hope is that these heuristics, and the implication of their susceptibility to bias and manipulation [30], may one day be harnessed so users may benefit from some form of positive nudge and thus mediation of the risks [6,8].

References

1. Acquisti, A.: Privacy and security of personal information. In: Camp, L.J., Lewis, S. (eds.) Economics of Information Security in Advances in Information Security, vol. 12, pp. 179–186. Springer, Heidelberg (2004). http://link.springer.com/content/pdf/10.1007/1-4020-8090-5_14.pdf
2. Acquisti, A.: Nudging privacy: the behavioral economics of personal information. Digit. Enlightenment Yearb. **2012**, 193–197 (2012)
3. Acquisti, A., Grossklags, J.: Privacy attitudes and privacy behavior. In: Camp, L.J., Lewis, S. (eds.) Economics of Information Security, pp. 1–15. Springer, Heidelberg (2004). http://link.springer.com/content/pdf/10.1007/1-4020-8090-5_13.pdf
4. Acquisti, A., Grossklags, J.: What can behavioral economics teach us about privacy? In: Digital Privacy, pp. 363–377. Auerbach Publications (2007). http://citeseerx.ist.psu.edu/viewdoc/download?doi=10.1.1.145.7609&rep=rep.1& type=pdf, http://www.crcnetbase.com/doi/abs/10.1201/9781420052183.ch18
5. Acquisti, A., John, L., Loewenstein, G.: The impact of relative standards on the propensity to disclose. J. Market. Res. **49**(2), 160–174 (2012). http://journals.ama.org/doi/abs/10.1509/jmr.09.0215
6. Adjerid, I., Acquisti, A., Brandimarte, L., Loewenstein, G.: Sleights of privacy. In: Proceedings of the Ninth Symposium on Usable Privacy and Security - SOUPS 2013, p. 1. ACM (2013). http://dl.acm.org/citation.cfm?id=2501604.2501613
7. Balebako, R., Jung, J., Lu, W., Cranor, L.F., Nguyen, C.: Little brothers watching you. In: Proceedings of the Ninth Symposium on Usable Privacy and Security - SOUPS 2013, p. 1. ACM (2013). http://dl.acm.org/citation.cfm?id=2501604.2501616%5Cnwww.scopus.com/inward/record.url?eid=2-s2.0-84883078013&partnerID=tZOtx3y1
8. Balebako, R., Leon, P.G., Almuhimedi, H., Kelley, P.G., Mugan, J., Acquisti, A., Cranor, L.F., Sadeh, N.: Nudging users towards privacy on mobile devices. In: CEUR Workshop Proceedings, vol. 722, pp. 23–26 (2011)
9. Cialdini, R., Trost, M.: Social influence: social norms, conformity and compliance. In: The Handbook of Social Psychology, vol. 2, pp. 151–192 (1998). http://psycnet.apa.org/psycinfo/1998-07091-021
10. Fereday, J., Muir-Cochrane, E.: Demonstrating rigor using thematic analysis: a hybrid approach of inductive and deductive coding and theme development. Int. J. Qual. Methods **5**(1), 80–92 (2006)
11. Fogg, B.J., Soohoo, C., Danielson, D.R., Marable, L., Stanford, J., Tauber, E.R.: How do users evaluate the credibility of web sites? A study with over 2,500 participants. In: Proceedings of the 2003 Conference on Designing for User Experiences (DUX 2003), pp. 1–15. ACM (2003). http://dl.acm.org/citation.cfm?id=997078.997097
12. Fogg, B.J.: Prominence-interpretation theory: explaining how people assess credibility online. In: Conference on Human Factors in Computing Systems - Proceedings, pp. 722–723. ACM (2003). http://dl.acm.org/citation.cfm?id=765951%5Cnwww.scopus.com/inward/record.url?eid=2-s2.0-84869039673&partnerID=40&md5=f36a1afb8a3a649f12e97c7d6b38854a
13. Furnell, S., Phippen, A.: Online privacy: a matter of policy? Comput. Fraud Secur. **2012**(8), 12–18 (2012). 10.1016/S1361-3723(12)70083-0
14. Gambino, A., Kim, J., Sundar, S.S., Ge, J., Rosson, M.B.: User disbelief in privacy paradox: heuristics that determine disclosure. In: Proceedings of the 2016 CHI Conference Extended Abstracts on Human Factors in Computing Systems, pp. 2837–2843. ACM (2016)

15. Gigerenzer, G., Gaissmaier, W.: Heuristic decision making. Ann. Rev. Psychol. **62**, 451–482 (2011)
16. Gigerenzer, G., Hoffrage, U., Goldstein, D.G.: Fast and frugal heuristics are plausible models of cognition: reply to Dougherty, Franco-Watkins, and Thomas. Psychol. Rev. **115**(1), 230–239 (2008)
17. Gigerenzer, G., Todd, P.M.: Fast and frugal heuristics: the adaptive toolbox. In: Simple Heuristics that make us Smart, pp. 3–34. Oxford University Press, Oxford (1999)
18. Goodman, M.: Future Crimes: Everything is Connected, Everyone is Vulnerable and What We can do about it. Anchor, Daman (2015)
19. Hansen, P.G., Jespersen, A.M.: Nudge and the manipulation of choice: a framework for the responsible use of the nudge approach to behaviour change in public policy. Eur. J. Risk Regul. **1**, 3–28 (2013). http://ssrn.com/abstract=2555337
20. Heikkinen, A., Wickström, G., Leino-Kilpi, H.: Understanding privacy in occupational health services. Nurs. Ethics **13**(5), 515–530 (2006). http://nej.sagepub.com/content/13/5/515.abstract
21. Higgins, E.: Promotion and prevention. Regulatory focus as a motivational principle.pdf. Adv. Exp. Soc. Psychol. **30**, 1–46 (1998)
22. Hollingsed, T., Novick, D.G.: Usability inspection methods after 15 years of research and practice. In: Proceedings of the 25th Annual ACM International Conference on Design of Communication, pp. 249–255. ACM (2007)
23. Holloway, I.: Basic Concepts for Qualitative Research. Wiley, Hoboken (1997)
24. Hoofnagle, C.J.: Identity theft: making the known unknowns known. Harvard J. Law Technol. **21**, 98–122 (2007). http://papers.ssrn.com/sol3/papers.cfm?abstract_id=969441
25. Kahn, C.M., Roberds, W.: Credit and identity theft. J. Monetary Econ. **55**(2), 251–264 (2008). http://linkinghub.elsevier.com/retrieve/pii/S0304393207001250
26. Kahneman, D.: Thinking, Fast and Slow. Macmillan, Basingstoke (2011)
27. Kehr, F., Wentzel, D., Mayer, P.: Rethinking the privacy calculus: on the role of dispositional factors and affect. In: The 34th International Conference on Information Systems, vol. 1, pp. 1–10 (2013). http://cocoa.ethz.ch/downloads/2013/11/1624_kehr_2013_privacy_icis.pdf
28. Knijnenburg, B.P.: On the dimensionality of information disclosure behavior in social networks. Int. J. Hum.-Comput. Stud. **71**(12), 1144–1162 (2013)
29. Komanduri, S., Shay, R., Kelley, P.G., Mazurek, M.L., Bauer, L., Christin, N., Cranor, L.F., Egelman, S.: Of passwords and people. In: Proceedings of the SIGCHI Conference on Human Factors in Computing Systems (CHI 2011), pp. 2595–2604. ACM (2011). http://dl.acm.org/citation.cfm?doid=1978942.1979321
30. Krasnova, H., Günther, O.: Privacy concerns and identity in online social networks. Identity Inf. Soc. **2**(1), 39–63 (2009)
31. Krasnova, H., Spiekermann, S., Koroleva, K., Hildebrand, T.: Online social networks: why we disclose. J. Inf. Technol. **25**(2), 109–125 (2010). http://www.palgrave-journals.com/doifinder/10.1057/jit.2010.6
32. Kruger, J., Wirtz, D., Van Boven, L., Altermatt, T.W.: The effort heuristic. J. Exp. Soc. Psychol. **40**(1), 91–98 (2004)
33. Metzger, M.J.: Privacy, trust, and disclosure: exploring barriers to electronic commerce. J. Comput.-Mediated Commun. **9**(4), 1–29 (2006)
34. Metzger, M.J., Flanagin, A.J.: Credibility and trust of information in online environments: the use of cognitive heuristics. J. Pragmatics **59**, 210–220 (2013). http://www.sciencedirect.com/science/article/pii/S0378216613001768

35. Metzger, M.J., Flanagin, A.J., Medders, R.B.: Social and heuristics approaches to credibility evaluation online. J. Commun. **60**(3), 413–439 (2010)
36. Nielsen, J.: Usability inspection methods. In: Conference Companion on Human Factors in Computing Systems, pp. 413–414. ACM (1994)
37. Norberg, P.A., Horne, D.R., Horne, D.A.: The privacy paradox: personal information disclosure intentions versus behaviors. J. Consum. Affairs **41**(1), 100–126 (2007)
38. Olivero, N., Lunt, P.: Privacy versus willingness to disclose in e-commerce exchanges: the effect of risk awareness on the relative role of trust and control. J. Econ. Psychol. **25**(2), 243–262 (2004)
39. Ryan, G.W., Bernard, H.R.: Techniques to identify themes. Field Methods **15**(1), 85–109 (2003)
40. Solove, D.J.: Introduction: privacy self-management and the consent dilemma. Harvard Law Rev. **126**, 1880–1903 (2012). http://papers.ssrn.com/abstract=2171018
41. Sundar, S.S., Kang, H., Wu, M., Go, E., Zhang, B.: Unlocking the privacy paradox: do cognitive heuristics hold the key? In: CHI 2013 Extended Abstracts on Human Factors in Computing Systems, pp. 811–816 (2013)
42. Sundar, S.S.: The MAIN model: a heuristic approach to understanding technology effects on credibility. In: Digital Media, Youth, and Credibility, pp. 73–100 (2008). http://www.mitpressjournals.org/doi/abs/10.1162/dmal.9780262562324.073
43. Tversky, A., Kahneman, D.: Availability: a heuristic for judging frequency and robability. Cogn. Psychol. **5**(2), 207–232 (1973). http://www.sciencedirect.com/science/article/pii/0010028573900339
44. Tversky, A., Kahneman, D.: Judgment under uncertainty: heuristics and biases. In: Wendt, D., Vlek, C. (eds.) Utility, Probability, and Human Decision Making, vol. 11, pp. 141–162. Springer, Heidelberg (1975). doi:10.1007/978-94-010-1834-0_8
45. Vila, T., Greenstadt, R., Molnar, D.: Why we can't be bothered to read privacy policies models of privacy economics as a lemons market. In: Proceeding ICEC 2003 Proceedings of the 5th International Conference on Electronic Commerce, pp. 403–407. ACM (2003). http://dl.acm.org/citation.cfm?id=948057&dl=ACM&coll=DL&CFID=304526782&CFTOKEN=23143651
46. Ward, R.: Physiological responses to different WEB page designs. Int. J. Hum.-Comput. Stud. **59**(1–2), 199–212 (2003). http://linkinghub.elsevier.com/retrieve/pii/S1071581903000193
47. Weitzner, D.J., Abelson, H., Berners-Lee, T., Feigenbaum, J., Hendler, J., Sussman, G.J.: Information accountability. Commun. ACM **51**(6), 82–87 (2008). http://dl.acm.org/ft_gateway.cfm?id=1349043&type=html
48. Westin, A.F.: Social and political dimensions of privacy. J. Soc. Issues **59**(2), 431–453 (2003)
49. Whitney, S., McCullough, L.B.: A typology of shared decision making, informed consent, and simple consent. Ann. Intern. Med. **140**(1), 54–59 (2004)

Tools and Methods

A Propagation-Based Method of Estimating Students' Concept Understanding

Rafael López-García[✉], Makoto P. Kato[✉], and Katsumi Tanaka[✉]

Department of Social Informatics, Graduate School of Informatics,
Kyoto University, Kyoto, Japan
{rafael.lopez,kato}@dl.kuis.kyoto-u.ac.jp,
tanaka.katsumi.85e@st.kyoto-u.ac.jp

Abstract. In this paper, we introduce a method to estimate the degree of students' understanding of concepts and relationships while they learn from digital text materials online. To achieve our goal, we first define a semantic network that represents the knowledge in a material. Second, we define students' behavior as the sequence of relationships they read in the material, and we create a probabilistic model for relationship understanding. We also create inference rules to include new relationships in the network. Third, we simulate the propagation of the new concept understanding through the network by using a method based on Biased PageRank, extending it with a method to represent prior knowledge and weighting the contribution of every concept according to the uniqueness of its relationships. Finally, we describe an experiment to compare our method against a method without propagation and a method in which propagation is inversely proportional to the distance between concepts. Our method shows significant improvement compared to the others, providing evidence that propagation of concept understanding through the entire network exists.

Keywords: Learning data analytics · Concept understanding · Biased PageRank

1 Introduction

The use of online digital text materials and Virtual Learning Environments (VLEs) like Moodle [1] in traditional classrooms has been increasing in the recent years. One advantage of such technologies is that we can capture students' behavior via network while they are learning. The analysis of this behavior allows instructors to evaluate students' learning as they read, allowing students with different prior knowledge and understanding to receive personalized materials [2] on the fly.

The main goal of this paper is to provide a method to estimate students' understanding from their behavior while they read digital learning materials, either uploaded by the teacher to a VLE or found in an arbitrary website. One advantage of using this method for students' evaluation is that it happens immediately, while traditional methods such as comprehensive quizzes or interviews consume much of instructors' and students' time and effort. Our idea is also applicable to Massive Open Online Courses (MOOCs) [3] as many of them include reading assignments as well.

© Springer International Publishing AG 2017
G.L. Ciampaglia et al. (Eds.): SocInfo 2017, Part I, LNCS 10539, pp. 611–627, 2017.
DOI: 10.1007/978-3-319-67217-5_36

For that purpose we must: (1) show in a knowledge model which information the student can acquire from those materials, (2) when a student reads an atomic unit of text (i.e.: sentence), reflect the immediate effect of this behavior in the corresponding region of the model, and (3) simulate how this change in a small region affects the rest of the model, this is, how the new understanding propagates through all the concepts.

The first problem is finding a method to represent the knowledge in the materials and the students' understanding. Terms such as "knowledge" and "understanding" are very broad, as they include facts, procedures, principles and some other categories [4]. In this research, we target a set of concepts and their relationships, as concepts are the base of many of the other categories and they have been widely studied in the research literature [5, 6] too. Moreover, well-known tools such as semantic networks are suitable to represent them.

The second problem is finding an accurate way to represent how the understanding of a relationship changes when the student reads an atomic unit of text that corresponds to it. A simple approach is marking in the network which relationships have been read. However, we cannot ensure that a student retains the relationship by reading it just once, so we discuss a probabilistic approach as an alternative.

The third problem is deciding how this change affects the understanding of the rest of the concepts and relationships in the network, this is, how understanding propagates through them. Piaget's constructivism describes how internal representations of knowledge are rebuilt by two operations: assimilation and accommodation [7]. In addition, Vygotsky's Zone of Proximal Development (ZPD) shows how new knowledge is better acquired when it is closely related to the one that the student already has [8]. Nevertheless, these theories do not include mathematical methods to represent those processes with numbers. In this paper, we try to solve this problem by using a variant of the Biased PageRank formula [9] that incorporates the idea of prior knowledge for some concepts in the graph.

Finally, we evaluate the effectiveness of our method by comparing it against a baseline in which propagation does not happen and another baseline in which propagation is naïvely calculated according to the shortest distance between concepts. For that purpose, we performed an experiment in which different people in a crowdsourcing system had to read some learning materials. We applied their data to our understanding models, and found that our method outperforms both baselines.

The main contribution of this paper is that, to the best of our knowledge, our method is the first in estimating the degree of concept and relationship understanding by using the sequence of the relationships read from a text document, as well as the first in proposing a method to measure the propagation of concept understanding and in setting the baselines for its evaluation.

The rest of this paper is as follows: Sect. 2 reviews the related work. In Sect. 3 we discuss our proposed method. In Sect. 4 we propose an experiment to evaluate the model, and we discuss the results. In Sect. 5 we conclude and in Sect. 6 we propose the future work.

2 Related Work

2.1 Predicting Students' Performance

For more than two decades, researchers have been publishing papers on using data mining techniques on learning data to predict students' performance [10, 11]. Much of that research uses classification methods to predict success after an academic year [12, 13] or finding what students will drop out [14]. They use demographic data such as sex and age, and academic data such as grades in exams or course subjects, rate of completion of activities, etc. However, our problem focuses on performance in a very short period and their data is not appropriate for our task.

The two major statistical models for estimating students' knowledge are Bayesian Knowledge Tracing [15] and Learning Factor Analysis [16], and they present several differences with our method. First, they focus on understanding procedural knowledge, while we focus on conceptual knowledge. Second, our method can be used in non-academic environments, as we only need to record the text that the student reads from a file or webpage (e.g. by mouse tracking), while theirs require interactions with an Intelligent Tutoring System. Third, their methods require long term interactions and repetitions of the same task, as they analyze data such as the number of mistakes before learning a skill, etc., while we can estimate the degree of understanding while the student is reading.

Actually, many approaches in the literature are non-viable in an actual higher education classroom as methods require (1) technology that is not common in most institutions, such as the Intelligent Tutoring System, or (2) input that is not always available. For instance, it is possible to use students' vocabulary to predict the quality of their answers [17], although this would require writing activities. Something similar happens in the estimation of reading comprehension. It can be achieved by using students' oral fluency [18], but that would require them to read aloud. Eye tracking can be used instead [19], although such technology is non-viable in a real classroom either.

2.2 Semantic Networks

A *semantic network* [20] is a way of knowledge representation formalized by a set of nodes representing concepts and a set of edges representing the relationships between those concepts. There are several types, such as *conceptual graphs* [21] and *simple concept graphs* [22]. In any case, semantic networks simply offer a picture of the knowledge in one instant, and therefore they are not sufficient to show the degree of students' understanding and its change. For that purpose, we use other mechanisms explained in Sect. 3.

Another problem of the semantic networks is the vast number of possible labels for the relationships. Some researchers addressed the need to restrict them [23]. In our work, we give a special treatment to IS_A relationships as their child nodes can always inherit the relationships of the parent, but we do not give any treatment to all the other labels.

3   Approach

3.1   Representation of Understanding

According to Gagné's instructional theory [5], a concept is a classification of things by using either physical features (concrete concept) or associations with other concepts (defined or relational concept). We understand concepts by building these associations (relationships), and this task involves linguistic operations and intensive use of prior knowledge.

In this research, we assume that the person or system assessing the student is interested in a set of concepts $C = \{c_1...c_n\}$ and a set of labeled, directed relationships R between them. Let L be the set of all the possible labels, we define the relationships as $R \subseteq C \times L \times C$. The triplet $(c_i, l, c_j) \in R$ with $c_i, c_j \in C$ is notated as r_{ij}.

There are several semantic networks capable of reflecting knowledge by using concepts and relationships. In this paper we define the Learning Material's Concept Graph (LMCG) as the representation of the knowledge expressed in the target learning materials. LMCGs are a variant of Simple Concept Graphs (SCG) [22] in which we do not include objects, hypergraphs or bipartite graphs, as these elements are unnecessary for our goal. Open relation extraction software [24] can be used to generate them automatically for arbitrary Web documents, although instructors can manually create more accurate ones for their own materials. We define a LMCG as $G = (C, R, L, W)$, where C is a set of nodes representing the concepts in the material, R is the set of labeled, directed edges representing the relationships between those concepts, and L is the set of labels. The set W, which does not exist in the original definition of SCG, assigns a weight to each relationship. Given a relationship $r_{ij} \in R$, w_{ij} represents how much c_i contributes to understand c_j. Figure 1 shows a small example of LMCG with four concepts (c_1 to c_4) connected by three relationships labeled as $l_{2,1}$, $l_{3,2}$ and $l_{4,3}$ and weighted by $w_{2,1}$, $w_{3,2}$ and $w_{4,3}$ respectively.

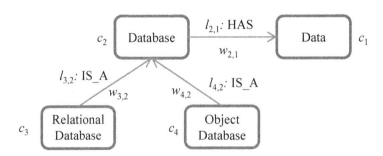

Fig. 1. Small example of LMCG.

Although relationships have direction, we assume that each relationship always has an "inverse" relationship that goes in the opposite direction, and if the student learns one, the inverse is automatically learned as well. For example, if we have the relationship "Database" HAS "Data", there is also the inverse relationship "Data" PART_OF "Database". We do not show these relationships in figures for simplicity.

Note that the content of a LMCG is completely independent from the actions of the students who read those materials. Therefore, it would only change if the instructor changes the materials themselves or the weights of the relationships.

Once concepts and relationships have been defined, we can mathematically define the degree of understanding of a concept as a function $u: C \times T \rightarrow [0, 1]$, in which T is a discrete representation of the time. This understanding degree changes as the student learns from a material. It is also possible that students had acquired some prior knowledge (pk) about the concepts in the past. We define the function pk: $C \rightarrow [0, 1]$ to represent it. One feature of pk is that it does not change during the reading process.

Regarding relationships, we cannot ensure that every student automatically understands every relationship they read in the text. Therefore, we need to define the function rund: $R \times T \rightarrow [0, 1]$ to estimate this relationship understanding. This relationship understanding changes as students read.

3.2   Assumptions on Understanding

Based on the characteristics of knowledge and understanding we stated in the previous sections, the first assumption of our method is that computation of the understanding of a concept must be based on (1) the prior knowledge on that concept, (2) the understanding of the relationships including that concept, and (3) the understanding of the other concepts included in those relationships. Since this method is recursive, we assume that understanding of a concept also depends on the understanding of concepts that are not directly connected to it. We call this effect propagation, and it leads to our first research question:

Research question 1: Does concept understanding propagate to concepts not directly connected in the concept graph, or does it only come from the prior knowledge of the given concept and the understanding of directly connected concepts?

Regarding relationship understanding, every relationship has a weight that changes its contribution to the understanding of a concept. This leads to our second question:

Research question 2: Do all the relationships in which a concept participates contribute in the same way to its understanding or is there a different contribution?

Furthermore, given a set of statements, humans often apply inference rules to them in order to obtain additional knowledge. Many of these rules depend on the domain of the text or on operators we do not provide in our LMCG (e.g.: complement of a set, choosing some elements of a set, etc. [25]). However, we can at least find two rules that are applicable to every domain. These are the two rules about relationship inheritance based on IS_A relationships:

$$\text{if } (c_i, l, c_j) \in R \wedge (c_h, IS_A, c_i) \in R \text{ then add } (c_h, l, c_j) \text{ to } R \tag{1}$$

$$\text{if } (c_i, l, c_j) \in R \wedge (c_h, IS_A, c_j) \in R \text{ then add } (c_i, l, c_h) \text{ to } R \tag{2}$$

For example, if we have $r_{1,2}$ "UNIX" IS_A "O.S." and $r_{2,3}$ = "O.S." MANAGES "Hardware", then we can add $r_{1,3}$ "UNIX" MANAGES "Hardware". By using these rules, we can create an extended version of the LMCG that includes every relationship of a parent concept in the successors of a hierarchy of IS_A relationships. Considering this, we formulate our third research question:

Research question 3: Do inference rules increase the accuracy of our prediction or should our model reflect the relationships explicitly written in the text?

3.3 Calculation of Relationship Understanding

As, in our model, relationship understanding is the previous step to concept understanding, we first present this part.

Most of the sentences in learning materials state relationships between concepts. Therefore, we can see the reading process as a sequence of steps in which the student understands these relationships. For example, let r be the relationship "Computer HAS C.P.U.". In a given instant t, the student did not know about it, so rund$(r, t) = 0$. Now, let us imagine that in the instant $t + 1$ the student reads r. Since students are not perfect at comprehension, we assume that this understanding is done with probability $p \in [0, 1]$. If this is the case, the equation of the relationship understanding for any relationship r_{ij} in the LMCG is as follows:

$$\text{rund}\left(r_{ij}, t+1\right) = 1 - \left(1 - \text{rund}\left(r_{ij}, t\right)\right)(1 - p) \tag{3}$$

If we assume that students are perfect at understanding relationships, we have $p = 1$ and therefore rund$(r_{ij}, t + 1) = 1$. If this is not the case, the students need to read again the same relationship in later instants until they can fully understand it.

Let us now consider the inference rules presented in the Eqs. (1) and (2). The added relationships must also be recursively updated accordingly by using Eq. (3), although the probability that they are understood is not exactly p, as it also depends on the understanding of the IS_A relationships. Let p_{ij}^t be the probability applied to relationship r_{ij} in an instant t, the probability to be applied to r_{hj} and r_{ih} is:

$$p_{hj}^t = p_{ij}^t \text{rund}(r_{hi}, t-1), \forall r\left(c_h, IS\_A, c_i\right) \in G \tag{4}$$

$$p_{ih}^t = p_{ij}^t \text{rund}\left(r_{hj}, t-1\right), \forall r\left(c_h, IS\_A, c_j\right) \in G \tag{5}$$

For example, if a student knows $r_{1,2} = $ "UNIX" IS_A "O.S." with rund$(r_{1,2}, t) = 0.5$ and she now reads $r_{2,3} = $ "O.S." MANAGES "Hardware" with probability of understanding $p_{2,3}^t = 0.75$, she also has a probability of understanding $r_{1,3} = $ "UNIX" MANAGES "Hardware" of $p_{1,3}^t = 0.75 \cdot 0.5 = 0.375$.

3.4 Calculation of Concept Understanding

Once a relationship has been read, we must simulate how this understanding propagates to the other concepts that the student has learned. For such simulation, we use a variant of the Biased PageRank formula [9], whose equation is as follows:

$$\mathbf{r} = \alpha\,\mathbf{Tr} + (1 - \alpha)\mathbf{d} \tag{6}$$

In this equation, $\mathbf{r}$ is the vector that contains the PageRank values, $\mathbf{T}$ is called the transition matrix and $\mathbf{d}$ is the vector containing the bias. The solution to this equation is often calculated by an iterative process called the Jacobi method [26].

In our case, the transition matrix is based on the relationship understanding we calculated in Sect. 3.3 and the weights of the relationships we explain in Sect. 3.5. The static part of the equation is based on the idea of prior knowledge we stated in Sect. 3.1. So our equation becomes as follows:

$$u\big(c_j, t'+1\big) = \alpha \sum_i \frac{\operatorname{rund}\big(r_{ij}, t'\big)w_{ij}u(c_i, t')}{\operatorname{in}(c_j)} + (1 - \alpha)\operatorname{pk}\big(c_j\big) \tag{7}$$

In this equation, in: $C \to N$ is a function that returns the number of relationships pointing to a given concept. The parameter $\alpha \in [0, 1]$ balances the contribution of the prior knowledge against the contribution of the propagation in the graph. In order to give more contribution to propagation than to the prior knowledge, we use $\alpha = 0.9$. Note that we use t' instead of t because relationship understanding and propagation of concept understanding happen in two different timelines.

One problem in the previous equation is that, in our model, the concepts that have been marked as previously known with $\operatorname{pk}(c_i) = 1$ should not be affected by the understanding propagation, as we know that students know them perfectly well. In order to achieve this, when we have a concept c_i with pre-established prior knowledge, we set $\operatorname{rund}(r_{ii}, t') = 1$ and $w_{ii} = 1$, and then $\operatorname{rund}(r_{ij}, t') = 0$ and $w_{ij} = 0$ for all $j \neq i$ and for all t'. With this, such concepts do not receive understanding from others, but they offer it. This also implies the weights of their relationships in our calculations are not exactly the ones initially defined in the LMCG.

Now, for $|C| = n$, let $\mathbf{u}^{t'}$ be $[u(c_1, t')...u(c_n, t')]$, let $\mathbf{k}$ be $[\operatorname{pk}(c_1)...\operatorname{pk}(c_n)]$, and $\mathbf{D}^{t'}$ be the matrix whose $d_{ij}^{t'} = \sum_i \operatorname{rund}\big(r_{ij}, t'\big)w_{ij}u(c_i, t')/\operatorname{in}\big(c_j\big)$, we can express Eq. (7) as matrices:

$$\mathbf{u}^{t'+1} = \alpha\mathbf{D}^{t'}\mathbf{u}^{t'} + (1 - \alpha)\mathbf{k} \tag{8}$$

One difference between Eqs. (8) and (6) is that we do not require $\sum_i^n u(c_i, t') = 1$, but $\sum_i^n u(c_i, t') \leq n$. For that purpose, we normalize the weights by forcing $\sum_i w_{ij} = 1$, although we do not require $\sum_i \operatorname{pk}(c_i) = 1$ or $\sum_i \operatorname{rund}(r_{ij}, t') = 1$. Therefore, we have that $\sum_i d_{ij}^{t'} \leq 1$. By allowing $\sum_i d_{ij} < 1$, we have a sub-stochastic transition matrix instead of a stochastic one. Hence, further analysis of convergence is necessary. This is done in the Appendix. A limitation of our method is that there has to be at least one concept c_i for which $\operatorname{pk}(c_i) = 1$, as smaller values do not grant convergence. This forces us to be conservative when setting the prior knowledge. In addition, if we start with $u(c_j, 0) = \operatorname{pk}(c_j) = 0$ for all j, we can verify that $u(c_j, t') = 0$ for all t', respecting the theory that we need to build on prior knowledge to learn [8].

3.5 Estimation of Weights

Up to this point, for a concept c_j we just required that $\sum_i w_{ij} = 1$, but we have not stated anything about how to establish the values of each w_{ij}. The basic approach followed by PageRank [27] is that all weights are equal, this is, $w_{ij} = 1/\text{in}(c_j)$. However, our intuition is that some relationships contribute to the understanding of the students more than the others, so we provide an alternative model that includes this idea.

The model we propose is based on the uniqueness of relationships. We assume that for a certain concept c_j, neighbor concepts with unique relationships are more relevant for the understanding of c_j than neighbors with relationships that are shared by other neighbors. The reason is that the information provided by the former is entirely new for c_j, while the latter just convey information c_j already has. For example, let us assume we want to calculate weights $w_{1,0}$, $w_{2,0}$ and $w_{3,0}$ in the LMCG in Fig. 2:

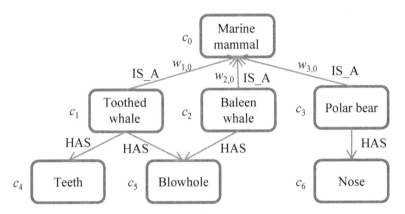

Fig. 2. A LMCG in which we calculate the weights of c_0. The neighbor of c_0 called c_1 has a unique relationship with c_4 and a non-unique one with c_5.

In Fig. 2, the relationship (c_1, HAS, c_5) is not carrying as much information for c_0 because (c_2, HAS, c_5) is also carrying similar information as (c_1, HAS, c_5). Therefore, c_1 and c_2 should distribute among themselves the contribution to the understanding of c_0 that comes from c_5.

Now, let neigh: $C \times G \to 2^C$ be the function that calculates the neighbors of a concept in a graph, and let edge: $C \times C \times G \to \{0, 1\}$ be the function that outputs 1 when there is an edge from the first to the second concept and 0 otherwise. Let G' be a version of G in which c_j does not exist. For a certain neighbor c_i, we define its degree of uniqueness δ_{ij} as:

$$\delta_{ij} = \prod_{c_h \in \text{neigh}(c_i, G')} \frac{1}{\sum_{c_x \in \text{neigh}(c_j, G)} \text{edge}(c_x, c_h, G')} \tag{9}$$

The division calculates the degree of uniqueness of a certain relationship r_{ih} among the neighbors of c_j, while the product aggregates the uniqueness of all the relationships of c_i without penalizing concepts with few relationships. We use G' instead of G to avoid counting c_j itself as one of the c_h. After calculating the aggregated uniqueness of each neighbor of c_j, we still need to normalize them, so we can have $\sum_i w_{ij} = 1$. To achieve this, we just divide the aggregated uniqueness of every neighbor of c_j by the summation of all the aggregated uniqueness of all the neighbors of c_j:

$$w_{ij} = \frac{\delta_{ij}}{\sum_{c_x \in \text{neigh}(c_j,G)} \delta_{xj}} \tag{10}$$

Back to the example in Fig. 2, we have that $\delta_{1,0} = \delta_{2,0} = 0.5$ because c_1 and c_2 share a relationship with c_5, but $\delta_{3,0} = 1$ because the only relationship of c_3 in G' is unique. As $\sum_x \delta_{x0} = 2$, the normalized weights would be $w_{1,0} = w_{2,0} = 0.25$, and $w_{3,0} = 0.5$.

4 Experiment

4.1 Experimental Setup

In order to answer our research questions, we performed an experiment in which we measure the understanding of several students in the Japanese crowdsourcing service Lancers [28], and we compared their results against two baselines and several variants of our method. This section explains the experiment.

Procedure. The main idea of our method is that concept understanding propagates through the graph according to the relationship understanding in every moment. Nevertheless, it is not feasible to ask every student about every relationship and concept as they read sentences of a text to observe the change. Furthermore, tracking the complete behavior of the students would require installing software in their computers, but this approach is non-viable in crowdsourcing. In order to solve these problems, we only ask about a few concepts and we simulate students do not understand some relationships by excluding them from their LMCG. We rewrote the text accordingly, so it does not lose coherence. We assume all the other relationships are read carefully and sequentially. We expect the answers of the students who read the original material to be better than the ones of the students who read the version we have modified.

As we want to generalize the result of our experiment, we repeat this procedure with 6 different learning materials of high school and first year university levels. We created materials about Computer Science, Biology and Chemistry because they focus on conceptual knowledge, while other topics such as Mathematics or Physics may focus too much on procedural knowledge. In addition, for reproducibility of the experiment, the topics we chose are cross-cultural, while other topics such as Literature or History may be localized to the place in which they are taught. For each topic, we chose two different "subtopics" in order to have LMCGs with different topology. We originally created the 6 texts in English with similar length, although the participants in the Japanese crowdsourcing site were shown a translation into their language, making the most technical documents a bit longer due to explanation of acronyms, etc.

For each subtopic, the procedure is as follows. We choose a target concept c_0 to evaluate its understanding. Then, we choose another 3 concepts c_1, c_2 and c_3, located in different points of the LMCG. With this, we can formulate 3 questions asking the relationships between c_1 and c_0, c_2 and c_0, and c_3 and c_0 respectively. This ensures that the student will have to traverse several relationships in the LMCG in order to answer correctly to all the questions, providing a more accurate estimation of the understanding of c_0. Now, given the original text t_0, we create a variant t_1 by removing relationships. These relationships are normally located between c_0 and c_1, c_2 or c_3, and we choose them trying to maximize the expectation of disconnecting a possible concept with prior knowledge from c_0, c_1, c_2 or c_3, or at least disabling the shortest path to these concepts. In order to traverse more relationships of a LMCG, we repeat this procedure for 3 different c_0. Therefore, apart from the original text t_0 we get 3 variants t_1, t_2 and t_3. Table 1 shows the statistics of the texts and LMCGs. Columns "$|C|$" and "$|R|$" contain the number of concepts and relationships in the LMCG, respectively, and the column "Rels. cut" shows the relationships removed in each variant of the original text. Both "$|R|$" and "Rels. cut" include inverse relationships.

Table 1. Statistics of the texts and the LMCGs

Subtopic	Words (Eng.)	Chars (Jap.)	$|C|$	$|R|$	Rels. cut ($t_1/t_2/t_3$)
Comp. Arch.	368	1162	34	110	4/18/10
Databases	363	1230	28	76	8/6/14
Genetics	396	976	25	66	6/8/6
Cetaceans	367	882	34	70	4/4/6
Compounds	389	883	33	92	10/16/6
Solutions	355	854	46	120	12/8/22

For our experiment, we created a web application in which the students are shown one of the above texts for 15 min, and they have to answer a questionnaire about it in another period of 15 min. In order to avoid cheating, the website does not let the students go back to the text when they reach the page of the questionnaire. Two "captcha" questions are also included in each questionnaire, in addition to the text areas in which the students have to write the relationship c_1-c_0, c_2-c_0 and c_3-c_0 respectively. Finally, if a student participated twice in the same subtopic the prior knowledge would be different, so we use a mechanism based on cookies in order to ensure that this does not happen, although one student can participate in the 6 subtopics.

Ground Truth. We let 90 students participate in each subtopic. We divided them in 3 groups of 30 depending on the target concept assigned to them. Each group is again sub-divided in two groups of 15, one receiving the original text and the other receiving the text in which relationships are removed.

In order to grade students' answers, we hired two evaluators for each topic. These evaluators are master and Ph.D. students majoring a related subject at our institution. Each evaluator was asked to grade each answer in a 5-level likert scale, where 1 is assigned to blank or completely unrelated answers, while 5 is assigned to perfect answers. Intermediate values are assigned according to the number of missing relationships between the target concept and the other concept. Another task we requested to each evaluator is grading the contribution of concepts c_1, c_2 and c_3 to the understanding of c_0. These values were also given in a 5-level likert scale, where 1 means no contribution and 5 means very high contribution. Let w_{i0}, where $i = 1..3$, be these weights, and let $\text{score}(c_i, c_0)$ be the score assigned to the answer about the relationship between c_i and c_0, we can calculate the ground truth of the understanding of a target concept as in Eq. (11). These values are normalized so $\hat{u}: C \rightarrow [0, 1]$.

$$\hat{u}(c_0) = \sum_{i=1}^{3} \text{score}(c_i, c_0) w_{i0} \tag{11}$$

Finally, since it is not viable to calculate the prior knowledge of each participant in every concept without unveiling the content of the text, we have decided to set it beforehand. For that purpose, we took a list of the 5000 most common words in English [29] and we decided that the terms appearing in that list would receive pk $(c_i) = 1$, while the others would receive $\text{pk}(c_i) = 0$. However, we found out that some of the terms appearing in the list are often used with a different meaning to the one in our text (e.g.: "class", "object", and so on in Object DBMS), so we had to apply human supervision to the concepts based on the following rules:

- If the concept has a meaning for daily life (e.g.: "class"), but the student probably has not studied the specialized meaning, set $\text{pk}(c_i) = 0$.
- If students may have studied the specialized meaning of the concept in school (e.g.: "character" in genetics), but it hardly ever appears in daily life, set $\text{pk}(c_i) = 0$.
- Otherwise, leave $\text{pk}(c_i) = 1$.

In addition we included some other terms because they are simple variants of the ones in the list (e.g.: "swimmer" does not appear but "swim" and "swimming" do).

Baseline. In order to know if propagation really affects understanding, we created the baseline in a way that the understanding of c_0 can only come from the prior knowledge of c_0 itself and the prior knowledge of the concepts that can reach c_0 in one hop, and we assume that the relationships between these concepts and c_0 have been read. Therefore, this baseline considers that propagation does not exist. Let $\text{points}: C \rightarrow 2^C$ be the function that calculates the concepts having an edge pointing to the given concept. We can define this baseline $u': C \rightarrow [0, 1]$ as:

$$u'(c_0) = \max\left(\text{pk}(c_0), \frac{\sum_{c_i \in \text{points}(c_0)} \text{pk}(c_i)}{|\text{points}(c_0)|}\right) \tag{12}$$

Notice that this baseline outputs the same value in the original LMCG and in the version in which we remove relationships, as these relationships are not neighbors of c_0 with prior knowledge.

We also created a naïve method in which understanding propagation is calculated based on the distance between the target concept and the concepts with prior knowledge. Let $\text{dist}: C \times C \rightarrow \mathbf{N}$ the function returning the distance in hops between two concepts and $\text{prior}: G \rightarrow 2^C$ be the function that returns all the concepts of a graph with some prior knowledge assigned. Our function $u'': C \rightarrow [0, 1]$ is as follows:

$$u''(c_0) = \max\left(\text{pk}(c_0), \frac{\sum_{c_i \in \text{prior}(G)} \frac{1}{\overline{\text{dist}}(c_0, c_i)}}{|\text{prior}(G)|}\right) \tag{13}$$

4.2 Experimental Results

We collected 540 answers from students, but we invalidated 5 of them because the students answered in English, remaining 535. As we have two evaluators per task, we have 1070 evaluations in total. Agreement between reviewers was measured by using Cohen's kappa with equal weights [30] in the statistical software R. The agreement for the evaluators was $\kappa = 0.68$ in Biology, $\kappa = 0.45$ in Computer Science and $\kappa = 0.28$ in Chemistry, meaning fair to substantial agreement. We observed that, when κ is low, the reason is that one evaluator gives higher scores than the other (average difference in the 5-level likert scale of 0.122 in Biology, 0.489 in CS and 0.985 in Chemistry).

We grouped all the normalized grades to the same question together by taking the average of the scores of all the students. This gives 36 values in total, with $\mu = 0.466$ and $\sigma = 0.088$. We cannot reject that the distribution of these values is normal (Shapiro-Wilk W = 0.947, p-value = 0.108).

We checked for a significant difference between the grades for the original texts ($\mu = 0.527$, $\sigma = 0.081$) and the grades for the texts in which relationships have been cut ($\mu = 0.425$, $\sigma = 0.061$). Student's T test found a significant difference between averages (t = 4.258, p-value = 0.000), while the Fisher's F-test did not find a significant difference of variances (F = 1.726, p-value = 0.270). Significant average differences are also found if we analyze independently for each topic.

The way in which we compare our method to the baseline is through the analysis of correlations with the ground truth. For each result, we calculated Pearson's coefficient r, Spearman's rank coefficient ρ and Kendall's rank coefficient τ. The baseline method without propagation performed quite poorly (r = −0.186, p-value = 0.278, $\rho = -0.129$, p-value = 0.445 and $\tau = -0.081$, p-value = 0.549), not only showing a negative correlation with the ground truth, but also returning p-values bigger than 0.1, so we cannot deny that there may not be any correlation. For the naïve propagation method based on distance, we can find that some correlation coefficients are bigger than 0 while others are not (r = −0.039, p-value = 0.821, $\rho = 0.040$, p-value = 0.734 and $\tau = 0.046$, p-value = 0.784), although with p-values bigger than 0.1 we cannot discard that there is no correlation either.

We tried 4 variants of our method by combining 2 features: equal weights vs. uniqueness-based weights (explained in Sect. 3.5) and using inference rules vs. no inference rules (explained in Sects. 3.2 and 3.3). We found out that all the methods achieve their best performance when relationship understanding is perfect ($p = 1$), although which variant performs the best (equal weights vs. uniqueness-based weights + inference rules) depends on the correlation coefficient we use, as shown in Table 2.

In order to verify whether these methods perform better than the others, we compared pairs of correlations by using Fisher's r-to-z transformation for dependent samples [31, 32] (only available for Pearson's r). Then, we corrected the p-values by

Table 2. Correlations of the variants of our method (rel. understanding probability $p = 1$)

Correlation coefficient	Equal weights	Uniqueness-based weights	Inferences + equal weights	Inferences + uniqueness-based weights
Pearson's r	0.392	0.436	0.304	0.459
(p-value)	(0.018)	(0.008)	(0.071)	(0.049)
Spearman's ρ	0.380	0.366	0.197	0.378
(p-value)	(0.025)	(0.030)	(0.245)	(0.026)
Kendall's τ	0.302	0.279	0.137	0.294
(p-value)	(0.010)	(0.017)	(0.241)	(0.012)

using the Holm-Bonferroni method [33]. Table 3 shows the test for the statistic z and the corrected p-values ($\alpha = 0.1$). All the variants of our method perform better than the baseline without propagation, and 3 of them (equal weights, uniqueness-based weights and uniqueness based weights + inference rules) perform better than the distance-based method. No significant difference occurs between two variants of our method.

Table 3. Differences between correlation pairs (statistic z)

Method	Equal weights	Uniqueness-based weights	Inferences + equal weights	Inferences + uniqueness-based weights
No propagation	−2.858	−3.158	−2.392	−3.316
(p-value)	(0.026)	(0.014)	(0.072)	(0.000)
Distance-based method (p-value)	−2.504 (0.060)	−2.752 (0.033)	−1.930 (0.216)	−2.954 (0,026)
Equal weights		−0.955	1.092	−0.712
(p-value)		(0.618)	(0.618)	(0.618)
Uniqueness weights (p-value)			1.393 (0.574)	−0.294 (0.618)
Inference + equal weights (p-value)				−1.242 (0.618)

As we have seen in the table, the variant with inference rules and uniqueness-based weights performs quite well, while using only inference rules does not outperform the distance-based propagation method. The reason is as follows. Given a concept c_i with $pk(c_i) = 1$, if we remove a relationship nearby, the concept may not be able to propagate its understanding anymore in the original concept graph. However, if we add new relationships by using inference rules, the concept may propagate understanding through them. Figure 3 illustrates this situation.

The problem now is that the amount of new relationships may be high, and if they all have equal weights, they may be propagating most of the understanding of c_i when

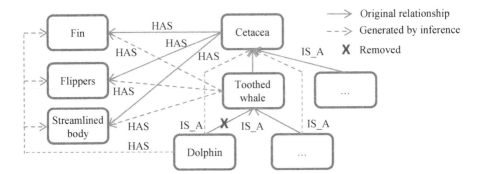

Fig. 3. A hierarchy in which inferred relationships allow propagation of understanding.

they should not propagate that much. Nevertheless, by applying the uniqueness-based weights, we decrease this propagation without removing it completely. This is especially true when there is a large hierarchy of IS_A relationships, as all the ancestors of c_i share most of the relationships that c_i got by inference, so their uniqueness is low.

5 Conclusions

This paper presented a method that allows the estimation of the degree of concept understanding of a student while reading a learning material (text). Our model first reflects the knowledge contained in the material in a semantic network called Learning Material Concept Graph (LMCG). Then, it estimates the understanding by two operations: (1) relationship understanding and (2) concept understanding propagation. The first follows a probabilistic model, and we also considered the addition of inference rules for its calculation. The second is based on the Biased PageRank formula [9]. In order to enhance this formula, we added the notion of prior knowledge and a weighting system to balance the contribution of each concept to the understanding of the others. This system is based on the uniqueness of the relationships of the neighbors of the target concept.

In order to validate our model we performed an experiment with real people in a Japanese crowdsourcing platform [28]. First, we created the ground truth by evaluating their answers to a questionnaire. Then, we proposed a baseline that does not consider propagation of understanding and another in which propagation is calculated based on the distance between the concepts with prior knowledge and the concepts to be evaluated. We also considered four variants of our method: (1) with equal weights, (2) with uniqueness-based weights, (3) with equal weights and inference rules and (4) with uniqueness-based weights and inference rules. Finally, we analyzed the correlation between the ground truth and each model and compared the correlations. The experimental results show that all the variants of our method outperform the baseline with no propagation, suggesting the existence of concept understanding propagation. Moreover, we found that three variants also outperform the distance-based propagation method, and we analyzed why the variant with equal weights and inference rules did not.

6 Future Work

Our future work is the development of a system that registers the prior knowledge and the behavior of each student when they read learning materials on the computer (e.g.: by using mouse tracking), so we can compute individual estimations of their concept understanding. Then we can focus on automatically finding the most suitable materials on the Web, personalizing the search according to each student's concept understanding.

Acknowledgements. This work was supported by JSPS KAKENHI Grant Numbers JP15H01718 and JP26700009.

We would also like to thank Profs. Masatoshi Yoshikawa and Roi Blanco for their inestimable advice to develop this research.

Appendix

In order to prove the convergence of our method, we remind that in case of having an iterative method with transition matrix $\mathbf{M}$, convergence is proven if $\lim_{y \to \infty} \mathbf{M}^y \mathbf{u} = \mathbf{u}$. Equivalently, to grant we will achieve a steady state distribution, we need to ensure that the biggest dominant eigenvalue of $\mathbf{M}$ is 1. In our case, we need to verify $\alpha \mathbf{D} \mathbf{u} + (1 - \alpha) \mathbf{k} = \mathbf{u}$. If we rewrite this equation as $\mathbf{u} = \mathbf{M} \mathbf{u}$, and we let $\mathbf{S}$ be the matrix that verifies $s_{ii} = \mathrm{pk}(c_i)$ and $s_{ij} = 0$ for $i \neq j$, we have that $\mathbf{M} = \alpha \mathbf{D} + (1 - \alpha) \mathbf{S}$. Since it is difficult to prove that the dominant eigenvalue of $\mathbf{M}$ is 1, we will prove that the dominant eigenvalue for $\mathbf{M}^{\mathrm{T}}$ is 1 instead. Then, we can use the Perron-Frobenius theorem, which states that the dominant eigenvalue is the same for $\mathbf{M}$ and $\mathbf{M}^{\mathrm{T}}$. We remember that in the concepts where the prior knowledge had been set, we had established that $\mathrm{rund}(r_{ii}, t) = 1$ and $\mathrm{rund}(r_{ij}, t) = 0$ for all $j \neq i$. By using this, we can see that the dominant eigenvector $\mathbf{u}$ for the matrix $\mathbf{M}^{\mathrm{T}}$ is precisely $\mathbf{k}$, the vector representing prior knowledge and the eigenvalue for that vector is 1.

As in the case of the original PageRank [27], convergence of is only granted if the transition matrix is (1) irreducible and (2) aperiodic. We know that matrices verifying that one diagonal element is non-zero are aperiodic [34]. This is our case because we had set the $\mathrm{pk}(c_i)$ for at least one concept c_i and we also stated that in such case $\mathrm{rund}(r_{ii}, t) = w_{ii} = 1$ for all t. The problem is that the transition matrix is not irreducible because we allowed $\mathrm{rund}(r_{ij}, t) = 0$ for all j in a concept whose prior knowledge has not been set. However, by using the principle "each relationship has its inverse" in Sect. 3.1, we have that if $\mathrm{rund}(r_{ij}, t) = 0$, then $\mathrm{rund}(r_{ji}, t) = 0$ too, so the concept c_i is completely isolated from the rest of the graph. In that case, we can just set $u(c_i, t) = 0$ for all t, and we can remove the concept from the graph, having that the remaining graph is strongly connected and therefore its matrix is irreducible.

References

1. Moodle. https://www.moodle.org. Accessed 15 Jan 2017
2. Dagger, D., Conlan, O., Wade, V.: Fundamental requirements of personalised eLearning development environments. In: World Conference on E-Learning in Corporate, Government, Healthcare, and Higher Education (2005)
3. Kaplan, A.M., Haenlein, M.: Higher education and the digital revolution: about MOOCs, SPOCs, social media, and the Cookie Monster. Bus. Horiz. **59**(4), 441–450 (2016)
4. Marzano, R.J., Kendall, J.S.: The New Taxonomy of Educational Objectives. Corwin Press, Thousand Oaks (2007)
5. Gagné, R.M.: The Conditions of Learning and Theory of Instruction. Holt, Rinehart and Winston, New York (1985)
6. Zentall, T.R., Galizio, M., Critchfied, T.S.: Categorization, concept learning, and behavior analysis: an introduction. J. Exp. Anal. Behav. **78**(3), 237–248 (2002)
7. Piaget, J.: L'equilibration des structures cognitives: Problème central du développement. Presses Universitaires de France (1975)
8. Vygotsky, L.S.: Interaction between learning and development. In: Mind in Society, pp. 79–91. Harvard University Press, Cambridge (1978)
9. Gyöngyi, Z., Garcia-Molina, H., Pedersen, J.: Combating web spam with TrustRank. In: Proceedings of the 30th VLDB Conference, pp. 576–587 (2004)
10. Shahiri, A.M., Husain, W., Rashid, N.A.: A review on predicting student's performance using data mining techniques. In: The Third Information Systems International Conference (2015). Procedia Comput. Sci. **72**, 414–422 (2015)
11. Thakar, P., Mehta, A., Manisha: Performance analysis and prediction in educational data mining: a research travelogue. Int. J. Comput. Appl. **110**(15), 60–68 (2015)
12. Kabakchieva, D.: Predicting student performance by using data mining methods for classification. Cybern. Inf. Technol. **13**(1), 61–71 (2013)
13. Kotsiantis, S., Pierrakeas, C., Pintelas, P.: Prediction of student's performance in distance learning using machine learning techniques. Appl. Artif. Intell. **18**(5), 411–426 (2004)
14. Dekker, G.W., Pechenizkiy, M., Vleeshouwers, J.M.: Predicting students drop out: a case study. In: Proceedings of 2nd International Conference on Educational Data Mining, pp. 41–50 (2009)
15. Corbett, A.T., Anderson, J.R.: Knowledge tracing: modeling the acquisition of procedural knowledge. User Model. User-Adap. Inter. **4**(4), 253–278 (1995)
16. Cen, H., Koedinger, K., Junker, B.: Learning factors analysis – a general method for cognitive model evaluation and improvement. In: Ikeda, M., Ashley, K.D., Chan, T.-W. (eds.) ITS 2006. LNCS, vol. 4053, pp. 164–175. Springer, Heidelberg (2006). doi:10.1007/11774303_17
17. Williams, C., D'Mello, S.: Predicting student knowledge level from domain-independent function and content words. In: Aleven, V., Kay, J., Mostow, J. (eds.) ITS 2010. LNCS, vol. 6095, pp. 62–71. Springer, Heidelberg (2010). doi:10.1007/978-3-642-13437-1_7
18. Fuchs, L.S., Fuchs, D., Hosp, M.K.: Oral reading fluency as an indicator of reading competency: a theoretical, empirical and historical analysis. Sci. Stud. Read. **5**(3), 239–256 (2001)
19. Copeland, L., Gedeon, T., Mendis, S.: Predicting reading comprehension scores from eye movements using artificial neural networks and fuzzy output error. Artif. Intell. Res. **3**(3), 35–48 (2014)
20. Sowa, J.F.: Semantic networks. In: Shapiro, S.C. (ed.) Encyclopedia of Artificial Intelligence (1987)

21. Sowa, J.F.: Conceptual graphs for a data base interface. IBM J. Res. Dev. **20**(4), 336–357 (1976)
22. Prediger, S.: Simple concept graphs: a logic approach. In: Mugnier, M.-L., Chein, M. (eds.) ICCS-ConceptStruct 1998. LNCS, vol. 1453, pp. 225–239. Springer, Heidelberg (1998). doi:10.1007/BFb0054917
23. Van der Riet, R.P., Meersman, R.A.: Linguistic Instruments in Knowledge Engineering. Imprint Elsevier Science Ltd., New York (1992)
24. Mesquita, F., Schmidek, J., Barbosa, D.: Effectiveness and efficiency of open relation extraction. In: Proceedings of the 2013 Conference on Empirical Methods in Natural Language Processing, pp. 447–457 (2013)
25. Atzeni, P., Parker Jr., D.S.: Set containment inference and syllogisms. Theor. Comput. Sci. **62**(1–2), 39–65 (1988)
26. Golub, G.H., Van Loan, C.F.: Matrix Computations. The Johns Hopkins University Press, Baltimore (1996)
27. Page, L., Brin, S., Motwani, R., Winograd, T.: The PageRank citation ranking: bringing order to the web. Technical report. Stanford InfoLab (1999)
28. Lancers. http://www.lancers.jp. Accessed 09 Jan 2017
29. Word frequency data. http://www.wordfrequency.info. Accessed 31 Jan 2017
30. Cohen, J.: Weighted kappa: nominal scale agreement with provision for scaled disagreement or partial credit. Psychol. Bull. **70**(4), 213–220 (1968)
31. Lenhard, W., Lenhard, A.: Hypothesis Tests for Comparing Correlations (2014). https://www.psychometrica.de/correlation.html. Accessed 15 Mar 2017
32. Eid, M., Gollwitzer, M., Schmitt, M.: Statistik und Forschungsmethoden Lehrbuch. Beltz, Weinheim (2011). (in German)
33. Holm, S.: A simple sequentially rejective multiple test procedure. Scand. J. Stat. **6**(2), 65–70 (1979)
34. Meyer, C.D.: Matrix Analysis and Applied Linear Algebra. SIAM, Philadelphia (2000). ISBN 0-89871-454-0

Seeds Buffering for Information Spreading Processes

Jarosław Jankowski[1]([envelope]), Piotr Bródka[2], Radosław Michalski[2],
and Przemysław Kazienko[2]

[1] Faculty of Computer Science for Information Technology,
West Pomeranian University of Technology, Szczecin, Poland
jjankowski@wi.zut.edu.pl
[2] Department of Computational Intelligence,
Wrocław University of Science and Technology, Wrocław, Poland
{piotr.brodka,radoslaw.michalski,kazienko}@pwr.edu.pl

Abstract. Seeding strategies for influence maximization in social networks have been studied for more than a decade. They have mainly relied on the activation of all resources (seeds) simultaneously in the beginning; yet, it has been shown that sequential seeding strategies are commonly better. This research focuses on studying sequential seeding with buffering, which is an extension to basic sequential seeding concept. The proposed method avoids choosing nodes that will be activated through the natural diffusion process, which is leading to better use of the budget for activating seed nodes in the social influence process. This approach was compared with sequential seeding without buffering and single stage seeding. The results on both real and artificial social networks confirm that the buffer-based consecutive seeding is a good trade-off between the final coverage and the time to reach it. It performs significantly better than its rivals for a fixed budget. The gain is obtained by dynamic rankings and the ability to detect network areas with nodes that are not yet activated and have high potential of activating their neighbours.

Keywords: Social network · Social network analysis · Spread of influence · Diffusion · Seed selection · Sequential seeding

1 Introduction

The growing complexity of problems which need to be solved daily is leading to increasingly complicated decision processes. In order to reduce risk and uncertainty, some decisions are naturally divided into a sequence of less complicated component decisions. Even though the decision can be taken and implemented immediately, [9,19], it is not always the most efficient strategy from the perspective of the final outcome, especially assuming that the process at hand bears some uncertainty. As an alternative, sequential analysis and decisions where introduced by Wald [31] and extended later [3,29]. Lower risk is usually assigned to series of many smaller decisions. As an outcome, dividing the decision or activity

© Springer International Publishing AG 2017
G.L. Ciampaglia et al. (Eds.): SocInfo 2017, Part I, LNCS 10539, pp. 628–641, 2017.
DOI: 10.1007/978-3-319-67217-5_37

into smaller chunks can be more profitable compared to the decisions that are taken immediately. In terms of acquiring knowledge and reducing risk, instead of using partial knowledge in the first stage, the strategy that performs better in many cases is gathering more knowledge about the nature of the process during its runtime, and using that knowledge in future decision-making. The same applies to marketing [30], cognitive science [14], medicine, especially for vaccination strategies [13,26], and the sequential nature of the process is also found in nature; for instance, in the way viral infections develop [4].

In this project, we investigate two seeding strategies built upon sequential seeding, which were initially proposed in [7]: (i) *sequential seeding with revival* and (ii) *sequential seeding with buffering*. Both are suited for the social influence maximisation problem [10], which was extended in various directions [18,21]. They are based on an independent cascades model and the concept of dynamic seed allocation, in which seeds are not used until the natural diffusion process stops. Yet, they differ on how the seeds are activated after the diffusion terminates. The proposed strategies are compared with typical single stage seeding when all seeds are used in the first stage, as in most typical seeding strategies [9–11,19]. The main goal of the work is to verify the performance of the proposed approach for different parameters related to network structures and characteristics of diffusion processes. The initial research on sequential seeding showed that the same number of seeds activated over time offers better results, i.e. a larger final coverage, compared to the single stage seeding [7], so the natural research question is whether there is any chance to outperform it by introducing some novel features. In this study, we carried out detailed research on better understanding this phenomenon, with the verification of several strategies that expand a typical sequential seeding strategy, which is using many parameters of diffusion processes.

2   Conceptual Framework

Earlier research showed a better outcome of the sequential seeding, compared to a single stage seeding, due to better usage of potential of natural diffusion processes. In this section, we further discuss methods for better exploitation of sequential seeding. Results from the single stage seeding (SS) are treated as a reference for evaluation of performance of sequential seeding. In the first stage, n initial seeds are selected with the use of a seed selection strategy, e.g., based on the structural characteristics of nodes like the degree, closeness, etc. The diffusion process starts and continues without any additional support, until it naturally stops at the time T_{SS}, (see Fig. 1. Its coverage is measured by a percentage of the naturally activated nodes in relation to all nodes in the network, and represented by C_{SS}. In the proposed generic sequential approach, splitting the seeds among several stages takes place in a form of sequence of seeds, which are used in several consecutive stages of the process [7]. The selection of seeds in each step is based on the ranks built using static measures, which were computed once before the process begins. The next evaluated approach is based on the highest

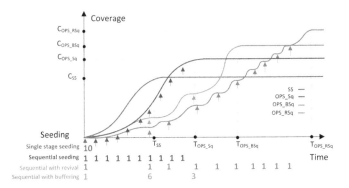

Fig. 1. Macroscopic view of diffusion process with various seeding strategies applied: single stage seeding SS, sequential seeding with one seed per stage activated OPS_Sq, sequential seeding with revival OPS_RSq and with buffering OPS_BSq. Only natural activations are contributing to the coverage.

decomposition of the seeding budget over time, and by activating a single node per stage (OPS_Sq).

The OPS_Sq approach is not dependent on the process characteristics and it leaves room for improvement, because the allocation of additional seeds takes place, even when natural diffusion processes are characterised with high dynamics. In order to use acquired knowledge about this dynamics, a sequential strategy with a revival mode is proposed, and this is named OPS_RSq. Additional seeding is used only when the diffusion process stops. In this approach, when natural activations are observed, additional seeds are not used. The proposed approach extends the total period of seeding because the number of seeds used to improve dynamics is the same as the ones present in generic strategies, and additional seeding is postponed to other periods if no further natural activations are detected. Here, only one seed is used per stage. Due to specifics of an independent cascades model, each node has only one chance to activate neighbours. Then, if the natural process stops, it will not be re-initiated in a natural way during future stages, so the only way to continue activations is by using additional seeding.

The second proposed method that extends the capabilities of sequential seeding is *sequential seeding with buffering* - OPS_BSq. Here, unlike with sequential seeding, if the activation process unfolds naturally and no additional seeding is performed. Yet, i for each stage that didnt require any seeding, a virtual counter increases the value of the amount of seeds which will be activated after the natural activation plateau is reached. If so, the number of seeds n which is equal to the value of this counter is activated and the counter is reset. All four seeding methods are depicted in Fig. 1 and the approaches which were based on sequential seeding are summarized in Table 1.

Table 1. Sequential seeding strategies

OPS_Sq	One per stage generic sequential seeding based on atomic decomposition with the one per stage seed used in each step of simulations and the length of sequence equals the number of seeds used
OPS_RSq	One per stage seeding with revival mode; an additional seed is used only when the natural diffusion process finishes
OPS_BSq	One per stage seeding with buffering mode where additional seeds are collected in the buffer while natural processes continues; the seeds from the buffer are used after the natural diffusion process stops

3 Related Work

The original influence maximization problem [10] considered static social networks, and researchers followed that path when proposing new algorithms for tackling it. Moreover, they focused on single stage seeding, i.e., the best allocation of the budget assuming its immediate spending [20] without any further support. However, in many realistic scenarios, this is not the only way of managing the budget and recent studies started to investigate how distributing a budget over time influences the outcome of the process. Starting with two-stage stochastic models [27] through more scalable approaches [6], it was shown that this research direction has a potential that was further explored in the area of social influence [28,34]. The most recent study [7] proposed sequential seeding as being a more effective way to allocate the budget, while showing its advantages over a single stage seeding in many network configurations. The potential of multi-period spraying algorithm for routing in delay-tolerant networks was also discussed [2]. Apart from that, some authors noticed the benefit of omitting the nodes that will be activated due to the natural diffusion process. As a result they proposed methods that avoid choosing as a new seed either a node that is a neighbour of the already chosen seed, [12,35], or a node that is in a local cluster that already contains another seed, which also reflects the observation on how information spreads across clusters [8]. In this assignment, we investigate sequential seeding [7] in detail, so as to answer the question about the extent to which this approach provides a better solution, compared to a single stage seeding.

4 Experimental Setting

Experimental research was conducted, using agent-based simulations within twenty networks, and including eleven real networks (N1 [22], N2 [22], N3 [24], N4 [22], N5 [1], N6 [33], N7 [23], N8 [25], N9 [17], N10 [16], N11 [15]) and nine artificially generated networks following the Watts-Strogatz and Barabsi-Albert models (N12-N20); these were done according to the specifications presented in Table 2. Networks were generated with the use of various parameters. For

Watts-Strogats model Parameter 1 represents the neighbourhood within which the vertices of the lattice will be connected and Parameter 2 represents rewiring probability. In the case of the Barabasi-Albert model, Parameter 1 represents the number of edges to be included in each time step and Parameter 2 shows the power of the preferential attachment.

Table 2. Specification of synthetic networks N12–N20

ID	Network model	Param. 1	Param. 2	Nodes	Edges
N12	Watts-Strogatz	nei = 1	r = 0.05	10,000	20,000
N13	Watts-Strogatz	nei = 2	r = 0.05	10,000	60,000
N14	Watts-Strogatz	nei = 3	r = 0.05	10,000	120,000
N15	Watts-Strogatz	nei = 2	r = 0.10	10,000	60,000
N16	Watts-Strogatz	nei = 2	r = 0.30	10,000	60,000
N17	Watts-Strogatz	nei = 2	r = 0.50	10,000	60,000
N18	Barabasi-Albert	m = 2	p = 0.50	10,000	19,997
N19	Barabasi-Albert	m = 4	p = 0.50	10,000	39,990
N20	Barabasi-Albert	m = 8	p = 0.50	10,000	79,964

The independent cascades model (IC) [10] was used for each edge (a, b), with the propagation probability $PP(a, b)$ that node a activates node b in the step $t + 1$, with the condition that node a was activated in the time t [32].

The main reason for the selection of IC model is that in the IC model, a single seed can induce diffusion and even a cascade, while in the linear threshold model [5], small seeds packages would not have any effect.

5   Results

5.1   Sequential Seeding with Revival and Buffering

Results achieved in sequential seeding were compared to the single stage seeding (SS) in the same conditions, i.e., for the same network and its parameters, such as propagation probability, seeding percentage and seed selection strategy based on a random selection (R), the degree (D), the second-level degree (D2), the closeness (CL), the clustering coefficient (CC) or the PageRank (PR) across twenty different networks. Reference values for comparison are based on the coverage achieved for single stage seeding (C_{SS}) and the duration of the single stage process representing the stage when the T_{SS} is achieved. Experiments showed that sequential seeding was almost always better than single stage seeding with the same parameters. An example of s simulation case is presented in Fig. 2.

Results for all networks, strategies and parameters showed that, in 91.94% of simulation cases, OPS_Sq delivered better results than single stage seeding.

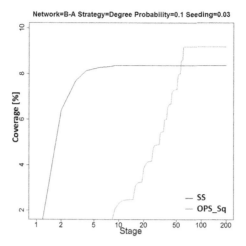

Fig. 2. Longer duration of sequential seeding with higher coverage

Even though the performance was dependent on the network characteristics and parameters of the process and the strategy used, the sequential seeding supported the diffusion in most cases. The improvement can even exceed 50% with the use of the same number of seeds, just like in single stage seeding. An average reach of diffusion processes based on the OPS_Sq with statistical significance ($p < 2.2e^{-16}$) achieved 8.43% better results than using the SS approach with the same conditions based on Wilcoxon signed-rank test.

The analysis of OPS_Sq showed that sequential seeding outperforms single stage seeding in most cases, and the performance of proposed methods is dependent on parameters of the diffusion process and network characteristics. Experiments were performed for a wide range of networks and parameters, including a very low performance, i.e., the propagation probability PP = 0.01 or seeding percentage 1% with a low number of activations and very difficult diffusion processes, no matter what strategy is applied. An opposite situation is observed within the networks, with a high degree and propagation probability PP = 0.25 and SP = 5%. Under these conditions, most strategies were performing very well, with diffusion processes leading to 100% activated nodes in a very short time, and they left a very small margin for improvements. Taking into account the above conditions, an average 8.43% or 6% of increase shows substantial growth, with much better results for conditions such as a higher activation probability. A substantial increase was obtained for degree -based strategies for both one (D) and second level degree (D2), and a propagation probability higher than 0.05.

For networks N2, N4, N10 and N19, a high performance average reaching higher 30% than in single stage seeding was observed for both sequential strategies, based on D and D2 selection, see Table 3 containing results compared with single stage seeding for each network. Low performance was observed for networks N12, N14, and at least in three strategies for networks N6, N8; however, it was still above 10% with only four cases with an increase which was smaller than 5% (N12, N14).

The first reason why sequential seeding (including its modifications outperforms single stage seeding is the fact that, in the case of sequential seeding, initial seeds used in a single stage approach are activated by a natural process, due to their high positions in the network, and they dont require seeding to be activated. When taking into account the seeds selected in the single stage seeding process, more than 60% of them can be activated in natural processes when sequential seeding is applied. Saved seeds can be used for activation of other nodes and unexplored segments of the network. This refers mostly to revival mode strategies, where the phenomena based on using natural diffusion processes is most visible, with additional seeding performed only when natural activations are stopped.

Table 3. Results for OPS_Sq based on D and D2 strategies with PP $= 0.1$ and SP $= 0.05$

Strategy	N1	N2	N3	N4	N5
OPS_Sq D	124.81	138.66	111.82	135.87	110.36
OPS_Sq D2	120.66	149.65	113.06	145.35	109.99
Strategy	N6	N7	N8	N9	N10
OPS_Sq D	107.47	126.21	113.05	109.05	130.22
OPS_Sq D2	113.89	137.28	111.33	114.01	145.41
Strategy	N11	N12	N13	N14	N15
OPS_Sq D	112.29	102.94	114.67	106.45	116.16
OPS_Sq D2	112.49	106.15	115.37	106.15	117.69
Strategy	N16	N17	N18	N19	N20
OPS_Sq D	119.59	114.94	114.44	130.78	114.28
OPS_Sq D2	118.84	119.24	119.33	130.59	114.60

In the next stage, an approach based on seeding with revival mode (with the presence of additional seeding) was used, and diffusion processes stops were observed. Results for compared strategies with the revival model showed statistical differences between OPS_Sq vs OPS_RSq with $p < 2.2e-16$. Results showed that the revival mode OPS_RSq achieved a 5.34% better reach than OPS_Sq for all cases linked to static rankings. In 2319 cases (64.42%), OPS_RSq delivered better results than OPS_Sq. For OPS_RSq, the best performance above median 4.66% was observed for networks N4, N5, N7, N8, N9, N10, N13, N14, N16, and N20; when compared to the non-revival mode, network parameters were not statistically significant. The results showed that, for networks with a higher degree, the performance of the revival mode was better. Diffusion processes within networks with a higher degree have higher dynamics and allocation of additional seeds when natural processes are continued is resulting in the waste of available resources. Results analysed for seeding percentages 1%, 2%, 3%, 4%, 5% showed an increase of OPS_RSq with values of 11.79%, 7.42%, 3.42%, 3.40%, 2.30%, and the relation between the seeding performance and revival mode showed the highest increase of performance for small proportion of seeds selected ($SP = 1\%$). While most of the analysis is performed on aggregated data obtained from all cases, Fig. 3 shows example results from a simulation performed within the network N2, with the propagation probability PP = 0.1 and seed selection strategy D2, and 5% of the initial selected seeds s. The revival mode is achieving better results, but the process is longer and dynamics are smaller than what is observed from the 75th stage of simulation.

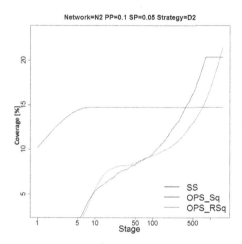

Fig. 3. Revival mode results within network N2 with PP = 0.1 and SP = 5% based on S = D2

The introduced approach to the revival mode increased the reach of processes, but the duration was increased as well, due to the delay of each additional seeding, until diffusion processes stopped. Results for compared strategies with the Wilcoxon signed rank and revival mode showed statistical differences between OPS_Sq vs. OPS_RSq and $p = 4.40e^{-09}$). The buffered mode OPS_BSq achieved 3.2% increase of reach when compared to OPS_Sq, and it represented 60% of value achieved with the revival mode (5.34%). The buffering mode, when compared to the revival mode without buffering, makes it possible to shorten the duration of processes achieved better results than in the case of generic sequential seeding. The average duration of OPS_BSq was only 21.92% longer than OPS_Sq, while the duration of OPS_RSq was 71.31% longer. Figure 4a illustrates the duration of OPS_BSq and OPS_RSq in relation to generic OPS_Sq approach.

The buffered approach showed an average increase when compared to OPS_Sq for propagation probabilities 0.01, 0.05, 0.1, 0.15, 0.2, 0.25 as follows:

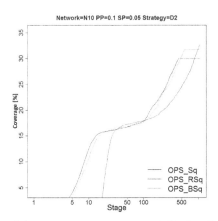

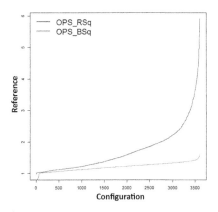

(a) Duration of difussion processes for OPS_BSq and OPS_RSq compared with generic OPS_Sq

(b) Strategies OPS_BSq and OPS_RSq compared with sequential seeding for network N10 with $PP = 0.1$, strategy D2 and $SP = 0.05$

Fig. 4. Comparison of seeding strategies

8.48%, 4.24%, 3.22%, 4.21%, 2.54% and 0.00%, with the best result being for lowest propagation probabilities. When compared to the revival mode, the buffering mode delivered improvements for PP = 0.01 with a 2.61% increase, while for probabilities 0.05, 0.1, 0.15, 0.2, 0.25, buffering results were worse. Average results from all propagation probabilities showed slightly better results than in the revival mode OPS_RSq for 6 networks: N1, N6, N12, N16, N17 and N15. Figure 4b shows an example OPS_BSq and OPS_RSq results from network N10 with the PP = 0.1 strategy D2 and SP = 0.05 with higher reach achieved for OPS_RSq and a lower reach of OPS_BSq, but with a shorter duration proposes.

Sequential strategies delivered better results than the single stage approach in terms of reach; however, the longer duration of diffusion processes is a disadvantage for the higher reach. It is a result of the smaller amount of seeds used in the first stages of processes and lower initial dynamics, due to spreading seeds over several periods of time. In an analysis presented in this section, the stage T_{SS} was used as a reference, where the maximal number of activations is achieved using a single stage approach. The cases in Fig. 5 show differences among generics per stage seeding strategy, as well as its extensions with the revival and buffering modes. The duration of one per stage seeding was increased by the revival mode, but cases from the buffering mode are concentrated between OPS_Sq and OPS_RSq.

5.2   Trade-Off Between the Coverage and Duration of the Process

The potential of sequential seeding can be evaluated as a trade-off between coverage and duration. The last stage of analysis includes connected effects of

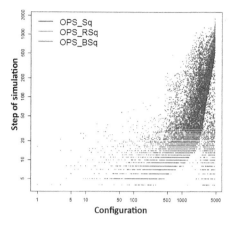

Fig. 5. Duration of one per stage strategies OPS_Sq, OPS_RSq and OPS_BSq

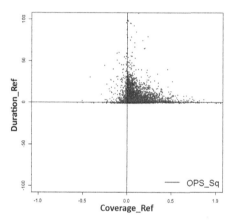

Fig. 6. Distribution of cases in generic sequential seeding approach OPS_Sq

increased coverage and longer duration of the diffusion processes with the reference to a single stage seeding, with integrated results for the same PP, SP, N and S. The distribution of reference values for OPS_Sq for all used strategies shows visual characteristics of obtained results in Fig. 6. The X axis represents the distance from the single stage reach, which was computed with the formula $Coverage_{Ref} = (Coverage_{Sq} - Coverage_{SS})/Coverage_{SS}$. Negative values represent cases with worse results than in a single stage seeding. Here, the Y axis is representing the distance between the stage when a maximal value was achieved according to the formula $Duration\_Ref = (Duration\_Sq - Duration\_SS)/Duration\_SS$. Each figure includes 3,600 cases for each sequential strategy. References for OPS_Sq are characterized by a bigger dispersion on the Y axis, including more cases with high values which are achieved in the X axis.

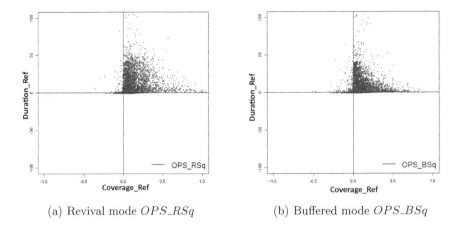

(a) Revival mode OPS_RSq (b) Buffered mode OPS_BSq

Fig. 7. Distribution of cases

The effect of the revival mode for OPS_RSq is presented in Fig. 7a with a growing dispersion and longer sequences, but with a shift that was observed on the X axis, and geared towards better reach. The reach and duration of diffusion processes and the relation between them in reference to single stage seeding were connected with results of a simulation with the same parameters. Cases with negative values on the X axis represent worse results in terms of reach than with single stage seeding. Cases with negative values on the Y-axis represent processes with SS_SS, which are achieved faster than in a single stage approach. Results for the buffered mode are presented in Fig. 7b. Buffered mode resulted in dispersion between OPS_Sq and OPS_RSq in terms of X and Y distribution.

Distribution of cases with used OPS_Sq shows a bigger dispersion and longer duration, especially for cases with low X values. Implementation of revival mode resulted in an increased number of cases, with a longer duration and an accompanied increase of reach.

6   Conclusions

The results revealed that the best result can be achieved by means of one per stage method with the revival mode, and it also lasts the longest. This observation is valid for all tested ranking methods: degree, second level degree, closeness, clustering coefficient and page rank If the process time span is limited, even from the duration of the single stage approach (the shortest possible), the length of the sequence may have to be reduced and the buffer-based consecutive seeding appears to be a good solution. The results show the potential of the buffering mode as being a suitable compromise, which enables us to extend coverage without high increase in duration. During the experiments, results from short sequences were compared with the longest sequences based on revival concepts.

The sequential seeding approaches with the longer duration usually yield better results in terms of the number of activated nodes, which is the final coverage. Hence, the trade-off between time and reach depends on individual preferences and the role of process coverage and duration in a given application domain. Further research will focus on various modifications of the buffering mode, as well as on other approaches for duration shortening. The general direction is leading towards finding clear dependencies between the length of sequences and the final coverage for different networks and strategies.

Acknowledgments. This work was partially supported by Wrocław University of Science and Technology statutory funds (PB) and by the National Science Centre, Poland, project nos. 2015/17/D/ST6/04046 (RM), 2016/21/B/ST6/01463 (PK), 2013/09/B/ST6/02317 and 2016/21/B/HS4/01562 (JJ); by European Union's Horizon 2020 research and innovation programme under the Marie Skłodowska-Curie grant no. 691152 (RENOIR); by the Polish Ministry of Science and Higher Education fund for supporting internationally co-financed projects in 2016–2019, no. 3628/H2020/2016/2.

References

1. Adamic, L.A., Glance, N.: The political blogosphere and the 2004 US election: divided they blog. In: Proceedings of the 3rd International Workshop on Link discovery, pp. 36–43. ACM (2005)
2. Bulut, E., Wang, Z., Szymanski, B.: Cost-effective multiperiod spraying for routing in delay-tolerant networks. IEEE/ACM Trans. Netw. **18**(5), 1530–1543 (2010)
3. Ghosh, B.K., Sen, P.K. (eds.): Handbook of sequential analysis. In: Statistics, Textbooks and Monographs. Marcel Dekker, New York (1991)
4. Jakab, G.J.: Sequential virus infections, bacterial superinfections, and fibrogenesis. Am. Rev. Respir. Dis. **142**(2), 374–9 (1990)
5. Granovetter, M.: Threshold models of collective behavior. Am. J. Sociol. **83**(6), 1420–1443 (1978)
6. Horel, T., Singer, Y.: Scalable methods for adaptively seeding a social network. In: Proceedings of the 24th International Conference on World Wide Web, pp. 441–451. ACM (2015)
7. Jankowski, J., Bródka, P., Kazienko, P., Szymanski, B., Michalski, R., Kajdanowicz, T.: Balancing speed and coverage by sequential seeding in complex networks. arXiv preprint (2016). arXiv:1609.07526
8. Jankowski, J., Kozielski, M., Filipowski, W., Michalski, R.: The diffusion of viral content in multi-layered social networks. In: Bădică, C., Nguyen, N.T., Brezovan, M. (eds.) ICCCI 2013. LNCS, vol. 8083, pp. 30–39. Springer, Heidelberg (2013). doi:10.1007/978-3-642-40495-5_4
9. Jankowski, J., Michalski, R., Kazienko, P.: Compensatory seeding in networks with varying availability of nodes. In: The 2013 IEEE/ACM International Conference on Advances in Social Networks Analysis and Mining - ASONAM 2013, pp. 1242–1249. IEEE (2013)
10. Kempe, D., Kleinberg, J., Tardos, E.: Maximizing the spread of influence through a social network. In: Proceedings of the Ninth ACM SIGKDD International Conference on Knowledge Discovery and Data Mining, KDD 2003, pp. 137–146. ACM, New York (2003)

11. Kempe, D., Kleinberg, J.M., Tardos, É.: Maximizing the spread of influence through a social network. Theory Comput. **11**(4), 105–147 (2015)
12. Kitsak, M., Gallos, L.K., Havlin, S., Liljeros, F., Muchnik, L., Stanley, H.E., Makse, H.A.: Identification of influential spreaders in complex networks. Nat. Phys. **6**(11), 888–893 (2010)
13. Kumar, A., Lifson, J.D., Li, Z., Jia, F., Mukherjee, S., Adany, I., Liu, Z., Piatak, M., Sheffer, D., McClure, H.M., Narayan, O.: Sequential immunization of macaques with two differentially attenuated vaccines induced long-term virus-specific immune responses and conferred protection against AIDS caused by heterologous simian human immunodeficiency virus (shiv89.6p). Virology **279**(1), 241–256 (2001)
14. de Lange, F.P., Jensen, O., Dehaene, S.: Accumulation of evidence during sequential decision making: the importance of top-down factors. J. Neurosci.: Off. J. Soc. Neurosci. **30**(2), 731–738 (2010)
15. Leskovec, J., Huttenlocher, D., Kleinberg, J.: Signed networks in social media. In: Proceedings of the SIGCHI conference on human factors in computing systems, pp. 1361–1370. ACM (2010)
16. Leskovec, J., Kleinberg, J., Faloutsos, C.: Graph evolution: densification and shrinking diameters. ACM Trans. Knowl. Discov. Data (TKDD) **1**(1), 2 (2007)
17. Leskovec, J., Mcauley, J.J.: Learning to discover social circles in ego networks. In: Advances in Neural Information Processing Systems, pp. 539–547 (2012)
18. Liu-Thompkins, Y.: Seeding viral content : the role of message and network factors (2012)
19. Michalski, R., Kajdanowicz, T., Bródka, P., Kazienko, P.: Seed selection for spread of influence in social networks: temporal vs. static approach. New Gener. Comput. **32**(3–4), 213–235 (2014)
20. Michalski, R., Kazienko, P.: Maximizing social influence in real-world networks—the state of the art and current challenges. In: Król, D., Fay, D., Gabryś, B. (eds.) Propagation Phenomena in Real World Networks. ISRL, vol. 85, pp. 329–359. Springer, Cham (2015). doi:10.1007/978-3-319-15916-4_14
21. Morone, F., Makse, H.A.: Influence maximization in complex networks through optimal percolation. Nature **524**(7563), 65–68 (2015)
22. Newman, M.E.: The structure of scientific collaboration networks. Proc. Nat. Acad. Sci. **98**(2), 404–409 (2001)
23. Newman, M.E.: Finding community structure in networks using the eigenvectors of matrices. Phys. Rev. E **74**(3), 036104 (2006)
24. Opsahl, T.: Triadic closure in two-mode networks: Redefining the global and local clustering coefficients. Soc. Netw. **35**(2), 159–167 (2013)
25. Opsahl, T., Panzarasa, P.: Clustering in weighted networks. Soc. Netw. **31**(2), 155–163 (2009)
26. Price, W.H.: Sequential immunization as a vaccination procedure against dengue viruses. Am. J. Epidemiol. **88**(3), 392–397 (1968)
27. Seeman, L., Singer, Y.: Adaptive seeding in social networks. In: 2013 IEEE 54th Annual Symposium on Foundations of Computer Science (FOCS), pp. 459–468. IEEE (2013)
28. Sela, A., Ben-Gal, I., Pentland, A., Shmueli, E.: Improving information spread through a scheduled seeding approach. In: The international conference on Advances in Social Network Analysis and Mining 2015 (2015)
29. Siegmund, D.: Sequential Analysis : Tests and Confidence Intervals. Springer Series in Statistics. Springer-Verlag, New York (1985)

30. Sridhar, S., Mantrala, M.K., Naik, P.A., Thorson, E.: Dynamic marketing budgeting for platform firms: theory, evidence, and application. J. Mark. Res. **48**(6), 929–943 (2011)
31. Wald, A.: Sequential Analysis. Wiley, Hoboken (1947)
32. Wang, C., Chen, W., Wang, Y.: Scalable influence maximization for independent cascade model in large-scale social networks. Data Min. Knowl. Discov. **25**(3), 545–576 (2012)
33. Watts, D.J., Strogatz, S.H.: Collective dynamics of small-worldnetworks. Nature **393**(6684), 440–442 (1998)
34. Zhang, H., Procaccia, A.D., Vorobeychik, Y.: Dynamic influence maximization under increasing returns to scale. In: Proceedings of the 2015 International Conference on Autonomous Agents and Multiagent Systems, pp. 949–957. International Foundation for Autonomous Agents and Multiagent Systems (2015)
35. Zhang, J.X., Duan-Bing Chen, Q.D., Zhao, Z.D.: Identifying a set of influential spreaders in complex networks. Sci. Rep. 6 (2016)

Author Index

Abbar, Sofiane II-74
Abisheva, Adiya II-301
Agathangelou, Pantelis I-162
Ahmad, Rehan II-101
Aker, Ahmet II-53
Aladhadh, Suliman II-316
Alani, Harith I-289
Aldarbesti, Hassan II-159
Alexandrov, Dimitar I-91
Alfifi, Majid I-218
Almeida, Virgilio I-341
An, Jisun I-124, II-159
Anai, Hirokazu II-419
Aragón, Pablo II-277, II-355
Araújo, Camila Souza I-341
Aroyo, Lora II-288
Atas, Müslüm II-368
Auxier, Brooke I-377

Bader, Robin II-458
Baggag, Abdelkader II-74
Banea, Carmen I-41
Baquerizo, Gabriela II-265
Barandiaran, Xabier E. II-277
Baratchi, Mitra II-443
Baronchelli, Andrea I-536
Barrat, Alain I-536
Bastas, Nikolaos II-121
Bauer, Travis L. I-257
Beelen, Kaspar II-288
Bengtsson, Linus II-14
Berger, Ryan I-440
Berti-Equille, Laure II-74
Bignotti, Enrico II-3
Binns, Reuben II-405
Bishop, Felicity I-591
Bison, Ivano II-3
Bjelland, Johannes II-14, II-41
Blekanov, Ivan S. I-360
Bodrunova, Svetlana S. I-360
Bontcheva, Kalina II-53
Boyd, Ryan L. I-323
Bracamonte, Vanessa II-347
Braesemann, Fabian II-31

Brian Pickering, J. II-491
Bródka, Piotr I-628
Brugman, Tristan II-443

Calleja-López, Antonio II-277
Carlson, Natalie A. I-3
Carro, Adrián I-17
Casiraghi, Giona II-111
Cattuto, Ciro I-536
Caverlee, James I-218
Cech, Florian II-527
Chan, Chi Ling I-499
Chandok, Srishti II-477
Chawla, Sanjay II-74
Chen, Zhouhan II-501
Choi, Jinho D. I-201

Daras, Petros II-121
Darwish, Kareem I-91, I-143
Davies, Todd I-499
Del Rio Chanona, R. Maria I-17
Dewan, Prateek II-477
Dickinson, Tom I-289
Doneda, Danilo I-341
Dubov, Mikhail II-391

Eguchi, Koji I-75
Elgesem, Dag I-178

Farmer, J. Doyne I-17
Farrahi, Katayoun II-89
Farzan, Rosta I-572
Felfernig, Alexander II-368
Feng, Yang I-440
Fernandez, Miriam I-289
Fisher, Andrew N. I-257

Gallego, Helena II-355
Garcia, David II-301
Gerla, Mario II-257
Giunchiglia, Fausto II-3
Gobbi, Elisa II-3
Golbeck, Jennifer I-377, II-469
Gómez, Vicenç II-277, II-355

Gribov, Alex   II-391
Gronas, Mikhail   II-391
Gunopulos, Dimitrios   I-162
Guo, Yike   II-513
Gupta, Nalin   II-477

Han, Jinyoung   II-257
Hartung, Pedro   I-341
Heijenk, Geert   II-443
Heinrich, Torsten   I-17
Hexter, Lindsay   I-201
Heydari, Babak   I-59
Hong, Zhe   I-440
Hooi, Bryan   I-499

Interdonato, Roberto   I-552
Iwao, Tadashige   II-419

Jahani, Eaman   II-14, II-41
Jain, Paridhi   II-477
Jankowski, Jarosław   I-628
Jarvis, Stephen   II-221
Jin, Hongshan   I-457
Joglekar, Sagar   I-237
Jurafsky, Dan   II-537
Jurgens, David   I-473, II-537

Kadar, Cristina   I-521, II-458
Kaltenbrunner, Andreas   II-277, II-355
Kamiyama, Naoyuki   II-419
Katakis, Ioannis   I-162
Kato, Makoto P.   I-611
Kaushal, Rishabh   II-477
Kazienko, Przemysław   I-628
Kim, Seungbae   II-257
Kira, Akifumi   II-419
Kolliakou, Anna   II-53
Koltcov, Sergei   II-431
Koltsova, Olessia   II-431
Kuhn, Tobias   II-288
Kuleva, Margarita   I-31
Kulshreshtha, Saurabh   II-391
Kumaraguru, Ponnurangam   II-477
Kunegis, Jérôme   I-277
Kwak, Haewoon   I-124, II-159

Lahiri, Shibamouli   I-41
Lai, Justin   I-499
Laniado, David   II-355

Lee, Roy Ka-Wei   II-245
Lepri, Bruno   I-536
Lertvittayakumjorn, Piyawat   II-513
Li, Cheng   II-141
Liakata, Maria   I-109, II-53, II-378
Litvinenko, Anna A.   I-360
Liu, Yue   II-513
Lo, David   I-426, II-245
López, Claudia   I-572
López-García, Rafael   I-611
Luo, Jiebo   I-409, I-440, II-65

Magdy, Walid   I-143
Maglevanaya, Daria   I-31
Magno, Gabriel   I-341
Marmion, Vincent   I-591
McCorriston, James   I-473
Meira Jr., Wagner   I-341
Mejova, Yelena   I-91
Mendieta, Jonathan   II-265
Mi, Hong   II-513
Michalski, Radosław   I-628
Mihalcea, Rada   I-41, I-323
Millard, David E.   I-591
Milne, Antony   II-89
Monterde, Arnau   II-277
Moro, Esteban   II-41
Mosleh, Mohsen   I-59
Murata, Tsuyoshi   I-75

Nakov, Preslav   I-91
Nanumyan, Vahan   II-111
Nguyen, Tu Ngoc   II-141
Nicolaou, Mihalis   II-89
Niederée, Claudia   II-141

Ohori, Kotaro   II-419
Okada, Hitoshi   II-347
Osorio, Carlos   I-391

Papagiannidis, Savvas   I-391
Pastor-Satorras, Romualdo   I-536
Pennebaker, James W.   I-323
Pentland, Alex 'Sandy'   II-41
Pereira, Andrés   II-277
Phethean, Chris   I-305
Piscopo, Alessandro   I-305
Pletikosa, Irena   I-521, II-458

Potash, Peter   II-391
Procter, Rob   I-109, II-53, II-221, II-378

Redi, Miriam   I-237
Reme, Bjørn-Atle   II-14
Richards, Barry   I-162
Romanov, Alexey   II-391
Roozenbeek, Jon   II-169, II-192
Rori, Lamprini   I-162
Rosés Brüngger, Raquel   I-521, II-458
Rumshisky, Anna   II-391
Ruths, Derek   I-473

Sabuco, Juan   I-17
Saint-Jacques, Guillaume   II-41
Salvador Palau, Adrià   II-192
Sanderson, Mark   II-316
Sastry, Nishanth   I-237
Schelter, Sebastian   I-277
Scholtes, Ingo   II-111
Schweitzer, Frank   II-111, II-301
Semertzidis, Theodoros   II-121
Shaban, Tarrek A.   I-201
Shadbolt, Nigel   II-405
Shah, Kushal   II-74
Simperl, Elena   I-305
Sinyavskaya, Yadviga   II-431
Smirnov, Ivan   II-24
Song, Yunya   II-230
Srinivasan, Sudharshan   II-329
Srivastava, Jaideep   II-74
Starnini, Michele   I-536
Stephany, Fabian   II-31
Stettinger, Martin   II-368
Stevenage, Sarah V.   I-591
Stoll, Richard   II-501
Straka, Mika J.   I-17
Subramanian, Devika   II-501
Sulistya, Agus   I-426
Sundararaman, Dhanasekar   II-329
Sundsøy, Pål   II-14, II-41

Tagarelli, Andrea   I-552
Taghawi-Nejad, Davoud   I-17
Tanaka, Katsumi   I-611
Tanash, Rima S.   II-501
Tanin, Rudy H.   I-17
Terentieva, Mariia   II-169
Thung, Ferdian   I-426
Timmermans, Benjamin   II-288
Ting, Christina L.   I-257
Tkachenko, Nataliya   II-221
Toyoda, Masashi   I-457
Tran, Thi Ngoc Trang   II-368
Tsvetkov, Yulia   II-537

Vaca, Carmen   II-265
Van Kleek, Max   II-405
van Steen, Maarten   II-443
Veale, Michael   II-405
Villavicencio, Mónica   II-265

Walland, Paul   II-491
Wang, Bo   II-378
Wang, Yu   I-409, I-440
Wendlandt, Laura   I-323
Wetter, Erik   II-14
Wilson, Rob   I-391
Wu, Chao   II-513

Xu, Kevin S.   II-101

Yamada, Hiroaki   II-419
Yoo, Seunghyun   II-257
Yoshida, Hiroaki   II-419
Yoshinaga, Naoki   I-457

Zanouda, Tahar   I-143, II-74
Zeni, Mattia   II-3
Zhan, Jingyao   II-65
Zhang, Xiuzhen   II-316
Zhang, Xiyang   I-409
Zhang, Yin   II-230
Zhou, Yiheng   II-65
Zubiaga, Arkaitz   I-109, II-53, II-378

Printed in the United States
By Bookmasters